TIM STRANG
JAN 2015
MGMT 480W

D0202439

Business and Society

Stakeholders, Ethics, Public Policy

Fourteenth Edition

Anne T. Lawrence
San José State University

James Weber
Duquesne University

McGraw-Hill Irwin

The McGraw·Hill Companies

McGraw-Hill
Irwin

BUSINESS AND SOCIETY: STAKEHOLDERS, ETHICS, PUBLIC POLICY, FOURTEENTH EDITION

Published by McGraw-Hill, a business unit of The McGraw-Hill Companies, Inc., 1221 Avenue of the Americas, New York, NY, 10020. Copyright © 2014 by The McGraw-Hill Companies, Inc. All rights reserved. Printed in the United States of America. Previous editions © 2011, 2008, and 2005. No part of this publication may be reproduced or distributed in any form or by any means, or stored in a database or retrieval system, without the prior written consent of The McGraw-Hill Companies, Inc., including, but not limited to, in any network or other electronic storage or transmission, or broadcast for distance learning.

Some ancillaries, including electronic and print components, may not be available to customers outside the United States.

This book is printed on acid-free paper.

2 3 4 5 6 7 8 9 0 DOW/DOW 1 0 9 8 7 6 5 4 3

ISBN   978-0-07-802947-9
MHID 0-07-802947-3

Senior Vice President, Products & Markets: *Kurt L. Strand*
Vice President, Content Production & Technology Services: *Kimberly Meriwether David*
Managing Director: *Paul Ducham*
Marketing Manager: *Elizabeth Trepkowski*
Senior Development Editor: *Trina Hauger*
Director, Content Production: *Terri Schiesl*
Project Manager: *Mary Jane Lampe*
Buyer: *Susan K. Culbertson*
Media Project Manager: *Prashanthi Nadipalli*
Cover Designer: *Studio Montage, St. Louis, MO*
Cover Image: *©Heath Korvola/Upper Cut Images/Getty Images*
Typeface: *10/12 Times LT Std*
Compositor: *Aptara®, Inc.*
Printer: *R. R. Donnelley*

All credits appearing on page or at the end of the book are considered to be an extension of the copyright page.

Library of Congress Cataloging-in-Publication Data
CIP has been applied for.

The Internet addresses listed in the text were accurate at the time of publication. The inclusion of a website does not indicate an endorsement by the authors or McGraw-Hill, and McGraw-Hill does not guarantee the accuracy of the information presented at these sites.

www.mhhe.com

To Our Fathers

Paul R. Lawrence
1922–2011

James F. Weber
1924–2009

About the Authors

Anne T. Lawrence   *San José State University*

Anne T. Lawrence is a professor of organization and management at San José State University. She holds a Ph.D. from the University of California, Berkeley, and completed two years of postdoctoral study at Stanford University. Her articles, cases, and reviews have appeared in many journals, including the *Academy of Management Review, Administrative Science Quarterly, Case Research Journal, Journal of Management Education, California Management Review, Business and Society Review, Research in Corporate Social Performance and Policy,* and *Journal of Corporate Citizenship.* Her cases in business and society have been reprinted in many textbooks and anthologies. She has served as guest editor of the *Case Research Journal* for two special issues on business ethics and human rights, and social and environmental entrepreneurship. She served as president of both the North American Case Research Association (NACRA) and of the Western Casewriters Association and is a Fellow of NACRA. She received the Emerson Center Award for Outstanding Case in Business Ethics (2004) and the Curtis E. Tate Award for Outstanding Case of the Year (1998 and 2009). At San José State University, she was named Outstanding Professor of the Year in 2005.

James Weber   *Duquesne University*

James Weber is a professor of management and business ethics at Duquesne University. He also serves as senior fellow and founding director of the Beard Center for Leadership in Ethics and coordinates the Masters of Science in Leadership and Business Ethics program at Duquesne. He holds a Ph.D. from the University of Pittsburgh and has taught at the University of San Francisco, University of Pittsburgh, and Marquette University. His areas of interest and research include managerial and organizational values, cognitive moral reasoning, business ethics, ethics training and education, eastern religions' ethics, and corporate social audit and performance. His work has appeared in *Organization Science, Human Relations, Business & Society, Journal of Business Ethics, Academy of Management Perspectives*, and *Business Ethics Quarterly*. He was recognized by the Social Issues in Management division of the Academy of Management with the Best Paper Award in 1989 and 1994 and received the Best Article Award from the International Association for Business and Society in 1998. He has served as division and program chair of the Social Issues in Management division of the Academy of Management. He has also served as president and program chair of the International Association of Business and Society (IABS).

Preface

In a world economy that is becoming increasingly integrated and interdependent, the relationship between business and society is becoming ever more complex. The globalization of business, the emergence of civil society organizations in many nations, and new government regulations and international agreements have significantly altered the job of managers and the nature of strategic decision making within the firm.

At no time has business faced greater public scrutiny or more urgent demands to act in an ethical and socially responsible manner than at the present. Consider the following:

- The global financial crisis and its continuing aftermath—highlighted by the failure of major business firms, unprecedented intervention in the economy by many governments, and the fall from grace of numerous prominent executives—have focused a fresh spotlight on issues of corporate responsibility and ethics. Around the world, people and governments are demanding that managers do a better job of serving shareholders and the public. Once again, policymakers are actively debating the proper scope of government oversight in such wide-ranging arenas as health care, financial services, and manufacturing. Management educators are placing renewed emphasis on issues of business leadership and accountability.

- A host of new technologies has become part of the everyday lives of billions of the world's people. Advances in the basic sciences are stimulating extraordinary changes in agriculture, telecommunications, and pharmaceuticals. Businesses can now grow medicine in plants, embed nanochips in tennis rackets, and communicate with customers overseas over the Internet and wireless networks. Technology has changed how we interact with others, bringing people closer together through social networking, instant messaging, and photo and video sharing. These innovations hold great promise. But they also raise serious ethical issues, such as those associated with genetically modified foods, stem cell research, or use of the Internet to exploit or defraud others or to censor free expression. Businesses must learn to harness new technologies, while avoiding public controversy and remaining sensitive to the concerns of their many stakeholders.

- Businesses in the United States and other nations are transforming the employment relationship, abandoning practices that once provided job security and guaranteed pensions in favor of highly flexible but less secure forms of employment. The recession that began in the latter part of the first decade of the 21st century caused job losses across broad sectors of the economy in the United States and many other nations. Many jobs, including those in the service sector, are being outsourced to the emerging economies of China, India, and other nations. As jobs shift abroad, transnational corporations are challenged to address their obligations to workers in far-flung locations with very different cultures and to respond to initiatives, like the United Nations' Global Compact, that call for voluntary commitment to enlightened labor standards and human rights.

- Ecological and environmental problems have forced businesses and governments to take action. An emerging consensus about the risks of climate change, for example, is leading many companies to adopt new practices, and once again the nations of the world have experimented with public policies designed to limit the emissions of greenhouse gases. Many businesses have cut air pollution, curbed solid waste, and designed products and buildings to be more energy-efficient. A better understanding of how human activities affect natural resources is producing a growing understanding that economic growth must be achieved in balance with environmental protection if development is to be sustainable.

• Many regions of the world are developing at an extraordinary rate. Yet, the prosperity that accompanies economic growth is not shared equally. Personal income, health care, and educational opportunity are unevenly distributed among and within the world's nations. The tragic pandemic of AIDS in sub-Saharan Africa and the threat of a swine or avian flu epidemic have compelled drug makers to rethink their pricing policies and raised troubling questions about the commitment of world trade organizations to patent protection. Many businesses must consider the delicate balance between their intellectual property rights and the urgent demands of public health, particularly in the developing world.

• In many nations, legislators have questioned business's influence on politics. Business has a legitimate role to play in the public policy process, but it has on occasion shaded over into undue influence and even corruption. In the United States, recent court decisions have changed the rules of the game governing how corporations and individuals can contribute to and influence political parties and public officials. Technology offers candidates and political parties new ways to reach out and inform potential voters. Businesses the world over are challenged to determine their legitimate scope of influence and how to voice their interests most effectively in the public policy process.

The new Fourteenth Edition of *Business and Society* addresses this complex agenda of issues and their impact on business and its stakeholders. It is designed to be the required textbook in an undergraduate or graduate course in Business and Society; Business, Government, and Society; Social Issues in Management; or the Environment of Business. It may also be used, in whole or in part, in courses in Business Ethics and Public Affairs Management. This new edition of the text is also appropriate for an undergraduate sociology course that focuses on the role of business in society or on contemporary issues in business.

The core argument of *Business and Society* is that corporations serve a broad public purpose: to create value for society. All companies must make a profit for their owners. Indeed, if they did not, they would not long survive. However, corporations create many other kinds of value as well. They are responsible for professional development for their employees, innovative new products for their customers, and generosity to their communities. They must partner with a wide range of individuals and groups in society to advance collaborative goals. In our view, corporations have multiple obligations, and all stakeholders' interests must be taken into account.

A Tradition of Excellence

Since the 1960s, when Professors Keith Davis and Robert Blomstrom wrote the first edition of this book, *Business and Society* has maintained a position of leadership by discussing central issues of corporate social performance in a form that students and faculty have found engaging and stimulating. The leadership of the two founding authors, and later of Professor William C. Frederick and James E. Post, helped *Business and Society* to achieve a consistently high standard of quality and market acceptance. Thanks to these authors' remarkable eye for the emerging issues that shape the organizational, social, and public policy environments in which students will soon live and work, the book has added value to the business education of many thousands of students.

Business and Society has continued through several successive author teams to be the market leader in its field. The current authors bring a broad background of business and society research, teaching, consulting, and case development to the ongoing evolution of the text. The new Fourteenth Edition of *Business and Society* builds on its legacy of market leadership by reexamining such central issues as the role of business in society, the nature of corporate responsibility and global citizenship, business ethics practices, and the complex roles of government and business in a global community.

For Instructors

For instructors, this textbook offers a complete set of supplements. An extensive instructor's resource manual—fully revised for this edition—includes lecture outlines, discussion case questions and answers, tips from experienced instructors, and extensive case teaching notes. A computerized test bank and PowerPoint slides for every chapter are also provided to adopters. A video supplement, compiled especially for the Fourteenth Edition, features recent segments from *PBS NewsHour,* produced by the Public Broadcasting Service. These videos may be used to supplement class lectures and discussions.

Business and Society is designed to be easily modularized. An instructor who wishes to focus on a particular portion of the material may select individual chapters or cases to be packaged in a Create custom product. Sections of this book can also be packaged with other materials from the extensive Create database, including articles and cases from the Harvard Business School, to provide exactly the course pack the instructor needs.

For instructors who teach over the Internet and for those who prefer an electronic format, this text may be delivered online, using McGraw-Hill's eBook technology. eBooks can also be customized with the addition of any of the materials in Create's extensive collection. Students may choose between an online product and a downloadable CourseSmart eBook.

For Students

Business and Society has long been popular with students because of its lively writing, up-to-date examples, and clear explanations of theory. This textbook has benefited greatly from feedback over the years from thousands of students who have used the material in the authors' own classrooms. Its strengths are in many ways a testimony to the students who have used earlier generations of *Business and Society.*

The new Fourteenth Edition of the text is designed to be as student-friendly as always. Each chapter opens with a list of key learning objectives to help focus student reading and study. Numerous figures, exhibits, and real-world business examples (set as blocks of colored type) illustrate and elaborate the main points. A glossary at the end of the book provides definitions for bold-faced and other important terms. Internet references and a full section-by-section bibliography guide students who wish to do further research on topics of their choice, and subject and name indexes help students locate items in the book.

Additional student resources are also available via the book's password-protected Online Learning Center at www.mhhe.com/lawrence14e, including self-grading quizzes and chapter review material.

New for the Fourteenth Edition

Over the years, the issues addressed by *Business and Society* have changed as the environment of business itself has been transformed. This Fourteenth Edition is no exception, as readers will discover. Some issues have become less compelling and others have taken their place on the business agenda, while others endure through the years.

The Fourteenth Edition has been thoroughly revised and updated to reflect the latest theoretical work in the field and the latest statistical data, as well as recent events. Among the new additions are:

- New discussion of theoretical advances in stakeholder theory, social and environmental entrepreneurship, corporate citizenship, public affairs management, corporate governance, corporate social auditing, social investing, reputation management, business partnerships, and corporate philanthropy.

- Treatment of practical issues, such as social networking, digital medical records, bottom of the pyramid, social entrepreneurship, political advertising and campaign contributions, as well as the latest developments in the regulatory environment in which businesses operate, including the Dodd-Frank Act and the Affordable Care Act.

- New discussion cases and full-length cases on such timely topics as conditions in Apple's Chinese supplier factories, the Upper Big Branch mine disaster, conflict minerals in cell phones, child sexual abuse in the global hotel industry, online piracy, Chiquita Brands in Latin America, working with bloggers in marketing, the campaign for clean cookstoves, the shareholder "say on pay" vote at Citigroup, the controversy over "pink slime," and undocumented immigrants in the workforce.

Finally, this is a book with a vision. It is not simply a compendium of information and ideas. The new edition of *Business and Society* articulates the view that in a global community, where traditional buffers no longer protect business from external change, managers can create strategies that integrate stakeholder interests, respect personal values, support community development, and are implemented fairly. Most important, businesses can achieve these goals while also being economically successful. Indeed, this may be the *only* way to achieve economic success over the long term.

Anne T. Lawrence

James Weber

Acknowledgments

We are grateful for the assistance of many colleagues at universities in the United States and abroad who over the years have helped shape this book with their excellent suggestions and ideas. We also note the feedback from students in our classes and at other colleges and universities that has helped make this book as user-friendly as possible.

We especially wish to acknowledge the assistance of several esteemed colleagues who provided detailed reviews for this edition. These reviewers were Shawn Berman of the University of New Mexico, Geoffrey Desa of San Francisco State University, Jennifer J. Griffin of George Washington University, Bernie Hayen of Kansas State University, Denise Kleinrichert of San Francisco State University, Cynthia M. Orms of Georgia College & State University, Alexia Priest of Post University, Joseph Petrick of Wright State University, and Ronald M. Roman of San José State University.

In addition, we are grateful to the many colleagues who over the years have generously shared with us their insights into the theory and pedagogy of business and society. In particular, we would like to thank Sandra Waddock of Boston College, Mary C. Gentile of Babson College, Margaret J. Naumes of the University of New Hampshire (retired), Michael E. Johnson-Cramer and Jamie Hendry of Bucknell University, John Mahon and Stephanie Welcomer of the University of Maine, Ann Svendsen of Simon Fraser University, Robert Boutilier of Robert Boutilier & Associates, Kathryn S. Rogers of Pitzer College, Anne Forrestel of the University of Oregon, Kelly Strong of Colorado State University, Daniel Gilbert of Gettysburg College, William Sodeman of Hawaii Pacific University, Gina Vega of Merrimack College, Craig Dunn and Brian Burton of Western Washington University, Lori V. Ryan of San Diego State University, Bryan W. Husted of York University, Sharon Livesey of Fordham University, Barry Mitnick of the University of Pittsburgh, Virginia Gerde and David Wasieleski of Duquesne University, Robbin Derry of the University of Lethbridge, Linda Ginzel of the University of Chicago, Jerry Calton of the University of Hawaii-Hilo, H. Richard Eisenbeis of the University of Southern Colorado (retired), Anthony J. Daboub of the University of Texas at Brownsville, Asbjorn Osland of San José State University, Linda Klebe Treviño of Pennsylvania State University, Mary Meisenhelter of York College of Pennsylvania, Stephen Payne of Georgia College and State University, Amy Hillman and Gerald Keim of Arizona State University, Jeanne Logsdon of the University of New Mexico (retired), Barbara Altman of Texas A&M University Central Texas, Craig Fleisher of the College of Coastal Georgia, Karen Moustafa Leonard of Indiana University-Purdue University Fort Wayne, Deborah Vidaver-Cohen of Florida International University, Lynda Brown of the University of Montana, Kathleen A. Getz of Loyola University Chicago, Gordon P. Rands of Western Illinois University, Paul S. Adler of the University of Southern California, Diana Sharpe of Monmouth University, Kathleen Rehbein of Marquette University, Harry Van Buren of the University of New Mexico, Bruce Paton and Peter Melhus of San Francisco State University, Heather Elms of American University, Jacob Park of Green Mountain College, Armand Gilinsky of Sonoma State University, Tara Ceranic of the University of San Diego, and Diane Swanson of Kansas State University.

These scholars' dedication to the creative teaching of business and society has been a continuing inspiration to us.

Thanks are also due to Murray Silverman and Tom E. Thomas of San Francisco State University; Pierre Batellier and Emmanuel Raufflet of HEC Montreal; Robyn Linde of Rhode Island College and H. Richard Eisenbeis of the University of Southern Colorado Pueblo (retired); and Steven M. Cox, Bradley W. Brooks, S. Cathy Anderson, and J. Norris Frederick of Queens University of Charlotte, who contributed cases to this edition.

A number of research assistants and former students have made contributions throughout this project for which we are appreciative. Among the special contributors to this project were Patricia Morrison of Grossmont College and Xi Yin of Duquesne University, who provided research assistance, and Emily DeMasi of Duquesne University, who provided research and assisted in preparing the instructor's resource manual and ancillary materials. Thanks are also due to Carolyn Roose and Nate Marsh for research assistance.

We wish to express our continuing appreciation to William C. Frederick, who invited us into this project many years ago and who has continued to provide warm support and sage advice as the book has evolved through numerous editions. James E. Post, another former author of this book, has also continued to offer valuable intellectual guidance to this project.

We continue to be grateful to the excellent editorial and production team at McGraw-Hill. We offer special thanks to Paul Ducham, our managing director, for his skillful leadership of this project. We also wish to recognize the able assistance of Trina Hauger, development editor, and Mary Jane Lampe and Manish Sharma, project managers, whose ability to keep us on track and on time has been critical. Elizabeth Trepkowski headed the excellent marketing team. Prashanthi Nadipalli, media project manager; Susan K. Culbertson, buyer; Richard Wright, copy editor; Susan Higgins, proofreader; and Jenny Lindeman, who designed the book cover, also played key roles. Each of these people has provided professional contributions that we deeply value and appreciate.

As always, we are profoundly grateful for the ongoing support of our spouses, Paul Roose and Sharon Green.

Anne T. Lawrence

James Weber

Online Learning Center (OLC)

www.mhhe.com/lawrence14e

Find a variety of online teaching and learning tools that are designed to reinforce and build on the text content. Students will have direct access to the learning tools while instructor materials are password protected.

EBOOK OPTIONS

eBooks are an innovative way for students to save money and to "go green." McGraw-Hill's eBooks are typically 55 percent off the bookstore price. Students may choose between an online and a downloadable CourseSmart eBook. Through CourseSmart, students have the flexibility to access an exact replica of their textbook from any computer that has Internet service without plugins or special software via the online version, or to create a library of books on their hard drive via the downloadable version. Access to the CourseSmart eBooks is for one year.

Features

CourseSmart eBooks allow students to highlight, take notes, organize notes, and share the notes with other CourseSmart users. Students can also search for terms across all eBooks in their purchased CourseSmart library. CourseSmart eBooks can be printed (five pages at a time).

More info and purchase

Please visit **www.coursesmart.com** for more information and to purchase access to our eBooks. CourseSmart allows students to try one chapter of the eBook, free of charge, before purchase.

CREATE

Craft your teaching resources to match the way you teach! With McGraw-Hill Create, **www.mcgrawhillcreate.com**, you can easily rearrange chapters, combine material from other content sources, and quickly upload content you have written, like your course syllabus or teaching notes. Find the content you need in Create by searching through thousands of leading McGraw-Hill textbooks. Arrange your book to fit your teaching style. Create even allows you to personalize your book's appearance by selecting the cover and adding your name, school, and course information. Order a Create book and you'll receive a complimentary print review copy in three to five business days or a complimentary electronic review copy (eComp) via e-mail in about one hour. Go to **www.mcgrawhillcreate.com** today and register. Experience how McGraw-Hill Create empowers you to teach *your* students *your* way.

Brief Contents

PART ONE
Business in Society 1

1. The Corporation and Its Stakeholders 2
2. Managing Public Issues and Stakeholder Relationships 24
3. The Corporation's Social Responsibilities 45

PART TWO
Business and Ethics 67

4. Ethics and Ethical Reasoning 68
5. Organizational Ethics and the Law 90

PART THREE
Business in a Globalized World 115

6. The Challenges of Globalization 116
7. Global Corporate Citizenship 137

PART FOUR
Business and Public Policy 159

8. Business–Government Relations 160
9. Influencing the Political Environment 183

PART FIVE
Business and the Natural Environment 209

10. Sustainable Development and Global Business 210
11. Managing Environmental Issues 234

PART SIX
Business and Technology 259

12. Technology, Organizations, and Society 260
13. Managing Technology and Innovation 285

PART SEVEN
Business and Its Stakeholders 307

14. Stockholder Rights and Corporate Governance 308
15. Consumer Protection 332
16. Employees and the Corporation 355
17. Managing a Diverse Workforce 378
18. The Community and the Corporation 402
19. Managing Public Relations 426

CASES IN BUSINESS AND SOCIETY 447

1. The Upper Big Branch Mine Disaster 448
2. The Carlson Company and Protecting Children in the Global Tourism Industry 458
3. Carolina Pad and the Bloggers 467
4. Moody's Credit Ratings and the Subprime Mortgage Meltdown 480
5. Merck, the FDA, and the Vioxx Recall 493
6. Kimpton Hotels' EarthCare Program 503
7. Ventria Bioscience and the Controversy over Plant-Made Medicines 511
8. The Solidarity Fund and Gildan Activewear, Inc. 522
9. Mattel and Toy Safety 531

GLOSSARY 541

BIBLIOGRAPHY 553

INDEXES
Name 559
Subject 563

Contents

PART ONE
BUSINESS IN SOCIETY   1

✗ Chapter 1
The Corporation and Its Stakeholders   2

Business and Society   4
A Systems Perspective   5
The Stakeholder Theory of the Firm   6
The Stakeholder Concept   7
Different Kinds of Stakeholders   8
Stakeholder Analysis   10
Stakeholder Interests   11
Stakeholder Power   12
Stakeholder Coalitions   13
Stakeholder Salience and Mapping   16
The Corporation's Boundary-Spanning
Departments   18
The Dynamic Environment of Business   19
Creating Value in a Dynamic Environment   21
Summary   21
Key Terms   22
Internet Resources   22
Discussion Case: A Brawl in Mickey's Backyard   22

✗ Chapter 2
Managing Public Issues and Stakeholder Relationships   24

Public Issues   25
Environmental Analysis   28
Competitive Intelligence   31
The Issue Management Process   32
Identify Issue   33
Analyze Issue   33
Generate Options   34
Take Action   35
Evaluate Results   35
Organizing for Effective Issue Management   35
Stakeholder Engagement   37
Stages in the Business–Stakeholder Relationship   37
Drivers of Stakeholder Engagement   38
Making Engagement Work Effectively   39
Stakeholder Networks   41
The Benefits of Engagement   41

Summary   42
Key Terms   42
Internet Resources   43
Discussion Case: Coca-Cola's Water Neutrality
Initiative   43

✗ Chapter 3
The Corporation's Social Responsibilities   45

Corporate Power and Responsibility   47
The Meaning of Corporate Social Responsibility   49
The Origins of Corporate Social Responsibility   50
Balancing Social, Economic, and Legal
Responsibilities   51
The Corporate Social Responsibility Debate   53
*Arguments for Corporate Social
Responsibility   53*
Arguments against Corporate Social Responsibility   56
The Social Enterprise   59
Social Entrepreneurship   60
The B Corporation   60
Serving the Bottom of the Pyramid   61
Award-Winning Corporate Social Responsibility
Practices   63
Summary   64
Key Terms   64
Internet Resources   65
Discussion Case: Timberland's Corporate Social
Responsibility—Under New Ownership   65

PART TWO
BUSINESS AND ETHICS   67

✗ Chapter 4
Ethics and Ethical Reasoning   68

The Meaning of Ethics   69
What Is Business Ethics?   70
Why Should Business Be Ethical?   71
Why Ethical Problems Occur in Business   75
Personal Gain and Selfish Interest   76
Competitive Pressures on Profits   77
Conflicts of Interest   77
Cross-Cultural Contradictions   78

The Core Elements of Ethical Character 78
  Managers' Values 78
  Spirituality in the Workplace 80
  Managers' Moral Development 81
Analyzing Ethical Problems in Business 83
  Virtue Ethics: Pursuing a "Good" Life 83
  Utility: Comparing Benefits and Costs 84
  Rights: Determining and Protecting Entitlements 85
  Justice: Is It Fair? 86
  Applying Ethical Reasoning to Business Activities 86
Summary 87
Key Terms 87
Internet Resources 87
Discussion Case: Chiquita Brands: Ethical Responsibility or Illegal Action? 88

Chapter 5
Organizational Ethics and the Law 90

Corporate Ethical Climates 91
Business Ethics across Organizational Functions 93
  Accounting Ethics 93
  Financial Ethics 95
  Marketing Ethics 96
  Information Technology Ethics 97
  Other Functional Areas 98
Making Ethics Work in Corporations 99
  Building Ethical Safeguards into the Company 99
  Comprehensive Ethics Programs 104
  Corporate Ethics Awards and Certifications 104
Ethics in a Global Economy 105
  Efforts to Curtail Unethical Practices 106
Ethics, Law, and Illegal Corporate Behavior 109
  Corporate Lawbreaking and Its Costs 109
Summary 110
Key Terms 111
Internet Resources 111
Discussion Case: Alcoa's Core Values in Practice 111

PART THREE
BUSINESS IN A GLOBALIZED WORLD 115

Chapter 6
The Challenges of Globalization 116

The Process of Globalization 117
  Major Transnational Corporations 118
  The Acceleration of Globalization 119
  International Financial and Trade Institutions 120
The Benefits and Costs of Globalization 122
  Benefits of Globalization 122
  Costs of Globalization 124
Doing Business in a Diverse World 126
  Comparative Political and Economic Systems 127
  Meeting the Challenges of Global Diversity 130
Collaborative Partnerships for Global Problem Solving 131
  A Three-Sector World 131
Summary 133
Key Terms 133
Internet Resources 133
Discussion Case: Conflict Coltan in the Global Electronics Industry Supply Chain 134

Chapter 7
Global Corporate Citizenship 137

Global Corporate Citizenship 138
  Citizenship Profile 140
  Management Systems for Global Corporate Citizenship 142
Stages of Corporate Citizenship 143
Assessing Global Corporate Citizenship 147
  Global Social and Environmental Audit Standards 147
  The Auditing Process 150
  Social and Environmental Reporting 151
  Triple Bottom Line 153
Summary 154
Key Terms 155
Internet Resources 155
Discussion Case: Apple's Supplier Code of Conduct and Foxconn's Chinese Factories 155

PART FOUR
BUSINESS AND PUBLIC POLICY 159

Chapter 8
Business–Government Relations 160

How Business and Government Relate 162
  Seeking a Collaborative Partnership 162
  Working at Arm's Length 163
  Legitimacy Issues 164
Government's Public Policy Role 164
  Elements of Public Policy 165
  Types of Public Policy 167
Government Regulation of Business 168
  Market Failure 169
  Negative Externalities 169

Natural Monopolies   *169*
Ethical Arguments   *170*
Types of Regulation   *170*
The Effects of Regulation   *175*
Regulation in a Global Context   178
Summary   179
Key Terms   180
Internet Resources   180
Discussion Case: Derivative Losses at JPMorgan
Chase   180

Chapter 9
Influencing the Political Environment   183

Participants in the Political Environment   185
Business as a Political Participant   *185*
Stakeholder Groups in Politics   *186*
Coalition Political Activity   *186*
Influencing the Business–Government
Relationship   187
Corporate Political Strategy   *187*
Political Action Tactics   188
Promoting an Information Strategy   *189*
Promoting a Financial-Incentive Strategy   *192*
Promoting a Constituency-Building Strategy   *199*
Levels of Political Involvement   202
Managing the Political Environment   203
Business Political Action: A Global Challenge   204
Summary   205
Key Terms   206
Internet Resources   206
Discussion Case: Stop Online Piracy Act—
A Political Battle between Old and New Media   207

PART FIVE
**BUSINESS AND THE NATURAL
ENVIRONMENT   209**

Chapter 10
**Sustainable Development and Global
Business   210**

Business and Society in the Natural
Environment   212
Sustainable Development   *213*
Threats to the Earth's Ecosystem   *214*
Forces of Change   *216*
The Earth's Carrying Capacity   *219*
Global Environmental Issues   221
Ozone Depletion   *221*
Climate Change   *222*

Decline of Biodiversity   *224*
Threats to Marine Ecosystems   *226*
Response of the International Business
Community   227
Codes of Environmental Conduct   *229*
Summary   231
Key Terms   231
Internet Resources   231
Discussion Case: Clean Cooking   232

Chapter 11
Managing Environmental Issues   234

Role of Government   236
Major Areas of Environmental Regulation   *236*
Alternative Policy Approaches   *242*
Costs and Benefits of Environmental Regulation   246
The Greening of Management   248
Stages of Corporate Environmental Responsibility   *248*
The Ecologically Sustainable Organization   249
Environmental Partnerships   *250*
Environmental Management in Practice   *250*
Environmental Audits   *251*
Environmental Management as a Competitive
Advantage   252
Cost Savings   *252*
Product Differentiation   *253*
Technological Innovation   *254*
Reduction of Regulatory Risk   *255*
Strategic Planning   *255*
Summary   256
Key Terms   256
Internet Resources   256
Discussion Case: Digging Gold   257

PART SIX
BUSINESS AND TECHNOLOGY   259

Chapter 12
Technology, Organizations, and Society   260

Technology Defined   262
Phases of Technology in Society   *262*
Fueling Technological Growth   *264*
Technology as a Powerful Force in Business   265
The Internet   *265*
E-Business   *267*
M-Commerce   *269*
Social Networking—Tools and Threats   271
Blogs and Vlogs   *272*
Spam and Unsolicited Commercial E-mail   *273*
Phishing   *274*

Government Censorship of the Internet   275
Socially Beneficial Uses of Technology   277
   Technology and Education   277
   Medical Information via the Internet   278
Special Issue: The Digital Divide in the United States and Worldwide   280
Summary   271
Key Terms   282
Internet Resources   282
Discussion Case: How Protected Is Your Online Privacy?   282

Chapter 13
Managing Technology and Innovation   285

Violations of Privacy: Causes and Costs   287
The Management of Information Security   291
   Businesses' Responses to Invasions of Information Security   291
   The Chief Information, Security, Technology Officer   292
Protecting Intellectual Property   294
   Business and Government Responses to Violations of Intellectual Property   294
Managing Scientific Breakthroughs   298
   Nanotechnology   298
   Human Genome   299
   Biotechnology and Stem Cell Research   300
   Cloning   301
   Genetically Engineered Foods   302
Summary   303
Key Terms   304
Internet Resources   304
Discussion Case: Cardholders' Information at Citigroup Hacked   305

PART SEVEN
BUSINESS AND ITS STAKEHOLDERS   307

Chapter 14
Stockholder Rights and Corporate Governance   308

Stockholders   309
   Who Are Stockholders?   310
   Objectives of Stock Ownership   312
   Stockholders' Legal Rights and Safeguards   312
Corporate Governance   313
   The Board of Directors   313
   Principles of Good Governance   315

Special Issue: Executive Compensation   317
Shareholder Activism   321
   The Rise of Institutional Investors   322
   Social Investment   322
   Stockholder Lawsuits   324
Government Protection of Stockholder Interests   325
   Securities and Exchange Commission   325
   Information Transparency and Disclosure   325
   Insider Trading   326
Stockholders and the Corporation   328
Summary   329
Key Terms   329
Internet Resources   329
Discussion Case: Citigroup Shareholders Say No on Pay   330

Chapter 15
Consumer Protection   332

Advocacy for Consumer Interests   334
   Reasons for the Consumer Movement   335
   The Rights of Consumers   336
How Government Protects Consumers   336
   Goals of Consumer Laws   336
   Major Consumer Protection Agencies   339
Consumer Privacy in the Digital Age   342
Special Issue: Product Liability   345
   Strict Liability   345
   Product Liability Reform and Alternative Dispute Resolution   346
Positive Business Responses to Consumerism   348
   Managing for Quality   348
   Voluntary Industry Codes of Conduct   349
   Consumer Affairs Departments   350
   Product Recalls   351
Consumerism's Achievements   351
Summary   352
Key Terms   352
Internet Resources   352
Discussion Case: Big Fat Liability   353

Chapter 16
Employees and the Corporation   355

The Employment Relationship   357
Workplace Rights   358
   The Right to Organize and Bargain Collectively   358
   The Right to a Safe and Healthy Workplace   359
   The Right to a Secure Job   362
Privacy in the Workplace   364
   Electronic Monitoring   365

Romance in the Workplace   367
Employee Drug Use and Testing   367
Alcohol Abuse at Work   368
Employee Theft and Honesty Testing   369
Whistle-Blowing and Free Speech in the
Workplace   370
Working Conditions around the World   372
Fair Labor Standards   372
Employees as Corporate Stakeholders   374
Summary   375
Key Terms   375
Internet Resources   375
Discussion Case: No Smoking Allowed—On the
Job or Off   376

Chapter 17
Managing a Diverse Workforce   378

The Changing Face of the Workforce   379
Gender and Race in the Workplace   381
Women and Minorities at Work   381
The Gender and Racial Pay Gap   383
Where Women and Persons of Color Manage   384
Breaking the Glass Ceiling   385
Women and Minority Business Ownership   387
Government's Role in Securing Equal Employment
Opportunity   388
Equal Employment Opportunity   388
Affirmative Action   390
Sexual and Racial Harassment   391
What Business Can Do: Diversity Policies and
Practices   393
Balancing Work and Life   395
Child Care and Elder Care   395
Work Flexibility   396
Summary   398
Key Terms   399
Internet Resources   399
Discussion Case: Unauthorized Immigrant Workers at
Chipotle Mexican Grill Restaurants   400

Chapter 18
The Community and the Corporation   402

The Business–Community Relationship   404
The Business Case for Community Involvement   405
Community Relations   407
Economic Development   408
Housing   408
*Aid to Minority, Women, and Disabled Veteran-Owned
Enterprises   409*
Disaster, Terrorism, and War Relief   409
Corporate Giving   410
Forms of Corporate Giving   413
Priorities in Corporate Giving   416
Corporate Giving in a Strategic Context   417
Measuring the Return on Social Investment   419
Building Collaborative Partnerships   420
Summary   422
Key Terms   422
Internet Resources   423
Discussion Case: Fidelity Investments' Partnership
with Citizen Schools   423

Chapter 19
Managing Public Relations   426

The General Public   427
Public Relations in an Emerging Digital World   428
Public Relations Department   429
*New Technology-Enhanced Channels for Public
Relations   430*
Global Public Relations   432
Influencing Public Opinion   433
Public Service Announcements   433
Image Advertisements   434
Protecting the Public through Government
Regulation   435
Crisis Management   437
Media Training of Employees   440
Summary   443
Key Terms   443
Internet Resources   443
Discussion Case: "Pink Sliming" the Processed Beef
Industry   444

CASES IN BUSINESS AND SOCIETY   447

1. **Upper Big Branch Mine Disaster   448**

2. **The Carlson Company and Protecting
    Children in the Global Tourism
    Industry   458**

3. **Carolina Pad and the Bloggers   467**

4. **Moody's Credit Ratings and the
    Subprime Mortgage Meltdown   480**

5. **Merck, the FDA, and the Vioxx
    Recall   493**

6.   **Kimpton Hotels' EarthCare Program   503**

7.   **Ventria Bioscience and the Controversy over Plant-Made Medicines   511**

8.   **The Solidarity Fund and Gildan Activewear, Inc.   522**

9.   **Mattel and Toy Safety   531**

Glossary   541

Bibliography   553

Indexes
Name   559
Subject   563

PART ONE

Business in Society

The Corporation and Its Stakeholders

Business corporations have complex relationships with many individuals and organizations in society. The term *stakeholder* refers to all those that affect, or are affected by, the actions of the firm. An important part of management's role is to identify a firm's relevant stakeholders and understand the nature of their interests, power, and alliances with one another. Building positive and mutually beneficial relationships across organizational boundaries can help enhance a company's reputation and address critical social and ethical challenges. In a world of fast-paced globalization, shifting public expectations and government policies, growing ecological concerns, and new technologies, managers face the difficult challenge of achieving economic results while simultaneously creating value for all of their diverse stakeholders.

This Chapter Focuses on These Key Learning Objectives:

- Understanding the relationship between business and society and the ways in which business and society are part of an interactive system.
- Considering the purpose of the modern corporation.
- Knowing what a stakeholder is and who a corporation's market and nonmarket and internal and external stakeholders are.
- Conducting a stakeholder analysis and understanding the basis of stakeholder interests and power.
- Recognizing the diverse ways in which modern corporations organize internally to interact with various stakeholders.
- Analyzing the forces of change that continually reshape the business and society relationship.

Walmart has been called "a template for 21st century capitalism." In each period of history, because of its size and potential impact on many groups in society, a single company often seems to best exemplify the management systems, technology, and social relationships of its era. In 1990, this company was U.S. Steel. In 1950, it was General Motors. Now, in the 2010s, it is Walmart.[1]

In 2012, Walmart was the largest private employer in the world, with 2.2 million employees worldwide. The company operated more than 10,000 facilities in 28 countries and had annual sales of $405 billion. The retailer was enormously popular with customers, drawing them in with its great variety of products under one roof and "save money, live better" slogan; 200 million customers worldwide shopped there every week. Economists estimated that Walmart had directly through its own actions and indirectly through its impact on its supply chain saved American shoppers $287 billion annually, about $957 for every person in the United States.[2] Shareholders who invested early were richly rewarded; the share price rose from 5 cents (split adjusted) when the company went public in 1970 to around $69 a share in 2012, near its all-time high.[3] Walmart was a major customer for 61,000 suppliers worldwide, ranging from huge multinationals to tiny one-person operations.

Yet, Walmart had become a lightning rod for criticism from many quarters, charged with corruption; driving down wages, benefits, and working conditions; and hurting local communities. Consider that:

- In 2012, the company confronted shocking charges that it had conducted a "campaign of bribery" to facilitate its rapid growth in Mexico. According to an investigation by *The New York Times,* Walmart had made $24 million in payments to government officials to clear the way for hundreds of new stores in what became the company's most important foreign subsidiary, in probable violation of both U.S. and Mexican law.[4]

- In 2011, Walmart announced that it would eliminate health insurance for part-timers working less than 24 hours a week. Other employees faced an increase in health care premiums of more than 40 percent, on top of deductibles that sometimes exceeded 20 percent of their annual pay.[5] Three years earlier, the company had settled a lawsuit, agreeing to pay at least $352 million, for violations of labor law. The retailer had allegedly forced employees to work off the clock, without pay.

- In 2012, local activists organized to block construction of a Walmart neighborhood market in Los Angeles's Chinatown. It was the latest of many incidents in which local communities resisted the arrival of the retail giant, saying it would hurt small businesses.[6] Economists studying Walmart's impact in Chicago, for example, found that about one quarter of neighborhood retailers near a new Walmart had gone out of business, causing a loss of 300 jobs.[7]

Lee Scott, then the company's CEO, commented in an interview with *BusinessWeek* in 2005, "We always believed that if we sat here in Bentonville [the company's headquarters

---

[1] Nelson Lichtenstein, "Wal-Mart: A Template for Twenty-First Century Capitalism," in *Wal-Mart: The Face of Twenty-First Century Capitalism,* ed. Nelson Lichtenstein (New York: The New Press, 2006), pp. 3–30.

[2] Global Insight, "The Price Impact of Wal-Mart: An Update through 2006," September 4, 2007.

[3] "Wal-Mart Stock Near All-Time High," *The Wall Street Journal,* June 28, 2012.

[4] "Wal-Mart Hushed Up a Vast Mexican Bribery Case," *The New York Times,* April 21, 2012.

[5] "Wal-Mart Cuts Some Health Care Benefits," *The New York Times,* October 20, 2011.

[6] "Chinatown Walmart Opponents Plan 10,000-Strong March," *NBC Southern California,* at *www.nbclosangeles.com.*

[7] Julie Davis et al., "The Impact of an Urban Wal-Mart Store on Area Businesses: An Evaluation of One Chicago Neighborhood's Experience," Center for Urban Research and Learning, Loyola University Chicago, December 2009.

in Arkansas] and took care of our customers and took care of associates that the world it-self would leave us alone." That, he acknowledged, was no longer the case. "We have to continue to evolve in how we operate and how we interface with society," he said.[8] In an effort to shore up its reputation, the company offered grants to small businesses, donated to wildlife habitat restoration, and announced a plan to lower the salt, fat, and sugar in many of its packaged foods.[9] It also pursued ambitious environmental goals to reduce waste, use more renewable energy, and sell more sustainable products, and began reporting to the public on its progress.[10] "Reputation is very important to Wal-Mart," said a historian who had studied the company. "They put a lot of money into building it."[11]

Walmart's experience illustrates, on a particularly large scale, the challenges of manag-ing successfully in a complex global network of stakeholders. The company's actions af-fected not only itself, but also many other people, groups, and organizations in society. Customers, suppliers, employees, stockholders, creditors, business partners, governments, and local communities all had a stake in Walmart's decisions. Walmart had to learn just how difficult it could be to simultaneously satisfy multiple stakeholders with diverse and, in some respects, contradictory interests.

Every modern company, whether small or large, is part of a vast global business system. Whether a firm has 50 employees or 50,000—or, like Walmart, more than 2 million—its links to customers, suppliers, employees, and communities are certain to be numerous, di-verse, and vital to its success. This is why the relationship between business and society is important to understand for both citizens and managers.

Business and Society

Business today is arguably the most dominant institution in the world. The term *business* refers here to any organization that is engaged in making a product or providing a service for a profit. Consider that in the United States today there are 6 million businesses, ac-cording to government estimates, and in the world as a whole, there are uncounted mil-lions more. Of course, these businesses vary greatly in size and impact. They range from a woman who helps support her family by selling handmade tortillas by the side of the road in Mexico City for a few pesos, to ExxonMobil, a huge corporation that employs 83,600 workers and earns annual revenues approaching $500 billion in 200 nations worldwide.

Society, in its broadest sense, refers to human beings and to the social structures they collectively create. In a more specific sense, the term is used to refer to segments of hu-mankind, such as members of a particular community, nation, or interest group. As a set of organizations created by humans, business is clearly a part of society. At the same time, it is also a distinct entity, separated from the rest of society by clear boundaries. Business is engaged in ongoing exchanges with its external environment across these dividing lines. For example, businesses recruit workers, buy supplies, and borrow money; they also sell products, donate time, and pay taxes. This book is broadly concerned with the relationship between business and society. A simple diagram of the relationship between the two appears in Figure 1.1.

[8] "Can Wal-Mart Fit into a White Hat?" *BusinessWeek*, October 3, 2005; and extended interview with Lee Scott available online at *www.businessweek.com*.

[9] "Wal-Mart Stores," November 15, 2011, at *www.nytimes.com*.

[10] "2011 Global Responsibility Report," *www.walmartstores.com/sustainability*.

[11] "Wal-Mart's Good-Citizen Efforts Face a Test," *The New York Times*, April 30, 2012.

FIGURE 1.1

Business and Society: An Interactive System

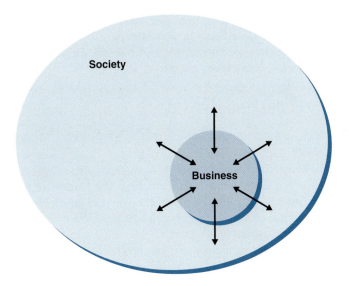

As the Walmart example that opened this chapter illustrates, business and society are highly interdependent. Business activities impact other activities in society, and actions by various social actors and governments continuously affect business. To manage these interdependencies, managers need an understanding of their company's key relationships and how the social and economic system of which they are a part affects, and is affected by, their decisions.

A Systems Perspective

General systems theory, first introduced in the 1940s, argues that all organisms are open to, and interact with, their external environments. Although most organisms have clear boundaries, they cannot be understood in isolation, but only in relationship to their surroundings. This simple but powerful idea can be applied to many disciplines. For example, in botany, the growth of a plant cannot be explained without reference to soil, light, oxygen, moisture, and other characteristics of its environment. As applied to management theory, the systems concept implies that business firms (social organisms) are embedded in a broader social structure (external environment) with which they constantly interact. Corporations have ongoing boundary exchanges with customers, governments, competitors, the media, communities, and many other individuals and groups. Just as good soil, water, and light help a plant grow, positive interactions with society benefit a business firm.

Like biological organisms, moreover, businesses must adapt to changes in the environment. Plants growing in low-moisture environments must develop survival strategies, like the cactus that evolves to store water in its leaves. Similarly, a long-distance telephone company in a newly deregulated market must learn to compete by changing the products and services it offers. The key to business survival is often this ability to adapt effectively to changing conditions. In business, systems theory provides a powerful tool to help managers conceptualize the relationship between their companies and their external environments.

Systems theory helps us understand how business and society, taken together, form an **interactive social system**. Each needs the other, and each influences the other. They are entwined so completely that any action taken by one will surely affect the other. They are both separate and connected. Business is part of society, and society penetrates far and often into business decisions. In a world where global communication is rapidly expanding, the connections are closer than ever before. Throughout this book we discuss examples of organizations and people that are grappling with the challenges of, and helping to shape, business–society relationships.

The Stakeholder Theory of the Firm

What is the purpose of the modern corporation? To whom, or what, should the firm be responsible?[12] No question is more central to the relationship between business and society.

In the **ownership theory of the firm** (sometimes also called property or finance theory), the firm is seen as the property of its owners. The purpose of the firm is to maximize its long-term market value, that is, to make the most money it can for shareholders who own stock in the company. Managers and boards of directors are agents of shareholders and have no obligations to others, other than those directly specified by law. In this view, owners' interests are paramount and take precedence over the interests of others.

A contrasting view, called the **stakeholder theory of the firm**, argues that corporations serve a broad public purpose: to create value for society. All companies must make a profit for their owners; indeed, if they did not, they would not long survive. However, corporations create many other kinds of value as well, such as professional development for their employees and innovative new products for their customers. In this view, corporations have multiple obligations, and all stakeholders' interests must be taken into account. This approach has been expressed well by the pharmaceutical company Novartis, which states in its code of conduct that it "places a premium on dealing fairly with employees, commercial partners, government authorities, and the public. Success in its business ventures depends upon maintaining the trust of these essential stakeholders."[13]

Supporters of the stakeholder theory of the firm make three core arguments for their position: *descriptive, instrumental,* and *normative.*[14]

The *descriptive argument* says that the stakeholder view is simply a more realistic description of how companies really work. Managers have to pay keen attention, of course, to their quarterly and annual financial performance. Keeping Wall Street satisfied by managing for growth—thereby attracting more investors and increasing the stock price—is a core part of any top manager's job. But the job of management is much more complex than this. In order to produce consistent results, managers have to be concerned with producing high-quality and innovative products and services for their customers, attracting and retaining talented employees, and complying with a plethora of complex government regulations. As a practical matter, managers direct their energies toward all stakeholders, not just owners.

The *instrumental argument* says that stakeholder management is more effective as a corporate strategy. A wide range of studies have shown that companies that behave responsibly toward multiple stakeholder groups perform better financially, over the long run, than those that do not. (This empirical evidence is further explored in Chapters 3 and 4.) These findings make sense, because good relationships with stakeholders are themselves a source

[12] One summary of contrasting theories of the purpose of the firm appears in Margaret M. Blair, "Whose Interests Should Corporations Serve?" in Margaret M. Blair and Bruce K. MacLaury, *Ownership and Control: Rethinking Corporate Governance for the Twenty-First Century* (Washington, DC: Brookings Institution, 1995), ch. 6, pp. 202–34. More recently, these questions have been taken up in James E. Post, Lee E. Preston, and Sybille Sachs, *Redefining the Corporation: Stakeholder Management and Organizational Wealth* (Palo Alto, CA: Stanford University Press, 2002).

[13] Novartis Corporation Code of Conduct, online at *www.novartis.com.*

[14] The descriptive, instrumental, and normative arguments are summarized in Thomas Donaldson and Lee E. Preston, "The Stakeholder Theory of the Corporation: Concepts, Evidence and Implications," *Academy of Management Review* 20, no. 1 (1995), pp. 65–71. See also, Post, Preston, and Sachs, *Redefining the Corporation,* ch. 1.

of value for the firm. Attention to stakeholders' rights and concerns can help produce motivated employees, satisfied customers, and supportive communities, all good for the company's bottom line.

The *normative argument* says that stakeholder management is simply the right thing to do. Corporations have great power and control vast resources; these privileges carry with them a duty toward all those affected by a corporation's actions. Moreover, all stakeholders, not just owners, contribute something of value to the corporation. A skilled engineer at Microsoft who applies his or her creativity to solving a difficult programming problem has made a kind of investment in the company, even if it is not a monetary investment. Any individual or group who makes a contribution, or takes a risk, has a moral right to some claim on the corporation's rewards.[15]

A basis for both the ownership and stakeholder theories of the firm exists in law. The legal term *fiduciary* means a person who exercises power on behalf of another, that is, who acts as the other's agent. In U.S. law, managers are considered fiduciaries of the owners of the firm (its stockholders) and have an obligation to run the business in their interest. These legal concepts are clearly consistent with the ownership theory of the firm. However, other laws and court cases have given managers broad latitude in the exercise of their fiduciary duties. In the United States (where corporations are chartered not by the federal government but by the states), most states have passed laws that permit managers to take into consideration a wide range of other stakeholders' interests, including those of employees, customers, creditors, suppliers, and communities. In addition, many federal laws extend specific protections to various groups of stakeholders, such as those that prohibit discrimination against employees or grant consumers the right to sue if harmed by a product.

In other nations, the legal rights of nonowner stakeholders are often more fully developed than in the United States. For example, a number of European countries—including Germany, Norway, Austria, Denmark, Finland, and Sweden—require public companies to include employee members on their boards of directors, so that their interests will be explicitly represented. Under the European Union's so-called harmonization statutes, managers are specifically permitted to take into account the interests of customers, employees, creditors, and others.

In short, while the law requires managers to act on behalf of stockholders, it also gives them wide discretion—and in some instances requires them—to manage on behalf of the full range of stakeholder groups. The next section provides a more formal definition and an expanded discussion of the stakeholder concept.

The Stakeholder Concept

The term **stakeholder** refers to persons and groups that affect, or are affected by, an organization's decisions, policies, and operations.[16] The word *stake*, in this context, means an interest in—or claim on—a business enterprise. Those with a stake in the firm's actions

---

[15] Another formulation of this point has been offered by Robert Phillips, who argues for a principle of stakeholder fairness. This states that "when people are engaged in a cooperative effort and the benefits of this cooperative effort are accepted, obligations are created on the part of the group accepting the benefit" [i.e., the business firm]. Robert Phillips, *Stakeholder Theory and Organizational Ethics* (San Francisco: Berrett-Koehler, 2003), p. 9 and ch. 5.

[16] The term *stakeholder* was first introduced in 1963 but was not widely used in the management literature until the publication of R. Edward Freeman's *Strategic Management: A Stakeholder Approach* (Marshfield, MA: Pitman, 1984). For more recent summaries of the stakeholder theory literature, see Thomas Donaldson and Lee E. Preston, "The Stakeholder Theory of the Corporation: Concepts, Evidence, Implications," *Academy of Management Review*, January 1995, pp. 71–83; Max B. E. Clarkson, ed., *The Corporation and Its Stakeholders: Classic and Contemporary Readings* (Toronto: University of Toronto Press, 1998); and Abe J. Zakhem, Daniel E. Palmer, and Mary Lyn Stoll, *Stakeholder Theory: Essential Readings in Ethical Leadership and Management* (Amherst, NY: Prometheus Books, 2008).

include such diverse groups as customers, employees, stockholders, the media, governments, professional and trade associations, social and environmental activists, and nongovernmental organizations. The term *stakeholder* is not the same as *stockholder*, although the words sound similar. Stockholders—individuals or organizations that own shares of a company's stock—are one of several kinds of stakeholders.

Business organizations are embedded in networks involving many participants. Each of these participants has a relationship with the firm, based on ongoing interactions. Each of them shares, to some degree, in both the risks and rewards of the firm's activities. And each has some kind of claim on the firm's resources and attention, based on law, moral right, or both. The number of these stakeholders and the variety of their interests can be large, making a company's decisions very complex, as the Walmart example illustrates.

Managers make good decisions when they pay attention to the effects of their decisions on stakeholders, as well as stakeholders' effects on the company. On the positive side, strong relationships between a corporation and its stakeholders are an asset that adds value. On the negative side, some companies disregard stakeholders' interests, either out of the belief that the stakeholder is wrong or out of the misguided notion that an unhappy customer, employee, or regulator does not matter. Such attitudes often prove costly to the company involved. Today, for example, companies know that they cannot locate a factory or store in a community that strongly objects. They also know that making a product that is perceived as unsafe invites lawsuits and jeopardizes market share.

Different Kinds of Stakeholders

Business interacts with society in many diverse ways, and a company's relationships with various stakeholders differ.

Market stakeholders are those that engage in economic transactions with the company as it carries out its purpose of providing society with goods and services. Each relationship between a business and one of its market stakeholders is based on a unique transaction, or two-way exchange. Stockholders invest in the firm and in return receive the potential for dividends and capital gains. Creditors loan money and collect payments of interest and principal. Employees contribute their skills and knowledge in exchange for wages, benefits, and the opportunity for personal satisfaction and professional development. In return for payment, suppliers provide raw materials, energy, services, and other inputs; and wholesalers, distributors, and retailers engage in market transactions with the firm as they help move the product from plant to sales outlets to customers. All businesses need customers who are willing to buy their products or services.

The puzzling question of whether or not managers should be classified as stakeholders along with other employees is discussed in Exhibit 1.A.

Nonmarket stakeholders, by contrast, are people and groups who—although they do not engage in direct economic exchange with the firm—are nonetheless affected by or can affect its actions. Nonmarket stakeholders include the community, various levels of government, nongovernmental organizations, the media, business support groups, competitors, and the general public. Nonmarket stakeholders are not necessarily less important than others, simply because they do not engage in direct economic exchange with a business. On the contrary, interactions with such groups can be critical to a firm's success or failure, as shown in the following example.

In 2001, a company called Energy Management Inc. (EMI) announced a plan to build a wind farm about six miles off the shore of Cape Cod, Massachusetts, to supply clean, renewable power to New England customers. The project, called Cape Wind, immediately generated intense opposition from socially prominent residents

Are managers, especially top executives, stakeholders? This has been a contentious issue in stakeholder theory.

On one hand, the answer clearly is "yes." Like other stakeholders, managers are impacted by the firm's decisions. As employees of the firm, managers receive compensation—often very generous compensation, as shown in Chapter 14. Their managerial roles confer opportunities for professional advancement, social status, and power over others. Managers benefit from the company's success and are hurt by its failure. For these reasons, they might properly be classified as employees.

On the other hand, top executives are agents of the firm and are responsible for acting on its behalf. In the stakeholder theory of the firm, their role is to integrate stakeholder interests, rather than to promote their own more narrow, selfish goals. For these reasons, they might properly be classified as representatives of the firm itself, rather than as one of its stakeholders.

Management theory has long recognized that these two roles of managers potentially conflict. The main job of executives is to act for the company, but all too often they act primarily for themselves. Consider, for example, the many top executives of Lehman Brothers, MF Global, and Merrill Lynch, who enriched themselves personally at the expense of shareholders, employees, customers, and other stakeholders. The challenge of persuading top managers to act in the firm's best interest is further discussed in Chapter 14.

of Cape Cod and nearby islands, who were concerned that its 130 wind turbines would spoil the view and get in the way of boats. Opponents of the project were able to block its progress for more than a decade. Finally, in 2011, Cape Wind secured its final permits and made plans to build the wind farm.[17]

In this instance, the community was able to block the company's plans for more than a decade, even though it did not have a market relationship with it.

Theorists also distinguish between **internal stakeholders** and **external stakeholders**. Internal stakeholders are those, such as employees and managers, who are employed by the firm. They are "inside" the firm, in the sense that they contribute their effort and skill, usually at a company worksite. External stakeholders, by contrast, are those who—although they may have important transactions with the firm—are not directly employed by it. Figure 1.2 shows the market and nonmarket, and internal and external, stakeholders of business. (Of note, firms have no internal, nonmarket stakeholders.)

FIGURE 1.2
The Stakeholders of Business

	Market Stakeholders	Nonmarket Stakeholders
Internal Stakeholders	Employees Managers	
External Stakeholders	Stockholders Customers Creditors Suppliers Wholesalers and Retailers	Governments Communities Nongovernmental Organizations Business Support Groups Media Competitors

[17] The website of the project is at *www.capewind.org*. The story of the opposition to Cape Wind is told in Robert Whitcomb and Wendy Williams, *Cape Wind: Money, Celebrity, Energy, Class, Politics, and the Battle for Our Energy Future* (New York: PublicAffairs, 2008).

The classification of government as a nonmarket stakeholder has been controversial in stakeholder theory. Most theorists say that government is a nonmarket stakeholder (as does this book) because it does not normally conduct any direct market exchanges (buying and selling) with business. However, money often flows from business to government in the form of taxes and fees, and sometimes from government to business in the form of subsidies or incentives. Moreover, some businesses—defense contractors for example—*do* sell directly to the government and receive payment for goods and services rendered. For this reason, a few theorists have called government a market stakeholder of business. And, in a few cases, the government may take a direct ownership stake in a company—as the U.S. government did after the financial crisis of 2008–09 when it invested in several banks and auto companies, becoming a shareholder of these firms. Government also has special influence over business because of its ability to charter and tax corporations, as well as make laws that regulate their activities. The unique relationship between government and business is discussed throughout this book.

Other stakeholders also have some market and some nonmarket characteristics. For example, the media is normally considered a nonmarket stakeholder. However, business buys advertising time on television and radio and in newspapers—a market transaction. Similarly, companies may pay dues to support groups, such as the Chamber of Commerce. Communities are a nonmarket stakeholder, but receive taxes, philanthropic contributions, and other monetary benefits from businesses. These subtleties are further explored in later chapters.

Modern stakeholder theory recognizes that most business firms are embedded in a complex web of stakeholders, many of which have independent relationships with each other.[18] In this view, a business firm and its stakeholders are best visualized as an interconnected network. Imagine, for example, an electronics company, based in the United States, that produces smartphones, tablets, and music players. The firm employs people to design, engineer, and market its devices to customers in many countries. Shares in the company are owned by investors around the world, including many of its own employees and managers. Production is carried out by suppliers in Asia. Banks provide credit to the company, as well as to other companies. Competing firms sell their products to some of the same customers and also contract production to some of the same Asian suppliers. Nongovernmental organizations may seek to lobby the government concerning the firm's practices and may count some employees among their members. A visual representation of this company and its stakeholders is shown in Figure 1.3.

As Figure 1.3 suggests, some individuals or groups may play multiple stakeholder roles. Some theorists use the term *role sets* to refer to this phenomenon. For example, one person may work at a company but also live in the surrounding community, own shares of company stock in his or her 401(k) retirement account, and even purchase the company's products from time to time. This person has several stakes in a company's actions.

Later sections of this book (especially Chapters 14 through 19) will discuss in more detail the relationship between business and its various stakeholders.

Stakeholder Analysis

An important part of the modern manager's job is to identify relevant stakeholders and to understand both their interests and the power they may have to assert these interests. This process is called **stakeholder analysis**. The organization from whose perspective the

[18] Timothy J. Rowley, "Moving Beyond Dyadic Ties: A Network Theory of Stakeholder Influence," *Academy of Management Review* 22, no. 4 (October 1997).

FIGURE 1.3
A Firm and Its Stakeholders

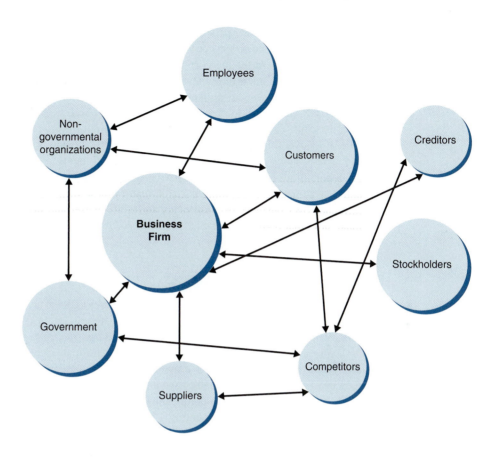

analysis is conducted is called the **focal organization**. Stakeholder analysis asks four key questions, as follows.

Who are the relevant stakeholders?

The first question requires management to identify and map the relevant stakeholders. Figure 1.2 provides a guide. However, not all stakeholders listed will be relevant in every management situation. For example, a privately held firm will not have stockholders. Some businesses sell directly to customers online and therefore will not have retailers. In other situations, a firm may have a stakeholder—say, a creditor that has loaned money—but this group is not relevant to a particular decision or action that management must take.

But stakeholder analysis involves more than simply *identifying* stakeholders; it also involves understanding the nature of their interests, power, legitimacy, and links with one another.

Stakeholder Interests

What are the interests of each stakeholder?

Each stakeholder has a unique relationship to the organization, and managers must respond accordingly. **Stakeholder interests** are, essentially, the nature of each group's stake. What are their concerns, and what do they want from their relationship with the firm?[19]

---

[19] A full discussion of the interests of stakeholders may be found in R. Edward Freeman, *Ethical Theory and Business* (Englewood Cliffs, NJ: Prentice Hall, 1994).

Stockholders, for their part, have an ownership interest in the firm. In exchange for their investment, stockholders expect to receive dividends and, over time, capital appreciation. The economic health of the corporation affects these people financially; their personal wealth—and often, their retirement security—is at stake. They may also seek social objectives through their choice of investments. Customers, for their part, are most interested in gaining fair value and quality in exchange for the purchase price of goods and services. Suppliers, likewise, wish to receive fair compensation for products and services they provide. Employees, in exchange for their time and effort, want to receive fair compensation and an opportunity to develop their job skills. Governments, public interest groups, and local communities have another sort of relationship with the company. In general, their stake is broader than the financial stake of owners, customers, and suppliers. They may wish to protect the environment, assure human rights, or advance other broad social interests. Managers need to understand these complex and often intersecting stakeholder interests.

Stakeholder Power

What is the power of each stakeholder?

Stakeholder power means the ability to use resources to make an event happen or to secure a desired outcome. Stakeholders have five different kinds of power: *voting power, economic power, political power, legal power,* and *informational power.*

Voting power means that the stakeholder has a legitimate right to cast a vote. Stockholders typically have voting power proportionate to the percentage of the company's stock they own. Stockholders typically have an opportunity to vote on such major decisions as mergers and acquisitions, the composition of the board of directors, and other issues that may come before the annual meeting. (Stockholder voting power should be distinguished from the voting power exercised by citizens, which is discussed below.)

> For example, Starboard Value LP, a New York–based hedge fund, used its voting power as a shareholder to force change in a company it had invested in. In 2011, Starboard bought more than 5 percent of the shares of the hair care company Regis Corporation. Starboard asserted that Regis, which owned or operated more than 12,000 hair salons under the Supercuts, Cost Cutters, and Hair Club for Men and Women brands, was "bloated with costs and lacked operational focus." The hedge fund reached out to other shareholders and won majority support in a contentious campaign to replace three members of the board of directors with its own nominees. Regis subsequently replaced several top executives and set out to cut expenses.[20]

Customers, suppliers, and retailers have *economic power* with the company. Suppliers can withhold supplies or refuse to fill orders if a company fails to meet its contractual responsibilities. Customers may refuse to buy a company's products or services if the company acts improperly. Customers can boycott products if they believe the goods are too expensive, poorly made, or unsafe. Employees, for their part, can refuse to work under certain conditions, a form of economic power known as a strike or slowdown. Economic power often depends on how well organized a stakeholder group is. For example, workers who are organized into unions usually have more economic power than do workers who try to negotiate individually with their employers.

Governments exercise *political power* through legislation, regulations, or lawsuits. While government agencies act directly, other stakeholders use their political power

[20] "Regis Investor Wins 3 Board Seats in Proxy Fight," *Twin Cities Business,* October 27, 2011; "Regis Ousts COO Following Board Shake-Up," *Twin Cities Business,* January 24, 2012, at *www.tcbmag.com;* and "Is Regis About to Bring Down the Hammer?" [Minnesota] *Star Tribune,* January 25, 2012.

indirectly by urging government to use its powers by passing new laws or enacting regulations. Citizens may also vote for candidates that support their views with respect to government laws and regulations affecting business, a different kind of voting power than the one discussed above. Stakeholders may also exercise political power directly, as when social, environmental, or community activists organize to protest a particular corporate action.

Stakeholders have *legal power* when they bring suit against a company for damages, based on harm caused by the firm; for instance, lawsuits brought by customers for damages caused by defective products, brought by employees for damages caused by workplace injury, or brought by environmentalists for damages caused by pollution or harm to species or habitat. After the mortgage lender Countrywide collapsed, many institutional shareholders, such as state pension funds, sued Bank of America (which had acquired Countrywide) to recoup some of their losses.

Finally, stakeholders have *informational power* when they have access to valuable data, facts, or details. The disclosure (or nondisclosure) of information can be used to persuade, mobilize, or threaten others. With the explosive growth of technologies that facilitate the sharing of information, this kind of stakeholder power has become increasingly important.

> Consumers' ability to use social networks to share information about businesses they like—and do not like—has given them power they did not previously have. For example, Yelp Inc. operates a website where people can search for local businesses, post reviews, and read others' comments. Since its launch in 2004, Yelp has attracted more than 50 million users. Its reviewers collectively have gained considerable influence. Restaurants, cultural venues, hair salons, and other establishments can attract customers with five-star ratings and "People Love Us on Yelp" stickers in their windows—but, by the same token, can be badly hurt when reviews turn nasty. A recent study in the *Harvard Business Review* reported that a one-star increase in an independent restaurant's Yelp rating led to a 5 to 9 percent increase in revenue. Some businesses have complained that Yelp reviewers have too much power. "My business just died," said the sole proprietor of a housecleaning business. "Once they locked me into the 3.5 stars, I wasn't getting any calls."[21]

Activists often try to use all of these kinds of power when they want to change a company's policy. For example, human rights activists wanted to bring pressure on Unocal Corporation to change its practices in Burma, where it had entered into a joint venture with the government to build a gas pipeline. Critics charged that many human rights violations occurred during this project, including forced labor and relocations. In an effort to pressure Unocal to change its behavior, activists organized protests at stockholder meetings (*voting power*), called for boycotts of Unocal products (*economic power*), promoted local ordinances prohibiting cities from buying from Unocal (*political power*), brought a lawsuit for damages on behalf of Burmese villagers (*legal power*), and gathered information about government abuses by interviewing Burmese refugees and publishing the results online (*informational power*). These activists increased their chances of success by mobilizing many kinds of power. This combination of tactics eventually forced Unocal to pay compensation to people whose rights had been violated and to fund education and health care projects in the pipeline region.[22]

Exhibit 1.B provides a schematic summary of some of the main interests and powers of both market and nonmarket stakeholders.

Stakeholder Coalitions

An understanding of stakeholder interests and power enables managers to answer the final question of stakeholder analysis.

---

[21] "Is Yelp Fair to Businesses?" *PC World,* November 15, 2011.

[22] Further information about the campaign against Unocal is available at *www.earthrights.org/unocal.*

Exhibit 1.B

Stakeholders: Nature of Interest and Power

Stakeholder	Nature of Interest— Stakeholder Wishes To:	Nature of Power—Stakeholder Influences Company By:
Market Stakeholders		
Employees	■ Maintain stable employment in firm ■ Receive fair pay for work ■ Work in safe, comfortable environment	■ Union bargaining power ■ Work actions or strikes ■ Publicity
Stockholders	■ Receive a satisfactory return on investments (dividends) ■ Realize appreciation in stock value over time	■ Exercising voting rights based on share ownership ■ Exercising rights to inspect company books and records
Customers	■ Receive fair exchange: value and quality for money spent ■ Receive safe, reliable products	■ Purchasing goods from competitors ■ Boycotting companies whose products are unsatisfactory or whose policies are unacceptable
Suppliers	■ Receive regular orders for goods ■ Be paid promptly for supplies delivered	■ Refusing to meet orders if conditions of contract are breached ■ Supplying to competitors
Retailers Wholesalers	■ Receive quality goods in a timely fashion at reasonable Cost ■ Offer reliable products that consumers trust and value	■ Buying from other suppliers if terms of contract are unsatisfactory ■ Boycotting companies whose goods or policies are unsatisfactory
Creditors	■ Receive repayment of loans ■ Collect debts and interest	■ Calling in loans if payments are not made ■ Utilizing legal authorities to repossess or take over property if loan payments are severely delinquent

How are coalitions likely to form?

Not surprisingly, stakeholder interests often coincide. For example, consumers of fresh fruit and farmworkers who harvest that fruit in the field may have a shared interest in reducing the use of pesticides, because of possible adverse health effects from exposure to chemicals. When their interests are similar, stakeholders may form coalitions, temporary

Stakeholder	Nature of Interest—Stakeholder Wishes To:	Nature of Power—Stakeholder Influences Company By:
Nonmarket Stakeholders		
Communities	■ Employ local residents in the company ■ Ensure that the local environment is protected ■ Ensure that the local area is developed	■ Refusing to extend additional credit ■ Issuing or restricting operating licenses and permits ■ Lobbying government for regulation of the company's policies or methods of land use and waste disposal
Nongovernmental organizations	■ Monitor company actions and policies to ensure that they conform to legal and ethical standards, and that they protect the public's safety	■ Gaining broad public support through publicizing the issue ■ Lobbying government for regulation of the company
Media	■ Keep the public informed on all issues relevant to their health, well-being, and economic status ■ Monitor company actions	■ Publicizing events that affect the public, especially those that have negative effects
Business support groups (e.g., trade associations)	■ Provide research and information which will help the company or industry perform in a changing environment	■ Using its staff and resources to assist company in business endeavors and development efforts ■ Providing legal or "group" political support beyond that which an individual company can provide for itself
Governments	■ Promote economic development ■ Encourage social improvements ■ Raise revenues through taxes	■ Adopting regulations and laws ■ Issuing licenses and permits ■ Allowing or disallowing commercial activity
The general public	■ Protect social values ■ Minimize risks ■ Achieve prosperity for society	■ Supporting activists ■ Pressing government to act ■ Condemning or praising individual companies
Competitors	■ Compete fairly ■ Cooperate on industry-wide or community issues ■ Seek new customers	■ Pressing government for fair competition policies ■ Suing companies that compete unfairly

alliances to pursue a common interest. **Stakeholder coalitions** are not static. Groups that are highly involved with a company today may be less involved tomorrow. Issues that are controversial at one time may be uncontroversial later; stakeholders that are dependent on an organization at one time may be less so at another. To make matters more complicated, the process of shifting coalitions does not occur uniformly in all parts of a large corporation.

Stakeholders involved with one part of a large company often have little or nothing to do with other parts of the organization.

In recent years, coalitions of stakeholders have become increasingly international in scope. Communications technology has enabled like-minded people to come together quickly, even across political boundaries and many miles of separation. Smartphones, blogs, e-mail, faxes, and social networking sites have become powerful tools in the hands of groups that monitor how multinational businesses are operating in different locations around the world.

> In 2000, the Mexican government cancelled plans for a salt plant in a remote area on the Pacific coast, after groups from around the world rallied to oppose it. The proposed plant was a joint venture of Mitsubishi (a multinational corporation based in Japan) and the Mexican government. Together, they wanted to create jobs, taxes, and revenue by mining naturally occurring salt deposits along the Baja California coast. Environmentalists attacked the venture on the grounds that it would hurt the gray whales that migrated every year to a nearby lagoon to give birth to their young. In the past, such objections would probably have attracted little attention. But critics were able to use the Internet and the media to mobilize over 50 organizations worldwide to threaten a boycott of Mitsubishi. One million people wrote the company, demanding that it "save the gray whale." Although Mitsubishi was convinced that the whales would continue to thrive near the salt works, it found its plans blocked at every turn.[23]

This example illustrates how international networks of activists, coupled with the media's interest in such business and society issues, make coalition development and issue activism an increasingly powerful strategic factor for companies. Nongovernmental organizations regularly meet to discuss problems such as global warming, human rights, and environmental issues, just as their business counterparts do. Today, stakeholder coalitions are numerous in every industry and important to every company.

Stakeholder Salience and Mapping

Some scholars have suggested that managers pay the most attention to stakeholders possessing greater **salience**. (Something is *salient* when it stands out from a background, is seen as important, or draws attention.) Stakeholders stand out to managers when they have power, legitimacy, and urgency. The previous section discussed various forms of stakeholder power. *Legitimacy* refers to the extent to which a stakeholder's actions are seen as proper or appropriate by the broader society. *Urgency* refers to the time-sensitivity of a stakeholder's claim, that is, the extent to which it demands immediate action. The more of these three attributes a stakeholder possesses, the greater the stakeholder's salience and the more likely that managers will notice and respond.[24]

Managers can use the salience concept to develop a **stakeholder map**, a graphical representation of the relationship of stakeholder salience to a particular issue. Figure 1.4 presents a simple example of a stakeholder map. The figure shows the position of various stakeholders on a hypothetical issue—whether or not a company should shut down an

---

[23] H. Richard Eisenbeis and Sue Hanks, "When Gray Whales Blush," case presented at the annual meeting of the North American Case Research Association, October 2002.

[24] Ronald K. Mitchell, Bradley R. Agle, and Donna J. Wood, "Toward a Theory of Stakeholder Identification and Salience: Defining the Principle of Who and What Really Counts," *Academy of Management Review* 22, no. 4 (1997), pp. 853–86.

FIGURE 1.4

Stakeholder Map of a Proposed Plant Closure

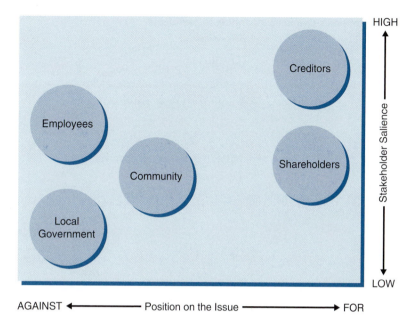

underperforming factory in a community. The horizontal axis represents each stakeholder's position on this issue—from "against" (the company should not shut the plant) to "for" (the company should shut the plant). The vertical axis represents the salience of the stakeholder, an overall measure of that stakeholder's power, legitimacy, and urgency. In this example, the company's creditors (banks) are pressuring the firm to close the plant. They have high salience, because they control the company's credit line and are urgently demanding action. Shareholders, who are powerful and legitimate (but not as urgent in their demands), also favor the closure. On the other side, employees urgently oppose shutting the plant, because their jobs are at stake, but they do not have as much power as the creditors and are therefore less salient. Local government officials and local businesses also wish the plant to remain open, but have lower salience than the other stakeholders involved.

A stakeholder map is a useful tool because it enables managers to see quickly how stakeholders feel about an issue and whether salient stakeholders tend to be in favor or opposed. It also helps managers see how stakeholder coalitions are likely to form and what outcomes are likely. In this example, company executives might conclude from the stakeholder map that those supporting the closure—creditors and shareholders—have the greatest salience. Although they are less salient, employees, local government officials, and the community all oppose the closure and may try to increase their salience by working together. Managers might conclude that the closure is likely, unless opponents organize an effective coaliton. This example is fairly simple; more complex stakeholder maps can represent network ties among stakeholders, the size of stakeholder groups, and the degree of consensus within stakeholder groups.[25]

---

[25] For two different approaches to stakeholder mapping, see David Saiia and Vananh Le, "Mapping Stakeholder Salience," presented at the International Association for Business and Society, June 2009; and Robert Boutilier, *Stakeholder Politics: Social Capital, Sustainable Development, and the Corporation* (Sheffield, UK: Greenleaf Publishing, 2009), chs. 6 and 7.

FIGURE 1.5   **The Corporation's Boundary-Spanning Departments**

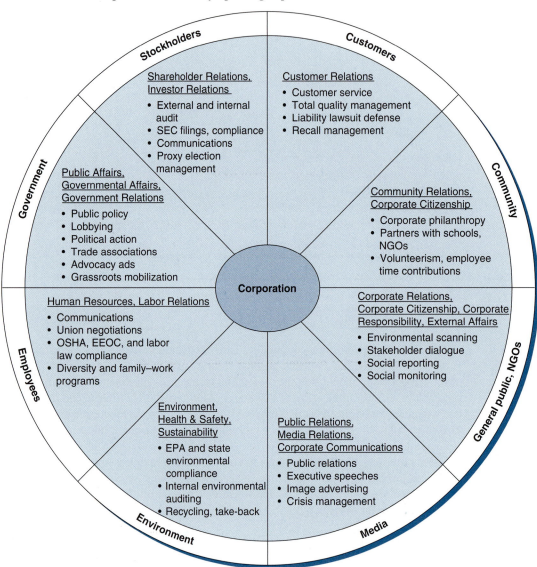

The Corporation's Boundary-Spanning Departments

How do corporations organize internally to respond to and interact with stakeholders?

Boundary-spanning departments are departments, or offices, within an organization that reach across the dividing line that separates the company from groups and people in society. Building positive and mutually beneficial relationships across organizational boundaries is a growing part of management's role.

Figure 1.5 presents a list of the corporation's market and nonmarket stakeholders, alongside the corporate departments that typically have responsibility for engaging with them. As the figure suggests, the organization of the corporation's boundary-spanning functions is complex. For example, in many companies, departments of public affairs or government relations interact with elected officials and regulators. Departments of investor relations interact with stockholders; human resources with employees; customer relations with customers; and community relations with the community. Specialized departments of environment, health, and safety may deal with environmental compliance and worker health and safety, and public relations or corporate communications with the media. Many of these specific departments will be discussed in more detail in later chapters.

The Dynamic Environment of Business

A core argument of this book is that *the external environment of business is dynamic and ever changing.* Businesses and their stakeholders do not interact in a vacuum. On the contrary, most companies operate in a swirl of social, ethical, global, political, ecological, and technological change that produces both opportunities and threats. Figure 1.6 diagrams the six dynamic forces that powerfully shape the business and society relationship. Each of these forces is introduced briefly below and will be discussed in more detail later in this book.

Changing societal expectations. Everywhere around the world, society's expectations of business are changing. People increasingly expect business to be more responsible, believing companies should pay close attention to social issues and act as good citizens in society. New public issues constantly arise that require action. Increasingly, business is faced with the daunting task of balancing its social, legal, and economic obligations, seeking to meet its commitments to multiple stakeholders. Modern businesses are increasingly exploring opportunities to act as social entrepreneurs often by focusing on those at the bottom of the pyramid. These changes in society's expectations of business, and how managers have responded, are described in Chapters 2 and 3.

FIGURE 1.6
Forces That Shape the Business and Society Relationship

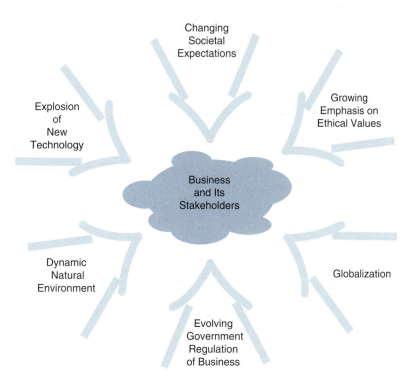

Growing emphasis on ethical reasoning and actions. The public also expects business to be ethical and wants corporate managers to apply ethical principles or values—in other words, guidelines about what is right and wrong, fair and unfair, and morally correct—when they make business decisions. Fair employment practices, concern for consumer safety, contribution to the welfare of the community, and human rights protection around the world have become more prominent and important. Business has created ethics programs to help ensure that employees are aware of these issues and act in accordance with ethical standards. The ethical challenges faced by business, both domestically and abroad—and business's response—are discussed in Chapters 4 and 5.

Globalization. We live in an increasingly integrated world economy, characterized by the unceasing movement of goods, services, and capital across national borders. Large transnational corporations do business in scores of countries. Products and services people buy every day in the United States or Germany may have come from Indonesia, Haiti, or Mexico. Today, economic forces truly play out on a global stage. A financial crisis on Wall Street can quickly impact economies around the world. Societal issues—such as the race to find a cure for HIV/AIDS, the movement for women's equality, or the demands of citizens everywhere for full access to the Internet—also cut across national boundaries. Environmental issues, such as ozone depletion and species extinction, affect all communities. Globalization challenges business to integrate their financial, social, and environmental performance. Chapters 6 and 7 address globalization and business firms' efforts to become better global citizens.

Evolving government regulations and business response. The role of government has changed dramatically in many nations in recent decades. Governments around the world have enacted a myriad of new policies that have profoundly constrained how business is allowed to operate. Government regulation of business periodically becomes tighter, then looser, much as a pendulum swings back and forth. Because of the dynamic nature of this force, business has developed various strategies to influence elected officials and government regulators at federal, state, and local levels. Business managers understand the opportunities that may arise from active participation in the political process. The changing role of government, its impact, and business's response are explored in Chapters 8 and 9.

Dynamic natural environment. All interactions between business and society occur within a finite natural ecosystem. Humans share a single planet, and many of our resources—oil, coal, and gas, for example—are nonrenewable. Once used, they are gone forever. Other resources, like clean water, timber, and fish, are renewable, but only if humans use them sustainably, not taking more than can be naturally replenished. Climate change now threatens all nations. The relentless demands of human society, in many arenas, have already exceeded the carrying capacity of the Earth's ecosystem. The state of the Earth's resources and changing attitudes about the natural environment powerfully impact the business–society relationship. These issues are explored in Chapters 10 and 11.

Explosion of new technology and innovation. Technology is one of the most dramatic and powerful forces affecting business and society. New technological innovations harness the human imagination to create new machines, processes, and software that address the needs, problems, and concerns of modern society. In recent years, the pace of technological change has increased enormously. From genetically modified foods to social networking via the Internet, from nanotechnology to wireless communications, change keeps coming. The extent and pace of technological innovation pose massive challenges for business, and sometimes government, as they seek to manage various privacy, security, and intellectual property issues embedded in this dynamic force. As discussed in Chapters 12 and 13, new technologies often force managers and organizations to examine seriously the ethical implications of their use.

Creating Value in a Dynamic Environment

These powerful and dynamic forces—fast-paced changes in societal and ethical expectations, the global economy, government policies, the natural environment, and new technology—establish the context in which businesses interact with their many market and nonmarket stakeholders, as discussed in Chapters 14 to 19. This means that the relationship between business and society is continuously changing in new and often unpredictable ways. Environments, people, and organizations change; inevitably, new issues will arise and challenge managers to develop new solutions. To be effective, corporations must meet the reasonable expectations of stakeholders and society in general. A successful business must meet *all* of its economic, social, and environmental objectives. A core argument of this book is that *the purpose of the firm is not simply to make a profit, but to create value for all its stakeholders.* Ultimately, business success is judged not simply by a company's financial performance but by how well it serves broad social interests.

Summary

- Business firms are organizations that are engaged in making a product or providing a service for a profit. Society, in its broadest sense, refers to human beings and to the social structures they collectively create. Business is part of society and engages in ongoing exchanges with its external environment. Together, business and society form an interactive social system in which the actions of each profoundly influence the other.

- According to the stakeholder theory of the firm, the purpose of the modern corporation is to create value for all of its stakeholders. To survive, all companies must make a profit for their owners. However, they also create many other kinds of value as well for their employees, customers, communities, and others. For both practical and ethical reasons, corporations must take all stakeholders' interests into account.

- Every business firm has economic and social relationships with others in society. Some are intended, some unintended; some are positive, others negative. Stakeholders are all those who affect, or are affected by, the actions of the firm. Some have a market relationship with the company, and others have a nonmarket relationship with it; some stakeholders are internal, and others are external.

- Stakeholders often have multiple interests and can exercise their economic, political, and other powers in ways that benefit or challenge the organization. Stakeholders may also act independently or create coalitions to influence the company. Stakeholder mapping is a technique for graphically representing stakeholders' relationship to an issue facing a firm.

- Modern corporations have developed a range of boundary-crossing departments and offices to manage interactions with market and nonmarket stakeholders. The organization of the corporation's boundary-spanning functions is complex. Most companies have many departments specifically charged with interacting with stakeholders.

- A number of broad forces shape the relationship between business and society. These include changing societal and ethical expectations; redefinition of the role of government; a dynamic global economy; ecological and natural resource concerns; and the transformational role of technology and innovation. To deal effectively with these changes, corporate strategy must address the expectations of all of the company's stakeholders.

Key Terms

boundary-spanning departments, *18*
business, *4*
external stakeholder, *9*
focal organization, *11*
general systems theory, *5*
interactive social system, *5*

internal stakeholder, *9*
ownership theory of the firm, *6*
society, *4*
stakeholder, *7*
stakeholder analysis, *10*
stakeholder coalitions, *15*
stakeholder interests, *11*
stakeholder map, *16*

stakeholder (market), *8*
stakeholder (nonmarket), *8*
stakeholder power, *12*
stakeholder salience, *16*
stakeholder theory of the firm, *6*

Internet Resources

www.businessweek.com
www.economist.com
www.fortune.com
www.nytimes.com
www.wsj.com
www.bloomberg.com
www.ft.com
www.cnnmoney.com

Bloomberg BusinessWeek
The Economist
Fortune
The New York Times
The Wall Street Journal
Bloomberg
Financial Times (London)
CNN Money

Discussion Case: *A Brawl in Mickey's Backyard*

Outside City Hall in Anaheim, California—home to the theme park Disneyland—dozens of protestors gathered in August 2007 to stage a skit. Wearing costumes to emphasize their point, activists playing "Mickey Mouse" and the "evil queen" ordered a group of "Disney workers" to "get out of town." The amateur actors were there to tell the city council in a dramatic fashion that they supported a developer's plan to build affordable housing near the world-famous theme park—a plan that Disney opposed.

"They want to make money, but they don't care about the employees," said Gabriel de la Cruz, a banquet server at Disneyland. De la Cruz lived in a crowded one-bedroom apartment near the park with his wife and two teenage children. "Rent is too high," he said. "We don't have a choice to go some other place."

The Walt Disney Company was one of the best-known media and entertainment companies in the world. In Anaheim, the company operated the original Disneyland theme park, the newer California Adventure, three hotels, and the Downtown Disney shopping district. The California resort complex attracted 24 million visitors a year. The company as a whole earned more than $35 billion in 2007, about $11 billion of which came from its parks and resorts around the world, including those in California.

Walt Disney, the company's founder, had famously spelled out the resort's vision when he said, "I don't want the public to see the world they live in while they're in Disneyland. I want them to feel they're in another world."

Anaheim, located in Orange County, was a sprawling metropolis of 350,000 that had grown rapidly with its tourism industry. In the early 1990s, the city had designated two square miles adjacent to Disneyland as a special resort district, with all new development restricted to serving tourist needs, and pumped millions of dollars into upgrading the area. In 2007, the resort district—5 percent of Anaheim's area—produced more than half its tax revenue.

Housing in Anaheim was expensive, and many of Disney's 20,000 workers could not afford to live there. The median home price in the community was more than $600,000, and a one-bedroom apartment could rent for as much as $1,400 a month. Custodians at the park earned around $23,000 a year; restaurant attendants around $14,000. Only 18 percent of resort employees lived in Anaheim. Many of the rest commuted long distances by car and bus to get to work.

The dispute playing out in front of City Hall had begun in 2005, when a local developer called SunCal had arranged to buy a 26-acre site in the resort district. (The parcel was directly across the street from land Disney considered a possible site for future expansion.) SunCal's plan was to build around 1,500 condominiums, with 15 percent of the units set aside for below-market-rate rental apartments. Because the site was in the resort district, the developer required special permission from the city council to proceed.

Affordable housing advocates quickly backed SunCal's proposal. Some of the unions representing Disney employees also supported the idea, as did other individuals and groups drawn by the prospect of reducing long commutes, a contributor to the region's air pollution. Backers formed the Coalition to Defend and Protect Anaheim, declaring that "these new homes would enable many . . . families to live near their places of work and thereby reduce commuter congestion on our freeways."

Disney, however, strenuously opposed SunCal's plan, arguing that the land should be used only for tourism-related development such as hotels and restaurants. "If one developer is allowed to build residential in the resort area, others will follow," a company spokesperson said. "Anaheim and Orange County have to address the affordable housing issue, but Anaheim also has to protect the resort area. It's not an either/or." In support of Disney's position, the chamber of commerce, various businesses in the resort district, and some local government officials formed Save Our Anaheim Resort District to "protect our Anaheim Resort District from non-tourism projects." The group considered launching an initiative to put the matter before the voters.

The five-person city council was split on the issue. One council member said that if workers could not afford to live in Anaheim, "maybe they can move somewhere else . . . where rents are cheaper." But another disagreed, charging that Disney had shown "complete disregard for the workers who make the resorts so successful."

Sources: "Disneyland Balks at New Neighbors," *USA Today,* April 3, 2007; "Housing Plan Turns Disney Grumpy," *The New York Times,* May 20, 2007; "In Anaheim, the Mouse Finally Roars," *Washington Post,* August 6, 2007; and "Not in Mickey's Backyard," *Portfolio,* December 2007.

Discussion Questions

1. What is the focal organization is this case, and what is the main issue it faces?
2. Who are the relevant market and nonmarket stakeholders in this situation?
3. What are the various stakeholders' interests? Please indicate if each stakeholder is in favor of, or opposed to, SunCal's proposed development.
4. What sources of power do the relevant stakeholders have?
5. Based on the information you have, draft a stakeholder map of this case. What conclusions can you draw from the stakeholder map?
6. What possible solutions to this dispute might emerge from dialogue between SunCal and its stakeholders?

Managing Public Issues and Stakeholder Relationships

Businesses today operate in an ever-changing external environment, where effective management requires anticipating emerging public issues and engaging positively with a wide range of stakeholders. Whether the issue is growing concerns about climate change, water scarcity, child labor, animal cruelty, or consumer safety, managers must respond to the opportunities and risks it presents. To do so effectively often requires building relationships across organizational boundaries, learning from external stakeholders, and altering practices in response. Effective management of public issues and stakeholder relationships builds value for the firm.

This Chapter Focuses on These Key Learning Objectives:

- Evaluating public issues and their significance to the modern corporation.
- Applying available tools or techniques to scan an organization's multiple environments.
- Describing the steps in the issue management process and determining how to make the process most effective.
- Identifying who is responsible for managing public issues and the skills required to do so effectively.
- Understanding how businesses can build collaborative relationships with stakeholders through engagement, dialogue, and network building.
- Identifying the benefits of stakeholder engagement to the business firm.

IKEA is the Scandinavian home furnishings retailer known for its distinctive yellow and blue big-box stores and stylish, inexpensive, and environmentally sound products. The firm's mission is "to create a better everyday life for the many people." In the late 1990s, the company's managers were startled by a documentary, broadcast on European television, showing young children in South Asia working under deplorable conditions making hand-woven rugs. The program named IKEA as one of several rug importers from that region. Shortly afterward, activists held protests outside several IKEA stores, demanding that it halt child labor in its supply chain. As the company's area manager for carpets later commented, "The use of child labor was not a high-profile public issue at the time. . . . We were caught completely unaware."

Rather than ignore the issue, IKEA responded by sending a legal team to Geneva to consult with the International Labour Organization. It promptly adopted a clause in all supply contracts stating that any supplier employing children under legal working age would be immediately terminated. The company also reached out to UNICEF (the United Nations Children's Fund) and Save the Children (a child-advocacy group) for further guidance about what actions to take.

After extensive consultation, IKEA decided to fund a community-development project in villages in the carpet-manufacturing region of northern India, which had been depicted in the documentary. Administered by UNICEF, the project provided alternative schooling, community loans, and vaccinations as a way to avoid the economic necessity for children to work. The company also integrated child labor issues into its established supplier auditing programs (set up initially to track environmental compliance), and instituted regular reviews of its rug suppliers. It later created a position of children's ombudsman to handle children's issues at the firm.

By 2012, IKEA, through its foundation, had donated more than $190 million to UNICEF for community development and child welfare in India. UNICEF commented on its website, "What makes IKEA a true partner is the company's deep commitment to social responsibility and their direct engagement with issues affecting children."[1]

IKEA's creative engagement with stakeholders on the issue of child labor went far beyond what was legally required. But it improved the firm's reputation with both customers and suppliers, avoided more serious conflict with activists, and produced positive outcomes that the company might not have been able to achieve on its own. IKEA had recognized an issue, reached out to stakeholders, and made a difference.

Public Issues

A **public issue** is any issue that is of mutual concern to an organization and one or more of its stakeholders. (Public issues are sometimes also called *social issues* or *sociopolitical issues*.) They are typically broad issues, often impacting many companies and groups, and of concern to a significant number of people. Public issues are often contentious—different groups may have different opinions about what should be done about them. They often, but not always, have public policy or legislative implications.

The emergence of a new public issue—such as concerns about child labor, mentioned in the opening example of this chapter—often indicates there is a *gap* between what the firm wants to do or is doing and what stakeholders expect. In the IKEA example, the company was sourcing products from suppliers who used child labor, a practice that offended many

[1] UNICEF, "International Partnerships: IKEA," at *www.unicef.org/corporate_partners*; and Christopher A. Bartlett, Vincent Dessain, and Anders Sjoman, "IKEA's Global Sourcing Challenge: Indian Rugs and Child Labor (A) and (B)," Cases # 9-906-414 and #9-906-415, 2006.

FIGURE 2.1

**The Performance–
Expectations Gap**

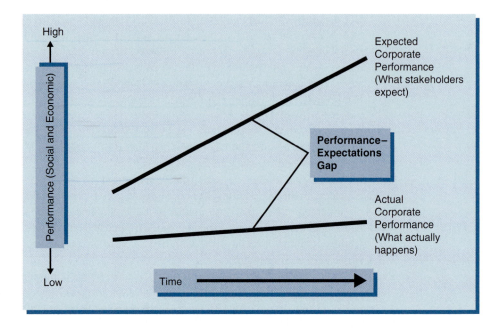

of its customers. Scholars have called this the **performance–expectations gap**. Stakeholder expectations are a mixture of people's opinions, attitudes, and beliefs about what constitutes reasonable business behavior. Managers and organizations have good reason to identify emergent expectations as early as possible. Failure to understand stakeholder concerns and to respond appropriately will permit the performance–expectations gap to grow: the larger the gap, the greater the risk of stakeholder backlash or of missing a major business opportunity. The performance–expectations gap is pictured in Figure 2.1.

Emerging public issues are both a risk and an opportunity. They are a risk because issues that firms do not anticipate and plan for effectively can seriously hurt a company. As the following examples show, sometimes a firm anticipates and addresses a public issue very well and other times it does not.

> Toyota, a Japanese automobile manufacturer with a history of attention to the safety of its automobiles, including the high-end Lexus model, was ill-prepared for the number and seriousness of the issues the firm encountered in 2010. A 911 call explained the problem: "We're in a Lexus . . . we're going north on 125 and our accelerator is stuck . . . we're in trouble . . . there's no brakes . . . we're approaching the intersection . . . hold on . . . hold on and pray. . . ." The call ended with the sound of a crash.
>
> By April 2010, Toyota had recalled more than 8 million vehicles because of a sticking gas pedal and a flaw in the design of the driver's side floor mats, both of which had apparently contributed to the sudden and uncontrolled acceleration experienced by some drivers. The firm also faced a $16.4 million fine from the U.S. National Highway Traffic Safety Administration with a threat of additional fines. Akio Toyoda, Toyota's president, admitted that the company lost sight of the importance of consumer safety and product quality, placing too much emphasis on market share and profitability.[2]

---

[2] "Toyota Faces $16.4 Million U.S. Fine," *The Wall Street Journal*, April 6, 2010, *online.wsj.com* and "Toyoda Concedes Profit Focus Led to Flaws," *The Wall Street Journal*, March 1, 2010, *online.wsj.com*.

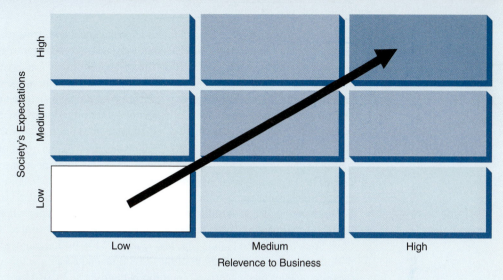

Source: Committee Encouraging Corporate Philanthropy, *Shaping the Future: Solving Social Problems through Business Strategy* (New York: CECP, 2010), Exhibit 11, p. 22. Used by permission.

On the other hand, correctly anticipating the emergence of an issue can confer a competitive advantage. The same firm, Toyota, was one of the first firms to recognize that growing public concern about the environment and related government regulations would spur demand for fuel-efficient and low-emission vehicles. As a result, the company got an early start on developing gas–electric engines and is today the leading producer of such vehicles. In 2011, Toyota announced that it had sold more than 3 million Priuses and other hybrid models since their introduction in 1989, exceeding all expectations.[3]

Understanding and responding to changing societal expectations is a business necessity. As Mark Moody-Stuart, former managing director of Royal Dutch/Shell, put it in an interview, "Communication with society . . . is a commercial matter, because society is your customers. It is not a soft and wooly thing, because society is what we depend on for our living. So we had better be in line with its wishes, its desires, its aspirations, its dreams."[4]

What issues should companies prioritize? Recent research suggests that issues become "ripe" for company action when two factors are present: society's expectations are high, and the issue is highly relevant to the business. This relationship is shown in Exhibit 2.A. Society's expectations may rise when people perceive an issue to be serious, believe the company is in some way responsible, and are willing to collaborate with other stakeholders to bring about change. An issue may be expecially relevant when it is likely to affect the company significantly, and the company has core competencies to address it. For example, the issue of water scarcity (explored in the discussion case at the end of this chapter) became ripe for action by the Coca-Cola Company when both society's expectations and its relevance to the firm became high.

Every company faces many public issues. Some emerge over a long period of time; others emerge suddenly. Some are predictable; others are completely unexpected. Some

[3] "Worldwide Sales of TMC Hybrids Top 3 Million," March 8, 2011, at *www.toyota.com.*

[4] Interview conducted by Anne T. Lawrence, "Shell Oil in Nigeria," interactive online case published by *www.icase.co.*

companies respond effectively; others do not. Consider the following recent examples of public issues and companies' responses:

- *Climate change*: Lafarge, a French multinational cement company, recognized that 5 percent of all man-made carbon dioxide emissions, a key contributor to global warming and a growing public concern, came from the cement industry. Lafarge partnered with the World Wildlife Foundation to reduce the levels of carbon dioxide emissions by 20 percent per ton by improving the energy efficiency of its plants and using locally available alternatives to fossil fuels, such as used tires and coffee husks. In 2010, the company achieved its goals ahead of schedule and adopted new, more aggressive targets.[5]

- *Executive pay and bonuses*: In 2010, Congress stepped in and questioned executive salaries and bonuses at Freddie Mac and Fannie Mae, government-sponsored financial institutions dealing with secondary mortgages and securities. "If $900,000 base salary isn't enough to get someone qualified in that position, I don't know what is. You don't have to bonus them another $2.3 million—it is just too much especially when those two entities owe the American taxpayers so much money," explained a member of Congress. At the time, Freddie Mac and Fannie Mae had received $170 billion in government bailout support, the most expensive bailout of the 2008 financial crisis, yet the top 10 executives at these companies made nearly $13 million in bonuses in 2010. After conducting hearings on this issue, Congress ruled that the salaries of the top 70 Fannie Mae and Freddie Mac executives would be limited to $500,000 per year and their annual bonuses eliminated.[6,7]

- *Food safety*: Outbreaks of E. coli, salmonella, and other food-borne illnesses were on the rise in the early years of the century. In 2011, 29 people died and nearly 3,000 were sickened by a virulent bacterial outbreak traced to organic sprouts from a farm in Germany. Urgent calls for action by consumer advocates, health care professionals, and political figures led to new and more stringent government standards for the processing and storage of vegetables and other food products in many countries. Growers, food companies, and restaurants scrambled to catch up with the new rules.[8]

- *Privacy*: Privacy advocates throughout Europe, where laws were more stringent than in the United States, protested the introduction of Google's Street View, an addition to the search firm's popular mapping service. Street View shows a driver's-eye view of the ground level of streets, buildings, and people. Google collected the images using specially equipped cameras mounted on cars. A Frenchman, who had decided to urinate in his front yard, was photographed by one of Google's Street View vehicles and sued Google for €10,000 ($13,300) in damages and demanded that Google remove the image.[9]

Environmental Analysis

As new public issues arise, businesses must respond. Organizations need a systematic way of identifying, monitoring, and selecting public issues that warrant organizational action because of the risks or opportunities they present. Organizations rarely have full control of

[5] "Sustainability 10th Report, 2010," at *www.lafarge.com.*

[6] Quote is by Congressman Darrell Issa, from "Fannie, Freddie CEOs Agree to Face Congress over Bonuses," *Housingwire,* November 14, 2011, *housingwire.com.* Other information is from "Fannie, Freddie Executive Pay Limited, Bonuses Cut," *Daily Herald,* March 9, 2012, *www.dailyherald.com.*

[7] "House Approves 90% Tax on Bonuses after Bailouts," *The New York Times,* March 20, 2009, *www.nytimes.com.*

[8] "Germany Says Bean Sprouts Are Likely E. Coli Source," *The New York Times,* June 10, 2011, *www.nytimes.com.*

[9] "Google Faces 'Street View Block,'" *BBC News,* July 4, 2008, *newsvote.bbc.co.uk;* "Google Pulls Some Street Images," *BBC News,* March 20, 2009, *newsvote.bbc.co.uk;* and "Google Street View Has Patent, Urination Problems," *Search Engine Watch,* March 5, 2012, *searchenginewatch.com.*

FIGURE 2.2
Eight Strategic Radar Screens

Source: Karl A. Albrecht, *Corporate Radar: Tracking the Forces That Are Shaping Your Business* (New York: American Management Association, 2000).

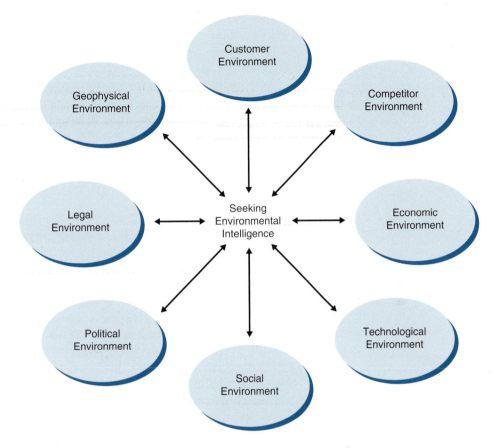

a public issue because of the many factors involved. But it is possible for the organization to create a management system that identifies and monitors issues as they emerge.

To identify those public issues that require attention and action, a firm needs a framework for seeking out and evaluating environmental information. (In this context, *environmental* means *outside the organization*; in Chapters 10 and 11, the term refers to the natural environment.) **Environmental analysis** is a method managers use to gather information about external issues and trends, so they can develop an organizational strategy that minimizes threats and takes advantage of new opportunities.

Environmental intelligence is the acquisition of information gained from analyzing the multiple environments affecting organizations. Acquiring this information may be done informally or as a formal management process. If done well, this environmental intelligence can help an organization avoid crises and spot opportunities.

According to management scholar Karl Albrecht, scanning to acquire environmental intelligence should focus on eight *strategic radar screens*,[10] Radar is an instrument that uses microwave radiation to detect and locate distant objects, which are often displayed on a screen; law enforcement authorities use radar, for example, to track the speed of passing cars. Albrecht uses the analogy of radar to suggest that companies must have a way of tracking important developments that are outside of their immediate view. He identifies eight different environments that managers must systematically follow. These are shown in Figure 2.2 and described next.

[10] Adapted from Karl Albrecht, *Corporate Radar: Tracking the Forces That Are Shaping Your Business* (New York: American Management Association, 2000).

- *Customer environment* includes the demographic factors, such as gender, age, marital status, and other factors, of the organization's customers as well as their social values or preferences. For example, the "graying" of the population as members of the baby boom generation age has created opportunities for developers that specialize in building communities for active older adults and for medical providers with a specialization in geriatric health care.

- *Competitor environment* includes information on the number and strength of the organization's competitors, whether they are potential or actual allies, patterns of aggressive growth versus static maintenance of market share, and the potential for customers to become competitors if they "insource" products or services previously purchased from the organization. (This environment is discussed further in the next section of this chapter.)

- *Economic environment* includes information about costs, prices, international trade, and any other features of the economic environment. The severe recession that hit the world's economy beginning in 2008 greatly shifted the behavior of customers, suppliers, creditors, and other stakeholders, dramatically impacting decision making in many firms.

- *Technological environment* includes the development of new technologies and their applications affecting the organization, its customers, and other stakeholder groups. Faster access to information through smartphones, PDAs, and other handheld electronic devices changed how people around the world were alerted to the devastation of natural disasters or terrorist actions and how they could be contacted regarding new job openings or the launching of innovative consumer products.

- *Social environment* includes cultural patterns, values, beliefs, trends, and conflicts among the people in the societies where the organization conducts business or might conduct business. Issues of civil or human rights, family values, and the roles of special interest groups are important elements in acquiring intelligence from the social environment.

- *Political environment* includes the structure, processes, and actions of all levels of government—local, state, national, and international. Awareness of the stability or instability of governments and their inclination or disinclination to pass laws and regulations is essential environmental intelligence for the organization. The emergence of strict environmental laws in Europe—including requirements to limit waste and provide for recycling at the end of a product's life—have caused firms all over the world that sell to Europeans to rethink how they design and package their products.

- *Legal environment* includes patents, copyrights, trademarks, and considerations of intellectual property, as well as antitrust considerations and trade protectionism and organizational liability issues. China's commitment in 2011 to dramatically increase its patent filings from 300,000 annually to one million by 2015 sent shock waves through the global business community. In comparison, about 500,000 patent applications are filed in the United States each year.

- *Geophysical environment* relates to awareness of the physical surroundings of the organization's facilities and operations, whether it is the organization's headquarters or its field offices and distribution centers, and the organization's dependency and impact on natural resources such as minerals, water, land, or air. Growing concerns about global warming and climate change, for example, have caused many firms to seek to improve their energy efficiency.

The eight strategic radar screens represent a system of interrelated segments, each one connected to and influencing the others.

Companies do not become experts in acquiring environmental intelligence overnight. New attitudes have to be developed, new routines learned, and new policies and action programs designed. Many obstacles must be overcome in developing and implementing the effective scanning of the business environments. Some are structural, such as the reporting relationships between groups of managers; others are cultural, such as changing traditional ways of doing things. In addition, the dynamic nature of the business environments requires organizations to continually evaluate their environmental scanning procedures.

Competitive Intelligence

One of the eight environments discussed by Albrecht is the competitor environment. The term **competitive intelligence** refers to the systematic and continuous process of gathering, analyzing, and managing external information about the organization's competitors that can affect the organization's plans, decisions, and operations. (As discussed in Chapter 1, competitors may be considered a nonmarket stakeholder of business.) The acquisition of this information benefits an organization by helping it better understand what other companies in its industry are doing. Competitive intelligence enables managers in companies of all sizes to make informed decisions ranging from marketing, research and development, and investing tactics to long-term business strategies. "During difficult times, excellent competitive intelligence can be the differentiating factor in the marketplace," explained Paul Meade, vice president of the research and consulting firm Best Practices. "Companies that can successfully gather and analyze competitive information, then implement strategic decisions based on that analysis, position themselves to be ahead of the pack."[11]

Clearly, numerous ethical issues are raised in the acquisition and use of competitive intelligence. Business managers must be aware of these issues, often clarified in the organization's code of ethics.[12] The importance of ethical considerations when collecting competitive intelligence cannot be understated, as illustrated by the following examples.

> In February 2011, Adrian Jones began a new job at Oracle after being the head of enterprise sales for Hewlett-Packard's Asia region. He allegedly took with him a USB drive that contained hundreds of files and thousands of e-mails with proprietary and valuable information about Hewlett-Packard's products and customers. Hewlett-Packard filed a lawsuit against Jones demanding the return of all documents.
>
> This incident closely paralleled a Ford Motor Company situation in 2009, in which a former Ford engineer allegedly stole thousands of sensitive documents, copied them onto a USB drive, and intended to deliver them to his new job at an unnamed company in China. The engineer was apprehended on his way to China at the Chicago O'Hare airport.
>
> Similar incidents also occurred at DuPont, Motorola, and Intel. A U.S. attorney said, "Employees and employers should be aware that stealing proprietary trade secrets to gain an economic advantage is a serious federal offense that will be prosecuted aggressively."[13]

---

[11] See Best Practices report at: *www.benchmarkingreports.com/competitiveintelligence.*

[12] For information about the professional association focusing on competitive intelligence, particularly with attention to ethical considerations, see the Strategic and Competitive Intelligence Professionals' website at: *www.scip.org.*

[13] "Hewlett-Packard Sues Former Exec at Oracle," *Reuters*, April 6, 2011, *www.reuters.com;* and "Ex-Ford Engineer Indicted for Allegedly Stealing Company Secrets," *Security Dark Reading*, October 16, 2009, *www.darkreading.com.* Also see "Engineer Gets 4 Years in Motorola Secrets Case," *The Wall Street Journal*, August 29, 2012, *online.wsj.com.*

As the Hewlett-Packard and Ford Motor Company attempted theft stories indicate, the perceived value of trade secrets or other information may be so great that businesses or their employees may be tempted to use unethical or illegal means to obtain such information (or provide it to others). However, competitive intelligence acquired ethically remains one of the most valued assets sought by businesses. A business must balance the importance of acquiring information about its competitors' practices with the need to comply with all applicable laws, domestic and international, and to follow the professional standards of fairness and honesty. Disclosure of all relevant information prior to conducting an interview and avoidance of conflicts of interest are just a few of the ethical guidelines promoted by the Strategic and Competitive Intelligence Professional's code of ethics.

The Issue Management Process

Once a company has identified a public issue and detects a gap between society's expectations and its own practices, what are its next steps? Proactive companies do not wait for something to happen; they actively manage issues as they arise. The process of doing so is called **issue management**. The **issue management process**, illustrated in Figure 2.3, has five steps or stages.[14] Each of these steps is explained below, using the example of McDonald's response to emerging stakeholder concerns about the humane treatment of farm animals raised for food. As the largest buyer of pork in the United States, McDonald's was vulnerable to stakeholder pressure on this issue, but also was well positioned to take action and move ahead of its competitors. But, as this example also illustrates, even a strong corporate response does not completely close an issue, since it may arise again in a new form. In McDonald's case, it had earlier responded to stakeholder concerns about its

FIGURE 2.3
The Issue Management Process

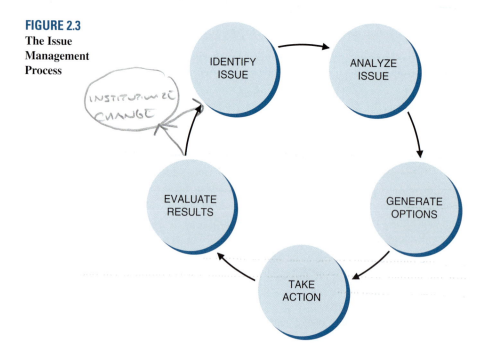

[14] Other depictions of the development and management of public issues may be found in Rogene Buchholz, *Public Issues for Management,* 2nd ed. (Englewood Cliffs, NJ: Prentice Hall, 1992); Robert Heath, *Strategic Issues Management* (Thousand Oaks, CA: Sage, 1997); and Eli Sopow, *The Critical Issues Audit* (Leesburg, VA: Issues Action Publications, 1994).

suppliers' treatment of cows and chickens, but that did not prevent the animal cruelty issue from arising again—this time, involving pigs.

Identify Issue

Issue identification involves anticipating emerging concerns, sometimes called "horizon issues" because they seem to be just coming up over the horizon like the first morning sun. Sometimes managers become aware of issues by carefully tracking the media, experts' views, activist opinion, and legislative developments to identify issues of concern to the public. Normally, this requires attention to all eight of the environments described in Figure 2.2. Organizations often use techniques of data searching, media analysis, and public surveys to track ideas, themes, and issues that may be relevant to their interests all over the world. They also rely on ongoing conversations with key stakeholders. Sometimes, awareness of issues is forced on companies by lawsuits or protests by activists who hold strong views about a particular matter.

> When McDonald's reintroduced its McRib sandwich in 2011, the U.S. Humane Society filed a legal complaint contending that McDonald's pork supplier was guilty of inhumane practices. According to a 2010 undercover Humane Society investigation, Smithfield Foods, the world's largest pork producer and a supplier to McDonald's, kept their female pigs in confined gestation crates. The crates were about 2 feet by 7 feet, too small for a pregnant pig to turn around. The crates were often coated in blood from pigs chewing the metal bars of the cages, prematurely born piglets fell through gate slates into a manure pit, and in one instance a pig was shot in the head with a bolt gun and thrown into a dumpster while still alive, as reported by *The Atlantic* magazine.
>
> The Humane Society's complaint was followed by an animated short film released online featuring the Coldplay song "The Scientist," sung by Willie Nelson. It featured a farmer who experienced a crisis of conscience, prompting him to abandon factory-like farming methods and free his pigs, chickens, and cows from confinement. Within months it had more than 4.6 million views on YouTube. "It's just wrong to immobilize animals for their whole lives in crates barely larger than their bodies," said the president of the U.S. Humane Society.[15]

McDonald's had been aware of animal welfare issues for some time, having proactively responded to questions of animal cruelty to cows and chickens a decade earlier. But the Humane Society's challenge elevated the urgency to the company of the issue of humane treatment of pigs and put it squarely on the agenda of managers.

Analyze Issue

Once an issue has been identified, its implications must be analyzed. Organizations must understand how the issue is likely to evolve, and how it is likely to affect them. For each company, the ramifications of the issue will be different.

How the animal welfare issue affected McDonald's was complex. On one hand, the company was concerned about public perception, and did not want customers to turn away because of concerns about the mistreatment of pigs used for food. On the other hand, it was also concerned about maintaining standards for food quality and keeping down costs. An added complexity was that McDonald's did not raise its own animals for slaughter, but

---

[15] "Humane Society Complaint Questions Conditions of McRib Pork Supplier," *Time Newsfeed*, November 3, 2011, *newsfeed.time.com;* and "McDonald's: Gestation Crates Have No Part in Pork Production," *Huffington Post*, February 13, 2012, *www.huffingtonpost.com.*

relied on a network of suppliers for its meat, including such major firms as Smithfield Foods, Hormel Food, and Cargill. In order to influence the treatment of animals, it would need to collaborate closely with companies in its supply chain and use lessons learned from earlier similar public issues.

> The pig-raising challenge paralleled the poultry industry's experience in the 1990s, which was attacked for their practices of keeping chickens in tight cages and other inhumane conditions. McDonald's aggressive response then helped jump-start changes in that industry. In 1999, McDonald's ordered their egg suppliers for the popular McMuffin sandwich to provide more space for laying hens. Shortly thereafter other fast-food chains followed suit.
>
> In response to the new issue of pig-raising, "there are alternatives that we think are better for the welfare of sows," McDonald's senior vice president said. In October 2011, in a joint statement with the Humane Society, the fast-food chain announced its decision to explore this issue and search for better practices. The Humane Society hailed this as a major victory in its fight against so-called gestation crates. "They do have the power to move an entire industry, to set an example that other food providers often follow," said the executive director of Mercy for Animals, a Chicago-based nonprofit animal rights group. "We hope it's a beginning of the end of these cruel and abusive practices."[16]

Generate Options

An issue's public profile indicates to managers how significant an issue is for the organization, but it does not tell them what to do. The next step in the issue management process involves generating, evaluating, and selecting among possible options. This requires complex judgments that incorporate ethical considerations, the organization's reputation and good name, and other nonquantifiable factors.

> Many of McDonald's competitors, including Burger King, Wendy's, and Hardee's, had already begun to move away from suppliers who used gestation crates. Alternative procedures for raising pigs included using larger and cleaner pens to house the pigs, permitting pigs more time outdoors for grazing and exercise, providing pigs with more nutritious diets, and a greater use of antibiotics to prevent diseases. McDonald's announcement to join in addressing this issue came a day after Chipotle Mexican Grill aired a nearly two-and-a-half-minute television commercial during the Grammy's televised award ceremony that touted Chipotle's ban on pork producers using the crates. "We're really looking to see a positive change regarding moving away from gestation stalls, and we think the best way to do that is working with our suppliers," a McDonald's spokeswoman said. "They're the ones that actually have to take action to make this happen."[17]

Selecting an appropriate response often involves a creative process of considering various alternatives and rigorously testing them to see how they work in practice.

---

[16] "McDonald's: Gestation Crates Have No Part in Pork Production," *Huffington Post*, February 13, 2012, *www.huffingtonpost.com;* and "McDonald's to Phase Out Pig Crates," *The Boston Globe*, February 14, 2012, *www.bostonglobe.com.*

[17] "McDonald's: Gestation Crates Have No Part in Pork Production," *Huffington Post*, February 13, 2012, *www.huffingtonpost.com;* and "Hog Heaven: Farmers Are Raising Pigs in Ways That Produce More Flavorful Meat and Are Better for the Pigs and the Environment," *Land Stewardship Project*, January 16, 2003, *www.landstewardshipproject.org.*

Take Action

Once an option has been chosen, the organization must design and implement a plan of action.

> McDonald's Corp. said in February 2012 that it would require five direct suppliers of bacon, Canadian bacon, sausage, and ribs to provide plans by May 2012 to phase out crates that tightly confined pregnant pigs, a move that one animal rights group predicted would have a "seismic impact" on the industry.[18]

Evaluate Results

Once an organization has implemented the issue management program, it must continue to assess the results and make adjustments if necessary. Many managers see issue management as a continuous process, rather than one that comes to a clear conclusion.

> After a review of the actions required in the February 2012 announcement, McDonald's said that it would explore all of its options to decide how to proceed. "It's a promising move," said the senior director of farm animal protection for the U.S. Humane Society. "No other fast-food company has done what McDonald's has done here."[19]

This example illustrates the complexity of the issue management process. Figure 2.3 is deliberately drawn in the form of a loop. When working well, the issue management process continuously cycles back to the beginning and repeats, pulling in more information, generating more options, and improving programmatic response. Such was the case with the concern over the treatment of pigs. McDonald's was committed to addressing the issue and knew that it needed to monitor the progress being made with its suppliers to fully address an emerging public issue.

Contemporary issue management is truly an interactive process, as forward-thinking companies must continually engage in a dialogue with their stakeholders about issues that matter, as McDonald's has learned. The new challenge from the Humane Society jump-started another round of discussions between company representatives and animal rights activists. As a result, all parties have continued to learn from one another. Managers must not only implement programs, but continue to reassess their actions to be consistent with both ethical practices and long-term survival.

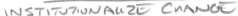

Organizing for Effective Issue Management

Who manages public issues? What departments and people are involved? There is no simple answer to this question. Figure 1.5, presented in Chapter 1, showed that the modern corporation has many boundary-spanning departments. Which part of the organization is mobilized to address a particular emerging issue often depends on the nature of the issue itself. For example, if the issue has implications for public policy or government regulations, the public affairs or government relations department may take a leadership role. (The public affairs department is futher discussed in Chapter 9.) If the issue is an environmental

---

[18] "McDonald's Teams Up with Humane Society to Phase Out Pig Crates," *National Public Radio: The Salt*, February 14, 2012, *www.npr.org/blogs/the salt*; and "McDonald's Set to Phase Out Suppliers' Use of Sow Crates," *The New York Times*, February 13, 2012, *www.nytimes.com*.

[19] "McDonald's Teams Up with Humane Society to Phase Out Pig Crates," *National Public Radio: The Salt*, February 14, 2012, *www.npr.org/blogs/the salt*.

one, the department of sustainability or environment, health, and safety may take on this role. Some companies combine multiple issue management functions in an office of external relations or corporate affairs. The following example illustrates how one company has organized to manage emerging public issues.

> BlueScope Steel, a flat steel product company based in Australia and New Zealand, created a Corporate Affairs office to manage relationships with a number of key external stakeholders. The office coordinates company efforts with the media, governments, industry bodies, and other steelmakers. Corporate Affairs produces regular media releases and announcements, and is responsible for managing the production of corporate reports, including the Annual Report and the Community, Safety and Environment Report. Corporate Affairs is also responsible for the management of communications with the company's 21,000 plus employees around the globe, including production of the company-wide employee newspaper, *Steel Connections*. BlueScope Steel maintains a sophisticated electronic communications system, including regular "Stop Press" e-mail announcements and an extensive corporate intranet site, in addition to the company's external Internet sites.

A corporation's issue management activities are usually linked to both the board of directors and to top management levels, because of their increasing importance. The Foundation for Public Affairs reported in 2011 that 70 percent of business executives say public affairs already plays an increasingly important or very important strategic role in their firms. Another 14 percent said that it was becoming more important. Despite widespread corporate budget cuts due to the recession, 80 percent of the corporate executives surveyed by the Foundation for Public Affairs reported that their firm's budgets for public issues had increased or remained the same between 2008 and 2011.[20]

What kinds of managers are best able to anticipate and respond effectively to emerging public issues? What skill sets are required? The European Academy of Business in Society (EABIS) undertook a major study of leaders in companies participating in the United Nations Global Compact. (This initiative, discussed in more detail in Chapter 7, is a set of basic principles covering labor, human rights, and environmental standards, to which companies can voluntarily commit.) The researchers were interested in the knowledge and skills required of what they called the "global leader of tomorrow."

They found that effective global leadership on these public issues required three basic capabilities, as schematically diagrammed in Exhibit 2.B. The first was an understanding of the changing business *context:* emerging environmental and social trends affecting the firm. The second was an ability to lead in the face of *complexity.* Many emerging issues, the researchers found, were surrounded by ambiguity; to deal with them, leaders needed to be flexible, creative, and willing to learn from their mistakes. The final capability was *connectedness:* the ability to engage with external stakeholders in dialogue and partnership. Although more than three-fourths of executives polled said that these skills were important, only 7 percent said their organization was developing them very effectively.[21]

We turn next to the topic of connectedness—how managers in today's corporations engage with stakeholders in the management of public issues.

---

[20] Public Affairs Goes Mainstream, *Public Affairs Council*, January 13, 2012, *pac/org/blog.*
[21] European Academy of Business in Society, *Developing the Global Leader of Tomorrow* (United Kingdom: Ashridge, December 2008). Based on a global survey of 194 CEOs and senior executives in September–October 2008.

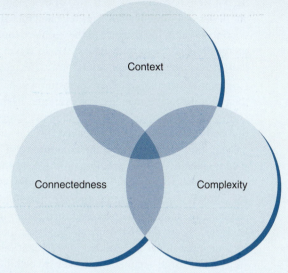

Source: Exhibit 3, "Three Clusters of Knowledge and Skills," p. 19, European Academy of Business in Society *Developing the Global Leader of Tomorrow* (United Kingdom: Ashridge, December 2008). Used by permission.

Stakeholder Engagement

One of the key themes of this book is that companies that actively engage with stakeholders do a better job of managing a wide range of issues than companies that do not. In the McDonald's example presented earlier in this chapter, one of the reasons that the company was quite successful in its response to the emerging issue of animal welfare was that it consulted widely with stakeholders such as the Humane Society. (This process is often ongoing, as McDonald's experienced when changing technology required the firm to re-establish critical dialogues with its stakeholders.) This section will further explore the various forms the business–stakeholder relationship takes, when stakeholder engagement is likely to occur, and how managers can engage with stakeholders most effectively.

Stages in the Business–Stakeholder Relationship

Over time, the nature of business's relationship with its stakeholders often evolves through a series of stages. Scholars have characterized these stages as *inactive, reactive, proactive,* and *interactive,* with each stage representing a deepening of the relationship. Sometimes, companies progress through this sequence from one stage to the next; other companies remain at one stage or another, or move backward in the sequence.[22]

- *Inactive* companies simply ignore stakeholder concerns. These firms may believe—often incorrectly—that they can make decisions unilaterally, without taking into consideration their impact on others. Stand 'n Seal Grout Sealer, a do-it-yourself home improvement product made by a company called BRTT, promised a "revolutionary fast way" to seal grout around tiles that was safe to use since any excess spray would

[22] This typology was first introduced in Lee Preston and James E. Post, *Private Management and Public Policy* (Englewood Cliffs, NJ: Prentice Hall, 1975). For a more recent discussion, see Sandra Waddock, *Leading Corporate Citizens: Visions, Values, and Value Added,* 2nd ed. (New York: McGraw-Hill, 2006), ch. 1.

"evaporate harmlessly." But the product was hardly harmless: dozens of people who used it were horribly sickened, two of them fatally, after breathing in dangerous chemical fumes. An investigation later revealed that BRTT tried to play down the hazard and contined to ship the product to the retailer Home Depot even after it had received numerous reports of serious illness. It said it had reformulated the product—although it had just changed the smell, not removed the hazardous ingredients.[23]

- Companies that adopt a *reactive* posture generally act only when forced to do so, and then in a defensive manner. For example, in the film *A Civil Action,* based on a true story, W. R. Grace (a company that was later bought by Beatrice Foods) allegedly dumped toxic chemicals that leaked into underground wells used for drinking water, causing illness and death in the community of Woburn, Massachusetts. The company paid no attention to the problem until forced to defend itself in a lawsuit brought by a crusading lawyer on behalf of members of the community.

- *Proactive* companies try to anticipate stakeholder concerns. These firms use the environmental scanning practices described earlier in this chapter to identify emerging public issues. They often have specialized departments, such as public affairs, community relations, consumer affairs, and government relations to manage stakeholder relationships. These firms are much less likely to be blindsided by crises and negative surprises. Stakeholders and their concerns are still, however, considered a problem to be managed, rather than a source of competitive advantage.

- Finally, an *interactive* stance means that companies actively engage with stakeholders in an ongoing relationship of mutual respect, openness, and trust. For example, in an effort to address continuing high unemployment rates, in 2011 Starbucks teamed with Opportunity Finance Network, a group of community development financial institutions, to launch "Create Jobs for USA." Donations from Starbucks customers, employees, and others were pooled into a nationwide fund to promote community business lending. The company also pledged $100,000 of profits annually from two stores located in low-income areas, the Harlem section of Manhattan, New York, and the Crenshaw neighborhood of Los Angeles, California, to create jobs and training for young adults living in those communities.[24] Firms with this approach recognize that positive stakeholder relationships are a source of value and competitive advantage for the company. They know that these relationships must be nurtured over time. The term **stakeholder engagement** is used to refer to this process of ongoing relationship building between a business and its stakeholders.

Drivers of Stakeholder Engagement

When are companies most likely to engage with stakeholders, that is, to be at the interactive stage? What drives companies further along in this sequence?

Stakeholder engagement is, at its core, a *relationship*. The participation of a business organization and at least one stakeholder organization is necessary, by definition, to constitute engagement. In one scholar's view, engagement is most likely when both the company and its stakeholders both have an urgent and important *goal,* the *motivation* to participate, and the *organizational capacity* to engage with one another. These three elements are presented in Figure 2.4.

Goals

For stakeholder engagement to occur, both the business and the stakeholder must have a problem that they want solved. The problem must be both important and urgent. Business

[23] "Dangerous Sealer Stayed on Shelves after Recall," *The New York Times,* October 8, 2008.

[24] "Starbucks Pushes to Create Jobs," *The Wall Street Journal*, October 5, 2011, *online.wsj.com.*

FIGURE 2.4
Drivers of
Stakeholder
Engagement

Source: Adapted from Anne
T. Lawrence, "The Drivers of
Stakeholder Engagement:
Reflections on the "Case of
Royal Dutch/Shell," *Journal of
Corporate Citizenship,* Summer
2002, pp. 71–85.

	Company	Stakeholder(s)
Goal	To improve corporate reputation; to earn a license to operate; to win approval of society	To change corporate behavior on an issue of concern
Motivation	Needs stakeholder involvement because of their expertise or control of critical resources	Governmental campaigns, protest perceived as inadequate to change corporate behavior
Organizational capacity	Top leaders committed to engagement; well-funded department of external (stakeholder) affairs	Experienced staff; core group of activists committed to dialogue with business

is often spurred to act when it recognizes a gap between its actions and public expectations, as discussed earlier. The company may perceive this gap as a reputational crisis or a threat to its license to operate in society. For their part, stakeholders are typically concerned about an issue important to them—whether child labor, animal cruelty, environmental harm, or something else—that they want to see addressed.

Motivation

Both sides must also be motivated to work with one another to solve the problem. For example, the company may realize that the stakeholder group has technical expertise to help it address an issue. Or, it needs the stakeholder's approval, because the stakeholder is in a position to influence policymakers, damage a company's reputation, or bring a lawsuit. Stakeholders may realize that the best way actually to bring about change is to help a company alter its behavior. In other words, both sides depend on each other to accomplish their goals; they cannot accomplish their objectives on their own. (Theorists sometimes refer to this as *interdependence.*)

Organizational Capacity

Each side must have the organizational capacity to engage the other in a productive dialogue. For the business, this may include support from top leadership and an adequately funded external affairs or comparable department with a reporting relationship to top executives. It may also include an issue management process that provides an opportunity for leaders to identify and respond quickly to shifts in the external environment. For the stakeholder, this means a leadership or a significant faction that supports dialogue and individuals or organizational units with expertise in working with the business community.

In short, engagement is most likely to occur where both companies and stakeholders perceive an important and urgent problem, see each other as essential to a solution, and have the organizational capacity to interact with one another.

Making Engagement Work Effectively

Companies have experimented with various engagement processes. These range from informal to formal, and from one-time-only interactions to fully institutionalized relationships. Engagement may take the form of focus groups, individual or small group interviews, surveys, key-person meetings, or advisory councils. In any event, the firm must invite stakeholders to participate, provide a forum for discussion, and sometimes offer financial or logistical support.

Sun Microsystems is an example of a company that has begun to institutionalize its stakeholder engagement process. The company has formed a Corporate Social Responsibility Stakeholder Committee, composed of representatives of major customers, investors, and environmental and human rights organizations. The company schedules regular telephone consultations, as well as face-to-face meetings, to air issues of common concern. During a discussion of the global nature of the business, one stakeholder team member suggested that the company adopt a human rights policy. After broad consultation, Sun did so—becoming one of just a few firms to have such a policy.

Sun's director of corporate sustainability and responsibility commented, "Working with external stakeholder groups allows Sun to get direct and meaningful feedback on the social and environmental aspects of our business performance. Admittedly, it isn't always easy to hear what they have to say, nor are we able to commit to all the things they ask of us. But every interaction we have with the stakeholder team so far has led to progress for Sun."[25]

The process of engagement can take many forms, but it often involves dialogue with stakeholders. One management theorist has defined dialogue as "the art of thinking together."[26] In **stakeholder dialogue**, a business and its stakeholders come together for face-to-face conversations about issues of common concern. There, they attempt to describe their core interests and concerns, define a common definition of the problem, invent innovative solutions for mutual gain, and establish procedures for implementing solutions. To be successful, the process requires that participants express their own views fully, listen carefully and respectfully to others, and open themselves to creative thinking and new ways of looking at and solving a problem. The promise of dialogue is that, together, they can draw on the understandings and concerns of all parties to develop solutions that none of them, acting alone, could have envisioned or implemented.[27]

PacifiCorp is a major electric utility, serving customers throughout the Pacific Northwest. In 2004, the company initiated the process of renewing the permits for seven hydroelectric dams it operated on the Klamath River, a massive waterway that ran 250 miles from southern Oregon into northern California and drained a 13,000 square mile watershed before emptying into the Pacific. Renewing the permits turned out to be highly contentious, as it impacted numerous stakeholders, including state and federal agencies, Native American tribes, fishermen, environmentalists, farmers, and recreational users, all with diverse interests. Finally, in 2010, after a lengthy collaborative process, the various stakeholders hammered out a historic pact, called the Klamath Basin Restoration Agreement, to remove the dams, restore habitat, and guarantee water for local farmers. PacifiCorp agreed to the plan when it realized that bringing the dams up to modern standards (the oldest had been built in 1903) would be more expensive than removing them. In 2012, the agreement—which one newspaper called "the equivalent of the Berlin wall coming down"—awaited congressional approval.[28]

[25] Author interview, July 8, 2009.

[26] William Isaacs, *Dialogue and the Art of Thinking Together* (New York: Doubleday, 1999).

[27] This section draws on the discussion in Anne T. Lawrence and Ann Svendsen, *The Clayoquot Controversy: A Stakeholder Dialogue Simulation* (Vancouver: Centre for Innovation in Management, 2002). The argument for the benefits of stakeholder engagement is fully developed in Ann Svendsen, *The Stakeholder Strategy: Profiting from Collaborative Business Relationships* (San Francisco: Berrett-Koehler, 1998).

[28] More information is available at: *www.pacificorp.com* and *www.sustainablenorthwest.org*.

Stakeholder Networks

Dialogue between a single firm and its stakeholders is sometimes insufficient to address an issue effectively. Corporations sometimes encounter public issues that they can address effectively only by working collaboratively with other businesses and concerned persons and organizations in **stakeholder networks**. One such issue that confronted Nike Inc. was a growing demand by environmentally aware consumers for apparel and shoes made from organic cotton.

> Cotton, traditionally cultivated with large quantities of synthetic fertilizers, pesticides, and herbicides, is one of the world's most environmentally destructive crops. In the late 1990s, in response both to consumer pressure and to its own internal commitments, Nike began for the first time to incorporate organic cotton into its sports apparel products. Its intention was to ramp up slowly, achieving 5 percent organic content by 2010. However, the company soon encountered barriers to achieving even these limited objectives. Farmers were reluctant to transition to organic methods without a sure market, processors found it inefficient to shut down production lines to clean them for organic runs, and banks were unwilling to loan money for unproven technologies. The solution, it turned out, involved extensive collaboration with groups throughout the supply chain—farmers, cooperatives, merchants, processors, and financial institutions—as well as other companies that were buyers of cotton, to facilitate the emergence of a global market for organic cotton. The outcome was the formation in 2003 of a new organization called the Organic Exchange, in which Nike has continued to play a leading role.[29]

In this instance, Nike realized that in order to reach its objective, it would be necessary to become involved in building a multi-party, international network of organizations with a shared interest in the issue of organic cotton.

The Benefits of Engagement

Engaging interactively with stakeholders—whether through dialogue, network building, or some other process—carries a number of potential benefits.[30]

Stakeholder organizations bring a number of distinct strengths. They often become aware of shifts in popular sentiment before companies do and thus are able to alert companies to emerging issues. For example, as described earlier in this chapter, the U.S. Humane Society brought the issue of animal cruelty to McDonald's attention and encouraged them to address it proactively. Stakeholders often operate in networks of organizations very different from the company's; interacting with them gives a firm access to information in these networks. Stakeholders often bring technical or scientific expertise in their area of concern. Finally, when a stakeholder agrees to work with a company on implementing a mutually agreed-upon solution, they can give the resulting work greater legitimacy in the eyes of the public. For example, when Coca-Cola partnered with the World Wildlife Fund and other nonprofit organizations to address stakeholder concerns about the company's impact on water quality and access—a story told in the discussion case at the end

---

[29] The website for the Organic Exchange is: *www.organicexchange.org*. Nike's description of its efforts is available online at: *www.nike.com/nikebiz*. This case is discussed in Ann C. Svendsen and Myriam Laberge, "Convening Stakeholder Networks: A New Way of Thinking, Being, and Engaging," *Journal of Corporate Citizenship* 19 (Autumn 2005), pp. 91–104.

[30] The following paragraph is largely based on the discussion in Michael Yaziji and Jonathan Doh, *NGOs and Corporations: Conflict and Collaboration* (Cambridge, UK: Cambridge University Press, 2009), ch. 7, "Corporate-NGO Engagements: From Conflict to Collaboration," pp. 123–45.

of this chapter—their efforts were more believable to many than if the company had undertaken this initiative on its own.

In short, stakeholder engagement can help companies learn about society's expectations, draw on outside expertise, generate creative solutions, and win stakeholder support for implementing them. It can also disarm or neutralize critics and improve a company's reputation for taking constructive action. On the other hand, corporations that do *not* engage effectively with those their actions affect may be hurt. Their reputation may suffer, their sales may drop, and they may be prevented from taking action. The need to respond to stakeholders has only been heightened by the increased globalization of many businesses and by the rise of technologies that facilitate fast communication on a worldwide scale.

Companies are learning that it is important to take a strategic approach to the management of public issues, both domestically and globally. This requires thinking ahead, understanding what is important to stakeholders, scanning the environment, and formulating action plans to anticipate changes in the external environment. Effective issue management requires involvement both by professional staff and leaders at top levels of the organization. It entails communicating across organizational boundaries, engaging with the public, and working creatively with stakeholders to solve complex problems.

Summary

- A public issue is an issue that is of mutual concern to an organization and one or more of the organization's stakeholders. Emerging public issues present a risk, but they also present an opportunity, because companies that correctly anticipate and respond to them can often obtain a competitive advantage.

- The eight strategic radar screens (the customer, competitor, economic, technological, social, political, legal, and geophysical environments) enable public affairs managers to assess and acquire information regarding their business environments. Managers must learn to look outward to understand key developments and anticipate their impact on the business.

- The issue management process includes identification and analysis of issues, the generation of options, action, and evaluation of the results.

- In the modern corporation, the issue management process takes place in many boundary-spanning departments. Some firms have a department of external affairs or corporate relations to coordinate these activities. Top management support is essential for effective issue management.

- Stakeholder engagement involves building relationships between a business firm and its stakeholders around issues of common concern. It may involve dialogue, network building, or partnerships.

- Engaging with stakeholders benefits businesses by bringing in expertise, enhancing legitimacy, and generating creative solutions to common problems.

Key Terms

competitive intelligence, *31*
environmental analysis, *29*
environmental intelligence, *29*

issue management, *32*
issue management process, *32*
performance–expectations gap, *26*

public issue, *25*
stakeholder dialogue, *40*
stakeholder engagement, *38*
stakeholder networks, *41*

Discussion Case: *Coca-Cola's Water Neutrality Initiative*

From approximately 2005 to the early 2010s, Coca-Cola faced an emerging issue: its corporate impact on water quality, availability, and access around the world.

The Coca-Cola Company (TCCC) was the world's largest beverage company. The company operated in more than 200 countries, providing 1.7 billion servings a day of carbonated beverages, juices and juice drinks, bottled water, and ready-to-drink coffees and teas. The company also partnered with more than 300 bottlers, independent companies that manufactured various Coca-Cola products under franchise. Seventy percent of the company's revenue came from outside the United States.

Water was essential to Coca-Cola's business. The company and its bottlers used around 82 billion gallons of water worldwide every year. Of this, about two-fifths went into finished beverages, and the rest was used in the manufacturing process—for example, to wash bottles, clean equipment, and provide sanitation for employees. Water supplies were also essential to the production of many ingredients in its products, such as sugar, corn, citrus fruit, tea, and coffee. Coca-Cola's chairman and CEO put it bluntly when he commented that unless the communities where the company operated had access to water, "we haven't got a business."

In 2003, Coca-Cola was abruptly reminded of the impact of its water use on local communities when the Center for Science and the Environment, a think tank in India, charged that Coca-Cola products there contained dangerous levels of pesticide residues. Other activists in India charged that the company's bottling plants used too much water, depriving local villagers of supplies for drinking and irrigation. Local officials shut down a Coca-Cola bottling plant in the state of Kerala, saying it was depleting groundwater, and an Indian court issued an order requiring soft-drink makers to list pesticide residues on their labels. In the United States, the India Resource Center took up the cause, organizing a grassroots campaign to convince schools and colleges to boycott Coca-Cola products.

Water was also emerging as a major concern to the world's leaders. In the early 21st century, more than 1 billion people worldwide lacked access to safe drinking water. Water consumption was doubling every 20 years, an unsustainable rate of growth. By 2025, one-third of the world's population was expected to face acute water shortages. The secretary general of the United Nations highlighted water stress as a major cause of disease, rising food prices, and regional conflicts, and called on national governments and corporations to take steps to address the issue.

Coca-Cola undertook a comprehensive study, surveying its global operations to assess its water management practices and impacts. It also reached out to other stakeholders, including the World Wildlife Fund, the Nature Conservancy, the humanitarian organization CARE, and various academic experts, to seek their advice. As the leader of TCCC's water stewardship initiative explained, the company also "sat down with each of our top bottlers, all of our operating groups, and really walked through all aspects of water and really understood where they were coming from and reached consensus though a very deliberate process."

In 2007, TCCC announced an aspirational goal of *water neutrality,* "to safely return to nature and to communities an amount of water equal to what we use in all our beverages and their production, by the year 2020." This goal would be accomplished in three ways: reduce, recycle, and replenish. The company said it would reduce its own use of water by running its operations more efficiently. It would discharge water used in manufacturing only if it were clean enough to support aquatic life—treating its wastewater itself where local authorities were unable to do so. Finally, the company would replenish the balance of the water it used (for example, as an ingredient in bottled beverages) by participating in various water conservation projects globally, such as river conservation, rainwater collection, and efficient irrigation.

As the water neutrality initiative proceeded, Coca-Cola moved to measure and publicly share its results. In 2011, the company reported that it had reduced its "water ratio" (the number of gallons of water used per gallon of product produced) by 13 percent from baseline levels. It estimated that 39 percent of its facilities were using recycled water, and 23 percent of the water used in finished products had been replenished through community water projects. The company also sought to measure the benefits of more than 300 partnerships with governments and nonprofit organizations around the world, ranging from building water treatment facilities in Colombia, to restoring watersheds in Thailand, to improving sugarcane irrigation in Australia. Coca-Cola estimated in 2011 that these conservation projects had replenished the equivalent of 31 percent of the water used in its finished beverages, although it acknowledged that its methodologies for accurately quantifying water benefits were still evolving.

Sources: The Coca-Cola Company, *The Water Stewardship and Replenish Report,* 2011, at *www.thecoca-colacompany .com/citizenship/pdf/replenish_2011.pdf,* and *2010/2011 Sustainability Report,* at *www.thecoca-colacompany.com /sustainabilityreport;* Business for Social Responsibility, "Drinking It In: The Evolution of a Global Water Stewardship Program at The Coca-Cola Company," March 2008; and "Coca-Cola in India," in Michael Yaziji and Jonathan Doh, *NGOs and Corporations* (Cambridge, UK: Cambridge University Press, 2009), pp. 115–19.

Discussion Questions

1. What was the public issue facing The Coca-Cola Company in this case? Describe the "performance–expectations gap" found in the case—what were the stakeholders' concerns, and how did their expectations differ from the company's performance?

2. If you applied the strategic radar screens model to this case, which of the eight environments would be most significant, and why?

3. Apply the issue management life cycle process model to this case. Which stages of the process can you identify in this case?

4. How did TCCC use stakeholder engagement and dialogue to improve its response to this issue, and what were the benefits of engagement to the company?

5. In your opinion, did TCCC respond appropriately to this issue? Why or why not?

CHAPTER THREE

The Corporation's Social Responsibilities

The idea that businesses bear broad responsibilities to society as they pursue economic goals is an age-old belief. Both market and nonmarket stakeholders expect businesses to be socially responsible, and many companies have responded by making social goals a part of their overall business operations. Some businesses have even integrated social benefit with economic objectives as their primary mission. With these dramatic changes in the mission and purpose of a business organization, what it means to act in socially responsible ways is not always clear, thus producing controversy about what constitutes such behavior, how extensive it should be, and what it costs to be socially responsible.

This Chapter Focuses on These Key Learning Objectives:

- Understanding the role of big business and the responsible use of corporate power in a democratic society.
- Knowing when the idea of corporate social responsibility originated and the phases through which it has developed.
- Investigating how a company's purpose or mission can integrate social objectives with economic objectives.
- Examining the key arguments for and against corporate social responsibility.
- Defining a social enterprise and understanding its role in solving social problems.
- Evaluating business's social obligations to help the world's poorest members.
- Recognizing socially responsible best practices.

Do managers have a responsibility to their stockholders? Certainly they do, because the owners of the business have invested their capital in the firm, exhibiting the ownership theory of the firm presented in Chapter 1. Do managers also have a responsibility, a *social* responsibility, to their company's other market and nonmarket stakeholders—the people who live where the firm operates, who purchase the firm's product or service, or who work for the firm? Does the stakeholder theory of the firm, described in detail in Chapter 1, expand a firm's obligations to include multiple stakeholders present in an interactive social system? Generally, yes, but while managers may have a clear responsibility to respond to all stakeholders, just how far should this responsibility go?

> Hewlett-Packard's vice president of Global Social Innovation stated, "It's no small feat to overcome the challenges we face as a global community. But at HP, we have the expertise, technology, and resources to make a real difference. And we're working with organizations around the world to innovate solutions that we believe will create lasting change for millions of people." HP followed up this pledge for global change by committing nearly $45 million in monetary contributions, product donations, and employee time. Employees volunteered more than 102,000 hours annually in communities worldwide. A half a million students, recent graduates, and young entrepreneurs were given help through HP's education and entrepreneurship assistance programs.
>
> In 2010, British pharmaceutical firm GlaxoSmithKline (GSK) announced that it was making thousands of drugs publicly available that potentially could lead to a cure for malaria, a disease that kills nearly one million children every year. Although GSK held the patents on these drugs and typically would keep the product away from its competitors and other scientists, "this is a chance to get thousands of researchers involved—just like software companies encourage thousands of people to contribute to their new ideas for software—and we'll see what comes of it," explained GSK's chief executive officer (CEO). GSK also announced that it had created an $8 million fund to pay scientists to explore these chemicals in an "open lab" at GSK's research center in Spain, which is dedicated to work on malaria and other diseases predominantly found in developing countries around the world.[1]

Are the efforts described above examples of a corporation's social responsibility, how businesses merge their social goals with solid economic objectives, or are these inappropriate uses of corporate assets—finances, personnel, and product? If these are examples of good business practice, how far should an organization go to help those in society in need of their support? How much is too much?

New, innovative methods are being created all the time to promote the corporation's social responsibilities, including using social media, as described in Exhibit 3.A.

This chapter describes the role business plays in society, introduces the notion of corporate social responsibility, and describes how this obligation began. How organizations should balance their multiple responsibilities—economic, legal, and social—is an ongoing challenge. What are the advantages and drawbacks of being socially responsible? Should the purpose or mission of the business integrate social objectives with economic objectives? What responsibility do businesses have to help those who are the poorest of the world? Whether businesses are large or small, make goods or provide services, operate at

[1] "Social Innovation," Hewlett-Packard's website, *www.hp.com;* and "Glaxo Offers Free Access to Potential Malaria Cures," *The Guardian,* January 19, 2010, *www.guardian.co.uk.*

In 2010, Pepsi-Cola committed $20 million to "doing well by doing good." The Pepsi Refresh Project asked Facebook and Twitter users to nominate programs worthy of the company's funding. The ideas for Pepsi Refresh grants were submitted each month to a website—refresheverything.com, where members of the public could vote for their favorite program using their cell phone or computer. Pepsi teamed with media partners AOL, Hulu, MTV Networks, Facebook, and Parade, and the project was featured on NBC, ABC, CBS, 30 cable channels, 10 print publications, and on websites like Yahoo!. The project was an extension of Pepsi's "Every generation refreshes the world—now it's your turn" campaign. According to the chief creative officer at Pepsi, "The goal is to develop a mechanism for young people to create ideas to make things better."

One of the first to receive a Pepsi Refresh grant was KIDDS Dance Project in Lithonia, Georgia. This program focused on teaching children the right moves on the dance floor and for their future. With help from a $50,000 Pepsi Refresh grant, they opened the doors of their Performing Arts and Youth Development Center to the community last year. Parents can sign their kids up to get tutoring, take dance lessons, participate in music workshops, and more. A different project funded by a Pepsi Refresh grant was Bikeloc, an initiative spearheaded by two young bicycle enthusiasts who used their $5,000 Pepsi Refresh Project grant to bike 4,000 miles. During their trek across the United States, the cyclists hosted community potlucks that engaged and educated 500 people across the country on the benefits of cycling and exercise. They documented all the action for a self-published book and website.

Pepsi also developed other innovative channels to promote this theme. The company launched the "If I Can Dream" reality show on hulu.com to promote the campaign. MTV Networks agreed to include the Pepsi campaign in their awards shows that aired on Comedy Central, Spike, and VH1. The campaign was prominently featured when Pepsi purchased the lead advertising position on face-book.com on Super Bowl Sunday.

Sources: "Pepsi Invites the Public to Do Good," *The New York Times,* February 1, 2010, *www.nytimes.com;* and "Check Out Past Pepsi Refresh Project Winners—And Vote to Fund the Next Inspiring Ideas!" *Huffington Post,* December 22, 2011, *www.huffingtonpost.com.*

home or abroad, willingly try to be socially responsible or fight against it all the way, there is no doubt that the public expects businesses to understand and act on their responsibility to all of their stakeholders in the society in which they operate.

Corporate Power and Responsibility

Undeniably, businesses, especially large corporations—whether by intention or accident, and whether for good or evil—play a major role in all that occurs in society. The power exerted by the world's largest business organizations is obvious and enormous. This influence, termed **corporate power**, refers to the capability of corporations to influence government, the economy, and society, based on their organizational resources.

One way to get a sense of the economic power of the world's largest companies is to compare them with nations. Figure 3.1 shows some leading companies alongside countries whose total gross domestic product is about the same as these companies' revenue. The revenues of automaker Toyota Motor, for example, are about equal to the entire economic output of Hong Kong; Walmart's are about the size of the economy of Norway; and BP's are about the size of the economy of Denmark.

The size and global reach of major transnational corporations such as Walmart and the others listed in Figure 3.1 give them tremendous power. Through their ever-present

FIGURE 3.1

Comparison of Annual Sales Revenue and the Gross Domestic Product for Selected Transnational Corporations and Nations, 2011, in $ Billions*

Sources: "*Fortune* Global 500," CNN Money.com, *oney .cnn.com/magazines/fortune /global500/2011/full_list*; and World Bank data, *data worldbank.org/indicator /NY.GDP.MKTP.CD.*

$ Billions of Sales (2011)	Gross Domestic Product, $ Billions (2011)
421.8 Walmart	Norway 413.0
354.7 ExxonMobil	South Africa 363.7
308.9 BP	Denmark 309.9
221.8 Toyota Motor	Hong Kong 224.4
196.3 Chevron	Nigeria 193.7
185.0 ConocoPhillips	Pakistan 176.9
135.6 General Motors	Ukraine 138.0

*2011 $ billions of sales compared to 2011 gross domestic product in $ billions.

marketing, they influence what people want and how they act around the world. We count on corporations for job creation; much of our community well-being; the standard of living we enjoy; the tax base for essential municipal, state, and national services; and our needs for banking and financial services, insurance, transportation, communication, utilities, entertainment, and a growing proportion of health care. These corporations have the resources to make substantial contributions to political campaigns, as discussed in Chapter 9, thus influencing the policies of governments. They dominate not only the traditional domains of product manufacture and service delivery, but also increasingly reach into such traditionally public sector activities as education, law enforcement, and the provision of social services.[2]

The following well-known quotation, frequently appearing in journals for business executives, challenges its readers to assume a responsible role for business in society:

> Business has become . . . the most powerful institution on the planet. The dominant institution in any society needs to take responsibility for the whole. . . . Every decision that is made, every action that is taken, must be viewed in light of that kind of responsibility.[3]

The tremendous power of the world's leading corporations has both positive and negative effects. A big company may have definite advantages over a small one. It can command more resources, produce at a lower cost, plan further into the future, and weather business fluctuations somewhat better. Globalization of markets can bring new

---

[2] For two classic analyses of corporate power, see Alfred C. Neal, *Business Power and Public Policy* (New York: Praeger, 1981); and Edwin M. Epstein and Dow Votaw, eds., *Rationality, Legitimacy, Responsibility: Search for New Directions in Business and Society* (Santa Monica, CA: Goodyear, 1978). More recent treatments may be found in David C. Korten, *When Corporations Rule the World* (San Francisco: Berrett-Koehler, 1996); Carl Boggs, *The End of Politics: Corporate Power and the Decline of the Public Sphere* (New York: Guilford Press, 2000); and Alastair McIntosh, *Soil and Soul: People versus Corporate Power* (London: Aurum Press, 2004).

[3] David C. Korten, "Limits to the Social Responsibility of Business," *The People-Centered Development Forum,* article 19, June 1, 1996.

products, technologies, and economic opportunities to developing societies, and help those in need. After Hurricane Katrina and the Haitian earthquake ravaged their respective regions, for example, Google's Person Finder provided emergency responders with a powerful tool with which to track missing persons. Google's global network enabled dozens of disaster relief organizations and government agencies to coordinate their work.[4]

Yet, the concentration of corporate power can also harm society. Huge businesses can disproportionately influence politics, shape tastes, and dominate public discourse. They can move production from one site to another, weakening unions and communities. These companies can also use their economic influence to collude to fix prices, divide markets, and quash competition in ways that can negatively affect consumer choices, employment opportunities, or the creation of new businesses. A United Nations report estimated that the world's largest 3,000 businesses were responsible for $2.2 trillion in environmental damage. That was one-third of the firms' annual profits in 2010.[5]

Many people are concerned about the enormous influence of business. Since 1994, between 80 and 90 percent of the Americans polled every year or so said that big business had too much power. The focused power found in the modern business corporation means that every action it takes can affect the quality of human life—for individuals, for communities, and for the entire globe.[6] The obligation this gives rise to is what is often referred to as the *iron law of responsibility*. The **iron law of responsibility** says that in the long run those who do not use power in ways that society considers responsible will tend to lose it.

Given the virtually immeasurable power in the hands of the leaders of large, global corporations, stakeholders throughout the social system expect business to take great care in wielding its power responsibly for the betterment of society. As a result, social responsibility has become a worldwide expectation.

The Meaning of Corporate Social Responsibility

Corporate social responsibility (CSR) means that a corporation should act in a way that enhances society and its inhabitants and be held accountable for any of its actions that affect people, their communities, and their environment. This concept is based in the root of the term *responsibility*, meaning "to pledge back," creating a commitment to give back to society and the organization's stakeholders.[7] It implies that harm to people and society should be acknowledged and corrected if at all possible. It may require a company to forgo some profits if its social impacts seriously hurt some of its stakeholders or if its funds can be used to have a positive social impact.

---

[4] The Google story is found in "Innovations in Corporate Global Citizenship: Responding to the Haiti Earthquake," *World Economic Forum*, 2010, p. 13.

[5] "World's Top Firms Cause $2.2tn of Environmental Damage, Report Estimates," *The Guardian*, February 18, 2010, *guardian .co.uk*.

[6] "Very Large Majorities of Americans Believe Big Companies, PACs, Political Lobbyists and the News Media Have Too Much Power and Influence in D.C.," *The Harris Poll*, Harris Interactive, March 12, 2009. The iron law of responsibility concept first appeared in Keith Davis and Robert Blomstrom, *Business and Its Environment* (New York: McGraw-Hill, 1966).

[7] For a more complete discussion of the roots of corporate social responsibility and how it is practiced, see Jerry D. Goldstein and Andrew C. Wicks, "Corporate and Stakeholder Responsibility: Making Business Ethics a Two-Way Conversation," *Business Ethics Quarterly* 17 (2007), pp. 375–98. Also see Florian Wettstein, "Beyond Voluntariness, beyond CSR: Making a Case for Human Rights and Justice," *Business and Society Review*, 2009, pp. 125–52.

Being socially responsible does not mean that a company must abandon its other missions. As discussed later in this chapter, a business has many responsibilities: economic, legal, and social; the challenge for management is to integrate them all into a coherent and comprehensive mission. In a worldwide survey of CEOs, for example, 72 percent of executives polled said they sought to *embed* social and environmental issues into the organization's core strategies and operations.[8] At times these responsibilities will be in tension; at other times they will blend together to better the firm and actually make it more profitable. Thus, having multiple and sometimes competing responsibilities does not mean that socially responsible firms cannot be as profitable as others that are less responsible; some are and some are not.

The Origins of Corporate Social Responsibility

In the United States, the idea of corporate social responsibility appeared around the start of the 20th century. Corporations at that time came under attack for being too big, too powerful, and guilty of antisocial and anticompetitive practices. Critics tried to curb corporate power through antitrust laws, banking regulations, and consumer protection laws.

Faced with this social protest, a few farsighted business executives advised corporations to use their power and influence voluntarily for broad social purposes rather than for profits alone. Some of the wealthiest business leaders—steelmaker Andrew Carnegie is a good example—became great philanthropists who gave much of their wealth to educational and charitable institutions. (A recent example of this was the "Giving Pledge" made by 16 billionaires, including Facebook's Mark Zuckerberg and Oracle's Larry Ellison, who publicly pledged to give away a majority of their wealth to charitable causes or organizations. Corporate philanthropy is discussed in more detail in Chapter 18.) Other business leaders, like automaker Henry Ford, developed paternalistic programs to support the recreational and health needs of their employees. These business leaders believed that business had a responsibility to society that went beyond or worked along with their efforts to make profits.[9]

William C. Frederick, a leading scholar and a coauthor of several earlier editions of this textbook, described in a recent book how business's understanding of corporate social responsibility has evolved over the past half century. During each of four historical periods, corporate social responsibility has had a distinct focus, set of drivers, and policy instruments, as shown in Figure 3.2. Corporate social responsibility is defined in its most basic form as "learning to live with, and respect, others" with deep roots in business. How corporate social responsibility was manifested evolved from a stewardship notion, then strategic responsiveness, to an ethics-based understanding found in culture to what Frederick calls the most recent phase of corporate social responsibility: *corporate citizenship*. (Chapter 7 will explore this concept more fully.)

---

[8] "CEOs on Strategy and Social Issues," *The McKinsey Quarterly*, October 2007, p. 7. The understanding of the interrelations among business's obligations is discussed in Jared D. Harris and R. Edward Freeman, "The Impossibility of the Separation Thesis," *Business Ethics Quarterly* 18 (2008), pp. 541–48. Michael E. Porter and Mark R. Kramer also discuss the link between competitive advantage and corporate social responsibility in "Strategy and Society," *Harvard Business Review*, December 2006, pp. 78–92.

[9] Harold R. Bowen, *Social Responsibility of the Businessman* (New York: Harper, 1953); and Morrell Heald, *The Social Responsibility of Business: Company and Community, 1900–1960* (Cleveland: Case Western Reserve Press, 1970). For a history of how some of these business philanthropists acquired their wealth, see Matthew Josephson, *The Robber Barons: The Great American Capitalists* (New York: Harcourt Brace, 1934).

FIGURE 3.2

Evolving Phases of Corporate Social Responsibility

	Phases of Corporate Social Responsibility	CSR Drivers	CSR Policy Instruments
CSR₁ Early in the 20th century but formally in the 1950s–1960s	**Corporate Social Stewardship** Corporate philanthropy—acts of charity Managers as public Trustee-stewards Balancing social pressures	Executive conscience Company image/reputation	Philanthropic funding Public relations
CSR₂ 1960s–1970s	**Corporate Social Responsiveness** Social impact analysis Strategic priority for social response Organizational redesign and training for responsiveness Stakeholder mapping and implementation	Social unrest/protest Repeated corporate misbehavior Public policy/government regulation Stakeholder pressures Think tank policy papers	Stakeholder strategy Regulatory compliance Social audits Public affairs function Governance reform Political lobbying
CSR₃ 1980s–1990s	**Corporate/Business Ethics** Foster an ethical corporate culture Establish an ethical organizational climate Recognize common ethical principles	Religious/ethnic beliefs Technology-driven value changes Human rights pressures Code of ethics Ethics committee/officer/audits Ethics training Stakeholder negotiations	Mission/vision/values Statements CEO leadership ethics
CSR₄ 1990s–present	**Corporate/Global Citizenship** Stakeholder partnerships Integrate financial, social, and environmental performance Identify globalization impacts Sustainability of company and environment	Global economic trade/investment High-tech communication networks Geopolitical shifts/competition Ecological awareness/concern NGO pressures	Intergovernmental compacts Global audit standards NGO dialogue Sustainability audits/reports

Source: Adapted from William C. Frederick, *Corporation, Be Good! The Story of Corporate Social Responsibility* (Indianapolis, IN: Dog Ear Publishing, 2006). Used with permission.

Balancing Social, Economic, and Legal Responsibilities

Being socially responsible by meeting the public's continually changing expectations requires wise leadership at the top of the corporation. Companies with the ability to recognize profound social changes and anticipate how they will affect operations have proven to be survivors. They get along better with government regulators, are more open to the needs of the company's stakeholders, and often cooperate with legislators as new laws are developed to cope with social problems.

Avon, the world's largest seller of cosmetics and beauty products for women, espouses the balancing of multiple responsibilities in their guiding principle: "To meet fully the obligations of corporate citizenship by contributing to the well-being of society and the environment in which it functions." Avon puts this principle into practice by being the leading corporate supporter globally of the fight against breast cancer. Starting in 1992, Avon has raised and donated nearly $700 million to breast cancer programs around the world. In addition, Avon and the Avon Foundation for Women responded swiftly to the September 11, 2001, disaster in the United States by providing $7 million in charitable aid and made available $1 million to the victims of the Haiti earthquake in 2010. Avon has supported people affected by natural disasters or other crises around the world by giving more than $17.7 million since 2001. The attention to corporate citizenship addressed the company's mission: "doing well by doing good." The company reported that revenues were up 4 percent at year-end 2011, along with other strong financial performance measures, while also maintaining its annual dividend for its investors.[10]

The actions taken by Avon are an example of a business organization's leaders being guided by **enlightened self-interest**. Avon recognizes the long-term rewards to the company from its global involvement, through an enhanced reputation, customer loyalty, employee satisfaction, and global community support. Avon's actions reflected the philosophy of the company's founder, who said in 1886 that the company would contribute to the well-being of society and the environment in which it functions and in doing so would be profitable. According to this view, it is in a company's self-interest in the long term to provide true value to its customers, to help its employees to grow, and to behave responsibly as a global corporate citizen.[11]

Do socially responsible companies sacrifice profits by working conscientiously to promote the social good? Do they make higher profits, better-than-average profits, or lower profits than corporations that ignore the public's desires for a high and responsible standard of social performance?

Scholars have explored this issue for decades, with mixed results. Researchers at the University of Iowa conducted a rigorous review of 52 prior studies of the relationship between corporate social responsibility and firm performance. They found that most of the time, more responsible companies also had solid financial results; the statistical association was highly to modestly positive across the range of all prior studies. The authors concluded, "Corporate virtue, in the form of social responsibility and, to a lesser extent, environmental responsibility is likely to pay off."[12] In short, most of the time, social responsibility and financial performance go together, although there may be some conditions under which this is not true.

Social responsibility is not a business organization's sole responsibility. In addition, as a member of a civil society, organizations have legal obligations, as well as economic responsibilities, to their owners and other stakeholders affected by the financial well-being of the firm. Any organization or manager must seek to juggle these multiple responsibilities—economic, legal, and social. The belief that the business of business is solely to attend to stockholders' return on investment and make a profit is no longer widely held, as discussed next in the

---

[10] See Avon's website for more information on its social responsibility activities and its social responsibility report at *www.avoncompany.com/corporate citizenship*.

[11] Jeff Frooman, "Socially Irresponsible and Illegal Behavior and Shareholder Wealth," *Business & Society*, September 1997, pp. 221–49, argues that the negative effects on shareholder wealth when a firm acts irresponsibly support the enlightened self-interest view: act responsibly to promote shareholders' interests.

[12] For various summaries of the research investigating this relationship see Mark Orlitzky, Frank Schmidt, and Sara Rynes, "Corporate Social and Financial Performance: A Meta-Analysis," *Organization Studies*, 2003, pp. 403–41; Joshua D. Margolis and James P. Walsh, "Misery Loves Companies: Rethinking Social Initiatives by Business," *Administrative Science Quarterly*, 2003, pp. 268–305; Pieter van Beurden and Tobias Gossling, "The Worth of Values—A Literature Review on the Relationship between Corporate Social and Financial Performance, *Journal of Business Ethics*, 2008, pp. 407–24; and Meng-Ling Wu, "Corporate Social Performance, Corporate Financial Performance, and Firm Size: A Meta-Analysis," *Journal of American Academy of Business*, 2006, pp. 163–71.

chapter. Rather, many business executives believe the key challenge facing their organizations today is to meet their multiple economic and social responsibilities simultaneously.

The Corporate Social Responsibility Debate

As we have seen, there are various views about business's social responsibilities and these views evolve over time. The arguments for and against corporate social responsibility are detailed next and summarized in Figure 3.3.

Arguments for Corporate Social Responsibility

Who favors the notion of corporate social responsibility? Many business executives believe that companies should make a profit but should balance this with their social responsibilities. Clearly, many groups that seek to preserve the environment, protect consumers, safeguard the safety and health of employees, prevent job discrimination, and forestall invasions of privacy through the Internet stress the importance of social responsibility by business, but so also do groups that look to business to maintain a strong return on their financial investments. Government officials also support CSR in that it ensures corporate compliance with laws and regulations that protect the general public from abusive business practices. In other words, both businesspeople and citizens, both supporters and critics of business, have reasons for wanting businesses to act in socially responsible ways.

Balances Corporate Power with Responsibility

Today's business enterprise possesses much power and influence. Most people believe that responsibility must accompany power, whoever holds it. This obligation, presented earlier in this chapter, is the *iron law of responsibility.* Businesses committed to social responsibility are aware that if they misuse the power they have, they might lose it. Corporations' reputations and to some extent even their independence have recently taken a hit in the economic downturn of 2008–09, as dozens of national governments rushed in to bolster their countries' economies and failing financial markets. This shows how managers' misuse of corporate power and their lack of responsibility as trustees of the public's wealth can result in their loss of power.

Discourages Government Regulation

One of the most appealing arguments in favor of CSR is that voluntary socially responsible acts may head off increased government regulation of business. Some regulation may reduce freedom for both business and society, and freedom is a desirable public good. In the case of business, regulations tend to add economic costs and restrict flexibility in decision

FIGURE 3.3
The Pros and Cons of Corporate Social Responsibility

Arguments for Corporate Social Responsibility	Arguments against Corporate Social Responsibility
Balances corporate power with responsibility.	Lowers economic efficiency and profit.
Discourages government regulation.	Imposes unequal costs among competitors.
Promotes long-term profits for business.	Imposes hidden costs passed on to
Improves stakeholder relationships.	stakeholders.
Enhances business reputation.	Requires skills business may lack.
	Places responsibility on business rather than individuals.

making. From business's point of view, freedom in decision making allows companies to maintain initiative in meeting market and social forces.

> Two scholars, Bryan Husted and Jose de Jesus Salazar, examined how well firms performed if they voluntarily developed a social responsibility strategy versus being coerced by government or some other external force to act to benefit society. They found that firms enjoyed significant strategic advantages and maximized social benefit to their communities when they voluntarily and freely developed a social strategy rather than acting under coercive pressure.[13]

This view is also consistent with political philosophy that wishes to keep power as decentralized as possible in a democratic society. From this perspective, government is already a massive institution whose centralized power and bureaucracy threaten the balance of power in society. Therefore, if business by its own socially responsible behavior can discourage new government restrictions, it is accomplishing a public good as well as its own private good. For example, the biotechnology industry may have prevented regulation when it voluntarily developed a program to monitor releases of genetically modified organisms, or GMOs.

> In the early 2000s an increasing number of genetically modified organisms (GMOs)—crops and seeds whose genes had been scientifically engineered—were unintentionally or accidentally released by companies in the agricultural biotechnology industry, initially in the United States. Eventually these GMOs made their way into the global food system via international product shipments. These potentially harmful, even lethal, organisms were not approved for human consumption or, in some cases, even commercial agricultural use. Bayer Corporation took the lead in creating a program called EcoCheck to better monitor and prevent such discharges of unapproved GMOs. Soon after, Monsanto, another leader in the biotechnology field, followed with their own corporate program. Within months this proactive effort to monitor discharges and develop an early warning system became the industry standard, forestalling the possibility of government intervention.[14]

Promotes Long-Term Profits for Business

At times, social initiatives by business produce long-run business profits. In 1951 a New Jersey judge ruled in a precedent-setting case, *Barlow et al. v. A.P. Smith Manufacturing,* that a corporate donation to Princeton University was an *investment* by the firm, and thus an allowable business expense. The rationale was that a corporate gift to a school, though costly in the present, might in time provide a flow of talented graduates to work for the company. The court ruled that top executives must take "a long-range view of the matter" and exercise "enlightened leadership and direction" when it comes to using company funds for socially responsible programs.[15]

> A classic example of the long-term benefits of social responsibility was the Johnson & Johnson Tylenol incident in the 1980s, when several people died after they ingested

---

[13] Bryan W. Husted and Jose de Jesus Salazar, "Taking Friedman Seriously: Maximizing Profits and Social Performance," *Journal of Management Studies* 43 (2006), pp. 75–91.

[14] See Jennifer Clapp, "Illegal GMO Releases and Corporate Responsibility: Questioning the Effectiveness of Voluntary Measures," *Ecological Economics* 66 (2008), pp. 348–58.

[15] *Barlow et al. v. A.P. Smith Manufacturing* (1951, New Jersey Supreme Court), discussed in Clarence C. Walton, *Corporate Social Responsibility* (Belmont, CA: Wadsworth, 1967), pp. 48–52.

Extra-Strength Tylenol capsules laced with the poison cyanide. To ensure the safety of its customers, Johnson & Johnson immediately recalled the product, an action that cost the firm millions of dollars in the short term. The company's production processes were never found defective. Customers rewarded Johnson & Johnson's responsible actions by continuing to buy its products, and in the long run the company once again became profitable.

In the opening examples of this chapter, the leadership at Hewlett-Packard believed that, in the long term, its commitment to improve the social and economic conditions around the world by targeting education and entrepreneurship could create a lasting change for millions of people. GlaxoSmithKline's executives believed that openly sharing their knowledge was the best strategy in addressing the world's most urgent health issues. These corporate social programs were investments in the future, and each firm hoped that their social responsibility efforts would also indirectly help their firm's financial bottom line.

Improves Stakeholder Relationships

Managers often believe that developing a strong social agenda and series of social programs will improve the firm's stakeholder relationships. Whether it improved the quality of people it attracted as employees, or appealed to consumers to purchase the firm's product or services, or built strong ties with the community residents in which it operated, or persuaded investors to purchase company stock, managers felt that social action by the firm was viewed positively by stakeholders. This belief was borne out in recent research where corporate social responsibility was linked to current and prospective employees' trust in the firm and desire to work for the firm, positive consumer purchasing decisions, and investors' decisions, especially during times of economic downturn. At Coca-Cola, 60,000 employees were surveyed and reported that corporate social responsibility was the second biggest driver of their commitment and loyalty to the firm, after leadership.[16]

Enhances Business Reputation

The social reputation of the firm is often viewed as an important element in establishing trust between the firm and its stakeholders. **Reputation** refers to desirable or undesirable qualities associated with an organization or its actors that may influence the organization's relationships with its stakeholders.[17] Rating Research, a British firm, created a "reputation index" to measure a company's social reputation. The index evaluates critical intangible assets that constitute corporate reputation and broadly disseminates these ratings to interested parties.

A firm's reputation is a valuable intangible asset, as it prompts repeat purchases by loyal consumers and helps to attract and retain better employees to spur productivity and enhance profitability. Employees who have the most to offer may be attracted to work for a firm that contributes to the social good of the community, or is more sensitive to the needs and safety of its consumers, or takes better care of its employees. Research has confirmed

---

[16] See S. Duane Hansen, Benjamin B. Dunford, Alan D. Boss, R. Wayne Boss, and Ingo Angermeier, "Corporate Social Responsibility and the Benefits of Employee Trust: A Cross-Disciplinary Perspective," *Journal of Business Ethics*, 2011, pp. 29–45; Russell Lacey and Pamela A. Kennett-Hensel, "Longitudinal Effects of Corporate Social Responsibility on Consumer Relationships," *Journal of Business Ethics*, 2010, pp. 581–97; and "Good Intentions," *The Wall Street Journal*, February 3, 2010, *online.wsj.com*.

[17] The definition of *reputation* is adapted from John F. Mahon, "Corporate Reputation: A Research Agenda Using Strategy and Stakeholder Literature," *Business & Society* 41, no. 4 (December 2002), pp. 415–45. For the "reputation index," see Charles Fombrun, *Reputation: Realizing Value from the Corporate Image* (Cambridge, MA: Harvard University Press, 1996) and Rating Research LLC, *www.ratingresearch.com*.

that a firm's "good deeds" or reputation increases its attractiveness to employees.[18] In 2012, Weber Shandwick, a public relations firm, reported that 6 in 10 executives said they would rather see their company in the news for "admired standing" than for financial accomplishments. The report, focusing on the United States, United Kingdom, China, and Brazil, also found that 70 percent of consumers said that they would not buy a product if they did not like the company behind it.[19] An example of a company that has embraced having a solid reputation when managing their stakeholders is described next.

Sodexo, a provider of integrated food and facilities management services throughout North America including many hospitals, senior living centers, colleges, universities, and school districts, was committed to developing a positive reputation. "Being a responsible corporate citizen is at the core of Sodexo's business," declared the company's website. "We set the benchmark in areas such as sustainability, diversity and inclusion, wellness, and the fight against hunger." Sodexo's "The Better Tomorrow Plan" impacted 80 countries at 30,600 locations and engaged the company's 380,000 employees. The program addressed 14 different issues, such as reducing the firm's carbon and water usage in all company operations and at all client's locations, providing and promoting varied and balanced food options to its clients, increasing the purchase of products sourced from fairly and responsibly certified sources, and ensuring compliance with a Global Sustainable Supply Chain Code of Conduct. Its attention to various social issues enhanced Sodexo's reputation as it was named to various "best" lists, including the "Best Company for Hourly Workers," the "Best Company for Multicultural Women," and *Fortune*'s "Most Admired Companies." The company was also ranked number one by DiversityInc for diversity inclusion and was recognized as one of the "World's Most Ethical Companies."[20]

Arguments against Corporate Social Responsibility

Who opposes corporate social responsibility? The economist Milton Friedman famously stated in 1970, "There is only one responsibility of business, namely to use its resources and engage in activities designed to increase its profits."[21] Some people in the business world—such as the 16 percent of CEOs in the survey (shown later in Figure 3.4) who believe that the appropriate role of business is to provide the highest possible returns to shareholders while obeying all laws and regulations—clearly agree with this view. Some fear that the pursuit of social goals by business will lower firms' economic efficiency, thereby depriving society of important goods and services. Others are skeptical about trusting business with social improvements; they prefer governmental initiatives and programs. According to some of the more radical critics of the private business system, social responsibility is nothing but a clever public relations smokescreen to hide business's true intentions to make as much money as possible. See Figure 3.3 again for some of the arguments against corporate social responsibility, discussed next.

---

[18] Rebecca A. Luce, Alison E. Barber, and Amy J. Hillman, "Good Deeds and Misdeeds: A Mediated Model of the Effect of Corporate Social Performance on Organizational Attractiveness," *Business & Society* 40, no. 4 (2001), pp. 397–415.

[19] "When It Comes to Company Reputation, Avoiding Scandal and Wrongdoing Trumps CSR, Survey Finds," *Ethikos*, January/February 2012, p. 15.

[20] The quotation and information about Sodexo is from the company's website, *www.sodexousa.com*.

[21] Milton Friedman, "The Social Responsibility of Business Is to Increase Its Profits," *The New York Times Magazine*, September 13, 1970.

Lowers Economic Efficiency and Profits

According to one argument, any time a business uses some of its resources for social purposes, it risks lowering its efficiency. For example, if a firm decides to keep an unproductive factory open because it wants to avoid the negative social effect that a plant closing would have on the local community and its workers, its overall financial performance may suffer. The firm's costs may be higher than necessary, resulting in lower profits. Stockholders may receive a lower return on their investment, making it more difficult for the firm to acquire additional capital for future growth. In the long run, the firm's efforts to be socially responsible by keeping the factory open may backfire.

Business managers and economists argue that the business of business is business. Businesses are told to concentrate on producing goods and services and selling them at the lowest competitive price. When these economic tasks are done, the most efficient firms survive. Even though corporate social responsibility is well-intended, such social activities lower business's efficiency, thereby depriving society of higher levels of economic production needed to maintain everyone's standard of living.[22]

Imposes Unequal Costs among Competitors

Another argument against social responsibility is that it imposes greater costs on more responsible companies, putting them at a competitive disadvantage. Consider the following scenario:

> A manufacturer operating in multiple countries wishes to be more socially responsible worldwide and decides to protect its employees by installing more safety equipment at its plants than local law requires. Other manufacturers in competition with this company do not take similar steps, choosing to install only as much safety equipment as required by law. As a result their costs are lower, and their profits higher. In this case, the socially responsible firm penalizes itself and even runs the risk of going out of business, especially in a highly competitive market.

This kind of problem becomes acute when viewed from a global perspective, where laws and regulations differ from one country to the next. If one nation requires higher and more costly pollution control standards, or stricter job safety rules, or more stringent premarket testing of prescription drugs than other nations, it imposes higher costs on business. This cost disadvantage means that competition cannot be equal. Foreign competitors who are the least socially responsible will actually be rewarded because they will be able to capture a bigger share of the market.

Imposes Hidden Costs Passed On to Stakeholders

Many social proposals undertaken by business do not pay their own way in an economic sense; therefore, someone must pay for them. Ultimately, society pays all costs. Some people may believe that social benefits are costless, but socially responsible businesses will try to recover all of their costs in some way. For example, if a company chooses to install expensive pollution abatement equipment, the air may be cleaner, but ultimately someone will have to pay. Stockholders may receive lower dividends, employees may be paid less, or consumers may be charged higher prices. If the public knew that it would eventually have to pay these costs, and if it knew how high the true costs were, it might not be so insistent that companies act in socially responsible ways. The same might be true of government regulations intended to produce socially desirable business behavior. By driving up business costs, these regulations often increase prices and lower productivity, in addition to making the nation's tax bill higher.

Requires Skills Business May Lack

Businesspeople are not primarily trained to solve social problems. They may know about production, marketing, accounting, finance, information technology, and personnel work, but what do they know about inner-city issues or world poverty or violence in schools? Putting businesspeople in charge of solving social problems may lead to unnecessarily expensive and poorly conceived approaches. A global survey of senior business executives on social responsibility found that "only 11 percent [of the companies who have developed a CSR strategy] have made significant progress in implementing the strategy in their organization."[23] Thus one might question the effectiveness and efficiency of businesspeople seeking to address social responsibility problems. Business analysts might be tempted to believe that methods that succeed in normal business operations will also be applicable to complex social issues, even though different approaches may work better in the social arena.

A related idea is that public officials who are duly elected by citizens in a democratic society should address societal issues. Business leaders are not elected by the public and therefore do not have a mandate to solve social problems. In short, businesspeople do not have the expertise or the popular support required to address what are essentially issues of public policy.

Places Responsibility on Business Rather Than Individuals

The entire idea of *corporate* responsibility is misguided, according to some critics. Only *individual persons* can be responsible for their actions. People make decisions; organizations do not. An entire company cannot be held liable for its actions, only those individuals who are involved in promoting or carrying out a policy. Therefore, it is wrong to talk about the social responsibility of *business* when it is the social responsibility of *individual businesspersons* that is involved. If individual business managers want to contribute their own personal money to a social cause, let them do so; but it is wrong for them to contribute their company's funds in the name of corporate social responsibility.[24] Together, the above arguments claim that the attempt to exercise corporate social responsibility places added burdens on both business and society without producing the intended effect of social improvement or produces it at excessive cost.

Some critics of corporate social responsibility argue that these efforts are merely superficial or cosmetic, not truly addressing the social problems claimed as targets or being responsive to the real objectives of business. Some of these opinions are presented in Exhibit 3.B.

What is the opinion of business executives on this debate? Of course, this group is not of one mind on this complex question. A survey by the consulting firm McKinsey showed, however, that a solid majority—84 percent—of business executives believed that companies should balance their responsibility to their investors with their responsibilities of other business stakeholders. A minority of 16 percent felt that companies should focus primarily on maximizing their investors' returns while staying within the law of society. These results are summarized in Figure 3.4.

---

[23] "Corporate Social Responsibility: Unlocking the Value," *www.ey.com/Global*.

[24] This argument, like the "lowers economic efficiency and profits" argument, often is attributed to Friedman, "Social Responsibility of Business."

Exhibit 3.B

The Limits of Corporate Social Responsibility

"It is easy to understand why big business has embraced corporate social responsibility with such verve. It makes for good press and reassures the public. . . . [B]ut the pressures operating on [corporations] to lure and keep consumers and investors haven't eased one bit. In supercapitalism, they *cannot* be socially responsible, at least not to any significant extent. . . . No company can 'voluntarily' take on an extra cost that its competitors don't also take on—which is why, under supercapitalism, regulations are the only means of getting companies to do things that hurt their bottom lines."—Robert B. Reich, *Supercapitalism: The Transformation of Business, Democracy, and Everyday Life* (New York: Alfred A. Knopf, 2007), pp. 170 and 204.

"Business leaders today say their companies care about more than profit and loss, that they feel responsible to society as a whole, not just to their shareholders. Corporate social responsibility is their new creed, a self-conscious corrective to earlier greed-inspired visions of the corporation. Despite this shift, the corporation itself has not changed. . . . Corporate social responsibility . . . holds out promises of help, reassures people, and sometimes works. We should not, however, expect very much from it. A corporation can do good only to help itself do well, a profound *limit* on just how much good it can do."—Joel Bakan, *The Corporation: The Pathological Pursuit of Profit and Power* (New York: The Free Press, 2004), pp. 28, 50.

"[P]recisely because CSR is voluntary and market-driven, companies will engage in CSR only to the extent that it makes business sense for them to do so. . . . Unlike government regulation, it cannot force companies to make unprofitable but socially beneficial decisions. In most cases, CSR only makes business sense if the costs of more virtuous behavior remain modest. This imposes important constraints on the resources that companies can spend on CSR, and limits the improvements in corporate social and environmental performance that voluntary regulation can produce."—David J. Vogel, *The Market for Virtue: The Potential and Limits of Corporate Social Responsibility* (Washington, DC: The Brookings Institution, 2005), p. 4.

The Social Enterprise

All modern businesses must take into account their impacts on all stakeholders. But one kind of business adopts social benefit as its core mission: a **social enterprise**. This term refers to an organization that uses business strategies for the purpose of improving human and environmental well-being. Although social enterprises often earn profit, their primary purpose is not to maximize returns to shareholders. Social enterprises can take a number of organizational forms. They can be large and established or small and new—like the social entrepreneurial ventures described next.

FIGURE 3.4

Business Executives' View of the Role of Business in Society

Source: For a more detailed discussion of these views, see "The McKinsey Global Survey of Business Executives: Business and Society," *McKinsey Quarterly*, January 2006. Based on a survey of 4,238 executives (more than a quarter are CEOs or other top executives) in 116 countries, conducted in December 2005.

Percentage of business executives who believe that business organizations should . . .

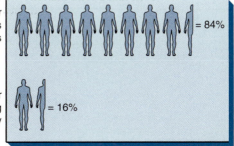

Balance their responsibility to their investors with their responsibilities to other business stakeholders = 84%

Primarily focus on maximizing their investors' returns while staying within the law of society = 16%

Social Entrepreneurship

Social entrepreneurs are individuals who—like traditional entrepreneurs—act boldly to pursue opportunities, attract support, and build new organizations. Unlike traditional entrepreneurs, however, these individuals are typically driven by a core mission to create and sustain social rather than economic value. When a person or group of people identify a social need and use their entrepreneurial skills to address this need, this process is called **social entrepreneurship**. Although their primary purpose is to achieve a social or environmental objective, this focus does not preclude these entrepreneurs from creating an economically viable organization that can continue to address social needs, as the following examples show.

> Rose Donna knew firsthand that medical data collection in developing nations involved piles of paperwork and tedious data entry. Envisioning a more efficient approach, she worked with DataDyne, a not-for-profit organization based in Washington, DC, to develop EpiSurveyor. This innovative software enabled public health workers in 15 sub-Saharan countries to digitize and streamline data collection and data entry processes. This social entrepreneurial venture was so successful that the World Health Organization, the United Nations Foundation, and the Vodafone Foundation partnered with Donna to disseminate the EpiSurveyor software to 22 additional African and Asian countries.
>
> Two University of Virginia business students, Chip Ransler and Manoj Sinha, noticed that 350 million people lived in India's Rice Belt region, where rice was plentiful but reliable electricity was scarce. The students launched their social entrepreneurial venture by devising a process to turn discarded rice husks into biogas, which could fuel mini power plants. Hundreds of homes in five rice-growing Indian communities acquired access to affordable power. In addition, the ash from generating the gas was not wasted but used as fertilizer or as a low-cost ingredient for cement.[25]

The goal of social entrepreneurs, like those illustrated here, is to use the power of enterprise to drive social change and help society.

The B Corporation

A specific kind of social enterprise is the **B Corporation**, or benefit corporation. This is a new type of corporation that seeks to blend its social objectives with financial goals. To qualify for B Corporation status, an organization must meet rigorous, independent social and environmental performance standards, assessed by the nonprofit organization B Lab. The company is assessed on the impact it has on its communities, employees, consumers, and the environment. The idea is that a business cannot just claim it is socially responsible, but it must prove it by meeting the B Lab standards. By 2012, this corporate status had been legally recognized in seven states: California, Hawaii, Virginia, Maryland, Vermont, New York, and New Jersey, and other states were considering this sort of legislation. More than 500 organizations in 60 industries, with a total of $2.9 billion in revenues, were registered as B Corporations.[26]

---

[25] These stories were found in Fast Company's "10 Best Social Enterprises" at *www.fastcompany.com*.

[26] See the B Corporation website at *bcorporation.net* and an in-depth description of B Corporations at *Trend Hunter*, January 4, 2012, *www.trendhunter.com* and Nellie Akalp, "B Corporations: Do They Really Indicate Good Companies?" *Yahoo! News*, December 8, 2011, *news.yahoo.com*.

Warby Parker is a B Corporation. Four college friends started the company to design, manufacture, and distribute high-quality eyeglasses that sold for around $95 rather than the more common $500 price tag. One of the company's founders, Neil Blumenthal, was the former director of VisionSpring, a New York nonprofit organization that provided glasses to impoverished people. Blumenthal provided Warby Parker with many manufacturing and distribution contacts. He also recommended Warby Parker's one-to-one donation practice—for every pair of eyeglasses sold, one pair would be donated to someone in need. Warby Parker also pledged to become one of the few carbon-neutral eyewear brands in the world. "It was important to the four of us that if we are going to dedicate our life savings and our time to building an organization, we wanted to have a positive impact," said Blumenthal. This combination of economic and social objectives qualified Warby Parker for B Corporation certification.[27]

The B Corporation's website and blog feature B Lab–certified businesses and help visitors understand the difference between "a good company and just good marketing." B Corporations are more likely to receive various government recognitions, such as the U.S. Drug Administration's organic seal, or to qualify for a LEED certification for their buildings (designating environmental excellence), or to be certified as engaging in fair trade. B Corporations are subjected to random audits, and these reports are made public, adding a layer of transparency to the process and certification. In addition, B Corporations must modify their company's bylaws in order to formalize their social mission.

Serving the Bottom of the Pyramid

Another way that business can carry out its responsibility to society is by bringing products and services to the many people in the world who have traditionally been beyond the reach of global commerce. The term **bottom of the pyramid** refers to the poorest people in the world—nearly 4 billion who earn less than $2.50 per day. As the scholar C. K. Prahalad argued in his book *The Fortune at the Bottom of the Pyramid*, this group, while often overlooked, represents an incredible business opportunity. Although the poor earn little individually, collectively they represent a vast market—and they often pay a "poverty premium," creating an opening for companies able to deliver quality products at lower prices. For example, there are nine countries—China, India, Brazil, Mexico, Russia, Indonesia, Turkey, South Africa, and Thailand—that are home to 3 billion people and represent 70 percent of the developing world population.[28]

Casas Bahia is a retail chain based in Brazil that specializes in durable goods such as refrigerators, televisions, and washing machines. The firm has carved out a profitable business by selling to poor residents of urban slums. Buyers are carefully screened, then required to come back monthly to their local store to make cash installment payments. The default rate is low, and Casas Bahia has fiercely loyal customers who often become repeat buyers.

Many businesses are learning that focusing on the bottom of the pyramid can foster social development and provide employment in underserved communities—and reap profits.

One product that people in poor countries often desperately need is loans with which to operate or expand their farms or small businesses. Commercial banks have historically

[27] Warby Parker was profiled in "Vision Quest," *Entrepreneur*, January 2012, pp. 56–57.

[28] C. K. Prahalad, *The Fortune at the Bottom of the Pyramid: Eradicating Poverty through Profits* (Upper Saddle River, NJ: Pearson Education, 2006); Stuart L. Hart, *Capitalism at the Crossroads*, 3rd ed. (Upper Saddle River, NJ: Pearson Education, 2010); and "The Fortune at the Bottom of the Pyramid," *Fast Company*, April 13, 2011, *www.fastcompany.com*.

Exhibit 3.C

The Grameen–Danone Foods Social Business Enterprise

In 2006, the Grameen Group, a network of financial institutions, and Groupe Danone, the French-based world leader in fresh dairy food products, agreed to form the Grameen–Danone Foods Social Business Enterprise based in Bangladesh. The goal of this partnership was to bring healthy nutrition to low-income, nutritionally deprived populations throughout Bangladesh and alleviate poverty in the country—a bold mission indeed.

The initial effort was to locally manufacture and market an easily affordable dairy product, a sweet version of yogurt, to satisfy the nutritional needs of Bangladeshi children, whose diet often consisted of only white rice. To maximize the social impact of the project, Grameen and Danone reinvested the profits from this enterprise back into the local and regional economy.

Muhammad Yunus, Grameen founder and Nobel Prize winner, commented, "This represents a unique initiative in creating a social business enterprise, that is, an enterprise created not to maximize profits, but created with a declared mission to maximize benefits to the people served, without incurring losses."

In 2008, raw material costs rose sharply, causing the enterprise board to approve an increase in the price of a cup of yogurt from 5tk to 8tk (6 to 9 cents in U.S. currency) to remain economically sustainable. Immediately, consumer demand collapsed. A month later a new formula was introduced in a smaller cup and at a price of 6tk (about 7 cents U.S.). After a number of promotional events and integration with school nutritional programs, sales recovered. A year later the program extended its outreach to other locations in the country. Television advertisements promoted the product and sales continued to rise. A new product was introduced—the Shokti+pocket, a 5tk pouch with the same nutrition, longer shelf life, and no need for refrigeration. Soon there were plans to expand throughout Bangladesh and into India.

Sources: "Launching of Grameen–Danone Foods Social Business Enterprise," Groupe Danone press release, March 16, 2006. There is a slide presentation describing the enterprise at *muhammadyunas.org*.

been reluctant to make small loans to people with little or no collateral. In response to this need, a new system has emerged called **microfinance**. This occurs when financial organizations provide loans to low-income clients or solidarity lending groups (a community of borrowers) who traditionally lack access to banking or related services. One of the most recognized microfinance institutions is the Grameen Bank in Bangladesh (which is also profiled in Chapter 18). Grameen Bank and its affiliated foundation and partners have had amazing results; by 2012, 1.1 million microloans had been made, nearly 10 million people had been helped, and $180 million had been leveraged to support projects in 13 countries.[29]

Microfinance has developed into a global trend, as evidenced by the annual Global Microcredit Summit, where thousands of business leaders and government representatives from more than 100 countries have gathered to meet since 1997. The Global Microcredit Summit began working with financial institutions to create access to microloans for 7.6 million of the world's poorest citizens and developed a proposal to serve 175 million families, especially the women of those families, by 2015. With an average family size of five people, this program could affect 875 million people around the world.[30] A partnership between the Grameen microfinancing network of organizations and Groupe Danone is described in Exhibit 3.C.

Businesses that sell products and services to the world's poor are, in their own way, promoting a social mission by enhancing economic development.

[29] See the Grameen Foundation website for dozens of success stories attributed to the foundation's microfinancing efforts at *www.grameenfoundation.org*. Also see Virgin Group CEO Richard Branson's opinion piece, "Britain Must Defend This Poverty-Busting Bank," *The Times*, August 24, 2012, p. 28, for a supportive view of Muhammad Yunass' contribution to society.

[30] See the Global Microcredit Summit website at *www.microcreditsummit.org*.

Award-Winning Corporate Social Responsibility Practices

Recognition of corporate social responsibility by business has increased dramatically in the past decade. Since 2000, academic scholars have teamed with KLD Research and Analytics to assess and score businesses' stakeholder relations to create a list of the "100 Best Corporate Citizens." In 2012, Bristol-Myers Squibb, IBM, Intel, Microsoft, and Johnson Controls topped the list. These companies earned the designation of "good corporate citizens" because of their attention to multiple stakeholder relations. The most heavily weighted categories focused on the environment, employees, climate change, human rights, and financial performance.[31]

A study of how Americans ranked companies' reputations, carried out by Harris Interactive, found in 2011 that 44 percent of those polled said that the reputation of corporate America was still falling. But according to the leader of the polling company, "We are seeing a more positive story beginning to develop."

Based on its financial performance and public admiration for its products, Google rose to first place in the Harris Interactive reputation rankings. Despite a year of more than a dozen product recalls, Johnson & Johnson retained its second-place position. In third place was 3M, followed by Berkshire Hathaway and Apple. Other companies got poor marks on the reputational index. Even though the public's view of the top banks improved slightly, the financial industry still placed second-to-last, ahead only of tobacco companies.[32]

Since 2009, the Center for Corporate Citizenship at Boston College has invited business organizations to submit their citizenship story in a one- to three-minute video. The FedEx video, announced as the winner of the first Corporate Citizenship Film Festival, demonstrated how the company used its transportation and logistics skills to meet the needs of communities around the world.[33] In 2010, the honor went to PricewaterhouseCoopers, which supported 100 college students and their service projects targeting areas suffering from the effects of Hurricane Katrina. Cummins received the Corporate Citizenship Film Festival award in 2011 for the company's video that showed its engineers working to bring an innovative power-generating system to a remote village in India.

Social entrepreneurs have also been recognized for their exemplary business practices. Each year *Bloomberg Businessweek* selects "America's Most Promising Social Entrepreneurs." These have included:

- University of California business students Nikhil Arora and Alex Velez, who created BTTR Ventures to turn nutrient-rich discarded coffee grounds into fertilizer for growing mushrooms and sold their mushrooms to Whole Foods.

- Todd Smith, Jess Lin, and Greg Wong, who started Hello Rewind and sold custom sleeves for laptops out of old T-shirts. The laptop sleeves sold for $49 and brought in more than $226,000 in 2010. The group's primary mission was to help victims of sex trafficking in New York break out of the cycle of prostitution and obtain jobs, so their company's profits were redirected to help people in need of job counseling and basic language proficiency.[34]

---

[31] For a complete listing of the 100 Best Corporate Citizens for 2012 and the methodology used for these rankings, see "CR's 100 Best Corporate Citizens 2012," *The CR Magazine*, March–April 2012, pp. 13–15 and *www.thecro.com.*

[32] "Google Leads Company-Reputation Poll as Berkshire Slips to No. 4," *Bloomberg*, May 2, 2011, *www.bloomberg.com.*

[33] To view all of the film festival's past winners and all of the current year's videos submissions, see *www.bcccc.net/index.*

[34] The stories of the more than two dozen "promising social entrepreneurs in 2010" can be found at *images.businessweek.com.*

These recognized companies—big and small—exemplify some of the best of corporate social responsibility practices in an era when firms are increasingly being called upon to move beyond rhetoric and put their commitment to social and environmental responsibility into action. They are meeting the public's expectations that the use of corporate power can enhance the well-being of the organization's stakeholders as well as serve the business organization's interests.

Summary

- The world's largest corporations are capable of wielding tremendous influence, at times even more than national governments, due to their economic power. Because of this potential influence, the organizations' stakeholders expect businesses to enhance society when exercising their power.

- The idea of corporate social responsibility in the United States was adopted by business leaders in the early 20th century. It has evolved from a notion of stewardship and strategic responsiveness to an ethics-based understanding found in culture and the practice of corporate citizenship.

- Socially responsible businesses should attempt to balance economic, legal, and social obligations. Following an enlightened self-interest approach, a firm may be economically rewarded while society benefits from the firm's actions.

- Corporate social responsibility is a debatable notion. Some argue that its benefits include discouraging government regulation, promoting long-term profitability for the firm, and enhancing the company's stakeholder relationships and business reputation. Others believe that it lowers efficiency, imposes undue costs, and shifts unnecessary obligations to business. Most executives believe that they should use their corporate power and influence to balance their response to multiple stakeholders rather than maximize stockholders' return alone.

- Social enterprises adopt social benefit as a core mission. These include B Corporations and a wide range of social entrepreneurial ventures around the world.

- Businesses have discovered that serving people at the bottom of the pyramid can be a profitable strategy, as well as help people in developing economies.

- Many organizations, large and small, have been recognized for their socially responsible or social entrepreneurship best practices. These practices have enhanced the organization's reputation with its stakeholders.

Key Terms

B Corporation, *60*
bottom of the pyramid, *61*
corporate power, *47*
corporate social responsibility, *49*

enlightened self-interest, *52*
iron law of responsibility, *49*
microfinance, *62*
reputation, *55*

social enterprise, *59*
social entrepreneur, *60*
social entrepreneurship, *60*

Discussion Case: *Timberland's Corporate Social Responsibility—Under New Ownership*

Timberland, a New Hampshire–based manufacturer of rugged outdoor boots, clothing, and accessories, was long known for its deep commitment to corporate social responsibility. When VF Corporation, a huge apparel and footwear conglomerate (and home to such brands as North Face, Wrangler, and Eagle Creek), acquired Timberland in 2011, many wondered whether VF would continue to support Timberland's many social initiatives.

Founded in 1918 in Boston by an immigrant shoemaker named Nathan Swartz, Timberland was run for almost a century by three generations of the Swartz family. Although the company was taken public in 1987, the Swartz family and its trusts and charitable foundations continued to hold about 48 percent of Timberland stock until the acquisition. The company's mission was ". . . to equip people to make a difference in their world. We do this by creating outstanding products and by trying to make a difference in the communities where we live and work." Jeffrey Swartz, the grandson of the founder and the last member of the family to serve as CEO, put the commitment this way:

> At Timberland, doing well and doing good are not separate or separable efforts. Every day, everywhere, we compete in the global economy. At the center of our efforts is the premise of service, service to a truth larger than self, a demand more pressing even than this quarter's earnings. While we are absolutely accountable to our shareholders, we also recognize and accept our responsibility to share our strength—to work, in the context of our for-profit business, for the common good.

Under the leadership of the Swartz family, the commitment to "doing good" took many forms. In 1992, the company launched the Path to Service program, which provided employees with numerous opportunities for community involvement—from engaging youth in art and cultural education in Kliptown, South Africa; to participating in rural medicine outreach in Santiago, Dominican Republic; to creating a 30-mile bike path along the seacoast of New England. As soon as they were hired, employees were granted up to 40 hours of paid time per year to participate in company-sponsored community service activities. Although participation was voluntary, almost 95 percent did so, and most cited the program as one of the most valuable benefits offered by the company.

Timberland contributed more than 4 percent of its operating income as charitable gifts. In 2010, it gave more than $1million in cash donations, with hundreds of gifts of in-kind contributions—tools and materials for service events—and nearly $2 million in product donations. Timberland sent 25,000 pairs of shoes to Afghanistan so that schoolchildren there would have proper footwear.

Timberland also focused on sustainability issues. By the end of 2010, Timberland had reduced its carbon emissions by 38 percent, from a 2006 baseline. The company had accomplished this by installing LED lighting in its stores in the United States and directing its European stores to purchase renewable energy. Shortly before its acquisition by VF, Timberland unveiled new sustainability goals for 2015, committing the company to reducing its carbon emissions by 50 percent and increasing its use of purchased energy from renewable sources to 39 percent of total energy consumption. Timberland established a baseline for its supply chain emissions and challenged all of its suppliers to meet Level 2 of the Global Social Compliance Program standards. "Setting aggressive goals challenge us to go to places we never would," said Timberland's CSR Strategy and Reporting Manager.

In September 2011, right after the acquisition, Timberland celebrated its centennial birthday with a service event called Serv-a-Palooza at its corporate headquarters in New Hampshire. Timberland employees volunteered for various activities, including:

- Touched by the suffering of families in tornado-devastated Joplin, Missouri, Timberland volunteers worked with Habitat for Humanity and framed four houses in its corporate parking lot to be shipped for final assembly in Missouri.
- Timberland volunteers created a new outdoor community gathering and performance space, built an outdoor classroom at a local elementary school, and improved the high school athletic facilities in Newmarket, New Hampshire—the birthplace of Timberland.
- Volunteers worked on "greening" a community center for local nonprofit organizations, transforming the meeting space for local disabled veterans, and knitting blankets for families affected by the Missouri tornados.

Many longtime Timberland employees were pleased to see that among the 566 volunteers were leaders of VF Corporation and their family members. "Their involvement was important as we're transitioning," said a Timberland executive. "People were wondering 'what now?' To have VF and some of their outdoor brands participate in our annual day of service symbolized their commitment to understanding and experiencing something that is uniquely Timberland."

Sources: Based on author interviews and information from the company's website at *www.timberland.com*. Both quotations by Jeff Swartz are from "Doing Well and Doing Good: The Business Community and National Service," *The Brookings Review* 20, no. 4 (Fall 2002). Other quotes are from the company's website.

Discussion Questions

1. How would you characterize Timberland's exercise of its corporate power in society? Is Timberland using its influence responsibly? If so, how?
2. Has Timberland balanced its economic and social responsibilities through its various programs, such as the annual Serv-a-Palooza event and sustainability goals? Are the company's programs examples of enlightened self-interest?
3. What are the arguments for and against Timberland's social responsibility initiatives?
4. If you were an executive of VF Corporation, would you support continuation of these initiatives? Why or why not?

PART TWO

Business and Ethics

Ethics and Ethical Reasoning

People who work in business frequently encounter and must deal with on-the-job ethical issues. Being ethical is important to the individual, the organization, and the global marketplace in today's business climate. Managers and employees alike must learn how to recognize ethical dilemmas and know why they occur. In addition, they need to be aware of the role their own ethical character plays in their decision-making process, as well as the influence of the ethical character of others. Finally, managers and employees must be able to analyze the ethical problems they encounter at work to determine an ethical resolution to these dilemmas.

This Chapter Focuses on These Key Learning Objectives:

- Defining ethics and business ethics.
- Evaluating why businesses should be ethical.
- Knowing why ethical problems occur in business.
- Identifying managerial values as influencing ethical decision making.
- Recognizing how people's spirituality influences their ethical behavior.
- Understanding stages of moral reasoning.
- Analyzing ethical problems using generally accepted ethics theories.

In 2011, Raj Rajaratnam, founder and former hedge-fund manager at the Galleon Group, was convicted of five counts of conspiracy and nine counts of insider trading. He was sentenced to serve more than 11 years in federal prison for his key role in a series of insider trading actions where Rajaratnam convinced other hedge-fund traders, industry consultants, and corporate directors to provide him with confidential corporate information so he could "get an edge" over other traders. He also was fined $10 million and ordered to forfeit $53.8 million in profits. "His crimes and the scope of his crimes reflect a virus in our business culture that needs to be eradicated," explained U.S. District Judge Richard Howell. A month later Rajaratnam was ordered to pay more than $92.8 million in fines resolving a separate civil case.

Other Galleon Group executives were caught up in the insider-trading case. Hedge-fund trader Michael Kimelman was sentenced to 2½ years in prison, joining Zvi Goffer, the alleged "ringleader" of the scheme, who was sentenced to 10 years in prison, and Zvi's brother, Emanuel, who received a three-year prison term. In addition, Rajat Gupta, a former Goldman Sachs board member, was found guilty of conspiracy and securities fraud for leaking boardroom secrets to Rajaratnam. Sixty other Wall Street traders and corporate executives involved in this insider-trading scandal pleaded guilty or were found guilty.[1]

With the Galleon Group insider-trading scandal as a backdrop, this chapter explores the meaning of ethics, explains why businesses should be ethical, identifies the different types of ethical problems that occur in business, and focuses on an ethical decision-making framework influenced by the core elements of an individual's ethical character. Then in Chapter 5 we will build on this with a discussion of how ethical performance in business can be improved by strengthening the organization's culture and climate and by providing organizational safeguards, such as policies, training, and reporting procedures.

The Meaning of Ethics

Ethics is a conception of right and wrong conduct. It tells us whether our behavior is moral or immoral and deals with fundamental human relationships—how we think and behave toward others and how we want them to think and behave toward us. **Ethical principles** are guides to moral behavior. For example, in most societies lying, stealing, deceiving, and harming others are considered to be unethical and immoral. Honesty, keeping promises, helping others, and respecting the rights of others are considered to be ethically and morally desirable behavior. Such basic rules of behavior are essential for the preservation and continuation of organized life everywhere.

These notions of right and wrong come from many sources. Religious beliefs are a major source of ethical guidance for many. The family institution—whether two parents, a single parent, or a large family with brothers and sisters, grandparents, aunts, cousins, and other kin—imparts a sense of right and wrong to children as they grow up. Schools and schoolteachers, neighbors and neighborhoods, friends, admired role models, ethnic groups, and the ever-present electronic media and the Internet influence what we believe to be right and wrong in life. The totality of these learning experiences creates in each person a

---

[1] Quotations and information for this example are from "Inside-Trade Sentencing Gets Tougher," *The Wall Street Journal*, October 12, 2011, *online.wsj.com*; "Ex-Trader Kimelman Sentenced in Insider Case," *The Wall Street Journal*, October 13, 2011, *online.wsj.com*; "Rajaratnam Gets 11 Years in Insider-Trading Case," *The Wall Street Journal*, October 13, 2011, *online.wsj.com*; "Rajaratnam Ordered to Pay Record SEC Penalty," *The Wall Street Journal*, November 9, 2011, *online.wsj.com*; and "Rajat Gupta Convicted of Insider Trading," *The New York Times Dealbook*, June 15, 2012, *dealbook.nytimes.com*.

concept of ethics, morality, and socially acceptable behavior. This core of ethical beliefs then acts as a moral compass that helps guide a person when ethical puzzles arise.

Ethical ideas are present in all societies, organizations, and individual persons, although they may vary greatly from one to another. Your ethics may not be the same as your neighbor's; one particular religion's notion of morality may not be identical to another's; or what is considered ethical in one society may be forbidden in another society. These differences raise the important and controversial issue of **ethical relativism**, which holds that ethical principles should be defined by various periods of time in history, a society's traditions, the special circumstances of the moment, or personal opinion. In this view, the meaning given to ethics would be relative to time, place, circumstance, and the person involved. In that case, the logical conclusion would be that there would be no universal ethical standards on which people around the globe could agree. However, for companies conducting business in several societies at one time, whether or not ethics is relevant can be vitally important; we discuss these issues in more detail in Chapter 5.

For the moment, however, we can say that despite the diverse systems of ethics that exist within our own society and throughout the world, all people everywhere do depend on ethical systems to tell them whether their actions are right or wrong, moral or immoral, approved or disapproved. Ethics, in this basic sense, is a universal human trait, found everywhere.

What Is Business Ethics?

Business ethics is the application of general ethical ideas to business behavior. Business ethics is not a special set of ethical ideas different from ethics in general and applicable only to business. If dishonesty is considered to be unethical and immoral, then anyone in business who is dishonest with stakeholders—employees, customers, stockholders, or competitors—is acting unethically and immorally. If protecting others from harm is considered to be ethical, then a company that recalls a dangerously defective product is acting in an ethical way. To be considered ethical, business must draw its ideas about what is proper behavior from the same sources as everyone else in society. Business should not try to make up its own definitions of what is right and wrong. Employees and managers may believe at times that they are permitted or even encouraged to apply special or weaker ethical rules to business situations, but society does not condone or permit such an exception. In a series of studies conducted by the Ethics Resource Center, researchers found that observations of unethical conduct in the workplace reached a peak in 2009 and then dropped slightly in 2011, although unethical behavior by employees remains a serious problem for businesses, as shown in Figure 4.1.

FIGURE 4.1
Observing Misconduct at Work, 2000–2011

Source: *2011 National Business Ethics Survey—Workplace Ethics in Transition,* Ethics Resource Center, Washington, DC, 2012.

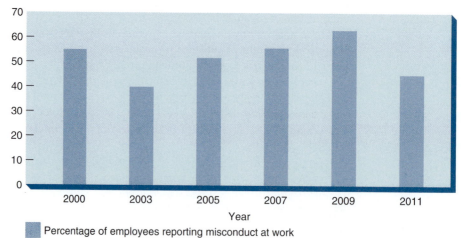

Year

 Percentage of employees reporting misconduct at work

FIGURE 4.2
**Why Should Business
Be Ethical?**

To meet demands of business stakeholders.
To enhance business performance.
To comply with legal requirements.
To prevent or minimize harm.
To promote personal morality.

The Ethics Resource Center reported that the combination of high rates of misconduct with low management awareness and few ethics and compliance programs led to a "treacherous ethics landscape." The top three types of observed misconduct were conflicts of interest, abusive or intimidating behavior, and lying to employees. Some positive findings were found in the 2011 report: employees increasingly reported bad behavior when they saw it at work—65 percent, a record high for the Ethics Resource Center's studies and up 2 percent from 2009. But there was some bad news, too. Retaliation against employees who reported bad behavior rose sharply, with 22 percent of employees who reported misconduct saying they experienced some sort of retaliation in return. The number of employees who reported pressure at work to compromise their ethical standards also rose in 2011, compared to 2009.[2]

Why Should Business Be Ethical?

Why should business be ethical? What prevents a business firm from piling up as much profit as it can, in any way it can, regardless of ethical considerations? Figure 4.2 lists the major reasons why business firms should promote a high level of ethical behavior.

Meet Demands of Business Stakeholders

In Chapter 3, we mentioned one reason businesses should be ethical when discussing social responsibility. Organizational stakeholders demand that businesses exhibit high levels of ethical performance and social responsibility. On a positive note, many employees believe that their firms are addressing these stakeholder demands. About three-fourths of employees surveyed believed their firms were considering the environment, employee well-being, and the interests of society and the community.[3] This positive attitude has a positive impact for business, too. If employees have an ethical view of their company, they likely have greater pride in working there, have higher overall work satisfaction, and are willing to recommend the company as a good place to work, according to a 2010 Kenexa Research Institute study in the U.K.[4]

Some businesses know that meeting stakeholders' expectations is good business. When a company upholds ethical standards, consumers may conduct more business with the firm and the stockholders may benefit as well, as illustrated by the Co-operative Bank, a retail bank based in Manchester, United Kingdom: "Living life and doing business in a socially responsible way isn't just good for the soul. It really does make a positive impact in the community and can save you money. Together we're stronger; together we can make a difference in your world."[5]

The Co-operative Bank first introduced its Ethics Policy in 1992. The bank's policy precluded it from lending funds to firms that were involved in animal testing, nuclear power, unfair labor practices, or weapons production. Since then it withheld

[2] *2011 National Business Ethics Survey*, Ethics Resource Center, Washington, DC, 2012, p. 12.
[3] Ibid., p. 19.
[4] "Only 40% of Employees Say Their Business Is Ethical," *HR Zone*, April 28, 2010, *www.hrzone.co.uk*.
[5] See Co-operative Bank's website at *www.co-operativebank.co.uk*.

over £1 billion of funding from businesses whose policies violated the bank's ethics standards. Yet, the bank reported that these losses were more than made up by income from consumers who supported the bank's strong ethical stand. During the same time period, Co-operative Bank increased its commercial lending sixteen-fold to almost £9 billion and experienced strong growth in profitability, increased customer deposits, and other positive financial measures.[6]

Enhance Business Performance

Some people argue that another reason for businesses to be ethical is that it enhances the firm's performance, or simply: *ethics pays.*

Empirical studies have supported the economic benefits of being perceived as an ethical company. *Ethisphere* also found a strong link between ethics and financial performance. Companies that were on *Ethisphere*'s list of the *World's Most Ethical Companies* have returned 53 percent to shareholders since 2005, significantly better than the Standard and Poor's benchmark return of only 4 percent. This positive relationship between ethics and profits can be seen in Figure 4.3.

Another way ethical performance is linked to financial performance is when considering the firm's **integrity capital**. The Corporate Executive Board defines integrity capital as "the financial benefit a company reaps from promoting a culture of integrity among its workforce." A Corporate Executive Board study of 130 companies found companies with the highest integrity capital outperformed those with the lowest integrity capital by more than 16 percentage points when it came to shareholder returns. In addition, companies with a culture of high integrity enjoyed a 12 percent advantage in employee productivity over other firms.[7]

Businesses increasingly are recognizing that ethics pays and are encouraging ethical behavior by their employees. Business executives recognize that ethical actions can directly affect their organization's bottom line.

FIGURE 4.3
World's Most Ethical Index versus S&P 500 and FTSE 100, 2005–2010

Source: See www.ethisphere .com/2011-worlds-most-ethical -companies/

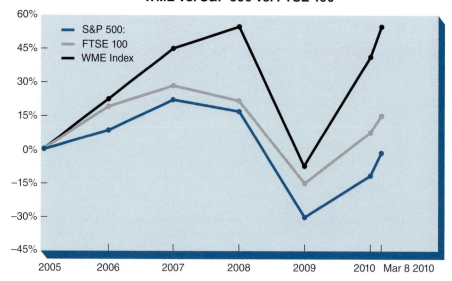

[6] For additional information about Co-operative Bank, *see www.goodwithmoney.co.uk.*

[7] "Is Your Company Building 'Integrity Capital'?", *Corporate Secretary*, June 2, 2011, *www.businessinsider.com.*

It is also clear that a lack of ethics has serious negative financial impact. Researchers have identified that costs to the company go far beyond the government's fines. In a study conducted by the University of Washington's business school, researchers found that "companies that have cooked their books [misstated accounting information] lose 41 percent of their market value after news spreads about their misdeeds." The reputational damage to the company is calculated to be 7.5 times the amount of the penalties imposed by government.[8] Unethical performance also may result in a loss of business. According to a Dow Jones survey of multinational companies, more than half of the firms were abandoning partnerships with agents, distributors, consultants, and joint ventures over concerns about liability arising from corruption activities and enforcement of anti-corruption regulations.[9]

Comply with Legal Requirements

Doing business ethically is also often a legal requirement. Two legal requirements, in particular, provide direction for companies interested in being more ethical in their business operations. Although they apply only to U.S.–based firms, these legal requirements also provide a model for firms that operate outside the United States.

The first is the **U.S. Corporate Sentencing Guidelines**, which provide a strong incentive for businesses to promote ethics at work.[10] The sentencing guidelines come into play when an employee of a firm has been found guilty of criminal wrongdoing and the firm is facing sentencing for the criminal act, since the firm is responsible for actions taken by its employees. To determine the sentencing, the judge computes a culpability (degree of blame) score using the guidelines, based on whether or not the company has:

1. Established standards and procedures to reduce criminal conduct.
2. Assigned high-level officer(s) responsibility for compliance.
3. Not assigned discretionary authority to "risky" individuals.
4. Effectively communicated standards and procedures through training.
5. Taken reasonable steps to ensure compliance—monitor and audit systems, maintain and publicize reporting system.
6. Enforced standards and procedures through disciplinary mechanisms.
7. Following detection of offense, responded appropriately and prevented reoccurrence.

Companies that have taken these steps, or most of them, typically receive lesser sentences or lower fines.

> The impact of the sentencing guidelines was felt by Hoffman-LaRoche. The multinational pharmaceutical company pleaded guilty to a price-fixing conspiracy in the vitamins market that spanned nine years and was fined $500 million. Although this was a significant financial blow to the firm, the government noted that the sentencing guidelines permitted a fine as high as $1.3 billion against Hoffman-LaRoche. The sentence was reduced because Hoffman-LaRoche had met many of the sentencing guidelines directives.

[8] "Cooked Books, Fried Reputation: Study," *Ethics Newsline*, Institute for Global Ethics, November 20, 2006, *www.globalethics .org*. Also see Jonathan M. Karpoff, D. Scott Lee, and Gerald S. Martin, "The Cost to Firms of Cooking the Books," *Journal of Financial and Quantitative Analysis*, 2008, pp. 581–611.

[9] "Corruption Concerns Cause Companies to Abandon Partners," *The Wall Street Journal*, March 30, 2011, *blogs.wsj.com*.

[10] For a thorough discussion of the U.S. Corporate Sentencing Guidelines, see Dan R. Dalton, Michael B. Metzger, and John W. Hill, "The 'New' U.S. Sentencing Commission Guidelines: A Wake-Up Call for Corporate America," *Academy of Management Executive*, 1994, pp. 7–13; and Dove Izraeli and Mark S. Schwartz, "What Can We Learn from the U.S. Federal Sentencing Guidelines for Organizational Ethics?" *Journal of Business Ethics*, 1998, pp. 1045–55.

Exhibit 4.A

Update to the Sarbanes-Oxley Act

Since the Sarbanes-Oxley Act was established in 2002, a number of provisions within the act have loosened. In 2006, rather than requiring elaborate, third-party audits of the company's financial records, the SEC developed more lenient guidelines on requiring companies to review their own systems for ensuring financial reports and then have them verified by outside auditors. Another round of regulation loosening occurred in 2007 when the SEC provided a more relaxed set of guidelines applied to small businesses and their compliance with the Sarbanes-Oxley Act. The new rules allow for more internal initiatives, rather than external auditing examinations, in discovering where financial controls are working or not and where areas of fraud or other financial violations are more likely to occur.

The most serious challenge to the act was in 2010 when critics questioned the constitutionality of the Public Company Accounting Oversight Board (PCAOB), created by the act. In *Free Enterprise Fund v. Public Company Accounting Oversight Board,* a group of business leaders and accounting firms questioned the PCAOB's authority since it was created by the Securities and Exchange Commission, rather than the president of the United States, and therefore violated the separation of powers in government by giving too much authority to regulators. In a 5 to 4 decision the U.S. Supreme Court upheld the Sarbanes-Oxley Act and the PCAOB's powers.

Sources: "Business Wins Its Battle to Ease a Costly Sarbanes-Oxley Rule," *The Wall Street Journal,* November 10, 2006, *online.wsj.com;* "SEC Revises Its Standards for Corporate Audits," *The New York Times,* May 24, 2007, *www.nytimes.com;* and "Supreme Court Upholds Sarbanes-Oxley Act," *The Washington Post,* June 29, 2010, p. A7.

The U.S. Sentencing Commission reviewed and made slight revisions to the Sentencing Guidelines in 2004 and 2010, yet the "seven steps" described above remain the blueprint for many businesses in designing their ethics and compliance program.[11]

Another legal requirement imposed upon U.S. businesses is the **Sarbanes-Oxley Act** of 2002.[12] Born from the ethics scandals at Enron, WorldCom, Tyco, and others, this law seeks to ensure that firms maintain high ethical standards in how they conduct and monitor business operations. For example, the Sarbanes-Oxley Act requires executives to vouch for the accuracy of a firm's financial reports and requires them to pay back bonuses based on earnings that are later proved fraudulent. The act also established strict rules for auditing firms. Recent changes in regulatory interpretation of the Sarbanes-Oxley Act are shown in Exhibit 4.A.

After the passage of the Sarbanes-Oxley Act, experts estimated that compliance costs were likely to total $7 billion annually for firms governed by the legislation. In fact, Sarbanes-Oxley compliance costs have been declining, partly due to the changes in the SEC rules described in Exhibit 4.A, and partly due to the need for fewer employee hours needed to handle compliance activities. In the first year of compliance, costs averaged $4.51 million per firm. By 2006, costs fell 23 percent, to an average of $2.92 million per company. In a 2010 study of 400 companies, firms generally reported that much of the cost burden for compliance was concentrated in the first few years, with costs trailing off over time.[13]

[11] For a discussion of the most recent Sentencing Guidelines amendments see Eric Moreland and Ryan McConnell, "The New Amendments: Examining the Latest Additions to the Organizational Sentencing Guidelines," *Ethisphere,* Q1, 2010, pp. 47–49.

[12] See Howard Rockness and Joanne Rockness, "Legislated Ethics: From Enron to Sarbanes-Oxley, the Impact on Corporate America," *Journal of Business Ethics,* 2005, pp. 31–54; and Alix Valenti, "The Sarbanes-Oxley Act of 2002: Has It Brought About Changes in the Boards of Large U.S. Corporations?" *Journal of Business Ethics,* 2008, pp. 401–12.

[13] "Costs to Comply with Sarbanes Decline Again," *The Wall Street Journal,* May 16, 2007, *online.wsj.com;* and "Sarbanes-Oxley Gains Some Acceptance, Survey Finds," *The New York Times,* June 17, 2010, *www.nytimes.com.*

Although costs are declining, most CEOs believe that the Sarbanes-Oxley Act was "an overreaction to the ethical failures of a handful of executives" and was unhealthy for the business environment. But, in 2010, Protiviti reported that 70 percent of the more than 400 firms who put in place accounting controls required by the act said that the benefits outweighed its costs. "What was once a compliance 'burden' for many companies . . . has evolved into something broader than its original objective," said Bob Hirth, head of Protiviti's global internal audit and financial control practice.[14]

Prevent or Minimize Harm

Another reason businesses and their employees should act ethically is to prevent harm to the general public and the corporation's many stakeholders. One of the strongest ethical principles is stated very simply: *Do no harm.* The notorious examples of outright greed and other unethical behavior by managers in the financial community contributed in part to the long-lasting Great Recession in the United States and around the world. These managers' unethical actions were responsible for significant harm to many stakeholders in society. Investors' portfolios dropped in value, retirees saw their nest eggs dwindle, hundreds of thousands of employees lost their jobs, and many small businesses failed. The costs of the financial sector's unethical behaviors devastated many in our society, and it will require years of effort and hard work to rebuild from this damage.

Promote Personal Morality

A final reason for promoting ethics in business is a personal one. Most people want to act in ways that are consistent with their own sense of right and wrong. Being pressured to contradict their personal values creates emotional stress. Knowing that one works in a supportive ethical climate contributes to one's sense of psychological security.

> More than one in three American employees reportedly have left their jobs because they disagreed with a company's business ethics. According to an LRN Corporation study, "A majority of workers—94 percent—say it is 'critical' or 'important' that the company they work for is ethical." Eighty-two percent said they would prefer to be paid less but work for a company with ethical business practices than receive higher pay at a company with questionable ethics. "Our findings confirm that companies with a commitment to ethical conduct enjoy distinct advantages in the marketplace, including attracting and retaining talent," said LRN's CEO Dov Seidman.[15]

Why Ethical Problems Occur in Business

If businesses have so many reasons to be ethical, why do ethical problems occur? Although not necessarily common or universal, ethical problems occur frequently in business. Finding out what causes them is one step toward minimizing their impact on business operations and on the people affected. Some of the main reasons are summarized in Figure 4.4 and are discussed next.

[14] *The National Survey of CEOs on Business Ethics,* Georgia State University's Center for Ethics and Corporate Responsibility and Clemson University's Robert J. Rutland Institute for Ethics, 2008, available online at *robinson.gsu.edu/files/ethics/2008CEO_Survey.pdf*; and "Sarbanes-Oxley Gains Some Acceptance, Survey Finds," *The New York Times*, June 17, 2010, *www.nytimes.com.*

[15] "Study: Workers Will Quit over Ethics," *LRN Corporation*, August 3, 2006, *www.centralvalleybusinesstimes.com.*

FIGURE 4.4
Why Ethical
Problems Occur in
Business

Reason	Nature of Ethical Problem	Typical Approach	Attitude
Personal gain and selfish interest	Selfish interest versus others' interests	Egotistical mentality	"I want it!"
Competitive pressures on profits	Firm's interest versus others' interests	Bottom-line mentality	"We have to beat the others at all costs!"
Conflicts of interest	Multiple obligations or loyalties	Favoritism mentality	"Help yourself and those closest to you!"
Cross-cultural contradictions	Company's interests versus diverse cultural traditions and values	Ethnocentric mentality	"Foreigners have a funny notion of what's right and wrong."

Personal Gain and Selfish Interest

Desire for personal gain, or even greed, causes some ethics problems. Businesses sometimes employ people whose personal values are less than desirable, who will put their own welfare ahead of all others, regardless of the harm done to other employees, the company, or society.

A manager or employee who puts his or her own self-interest above all other considerations is called an **ethical egoist**.[16] Self-promotion, a focus on self-interest to the point of selfishness, and greed are traits commonly observed in an ethical egoist. The ethical egoist tends to ignore ethical principles accepted by others, believing that ethical rules are made for others. Altruism—acting for the benefit of others when self-interest is sacrificed—is seen to be sentimental or even irrational. "Looking out for number one" is the ethical egoist's motto, as the Rajaratnam example at the beginning of this chapter and the following stories show:

> Gary Foster, a former Citigroup vice president, embezzled nearly $23 million from the bank by wiring company funds to his personal account at JPMorgan. Foster used the company money to purchase a Ferrari, a Maserati, and residences in Manhattan, Brooklyn, and New Jersey. "The defendant violated his employer's trust and stole a stunning amount of money over an extended period of time to finance his personal lifestyle," explained U.S. Attorney Loretta Lynch. Foster pleaded guilty to bank fraud in 2011.
>
> New York prosecutors charged Dennis Kozlowski, former CEO of Tyco, with stealing more than $170 million from the company. Kozlowski was also accused of borrowing $270 million from a company loan program intended to help him pay taxes, but he improperly used 90 percent of this money for personal expenses, such as yachts, jewelry, fine art, and real estate. Kozlowski was sentenced to up to 25 years in a New York state prison.[17]

---

[16] For a compact discussion of ethical egoism, see Tom L. Beauchamp and Norman E. Bowie, *Ethical Theory and Business*, 7th ed. (Upper Saddle River, NJ: Prentice Hall, 2004), pp. 12–16; and Laura P. Hartman and Joe DesJardins, *Business Ethics: Decision-Making for Personal Integrity and Social Responsibility*, 2nd ed. (New York: McGraw-Hill, 2011), p. 102.

[17] "Ex-Citigroup Executive Foster Pleads Guilty to Bank Fraud," *Bloomberg*, September 6, 2011, *www.bloomberg.com*; and "Kozlowski, Swartz Sentenced to Up to 25 Years in Prison," *The Wall Street Journal*, September 19, 2005, *online.wsj.com*.

Competitive Pressures on Profits

When companies are squeezed by tough competition, they sometimes engage in unethical activities to protect their profits. This may be especially true in companies whose financial performance is already substandard. Research has shown that managers of poor financial performers and companies with financial uncertainty are more prone to commit illegal acts. In addition, intense competitive pressure in the global marketplace has resulted in unethical activity, such as the practice of price fixing or a violation of competition law.

> German antitrust regulators fined three coffee roaster firms and six managers a total of €159.5 million ($229 million) for creating a scheme to fix prices of beans, espresso, and filtered bags. The price-fixing system was in place for nearly a decade and "the price fixing was directly burdening consumers, because retailers as a rule immediately passed on higher prices (set by the coffee makers)," reported the German Federal Cartel Office.
>
> In 2010, the U.K. competition authorities stepped in and ordered the Royal Bank of Scotland (RBS) to pay £28.59 million ($42.8 million) for colluding with rival Barclays PLC on loan pricing. According to the Office of Fair Trading, confidential loan-pricing information was given by RBS employees to Barclays on general lending as well as specific loans.[18]

Conflicts of Interest

Ethical challenges in business often arise in the form of conflicts of interest. A **conflict of interest** occurs when an individual's self-interest conflicts with acting in the best interest of another, when the individual has an obligation to do so.[19] For example, if a purchasing agent directed her company's orders to a firm from which she had received a valuable gift, regardless if this firm offered the best quality or value, she would be accused of unethical behavior because of a conflict of interest. In this situation, she would have acted to benefit herself, rather than in the best interests of her employer. A failure to disclose a conflict of interest represents deception in and of itself and may hurt the person or organization on whose behalf judgment has been exercised. Many ethicists believe that even the *appearance* of a conflict of interest should be avoided because it undermines trust.

Both individuals and organizations can be in a conflict of interest. In recent years, much attention has been focused on organizational conflicts of interest in the accounting profession. When an accounting firm audits the books of a public company, it has an obligation to shareholders to provide an honest account of the company's financial health. Sometimes, though, accounting firms may be tempted to overlook irregularities to increase their chances of attracting lucrative consulting work from the same company. This conflict is now significantly curtailed by provisions in the Sarbanes-Oxley Act, which restricts accounting firms from providing both auditing and consulting services to the same client.

Many cases of financial fraud illustrate conflicts of interest, in which opportunities for self-enrichment by senior managers conflict with the long-term viability of the firm and the best interests of employees, customers, suppliers, and stockholders. The case "Moody's Credit Ratings and the Subprime Mortgage Meltdown," which appears at the end of this book, describes an organizational conflict of interest in which a company was paid by the firms whose bonds it rated, rather than by the buyers of these bonds. Many firms seek to

---

[18] "German Coffee Roasters Fined $229 Million in Price-Fixing Case," *Bloomberg.com*, December 21, 2009, *www.bloomberg.com*; and "RBS Fined for Breaching Competition Law," *The Wall Street Journal*, March 30, 2010, *online.wsj.com*.

[19] Based on John R. Boatright, *Ethics and the Conduct of Business,* 6th ed. (Upper Saddle River, NJ: Prentice Hall, 2009), pp. 123–24.

guard against the dangers inherent in conflicts of interest by including prohibitions of any such practices in their codes of ethics, as discussed in Chapter 5.

Cross-Cultural Contradictions

Some of the knottiest ethical problems occur as corporations do business in other societies where ethical standards differ from those at home. Today, the policymakers and strategic planners in all multinational corporations, regardless of the nation where they are headquartered, face this kind of ethical dilemma. Consider the following situation:

> PPG Industries, the global leader in coatings and specialty products operating in more than 60 countries around the world, has sold high lead content paint to the African nation of Cameroon for many years. The United States banned interior and exterior household paint with lead content above 600 parts per million in 1978 and tightened this standard to 90 parts per million in 2008 to reduce the risk of lead poisoning in children who can ingest paint chips, flakes, or peelings or inhale lead paint dust. But as far as international sales, the company maintained that it "initiated its own action to review its consumer coatings to ensure the lead content conforms to applicable legal requirements." Cameroon has no lead paint limits, and PPG's product on the shelves in stores in this country have lead paint levels of well above the U.S. legal limit. Studies have shown that even low-level lead exposure can significantly affect mental capacity, and higher exposures can cause behavioral problems, learning disabilities, even seizures and death. PPG stopped short of requiring its newly acquired Cameroon subsidiary, Seigneurie, to recall the lead-based paint already on the market in Cameroon or label it as containing lead but has agreed to exchange lead-free paint for previously sold paint containing lead.[20]

This episode raises the issue of *ethical relativism,* which was defined earlier in this chapter. Although the sale of lead-based paint in Cameroon was *legal,* was it *ethical?* Is the selling of unsafe products by any measure *ethical* if it is not forbidden by the receiving nation, especially if the company knows that the products are exported to another country where others are exposed to serious health risks? *Are multinational companies ethically responsible for what happens to their products, even though they are being sold legally? Which standards or whose ethical standards should be the guide?*

As business becomes increasingly global, with more and more corporations penetrating overseas markets where cultures and ethical traditions vary, these cross-cultural questions will occur more frequently.

The Core Elements of Ethical Character

The ethical analysis and resolution of ethical dilemmas in the workplace significantly depend on the ethical character and moral development of managers and other employees. Good ethical practices not only are possible, but also become normal with the right combination of these components.

Managers' Values

Managers are key to whether a company and its employees will act ethically or unethically. As major decision makers, they have more opportunities than others to create an ethical

---

[20] "PPG Refuses to Recall Leaded Paint in Cameroon," *Pittsburgh Post-Gazette*, February 6, 2012, *www.post-gazette.com.*

tone for their company. The values held by managers, especially the top-level managers, will serve as models for others who work at the company.

Unfortunately, according to a 2009 opinion poll, Americans hold a dim view of business executives' and managers' values. A majority—60 percent—of the 2,000 American adults polled gave Wall Street executives poor grades when it came to honesty and ethics. Other executives did not fare much better, with 49 percent receiving poor grades. One-third of American employees surveyed in July 2010 said they planned to look for a new job as soon as the economy got better, citing a loss of trust in their employer and a lack of transparency by their company's leadership as the primary reasons for pursuing new employment.[21]

In an annual Gallup poll that rated 21 occupations for honesty and ethics, nurses—for the 10th straight year—came out on top. In 2011, only 18 percent of those surveyed saw business executives as having "very high" or "high" ethical standards or honesty. This placed executives below real estate agents and lawyers on this list. Stockbrokers ranked lower than business executives, with lobbyists and members of Congress at the bottom of the list.[22]

How do executives view their own values? Studies generally show that most U.S. managers focus on themselves and are primarily concerned about being competent. They place importance on values such as having a comfortable and exciting life. Researchers also found that new CEOs tend to be more self-interested and short-term focused, possibly in an effort to immediately drive up company profits, rather than valuing long-term investments in research and development or capital expenditures. However, one out of four managers shows a strong concern for moral values that include others, such as living in a world at peace, or seeking equality among people. These managers place greater importance on the value of forgiving others, being helpful, and acting honestly.[23]

The challenge for many moral managers is acting effectively on their beliefs in the day-to-day life of their organizations. Educator Mary Gentile tries to empower business leaders and managers by enabling them to give voice to—and to act on—their values at work. Gentile's "Giving Voice to Values" program believes that the key is knowing how to act on your values despite opposing pressure, and she "offers advice, practical exercises, and scripts for handling a wide range of ethical dilemmas" through her innovative curriculum for values-driven management and leadership.[24]

But what about future managers? A survey of 759 graduating MBA students from 11 top American business schools reported that "a company's CSR performance is a major factor when selecting a new employer." These MBA students said they were willing to sacrifice a portion of their salary to work for a firm that shares their outlook. These results mirror another study, undertaken by Net Impact, an international group of MBA and graduate students, who believe corporations should work for social good. Of the more than 2,000 MBA students surveyed, nearly 80 percent said they wanted to find socially responsible employment in their careers. Seventy-eight percent believed that classes in ethics and social responsibility should be a part of their business school training.

---

[21] "Fortune 1000 Executives Say Loss of Trust Is an Issue," *PR Newswire*, July 26, 2010, *www.prnewswire.com.*

[22] "37% of People Say Lawyers Have 'Very Low' Ethical Standards," *InsideCounsel.com*, December 12, 2011, *www.insidecounsel.com.*

[23] See James Weber, "Managerial Value Orientations: A Typology and Assessment," *International Journal of Value-Based Management*, 1990, pp. 37–54; and Jeffrey S. Harrison and James O. Fiet, "New CEOs Pursue Their Own Self-Interests by Sacrificing Stakeholder Value," *Journal of Business Ethics*, 1999, pp. 301–8.

[24] To learn more about Mary Gentile's "Giving Voice to Values" program, see *www.marygentile.com* or *www.GivingVoicetoValues.com.* at Babson College.

Spirituality in the Workplace

A person's **spirituality**—that is, a personal belief in a supreme being, religious organization, or the power of nature or some other external, life-guiding force—has always been a part of the human makeup. In 1953, *Fortune* published an article titled "Businessmen on Their Knees" and claimed that American businessmen (women generally were excluded from the executive suite in those days) were taking more notice of God. More recently, cover stories in *Fortune, Bloomberg Businessweek,* and other business publications have documented a resurgence of spirituality or religion at work.

As far back as 1976, scholars have found a positive relationship between an organization's economic performance and attention to spiritual values. Scholars have found that spirituality positively affects employee and organizational performance by enhancing intuitive abilities and individual capacity for innovation, as well as increasing personal growth, employee commitment, and responsibility. Best-selling books have touted the importance of managers being sensitive to employees' values and spirituality as a success path. Ethical leadership and ethical cultures in organizations based on a strong sense of spirituality are seen as necessary and productive. As Jack Hawley explains, "All leadership is spiritual because the leader seeks to liberate the best in people and the best is always linked to one's higher self."[25]

Organizations have responded to the increased attention to spirituality and religion at work by attempting to accommodate their employees.

> The chief diversity officer at PricewaterhouseCoopers found office space in their Asia-Pacific region facility to provide a prayer room for their Muslim employees. In the United States, employers are required by law to make substantial accommodations for their employees' religious practices, as long as it does not create major hardships for the organization. Ford's Interfaith Network, a group of employees focusing on religious issues, successfully lobbied the company to install sinks designed for the religious washings that Muslim employees perform.[26]

Most companies use chaplains on an outsourced basis from employee assistance programs or from chaplaincy providers such as Marketplace Ministries, a nonprofit concern that provides about 21,500 Protestant chaplains to more than 400 companies nationwide. Other firms, such as Tyson Foods, have found it worthwhile to have a chaplain on staff full-time. When a Tyson employee told his boss that he had a drug problem, the supervisor sent the employee to the chaplain. The employee thought, "What could he do? Offer me a prayer?" The chaplain met with the employee and over the next few months helped the employee enroll in a drug rehabilitation program, find a drug counselor, and attend Narcotics Anonymous meetings. The spread of the practice of including chaplains within the organization demonstrates the understanding that firms need to embrace their employees' religious or spiritual characteristics as part of who they are as employees, not something relegated to places of worship alone.[27]

[25] The quotation is from Jack Hawley, *Reawakening the Spirit at Work: The Power of Dharmic Management* (San Francisco: Berrett-Koehler, 1993), p. 5. Studies establishing a link between spirituality and spiritual values and economic performance include J. Richard Hackman and Greg Oldham, "Motivation through the Design of Work: A Test of a Theory," *Organizational Behavior and Human Performance* 16 (1976), pp. 250–79; Melvin W. Reder, "Chicago Economics: Permanence and Change," *Journal of Economic Literature,* 1982, pp. 1–38; and Christopher P. Neck and John F. Milliman, "Thought Self-Leadership: Finding Spiritual Fulfillment in Organizational Life," *Journal of Managerial Psychology,* 1994, pp. 9–16.

[26] "When Religious Needs Test Company Policy," *The New York Times,* February 25, 2007, *www.nytimes.com.*

[27] For additional information, see "UNT Faculty Member Researches Workplace Spirituality, Duties of Corporate Chaplains," *University of North Texas News Service,* July 14, 2009, *web3.unt.edu;* "More Businesses Turning to Workplace Chaplains," *The Virginian-Pilot,* October 30, 2011, *hamptonroads.com/2011/10;* and, "The Rise of the Corporate Chaplain," *Bloomberg Businessweek,* August 23, 2012, *www.businessweek.com.* For a list of companies considered "religious," see "10 Religious Companies (Besides Chick-fil-A)," *CNN Belief Blog,* February 7, 2011, *religion.blogs.cnn.com.*

However, others disagree with the trend toward a stronger presence of religion in the workplace. They hold the traditional belief that business is a secular—that is, nonspiritual—institution. They believe that business is business, and spirituality is best left to churches, synagogues, mosques, and meditation rooms, not corporate boardrooms or shop floors. This, of course, reflects the separation of church and state in the United States and many other countries.

Beyond the philosophical opposition to bringing spirituality into the business environment, procedural or practical challenges arise. Whose spirituality should be promoted? The CEO's? *With greater workplace diversity comes greater spiritual diversity, so which organized religion's prayers should be cited or ceremonies enacted? How should businesses handle employees who are agnostics or atheists (who do not follow any religion)?*

Just as personal values and character strongly influence employee decision making and behavior in the workplace, so does personal spirituality, from all points on the religious spectrum, impact how businesses operate.

Managers' Moral Development

People's values and spirituality exert a powerful influence on the way ethical work issues are treated. Since people have different personal histories and have developed their values and spirituality in different ways, they are going to think differently about ethical problems. This is as true of corporate managers as it is of other people. In other words, the managers in a company are likely to be at various **stages of moral development**. Some will reason at a high level, others at a lower level.

A summary of the way people grow and develop morally is diagrammed in Figure 4.5. From childhood to mature adulthood, most people move steadily upward in their moral reasoning capabilities from stage 1. Over time, they become more developed and are capable of more advanced moral reasoning, although some people never use the most advanced stages of reasoning in their decision processes.

At first, individuals are limited to an ego-centered focus (stage 1), fixed on avoiding punishment and obediently following the directions of those in authority. (The word *ego* means "self.") Slowly and sometimes painfully, the child learns that what is considered to

FIGURE 4.5
Stages of Moral Development and Ethical Reasoning

Source: Adapted from Lawrence Kohlberg, *The Philosophy of Moral Development* (New York: Harper & Row, 1981).

Age Group	Development Stage and Major Ethics Referent	Basis of Ethics Reasoning
Mature adulthood	**Stage 6** Universal principles: justice, fairness, universal human rights	Principle-centered reasoning
Mature adulthood	**Stage 5** Moral beliefs above and beyond specific social custom: human rights, social contract, broad constitutional principles	Principle-centered reasoning
Adulthood	**Stage 4** Society at large: customs, traditions, laws	Society- and law-centered reasoning
Early adulthood, adolescence	**Stage 3** Social groups: friends, school, coworkers, family	Group-centered reasoning
Adolescence, youth	**Stage 2** Reward seeking: self-interest, own needs, reciprocity	Ego-centered reasoning
Childhood	**Stage 1** Punishment avoidance: avoid harm, obedience to power	Ego-centered reasoning

be right and wrong is pretty much a matter of reciprocity: "I'll let you play with my toy if I can play with yours" (stage 2). At both stages 1 and 2, however, the individual is mainly concerned with his or her own pleasure. The self-dealings of Raj Rajaratnam, Gary Foster, and Dennis Kozlowski, described earlier in this chapter, exemplify ego-centered reasoning. By taking money from their companies for personal use, they benefited themselves and their immediate families, without apparent concern for others.

In adolescence the individual enters a wider world, learning the give-and-take of group life among small circles of friends, schoolmates, and similar close-knit groups (stage 3). Studies have reported that interaction within groups can provide an environment that improves the level of moral reasoning. This process continues into early adulthood. At this point, pleasing others and being admired by them are important cues to proper behavior. Most people are now capable of focusing on other-directed rather than self-directed perspectives. When a manager "goes along" with what others are doing or what the boss expects, this would represent stage 3 behavior. On reaching full adulthood—the late teens to early 20s in most modern, industrialized nations—most people are able to focus their reasoning according to society's customs, traditions, and laws as the proper way to define what is right and wrong (stage 4). At this stage, a manager would seek to follow the law; for example, he or she might choose to curtail a chemical pollutant because of government regulations mandating this.

Stages 5 and 6 lead to a special kind of moral reasoning. At these highest stages, people move above and beyond the specific rules, customs, and laws of their own societies. They are capable of basing their ethical reasoning on broad principles and relationships, such as human rights and constitutional guarantees of human dignity, equal treatment, and freedom of expression. In the highest stage of moral development, the meaning of right and wrong is defined by universal principles of justice, fairness, and the common rights of all humanity. For example, at this stage, an executive might decide to pay wages above the minimum required by law because this is the morally just thing to do.[28]

Researchers have consistently found that most managers typically rely on criteria associated with reasoning at stages 3 and 4, although some scholars argue that these results may be slightly inflated.[29] Although they may be capable of more advanced moral reasoning that adheres to or goes beyond society's customs or law, managers' ethical horizons most often are influenced by their immediate work group, family relationships, or compliance with the law. Another study found that CEOs of automakers in Asia demonstrated higher stages of moral reasoning and focused on the societal impacts of the company's attention to sustainability when compared to their CEO counterparts in the United States and Europe.[30]

The development of a manager's moral character can be crucial to a company. Some ethics issues require managers to move beyond selfish interest (stages 1 and 2), beyond company interest (stage 3 reasoning), and even beyond sole reliance on society's customs and laws (stage 4 reasoning). Needed is a manager whose personal character is built on a caring attitude toward all affected, recognizing others' rights and their essential humanity (a combination of stage 5 and 6 reasoning). The moral reasoning of upper-level managers, whose decisions affect companywide policies, can have a powerful and far-reaching impact both inside and outside the company.

[28] For details and research findings, see Lawrence Kohlberg, *The Philosophy of Moral Development* (San Francisco: Harper & Row, 1981); and Anne Colby and Lawrence Kohlberg, *The Measurement of Moral Judgment, Volume I: Theoretical Foundations and Research Validations* (Cambridge: Cambridge University Press, 1987).

[29] James Weber and Janet Gillespie, "Differences in Ethical Beliefs, Intentions, and Behaviors," *Business & Society*, 1998, pp. 447–67; and James Weber and David Wasieleski, "Investigating Influences on Managers' Moral Reasoning," *Business & Society*, 2001, pp. 79–111.

[30] James Weber, "Assessing the 'Tone at the Top': The Moral Reasoning of CEOs in the Automobile Industry," *Journal of Business Ethics*, 2010, pp. 167–82.

Analyzing Ethical Problems in Business

Underlying an ethical decision framework is a set of universal ethical values or principles, notions that most people anywhere in the world would hold as important. While a list of ethical principles may be exhaustive, these five values seem to be generally accepted and are present in most ethical dilemmas: do no harm, be fair and just, be honest, respect others' rights, and do your duty/act responsibly. Business managers and employees need a set of decision guidelines that will shape their thinking when on-the-job ethics issues occur. The guidelines should help them (1) identify and analyze the nature of an ethical problem and (2) decide which course of action is likely to produce an ethical result. The following four methods of ethical reasoning can be used for these analytical purposes, as summarized in Figure 4.6.

Virtue Ethics: Pursuing a "Good" Life

Some philosophers believe that the ancient Greeks, specifically Plato and Aristotle, developed the first ethical theory, which was based on values and personal character. Commonly referred to as **virtue ethics**, it focuses on character traits that a good person should possess, theorizing that moral values will direct the person toward good behavior. Virtue ethics is based on a way of being and on valuable characteristics rather than on rules for correct behavior. Moral virtues are habits that enable a person to live according to reason, and this reason helps the person avoid extremes. Aristotle argued, "Moral virtue is a mean between two vices, one of excess and the other of deficiency, and it aims at hitting the mean in feelings, desires, and action."[31] A variety of people have suggested lists of moral values over the years as shown in Figure 4.7.

As indicated in Figure 4.7, Plato, Aristotle, Aquinas, Franklin, and Solomon have slightly different views of what guides a moral or virtuous person. This suggests that to some extent what counts as a moral virtue depends on one's personal beliefs. However, most scholars believe that there is a great deal of agreement on the question of who is

FIGURE 4.6
Four Methods of Ethical Reasoning

Method	Critical Determining Factor	An Action Is Ethical When ...	Limitations
Virtues	Values and character	It aligns with good character	Subjective or incomplete set of good virtues
Utilitarian	Comparing benefits and costs	Net benefits exceed net costs	Difficult to measure some human and social costs; majority may disregard rights of the minority
Rights	Respecting entitlements	Basic human rights are respected	Difficult to balance conflicting rights
Justice	Distributing fair shares	Benefits and costs are fairly distributed	Difficult to measure benefits and costs; lack of agreement on fair shares

[31] For discussions of virtue ethics, see Richard DeGeorge, *Business Ethics,* 6th ed. (Upper Saddle River, NJ: Prentice Hall, 2008), pp. 106–11; and Laura P. Hartman and Joe DesJardins, *Business Ethics: Decision-Making for Personal Integrity and Social Responsibility,* 2nd ed. (New York: McGraw-Hill, 2011), pp. 116–21.

FIGURE 4.7

Lists of Moral Values across Time

Plato and Aristotle, 4th century BC	St. Thomas Aquinas, 1225–1274	Benjamin Franklin, 1706–1790	Robert Solomon, 1942–2007
• Courage • Self-control • Generosity • Magnificence • High-mindedness • Gentleness • Friendliness • Truthfulness • Wittiness • Modesty	• Faith • Hope • Charity • Prudence • Justice • Temperance • Fortitude • Humility	• Cleanliness • Silence • Industry • Punctuality • Frugality	• Honesty • Trust • Toughness

Sources: Plato and Aristotle's values are from Steven Mintz, "Aristotelian Virtue and Business Ethics Education," *Journal of Business Ethics*, 1996, pp. 827–38; St. Thomas Aquinas's values are from Manuel G. Velasquez, *Business Ethics: Concepts and Cases*, 6th ed. (Upper Saddle River, NJ: Prentice Hall, 2006), pp. 110–11; Benjamin Franklin's values, from the American Industrial Revolution era, are from Peter McMylor, *Alisdair MacIntyre: Critic of Modernity* (London: Routledge, 1994); and Robert Solomon's moral values can be found in Robert C. Solomon, *Ethics and Excellence: Cooperation and Integrity in Business* (New York: Oxford University Press, 1992), pp. 207–16.

acting as the virtuous person, as summed up by business ethicist Manuel Velasquez: "An action is morally right if in carrying out the action the agent exercises, exhibits, or develops a morally virtuous character, [as opposed to] develops a morally vicious character."[32]

When placing virtue ethics in a business context, ethicist Robert Solomon explains, "The bottom line of the Aristotelian approach to business ethics is that we have to get away from 'bottom line' thinking and conceive of business as an essential part of the good life, living well, getting along with others, having a sense of self-respect, and being a part of something one can be proud of."[33]

However, others argue that virtue ethics is not really an ethics at all, not a thoroughly developed ethical system of rules and guidelines, but rather a system of values that form good character. Virtue ethics also suffers from this challenge: whose values? As noted in Figure 4.7, different people offer different sets of values to define virtue ethics. What if these values conflict or the list is incomplete? Does a set of values provide a sufficient framework to resolve the most complex ethical dilemmas found in global business? Does a manager sometimes have to be or seem to be "the bad person" or do or seem to do "a bad thing" for the sake of some ultimate ethical good? Would this be virtuous or vicious?[34]

Applying this ethical framework to a commonplace business example—how would a moral person decide to close a plant? Would the decision maker, using values espoused by Aristotle or Franklin or Solomon, shut down a plant and lay off workers? Would virtue ethics help a manager close a plant in a way that is virtuous and supportive of the workers about to be laid off?

Utility: Comparing Benefits and Costs

Another approach to ethics emphasizes *utility*, or the overall amount of good that can be produced by an action or a decision. This ethical approach is called **utilitarian reasoning**.

[32] Manuel G. Velasquez, *Business Ethics: Concepts and Cases,* 7th ed. (Upper Saddle River, NJ: Pearson, 2012), p. 132.

[33] Robert C. Solomon, *Ethics and Excellence: Cooperation and Integrity in Business* (New York: Oxford University Press, 1992), p. 104.

[34] For a critique of virtue ethics, see Boatright, *Ethics and the Conduct of Business*, pp. 80–81.

It is often referred to as cost–benefit analysis because it compares the costs and benefits of a decision, a policy, or an action, as shown in Figure 4.6. These costs and benefits can be economic (expressed in dollar amounts), social (the effect on society at large), or human (usually a psychological or emotional impact). After business managers add up all the costs and benefits and compare them with one another, the net cost or the net benefit should be apparent. For a utilitarian, the alternative where the benefits most outweigh the costs is the ethically preferred action because it produces the greatest good for the greatest number of people in society.

The main drawback to utilitarian reasoning is the difficulty of accurately measuring both costs and benefits. Some things can be measured in monetary terms—goods produced, sales, payrolls, and profits—but others that are less tangible, such as employee morale, psychological satisfaction, or the worth of a human life, are trickier. Human and social costs are particularly difficult to measure with precision. But unless they can be measured, the cost–benefit calculations will be incomplete, and it will be difficult to know whether the overall result is good or bad, ethical or unethical. Another limitation of utilitarian reasoning is that the majority may override the rights of those in the minority. Since utilitarian reasoning is primarily concerned with the end results of an action, managers using this reasoning process often fail to consider the means taken to reach the end.

Despite these drawbacks, cost–benefit analysis is widely used in business. Because this method works well when used to measure economic and financial outcomes, business managers sometimes are tempted to rely on it to decide important ethical questions without being fully aware of its limitations or the availability of still other methods that may improve the ethical quality of their decisions.

How would a utilitarian decision maker decide to close a plant? Using utilitarian reasoning, the decision maker must consider all the benefits (improving the company bottom line, higher return on investment to the investors, etc.) versus the costs (employee layoffs, reduced economic activity to the local community, etc.).

Rights: Determining and Protecting Entitlements

Human rights are another basis for making ethical judgments. A right means that a person or group is entitled to something or is entitled to be treated in a certain way, as shown in Figure 4.6. The most basic human rights are the rights to life, safety, free speech, freedom, being informed, due process, and property, among others. Denying those rights or failing to protect them for other persons and groups is normally considered to be unethical. Respecting others, even those with whom we disagree or dislike, is the essence of human rights, provided that others do the same for us. This approach to ethical reasoning holds that individuals are to be treated as valuable ends in themselves just because they are human beings. Using others for your own purposes is unethical if, at the same time, you deny them their goals and purposes.

The main limitation of using rights as a basis of ethical reasoning is the difficulty of balancing conflicting rights. For example, an employee's right to privacy may be at odds with an employer's right to protect the firm's assets by testing the employee's honesty. Rights also clash when U.S. multinational corporations move production to a foreign nation, causing job losses at home but creating new jobs abroad. In such cases, whose job rights should be respected?[35]

Despite this kind of problem, the protection and promotion of human rights is an important ethical benchmark for judging the behavior of individuals and organizations. Surely most people would agree that it is unethical to deny a person's fundamental right to life,

---

[35] For a discussion of ethical rights, see ibid., pp. 36–39; and Velasquez, *Business Ethics: Concepts and Cases*, pp. 90–98.

freedom, privacy, growth, and human dignity. By defining the human condition and pointing the way to a realization of human potentialities, such rights become a kind of common denominator of ethical reasoning, setting forth the essential conditions for ethical actions and decisions.

Would someone using human rights reasoning decide to close a plant? When using human rights reasoning, the decision maker must consider the rights of all affected (the right to a livelihood for the displaced workers or business owners in the local community versus the right of the employees to be informed of the layoffs and plant closing versus the right of the managers to the freedom to make decisions they believe are within their duty to the company, etc.).

Justice: Is It Fair?

A fourth method of ethical reasoning concerns **justice**. As shown in Figure 4.6, a common question in human affairs is, Is it fair or just? Employees want to know if pay scales are fair. Consumers are interested in fair prices when they shop. When new tax laws are proposed, there is much debate about their fairness—where will the burden fall, and who will escape paying their fair share?[36] After the U.S. government bailed out several big banks and insurance companies in 2008–2009, many people wondered if it was fair that some of their top executives continued to receive big bonuses while their employees, shareholders, and bondholders suffered—and taxpayers absorbed the cost. The Occupy Wall Street protests, which began in 2010, called attention to the perceived lack of fairness in the distribution of income and assets between wealthy bankers and ordinary Americans.

Justice, or fairness, exists when benefits and burdens are distributed equitably and according to some accepted rule. For society as a whole, social justice means that a society's income and wealth are distributed among the people in fair proportions. A fair distribution does not necessarily mean an equal distribution. Most societies try to consider people's needs, abilities, efforts, and the contributions they make to society's welfare. Since these factors are seldom equal, fair shares will vary from person to person and group to group. Justice reasoning is not the same as utilitarian reasoning. A person using utilitarian reasoning adds up costs and benefits to see if one is greater than the other; if benefits exceed costs, then the action would probably be considered ethical. A person using justice reasoning considers who pays the costs and who gets the benefits; if the shares seem fair (according to society's rules), then the action is probably just.

Is it just to close a plant? Using justice reasoning, a decision maker must consider the distribution of the benefits (to the firm, its investors, etc.) versus the costs (to the displaced employees, local community, etc.). To be just, the firm closing the plant might decide to accept additional costs for job retraining and outplacement services for the benefit of the displaced workers. The firm might also decide to make contributions to the local community over some period of time to benefit the local economy, in effect to balance the scales of justice in this situation.

Applying Ethical Reasoning to Business Activities

Anyone in the business world can use these four methods of ethical reasoning to gain a better understanding of ethical issues that arise at work. Usually, all four can be applied at the same time. Using only one of the four methods is risky and may lead to an incomplete understanding of all the ethical complexities that may be present. It also may produce a lopsided ethical result that will be unacceptable to others.

[36] For an interesting discussion of "what is fair?" see Patrick Primeaux and Frank P. LeVeness, "What Is Fair: Three Perspectives," *Journal of Business Ethics* 84 (2009), pp. 89–102.

Once the ethical analysis is complete, the decision maker should ask this question: Do all of the ethics approaches lead to the same decision? If so, then the decision or policy or activity is probably ethical. If the application of all ethics theories results in a "no, this is not ethical," then you probably are looking at an unethical decision, policy, or activity. The reason you cannot be *absolutely* certain is that different people and groups (1) may honestly and genuinely use different sources of information, (2) may rely on different values or definitions of what is a virtuous character, (3) may measure costs and benefits differently, (4) may not share the same meaning of justice, or (5) may rank various rights in different ways. Nevertheless, any time an analyst obtains a consistent result when using all of the approaches, it indicates that a strong case can be made for either an ethical or an unethical conclusion.

What happens when the application of the four ethical approaches does not lead to the same conclusion? A corporate manager or employee then has to assign priorities to each method of ethical reasoning. What is most important to the manager, to the employee, or to the organization—virtue, utility, rights, or justice? What ranking should they be given? A judgment must be made, and priorities must be determined. These judgments and priorities will be strongly influenced by a company's culture and ethical climate. Some will be sensitive to people's needs and rights; others will put themselves or their company ahead of all other considerations.

The importance of being attentive to ethical issues at work and the ability to reason to an ethical resolution of these knotty dilemmas have always been important but today are essential given the increasing ethical scrutiny of business and the grave consequences for unethical behavior in the workplace. Employees do not work in a vacuum. The organization where they work and the culture that exists within any organization exert significant influence on the individual as an ethical decision maker. Businesses are making significant efforts to improve the ethical work climates in their organizations and are providing safeguards to encourage ethical behavior by their employees, as the next chapter discusses.

Summary

- Ethics is a conception of right and wrong behavior, defining for us when our actions are moral and when they are immoral. Business ethics is the application of general ethical ideas to business behavior.

- Ethical business behavior is demanded by business stakeholders, enhances business performance, complies with legal requirements, prevents or minimizes harm, and promotes personal morality.

- Ethics problems occur in business for many reasons, including the selfishness of a few, competitive pressures on profits, the clash of personal values and business goals, and cross-cultural contradictions in global business operations.

- Managers' on-the-job values tend to be company-oriented, assigning high priority to company goals. Managers often value being competent and place importance on having a comfortable or exciting life, among other values.

- Individual spirituality can greatly influence how a manager understands ethical challenges; increasingly, it is recognized that organizations must acknowledge employees' spirituality in the workplace.

- Individuals reason at various stages of moral development, with most managers focusing on personal rewards, recognition from others, or compliance with company rules as guides for their reasoning.

- People in business can analyze ethics dilemmas by using four major types of ethical reasoning: virtue ethics, utilitarian reasoning, rights reasoning, and justice reasoning.

Key Terms

business ethics, *70*
conflict of interest, *77*
ethical egoist, *76*
ethical principles, *69*
ethical relativism, *70*
ethics, *69*
human rights, *85*

integrity capital, *72*
justice, *86*
Sarbanes-Oxley
Act, *74*
spirituality, *80*
stages of moral
development, *81*

U.S. Corporate Sentencing
Guidelines, *73*
utilitarian reasoning, *84*
virtue ethics, *83*

Internet Resources

www.ethics.org
www.ibe.org.uk
www.business-ethics.org
www.charactercounts.org
www.soxlaw.com
www.usoge.gov
www.ussc.gov
www.workplacespirituality.info

Ethics Resource Center
Institute for Business Ethics
International Business Ethics Institute
Josephson Institute
Sarbanes-Oxley Act
United States Office of Government Ethics
United States Sentencing Commission
Workplace Spirituality

Discussion Case: *Chiquita Brands:* *Ethical Responsibility or Illegal Action?*

In the early 2000s, Chiquita Brands International, a Cincinnati–based multinational marketer and distributor of food products—widely known for its Chiquita banana brand—found itself in the middle of a crisis in its Latin American operations. The company was confronted by a local armed paramilitary group, the United Defense Forces of Colombia, which attempted to extort substantial payments from the company to help fund the group's operations. The paramilitary group made it clear that if the company did not make the payments Chiquita's employees would be at risk. The company's managers took these threats seriously, because they believed that, in 1995, the paramilitary group had been responsible for bombing Chiquita's operations and murdering 17 banana workers, who had been gunned down on a muddy soccer field.

Chiquita's mission emphasized a strong sense of ethical performance and social responsibility. It stated that it wanted "to help the world's consumers broaden mindsets about nutrition and bring healthy, nutritious, and convenient foods that taste great and improve people's lives." Therefore, it was not surprising that Chiquita's management also wanted to protect its employees and ensure their safety while working for the company. In a handwritten note, a Chiquita executive said that such payments were the "cost of doing business in Colombia." The company agreed to make the payments demanded by the paramilitary group, but hid the payments through a series of questionable accounting actions. From 1997 through 2004 Chiquita paid monthly "protection payments" totaling more than $1.7 million.

After the September 11, 2001, terrorist attack in the United States, the U.S. Government declared the Colombian paramilitary group to be a terrorist organization. In February 2003, a Chiquita employee informed a senior Chiquita officer that the company's protection payments were illegal under the new U.S. terrorism laws. Chiquita officials met with their attorneys in Washington, DC, and were advised to stop the payments to the terrorist group. Yet the company continued to make the protection payments, amounting to an additional $825,000.

In the minds of the Chiquita's executives, stopping the payments would risk the lives of their employees. Chiquita's executives also considered but rejected the option of withdrawing operations from Colombia. But in a surprising move in April 2003, Chiquita decided to disclose to the Department of Justice that the company was still making payments to the Colombian paramilitary group. The company told the government that the payments were made under the threat of violence against them and their employees.

The Justice Department informed Chiquita that these payments were illegal, yet the company continued to make the payments. In 2007 Chiquita Brands International pleaded guilty to one count of the criminal charge of engaging in transactions with a designated global terrorist group and agreed to pay a $25 million fine.

Chiquita's troubles did not end when it settled the charges filed by the Justice Department. In 2007, new lawsuits were filed under the Alien Tort Statute, a 222-year-old law that allows foreigners to sue a U.S.–based company in American federal courts if their claims involve violations of U.S. treaties. The lawsuit claimed that Chiquita was responsible for the deaths of 393 victims at the hands of the Colombian terrorist group that Chiquita funded through their payments and demanded damages of $20 million per victim, a total of $7.86 billion. The lawsuits pointed specifically to a 1997 massacre in which 49 people were tortured, dismembered, and decapitated and another incident in 2000 in which 36 more people were killed. "The principle upon which this lawsuit is brought is that when you put money into the hands of terrorists, when you put guns into the hands of terrorists, then you are legally responsible for the atrocities, the murders and the tortures that those terrorists commit," said attorney Jonathan Reiter.

Additional lawsuits were filed in 2011, where the names of 4,000 victims were submitted, each targeting Chiquita due to the company's support of the Colombian terrorist paramilitary group. Attorney Terry Collingsworth, who helped file the lawsuits on behalf of the Colombians, said, "A company that pays a terrorist organization that kills thousands of people should get the capital punishment of civil liability and be put out of business by punitive damages."

A Chiquita spokesperson responded, "We reiterate that Chiquita and its employees were victims and that the actions taken by the company were always motivated to protect the lives of our employees and their families." Michael Mitchell, Chiquita's director of communications added, "Our company had been forced to make protection payments to safeguard our workforce. It is absolutely untrue for anyone to suggest that these payments were made for any other purpose. Chiquita has already been the victim of extortion in Colombia. We will not allow ourselves to become extortion victims in the United States."

Sources: "Chiquita Brands International Pleads Guilty to Making Payments to a Designated Terrorist Organization and Agrees to Pay $25 Million Fine," *U.S. Department of Justice Press Release*, March 19, 2007, *www.justice.gov/opa/pr/2007 /March/07_nsd_161.html*; "Colombian Families' Suit Says Chiquita Liable for Torture, Murder," *CNN.com*, February 14, 2007, *www.cnn.com/2007/US/law/11/14/chiquita.lawsuit*; and "Chiquita Sued over Colombian Paramilitary Payments," *The Sacramento Bee*, May 30, 2011, *www.sacbee.com*.

Discussion Questions

1. Should Chiquita have agreed to make the payments to the terrorist group to protect its employees? What ethical principles support your opinion?

2. Is there anything that Chiquita could have done to protect its employees adequately without paying the terrorists?

3. Using each of the four methods of ethical reasoning, see Figure 4.6, was it ethical or not for Chiquita to pay the terrorist organization?

4. How should Chiquita respond to the new lawsuits claiming that the company is responsible for the deaths of victims at the hands of the terrorist group the company helped fund?

5. Should Chiquita be given the "civil death penalty" and be put out of business for their actions?

Organizational Ethics and the Law

Faced with increasing pressure to create an ethical and law-abiding environment at work, businesses can take tangible steps to improve their ethical performance. The organization's culture and ethical work climate play a central role in promoting ethics at work. Ethical situations arise in all areas and functions of business, and often professional associations seek to guide managers in addressing these challenges. Corporations can also implement ethical safeguards to create a comprehensive ethics program, and corporations must of course follow the laws of the nation. This can become a complex challenge when facing different customs and regulations around the world. Although ethics and the law are not exactly the same, both are important emphases for businesses, especially when operating in the global marketplace.

This Chapter Focuses on These Key Learning Objectives:

- Classifying an organization's culture and ethical climate.
- Recognizing ethics challenges across the multiple functions of business.
- Creating effective ethics policies, ethics training programs, ethics reporting mechanisms, and similar safeguards.
- Assessing the strengths and weaknesses of a comprehensive ethics program.
- Understanding how to conduct business ethically in the global marketplace.
- Identifying the differences between ethics and the law.

In 2009, Spanish regulators fined six European insurance companies a total of €120.7 million ($180 million) for price fixing. From 2002 to 2007, these firms had colluded to set minimum premiums that they would charge to insure builders and their re-insurers against building defects during the Spanish housing boom. The Spanish National Competition Commission explained that the companies had simply agreed among themselves what the rates would be, eliminating competition.

Two former top executives at Value Line Inc. and an affiliated broker agreed to pay $45 million to settle charges of fraud brought against them by the U.S. Securities and Exchange Commission (SEC). The SEC claimed that these executives charged more than $24 million in bogus commissions on phantom trades and brokerage services from 1986 through 2004. Although the executives did not admit to any wrongdoing, Value Line's CEO resigned in 2009, and both he and the former chief compliance officer were barred from associating with any broker, dealer, investment adviser, or investment company or from acting as an officer or director of any public company in the future.[1]

In the United States, Europe, and around the world, dozens and dozens of other companies have been charged with accounting fraud, mishandling investors' funds, market improprieties, and many other illegal activities. *Why are business executives, managers, and employees repeatedly being caught conducting illegal and unethical activities? What can firms do to minimize or prevent the unethical activities perpetrated by their executives and employees? Could companies set in place systems or programs to monitor workplace activities to detect illegal or unethical behavior?*

Corporate Ethical Climates

Personal values and moral character play key roles in improving a company's ethical performance, as discussed in Chapter 4. However, they do not stand alone, because personal values and character can be affected by a company's culture and ethical climate.

The terms *culture* and *climate* are often used interchangeably and, in fact, are highly interrelated. **Corporate culture** is a blend of ideas, customs, traditional practices, company values, and shared meanings that help define normal behavior for everyone who works in a company. Culture is "the way we do things around here." Two experts testify to its overwhelming influence:

> Every business—in fact every organization—has a culture . . . [and it] has a powerful influence throughout an organization; it affects practically everything—from who gets promoted and what decisions are made, to how employees dress and what sports they play. . . . When [new employees] choose a company, they often choose a way of life. The culture shapes their responses in a strong but subtle way.[2]

The Ethics Resource Center (ERC) observed that a "strong ethical culture in a company has a profound impact on the kinds of workplace behavior that can put a business in jeopardy." According to an ERC study, organizations with strong ethical cultures find that fewer than 5 percent of their employees feel pressure to commit misconduct, compared with 15 percent in organizations with weak ethical cultures. Nearly twice as many employees

[1] "Spain Fines Insurers for Price-Fixing," *The Associated Press*, November 12, 2009, *www.businessweeki.com;* and "Value Line, Execs to Pay $45mln in SEC Case," *Reuters*, November 4, 2009, *www.reuters.com*.

[2] Terrence E. Deal and Allan A. Kennedy, *Corporate Cultures: The Rites and Rituals of Corporate Life* (Reading, MA: Addison-Wesley, 1982), pp. 4, 16.

FIGURE 5.1
The Components of Ethical Climates

Ethical Criteria	Focus of Individual Person	Organization	Society
Egoism (self-centered approach)	Self-interest	Company interest	Economic efficiency
Benevolence (concern-for-others approach)	Friendship	Team interest	Social responsibility
Principle (integrity approach)	Personal morality	Company rules and procedures	Laws and professional codes

Source: Adapted from Bart Victor and John B. Cullen, "The Organizational Bases of Ethical Work Climates," *Administrative Science Quarterly* 33 (1988), p. 104.

observe misconduct by coworkers in weak ethical cultures companies (76 percent) as in strong ethical cultures (39 percent).[3]

Most companies have a kind of moral atmosphere. People can feel which way the ethical winds are blowing. They pick up subtle hints and clues that tell them what behavior is approved and what is forbidden. The unspoken understanding among employees of what is and is not acceptable behavior is called an **ethical climate**. It is the part of corporate culture that sets the ethical tone in a company. One way to view ethical climates is diagrammed in Figure 5.1. Three distinct ethical criteria are *egoism* (self-centeredness), *benevolence* (concern for others), and *principle* (respect for one's own integrity, for group norms, and for society's laws). (These parallel the levels of moral development were developed by Lawrence Kohlberg and discussed in Chapter 4.) These ethical criteria can be used to describe how individuals, a company, or society at large approach various moral dilemmas.

For example, if a company approaches ethics issues with benevolence in mind, it would emphasize friendly relations with its employees, stress the importance of team play and cooperation for the company's benefit, and recommend socially responsible courses of action. However, a company using egoism would be more likely to think first of promoting the company's profit and striving for efficient operations at all costs, perhaps at the sake of others or the environment, as illustrated by the following example:

> Barrick, a Toronto-based gold-mining corporation, was listed as one of the least ethical companies according to Covalence, a Swiss research firm. Allegations against the company included charges that it participated in the burning of at least 130 homes near its Porgera Mine in Papua New Guinea and that it manipulated land titles in Australia and Chile. The company was also blamed in a toxic spill in Tanzania that left dangerous levels of arsenic in the area around its North Mara mine. Barrick's attempts to mine along the Argentina-Chile border were associated with a significant shrinking of nearby glaciers. These allegations would point to a company placing its own interests ahead of others.[4]

Researchers have found that multiple ethical climates, or subclimates, may exist within one organization. For example, one company might include managers who often interact with the public and government regulators, using a principle-based approach, compared to

---

[3] "A Strong Culture Is a Key to Cutting Misconduct on the Job," *Ethics Resource Center*, June 23, 2010, *www.ethics.org/files/u5/CultureSup4.pdf.*

[4] "The 12 Least Ethical Companies in the World: Covalence's Ranking," *The Huffington Post*, May 25, 2011, *www.huffingtonpost.com.*

another group of managers, whose work is geared toward routine process tasks and whose focus is mainly egotistic—higher personal pay or company profits.[5]

Corporate ethical climates can also signal to employees that ethical transgressions are acceptable. By signaling what is considered to be right and wrong, corporate cultures and ethical climates can pressure people to channel their actions in certain directions desired by the company. This kind of pressure can work both for and against good ethical practices.

Business Ethics across Organizational Functions

Not all ethics issues in business are the same. Because business operations are highly specialized, ethics issues can appear in any of the major functional areas of a business firm. Accounting, finance, marketing, information technology, and other areas of business all have their own particular brands of ethical dilemmas. In many cases, professional associations in these functional areas have attempted to define a common set of ethical standards, as discussed next.

Accounting Ethics

The accounting function is a critically important component of every business firm. By law, the financial records of publicly held companies are required to be audited by a certified professional accounting firm. Company managers, external investors, government regulators, tax collectors, and labor unions rely on such public audits to make key decisions. Honesty, integrity, and accuracy are absolute requirements of the accounting function, and the impact can be devastating for organizations when these values are absent.

> The dismissal of Michael Woodford, president of the Japanese camera-maker Olympus, sparked an inquiry that uncovered evidence of a multi-million dollar accounting fraud. The cover-up at Olympus spanned three generations of chief executives who spent nearly $2 billion (¥135 billion) to hide corporate losses using a complex web of offshore companies in the Cayman Islands and British Virgin Islands. An independent panel charged with the investigation called the three chief executives "rotten to the core." In 2012, the three executives pleaded guilty to the charges of accounting fraud. Olympus stock lost more than half of its value in less than two months after the scandal broke, and the company was threatened with delisting from the Tokyo Stock Exchange if executives did not comply with investigation deadlines.[6]

Accountants often are faced with conflicts of interest, introduced in Chapter 4, where loyalty or obligation to the company (the client) may be divided or in conflict with self-interest (of the accounting firm) and the interests of others (shareholders and the public). For example, while conducting an audit of a company, should the auditor look for opportunities to recommend to the client consulting services that the auditor's firm can provide? Sometimes, accounting firms may be tempted to soften their audit of a company's financial statements if the accounting firm wants to attract the company's nonaudit business. For this

---

[5] James Weber, "Influences upon Organizational Ethical Subclimates: A Multi-departmental Analysis of a Single Firm," *Organization Science* 6 (1995), pp. 509–23.

[6] "Olympus Report Clears Way for Clean Sweep of Board That Failed to Stop Rot," *Bloomberg*, December 6, 2011, *www.bloomberg.com*; "Panel Releases Findings in Olympus Case," *The Wall Street Journal*, December 6, 2011, *online.wsj.com*; "Tokyo Makes Arrests in Olympus Scandal," *The Wall Street Journal*, February 17, 2012, *online.wsj.com*; and "Olympus and Ex-Executives Plead Guilty in Accounting Fraud," *The New York Times*, September 25, 2102, *www.nytimes.com*.

Exhibit 5.A

Professional Codes of Conduct in Accounting and Finance

AMERICAN INSTITUTE OF CERTIFIED PUBLIC ACCOUNTANTS (AICPA)

Code of Professional Conduct

These Principles of the Code of Professional Conduct of the American Institute of Certified Public Accountants express the profession's recognition of its responsibilities to the public, to clients, and to colleagues. They guide members in the performance of their professional responsibilities and express the basic tenets of ethical and professional conduct. The Principles call for an unswerving commitment to honorable behavior, even at the sacrifice of personal advantage.

- Responsibilities—In carrying out their responsibilities as professionals, members should exercise sensitive professional and moral judgments in all their activities. . . .
- The Public Interest—Members should accept the obligation to act in a way that will serve the public interest, honor the public interest, and demonstrate commitment to professionalism. . . .
- Integrity—To maintain and broaden public confidence, members should perform all professional responsibilities with the highest sense of integrity. . . .
- Objectivity and Independence—A member should maintain objectivity and be free of conflicts of interest in discharging professional responsibilities. . . .
- Due Care—A member should observe the profession's technical and ethical standards, strive continually to improve competence and the quality of services, and discharge professional responsibility to the best of the member's ability. . . .
- Scope and Nature of Services—A member in public practice should observe the Principles of the Code of Professional Conduct in determining the scope and nature of services to be provided.*

reason, the Sarbanes-Oxley Act severely limits the offering of nonaudit consulting services by the auditing firm.

Recently, there was an appeal to adopt the International Financial Reporting Standards (IFRS), including from the Obama administration, since many believed these standards should replace the Generally Accepted Accounting Principles (GAAP) that currently govern U.S. accounting practices. At a time when corporate financial mismanagement had shaken the American public's confidence in the American business system, the desire for greater company oversight, accountability, and transparency gave support for a new international accounting system. Others argued, however, that the rush to adopt international accounting standards by the United States would hurt the standing of the United States in the world's capital markets by undermining the U.S. regulatory system and negatively impact securities issuers.[7]

Examples of the U.S. accounting profession's efforts promoting ethics are shown in Exhibit 5.A. Spurred by a growing threat of liability suits filed against accounting firms and a desire to reaffirm professional integrity, these standards go far toward ensuring a high level of honest and ethical accounting behavior.[8]

---

[7] See the *International Accounting Standards*, The European Commission, *europa.eu.int*. For a discussion of the proposed International Financial Reporting Standards, see "The Rush to International Accounting," *The New York Times* blog, September 11, 2008, *norris.blogs.nytimes.com;* "Ready for Global Financial Standards?" *Pittsburgh Post-Gazette*, March 22, 2009, *www.post-gazette.com;* and the International Financial Reporting Standards website at *www.ifrs.com*.

[8] For several excellent examples of ethical dilemmas in accounting, see Leonard J. Brooks and Paul Dunn, *Business & Professional Ethics for Directors, Executives, and Accountants*, 5th ed. (Mason, OH: South-Western Cengage Learning, 2010); and Ronald Duska and Brenda Duska, *Accounting Ethics* (Malden, MA: Blackwell, 2003).

CHARTERED FINANCIAL ANALYST (CFA)®

Summary from CFA Institute Code of Ethics and Standards of Professional Conduct

Members of CFA Institute (including Chartered Financial Analyst® (CFA®) charterholders) and candidates for the CFA designation ("Members and Candidates") must:

- Act with integrity, competence, diligence, respect, and in an ethical manner with the public, clients, prospective clients, employers, employees, colleagues in the investment profession, and other participants in the global capital markets.
- Place the interests of clients, the interests of their employer, and the integrity of the investment profession above their own personal interests.
- Use reasonable care and exercise independent professional judgment when conducting investment analysis, making investment recommendations, taking investment actions, and engaging in other professional activities.
- Practice and encourage others to practice in a professional and ethical manner that will reflect credit on themselves and the profession.
- Promote the integrity of, and uphold the rules governing, global capital markets.
- Maintain and improve their professional competence and strive to maintain and improve the competence of other investment professionals.[†]

*Reprinted from the AICPA Code of Professional Conduct, copyright © 2011. American Institute of CPAs. All rights reserved. Used with permission. For a full text of the professional code, see *www.aicpa.org*.

[†] Copyright 2012, CFA Institute. Reproduced with permission from CFA Institute. All Rights Reserved. For full text see *www.cfapubs.org/doi/pdf/10.2469/ccb.v2010.n14.1*.

Financial Ethics

Within companies, the finance department and its officers are typically responsible for managing the firm's assets and raising capital—for example, by issuing stocks and bonds. Financial institutions, such as commercial banks, securities firms, and so forth, assist in raising capital and managing assets for both individuals and institutions. Whether working directly for a business or in a firm that provides financial services, finance professionals face a particular set of ethical issues. Consider the following ethical lapses in corporate finance:

- Kweku Adoboli, a London trader at the Swiss bank UBS, was charged with making trades using the firm's money without its authorization—a practice known as "rogue trading." Adoboli's trades resulted in more than $2 billion in losses. The effect on the Swiss bank was profound: UBS profits fell 39 percent in the period immediately following the scandal compared to the same period a year earlier, and several top executives, including the CEO, resigned.
- As MFGlobal's management was attempting to sell the firm, roughly $900 million was discovered missing from its client's accounts. A month later, after a government investigation, this figure was revised to $1.2 billion, presenting one of the largest financial fraud scandals in history. MFGlobal had systematically violated established regulatory rules and merged client money with its broker's funds so that the brokers could meet various financial obligations.
- In 2010, the U.K.'s Financial Services Authority (FSA) ordered Goldman Sachs to pay a fine of nearly £20 million ($31 million) due to errors made in their regulatory disclosures regarding a trader's activities. In the same year, the FSA levied its largest fine—£33.32 million

($48.8 million)—on JPMorgan Chase & Co. for failing to separate client money from the firm's money.[9]

These and other lapses in ethical conduct occurred despite efforts by the finance professions to foster an ethical environment. As shown in Exhibit 5.A, the highly regarded Chartered Financial Analyst Institute, which oversees financial executives performing many different types of jobs in the financial discipline, emphasizes self-regulation as the best path for ethical compliance. There are, however, skeptics who do not believe the industry can self-regulate when it comes to the type of ethical violations that are reported ealrier in this chapter.[10] "The financial meltdown that took place from 2007 to 2009 uncovered all the skeletons, what was taking place in the marketplace, from mortgage financing to Ponzi schemes," explained a mortgage and real estate expert. After the financial crisis of 2008–2009, many felt that self-regulation in the financial sector was insufficient to curb ethical abuses and called for stronger regulatory standards, as discussed in detail in Chapters 8 and 14.

Marketing Ethics

Marketing refers to advertising, distributing, and selling products or services. Within firms, the marketing department is the functional area that typically interacts most directly with customers. Outside the firm, advertising agencies and other firms provide marketing services to businesses. The complex set of activities involved in marketing generates its own distinctive ethical issues.

One issue in marketing ethics emphasizes honesty and fairness in advertising. When it comes to pharmaceutical products, honesty and fairness in advertising are paramount, but not always practiced, as the following example illustrates.

In 2012, GlaxoSmithKline pleaded guilty to criminal charges and agreed to pay $3 billion for illegally marketing three different drugs and withholding safety data from the U.S. Food and Drug Administration (FDA). In the past several years, the U.S. government has also fined several well-known pharmaceutical companies, including Pfizer, Schering-Plough, and Eli Lilly for illegally promoting drugs for uses other than those approved by the FDA, often known as "off-label" marketing.[11]

In addition to the general ethical questions that surround the marketing or advertising of products to consumers, consumer health and safety are another key ethics issue in marketing. Chapter 15 discusses several other issues in marketing ethics, including deceptive advertising, firm liability for consumer injury, and a firm's responsibility for the unethical use of products by buyers.

To improve the ethics of the marketing profession, the American Marketing Association (AMA) has adopted a code of ethics for its members, as shown in Exhibit 5.B. The AMA

---

[9] "UBS Trader Charged with Fraud," *The Wall Street Journal*, September 16, 2011, *online.wsj.com;* "UBS Profit Falls after Trading Scandal," *The New York Times*, October 25, 2011, *dealbook.nytimes.com;* "The MF Global Scandal," *Finance Careers*, n.d. (accessed March 3, 2012), *financecareers.about.com;* and "Goldman Sachs Is Fined in the U.K.," *The Wall Street Journal*, September 8, 2010, *online.wsj.com.*

[10] "Party Tab: Wall Street to Set Limits on Gifts," *The Wall Street Journal*, January 24, 2006, *online.wsj.com.* For several good examples of other financial ethics issues, see Larry Alan Bear and Rita Maldonado-Bear, *Free Markets, Finance, Ethics, and Law* (Englewood Cliffs, NJ: Prentice Hall, 1994); and John R. Boatright, ed., *Ethics in Finance* (Malden, MA: Blackwell, 1999). Quotation is from "2011 Was Worst Year for Suspected Financial Crimes on Record," *ABC News*, March 27, 2012, *abcnews.go.com.*

[11] "Glaxo in $3 Billion Settlement," *The Wall Street Journal*, July 2, 2012, *online.wsj.com;* and "Drug Makers to Pay Fine of $81 Million," *The New York Times*, April 29, 2010, *www.nytimes.com.* For a complete listing of the pharmaceutical firms fined by the FDA in the early 2000s, see "Big Pharma's Crime Spree," *Bloomberg Markets*, December 2009, p. 78)

AMERICAN MARKETING ASSOCIATION (AMA)

Statement of Ethics

The American Marketing Association commits itself to promoting the highest standard of professional ethical norms and values for its members (practitioners, academics, and students).

As Marketers, we must:

1. **Do no harm.** This means consciously avoiding harmful actions or omissions by embodying high ethical standards and adhering to all applicable laws and regulations in the choices we make.
2. **Foster trust in the marketing system.** This means striving for good faith and fair dealing so as to contribute toward the efficacy of the exchange process as well as avoiding deception in product design, pricing, communication, and delivery of distribution.
3. **Embrace ethical values.** This means building relationships and enhancing consumer confidence in the integrity of marketing by affirming these core values: honesty, responsibility, fairness, respect, transparency, and citizenship.

We expect AMA members to be courageous and proactive in leading and/or aiding their organizations in the fulfillment of the explicit and implicit promises made to those stakeholders.*

ASSOCIATION FOR COMPUTING MACHINERY (ACM)

Code of Ethics and Professional Conduct

This code, consisting of 24 imperatives formulated as statements of personal responsibility, identifies the elements of such a commitment. It contains many, but not all, issues professionals are likely to face. . . . The code and its supplemental guidelines are intended to serve as a basis for ethical decision making in the conduct of professional work. Secondarily, they may serve as a basis for judging the merit of a formal complaint pertaining to violation of professional ethical standards.

The general imperatives for ACM members include contribute to society and human well-being, avoid harm to others, be honest and trustworthy, be fair and take action not to discriminate, honor property rights including copyrights and patents, give proper credit for intellectual property, respect the privacy of others, and honor confidentiality.

Adherence of professionals to a code of ethics is largely a voluntary matter. However, if a member does not follow this code by engaging in gross misconduct, membership in ACM may be terminated.†

* Adapted with permission from the American Marketing Association's Statement of Ethics. For a full text of the professional marketing code, see *www.marketingpower.com/AboutAMA/Pages/Statement%20of%20Ethics.aspx*.

† Copyright © 1997, Association for Computing Machinery, Inc. A full text of the ACM code of ethics can be found at *www.acm.org/constitution/code*.

code advocates professional conduct guided by ethics, adherence to applicable laws, and honesty and fairness in all marketing activities. The code seeks to help marketing professionals translate general ethical principles into specific working rules.[12]

Information Technology Ethics

One of the most complex and fast-changing areas of business ethics is in the field of information technology. Ethical challenges in this field involve invasions of privacy; the collection and storage of, and access to, personal and business information, especially through

[12] The AMA Code for Market Researchers and a discussion of numerous marketing ethics issues can be found in Patrick E. Murphy and Gene R. Laczniak, *Ethical Marketing: Cases and Readings* (Upper Saddle River, NJ: Prentice Hall, 2006); and D. Kirk Davidson, *The Moral Dimension of Marketing: Essays on Business Ethics* (Mason, OH: Thomson, 2002).

e-commerce transactions; confidentiality of electronic mail communication; copyright protection regarding software, music, and intellectual property; and numerous others.

New advances in information technology played a role in the Bernie Madoff multi-billion-dollar Ponzi scheme. Federal prosecutors filed charges against two former computer programmers, Jerome O'Hara and George Perez, as co-conspirators in the Madoff scheme. The government alleged that O'Hara and Perez filled in the blanks in the timeline of Madoff's masterminded scheme that cost investors more than $20 billion. Programs were developed to generate records showing Madoff's new "split-strike conversion" trading strategy for investment clients that used sophisticated algorithms to generate random, fictitious trading data even though no actual trades were being made.[13]

Ethical breaches challenging IT professionals are expanding to include the global community. In one incident, a vast electronic spying operation infiltrated computers around the world and stole documents from hundreds of government and private corporate offices, including files from the computer belonging to the Dalai Lama, the religious leader of Buddhism. Investigators believed that although the spy ring had operated for less than two years, at least 1,295 computers in 103 countries were infiltrated. The operating system, called GhostNet, focused mostly on governments of South Asian and Southeast Asian countries.[14]

As discussed in later chapters of this book, the explosion of information technology has raised serious questions of trust between individuals and businesses. In response to calls by businesspeople and academics for an increase in ethical responsibility in the information technology field, professional organizations have developed or revised professional codes of ethics, as shown in Exhibit 5.B.[15]

Other Functional Areas

Production and operations functions, which may seem remote from ethics considerations, have also been at the center of some ethics storms.

Mylan Inc., the world's third largest manufacturer of generic pharmaceuticals, abruptly halted production at its Morgantown, West Virginia, plant and privately informed workers that two employees had violated government-mandated quality control procedures. These procedures were intended to ensure the safety and effectiveness of their manufactured prescription drugs. A confidential internal report leaked to a local newspaper said that workers routinely overrode computer-generated warnings about potential problems with the medications they were producing. The report said that this practice was "pervasive," occurring on all three shifts at the plant for at least two years.[16]

Similar to the other professional associations, whose codes of ethical conduct are presented in Exhibits 5.A and 5.B, the Institute for Supply Management (ISM) developed a professional code of ethics that advocates "loyalty to your organization, justice to those

---

[13] "U.S. Charges Madoff Programmers," *The Wall Street Journal*, November 14, 2009, *online.wsj.com.*

[14] "AOL Worker Is Accused of Selling 93 Million E-Mail Names," *The New York Times*, June 24, 2004, *www.nytimes.com;* and "Vast Spy System Loots Computers in 103 Countries," *The New York Times*, March 29, 2009, *www.nytimes.com.*

[15] For further discussion of ethics in information technology, see Sara Baase, *A Gift of Fire: Social, Legal, and Ethical Issues for Computing and the Internet,* 3rd ed. (Upper Saddle River, NJ: Prentice Hall, 2008); and Richard Spinello, *Cyber Ethics: Morality and Law in Cyberspace,* 3rd ed. (Sudbury, MA: Jones and Bartlett, 2006).

[16] "Mylan Workers Overrode Drug Quality Controls," *Pittsburgh Post-Gazette*, July 26, 2009, *www.post-gazette.com.*

with whom you deal, and faith in your profession." The professional code denotes 12 principles and standards "to encourage adherence to an uncompromising level of integrity."[17]

Efforts by professional associations to guide their members toward effective resolution of ethical challenges make one point crystal clear: All areas of business, all people in business, and all levels of authority in business encounter ethics dilemmas from time to time. Ethics issues are a common thread running through the business world. Specific steps that businesses can take to make ethics work are discussed next.

Making Ethics Work in Corporations

Any business firm can improve the quality of its ethical performance. Doing so requires a company to build ethical safeguards into its everyday routines. This is sometimes called *institutionalizing ethics.* The proportion of the world's largest firms (the *Fortune 500* or *1000* as reported in *Fortune* magazine each year) that have adopted these safeguards since the 1980s is shown in Figure 5.2.

Building Ethical Safeguards into the Company

Managers and employees need guidance on how to handle day-to-day ethical situations; their own personal ethical compass may be working well, but they need to receive directional signals from the company. Several organizational steps can be taken to provide this kind of ethical awareness and direction.

Lynn Sharp Paine, a Harvard Business School professor, has described two distinct approaches to ethics programs: a compliance-based approach and an integrity-based approach. A compliance-based program seeks to avoid legal sanctions. This approach emphasizes the threat of detection and punishment in order to channel employee behavior in a lawful direction. Paine also described an integrity-based approach to ethics programs. Integrity-based ethics programs combine a concern for the law with an emphasis on employee responsibility for ethical conduct. Employees are told to act with integrity and conduct their business dealings in an environment of honesty and fairness. From these values a company will nurture and maintain business relationships and will be profitable.[18]

FIGURE 5.2
Percentage of Firms Reporting They Have the Ethical Safeguard

Ethical Safeguard	1986	1992	1994	2005	2011
Developed code of ethics	93%	93%	60%	86%	98%
Offered ethics training	44	52	33	69	98
Created ethics office/officer			33	65	100
Established ethics hotline				73	95
Conducted an ethics audit	44			67	67

Sources: Center for Business Ethics, "Are Corporations Institutionalizing Ethics?" *Journal of Business Ethics* 5 (1986), pp. 85–91; Center for Business Ethics, "Instilling Ethical Values in Large Corporations," *Journal of Business Ethics* 11 (1992), pp. 863–67; Ethics Resources Center, *Ethics in American Business: Policies, Programs, and Perceptions* (Washington, DC: Ethics Resource Center, 1994); Ethics Resource Center, *National Business Ethics Survey: How Employees View Ethics in Their Organizations 1994–2005* (Washington, DC: Ethics Resource Center, 2005); and James Weber and David Wasieleski, "Corporate Ethics and Compliance Programs: A Report, Analysis, and Critique," *Journal of Business Ethics*, forthcoming.

[17] All quotations are from the Institute for Supply Management's Principles and Standards of Ethical Supply Management Conduct, available to members of the association at *www.ism.ws.*

[18] Lynn Sharp Paine, "Managing for Organizational Integrity," *Harvard Business Review,* March–April 1994, pp. 106–17.

Researchers found that both approaches lessened unethical conduct, although in somewhat different ways. Compliance-based ethics programs increased employees' willingness to seek ethical advice and sharpened their awareness of ethical issues at work. Integrity-based programs, for their part, increased employees' sense of integrity, commitment to the organization, willingness to deliver bad news to supervisors, and their perception that better decisions were made.[19]

Top Management Commitment and Involvement

Research has consistently shown that the "tone at the top"—the example set by top executives—is critical to fostering ethical behavior. When senior-level managers and directors signal employees, through their own behavior, that they believe ethics should receive high priority in all business decisions, they have taken a giant step toward improving ethical performance throughout the company.

Whether the issue is sexual harassment, honest dealing with suppliers, or the reporting of expenses, the commitments (or lack thereof) by senior management and the employees' immediate supervisor and their involvement in ethics as a daily influence on employee behavior are the most essential safeguards for creating an ethical workplace.

Ethics Policies or Codes

As shown in Figure 5.2, many U.S. businesses, especially large firms, have **ethics policies or codes**. An example of one of the first corporate ethics codes is shown in Exhibit 5.C. The purpose of such policies and codes is to provide guidance to managers and employees when they encounter an ethical dilemma. Research has shown significant differences among countries. In the United States and Latin America, ethics policies were found to be primarily *instrumental*—that is, they provided rules and procedures for employees to follow in order to adhere to company policies or societal laws. In Japan, most policies were a mixture of *legal compliance* and *statements of the company's values and mission*. *Values and mission* policies were also popular with European and Canadian companies.[20] Despite some differences in orientation, codes of ethics are clearly becoming more common, as seen recently in Russia.

The Moscow Times reported that since 2008 many companies have adopted ethics codes for their workers as part of the Russian president's initiative to improve transparency. "It is good for the image and clients, investors and partners respond with trust," said Econika chief executive Andrei Ilioipulo. Some experts saw the ethics code trend as part of the transformation of the Russian economic model from wild capitalism to socially responsible business. "Business feels this need and tried to fulfill it," said a Russian economics professor. "It might seem strange, but people like to live by the rules."[21]

Typically, ethics policies cover issues such as developing guidelines for accepting or refusing gifts from suppliers, avoiding conflicts of interest, maintaining the security of proprietary information, and avoiding discriminatory personnel practices. Yet, researchers have found that a written ethics policy, while an important contributor, is insufficient by itself to bring about ethical conduct. Companies must circulate ethics policies frequently and widely among employees and external stakeholder groups (for example, customers, suppliers, or

---

[19] Gary R. Weaver and Linda Klebe Trevino, "Compliance and Values Oriented Ethics Programs: Influences on Employees' Attitudes and Behavior," *Business Ethics Quarterly* 9 (1999), pp. 315–35.

[20] Ronald C. Berenbeim, *Global Corporate Ethics Practices: A Developing Consensus* (New York: Conference Board, 1999).

[21] "Business Ethics Get Codified," *The Moscow Times*, February 24, 2011, *www.themoscowtimes.com*.

Drafted by Judge Elbert Gary, the first chairman of United States Steel Corporation, and distributed throughout the company in 1909, The Gary Principles stated the following:

- I believe that when a thing is right, it will ultimately and permanently succeed.
- The highest rewards come from honest and proper practice. Bad results come in the long run from selfish, unfair, and dishonest conduct.
- I believe in competition . . . that the race should be won by the swiftest, and that success should come to him who is most earnest and active and persevering.
- I believe that no industry can permanently succeed that does not treat its employees equitably and humanely.
- I believe thoroughly in publicity. The surest and wisest of all regulation is public opinion.
- If we are to succeed in business, we must do it on principles that are honest, fair, lawful, and just.
- We must put and keep ourselves on a platform so fair, so high, so reasonable, that we will attract the attention and invite and secure the approval of all who know what we are doing.
- We do not advocate combinations or agreements in restraint of trade, nor action of any kind which is opposed to the laws or to the public welfare.
- We must never forget that our rights and interests are and should be subservient to the public welfare, that the rights and interests of the individual must always give way to those of the public.

Reproduced with permission of United States Steel Corporation.

competitors). The creation of an ethics policy must be followed up with employee training so that the policy's provisions actually influence day-to-day company activities.[22]

Ethics and Compliance Officers

Ethical lapses in large corporations throughout the 1980s prompted many firms to create a new position: the **ethics and compliance officer**. A second surge of attention to ethics and the creation of ethics offices came in response to the 1991 U.S. Corporate Sentencing Guidelines, discussed in Chapter 4. Finally, the recent wave of corporate ethics scandals and the passage of the Sarbanes-Oxley Act have again turned businesses' attention toward entrusting ethical compliance and the development and implementation of ethics programs to an ethics or compliance officer. From 2000 to 2004, the number of members in the Ethics Officers Association doubled from 632 to more than 1,200 members and remained at that level through 2012. To reflect the growing number of compliance officers heading companies' ethics programs, this association changed its name to the Ethics and Compliance Officers Association (ECOA).

Keith Darcy, executive director of the ECOA, explained, "Organizations are increasingly recognizing the importance of their ethics and compliance office [and officers], not just in a time of crisis, but as an integral part of day-to-day business." An ECOA study found that top ethics executives received compensation, including stock options, that was comparable to individuals in other executive-level jobs.[23]

[22] Betsy Stevens, "Communicating Ethical Values: A Study of Employee Perceptions," *Journal of Business Ethics* 20 (1999), pp. 113–20. For examples of codes, see Ivanka Mamic, *Implementing Codes of Conduct* (Sheffield, UK: Greenleaf Publishing, 2004); and Oliver F. Williams, C.S.C., ed., *Global Codes of Conduct: An Idea Whose Time Has Come* (Notre Dame, IN: University of Notre Dame Press, 2000).

[23] "EOA Survey: Companies Seeking to Integrate Ethics through the Whole Organization," *Ethikos*, July–August 2001, pp. 1–3, 16; and "Pay for Top Corporate Ethics Officers Rising Quickly," *Ethics Newsline*, Institute for Global Ethics, October 10, 2006, www.globalethics.org. For additional information, see *The Business Case for Creating a Standalone Chief Compliance Officer Position*, Ethisphere, www.ethisphere.com.

Ethics Reporting Mechanisms

In most companies, when employees are troubled about some ethical issue they seek out their immediate supervisor or someone else in senior management. The Ethics Resource Center reported that 43 percent of employees informed their supervisor of a possible ethical violation and 34 percent told someone else in higher management.[24] But what if the employee is reluctant, for whatever reason, to raise the issue with their immediate supervisor? In that case, they can turn to their company's **ethics reporting mechanisms** and call a "helpline" or send an e-mail expressing their concerns, anonymously if they wish. Ethics reporting systems typically have three uses: (1) to provide interpretations of proper ethical behavior involving conflicts of interest and the appropriateness of gift giving, (2) to create an avenue to make known to the proper authorities allegations of unethical conduct, and (3) to give employees and other corporate stakeholders a way to discover general information about a wide range of work-related topics.

Ethics officers say more and more employees are willing to use their companies' ethical reporting mechanisms, but a number of challenges remain. Executives tend to use the helpline more often than those farther down the organizational chart. The Ethics Resource Center study found that middle managers were "an area of vulnerability within companies" since they were less likely to use the helpline. The report also discovered that rates of helpline usage were lower in foreign-owned companies than in their U.S. counterparts. Yet, many businesses described greater success when employees use the company's helpline/hotline and were better able to avoid more serious ethical violations. Technology seemed to be the key.

Medtronics' global chief ethics and compliance officer, Tom Schumacher, received hotline reports quicker and more frequently through his handheld device. Employees can report possible violations online. For some firms, 60 to 70 percent of all reports arrived via the Internet. A web-based reporting system can be designed to solicit information from the employee for a more detailed and helpful report. According to Schumacher, "I really like the [enhanced] ability to communicate with an anonymous reporter" since the system is more secure than in the past.[25]

But no matter how advanced is the technology used in an ethics and compliance program, the ethics and compliance officer never really knows what to expect when monitoring calls to the helpline, as the following example showed:[26]

"Oh, boy, this is one of those days," thought the ethics officer at a midsized manufacturing firm when she received a call on the ethics helpline that a toilet in the company's administration building was overflowing. She called maintenance and they found that someone had clogged up the toilet drain. When the same call was received a week later, the ethics officer knew she had to investigate. Through interviews with personnel who worked on that floor, she discovered that the supervisor had refused to allow workers to take bathroom breaks when needed, and an employee had boasted that "he was going to get even with his supervisor and plug up the toilet" to attract attention to unsafe working conditions. The call about the overflowing toilet and subsequent investigation allowed the ethics officer to address the real issue, counsel the supervisor, and repair the deteriorating working conditions at her company.[27]

[24] Ethics Resource Center, *2009 National Business Ethics Survey: Reporting—Who's Telling You What You Need to Know, Who Isn't, and What You Can Do About It* (Washington, DC: Ethics Resource Center, 2009), p. 15.

[25] For a more detailed description of Medtronics' ethics and compliance program, see Andrew Singer, "Going Beyond Devices: Medtronics Urges Employees to 'Speak Up,'" *Ethikos*, May/June 2011, pp. 1–3, 16.

[26] *2007 Corporate Governance and Compliance Hotline Benchmarking Report*, Security Executive Council, p. 10.

[27] Based on an interview with an ethics and compliance officer who requested that her firm and her identity remain anonymous.

Ethics Training Programs

Another step companies can take to build in ethical safeguards is to offer **employee ethics training**. This is generally the most expensive and time-consuming element of an ethics program. Studies have shown that only 20 to 40 percent of small businesses formally offer ethics training to their employees, often using less formal ways to communicate ethical values and procedures. Larger businesses, by contrast, usually conduct regular ethics training, as shown in Figure 5.2. Most ethics and compliance training programs focus on making sure employees know what the law requires and the company expects. Few firms, however, systematically measure the effectiveness of this effort or consider the impact of new training approaches. Some experts argued that the explosion of web-based ethics training may not be as effective as the more traditional but expensive face-to-face training.[28] A new approach to employee ethics training emphasizes the importance of varied yet frequent efforts at ethics training, as seen at Raytheon.

> At Raytheon, ethics training tried to guide employees' ethical decision making and communicate important ethics messages throughout the organization. In 2010, 82 percent of employees favorably rated the company's ethics training efforts. The company attributed this high satisfaction rate due to the delivery of ethics training through numerous vehicles. All employees participated in small-group sessions to study ethical dilemmas based on real workplace situations, watched videos that presented meaningful and relevant ethical issues in an entertaining way, and studied online learning modules on a wide range of topics. Follow-up assessment of the ethics training program revealed that employees were more likely to report alleged misconduct to the ethics office.[29]

Ethics Audits

Some firms have attempted to assess the effectiveness of their ethical safeguards by documenting evidence of increased ethical employee behavior. One technique used is an **ethics audit**. In such an audit, the auditor—either a hired outside consultant or an internal employee—is required to note any deviations from the company's ethics standards and bring them to the attention of the audit supervisor. Ethics audits are becoming more common as an ethical safeguard, as shown in Figure 5.2, but exactly what goes into an ethics audit is very different for each organization.

> *HR Magazine* provided the following "Six Steps to Highly Effective Ethics Audits" as a guide for organizations seeking to create and conduct an ethics audit:
>
> 1. Start with a detailed foundation—the more descriptive and specific the ethics code is, the easier it is to compare the firm's policy with actual practice.
> 2. Develop metrics—audits run more smoothly when tangible ethics measures are in place.
> 3. Create a cross-functional team—include someone from human resources, the ethics and compliance office, the internal auditor staff, and the legal department.
> 4. Audit efficiently—since audits can disrupt normal business operations, it is important to avoid conflicting with other audits being conducted in the company and to have a clear timeline plan for interviews, collection of information, and so on.

[28] See "Is Your Ethics and Compliance Training Really Preparing Your Employees?" *Compliance and Ethics Professional,* March–April 2012, *www.corporatecompliance.org.*

[29] "Ethics: Demonstrating Our Values through Our Actions," *Raytheon's 2010 Corporate Responsibility Report,* p. 7.

5. Look for other issues—always keep an eye out for unexpected improvement opportunities while conducting the audit.

6. Respond consistently and communicate—make sure that the punishment for the ethical violations is in line with the company's policies every time, and try to use these situations as "lessons learned" in subsequent ethics training or communications.[30]

Comprehensive Ethics Programs

Experts believe that integrating various ethics safeguards into a comprehensive program is critically important. When all six components discussed in this chapter—top management commitment, ethical policies or codes, compliance officers, reporting mechanisms, training programs, and audits—are used together, they reinforce each other and become more effective. In an Ethics Resource Center survey of U.S. employees, only 26 percent reported that their employer had developed a comprehensive, six-element ethics program. The startling discovery, however, was the dramatic impact a comprehensive ethics program, along with a strong ethical culture, had in creating an ethical work environment for employees. People working at a firm that did have a comprehensive ethics program were more likely to report ethical misconduct in the workplace to the appropriate company authority and to be satisfied with the company's investigation of and response to charges of ethical misconduct. In contrast, firms with only an ethics policy or code were often perceived as less ethically responsible and less able to address ethical misconduct in the workplace than firms without any ethical safeguards.[31] An example of a strong values-based ethics program at Alcoa is described in the discussion case at the end of this chapter.

Corporate Ethics Awards and Certifications

Firms are recognized for their efforts to create an ethical climate and improve ethical performance by various groups and associations.

Ethisphere Magazine honors ethical leadership and business practices worldwide based on an Ethical Quotient (EQ) score. The EQ score considers corporate responsibility performance; governance adherence; innovation that contributes to the public's well-being; exemplary leadership to the industry; executive leadership; the firm's legal, regulatory, and reputation track record; and the internal systems and ethics and compliance program developed at the firm. As seen in Chapter 4, Figure 4.3, *Ethisphere*'s "the world's most ethical companies" financially outperformed the S&P 500 and FTSE 1000 every year since 2005. Figure 5.3 shows the 25 companies that have made the World's Most Ethical Companies list each year since 2007.

The Foundation for Financial Service Professionals sponsored the American Business Ethics Awards (ABEA). Established in 1994, the ABEA "recognizes companies that exemplify high standards of ethical behavior in their everyday business conduct and in response to specific crises or challenges." Kimberly-Clark, producer of many well-known household consumer brands such as Kleenex, Huggies, Scott, and Depend, received the award in 2011 in the large-company category. Corgan Associates, an international architectural and interior design company headquartered in Dallas, Texas, received the award for a midsized company, and The Eye & Laser Center, based in South Carolina, was honored as the small-company awardee.[32]

---

[30] Eric Krell, "How to Conduct an Ethics Audit," *HR Magazine*, April 2010, p. 49. For a good example of an internal ethics audit, see Andrew Singer, "Global Expansion Raises the Stakes for Kimberly-Clark Corp.," *Ethikos*, July/August 2011, pp. 1–3, 16.

[31] See Joshua Joseph, *2000 National Business Ethics Survey, Volume I: How Employees Perceive Ethics at Work* (Washington, DC: Ethics Resource Center, 2000).

[32] A full description of the ABEA program can be found at *www.financialpro.org/foundation/ABEA* and additional information about Kimberly-Clark's ABEA award is available at *www.csrwire.com*.

FIGURE 5.3
The World's Most Ethical Companies and Their Industries, According to *Ethisphere*

Source: Information is from the *Ethisphere* website at *ethisphere.com/past-wme-honorees.*

These firms were ranked among the highest ethical firms each year from 2007 through 2011.	
AFLAC (insurance)	Kao Corporation (consumer products)
American Express (financial services)	Milliken & Company (industrial manufacturing)
Becton Dickinson (medical devices)	Patagonia (apparel)
Caterpillar (industrial manufacturing)	PepsiCo (food & beverage)
Deere and Company (industrial manufacturing)	Rabobank (banking)
	Royal Phillips (electronics)
Eaton Corporation (industrial manufacturing)	Salesforce.com (software)
Ecolab (chemicals)	Standard Chartered (banking)
Fluor Corporation (engineering)	Starbucks Coffee Company (restaurants)
The Gap (apparel)	Target (retail)
General Electric (diversified)	Texas Instrument (computers)
International Paper (paper products)	UPS (transportation)
Johnson Controls (automotive)	Xerox (computers)

These and other award-winning firms provide the foundation for a collection of corporate ethics role models. Their commitment to ethical values and efforts to establish effective ethics programs demonstrate that firms can be financially successful and ethically focused.

Ethics in a Global Economy

Doing business in a global context raises a host of complex ethical challenges. Examples of unethical conduct by business employees are reported from nearly every country. One example of unethical activity is **bribery**, a questionable or unjust payment often to a government official to ensure or facilitate a business transaction. Bribery is found in nearly every sector of the global marketplace.

A Berlin-based watchdog agency, Transparency International, annually publishes a survey that ranks corruption by country according to perceptions of executives and the public. Countries where having to pay a bribe is least likely included New Zealand, Denmark, Finland, Sweden, Singapore, Norway, and the Netherlands. At the other end of the index, North Korea and Somalia are considered the world's most corrupt countries, along with Afghanistan, Myanmar, Uzbekistan, Turkmenistan, Sudan, and Iraq. The United States ranked 24th on the list of 182 countries, with the United Kingdom tied for 16th, Canada 10th, Germany and Japan tied for 14th, France 25th, Italy 69th, China 75th, India 95th, and Russia 143rd.[33]

An analysis of Transparency International's Corruption Perceptions Index (CPI) by a business scholar revealed that bribe-taking was more likely in countries with low per capita income, low salaries for government officials, and less variation in income distribution. The report also argued that "a legalistic approach, by itself, is unlikely to be effective in curbing bribery," since the culture of the society plays an important role in the occurrence of bribery. What may be effective in combating bribery is an integrative approach of economic advancement policies, social investment in education, and friendly business policies to foster economic growth, in addition to anticorruption laws and punishments to combat bribery while seeking to enhance economic development and gradual cultural adjustments.[34]

[33] For a complete list of all countries according to their perceived level of corruption, see *cpi.transparency.org/cpi2011*.

[34] Rajib Sanyal, "Determinants of Bribery in International Business: The Cultural and Economic Factors," *Journal of Business Ethics 59* (2005), pp. 139–45.

Bribery has significant economic, as well as ethical, consequences. U.S. Vice President Joseph Biden told a Russian audience, "Corruption is the number one impediment to better economic relations." The United Nations reported that corruption costs governments about $1.6 trillion every year. Economists estimated, based on polls conducted in 86 countries, that one businessperson in every four worldwide paid a bribe in the past year.[35]

Bribery is particularly prevalent in Russia. According to a PricewaterhouseCoopers study, "Russia is the worst country in the world for companies in terms of employee theft and extortion by officials." Economists estimated that Russian corruption generated at least 50 percent of the country's gross domestic product, or around $650 billion annually. And it seems that things are getting worse. "The average size of a bribe has risen to 300,000 rubles (more than $10,000 US) in Russia," according to a high-ranking Russian official, compared to the average of 44,000 rubles just a year earlier. Moreover, in a survey of Russian citizens, many accept that corruption is "Russia's own special way" of conducting business.[36]

Some people, however, believed that corruption was necessary, even beneficial, to global commerce. More than half of the Russians surveyed thought bribing officials was the best way to solve problems, according to a *Reuters* poll. In Australia, 9 out of 10 people thought bribery and corruption were wrong but unavoidable. A German newspaper columnist said his business had paid bribes on several occasions, "because there are certain countries where there is no other way to do it." These attitudes may cause global efforts to reduce bribery, discussed next, to become even more difficult.[37]

Efforts to Curtail Unethical Practices

Numerous efforts are under way to curb unethical business practices throughout the world. The most common control is through government intervention and regulation. Efforts to address unethical business behavior often begin with national governments, which can enact stiff legislative controls, but also include efforts by international organizations.

One of the most widespread and potentially powerful efforts to combat bribery was initiated by the Organization for Economic Cooperation and Development (OECD). The OECD treaty called on member countries to take steps to deter, prevent, and combat the bribery of public officials in foreign countries. Nearly 40 countries ratified the treaty, meaning that bribery is a crime and punishable by the country's courts.

To support the trend toward anticorruption efforts, the OECD Working Group on Bribery called on businesses to adopt a clear and visible antibribery policy, instill a sense of responsibility for compliance at all levels of the company, conduct regular communication and training on foreign bribery for all employees, and encourage observance of antibribery compliance measures and disciplinary procedures to address their violations.[38] After suffering global embarrassment and potential loss of business due to governmental corruption, the Chinese government launched an effort to combat corruption, as shown in Exhibit 5.D.

[35] "Corruption: The Biggest Threat to Developing Economies," *CNN Money.com*, April 20, 2011, *money.cnn.com;* "Corruption Costs $1.6tn, UN Says," *BBC News*, November 9, 2009, *newsvote.bbc.co.uk;* and "One in Four Worldwide Pays Bribes: Study," *The Age*, December 9, 2010, *news.theage.com.au.*

[36] "Russia Leads World in Company Fraud, State Extortion, PwC Says," *Bloomberg.com*, November 19, 2009, *www.bloomberg.com;* "Russia's Corruption Generates Equivalent of 50% GDP—Watchdog," *Dow Jones Newswires*, August 2, 2010, *www.nasdaq.com;* "Average Bribe Grows to about $10,000 in Russia, Says Police," *Kyiv Post*, August 10, 2010, *www.kyivpost.com;* "For Russians, Corruption Is Just a Way of Life," *The New York Times*, August 18, 2012, *www.nytimes.com.* For an in-depth look at Russian corruption, see "Deadly Business in Moscow," *Bloomberg Businessweek*, March 1, 2010, pp. 22–23.

[37] "Half of Russians Believe Bribery Solves 'Problems,'" *Reuters*, May 13, 2010, *www.reuters.com;* "Bribery 'Wrong but Unavoidable' in Oz, Claim Managers," *Sify*, June 20, 2010, *sify.com;* and "Police Raid German Pipeline Contractor over Kickback Claim," *Earthtimes.org*, August 20, 2010, *www.earthtimes.org.*

[38] "OECD Calls on Businesses to Step Up Their Fight against Bribery," *OECD*, March 3, 2010, *www.oecd.org.*

Anticorruption experts and global business executives pointed out that corruption and bribery were at epidemic proportions in China. During a one-year period, 148 bribery attempts were reported. The Carnegie Endowment for Peace concluded that corruption in China imposes crippling costs on the country's economy and threatens to undermine its political stability. In 2011, the Chinese National People's Congress responded by declaring that paying bribes to foreign officials or government officials receiving bribes are criminal acts.

The Chinese government also created a new National Corruption Prevention Bureau, charged with fighting corruption. China's President Hu Jinto helped launch the anticorruption campaign by saying that his government "would focus on improving ethics education, reforming legal procedures, arresting high-profile offenders, and cracking down on crimes that most affect the public interest." This initiative enabled China to meet commitments to the United Nations Convention Against Corruption—which led some critics to speculate that these efforts were mostly political posturing on the world stage.

But the Chinese government showed its seriousness toward combating bribery in a number of ways:

- Zheng Xiaoyu, the former head of the State Food and Drug Administration, was executed after admitting to accepting $850,000 in bribes to grant approval for hundreds of medicines. Some drugs were proven to be fakes and others did not pass regulatory standards for safety.

- Cao Wenzhuang, who was in charge of drug registration approvals at the same government agency, was also sentenced to death for accepting more than $300,000 in bribes. Cao was given a two-year reprieve and later received the lighter sentence of life in prison.

- Li Hua, former chairman and general manager of China Mobile, was sentenced to death after being convicted of accepting more than $2.5 million in bribes, but was later given a two-year reprieve and his sentence was commuted to life in prison.

- Former Chongqing Energy Investment Group president was sentenced to life in prison for paying 6.25 million yuan ($992,000) between 1996 and 2011.

Sources: "China Criminalizes Foreign Bribery," *The Wall Street Journal*, March 23, 2011, *blogs.wsj.com*; "China May Create a National Anti-Corruption Bureau," *Ethics Newsline*, Institute for Global Ethics, February 20, 2007, *www.globalethics.org*; "China Sentences Official to Death for Corruption," *The New York Times*, July 7, 2007, *www.nytimes.com*; "China Quick to Execute Drug Official," *The New York Times*, July 11, 2007, *www.nytimes.com*; "Chinese Telecom Executive Sentenced to Death for Bribery," *The New York Times*, August 30, 2011, *www.nytimes.com*; "Bribery Is Losing Its Charm in China," *Bloomberg Businessweek*, July 12–18, 2010, pp. 11–12; and "Corrupt Former President of Chongqing Energy Handed a Life Sentence," *Xinhuanet.com*, December 19, 2011, *news.xinhuanet.com*.

Since 1977, executives representing U.S.-based companies have been prohibited by the **U.S. Foreign Corrupt Practices Act** (FCPA) from paying bribes to foreign government officials, political parties, or political candidates. To achieve this goal, the FCPA requires U.S. companies with foreign operations to adopt accounting practices that ensure full disclosure of the company's transactions. The FCPA received greater enforcement attention recently, and the more than $3 billion in settlements most often involve non-U.S. companies who operate in the United States, as shown in these examples:[39]

- The German automaker Daimler AG (which was subject to the FCPA because it had business operations in the United States) agreed to pay $185 million to end a U.S. investigation into allegations that it had paid tens of millions of dollars in bribes to secure business overseas.

[39] "More Heat Coming," *Foreign Corrupt Practices Act blog*, August 10, 2009, *fcpablog.blogspot.com*.

- Six oil and gas service companies and a freight-forwarding company agreed to pay $236 million in penalties to settle a bribery case that spanned seven countries in Eastern Europe, Africa, and South America. One of the largest companies in this group, Panalpina, based in Switzerland, admitted that it paid $27 million to foreign officials.
- Terra Telecommunications former president Joel Esquenazi was sentenced to 15 years in prison for his role in bribing officials at Haiti Teleco, a state-owned telecommunications company. Former executive vice president, Carlos Rodriguez, was sentenced to seven years in prison, and both were ordered to forfeit more than $3 million.

Given the magnitude of the illegal operations involving bribery, enforcement of the FCPA was increased and resulted in an 85 percent jump in the number of FCPA enforcement actions in 2010 from the prior year. The Department of Justice and the Securities and Exchange Commission brought a combined 122 FCPA enforcement actions in 2010 and 2011, far surpassing any prior 2-year period in the statute's 33-year history. Eight of the top 10 monetary settlements in FCPA history occurred in 2010.[40]

The United Kingdom's Bribery Act was passed in 2010. Some believed it was even more stringent than the U.S.'s FCPA. The U.K. Bribery Act differs from the FCPA in that:

- The Bribery Act prohibits the bribery of another person and receiving or accepting a bribe, whereas the FCPA only prohibits bribery of non-U.S. government officials. Bribery of a private business executive would be illegal under British, but not U.S., anticorruption law.
- The Bribery Act does not require that the improper offer, promise, or payment be made "corruptly," but the FCPA does require evidence of the intent to corrupt.
- The Bribery Act does not provide exemptions for "facilitating payments" or the defense that there are reasonable and bona fide contractual or promotional expenses, as the FCPA does.
- The Bribery Act contains a strict liability offense for failure to prevent bribery by commercial organizations; the FCPA does not.[41]

The initial efforts to implement the Bribery Act were met with many challenges. Just weeks before the new law was to go into effect, 73 percent of U.K. business professionals said they were not familiar with provisions of the Bribery Act, and many felt that the law would not apply to their business, even though it would. The act left many companies scrambling to develop ethical safeguards to ensure compliance with the new bribery standard. A year after the law went into effect 24 percent of U.K. managers surveyed believed that the bribery law was negatively affecting the U.K.'s global competitiveness.

Antibribery laws and enforcement, however, was more the norm than the exception, particularly in Europe. In Germany there were more antibribery corruption enforcement cases in 2010 than in the United States. Transparency International acknowledged that

---

[40] "Foreign Firms Most Affected by a U.S. Law Barring Bribes," *The New York Times*, September 3, 2012, *www.nytimes.com;* "Daimler to Settle with U.S. on Bribes," *The Wall Street Journal*, March 24, 2010, *online.wsj.com;* "Oil and Gas Bribery Case Settled for $236 Million," *The New York Times*, November 4, 2010, *www.nytimes.com;* "Ex-Terra President Gets Longest Foreign Bribery Sentence of 15 Years," *Bloomberg*, October 26, 2011, *www.bloomberg.com;* "2010 FCPA Enforcement Shatters Records," *Compliance Week*, January 4, 2011, *www.compliance week.com;* and "2011 Was a Banner Year for FCPA Enforcements and Trials," *Corporate Counsel*, January 6, 2012, *www.law.com.* It should be noted that if a firm is listed on an American stock exchange or is acting as an agent for a U.S.-based firm, then the action of that firm is subject to U.S. law, specifically the Foreign Corrupt Practices Act, as is the case for each example here.

[41] "FCPA vs. the UK Bribery Act," *Ethisphere*, Quarter 3, 2010, pp. 38–41. Also see "Parallels between the UK Bribery Act and the U.S. Foreign Corrupt Practices Act," *Boardmember.com*, July 9, 2010, *www.boardmember.com.*

Germany had joined the United States as the most active government fighting corporations paying bribes. Other countries also aggressively attacked bribery through law enforcement, such as in Italy, France, the Netherlands, and Brazil.[42]

Ethics, Law, and Illegal Corporate Behavior

It is important when discussing specific ways to improve business's ethical performance to consider the relationship of laws and ethics. Some people have argued that the best way to assure ethical business conduct is to insist that business firms obey society's laws. However, this approach is not as simple as it seems.

Laws and ethics are not quite the same. Laws are similar to ethics because both define proper and improper behavior. In general, laws are a society's attempt to formalize—that is, to reduce to written rules—the general public's ideas about what constitutes right and wrong conduct in various spheres of life. Ethical concepts—like the people who believe in them—are more complex than written rules of law. Ethics deal with human dilemmas that frequently go beyond the formal language of law and the meanings given to legal rules. Sometimes businesses or industries preempt legislation and voluntarily adopt ethically based practices:

> The Interactive Digital Software Association, which represents video game makers, established a five-category system that was voluntarily adopted by the industry to inform consumers of the intended target audience. The video game industry also agreed to provide content warnings, such as mild profanity, and to use warning symbols.

Following laws cannot always define proper action—that is, what is ethical or unethical. Although laws attempt to codify a society's notions of right and wrong, they are not always able to do so completely. Obeying laws is usually one way of acting ethically, and the public generally expects business to be law-abiding. But at times, the public expects business to recognize that ethical principles are broader than laws. Because of the imperfect match between laws and ethics, business managers who try to improve their company's ethical performance need to do more than comply with laws.

Corporate Lawbreaking and Its Costs

Although estimates vary, lawbreaking in business may cause serious financial losses to the firms, often inflicted by the company's own employees.

White-collar crime, illegal acts committed by individuals, employees, or business professionals such as fraud, insider trading, embezzlement, or computer crime, accounts for more than 330,000 arrests each year in the United States, despite significant attention to prevent this type of crime. The Association of Certified Fraud Examiners (ACFE) reported in 2012 that the typical organization lost 5 percent of its revenues to fraud each year. This translated to a potential global fraud loss of more than $3.5 trillion. The most commonly reported white-collar crime is credit card fraud, followed by price misrepresentation, unnecessary repairs, monetary loss when using the Internet, and identity theft. One in four

[42] "Deloitte Poll: 73% Are Unfamiliar with Bribery Act Provisions," *The Wall Street Journal*, April 19, 2011, *blogs.wsj.com;* "Nearly a Year On, One in Four Worry That Bribery Act Is Affecting UK Competitiveness," *Ernest & Young*, April 30, 2012, *www.ey.com;* "Kroll: Only One-Third of Companies Believe They Have to Abide by Bribery Laws," *The Wall Street Journal*, October 21, 2010, *blogs.wsj.com;* "Transparency International: US and Germany Most Active in Fighting Corporations Paying Bribes," *Washington Post*, September 6, 2012, *www.washingtonpost.com;* and "Anti-Corruption Enforcement Gains Traction on a Global Scale," *Ethikos*, January–February 2012, p. 13.

Americans reported that they were victims of some type of white-collar crime and nearly half of the victims did not recover any of their fraud losses, according to the ACFE report.[43]

The United States is not the only nation suffering losses from illegal acts. German officials believe that more than 50 billion marks (about $29 billion) a year is lost from the German economy as a result of inflated accounting, tax evasion, and illegal kickbacks. The PricewaterhouseCoopers global survey on crime reported that total fraud loss incurred by businesses in the United Kingdom doubled to £1.75 million (about $2.75 million). Businesses in the United Kingdom that experienced fraud were hit on average 15 times in a 24-month period, twice the global average and three times more than the average across Western Europe.[44]

But there is still an unanswered question: "Does crime pay?" Although many executives received severe prison sentences, as discussed throughout this chapter, in a Conference Board–supported survey of executives, 62 percent of respondents said that executives who leave their firm because of major violations of ethics and compliance codes "get a financial package and go." So, while the risks are great, some evidence supports the adage "crime does pay," although governmental and business efforts may seek to change this situation in the future.

Yet the more likely lesson to be learned from recent business ethics scandals is that "crime does *not* pay." The consequences for acting unethically and illegally are serious, as the "perp walks" portrayed in the media of business executives going off to jail in handcuffs would indicate. Therefore, businesses have taken significant measures to foster an ethical environment in the workplace and to provide mechanisms to ensure their employees know what is the "right thing to do" and consistently act in an ethical manner.

Summary

- A company's culture and ethical climate tend to shape the attitudes and actions of all who work there, sometimes resulting in high levels of ethical behavior and at other times contributing to less desirable ethical performance.

- Not all ethical issues in business are the same, but ethical challenges occur in all major functional areas of business. Professional associations for each functional area often attempt to provide a standard of conduct to guide practice.

- Companies can improve their ethical performance by creating a values-based ethics program that relies on top management leadership and organizational safeguards, such as ethics policies or codes, ethics and compliance offices and officers, ethics training programs, ethics reporting mechanisms, and ethics audits.

- Companies that have a comprehensive, or multifaceted, ethics program often are better able to promote ethical behavior at work and avoid unethical action by employees.

- Ethical issues, such as bribery, are evident throughout the world, and many international agencies and national governments are actively attempting to minimize such unethical behavior through economic sanctions and international codes.

- Although laws and ethics are closely related, they are not the same; ethical principles tend to be broader than legal principles. Illegal behavior by businesses and employees imposes great costs on business generally and the general public.

[43] *The 2010 National Public Survey on White-Collar Crime,* National White Collar Crime Center, *www.nw3c.org;* and the *2012 Report to the Nations,* Association of Certified Fraud Examiners, *www.acfe.com.*

[44] See the PricewaterhouseCoopers Global Economic Crime Survey at *www.pwc.com.*

Key Terms

bribery, *105*
corporate culture, *91*
employee ethics training, *103*
ethical climate, *92*
ethics and compliance officer, *101*

ethics audit, *103*
ethics policies or codes, *100*
ethics reporting mechanisms, *102*
laws, *109*

U.S. Foreign Corrupt Practices Act, *107*
white-collar crime, *109*

Internet Resources

www.TheCRO.com	*CR: Corporate Responsibility Magazine*
www.dii.org	Defense Industry Initiative on Business Ethics and Conduct
www.theecoa.org	Ethics & Compliance Officers Association
www.ethicaledge.com	Ethics and Policy Integration Centre
ethisphere.com	Ethisphere Institute
www.ethics.org/resources	Ethics Resource Center
www.globalethics.org	Institute for Global Ethics
www.saiglobal.com	SAI Global
www.business-ethics.org	International Business Ethics Institute
www.corporatecompliance.org	Society of Corporate Compliance and Ethics
www.transparency.org	Transparency International
www.nw3c.org	National White Collar Crime Center

Discussion Case: *Alcoa's Core Values in Practice*

Alcoa began under the name of the Pittsburgh Reduction Company in 1888, changing its name to the Aluminum Company of America (Alcoa) in 1907. The company was originally founded on a $20,000 investment to capitalize on Charles Martin Hall's invention to smelt bauxite ore into the metal known as aluminum. Within a few years, Alcoa had developed into a model of large-scale vertical integration with control over all the inputs to aluminum production.

Since its inception, Alcoa has had a very strong values-based culture. Employees learned early in their careers that every decision they made and everything they did must be aligned with the company's values. In 1985, Fred Fetterolf, then president, decided the company needed to document the values that all employees must live by: Integrity; Environment, Health, and Safety; Customer; Accountability; Excellence; People; and Profitability. (In 2012, Alcoa slightly revised its core values—Integrity; Environmental, Health and Safey; Excellence; Respect; and Innovation.)

In the 1990s Alcoa's CEO, Paul O'Neill, communicated his unswerving belief in the importance of health and safety—one of the company's core values. As is the case with many large organizations, Alcoa had implemented a global ethics and compliance program, and the focus on health and safety was interwoven through the company's program. The Alcoa program included all the basic elements specified in the U.S. Federal Sentencing Guidelines and Sarbanes-Oxley Act. Alcoa had an ethics and compliance officer who reported to the company's CEO and board of directors, a global code of conduct, continuous ethics and compliance training for all employees, and a global helpline reporting system, to name just a few. Overall, the company emphasized that the program's tools must be understandable by all employees, must support the company's strong value system, and must be continually reinforced by management.

For example, in addition to continuous safety training and education programs, it was the norm at Alcoa to start all business meetings with an identification of exits, the evacuation plans in the event of an emergency, and other safety procedures. Although specific safety procedures differed among Alcoa's various businesses, corporate headquarters required all of its units to meet the same overall goal: zero work-related injuries and illnesses. O'Neill took this message outside of Alcoa, as well. In meetings with analysts and other outside parties, he always highlighted Alcoa's progress in health and safety. O'Neill explained that Alcoa's emphasis on safety and the reduction of workplace injuries was not based on grandstanding or self-promotion, but rather on a genuine concern for employees.

The emphasis on safety had deep meaning to Alcoa's management team. The company's management firmly believed that no employees should be forced to work in an environment where their safety and the safety of other employees might be jeopardized. Alcoa's management supported the ethical principle that no employees should leave work in a worse condition than when they arrived. Once the change toward safety at work became "the way we do things around here" and was embedded in the Alcoa culture, the process used to achieve this culture could be duplicated throughout Alcoa's value chain. O'Neill's point was simply that the processes used to achieve success in safety were not grand initiatives or episodic programs but rather were the result of persistent attention to changing behaviors and could be duplicated throughout the organization. Alcoa's vision was "Alcoa Aspires to Be the Best Company in the World." Being the best at everything, for O'Neill and Alcoa employees, required continuous improvement as everyone strove toward an ideal goal of perfection.

In 1996, activist shareholders raised allegations at the annual meeting that health and safety conditions at one of Alcoa's Mexican facilities had deteriorated. The Catholic Sister who spoke at the meeting concluded by saying that "the company's behavior in Mexico was inconsistent with its widely publicized values." The company promptly launched an investigation, and O'Neill himself personally visited the plant. Although the company learned that many of the issues raised at the annual meeting were unfounded, it also discovered that a few injury incidents and the subsequent actions taken by local managers were not reported to corporate headquarters, as required by company policy. Meetings held with local government officials over safety incidents at the facility were also not reported, even though the results of these meetings indicated Alcoa was in compliance with all appropriate laws and regulations.

Given these facts, O'Neill concluded that although the business unit management's response to the safety incidents uncovered in the investigation was adequate, there was "a breach of the letter and spirit of our communication practices with respect to major incidents." O'Neill further noted "there was a serious lack of understanding when it came to incident classification, reporting, and recordkeeping of occupational illnesses." The lack of reporting these safety incidents to others in the company was critical to O'Neill, since others in the company were denied the opportunity to learn and possibly prevent similar occurrences at other Alcoa facilities.

O'Neill decided that a change of leadership at the facility was necessary, and he fired the facility's manager. He did so in spite of the manager's stellar record of increased sales and profitability and high marks for quality and customer satisfaction. In an open letter to the entire company, O'Neill concluded by saying, "It is imperative that there be no misperceptions about our values. It is equally imperative that we all learn from this. Full compliance with both the letter—and spirit—of our policies is imperative. Anything less is unacceptable."

Over time, Alcoa's tenacious focus on safety has paid off. In 2012, Alcoa's lost workday rate was 0.036. (This number represents the number of injuries and illnesses resulting in one or more days away from work per 100 full-time workers.) In the 12-month period ending December 31, 2011,

- 47.8 percent of Alcoa's 242 locations worldwide had zero recordable injuries.
- 79.2 percent of Alcoa's 242 locations worldwide had zero lost workdays.
- 99.9 percent of Alcoa employees had zero lost workdays.

Alcoa was rapidly closing the gap between its safety record and that of DuPont, which had long been the benchmark for safety among American industrial companies. This achievement was especially significant since Alcoa had completed several substantial acquisitions during this time in many countries whose safety regulations had not yet matured to the level of those in the United States.

Sources: Quotations by Paul O'Neill are from his July 3, 1996, memo to all Alcoa business unit presidents and subsequently distributed to all Alcoa managers. The new Alcoa values are from an internal company memo from Klaus Kleinfeld, Alcoa's CEO, to his employees on July 2, 2012, and is used with permission. This case was developed with the assistance of long-time Alcoa employee Perry Minnis, formerly the Global Director of Ethics, Compliance, and Advisory Services at Alcoa before his retirement from the company.

Discussion Questions

1. How would you classify Alcoa's ethical work climate? Which ethical criterion, as shown in Figure 5.1, was used by the company: egoism (self-centered), benevolence (concern for others), or principles (integrity approach)? Or, using Professor Paine's two distinct ethics approaches, as discussed in this chapter, was Alcoa's approach more compliance or integrity?

2. What role did top management commitment play in developing the ethical work climate and organizational performance seen at Alcoa? What other ethical safeguards are mentioned in the case to support the company's efforts at developing a strong ethical culture?

3. Was O'Neill justified in terminating the manager for his lack of reporting the workplace accidents, even though no serious harm resulted from the workplace incident?

4. Can Alcoa's "values in practice" be adopted by other organizations as a universal set of ethical standards leading to ethical employee behavior?

PART THREE

Business in a Globalized World

The Challenges of Globalization

The world economy is becoming increasingly integrated, and many businesses have extended their reach beyond national borders. Yet the process of globalization is controversial, and the involvement of corporations in other nations is not always welcome. Doing business in diverse political and economic systems poses difficult challenges. When a transnational corporation buys resources, manufactures products, or sells goods and services in multiple countries, it is inevitably drawn into a web of global social and ethical issues. Understanding what these issues are and how to manage them through collaborative action with governments and civil society organizations is a vital skill for today's managers.

This Chapter Focuses on These Key Learning Objectives:

- Defining globalization and classifying the major ways in which companies enter the global marketplace.
- Recognizing the major drivers of the globalization process and the international financial and trade institutions that have shaped this process in recent decades.
- Analyzing the benefits and costs of the globalization of business.
- Identifying the major types of political and economic systems in which companies operate across the world and the special challenges posed by doing business in diverse settings.
- Assessing how businesses can work collaboratively with governments and the civil sector to address global social issues.

In 2012, Newmont Mining Corp. struggled with how to move forward with plans to develop a major gold and copper project in Peru. Since 1993, in partnership with the World Bank's International Finance Corporation, Newmont had operated three open-pit gold mines high in the Andes Mountains, six miles from the city of Cajamarca. The company planned to develop a new surface mine about 15 miles away, to be called Minas Conga, in what would be Peru's biggest-ever mining operation. In 2011, the company's board of directors approved funding for the $4.8 billion project, which was scheduled to begin production in 2015. But violent protests broke out, involving thousands of local residents concerned that the new mine would require draining four natural lakes, drying up and polluting the community's water supplies. Newmont then suspended the project, saying it could not proceed without "tranquility and social peace," and noting that its global portfolio enabled it to consider alternative development sites in Ghana, Canada, Indonesia, and elsewhere. In early 2012, the Peruvian government brought in outside experts to study the project's environmental impact, in an apparent effort to restart the stalled project. If it went forward, the Minas Conga project would employ five to seven thousand workers during its construction, in a nation that was home to 8 million people who lived in extreme poverty. In the 2010s, mining provided 60 percent of Peru's exports and 30 percent of its tax revenue.[1]

This complex episode captures much of the turmoil and controversy that surrounds the globalization of business and its far-reaching social impacts. We live in a world that seems increasingly small, more connected, and highly interdependent. It is a world in which transnational companies such as Newmont Mining often bring much-needed technical know-how, capital, managerial experience, and jobs to poorer nations deeply in need of them. Yet corporate involvement abroad often involves challenging social, ethical, and environmental issues. How companies can best negotiate the difficult challenges of doing business in a global world is the subject of this chapter.

The Process of Globalization

Globalization refers to the increasing movement of goods, services, and capital across national borders. Globalization is a *process*, that is, an ongoing series of interrelated events. International trade and financial flows integrate the world economy, leading to the spread of technology, culture, and politics. Thomas Friedman, a columnist for *The New York Times* and a well-known commentator, has described globalization as a *system* with its own internal logic:

> Globalization is not simply a trend or a fad but is, rather, an international system. It is the system that has now replaced the old Cold War system, and, like that Cold War system, globalization has its own rules and logic that today directly or indirectly influence the politics, environment, geopolitics, and economics of virtually every country in the world.[2]

The process of globalization is so pervasive that it affects all businesses—whether they are small or large, local or multinational, or an employer of one or many.

Firms can enter and compete in the global marketplace in several ways. Many companies first build a successful business in their home country, and then export their products or services to buyers in other countries. In other words, they develop *global market channels* for their products. Nokia, for example, began in Finland but now sells its cellular

[1] "Newmont Mining Halts Big Gold Project in Peru," *San Francisco Chronicle,* December 1, 2011; "Newmont Project Suspension May Raise Risks for Peru," *The Wall Street Journal,* November 30, 2011; and *www.newmont.com/south-america.*

[2] Thomas L. Friedman, *The Lexus and the Olive Tree* (New York: Anchor Books, 2000), p. ix.

phones and other products all over the world. Other firms begin in their home country but realize that they can cut costs by locating some or all of their *global operations* in another country. This decision leads to establishing manufacturing plants or service operations abroad. For example, the Ford Fusion is manufactured in Mexico; the Ford F-150 pickup is manufactured in Kansas City, Missouri, but almost half of its parts are made in other countries. Finally, a third strategy involves subcontracting manufacturing to suppliers located abroad. In other words, these companies develop *global supply chains*. For example, in the apparel and shoe industries, companies such as Nike, Gap, and Abercrombie & Fitch have extensive networks of subcontractors outside the United States—mostly in Asia—that make products of their design. Some of these suppliers are major multinational firms in their own right. Chapter 7 includes a discussion case about Apple's relationship with Foxconn, a Taiwanese supplier that manufactures many of the company's products in mainland China.

These three strategies of globalization can be summarized in three words: *sell, make,* and *source.* Today, many companies have all three elements of global business—market channels, manufacturing operations, and supply chains.

Major Transnational Corporations

According to United Nations estimates, there are almost 104,000 **transnational corporations (TNCs)** operating in the modern global economy (defined by the United Nations as firms that control assets abroad). These corporations, in turn, have about 9 times that number of *affiliates*, meaning suppliers, subcontractors, retailers, and other entities with which they have some business relationship. These affiliates collectively produce more than 10 percent of global gross domestic product (GDP) and employ 80 million workers.[3] The interconnectedness of the world's businesses is a major reason why the financial crisis that began in 2008 spread so quickly to almost all corners of the globe.

Although many firms conduct business across national boundaries, most global commerce is carried out by a small number of powerful firms. Who are these leading transnational corporations? Figure 6.1 lists the top 10 nonfinancial transnational corporations, ranked in order of the value of the foreign assets they control. Leading the list is General Electric, the American electrical equipment and electronics conglomerate. Rounding out the group are several of the world's leading oil companies, automakers, telecommunications firms, and utilities. The world's major financial institutions also extend across the globe; Citigroup, the largest of these, has 664 foreign affiliates in 77 host countries.[4]

Another important aspect of globalization is the worldwide flow of capital. **Foreign direct investment (FDI)** occurs when a company, individual, or fund invests money in another country, for example, by buying shares of stock in or loaning money to a foreign firm. The world economy is increasingly bound together by such cross-border flows of capital. In 2010, FDI was $1.24 trillion, 15 percent below its pre-crisis average.[5] An emerging trend in foreign direct investment is the rise of *sovereign wealth funds*. These are funds operated by governments to invest their foreign currency reserves. They are most commonly operated by nations that export large amounts of oil and manufactured goods; the largest are run by the United Arab Emirates (Abu Dhabi), Kuwait, Norway, China, and Singapore. In recent years, sovereign wealth funds have made significant cross-border investments.

---

[3] United Nations Conference on Trade and Development, Web Table 34, at *www.unctad.org*. Data are for 2010.

[4] United Nations Conference on Trade and Development, Web Table 298, at *www.unctad.org*. Data are for 2010.

[5] UNCTAD, *World Investment Report 2011: Non-Equity Modes of International Production and Development,* at *www.unctad.org*.

FIGURE 6.1

The World's Top 10 Nonfinancial Transnational Corporations, Ranked by Foreign Assets

Source: United Nations, "The World's Top 100 Non-Financial TNCs, Ranked by Foreign Assets, 2010," *www.unctad.org.* All data are for the year 2010.

Corporation	Home Economy	Industry	Foreign Assets (in $ millions)
General Electric	United States	Electrical equipment	$551,585
Royal Dutch/Shell	UK/Netherlands	Petroleum	271,672
BP	United Kingdom	Petroleum	243,950
Vodafone	United Kingdom	Petroleum	224,449
Toyota Motor	Japan	Motor vehicles	211,153
ExxonMobil	United States	Petroleum	193,743
Total	France	Petroleum	175,001
Volkswagen Group	Germany	Motor Vehicles	167,773
Électricité de France	France	Electricity, gas, and water	165,413
GDF Suez	France	Utilities	151,984

The Acceleration of Globalization

Global commerce has taken place for hundreds of years, dating back to the exploration and colonization of Africa, Asia, and the Americas by Europeans beginning in the 15th century. But it is during the past 70 years or so, since the end of World War II, that global commerce has truly transformed the world's economy. About one-fifth of all goods and services produced worldwide are sold to other nations, rather than domestically; this is almost double the percentage in 1960. In other words, the world's economy is becoming increasingly integrated, as an ever-higher share of output is being exported across national borders.[6] In earlier years, most exports were of goods; an important recent trend is the globalization of services, such as travel, insurance, financial, and information services.

The acceleration of globalization has been driven by several factors:

- *Technological innovation:* Sophisticated software, Internet, fiber optics, wireless, and satellite technologies, among others, have made it easier and faster for companies to communicate with employees, partners, and suppliers all over the globe in real time. In the words of Thomas Friedman, the world has become increasingly "flat," as technology has leveled the playing field and allowed all to participate on an equal footing in global commerce.[7]

- *Transportation systems:* Improvements in transportation—from air freight, to high-speed rail, to new generations of oceangoing vessels—enable the fast and cheap movement of goods and services from one place to another.

- *The rise of major transnational corporations:* Big, well-capitalized firms are better equipped to conduct business across national borders than smaller, local companies.

- *Cultural convergence:* The spread of popular culture has increased demand for products with universal appeal, from Apple iPods to Nike sneakers.

- *Social and political reforms:* Critical changes, including the rise of dynamic growth economics on the Pacific Rim and the collapse of the former communist states of central and eastern Europe, have opened new regions to world trade.

[6] Current data on exports of goods and services as a percentage of gross domestic product are available at *www.devdata.worldbank.org.*

[7] Thomas Friedman, *The World Is Flat: A Brief History of the Twenty-First Century* (New York: Farrar, Straus and Giroux, 2005).

Volkswagen, Renault, Audi, and other European car companies have shifted much of their production across the former Iron Curtain that divided communist and non-communist Europe, drawn by the availability of cheap skilled labor, from assemblers to engineers. The VW Touareg, Audi Q7, and Porsche Cayenne are now made in Slovakia, the Renault Logan in Romania, and the Audi TT roadster in Hungary. The Asian companies Toyota, Kia, and Suzuki have followed suit, also building cars in central and eastern Europe. The concentration of auto factories in the region has gone so far that some have begun to call it "Detroit East."

Finally, the process of globalization has also been spurred by the rise of international financial and trade institutions that stabilize currencies and promote free trade. These institutions are discussed in the next section.

International Financial and Trade Institutions

Global commerce is carried out in the context of a set of important **international financial and trade institutions (IFTIs)**. The most important of these are the World Bank, the International Monetary Fund, and the World Trade Organization. By setting the rules by which international commerce is transacted, these institutions increasingly determine who wins and who loses in the global economy.

The **World Bank (WB)** was set up in 1944, near the end of World War II, to provide economic development loans to its member nations. Its main motivation at that time was to help rebuild the war-torn economies of Europe. Today, the World Bank is one of the world's largest sources of economic development assistance; it provided almost $47 billion in loans in 2011 for roads, dams, power plants, and other infrastructure projects, as well as for education, health, and social services. The bank gets its funds from dues paid by its member countries and from money it borrows in the international capital markets. Representation on the bank's governing board is based on economic power; that is, countries have voting power based on the size of their economies. Not surprisingly, the United States and other rich nations dominate the bank.

The World Bank often imposes strict conditions on countries that receive its loans, to make sure the debtor countries can pay back what they owe. These conditions may include demands that governments cut spending, devalue their currencies, increase exports, liberalize financial markets, reduce wages, and remove agricultural price subsidies. These conditions often lead to hardship, particularly for the poor. Critics have charged that developing countries are unfairly burdened by these conditions. In recent years, the World Bank has responded by encouraging borrowing nations to participate more fully in determining the terms of the loans and to use the money to reduce poverty.

The World Bank's sister organization is the **International Monetary Fund (IMF)**. Founded at the same time as the bank (and today residing across the street from it in Washington, DC), the IMF has a somewhat narrower purpose: to make currency exchange easier for member countries so that they can participate in global trade. It does this by lending foreign exchange to member countries. Like the World Bank, the IMF sometimes imposes strict conditions on governments that receive its loans, although it has shown more flexibility in the wake of the global financial crisis.

One country that was particularly hard hit by IMF conditions was Jamaica, a developing island nation in the Caribbean. In exchange for IMF loans, Jamaica agreed to a number of conditions, including opening up its borders to free trade with other nations. The problem was that Jamaican dairy, poultry, vegetable, and fruit farmers were unable to compete with the United States, whose meat and produce were produced more efficiently by large agribusiness companies. The result was that many Jamaican farms failed, and the country became increasingly reliant on imports to feed its people. Jamaica fell into an increasing spiral of debt, its citizens became poorer, and the country found it increasingly difficult to repay its IMF loans.[8]

By the mid-2000s, many developing countries had accumulated huge debts to the World Bank, the IMF, and other lenders. The total amount of money owed was almost $3 trillion. One of the unintended consequences of past loans was persistent poverty, because a large share of many nations' earnings went to pay off debt rather than to develop the economy or improve the lives of citizens. In response, many industrialized nations extended aid to heavily indebted countries to enable them to pay down loans to the World Bank, IMF, and other lenders. By 2009, more than $70 billion in **debt relief** had been extended to 33 heavily indebted countries, and these nations' payments had been cut in half.

However, problems remained. Poor countries still owed billions more, and the world financial crisis weakened their ability to pay—and the ability of developed countries to offer aid. And, so-called *vulture funds* sought to take advantage of the indebted countries, a situation that is profiled in Exhibit 6.A.

The final member of the triumvirate of IFTIs is the **World Trade Organization (WTO)**. The WTO, founded in 1995 as a successor to the General Agreement on Tariffs and Trade (GATT), is an international body that establishes the ground rules for trade among nations. Most of the world's nations are members of the WTO, which is based in Switzerland. Its major objective is to promote free trade; that is, to eliminate barriers to trade among nations, such as quotas, duties, and tariffs. Unlike the WB and the IMF, the WTO does not lend money or foreign exchange; it simply sets the rules for international trade. The WTO conducts multi-year negotiations, called *rounds,* on various trade-related topics, rotating its meetings among different cities. The most recent negotiations—called the Doha round, because they were launched in Doha, Quatar—collapsed in 2008, after negotiators were unable to reach agreement on a number of proposals to help the world's poor. More recent efforts to restart the talks have failed. An issue of great contention in the Doha round, involving agricultural subsidies, is profiled in Exhibit 6.B.

Under the WTO's most favored nation rule, member countries may not discriminate against foreign products for any reason. All import restrictions are illegal unless proven scientifically, for example, on the basis that a product is unsafe. If countries disagree about the interpretation of this or any other WTO rule, they can bring a complaint before the WTO's Dispute Settlement Body (DSB), a panel of appointed experts, which meets behind closed doors. For example, China complained to the DSB that India had tried to ban imports of Chinese toys to protect its own toy industry, a possible violation of WTO rules.[9] Usually, member countries comply voluntarily with the DSB's rulings. If they do not, the DSB can allow the aggrieved nation to take retaliatory measures, such as imposing tariffs. Rulings are binding; the only way a decision can be overruled is if every member country opposes it.

These three international financial and trade institutions are important because no business can operate across national boundaries without complying with the rules set by the WTO, and many businesses in the developing world are dependent on World Bank and IMF loans for their very lifeblood. The policies these institutions adopt, therefore, have much to do with whether or not globalization is perceived as a positive or negative force, a subject to which we turn next.

---

[8] *Life and Debt,* a film by Stephanie Black. For more information, see *www.lifeanddebt.org.*

[9] Information about this and other cases heard by the Dispute Settlement Body is available at *www.wto.org.*

Exhibit 6.A

Vulture Funds and Heavily Indebted Nations

A "vulture fund" is a private equity fund that buys the debt of weak companies or heavily indebted countries with the intention of making a profit. (The term analogizes these investors to vultures, birds of prey that feed on dead or dying animals.) In the late 2000s and early 2010s, a number of vulture funds bought loans made to very poor countries at a deep discount and then sued in international courts demanding that these countries pay back the loans at full face value. A World Bank study found $1.8 billion in pending lawsuits against countries where people lived on less than $1 a day. In one particularly stark example, a vulture fund called Donegal International bought a Zambian loan for around $3 million, and then sued successfully in British courts. Zambia had to pay Donegal International $15 million—which was more than 60 percent of the debt relief it had received that year—creating windfall profits for the investors. "When vulture funds sue for such exorbitant amounts, it's clearly taking away money that should be invested in health, education, infrastructure, and other social problems, and goes to line the pockets of already wealthy investors," said a representative of the nongovernmental organization (NGO) Africa Action. Activists called for laws banning such practices.

Sources: *Jubilee Network,* "The Responsible Lending and Borrowing Imperative: Addressing the Root Causes of Poverty," Winter 2012; and "Vulture Funds Prey on Poor Debtor Nations," *Inter Press Service (Johannesburg, South Africa),* August 19, 2009.

The Benefits and Costs of Globalization

Globalization is highly controversial. One need only look at television coverage of angry protests at meetings of the World Trade Organization, World Bank, and International Monetary Fund in the late 1990s and the early 2000s to see that not all people and organizations believe that globalization—at least as currently practiced—is a positive force. Yet, many others feel that globalization holds tremendous potential for pulling nations out of poverty, spreading technological innovation, and allowing people everywhere to enjoy the bounty generated by modern business. Clearly, some benefit from globalization, while others do not. In this section, we present some of the arguments advanced by both sides in the debate over this important issue.

Benefits of Globalization

Proponents of globalization point to its many benefits. One of the most important of these is that globalization tends to increase economic productivity. That means, simply, that more is produced with the same effort.

Why should that be? As the economist David Ricardo first pointed out, productivity rises more quickly when countries produce goods and services for which they have a natural talent. He called this the *theory of comparative advantage.* Suppose, for example, that one country had a climate and terrain ideally suited for raising sheep, giving it an advantage in the production of wool and woolen goods. A second country had a favorable combination of iron, coal, and water power that allowed it to produce high-grade steel. The first country would benefit from trading its woolen goods for the second country's steel, and vice versa; and the world's economy overall would be more productive than if both countries had tried to make everything they needed for themselves. In other words, in the context of free trade, specialization (everyone does what they are best at) makes the world economy as a whole more efficient, so living standards rise.

Many countries today have developed a specialization in one or another skill or industry. India, with its excellent system of technical education, has become a

Is trade among nations really free when governments aid their own producers? This issue has been at the heart of an ongoing dispute within the World Trade Organization over farm subsidies.

The European Union, the United States, and Japan all provide generous agricultural subsidies. In 2011, for example, the U.S. government paid farmers around $16 billion to support production of a range of commodities, including cotton, corn, wheat, rice, soybeans, and peanuts. The farm lobby strongly backed these subsidies, which it said were necessary to protect the rural way of life. Critics, however, said that subsidies allowed farmers to "dump" their products on world markets at artificially reduced prices, competing unfairly with agricultural products from poor countries that could not afford similar support payments—not to mention that they added to the U.S. deficit.

In the cotton industry, for example, every acre under cultivation in the United States received an annual government payment of around $230. Elimination of these payments, according to one economic analysis, would raise the world price of cotton by 26 percent. Particularly hurt by U.S. cotton subsidies were poor farmers in west and central Africa, where more than 10 million people depended on this crop for their livelihoods. In a painful irony, the U.S. government provided more dollars to its own cotton farmers than to all of Africa in the form of development aid.

In 2005, ruling in a complaint brought by Brazil with support from several African nations, the WTO declared the United States and other countries would have to end their cotton subsidies. When the United States failed to do so, the WTO said that Brazil could retaliate by imposing tariffs on American products. Rather than accept this, the United States simply agreed to pay Brazil $147 million a year to settle the dispute. A group of legislators—both Republicans and Democrats—protested strongly, saying in a letter to the president that the cotton subsidies were "quickly becoming a liability for future trade growth" and needed to be ended.

Ongoing disagreements between rich and poor nations over the terms of agriculture trade were a main reason that the Doha round of WTO negotiations collapsed—and why it has been so difficult to restart the talks.

Sources: "Farm Subsidies Become Target Amid Spending Cuts," *The New York Times,* May 6, 2011; "Brazil's Victory in Cotton Trade Case Exposes America's Wasteful Subsidies," *Washington Post,* June 3, 2010; "The Doha Round . . . and Round . . . and Round," *The Economist,* August 2, 2008; "Busted: World Trade Watchdog Declares EU and U.S. Farm Subsidies Illegal," *Oxfam International,* September 9, 2004; "WTO Agreement on Agriculture: A Decade of Dumping," Institute for Agriculture and Trade Policy, 2005, available online at *www.globalpolicy.org.*

world powerhouse in the production of software engineers. China has become expert in electronics manufacturing. France and Italy, with their strong networks of skilled craftspeople and designers, are acknowledged leaders in the world's high fashion and footwear design industries. The United States, with its concentration of actors, directors, special effects experts, and screenwriters, is the global headquarters for the movie industry.

Comparative advantage can come from a number of possible sources, including natural resources; the skills, education, or experience of a critical mass of people; or an existing production infrastructure.

Globalization also tends to reduce prices for consumers. If a shopper in the United States goes into Walmart to buy a shirt, he or she is likely to find one at a very reasonable price. Walmart sources its apparel from all over the world, enabling it to push down production costs. Globalization also benefits consumers by giving them access to a wide range of diverse goods and the latest "big thing." Teenagers in Malaysia can enjoy the latest Johnny Depp or Will Smith movie, while American children can play with new Nintendo Wii games from Japan.

For the developing world, globalization also brings benefits. It helps entrepreneurs the world over by giving all countries access to foreign investment funds to support economic development. Globalization also transfers technology. In a competitive world marketplace, the best ideas and newest innovations spread quickly. Multinational corporations train their employees and partners how to make the fastest computer chips, the most productive food crops, and the most efficient lightbulbs. In many nations of the developing world, globalization has meant more manufacturing jobs in export sectors and training for workers eager to enhance their skills.

The futurist Allen Hammond identifies two additional benefits of globalization. First, he says that world trade has the potential of supporting the spread of democracy and freedom.

> The very nature of economic activity in free markets . . . requires broad access to information, the spread of competence, and the exercise of individual decision making throughout the workforce—conditions that are more compatible with free societies and democratic forms of government than with authoritarian regimes.[10]

Second, according to Hammond, global commerce can reduce military conflict by acting as a force that binds disparate peoples together on the common ground of business interaction. "Nations that once competed for territorial dominance," he writes, "will now compete for market share, with money that once supported military forces invested in new ports, telecommunications, and other infrastructure." In this view, global business can become both a stabilizing force and a conduit for Western ideas about democracy and freedom.

Costs of Globalization

If globalization has all these benefits, why are so many individuals and organizations so critical of it? The answer is complex. Just as some gain from globalization, others are hurt by it. From the perspective of its victims, globalization does not look nearly so attractive.

One of the costs of globalization is job insecurity. As businesses move manufacturing across national borders in search of cheaper labor, workers at home are laid off. Jobs in the domestic economy are lost as imports replace homemade goods and services. In the American South, for example, tens of thousands of jobs in the textile industry have been lost, as jobs have shifted to low-labor cost areas of the world, leaving whole communities devastated. In the past, mainly manufacturing was affected by the shift of jobs abroad; more recently, clerical, white-collar, and professional jobs have also been "offshored." Many customer service calls originating in the United States are now answered by operators in the Philippines and India. The back office operations of many banks—sorting and recording check transactions, for example—are done in India and China. Aircraft manufacturers are using aeronautical specialists in Russia to design parts for new planes. Economists have estimated that around one in four jobs in the United States may be potentially "offshorable."[11] Even when jobs are not actually relocated, wages may be driven down because companies facing foreign competition try to keep their costs in check. Much of the opposition to globalization in affluent nations comes from people who feel their own jobs, pay, and livelihoods threatened by workers abroad who can do their work more cheaply.

> Recently, some evidence suggests the trend to move U.S. jobs overseas has begun to reverse. Wages have increased in China and many other developing nations, while wages gains in the United States have stagnated. Productivity is considerably higher in the United States than in China. And, small businesses in particular have found that solving everyday production problems with a contractor halfway around

[10] Allen Hammond, *Which World? Scenarios for the 21st Century* (Washington, DC: Island Press, 1998), p. 30.

[11] "Offshoring (or Offshore Outsourcing) and Job Loss among U.S. Workers," *Congressional Research Service,* January 21, 2011.

the globe can be daunting. "If we have an issue in manufacturing, in America we can walk down to the plant floor," explained the founder of a business that made emergency lights for homeowners. "We can't do that in China." The company had recently relocated production from China to a facility near its headquarters in California.[12]

Not only workers in rich countries are affected by globalization. When workers in Indonesia began organizing for higher wages, Nike Corporation moved much of its production to Vietnam and China. Many Indonesian workers lost their jobs. Some call this feature of global capitalism the "race to the bottom."

Another cost of globalization is that environmental and labor standards may be weakened as companies seek manufacturing sites where regulations are most lax. Just as companies may desire locations offering the cheapest labor, they may also search for locations with few environmental protections; weak regulation of occupational health and safety, hours of work, and discrimination; and few rights for unions. For example, the so-called gold coast of southeastern China has become a world manufacturing center for many products, including electronics and toys. An undercover team investigating conditions there in 2011 found that many workers were paid up to a month late, were expected to work with dangerous machines without training or safety equipment, and were fined for using the toilet without permission.[13] Low wages, long hours, and weak health and safety and environmental regulations—and lax enforcement of the laws that do exist—are a major draw for the companies that manufacture in factories in China's industrial zones.

A related concern is that the World Trade Organization's most favored nation rules make it difficult for individual nations to adopt policies promoting environmental or social objectives, if these have the effect of discriminating against products from another country.

> For example, in 2009 the United States banned the importation of Indonesian clove cigarettes under newly strengthened tobacco control laws. The United States said that the sweet-flavored cigarettes attracted younger smokers, drawing them into nicotine addiction. Indonesia brought a complaint before the WTO's dispute settlement body. In 2012, the WTO ruled in Indonesia's favor, saying that since the United States permitted the sale of another flavored cigarette—menthols—it had acted in a discriminatory way by excluding Indonesian clove cigarettes. The United States said it would appeal.[14]

Critics of globalization say that incidents such as this one show that free trade rules are being used to restrict the right of sovereign nations to make their own laws setting health or environmental standards for imported products.

Another cost of globalization is that it erodes regional and national cultures and undermines cultural, linguistic, and religious diversity. In other words, global commerce makes us all very much the same. Is a world in which everyone is drinking Coke, watching Hollywood movies, texting on an iPhone, and wearing Gap jeans a world we want, or not? Some have argued that the deep **anti-Americanism** present in many parts of the world reflects resentment at the penetration of the values of dominant U.S.-based transnational corporations into every corner of the world.

With respect to the point that globalization promotes democracy, critics charge that market capitalism is just as compatible with despotism as it is with freedom. Indeed, transnational corporations are often drawn to nations that are governed by antidemocratic or

---

[12] "Small U.S. Manufacturers Give Up on 'Made in China,'" *Bloomberg Businessweek*, June 21, 2012.

[13] "Revealed: True Cost of the Christmas Toys We Buy from China's Factories," *The Observer [London]*, December 3, 2011.

[14] Details on this and other cases before the WTO's dispute settlement body are available at *www.wto.org*.

FIGURE 6.2
Benefits and Costs of Globalization

Benefits of Globalization	Costs of Globalization
Increases economic productivity.	Causes job insecurity.
Reduces prices for consumers.	Weakens environmental and labor standards.
Gives developing countries access to foreign investment funds to support economic development.	Prevents individual nations from adopting policies promoting environmental or social objectives, if these discriminate against products from another country.
Transfers technology.	Erodes regional and national cultures and undermines cultural, linguistic, and religious diversity.
Spreads democracy and freedom, and reduces military conflict.	Is compatible with despotism.

military regimes, because they are so effective at controlling labor and blocking efforts to protect the environment. For example, Unocal's joint-venture collaboration to build a gas pipeline with the military government of Myanmar (Burma), a notorious abuser of human rights, may have brought significant financial benefits to the petroleum company.

Figure 6.2 summarizes the major points in the discussion about the costs and benefits of globalization.

What is public opinion on these issues? A survey of almost 13,000 people in 25 countries around the world in 2010 found that people in 19 countries thought that the free market economic system was best (people in Turkey, France, Chile, Peru, Ecuador, and Japan disagreed). Although a majority (59 percent) of Americans favored free enterprise, this proportion had fallen 15 percent in just a single year, perhaps reflecting turmoil in the world economy. Support was highest in the emerging economies of China and Brazil. At the same time, solid majorities in most countries also favored governments playing an active role in regulating their economies. Although consensus about the free market system remained, most people polled felt it worked best when coupled with strong government oversight.[15]

This discussion raises the very real possibility that globalization may benefit the world economy as a whole, while simultaneously hurting many individuals and localities. An ongoing challenge to business, government, and society is to find ways to extend the benefits of globalization to all, while mitigating its adverse effects.[16]

Doing Business in a Diverse World

Doing business in other nations is much more than a step across a geographical boundary; it is a step into different social, political, cultural, and economic realities. As shown in Chapters 1 and 2, even businesses operating in one community or one nation cannot function successfully without considering a wide variety of stakeholder needs and interests. When companies operate globally, the number of stakeholders to be considered in decision making, and the diversity of their interests, increases dramatically.

[15] "Sharp Drop in American Enthusiasm for Free Market, Poll Shows," April 6, 2011; and "Global Poll Shows Support for Increased Government Spending and Regulation," September 13, 2009, at *www.worldpublicopinion.org.*

[16] For arguments for and against globalization, and on strategies to make the world's governing institutions more effective, see Jagdish Bhagwati, *In Defense of Globalization* (New York: Oxford University Press, 2007); and Joseph E. Stiglitz, *Making Globalization Work* (New York: W.W. Norton, 2007).

Comparative Political and Economic Systems

The many nations of the world differ greatly in their political, social, and economic systems. One important dimension of this diversity is how power is exercised, that is, the degree to which a nation's people may freely exercise their democratic rights. **Democracy** refers broadly to the presence of political freedom. Arthur Lewis, a Nobel laureate in economics, described it this way: "The primary meaning of democracy is that all who are affected by a decision should have the right to participate in making that decision, either directly or through chosen representatives." According to the United Nations, democracy has four defining features:[17]

- Fair elections, in which citizens may freely choose their leaders from among candidates representing more than one political party.
- An independent media, in which journalists and citizens may express their political views without fear of censorship or punishment.
- Separation of powers among the executive, legislative, and judicial branches of government.
- An open society where citizens have the right to form their own independent organizations to pursue social, religious, and cultural goals.

One of the truly remarkable facts about the past century has been the spread of democratic rights for the first time to many nations around the world. Consider, for example, that at the beginning of the 20th century *no* country in the world had universal suffrage (all citizens can vote); today, the majority of countries do. One hundred and forty of the world's nearly 200 countries now hold multiparty elections, the highest number ever. The collapse of communist party rule in the former Soviet Union and its satellites in eastern and central Europe in the early 1990s was followed by the first open elections ever in these countries. These changes led some observers to call the end of the 20th century the "third wave of democracy."

> In an extraordinary development, popular movements that became known as the "Arab Spring" swept through much of northern Africa, the Persian Gulf region, and the Middle East in 2011 and 2012, as ordinary people demanded full political rights. In Egypt, Tunisia, and Libya, longtime strongmen were deposed, and people demanded free elections to choose their successors. Widespread civil resistance occurred in Morocco, Algeria, Bahrain, and Yemen; and Syria teetered on the brink of full civil war when its dictatorial leader refused to give up power. In a speech in Israel in 2012, Ban Ki Moon, secretary-general of the United Nations, declared, "It is hard not to view the dramatic events of the past year as a fulfillment of our most noble aspirations. . . . Everywhere people are experiencing a fundamental human yearning; a universal hunger for freedom, dignity, and human rights.[18]

Despite these developments, many countries still lack basic democratic rights. Single-party rule by communist parties remains a reality in China, Vietnam, Cuba, and the People's Democratic Republic of Korea (North Korea). **Military dictatorships**, that is, repressive regimes ruled by dictators who exercise total power through control of the armed forces, are in place in, among others, Zimbabwe, Uzbekistan, and Eritrea.[19] The rights of women to full societal participation—and the rights of all citizens to organize in support of cultural

---

[17]United Nations Development Programme, *Human Development Report 2000* (New York: Oxford University Press, 2000), ch. 3, "Inclusive Democracy Secures Rights," pp. 56–71. The quotation from Arthur Lewis appears on p. 56.

[18] "All Hail the Arab Spring," February 2, 2012, at *www.israelnationalnews.com.*

[19] For profiles of the dictators of these nations, see *Parade Magazine,* "The World's 10 Worst Dictators," February 7, 2012, at *www.parade.com.*

and religious goals—are restricted in a number of Arab states, including Iran, Syria, and Saudi Arabia. According to United Nations estimates, 106 countries still limit important civil and political freedoms.

The degree to which human rights are protected also varies widely across nations. *Human rights*, introduced in Chapter 4, refer broadly to the rights and privileges accorded to all people, simply by virtue of being human, for example, the rights to a decent standard of living, free speech, religious freedom, and due process of law, among others. Fundamental human rights have been codified in a number of international agreements, the most important of which is the Universal Declaration of Human Rights of 1948.[20] The second half of the 20th century was a period of great advances in human rights in many regions, and over half of the world's nations have now ratified *all* of the United Nations' human right covenants. Nonetheless, many human rights problems remain. Consider the following examples:

- Almost 8 million children die each year before their fifth birthday. Most of these deaths are preventable.[21]

- Gross violations of human rights have not been eliminated. *Genocide,* mass murder of innocent civilians, has occurred all too recently in Rwanda, Iraq, Bosnia and Herzegovina, the Congo, and Sudan.

- Close to 1 million people are trafficked into forced labor every year. Eighty percent of these are women and girls, most of whom are forced into prostitution.[22] The efforts of a major hotel chain, The Carlson Companies, to prevent the use of their facilities for prostitution or child trafficking is described in a case at the end of this book.

- Minority groups and indigenous peoples in many nations still lack basic political and social rights. In Nepal, the life expectancy of "untouchables," the lowest caste, is fully 15 years less than that of Brahmins, the highest caste.

The absence of key human rights in many nations remains a significant issue for companies transacting business there.

Another dimension of difference among nations today is how economic assets are controlled, that is, the degree of economic freedom. On one end of the continuum are societies in which assets are privately owned and exchanged in a free and open market. Such **free enterprise systems** are based on the principle of voluntary association and exchange. In such a system, people with goods and services to sell take them voluntarily to the marketplace, seeking to exchange them for money or other goods or services. Political and economic freedoms are related: as people gain more control over government decisions they often press for greater economic opportunity; open markets may give people the resources to participate effectively in politics. But this is not always the case. The particular situation of China with respect to political and economic freedom is explored in Exhibit 6.C.

At the other end of the continuum are systems of **central state control**, in which economic power is concentrated in the hands of government officials and political authorities. The central government owns the property that is used to produce goods and services. Private ownership may be forbidden or greatly restricted, and most private markets are illegal. Very few societies today operate on the basis of strict central state control of the economy. More common is a system of mixed free enterprise and central state control in which some industries are state controlled, and others are privately owned. For example, in Nigeria, the oil industry is controlled by a government-owned enterprise that operates in partnership

---

[20] For more information on the Universal Declaration of Human Rights and other United Nations agreements on human rights, see the website of the UN High Commissioner for Human Rights at *www.unhchr.org.*

[21] United Nations Children's Fund (UNICEF) data on child mortality are available online at *www.childinfo.org.*

[22] Data are available at *www.humantrafficking.org, www.ungift.org,* and *www.state.gov/j/tip.*

Democracy, a *political* system in which citizens choose their own leaders and may openly express their ideas, and capitalism, an *economic* system in which the means of creating wealth are privately owned and controlled, have historically often developed in tandem. The two are not always coupled, however. During the early years of the 20th century, for example, capitalism coexisted with nondemocratic, fascist governments in Germany, Spain, and Japan. More recently, scholars have coined the term "authoritarian capitalism" to refer to modern states that combine elements of a market economy with political control by nonelected elites. A prime example is China. In its drive for economic development, the Chinese government has granted considerable freedom to private individuals to own property, invest, and innovate. The result has been very rapid growth in much of the country over the past two decades. At the same time, the Chinese communist authorities have vigorously held on to political power and suppressed dissent. The government has also held on to ownership of some big companies, such as the China National Petroleum Corporation and China Mobile. In what direction will China and other authoritarian capitalist nations evolve in the future? "Some believe these countries could ultimately become liberal democracies through a combination of internal development, increasing affluence, and outside influence," commented the political scientist Azar Gat. "Alternatively, they may have enough weight to create a new nondemocratic but economically advanced Second World."

Sources: "The Rise of State Capitalism," *The Economist,* January 21, 2012; Azar Gat, "The Return of the Authoritarian Capitalists," *International Herald Tribune,* June 14, 2007; and "The Return of Authoritarian Great Powers," *Foreign Affairs,* July/August 2007.

with foreign companies such as Shell and Chevron, but many other industries are privately controlled. In the social democracies of Scandinavia, such as Norway, the government operates some industries but not others. In the United States, the government temporarily took partial ownership in some banks, including Citigroup, as they faltered during the financial crisis.

> The Heritage Foundation, a conservative think tank, has scored the nations of the world according to an *index of economic freedom* defined as "the fundamental rights of every human being to control his or her own labor and property." In economically free societies, governments "refrain from coercion or restraint of liberty beyond the extent necessary to protect and maintain liberty itself." Among the freest nations in 2012, by this measure, were Hong Kong, Singapore, and Australia; among the most repressed were Cuba, Zimbabwe, and—the least free in the world—North Korea. The United States ranked tenth out of 179 countries.[23]

Nations also differ greatly in their overall levels of economic and social development. Ours is a world of great inequalities. To cite just one simple measure, the richest 1 percent of people in the world receives as much income annually as the poorest 57 percent. The lives of a software engineer in Canada, say, and a subsistence farmer in Mali (in central Africa) could not be more different. The engineer would have a life expectancy of 81 years, access to excellent medical care, and a comfortable home in an affluent suburb. His children would likely be healthy, and they could look forward to a college education. The farmer, by contrast, could expect to live only to age 52, probably could not read or write, and would earn an annual income of around $1,000 (U.S.)—in good years when his crops did not fail. He would likely not have access to clean drinking water, and his children would be poorly nourished and unprotected by vaccination against common childhood illnesses. Several of

[23] Available at *www.heritage.org.*

his children would die before reaching adulthood.[24] Even as the world has become freer politically and economically, inequality has grown; the gaps between the richest and poorest nations are rising, as are gaps between the richest and poorest people in many nations.

Meeting the Challenges of Global Diversity

As the preceding discussion suggests, transnational corporations today do business in a world of staggering diversity and complexity. Not surprisingly, the wide range of political, social, and economic environments in which business operates poses complex and challenging questions for managers, such as the following:

- If a company does business in a nation that does not grant women equal rights, such as Saudi Arabia, for example, should that company hire and promote women at work, even if this violates local laws or customs?

- Should a company enter into a business joint venture with a government-owned enterprise if that government has a reputation for violating the human rights of its own citizens? For example, Unocal, mentioned earlier in this chapter, was criticized and later successfully sued for entering into a joint venture with the repressive military government of Myanmar.

- Does a company have a duty to offer its products or services—say, life-saving medication—at a lower price in poor countries like Mali, or to customers who desperately need them?

- If a government fails to provide basic services to its citizens, such as primary education, decent housing, and sanitation services, is it the duty of a company to provide these things for its own employees or for members of the community in which it is located? This question is particularly likely to arise for companies in extractive industries, such as oil, natural gas, and metal mining, where production may be located far from established communities.

Many people believe that when transnational corporations operate according to strong moral principles, they can become a force for positive change in other nations where they operate. This is known as **constructive engagement**. In some situations, however, constructive engagement may not be possible. At what point do violations of political, human, and economic rights become so extreme that companies simply cannot morally justify doing business in a country anymore?

> The experience of Shell Oil in Nigeria illustrates this dilemma. Shell entered into a joint venture with the Nigerian government, then ruled by a military dictator, to produce and export oil. Citizens of the oil-producing regions organized to protest Shell's behavior, charging that the company had despoiled the environment, failed to provide adequate services to the community, and not hired enough indigenous people from the local area. In response, the Nigerian government imposed martial law and arrested the leaders of the protest. Civilians were killed, and several leaders of the protest were executed after military tribunals where they were not given the right to defend themselves. Was Shell responsible for what the government did? Should Shell have provided basic services in the oil-producing regions that the government had not? Should Shell leave Nigeria, or try to work with the government and communities there to improve conditions in the oil-producing regions?

In this situation, Shell decided not to take a public stance against the government's actions, on the grounds that it should "stay out of politics." The company was strenuously criticized for this. Eventually, Shell announced that it had changed its view and was prepared

---

[24] Profiles derived from human development statistics published annually by the United Nations Development Programme.

to make known to governments its position on political matters, such as this one, that affected the company or its stakeholders. It also took action to better protect the environment and to train its managers in human rights principles.

Like Shell, many companies face ongoing dilemmas deciding how to respond to conditions in repressive nations. The next chapter discusses a number of codes of conduct that transnational companies have used to help guide their actions.

Collaborative Partnerships for Global Problem Solving

As the preceding section suggested, doing business in a diverse world is exceptionally challenging for businesses. One solution to the challenging questions facing transnational corporations is to approach them collectively, through a collaborative process. An emerging trend is the development of collaborative, multi-sector partnerships focused on particular social issues or problems in the global economy. These partnerships have been termed **global action networks (GANs)**.[25] This final section of Chapter 6 describes this approach.

A Three-Sector World

The term *sector* refers to broad divisions of a whole. In this context, it refers to major parts or spheres of society, such as business (the private sector), government (the public sector), and civil society. **Civil society** comprises nonprofit, educational, religious, community, family, and interest-group organizations; that is, social organizations that do not have a commercial or governmental purpose.

The process of globalization has spurred development of civil society. In recent decades, the world has witnessed the creation and growth of large numbers of **nongovernmental organizations (NGOs)** concerned with such issues as environmental risk, labor practices, worker rights, community development, and human rights. (NGOs are also called *civil society organizations* or *civil sector organizations*.) The number of NGOs accredited by the United Nations has soared in recent years, rising from 1,000 in 1996 to around 3,500 in 2012. This figure counts just major organizations.[26] Worldwide, the total number of international NGOs is estimated to be around 55,000.[27] (Many more NGOs operate regionally or locally.)

Experts attribute the growth of NGOs to several factors, including the new architecture of global economic and political relationships. As the Cold War has ended, with democratic governments replacing dictatorships, greater openness has emerged in many societies. More people, with more views, are free to express their pleasure or displeasure with government, business, or one another. NGOs form around specific issues or broad concerns (environment, human rights) and become voices that must be considered in the public policy debates that ensue.

Each of the three major sectors that participate in global action networks—business, government, and civil society—has distinctive resources and competencies, as well as weaknesses. For example, businesses have access to capital, specialized technical knowledge, networks of commercial relationships, and the management skills to get projects completed on time and on budget. On the other hand, businesses tend to disregard the impacts of their actions on others, especially in the long term. For their part, government agencies have knowledge of public policy, an ability to enforce rules, and revenue from taxation, but are often inflexible, slow to mobilize, and poorly coordinated. Finally, NGOs often enjoy strong community knowledge, volunteer assets, and inspirational leaders,

---

[25] Steve Waddell, *Global Action Networks: Creating Our Future Together* (New York: Palgrave Macmillan, 2011).

[26] Data available at *http://csonet.org/*.

[27] *Global Civil Society 2012* (London: Palgrave Macmillan, 2012).

FIGURE 6.3

Distinctive Attributes of the Three Major Sectors

Source: Adapted from Steven Waddell, "Core Competencies: A Key Force in Business-Government-Civil Society Collaborations," *Journal of Corporate Citizenship,* Autumn 2002, pp. 43–56, Tables 1 and 2. Used by permission.

	Business	**Government**	**Civil Society**
Organizational form	For-profit	Governmental	Nonprofit
Goods produced	Private	Public	Group
Primary control agent	Owners	Voters/rulers	Communities
Primary power form	Money	Laws, police, fines	Traditions, values
Primary goals	Wealth creation	Societal order	Expression of values
Assessment frame	Profitability	Legality	Justice
Resources	Capital assets, technical knowledge, production skills	Tax revenue, policy knowledge, regulatory and enforcement power	Community knowledge, inspirational leadership
Weaknesses	Short-term focus, lack of concern for external impacts	Bureaucratic, slow-moving, poorly coordinated internally	Amateurish, lack of financial resources, parochial perspective

but may lack financial resources and technical skill and may suffer from a narrow, parochial focus.[28] One model highlighting various attributes of actors in the business, government, and civil society sectors is presented in Figure 6.3.

Many businesses have realized that these differences across sectors can be a resource to be exploited. In this view, global action networks—alliances among organizations from the three sectors—can draw on the unique capabilities of each and overcome particular weaknesses that each has.

> One example of a global action network was the Kimberley Process, an initiative to end the trade in *conflict diamonds*—gemstones that had been mined or stolen by rebels fighting internationally recognized governments. The problem was that combatants in civil wars in Africa had seized control of diamond mines in Sierra Leone, Angola, and the Congo, and were selling uncut diamonds to fund their operations. Concerned that the image of diamonds as a symbol of romance would be tarnished, the World Diamond Congress and the international diamond company DeBeers joined forces with the governments of nations with legitimate diamond industries and NGOs campaigning to end civil violence. Together, these parties developed the Kimberley Process, a system for tracking diamonds all the way from the mine to the jewelry shop, so that consumers could be assured that their gem was "conflict-free."

In this case, although the interests of the parties were somewhat different, they were each able to bring their distinctive capabilities to bear to accomplish a common objective. A similar multi-party effort to ban conflict minerals—ones mined in war-torn areas of the Congo, is profiled in the discussion case at the end of this chapter. Other applications of the principle of cross-sector networks and collaborations are explored in Chapters 11 and 18.

The process of globalization presents today's business leaders with both great promise and great challenge. Despite the global economic downturn and the ever-present threat of war and terrorism, the world's economy continues to become more integrated and interdependent. Transnational corporations, with their financial assets and technical and managerial skills, have a great contribution to make to human betterment. Yet, they must operate in a world of great diversity, and in which their presence is often distrusted or feared. Often, they must confront situations in which political and economic freedoms are lacking and human rights

---

[28] This paragraph draws on Steven Waddell, "Core Competencies: A Key Force in Business-Government-Civil Society Collaborations," *Journal of Corporate Citizenship,* Autumn 2002, pp. 43–56.

are routinely violated. The challenge facing forward-looking companies today is how to work collaboratively with stakeholders to promote social and economic justice, while still achieving strong bottom-line results.

Summary

- Globalization refers to the increasing movement of goods, services, and capital across national borders. Firms can enter and compete in the global marketplace by exporting products and services; locating operations in another country; or buying raw materials, components, or supplies from sellers abroad.

- The process of globalization is driven by technological innovation, improvements in transportation, the rise of major multinational corporations, and social and political reforms.

- Globalization brings both benefits and costs. On one hand, it has the potential to pull nations out of poverty, spread innovation, and reduce prices for consumers. On the other hand, it may also produce job loss, reduce environmental and labor standards, and erode national cultures. An ongoing challenge is to extend the benefits of globalization to all, while mitigating its adverse effects.

- Multinational corporations operate in nations that vary greatly in their political, social, and economic systems. They face the challenge of deciding how to do business in other nations, while remaining true to their values.

- Businesses can work with governments and civil society organizations around the world in collaborative partnerships that draw on the unique capabilities of each to address common problems.

Key Terms

anti-Americanism, *125*
central state control, *128*
civil society, *131*
constructive engagement, *130*
debt relief, *121*
democracy, *127*
foreign direct investment (FDI), *118*
free enterprise system, *128*

global action network (GAN), *131*
globalization, *117*
international financial and trade institution (IFTI), *120*
International Monetary Fund (IMF), *120*
military dictatorships, *127*

nongovernmental organizations (NGOs), *131*
transnational corporation (TNC), *118*
World Bank (WB), *120*
World Trade Organization (WTO), *121*

Internet Resources

www.wto.org	World Trade Organization
www.imf.org	International Monetary Fund
www.worldbank.org	World Bank
www.ifg.org	International Forum on Globalization
www.globalpolicy.org	Global Policy Forum
www.un.org/en/civilsociety	United Nations and Civil Society
www.unglobalcompact.org/Participants AndStakeholders/civil_society	United Nations Global Compact and Nongovernmental Organizations
www.thomaslfriedman.com	Website of author and columnist Thomas L. Friedman
http://en.wordpress.com/tag/globalization	Blogs on globalization and related topics

Discussion Case: *Conflict Coltan in the Global Electronics Industry Supply Chain*

Most people have never heard of coltan, although it is an essential ingredient in electronic products they use every day. Columbite-tantalite, or "coltan" as it is commonly known, is a black metallic ore. When refined, it produces tantalum, which is used to regulate electricity in portable consumer electronics, such as smartphones, laptops, play stations, and digital cameras. The largest share of coltan comes from Africa; other sources include Australia, Brazil, and Canada.

In the late 2000s, a common concern emerged among members of an oddly matched group—the electronics industry, the United Nations, governments, and human rights organizations. All wished to ban *conflict coltan*—ore that had been traded by warring groups to fund horrific civil conflict in the Democratic Republic of the Congo (DRC). Their efforts led, ultimately, to a set of international guidelines, national laws, and voluntary initiatives whose goal was to keep the electronics industry and its customers from inadvertently supporting killing, sexual assault, and labor abuses.

The Democratic Republic of the Congo is a nation of 71 million people in central Africa, covering a vast region the size of Western Europe. Since the late 1990s, the DRC has been the site of a brutal regional conflict, in which armed militias, including some from neighboring states, have fought for control. Despite the presence of United Nations troops, as many as 5 million people have died—the most in any conflict since World War II. Warring groups have used sexual assault as a weapon to control the population; an estimated 200,000 Congolese women and girls have been raped, often in front of their husbands and families.

The United Nations and several NGOs reported that militias had systematically looted coltan and other minerals from eastern Congo, using the profits to fund their operations. According to the human rights group Global Witness:

> In the course of plundering these minerals, rebel groups and the Congolese army have used forced labor (often in extremely harsh and dangerous conditions), carried out systematic extortion, and imposed illegal "taxes" on the civilian population. They have also used violence and intimidation against civilians who attempt to resist working for them or handing over the minerals they produce.

Said a representative of The Enough Project, another human rights group, "In eastern Congo, you see child miners [with] no health or safety standards. Minerals are dug by hand, traded in sacks, smuggled across borders."

Once mined—whether in the Congo or elsewhere—raw coltan made its way through a complex, multi-step global supply chain. Local traders sold to regional traders, who shipped the ore to processing companies such as H.C. Starck (Germany), Cabot Corporation (U.S.), and Ningxia (China). Their smelters produced refined tantalum powder, which was then sold to parts makers such as Kemet (U.S.), Epcos (Germany), and Flextronics (Singapore). They sold, in turn, to original equipment manufacturers such as Dell (U.S.), Sony (Japan), and Nokia (Finland).

By the time coltan reached the end of this convoluted supply chain, determining its source was nearly impossible. The late Steve Jobs, then CEO of Apple, commented in an e-mail in 2010, "We require all of our suppliers to certify in writing that they use conflict-free materials. But honestly there is no way for them to be sure. Until someone invents a way to chemically trace minerals from the source mine, it's a very difficult problem."

As public awareness of atrocities in the Congo grew, governments and companies began to take action. The Organization for Economic Cooperation and Development, an alliance of mostly European nations, issued guidance for companies that wished to responsibly source minerals. A group of electronics firms, collaborating under the banner of the Electronic Industry Citizenship Coalition (EICC), developed a Conflict-Free Smelter Assessment Program, a voluntary system in which an independent third-party auditor would evaluate processors and designate them as "conflict-free." Minerals originating from responsibly operated mines would be "bagged and tagged" and then tracked through each step of the supply chain.

In 2010, the U.S. Congress passed the Wall Street Reform and Consumer Protection Act (also known as the Dodd-Frank Act, and further discussed in Chapters 8 and 14). This law included a provision, Section 1502, which required companies to disclose whether certain minerals and metals used in their products, including tantalum, had come from the DRC or adjoining countries. It was scheduled to go into effect in 2012. Supporters said that by shining a spotlight on conflict minerals, this law would help drive them out of the supply chain.

Others, however, thought the law could unintentionally hurt the very people it was meant to help. A journalist traveling in eastern Congo posted this report in late 2011:

> The smelting companies that used to buy from eastern Congo have stopped. No one wants to be tarred with financing African warlords—especially the glamorous high-tech firms like Apple and Intel that are often the ultimate buyers of these minerals. It's easier to sidestep Congo than to sort out the complexities of Congolese politics—especially when minerals are readily available from other, safer countries. . . .
> For locals, however, the law has been a catastrophe.

In an effort to address this concern, two companies, AVX and Motorola, joined forces to create an initiative called Solutions for Hope. Their aim was to begin using coltan from the DRC that could be verified as conflict-free, in order to support legitimate exports from that nation as it struggled to recover from years of civil conflict. In one of the first shipments, in late 2011, coltan was shipped from a licensed concession holder in the DRC to a certified conflict-free smelter in South Africa. During the next year, the initiative planned audits by key stakeholders.

Despite progress on many fronts, some called for a higher level of collaboration among companies, governments, and NGOs. The Enough Project said that the "missing link" was a common certification program for conflict minerals. It called for a "high-level negotiation process . . . aimed at building multi-stakeholder consensus for a scheme to unite current initiatives around common standards and certify conflict-free minerals from Congo from mine to end product."

Sources: Peter Eichstaedt, *Consuming the Congo* (Chicago: Lawrence Hill, 2011); Michael Nest, *Coltan* (Cambridge, UK: Polity Press, 2011); "EICC-GeSI Conflict-Free Smelter (CFS) Assessment Program," January 30, 2012, at *http://solutions-network .org/site-solutionsforhope;* "AVX Is Industry's First to Guarantee Conflict-Free Tantalum Capacitors," *Business Wire,* December 14, 2011; "Conflict Minerals: Dodd-Frank Section 1502 and Proposed SEC Rule," Ernst & Young, 2011; "U.S. Congo Policy: Matching Deeds to Words to End the World's Deadliest War," The Enough Project, October 4, 2011, at *www .enoughproject.org;* "How Congress Devastated Congo," *The New York Times,* August 7, 2011; "Conflict Minerals: Genocide in Your Gadgets?" *Christian Science Monitor,* February 24, 2011; "Conflict Minerals Law Spotlights Electronics Supply Chain," *Electronics Design, Strategy, News (EDN),* October 7, 2010; "Tracing a Path Forward: A Study of the Challenges of the Supply Chain for Target Markets Used in Electronics," *RESOLVE,* April 2010, at *http://eicc.info/documents /RESOLVEReport4.10.10.pdf;* "The New Blood Diamonds," *Foreign Policy,* January/February 2010; and Global Witness, *Faced with a Gun, What Can You Do?* July 2009, at *www.globalwitness.org.*

Discussion Questions

1. What is conflict coltan? What groups benefited from the trade in conflict coltan? What groups were hurt by it?

2. What three sectors were concerned with the problem of conflict coltan? What were the interests of each, and in what ways did their interests converge?

3. What steps could be taken by governments, NGOs, and companies to strengthen the process to exclude conflict minerals from the global supply chain?

4. Could conflict minerals be excluded from the global supply chain without hurting the noncombatant citizens of the DRC?

Global Corporate Citizenship

As businesses have become increasingly global, so have their interactions with society. Global corporate citizenship refers to putting an organization's commitment to social and environmental responsibility into practice worldwide, not only locally or regionally. Like corporate social responsibility, discussed in Chapter 3, global corporate citizenship involves building positive relationships with stakeholders, discovering business opportunities in serving society, and transforming a concern for financial performance into a vision of integrated financial *and* social and environmental performance, but on a much broader scale. Establishing effective structures and processes to meet a company's global corporate citizenship responsibilities, assess the results of these efforts, and the report on the firm's performance to the public are important challenges facing today's global manager.

This Chapter Focuses on These Key Learning Objectives:

- Defining global corporate citizenship and observing it in practice.
- Recognizing the many different approaches to managing corporate citizenship.
- Understanding how the multiple dimensions of corporate citizenship progress through a series of stages.
- Understanding how business or social groups can audit corporate citizenship activities and report their findings to stakeholders.
- Recognizing how an organization communicates its corporate citizenship practices and manifests its attention to various social performance standards, such as the triple bottom line.

Novo Nordisk is a multinational health care company, based in Denmark, dedicated to the treatment of diabetes. It conducts research and markets a range of products, including synthetic insulin and delivery devices—such as the "FlexPen" and "NovoPen"—that diabetics can use to inject medicine more comfortably. In 2012, Novo Nordisk continued to develop new products, such as the "NovoTwist" allowing for easier injections, and, despite the global recession, had experienced increased revenue each year since 2008. Novo Nordisk has publicly committed "to conduct its activities in a financially, environmentally, and socially responsible way." The company reports its financial results along with its social and environmental impacts in an integrated annual report, one of the first of its kind. Novo Nordisk's corporate strategy is guided by the Global Reporting Initiative and United Nations Global Compact, discussed later in this chapter. Many of the company's citizenship initiatives are linked to its core mission of fighting diabetes. For example, on World Diabetes Day more than 7,500 Novo Nordisk employees in 50 countries engaged over 1 million people in activities to raise awareness about the diabetes pandemic. The company constantly monitors its environmental impacts; for example, an initiative was designed to reduce the adverse effects of pharmaceuticals excreted in the urine—potentially a danger to aquatic life when these chemicals enter the sewage system and are eventually discharged into waterways. The company calls its holistic approach the "Novo Nordisk Way of Management."[1]

CEMEX, founded in Mexico in 1906, is a global building materials company that provides high-quality products and reliable service to customers and communities throughout the Americas, Europe, Africa, the Middle East, Asia, and Australia, maintaining trade relationships in more than 100 countries. Embedded in its mission is a commitment to be an exemplary global citizen by advancing the quality of life of those served through its efforts. CEMEX developed Rizal Green cement, used in residential construction, which produces 32 percent less carbon dioxide emissions than traditional cement. Its U.K. affiliate was the first cement company in the world to provide certified carbon labels for its product. CEMEX employees said that work–life balance was the greatest reason they volunteer and work in their communities. In Poland, the company was honored as a "leader in responsible business" in the construction industry. CEMEX stated, "We aim to be leaders not only in the building materials industry, but also in all of our relationships. We are a company with a sound vision for the future based on sustainability, excellence and innovation."[2]

This chapter introduces the concept of global corporate citizenship and explains how companies around the world, such as Novo Nordisk and CEMEX, have organized themselves to carry out their citizenship responsibilities. It provides examples of what leading-edge companies are doing to put social and environmental responsibility into practice. This chapter also addresses the emerging practice of social auditing, a method for measuring and assessing corporate social performance, and reporting these results to the public.

Global Corporate Citizenship

The term **global corporate citizenship** refers to putting an organization's commitment to social and environmental responsibility into practice worldwide, not only locally or regionally. Companies demonstrate this commitment by proactively building stakeholder partnerships, discovering business opportunities in serving society, and transforming a concern for

[1] More information about Novo Nordisk's Way of Management and a copy of the company's integrated annual report are available online at *www.novonordisk.com.*

[2] This information and quotation are from CEMEX's website at www.cemex.com.

financial performance into a vision of integrated financial *and* social performance.[3] Corporate citizenship has become increasingly global in scope, reflecting the global nature of commerce and emerging awareness of the worldwide scope of many social issues. Since corporations are not *global* citizens, but citizens of a single country, the notion of citizenship takes on more all-encompassing meanings ranging from indirect involvement in various community or environmental organizations to explicit and aggressive leadership in addressing societal problems on a global scale.[4]

Roberto Civita, chairman and chief executive officer of the Brazilian Abril Group, has defined global corporate citizenship as "capitalism with a social conscience." According to many business leaders, global corporate citizenship used to be simple and optional. Now, a decade into the 21st century, it has become complicated and mandatory. This is because global markets, lightning-quick access to information, and heightened stakeholder expectations have compelled organizations of all sizes to establish an "integrated global corporate citizenship strategy" as part of their overall business plan.[5]

The Economist Intelligence Unit investigated the notion of corporate citizenship by interviewing dozens of senior executives and surveying managers at 566 companies. They concluded that "corporate citizenship is becoming increasingly important for the long-term health of companies . . . 74 percent of respondents to the survey say corporate citizenship can help increase profits at their company . . . Survey respondents who say effective corporate citizenship can help to improve the bottom line are also more likely to say their strategy is 'very important' to their business (33 percent) compared with other survey respondents (8 percent)."[6]

A research report from a leading academic center defines global corporate citizenship in these terms:

> Global corporate citizenship is the process of identifying, analyzing, and responding to the company's social, political, and economic responsibilities as defined through law and public policy, stakeholder expectations, and voluntary acts flowing from corporate values and business strategies. Corporate citizenship involves actual results (what corporations do) and the processes through which they are achieved (how they do it).[7]

This definition of global corporate citizenship is consistent with several major themes discussed throughout this book:

- Managers and companies have responsibilities to all of their stakeholders.
- Corporate citizenship or responsibility involves more than just meeting legal requirements.

---

[3] See Barbara W. Altman and Deborah Vidaver-Cohen, "A Framework for Understanding Corporate Citizenship," *Business and Society Review,* Spring 2000, pp. 1–7. An understanding of corporate citizenship as embedded in a "liberal view of citizenship" is presented by Dirk Matten and Andrew Crane in "Corporate Citizenship: Toward an Extended Theoretical Conceptualization," *Academy of Management Review,* 2005, pp. 166–79. The concept of global citizenship grounded in voluntary codes of conduct is developed by Jeanne M. Logsdon and Donna J. Wood in "Global Business Citizenship and Voluntary Codes of Ethical Conduct," *Journal of Business Ethics,* 2005, pp. 55–67.

[4] See Jeremy Moon, Andrew Crane, and Dirk Matten, "Can Corporations Be Citizens?" *Business Ethics Quarterly,* 2005, pp. 429–53. Also see Donna J. Wood, Jeanne Logsdon, Patsy G. Lewellyn, and Kim Davenport, *Global Business Citizenship: A Transformative Framework for Ethics and Sustainable Capitalism* (Armonk, NY: M.E. Sharpe, 2006).

[5] "Corporate Citizenship on the Rise," New Futures Media, *www.NewFuturesMedia.com.*

[6] "Corporate Citizenship: Profiting from a Sustainable Business," *The Economist,* November 2008, *www.eiu.com.*

[7] James E. Post, "Meeting the Challenge of Global Corporate Citizenship," *Center Research Report* (Chestnut Hill, MA: Boston College Center for Corporate Community Relations, 2000), p. 8.

- Corporate citizenship requires that a company focus on, and respond to, stakeholder expectations and undertake those voluntary acts that are consistent with its values and business mission.
- Corporate citizenship involves both what the corporation does and the processes and structures through which it engages stakeholders and makes decisions, a subject to which this chapter next turns.

What are the core elements of global corporate citizenship? One scholar's answer to this question is shown in Exhibit 7.A.

Citizenship Profile

What are the benefits of global corporate citizenship? When businesses invest time, money, and effort in citizenship activities, they often reap rewards in the form of enhanced reputation and legitimacy. Recent research by Naomi A. Gardberg and Charles J. Fombrun argues that corporate citizenship programs, particularly those of global firms, should be viewed as "strategic investments comparable to R&D [research and development] and advertising." This is because such programs "create intangible assets for companies that help them overcome nationalistic barriers, facilitate globalization, and build local advantage." (A *tangible* asset is something that can be seen and counted, such as machinery, buildings, or money. An *intangible* asset, by contrast, is something that cannot be seen or counted, but that nevertheless has value—such as a good reputation, trusting relationships, or customer loyalty.)

In this respect, global corporate citizenship activities are considered to be important contributors to "a reinforcing cycle through which global companies create legitimacy, reputation, and competitive advantage." Gardberg and Fombrun suggest this effect is most likely where companies choose a configuration of citizenship activities—they call this a **citizenship profile**—that fits the setting in which the company is working. For example, the public's expectations of corporate philanthropy, management of environmental risk, and worker rights vary across nations and regions. Companies whose citizenship profile best matches public expectations are most likely to benefit from strategic investments in corporate citizenship.[8]

Accenture, a global management consulting, technology services, and outsourcing company, encourages its employees to become involved in, and make a difference through, a variety of community and environmental programs. The Accenture Development Partnerships program offers world-class management and technology consulting services free of charge to address international challenges by working with nonprofit and nongovernmental organizations. Voluntary Services Overseas offers Accenture employees the opportunity to take a leave of absence from work to volunteer their time and professional skills to help communities in developing countries.[9]

CEOs increasingly have accepted the multiple roles of business that make up the citizenship profile. The McKinsey Group interviewed 400 CEOs and senior executives of companies that participate in the United Nations Global Compact program (discussed later in this chapter), and found that more than 9 out of 10 corporate leaders are "doing more than they did five years ago to incorporate environmental, social, and political issues into their firms' core strategies." Some visionary CEOs see citizenship as an opportunity to create value for

---

[8] Naomi A. Gardberg and Charles Fombrun, "Corporate Citizenship: Creating Intangible Assets across Institutional Environments," *Academy of Management Review* 31, no. 2 (2006), pp. 329–46.

[9] For more information on these programs, see Accenture's website at *careers.accenture.com*.

Exhibit 7.A

Principles of [Global] Corporate Citizenship

Good corporate citizens strive to conduct all business dealings in an ethical manner, make a concerted effort to balance the needs of all stakeholders, and work to protect the environment. The principles of corporate citizenship include the following:

Ethical Business Behavior

1. Engages in fair and honest business practices in its relationship with stakeholders.
2. Sets high standards of behavior for all employees.
3. Exercises ethical oversight of the executive and board levels.

Stakeholder Commitment

4. Strives to manage the company for the benefit of all stakeholders.
5. Initiates and engages in genuine dialogue with stakeholders.
6. Values and implements dialogue.

Community

7. Fosters a reciprocal relationship between the corporation and community.
8. Invests in the communities in which the corporation operates.

Consumers

9. Respects the rights of consumers.
10. Offers quality products and services.
11. Provides information that is truthful and useful.

Employees

12. Provides a family-friendly work environment.
13. Engages in responsible human resource management.
14. Provides an equitable reward and wage system for employees.
15. Engages in open and flexible communication with employees.
16. Invests in employee development.

Investors

17. Strives for a competitive return on investment.

Suppliers

18. Engages in fair trading practices with suppliers.

Environment Commitment

19. Demonstrates a commitment to the environment.
20. Demonstrates a commitment to sustainable development.

Source: Kimberly Davenport, "Corporate Citizenship: A Stakeholder Approach for Defining Corporate Social Performance and Identifying Measures for Assessment," 1998, doctoral dissertation, Fielding Graduate University, *http://www.fielding.edu/library/dissertations/default.asp.* Used by permission.

their organization, gain a competitive advantage, and help address some of the world's biggest challenges.[10]

[10] "Shaping the New Rules of Competition: UN Global Compact Participant Mirror," McKinsey & Company, July 2007, *www.unglobalcompact.org/docs;* and "Valuing Corporate Social Responsibility: McKinsey Global Survey Results," *McKinsey Quarterly,* February 2009, *www.mckinseyquarterly.com.*

As companies expand their sphere of commercial activity around the world, expectations grow that they will behave in ways that enhance the benefits and minimize the risk to all stakeholders, wherever they are. This is the essence of legitimacy in a global economy. A company must earn—and maintain—its "license to operate" in every country in which it does business through its efforts to meet stakeholder expectations. (This concept is further explained in Chapter 18.)

Management Systems for Global Corporate Citizenship

Global corporate citizenship is more than espoused values; it requires action. In order to become leading citizens of the world, companies must establish management processes and structures to carry out their citizenship commitments. This section describes some of the ways forward-thinking companies are changing to improve their ability to act as responsible citizens.

BSR, formerly Businesses for Social Responsibility, represents more than 300 member companies seeking to develop sustainable business strategies. When surveying its members to determine how companies had organized to carry out their citizenship functions, BSR observed great variation in what they termed corporate social responsibility (CSR) or corporate citizenship management systems. BSR found that the goal of a global citizenship management system is to integrate corporate responsibility and citizenship concerns into a company's values, culture, operations, and business decisions at all levels of the organization. Many companies have taken steps to create such a system by assigning responsibility to a committee of the board, an executive level committee, or a single executive or group of executives who can identify key CSR or corporate citizenship issues and evaluate and develop a structure for long-term integration of social values throughout the organization. One important observation is that there is no single universally accepted method for designing a global corporate citizenship management structure. This is definitely not a "one size fits all" exercise.[11]

Corporate citizenship, as this study recognized, is a rapidly evolving area of managerial practice in many organizations. In some cases companies have broadened the job of the public relations office to include a wider range of tasks, discussed in Chapter 19. In other situations, the corporate citizenship function is *centralized* under a **department of corporate citizenship** to concentrate the leadership of the wide-ranging corporate citizenship functions. Yet, in other companies it is a *decentralized* function, involving many different managers and skill sets, confirming the "one size does not fit all" observation by Business for Social Responsibility.

An example of a firm centralizing their corporate citizenships activities under one department can be found at Pfizer.

> In 2012, at Pfizer—the world's largest biopharmaceutical company—Sally Susman served as executive vice president for policy, external affairs, and communications. A member of Pfizer's executive leadership team, she also was vice chair of the Pfizer Foundation, which promoted access to quality health care, nurtured innovation, and supported the volunteerism of Pfizer's 100,000 employees. Susman also directed Pfizer's global communications and its public affairs activities, including high-level relations with the governments of all nations in which Pfizer had operations or marketed products. Susman also provided oversight for the firm's auditing and social reporting activities, headed the firm's corporate responsibility group, and played a key role in shaping the company's social responsibility and sustainability policy initiatives.[12]

[11] For additional information about BSR, see *www.bsr.org*.

[12] See *www.pfizer.com/about/leadership_and_structure/leadership_executives_susman.jsp*.

One emerging trend is the consolidation of corporate citizenship efforts, like the ones at Pfizer, into a single office that may encompass community relations, philanthropy, stakeholder engagement, social auditing and reporting, and other functions. According to a recent study, almost all—94 percent—of *Fortune* 250 companies (the largest corporations in the United States, published annually in *Fortune* magazine) had a department of corporate citizenship, global citizenship, corporate social responsibility, or a similar name. Many of these departments had been recently established. The heads of many of them were senior vice presidents or vice presidents.[13]

Alternatively, some organizations believe that decentralizing the corporate citizenship function allows specialists to develop their skills to address specific elements of the corporate citizenship strategy. For example, Alliance Boots, an international pharmacy-led health and beauty company, has split the corporate citizenship function into four strands: community, environment, marketplace, and workplace functions. The company started "CR Action Groups" within each function to enable its specialists to better respond to local government requirements and community needs.[14]

Regardless of the structural form, the importance of corporate citizenship is clear and connected to the upper levels of the organization. A survey by the Corporate Responsibility Officer Association (CROA) found that 43 percent of the managers entrusted with the company's corporate citizenship function reported directly to the CEO or board of directors. The company's CEO and board of directors were also involved in corporate citizenship. The CROA reported that 51 percent of the CEOs had recently led a corporate citizenship initiative and 41 percent of boards of directors had designated one or more members to lead corporate citizenship-related topics or activities.[15]

As businesses have become more committed to citizenship, specialized consultancies and professional associations for managers with responsibility in this area have emerged. Many of these organizations, including BSR, whose study is cited earlier, are profiled in Exhibit 7.B.

Stages of Corporate Citizenship

Companies do not become good corporate citizens overnight. The process takes time. New attitudes have to be developed, new routines learned, new policies and action programs designed, and new relationships formed. Many obstacles must be overcome. What process do companies go through as they proceed down this path? What factors push and pull them along?

Philip H. Mirvis and Bradley K. Googins of the Center for Global Citizenship at Boston College developed a five-stage model of global corporate citizenship, based on their work with hundreds of practitioners in a wide range of companies.[16] In their view, firms typically pass through a sequence of five stages as they develop as corporate citizens. Each stage is

---

[13] Anne T. Lawrence, Gordon Rands, and Mark Starik, "The Role, Career Path, Skill Set, and Reporting Relationships of the Corporate Social Responsibility/Citizenship/Sustainability Officer in *Fortune* 250 Firms," presented at the annual meeting of the International Association for Business and Society, 2009.

[14] "How to Embed Corporate Responsibility across Different Parts of Your Company," *Ethical Corporation,* October 2009, *www.ethicalcorp.com/csr.*

[15] "Corporate Responsibility Best Practices: Setting the Baseline," Corporate Responsibility Officer Association, April 2010, pp. 10–11.

[16] Philip H. Mirvis and Bradley K. Googins, *Stages of Corporate Citizenship: A Developmental Framework* (Chestnut Hill, MA: Center for Corporate Citizenship at Boston College, 2006). For a contrasting stage model, based on the experience of Nike, see Simon Zadek, "The Path to Corporate Responsibility," *Harvard Business Review,* December 2004, pp. 125–32.

As the practice of corporate citizenship has spread, so have professional associations and consultancies serving managers active in this arena. Among the leading organizations are these:

- In the United States, *BSR* (formerly Business for Social Responsibility), based in San Francisco but with regional offices around the world, functions as a membership organization for companies and provides consulting services to its members and others. The organization, which was founded in 1992, describes itself as a "global resource for companies seeking to sustain their commercial success in ways that demonstrate respect for ethical values, people, communities, and the environment." The organization provides hands-on guidance in setting up social programs, as well as providing useful research and best-practices examples for its member organizations.

- *Canadian Business for Social Responsibility* (CBSR) is seeking to change the way that business does business by supporting Canadian companies to advance their social, environmental, and financial performance. Founded in 1995, CBSR addresses issues of poverty, climate change, and related issues to promote business performance and contribute to a better world.

- *Corporate Social Responsibility Europe* provides a unique service delivery model that focuses on supporting companies in building sustainable competitiveness, fostering close cooperation between companies and their stakeholders, and strengthening Europe's global leadership on CSR. Based in Brussels, Belgium, it is the largest CSR network in Europe, including 33 membership-based, business-led CSR organizations with ties to approximately 4,000 companies throughout Europe.

- *Forum Empresa* was created in 1997 as an inter-American organization (North and South America) to unite organizations focusing on corporate social responsibility from Canada to Chile. The network is dedicated to strengthening national or regional organizations committed to corporate social responsibility. More than 3,000 businesses belonged to this network in 2012.

- *The African Institute of Corporate Citizenship*, or AICC Africa, broadly defines its role of corporate citizenship from assisting Western businesspeople in the proper etiquette when doing business in Africa to fighting for a minimum wage for workers in South Africa.

- Founded in 2004, *CSR—Asia* is the leading provider of information, training, research, and consulting services on sustainable business practices in Asia. It offers a wide range of programs: providing CSR intelligence to interested businesses, assistance with reporting social and environmental programs to the company's stakeholders, and offering one- and two-day training courses on sustainable initiatives.

- *Asian Forum on Corporate Social Responsibility*, based in the Philippines, sponsors conferences to provide CSR practitioners in Asia an opportunity to learn, collaborate, and share insights. The organization also gives awards for excellence in environmental management, education, poverty alleviation, workplace practices, and health care.

Source: More information about these organizations is available online at *www.bsr.org, www.cbsr.ca, www.csreurope .org, empresa.org, www.aiccafrica.org, csr-asia.com,* and *www.asianforumcsr.com.*

characterized by a distinctive pattern of concepts, strategic intent, leadership, structure, issues management, stakeholder relationships, and transparency, as illustrated in Figure 7.1.

Elementary Stage. At this stage, citizenship is undeveloped. Managers are uninterested and uninvolved in social issues. Although companies at this stage obey the law, they do not move beyond compliance. Companies tend to be defensive; they react only when threatened. Communication with stakeholders is one-way: from the company to the stakeholder.

Engaged Stage. At this second stage, companies typically become aware of changing public expectations and see the need to maintain their license to operate. Engaged companies may adopt formal policies, such as governing labor standards or human rights.

FIGURE 7.1　The Stages of Global Corporate Citizenship

	Citizenship Content	Strategic Intent	Leadership	Structure	Issues Management	Stakeholder Relationships	Transparency
Stage 5: Transforming	Change the game	Market creation or social change	Visionary, ahead of the pack	Mainstream: business driven	Defining	Multi-organization	Full disclosure
Stage 4: Integrated	Sustainability or triple bottom line	Value proposition	Champion, in front of it	Organizational alignment	Proactive, systems	Partnership alliance	Assurance
Stage 3: Innovative	Stakeholder management	Business case	Steward, on top of it	Cross-functional coordination	Responsive, programs	Mutual influence	Public reporting
Stage 2: Engaged	Philanthropy, environmental protection	License to operate	Supporter, in the loop	Functional ownership	Reactive, policies	Interactive	Public relations
Stage 1: Elementary	Jobs, profits, and taxes	Legal compliance	Lip service, out of touch	Marginal, staff-driven	Defensive	Unilateral	Flank protection

Source: Philip H. Mirvis and Bradley K. Googins, *Stages of Corporate Citizenship: A Developmental Framework,* Center for Corporate Citizenship at Boston College Monograph (Chestnut Hill, MA: Boston College, 2006). Adapted from material on pp. 3–5. Used by permission.

They begin to interact with and listen to stakeholders, although engagement occurs mainly through established departments. Top managers become involved. Often, a company at this stage will step up its philanthropic giving or commit to specific environmental objectives. When Home Depot announced that it would sell only environmentally certified wood products, this was an example of a company at the engaged stage of corporate citizenship.

Innovative Stage. At this third stage, organizations may become aware that they lack the capacity to carry out new commitments, prompting a wave of structural innovation. Departments begin to coordinate, new programs are launched, and many companies begin reporting their efforts to stakeholders. (Social auditing and reporting are further discussed later in this chapter.) External groups become more influential. Companies begin to understand more fully the business reasons for engaging in citizenship. The actions taken by Accenture, described earlier in this chapter, illustrate a company at this stage.

Integrated Stage. As they move into the fourth stage, companies see the need to build more coherent initiatives. Mirvis and Googins cite the example of Asea Brown Boveri (ABB), a Switzerland-based multinational producer of power plants and automation systems, which carefully coordinates its many sustainability programs from the CEO level down to line officers in more than 50 countries where the company has a presence. Integrated companies may adopt triple bottom line measures (explained later in this chapter), turn to external audits, and enter into ongoing partnerships with stakeholders.

Transforming Stage. This is the fifth and highest stage in the model. Companies at this stage have visionary leaders and are motivated by a higher sense of corporate purpose. They partner extensively with other organizations and individuals across business, industry, and national borders to address broad social problems and reach underserved markets.

Ajinomoto, a Japanese-based manufacturer of food spices and amino acids, is committed to enhancing the taste of food while supporting healthy living. Led by president and CEO Masatoshi Ito, the company celebrated its 100-year anniversary by creating the "Ajinomoto Way," a set of shared values that included creating new value, having a pioneer spirit, making a social contribution, and valuing people. The firm revealed elements of the transforming stage of corporate citizenship by reaching out with food and other aid to disaster victims, providing plant tours to demonstrate its commitment to a healthy and safe work environment, conducting nutrition education programs for school children, and committing to sustainable business operations wherever it operated.[17]

The model's authors emphasize that individual companies can be at more than one stage at once, if their development progresses faster in some areas than in others. For example, a company might audit its activities and disclose the findings to the public in social reports (transparency, stage 5), but still be interacting with stakeholders in a pattern of mutual influence (stakeholder relationships, stage 3). This is normal, the authors point out, because each organization evolves in a way that reflects the particular challenges it faces. Nevertheless, because the dimensions of global corporate citizenship are linked, they tend to become more closely aligned over time.

As corporate citizenship commitments have become more widespread in the global business community, they have attracted critics as well as admirers. Citizenship initiatives have been challenged on the grounds either that they represent superficial attempts to enhance reputation, without real substance, or that they are inherently limited by the corporation's profit-maximizing imperative, or both.

Some allege that companies may be involved in corporate citizenship to distract the public from ethical questions posed by their core operations. The Ronald McDonald House charity, operated by McDonald's, provides homes-away-from-home for the families of seriously ill children being treated in hospitals. Many view the initiative as a wonderful social gesture by the company and its franchisees. Others, though, have criticized it as a diversion from other aspects of McDonald's operations that may be less praiseworthy—such as the company's contributions to the nation's obesity epidemic, its treatment of animals slaughtered for food, or the low wages of its employees. Yet, McDonald's defends its actions and offers a long list of socially minded programs.[18]

Whether firms embrace corporate citizenship for altruistic reasons or simply to deflect negative publicity remains a lively debate.

While there remains regional differences in the corporate citizenship challenges facing businesses due to differences in attitudes, beliefs, and culture, according to a report from a recent conference on corporate citizenship, in recent years this phenomenon has developed into a global initiative. This notion of a globally integrated CSR approach was discussed at various conferences throughout Europe and North America. And most experts conclude that as issues of sustainability, human rights, and concern for the bottom of the pyramid continue to dominate the corporate citizenship conversation, global initiatives, not selective regional solutions, are needed. Examples of global corporate citizenship approaches are shown by diverse businesses, from those in the brewing industry (the Worldwide Brewing Alliance) to an automobile manufacturer (Toyota).[19]

[17] Ajinomoto's vision, values, and citizenship programs can be found at their website, *www.ajinomoto.com.*

[18] See "McDonald's Corporate Responsibility: Values in Practice" at *www.crmcdonalds.com.*

[19] For a more detailed discussion of corporate citizenship as a global initiative, see *csr-net.org* and *csrvadergio.net.* For examples of global initiatives, see *gsri.worldwidebrewingalliance.org* and *www.toyota-global.com/sustainability/csr_initiatives.*

Assessing Global Corporate Citizenship

As companies around the world expand their commitment to corporate citizenship, they have also improved their capacity to measure performance and assess results. A **social audit** is a systematic evaluation of an organization's social, ethical, and environmental performance.[20]

In a social audit, a company's performance is evaluated relative to a set of externally imposed standards. The results of the audit are used to improve the firm's performance and to communicate with stakeholders and the public. The scholar Simon Zadek has identified six benefits of social audits. They help businesses know what is happening within their firm, understand what stakeholders think about and want from the business, tell stakeholders what the business has achieved, strengthen the loyalty and commitment of stakeholders, enhance the organization's decision making, and improve the business's overall performance.[21]

Today, many businesses use social audits to measure the **social equity** produced by their actions. In a world where the use of company resources must be justified, the greater the social equity documented, the stronger the argument a business can make that it is meeting its social obligations. Businesses also used their social audit results to minimize risks or capitalize on opportunities. They see the process as fostering innovation within the company. Some believe that to communicate with the organization's stakeholders in a transparent manner is simply the ethical thing to do.

This section will describe the standards against which audits are performed, different kinds of auditing processes, and how results are reported to stakeholders and the public.

Global Social and Environmental Audit Standards

In response to the emerging efforts by governments to promote global citizenship, a number of different corporate citizenship standards have been developed that establish measures or benchmarks against which a firm's citizenship activities (or those of its suppliers or partners) can be compared in a social audit. (One such list of principles appears in Exhibit 7.A, presented earlier in this chapter.) Social audits look not only at what an organization does, but also at the results of these actions. For example, if a company supports a tutorial program at a local school, the audit might not only look at the number of hours of employee volunteerism, but also assess changes in student test scores as an indicator of the program's social impact.

Audit standards can be created in three different ways. Companies can develop standards designed to set expectations of performance for their suppliers or partners. For example, Apple developed its own supplier code—a development described in the discussion case at the end of this chapter. Or, companies within an industry can agree on a common industry-wide standard, as several high technology companies did when they agreed on an Electronics Industry Citizenship Coalition Code of Conduct, further described in Chapter 16. Another example of an industry-wide social performance standard was developed by the Fair Labor Association, when setting expectations for worker safety and pay in the apparel and footwear industries. Finally, audit standards can be developed by global nongovernmental organizations or standard-setting organizations.

A number of such organizations have developed standards to judge corporate performance. These include the International Organisation for Standards (ISO 14001, 14063, and 26000), the Global Reporting Initiative, Social Accountability 8000, the Institute of Social

---

[20] The concept of a social audit was first introduced in Howard R. Bowen, *Social Responsibilities of the Businessman* (New York: Harper, 1953).

[21] Simon Zadek, "Balancing Performance, Ethics, and Accountability," *Journal of Business Ethics* 17 (1998), pp. 1421–42.

FIGURE 7.2 **Summary of Global Social and Environmental Audit Standards**

	ISO 14001	Global Reporting Initiative	SA 8000
Origin	1996	1997	1997
Scope	Environmental management standards	Economic, environmental, and social sustainability	Improved working conditions through eight core labor elements
Governance	ISO council, technical management board, technical committees	Multi-stakeholder board of directors, technical advisers, stakeholder councils	SAI multi-stakeholder advisory board—experts from business, NGOs, government, and trade unions
Participants	ISO member countries, environmental NGOs, technical experts	Businesses; United Nations; human rights, environmental, labor groups; industry associations; governments	Businesses and their suppliers, trade associations, unions, auditing firms, NGOs, government
Funding	ISO member dues, document sales, volunteer efforts	Foundations, companies, Dutch government	Foundations, government grants, income from services and programs

	ISEA AA 1000	United Nations Global Compact	ISO 14063	ISO 26000
Origin	1999	1999	2001	2010
Scope	Help organizations to become more accountable, responsible, and sustainable, emphasizing low carbon and green economy	Business operating principles: human rights, labor, environment	Guidance on environmental communication	Seven core subjects of social responsibility
Governance	ISEA; business members; nonprofits, academic, and consultancy organizations	UN Secretary General, Global Issues Network, ILO, stakeholder groups	ISO technical committee, working group	ISO technical management board, working group
Participants	Multi-stakeholder membership	Businesses, labor organizations, NGOs	ISO member countries experts: business, NGOs, standards organizations, consultants	ISO member countries, public and private sectors
Funding	Membership income, commissioned research, foundations	Voluntary government and foundation contributions	ISO member dues, document sales, volunteer efforts	ISO member dues, document sales, volunteer efforts

Sources: International Organisation for Standards, ISO14001, *www.iso.org;* Global Reporting Initiative, *www.globalreporting.org;* Social Accountability International, SA 8000, *www.sa-intl.org;* AccountAbility, AA 1000, *www.accountability.org.uk;* United Nations Global Compact, *www.unglobalcompact.org;* International Organisation for Standards, ISO14063, *www.iso.org;* and International Organisation for Standards, ISO 26000, *www.iso.org.*

and Ethical Accountability (ISEA), AccountAbility (or AA 1000), and the more general guidelines promulgated in the United Nations Global Compact (discussed earlier in this chapter).[22] The major characteristics of these global audit standards are summarized in Figure 7.2.

[22] Another comprehensive list of major business-related standards is in Sandra Waddock's "Building a New Institutional Infrastructure for Corporate Responsibility," *Academy of Management Perspectives,* 2008, p. 92, Table 2.

Exhibit 7.C

Implementing the Global Compact at Novartis

An early endorser of the United Nations Global Compact was Novartis, a major pharmaceutical firm based in Switzerland.

In 2000, CEO Daniel Vasella publicly signed the Global Compact, saying, "Novartis would like to see [it] become a catalyst for concrete action of enterprises and nations . . . furthering worldwide acceptance of fundamental human rights, labor and environmental standards." The company reworked its own code of conduct to include the Compact's principles. It established a steering committee made up of representatives from its major operating divisions and functional areas. A senior member of the executive committee (board of directors) was put in charge, and the process was named the Novartis Corporate Citizenship Initiative.

One major challenge faced by the committee was to apply the Compact's very general prescriptions to specific business circumstances. For example, Principle 1 calls on companies to "support and respect the protection of international human rights." The committee quickly concluded that some human rights principles, such as protecting people from such acts as murder, arbitrary imprisonment, and torture, had nothing to do with corporate reality and could be dismissed as irrelevant.

Applying other human rights principles, however, proved more complex. The Universal Declaration of Human Rights states that each person has "the right to a standard of living adequate for the health and well-being of himself and of his family." What did this mean for Novartis?

The committee took its job seriously, consulting widely within the company, writing briefs on various topics, engaging in dialogue with stakeholders, and consulting with outside experts. As a result of this process, Novartis undertook several health care initiatives. Among other things, the company agreed to provide antimalarial drugs at cost for use in poor countries, to subsidize research on diseases of poverty such as dengue fever, and to donate thousands of treatments for tuberculosis. It also committed to provide prevention, diagnosis, treatment, and counseling services for its employees and their immediate family members for HIV/AIDS, TB, and malaria in developing countries. Later, the company committed to provide a living wage—sufficient to provide an adequate standard of living—to all employees. By 2006, it had completed wage studies in all countries where it did business and had made adjustments where necessary to bring up worker pay to the living wage standard.

One researcher who examined the process at Novartis concluded, "[Making] the general commitment is probably the easiest part of the Global Compact adventure for a company. The real challenge is to translate the top management's signature into an organizational commitment for concrete action and into the sustained motivation of employees that it is the right thing to do."

Sources: Klaus M. Leisinger, "Opportunities and Risks of the United Nations Global Compact: The Novartis Case Study," *Journal of Corporate Citizenship* 11 (Autumn 2003), pp. 113–31; and Juegen Brotatzky-Geiger et al., "Implementing a Living Wage Globally—The Novartis Approach," April 4, 2007. For a full description of Novartis's efforts to meet the challenges of the United Nations Global Compact, see *Novartis and the Global Compact: An Inspirational Guide to Implementing the Commitment* at *www.novartisfoundation.org/platform/content/element/3709/Novartis_Global_Compact_FINAL.pdf.*

The acceptance and use of all of these audit standards by companies have grown since their inception. Each standard recognizes and concentrates on a combination of internally focused economic benefits for the firm, as well as externally focused social benefits for the environment and key stakeholders. The standards utilize a multiple stakeholder governance structure so that the firm interacts with many of the stakeholders it seeks to serve through its multiple performance targets. Many companies committed to socially responsive practices have used these and other standards and have made their reports available online for their stakeholders and the general public. While most of the standards are voluntary, some businesses have incorporated the standards into their strategic plans, and more stakeholders are expecting firms to adhere to these global standards. The experience of one company that has endorsed the United Nations Global Compact, Novartis, is profiled in Exhibit 7.C.

The Auditing Process

Once a company has agreed to comply with an industry or global set of standards, it must determine what **auditing process** to use. In a simpler time, when a firm operated its own manufacturing facilities in a limited geographical area, monitoring its own compliance with an established set of standards was straightforward. But in today's more complex world, obtaining this information can be extraordinarily difficult. As described in Chapter 6, many corporations are embedded in far-flung global supply chains, and they source from factories around the world, which they do not manage directly. These factories, in turn, may subcontract work to others. A company can commit, for example, that all workers making its products are paid at least the minimum wage, but how can it assure that this is actually true?

Companies have several choices in carrying out an audit. One is to hire and train its own staff of auditors whose job is to inspect factories—either its own or those operated by contractors—to determine whether or not they are in compliance. This is similar to conducting an ethics audit, discussed in Chapter 5, and is sometimes called an *internal audit*.

An example of a company that has conducted its own internal audits is The Gap, Inc. This specialty retailer of clothing, accessories, and personal care products adopted a code of vendor conduct. In order to obtain a contract with The Gap, suppliers had to agree to pay at least the minimum wage, respect human rights, and refrain from discrimination, among other commitments. To assure that its suppliers were following the code, The Gap hired more than 90 vendor compliance officers, or VCOs. These individuals came from the communities where they worked, so they would be able to communicate well and understand the culture of the contractors they audited. These VCOs visited thousands of factories annually in the 50 or so countries where Gap products were made. Their work was overseen by a chief compliance officer, who reported directly to the CEO.[23]

An advantage of an internal audit is that the company controls and manages the process. It can train its own compliance officers, determine what factories need to be audited, and learn immediately about any problems uncovered. On the other hand, a disadvantage is that stakeholders might view reports based on an internal audit as less than credible, because the company would have an interest in casting itself and its suppliers in a favorable light.

A second option is to hire another organization to carry out the audit and report back to the company. This is called an *external audit* or a *third-party audit* because it is carried out by someone who does not work for the company or the managers of the factories that produce its goods. External audits may be carried out by an organization (such as the Fair Labor Association) that specializes in a particular set of standards, or by one that will work with any standard specified by the company. For example, the International Center for Corporate Accountability (ICCA) is an independent auditing firm that conducts audits on behalf of corporate clients. The ICCA conducted an investigation of toy product safety in China, as discussed in the Mattel case at the end of the book. Recently, a number of big accounting firms have developed specialized services in which they will conduct not a financial audit, which is their traditional specialty, but rather a social or environmental audit for clients. The advantage of an external audit is that it is often perceived as more objective and reliable by stakeholders. The audited company may find, however, that the information is delayed, and it does not directly control the quality of the audit.

---

[23] "Closing the Gap: Quality and Standards in Ethical Supply Chains," *International Trade Forum Magazine,* March 2010. The Gap's corporate social responsibility reports are available at *www.thegap.com.*

Finally, an emerging approach to auditing involves bypassing the factory inspection process entirely and, instead, crowd-sourcing information directly from workers using their mobile phones. In this approach, rather than relying on inspectors—who may be deceived by factory managers who want conditions to appear better than they really are—workers provide information directly by responding to questions generated by a recorded voice on their mobile phones when they are away from work. For example, LaborVoices, a recently established social enterprise, has piloted such an approach in the garment industry in India.[24] Workers must trust the process and participate widely for crowd-sourced data to be reliable and useful.

Once a company has collected compliance data, using any one of these processes, the next step is to decide what to do with it. Most audits turn up at least some instances in which a company's global operations are not in compliance with the relevant expectations. For example, inspectors may uncover underage workers, violations of environmental commitments, or discriminatory hiring practices. When this happens, most companies try to work with suppliers to correct any problems. But, sometimes, a company will terminate a supplier if a supplier is unwilling to change or the deficiencies are egregious. For example, when The Gap's auditors found an unauthorized, makeshift factory operated by a subcontractor in India, where children were embroidering a product for GapKids, the company immediately canceled the order and banned the subcontractor from any future work. It also cooperated with a child welfare organization to care for the children and reunited them with their families.

In addition to acquiring information that can be used to improve a firm's operations and policies, or even terminate a business relationship, companies must decide if they want to report this information to others, and if so, how or to which stakeholders. This topic is described next.

Social and Environmental Reporting

When a company decides to publicize information collected in a social audit, this is called **corporate social reporting**. While there is a risk of incurring reputational damage from exposing any problems publicly, many companies see value in practicing **transparency**. The term transparency refers to a quality of complete clarity; a clear glass window, for example, is said to be transparent. When companies clearly and openly report their performance—financial, social, and environmental—to their various stakeholders, they are acting with transparency. One company that has raised the bar for transparency in social auditing is Freeport-McMoran Copper and Gold, one of the world's largest metal mining companies.

> In Indonesia, Freeport-McMoran operates the largest gold mine and the third-largest copper mine in the world. The company's mines there have long been criticized by human rights, shareholder, and environmental activists for abuses ranging from cooperation with the repressive military government to dumping toxic mining waste into rivers. The company responded by developing social and human rights policies and hiring an independent organization, the International Center for Corporate Accountability (ICCA), to carry out an audit of its Indonesian operations. ICCA's report, issued in 2005, revealed many problems, including some that surprised the company, such as the fact that its security personnel were serving as drivers for the Indonesian military. What shocked many observers then was that the company, instead of hiding the auditor's report, posted it to the web for all to see. Commented

---

[24] For more information, see *www.laborvoices.com*.

FIGURE 7.3

Trend in Corporate Social Reporting, 1993–Present

Source: *KPMG International Corporate Responsibility Reporting Survey 2011* at *www.kpmg.com.*

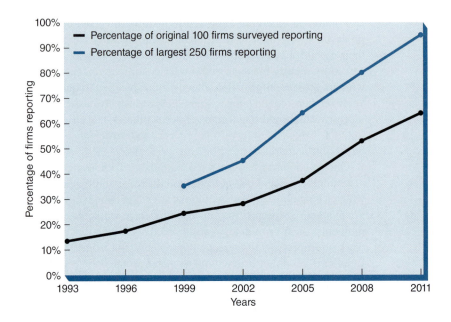

BusinessWeek, "The company's willingness to open up so wide is a major development in the corporate responsibility movement. Certainly, no other global mining or oil company has come close to such transparency, long a key demand by human rights groups."[25]

A 2011 survey of business firms by KPMG, an accounting and consulting firm, showed a steep increase in corporate social reporting in recent years, as shown in Figure 7.3.

KPMG found that 95 percent of the world's largest 250 companies disclosed environmental, social, and governance data, and 77 percent of those used the Global Reporting Initiative framework (discussed earlier in Figure 7.2). Of the original 100 firms surveyed since 1993, the number of firms reporting rose to an all-time high of 64 percent in 2011. KPMG concluded, "where [corporate citizenship and responsibility] reporting was once merely considered an 'optional but nice' activity, it now appears to have become virtually mandatory for most multinational companies, almost regardless of where they operate around the world."[26]

Since the early 2000s, the emergence of corporate social reporting regulation or governmental guidelines gained momentum in Europe and the United States, and to a more limited degree in Asia and Africa. In a 2010 investigation of global social performance and reporting that targeted 30 key countries,[27] a total of 142 country standards or laws were

[25] "Freeport's Hard Look at Itself: The Mining Giant's Gutsy Human-Rights Audit May Set a Standard for Multinationals," *BusinessWeek,* October 24, 2005, pp. 108ff; "So Much Gold, So Much Risk," *BusinessWeek,* May 29, 2006, pp. 52ff; and "Audit Report on Freeport McMoran's Mining Operation in Papua," *Free West Papua,* December 4, 2007, *www.freewestpapua.org.* The audit report may be found at SICCA's website at *www.icca-corporateaccountability.org.*

[26] *Carrots and Sticks—Promoting Transparency and Sustainability: An Update on Trends in Voluntary and Mandatory Approaches to Sustainable Reporting,* Project Partners: KPMG; University of Stellenbosch Business School, South Africa; United Nations Environment Programme; and, The Global Reporting Initiative, 2010, *www.governance.usb.ac.za.*

[27] These countries included Australia, Austria, Belgium, Brazil, Canada, Chile, Denmark, Ecuador, Finland, France, Germany, Hungary, India, Indonesia, Italy, Japan, Luxembourg, Mexico, Netherlands, Norway, Portugal, South Africa, South Korea, Spain, Sweden, Switzerland, the United Kingdom, and the United States. In addition, the CorporateRegister.com conducts an annual reporting awards competition based on a variety of criteria. See *www.corporateregister.com.*

found having some form of sustainability-related reporting requirement or guidance. Approximately two-thirds of these standards were classified as mandatory compliance for companies operating in the country. Sixteen other standards required some form of reporting at both the global and regional levels.

An emerging trend in corporate reporting is the integration of legally required financial information with social and environmental information into a single report. More than 15 percent of the 2,189 firms surveyed by KPMG in 2011 integrated their two reports—financial and social/environmental—into one report. However, KPMG comments that "while this has been a valuable stepping stone in building a holistic understanding of how [corporate reporting] impacts the business, we believe that greater value will be gained once both sets of information are treated as part of the company's comprehensive business performance reporting, both to internal management and external stakeholders."[28]

The International Integrated Reporting Council (IIRC) launched a new global effort in 2011 to provide a select group of companies the opportunity to demonstrate global leadership in the area of social reporting. Over 60 companies from around the world were invited to participate in the pilot program from a broad range of industry groups: AB Volvo (automobiles), CLP Holdings (utilities), DANONE (food producers), Marks and Spencer (retailers), Solvay (chemicals), Microsoft (software and computer services), HSBC (banking), and Gold Fields (mining) and from many countries: Australia, Belgium, Brazil, Canada, Chile, China, Denmark, France, Germany, Italy, Japan, Netherlands, Russia, South Africa, Spain, Sri Lanka, Sweden, Switzerland, the United Kingdom, and the United States. "The aim of the Integrated Reporting was to demonstrate the linkage between the organization's strategy, governance and financial performance and the social, environmental and economic context within which it operates."[29]

Why do companies publish these reports? According to one study, most firms (80 percent) are motivated by ethical concerns when publishing their social responsibility reports. Ethical drivers replaced economic considerations (80 percent versus 50 percent) as the primary motivator for publishing these reports, a complete reverse from a few years ago when economic considerations were viewed as the most important. Nearly two-thirds of the 250 firms worldwide reported that they engaged with their stakeholders in a structured way, up from 33 percent in 2005. One of the most pressing issues, climate change, was discussed in about 85 percent of the reports.[30]

Triple Bottom Line

Another approach to reporting corporate social performance is captured by the term **triple bottom line**.[31] Bottom line refers, of course, to the figure at the end of a company's financial statement that summarizes its earnings, after expenses. Triple bottom line reporting occurs when companies report to stakeholders not just their financial results—as in the traditional annual report to shareholders—but also their environmental and social impacts.

---

[28] Both quotations and the survey data are from *KPMG International Corporate Responsibility Reporting Survey 2011,* www.kpmg.com.

[29] See International Integrated Reporting Council's website at *theiirc.org* for a full description of this program.

[30] "Socially Responsible Investment Analysts Find More Large U.S. Companies Reporting on Social and Environmental Issues," Social Investment Research Analysts Network report, *www.kld.com.*

[31] One of the more popular books on this topic is John Elkington, *Cannibals with Forks: The Triple Bottom Line of 21st Century Business—Conscientious Commerce* (Gabriola Island, British Columbia: New Society Publishers, 1998). For a critique of triple bottom line accounting, see Wayne Norman and Chris MacDonald, "Getting to the Bottom of 'Triple Bottom Line,'" *Business Ethics Quarterly,* 2004, pp. 243–62.

Financial, social, and environmental results, taken together as an integrated whole, constitute a company's *triple* bottom line. Novo Nordisk, described in an opening example in this chapter, is one company that has adopted this approach.

As in the trend toward social reporting, firms in Europe have more quickly accepted triple bottom line than have those in the United States. European executives have seized on this notion as both a proactive way to provide stakeholders with increased transparency and a broader framework for decision making. A few American executives have also begun to see the appeal of the idea. "Triple bottom line reporting as it currently stands has its limitations, but it's a great way for companies to disclose meaningful nonfinancial information that impacts their financial results," said Sunny Misser, global and U.S. leader of PricewaterhouseCoopers' sustainability practice. "This is the time for companies, especially in the U.S., to seize the opportunity."[32]

An example of a firm embracing the triple bottom line approach to business operations and disclosure to the public is shown next.

> Triple bottom line is not just for large, multinational firms. Sanford Limited, a fishing company with more than 100 years of sustained growth, is devoted to the harvesting, farming, processing, storage, and marketing of quality New Zealand seafood.
>
> Sanford's first triple bottom line report was released in 2007 and made the following commitments: "to ensure that our operations are sustainable, to maximize positive social outcomes from both the employee and general community perspectives, and to maximize the economic growth and prosperity of the company for the benefits of shareholders, staff, customers, suppliers, and the general community." To further elaborate, Sanford provides an extensive performance scorecard emphasizing its commitments to areas of corporate governance, shareholder value, stakeholder satisfaction, employee orientation, and environmental performance. Sanford has "adopted a wider meaning to the term sustainability—achieving economic growth in an environmentally and socially responsible manner." Sanford Limited acknowledged and practices the interconnection between a concern for people, a pursuit of profitability, and sensitivity to the natural environment and report on their performance in the quest to balance these three business objectives.[33]

As social audits continue to develop and become more focused on the impact of the firm's performance affecting various stakeholders, the projected performance targets can be better assessed. By adjusting existing strategies or creating new ones as needed, firms will be able to "close the loop" on social performance assessment. As firms accept the importance of stakeholders in their quest for financial viability, companies have discovered and welcomed new approaches for disclosure of information such as social auditing, triple bottom line reporting, and other measures.

Summary

- Global corporate citizenship refers to putting a commitment to serving various stakeholders into practice by building stakeholder partnerships, discovering business opportunities in serving society, and transforming a concern for financial performance into a vision of integrated financial *and* social performance worldwide. Global corporate citizenship programs can be considered a strategic investment by the firm.

[32] "Europe Leads International Trend in 'Triple Bottom Line' Reporting," *Ethics Newsline*, Institute for Global Ethics, October 7, 2002, www.globalethics.org.

[33] All quotations and other information are taken from www.sanford.co.nz.

- One size does not fit all when it comes to managing corporate citizenship. Some firms centralize this function under one manager or department; while others decentralize the functions into multiple areas.

- Companies progress through five distinct stages as they develop as global corporate citizens; these are termed the elementary, engaged, innovative, integrated, and transforming stages. A particular company may be at more than one stage at once, as it may be progressing more quickly on some dimensions than on others.

- Many companies have experimented with systemic audits of their social, ethical, and environmental performance, measured against industry-wide performance expectations as well as auditing standards developed by global standard-setting organizations.

- An emerging trend is the practice of communicating social, environmental, and financial results to stakeholders through an integrated corporate report or in an integrated triple bottom line report.

Key Terms

auditing process, *150*	department of corporate	social audit, *147*
citizenship profile, *140*	citizenship, *142*	social equity, *147*
corporate social reporting, *151*	global corporate citizenship, *138*	transparency, *151*
		triple bottom line, *153*

Internet Resources

www.accountability.org.uk	AccountAbility: Institute for Social and Ethical Accountability
www.asianforumcsr.com	Asian Forum on Corporate Social Responsibility
www.bsr.org	Businesses for Social Responsibility
www.corporateresponsibility.net	Corporate Responsibility.Net
www.thecro.com	Corporate Responsibility Magazine
www.csreurope.org	CSR Europe
www.globalreporting.org	Global Reporting Initiative
www.iso.org	International Organization for Standardization
www.sa-intl.org	Social Accountability International
www.unglobalcompact.org	United Nations Global Compact

Discussion Case: *Apple's Supplier Code of Conduct and Foxconn's Chinese Factories*

In March 2012, the Fair Labor Association (FLA) released the results of an independent, month-long investigation, commissioned by Apple, on labor conditions at three enormous Chinese factories where the company's iPhones, iPads, and other popular consumer electronics were manufactured. The FLA, a nongovernment organization committed to promoting fair labor practices globally, found a number of serious violations of Apple's supplier code of conduct, as well of its own standards. Among the key findings of the audit were these:

- During peak production periods, all three factories, which were operated by the Taiwanese firm Foxconn, had exceeded the mandated limit of 60 hours of work per week, and many employees had been required to work more than seven days in a row.
- Fourteen percent of workers had not received fair pay for overtime. Workers were paid in 30-minute increments, so if an employee worked 55 minutes of overtime, for example, she would be paid for one half hour, not for the full period worked.
- Almost two-thirds of workers said that their pay did not meet their basic needs. Average wages at Foxconn's plants, the report said, were about $426 to $455 a month, including overtime.
- Almost half said they had experienced an accident or injury at work or had personally witnessed one. Many workers said they were in pain by the end of their workday.

Particularly worrisome was the FLA's discovery that Foxconn had instructed employees on how to respond to questions during earlier audits conducted by Apple, using what the FLA called a "cheat sheet" to avoid detection of code violations.

At the time of the report, Apple was riding a wave of business success, lifted by a series of innovative products and services. In 2012, Apple was the largest publicly traded company in the world by market capitalization, with revenues exceeding those of Google and Microsoft combined. The company directly employed more than 60,000 people and operated more than 350 stores in 10 countries, as well as its iTunes online music store. *Fortune* magazine had named Apple the most admired company in the world for four years in a row.

But there was a dark side to the company's success. Since the 1990s, Apple had outsourced almost all of its manufacturing, mostly to China. The company's biggest supplier was Foxconn, which by 2012 had become the largest manufacturer of consumer electronics in the world. Foxconn's facility in Shenzhen, China—one of three audited by the FLA—operated like a good-sized city, with its own dormitories, cafeterias, hospital, swimming pool, and stores. In its complex of factories, 300,000 workers—many of them young women and men from rural areas—churned out electronics for Sony, Dell, IBM, and other major brands, as well as Apple.

In 2006, a British newspaper ran a story alleging mistreatment of workers at the Shenzhen facility. Apple investigated and found some violations of its supplier code of conduct, which it had introduced in 2005. The following year, the company published its first annual supplier responsibility progress report. By 2011, Apple had inspected nearly 400 suppliers and had terminated 11 for serious violations.

In 2010, a series of developments focused a fresh spotlight on harsh conditions in Foxconn's factories. In a few short months, nine workers committed suicide by throwing themselves from the upper floors of company dormitories. (Foxconn responded by putting up nets to catch jumpers, raising wages, and opening a counseling center.) In 2011, two separate explosions at factories where iPads were being made (one was Foxconn's facility in Chengdu), apparently caused by a buildup of combustible aluminum dust, injured 77 and killed four. At Wintek, another Chinese supplier, 137 workers were sickened after using a toxic chemical called n-hexane to clean iPhone screens.

In January 2012, the public radio show *This American Life* broadcast a feature by monologist Mike Daisey about his interviews with workers leaving their shifts at Foxconn's Shenzhen facility, which related in dramatic fashion their disturbing stories. Although Daisey's piece was later criticized for not being entirely factual, it prompted some listeners to launch a petition drive on *www.change.org* that quickly garnered more than a quarter million signatures calling on Apple to protect workers that made their iPhones.

Just one week later, Apple announced it had joined the Fair Labor Association, the first electronics company to do so. The FLA, founded in 1999, was a nonprofit alliance of companies, universities, and human rights activists committed to ending sweatshop conditions. At Apple's request and with the company's financial support, the FLA immediately undertook the most extensive audit ever conducted of conditions in China's electronics supply chain. Auditors spent weeks inspecting Foxconn's three big Chinese factories, and 35,000 workers filled out anonymous questionnaires—on iPads—about their experiences.

In response to the FLA's findings, Apple issued a statement saying, "Our team has been working for years to educate workers, improve conditions and make Apple's supply chain a model for the industry, which is why we asked the FLA to conduct these audits." For its part, Foxconn agreed to reduce overtime from 80 to 36 hours per month by July 2013, while raising wages to prevent workers from losing income. It also agreed to pay workers retroactively for unpaid overtime and to improve health and safety protections. "That's a major commitment," said the head of the FLA. "If Apple and Foxconn can achieve that, they will have set a precedent for the electronics sector."

Sources: "The Forbidden City of Terry Guo," *The Wall Street Journal,* August 11, 2007; "The Man Who Makes Your iPhone," *Bloomberg Businessweek,* September 9, 2010; "Fair Labor Association Secures Commitment to Limit Workers' Hours, Protect Pay at Apple's Largest Supplier" [press release], March 29, 2012, *www.fairlabor.org;* "A Trip to the iFactory: 'Nightline' Gets an Unprecedented Glimpse Inside Apple's Chinese Core," February 20, 2012, *www.abcnews.go.com;* "How the U.S. Lost Out on iPhone Work," *The New York Times,* January 21, 2012; "Electronics Giant Vowing Reforms in China Plants," *The New York Times,* March 29, 2012; "Apple's Chief Puts Stamp on Labor Issues," *The New York Times,* April 1, 2012; and "Apple Moves from Laggard to Sector Leader on Transparency," March 30, 2012, *www.socialfunds.com.* Apple's Supplier Responsibility Progress Reports are available at *www.apple.com/supplierresponsibility.* The Fair Labor Association report is available at *www.fairlabor.org/transparency/complaints-investigations.*

Discussion Questions

1. Do you think that Apple has demonstrated global corporate citizenship, as defined in this chapter? Why or why not?

2. In its response to problems in its contractor factories, do you think Apple moved through the stages of corporate citizenship presented in this chapter, or not? Why do you think so?

3. What are the advantages and disadvantages to Apple of using its own company-specific supplier code of conduct, rather than a global code, such as those discussed in this chapter?

4. What are the advantages and disadvantages to Apple of using an independent third-party auditor, rather than rely solely on its own internal audits?

PART FOUR

Business and Public Policy

Business–Government Relations

Governments seek to protect and promote the public good and in these roles establish rules under which business operates in society. Therefore, a government's influence on business through public policy and regulation is a vital concern for managers. Government's relationship with business can be either cooperative or adversarial. Various economic or social assistance policies significantly affect society, in which businesses must operate. Many government regulations also impact business directly. Managers must understand the objectives and effects of government policy and regulation, both at home and abroad, in order to conduct business in an ethical and legal manner.

This Chapter Focuses on These Key Learning Objectives:

- Understanding why sometimes governments and business collaborate and other times work at arm's length from each other.
- Defining public policy and the elements of the public policy process.
- Explaining the reasons for regulation.
- Knowing the major types of government regulation of business.
- Identifying the purpose of antitrust laws and the remedies that may be imposed.
- Comparing the costs and benefits of regulation for business and society.
- Examining the conditions that affect the regulation of business in a global context.

In early 2009, the International Monetary Fund and the World Bank projected that the global economic crisis would result in an unprecedented worldwide economic recession. Governments around the world—Argentina, Australia, Canada, China, Germany, Ireland, Japan, Russia, Spain, the United Kingdom, and the United States, among others— responded in ways that significantly affected, and possibly will forever affect, the business–government relationship and the involvement of government in free market systems. Sometimes government stepped in to assist businesses and at other times the government itself needed assistance from the international community, as the following two examples show.

The United States decided to help the U.S. automobile industry and provided General Motors and Chrysler with $25 billion in loans. (Ford Motor Company did not seek bailout loans from the U.S. government.) The auto companies argued that the 37 percent drop in auto sales from a year earlier, or 400,000 fewer vehicles, would lead to a complete collapse without government assistance. These loans allowed them to keep an estimated three million workers on the job, provided them with operating cash, and enabled car-buying consumers to acquire auto loans. In 2010, General Motors declared that it had paid back the loans, in full and with interest. Yet, the U.S. government still owned about one-third of all GM shares of stock, taken as collateral, due to its devaluation. A year later, Chrysler paid back $11.2 billion of the government loans to allow Fiat, an Italian auto company, to acquire controlling interest in Chrysler. Some argued that the remaining $1.3 billion owed by Chrysler, which was absorbed by the U.S. government as debt, and the General Motors stock still held by the U.S. government were worth avoiding a Chrysler and General Motors bankruptcy, while others disagreed.

Throughout Europe the recession also had a serious impact. Greece had enjoyed a spending spree during the early 2000s, and the global economic crisis hit this country's economy particularly hard. Its dominant national party's leaders were ousted in an election, increasing social unrest spilled into the streets, and the country's economic instability began to negatively impact the European Union and the value of the euro. The Greek government needed help, and quickly. After two years of struggle, Greek government leaders negotiated a debt-restructuring deal with private lenders, who agreed to swap €61.5 billion, or $77 billion, in Greek debt for new bonds worth 75 percent less. A newly created troika—the European Union, the European Central Bank, and the International Monetary Fund—began to release funds from a second bailout package of nearly €120 billion, or $150 billion, to avoid uncontrolled default with ramifications that likely would have rippled through Europe. This enabled the Greek government to provide €18 billion, about $23 billion, to the country's four largest banks to guard against losses and improve the banks' ability to raise additional money. These measures provided some short-term relief, yet experts wondered if Greece and its banking community would ever fully recover.[1]

What prompted or compelled governments to become more involved in their nations' free market systems and heighten the level of government participation in the economy? How do these government's actions affect businesses and what they are permitted to do? Did government's involvement save some companies and allow them to re-enter the free market system, or did the action increase the dependence of business on government assistance? Were these efforts by the governments necessary and effective, or can this only be answered in time?

[1] "Chrysler Pays Back Rescue Loan," *The New York Times*, May 24, 2011, www.nytimes.com; "U.S. Loses $1.3 Billion in Exiting Chrysler," *CNN Money*, July 21, 2011, money.cnn.com; "The Auto Industry Bailout," *About.com—The U.S. Economy*, March 28, 2012, useconomy.about.com; "A Bailout Success?" *Times Free Press*, May 11, 2012, timesfreepress.com; "Greece," *New York Times Topics*, May 22, 2012, topics.nytimes.com; and "Largest Greek Banks to Receive Financing," *The New York Times*, May 22, 2012, www.nytimes.com.

Governments create the conditions that make it possible for businesses to compete in the modern economy. As shown in the opening examples, governments can act in dramatic ways to prevent the failure of banks, stimulate job creation, and promote lending. In good times and bad, government's role is to create and enforce the laws that *balance* the relationship between business and society. Governments become involved when unintended costs of manufacturing a product are imposed on others and government is needed to control or redirect these costs, or when the confidence in the country's stock market or financial services industry drops to the point where a recession impedes productivity and economic growth. Governments also hold the power to grant or refuse permission for many types of business activity. Even the largest multinational companies, which operate in dozens of countries, must obey the laws and public policies of national governments.

This chapter considers the ways in which government actions impact business through the powerful twin mechanisms of public policy and regulation. The next chapter addresses the related question of actions business may take to influence the political process.

How Business and Government Relate

The relationship between business and government is dynamic and complex. The stability of a government can be shaky or solid, as shown in the opening examples. Even within a stable government, different individuals or groups can acquire or lose power through elections, the natural death of a public official, or other means. Understanding the government's authority and its relationship with business is essential for managers in developing their strategies and achieving their organization's goals.

Seeking a Collaborative Partnership

In some situations, government may work closely with business to build a collaborative partnership and seek mutually beneficial goals. They see each other as key partners in the relationship and work openly to achieve common objectives.

The basis for this cooperation may be at the core of the nation's societal values and customs. In some Asian countries, society is viewed as a collective family that includes both government and business. Thus, working together as a family leads these two powers to seek results that benefit both society and business. In Europe, the relationship between government and business often has been collaborative. European culture includes a sense of teamwork and mutual aid. Unions, for example, are often included on administrative boards with managers to lead the organization toward mutual goals through interactive strategies.

A crisis can sometimes join government and business forces, as described at the beginning of this chapter when the U.S. government stepped in to provide financial assistance to the automobile industry or when the Greek government took steps to bolster the country's failing banking system. In other situations, the government can provide subsidies, grants, or other forms of assistance to help businesses expand, stabilize, or fight off threats. For example, Partnerships for a Skilled Workforce merged government assistance with business employment and training needs. The National Conference of State Legislatures targeted transportation and offered businesses involved in the road construction industry with a toolkit on how to create a public–private partnership that could lead to being awarded public contracts to improve states' infrastructure and roadway systems.[2]

---

[2] See Partnerships for a Skilled Workforce at *pswinc.org* and the National Conference of State Legislatures at *ncsl.org*.

Working at Arm's Length

In other situations, government's goals and business's objectives are at odds, and these conflicts result in an adversarial relationship where business and government tend to work at arm's length from each other.[3] While General Motors was seeking government support, as discussed earlier, other businesses and industries were rejecting offers of government intervention and assistance, believing that they could weather the financial storm themselves and operate quite well without government meddling.

Small businesses also tend to dislike government regulation. In a 2011 Wells Fargo/Gallup small business poll, small business owners indicated that "complying with government regulation" was the number one problem they faced. Looking ahead to 2012, approximately one in three small business owners said they were very or moderately worried about staying in business, and "fewer government regulations" was listed as the third most important influence on their businesses' survival.[4]

> For nearly 40 years, William John Woods made wooden toys for children in his shop in Ogunquit, Maine. He proudly reported that no child had ever been hurt by one of his small boats, cars, helicopters, or rattles. But the recent scandal involving the manufacturing of toys in China led to a massive recall in the United States, as detailed in the Mattel and Toy Safety case at the end of the book. This resulted in the Consumer Product Safety Improvement Act in 2008, which would have put Woods out of business. Woods explained that the new requirements for extensive testing for toxic materials in toys would cost him an additional $400 per toy, a cost he simply could not afford. "I use beeswax. The law was targeted at large toymakers using lead. There was no exclusion for benign [nontoxic] products." Woods and other small business toymakers challenged the new legislation, and the Consumer Product Safety Commission pledged to consider an exemption for certain toys in an effort to "have enough flexibility to address the legitimate concerns of toy handicrafters while still upholding the new law."[5]

Why do businesses sometimes welcome government regulation and involvement in the private sector, and other times oppose it? Companies often prefer to operate without government constraints, which can be costly or restrict innovation. But regulations can also help business, by setting minimum standards that all firms must meet, building public confidence in the safety of a product, creating a fair playing field for competition, or creating barriers to entry to maintain a business's competitive advantage. How a specific company reacts to a specific government policy often depends on their assessment of whether they would be helped or hurt by that rule.

In short, the relationship between government and business can range from one of cooperation to one of conflict, with various stages in between. Moreover, this relationship is constantly changing. A cooperative relationship on one issue does not guarantee cooperation on another issue. In some countries the stability of a particular form of government may appear to be quite shaky and signal to businesses to be wary of the potential for change. However, in other countries the form of government appears static yet unexpected changes in government or rulers may occur without warning. The business–government relationship is one that requires managers to keep a careful eye trained toward significant

---

[3] The "collaborative partnership" and "at arm's length" models for business–government relations is discussed in "Managing Regulation in a New Era," *McKinsey Quarterly*, December 2008, www.mckinseyquarterly.com.

[4] "Government Regulations at Top of Small-Business Owners' Problem List," *Gallup Poll*, October 24, 2011, www.gallup.com.

[5] "Burden of Safety Law Imperils Small Toymakers," *The New York Times*, October 31, 2009, www.nytimes.com.

forces that might alter this relationship or to promote forces that may encourage a positive business–government relationship.[6]

Legitimacy Issues

When dealing with a global economy, business may encounter governments whose authority or right to be in power is questioned. Political leaders may illegally assume lawmaking or legislative power, which can become economic power over business. Elections can be rigged, or military force can be used to acquire governmental control.

Business managers may be challenged with the dilemma of doing business in such a country where their business dealings would support this illegitimate power. Sometimes, they may choose to become politically active, or refuse to do business in this country until a legitimate government is installed.

Businesses can also influence the ability of a government leader or group of leaders to maintain political power. For example, companies can decide to withdraw operations from a country, as many U.S. firms did from South Africa in the 1970s to protest the practice of apartheid (institutionalized racial segregation). Some believe that the economic isolation of South Africa contributed to the eventual collapse of the apartheid regime. Governments may also order companies not to conduct business in another country because of a war, human rights violations, or lack of a legitimate government. These orders are called *economic sanctions.* As of 2011, the United States had imposed economic sanctions on Kuwait, Lebanon, Libya, Qatar, Saudi Arabia, Syria, the United Arab Emirates, and the Republic of Yemen because of political and human rights concerns. Iran's status on this list was under review by the Department of Defense.[7]

Government's Public Policy Role

Government performs a vital and important role in modern society. Although vigorous debates occur about the proper size of programs government should undertake, most people agree that a society cannot function properly without some government activities. Citizens look to government to meet important basic needs. Foremost among these are safety and protection provided by homeland security, police, and fire departments. These are collective or public goods, which are most efficiently provided by government for everyone in a community. In today's world, governments are also expected to provide economic security and essential social services, and to deal with the most pressing social problems that require collective action, or public policy.

Public policy is a plan of action undertaken by government officials to achieve some broad purpose affecting a substantial segment of a nation's citizens. Or as the late U.S. Senator Patrick Moynihan said, "Public policy is what a government chooses to do or not to do." In general, these ideas are consistent. Public policy, while differing in each nation, is the basic set of goals, plans, and actions that each national government follows in achieving its purposes. Governments generally do not choose to act unless a substantial segment of the public is affected and some public purpose is to be achieved. This is the essence of the concept of governments acting in the public interest.

The basic power to make public policy comes from a nation's political system. In democratic societies, citizens elect political leaders who can appoint others to fulfill defined public functions ranging from municipal services (e.g., water supplies, fire protection)

---

[6] See George Lodge, *Comparative Business–Government Relations* (Englewood Cliffs, NJ: Prentice Hall, 1990).

[7] For the 2011 country boycott list, see CPA Global Tax Blog at *cpaglobaltax.wordpress.com.*

to national services, such as public education or homeland security. Democratic nations typically spell out the powers of government in the country's constitution.

Another source of authority is *common law*, or past decisions of the courts, the original basis of the U.S. legal system. In nondemocratic societies, the power of government may derive from a monarchy (e.g., Saudi Arabia), a military dictatorship (e.g., Eritrea or Zimbabwe), or religious authority (e.g., the mullahs in Iran). These sources of power may interact, creating a mixture of civilian and military authority. The political systems in Russia, Libya, Tunisia, and other nations have undergone profound changes in recent times. And democratic nations can also face the pressures of regions that seek to become independent nations exercising the powers of a sovereign state, as does Canada with Quebec.

Elements of Public Policy

The actions of government in any nation can be understood in terms of several basic elements of public policy. These are inputs, goals, tools, and effects.

Public policy inputs are external pressures that shape a government's policy decisions and strategies to address problems. Economic and foreign policy concerns, domestic political pressure from constituents and interest groups, technical information, and media attention all play a role in shaping national political decisions. For example, a growing recognition of the dangers of cell phone use—especially texting—while driving has pressured many state and local governments to ban or regulate their use by drivers.

> According to a National Highway Traffic Safety Administration study released in December 2011, at any given time, 660,000 drivers were holding phones to their ears. Nearly 15 people reportedly died each day in the United States in crashes that involved distracted driving (which included using a cell phone, texting, eating, drinking, and talking with passengers) and another 1,200 people were injured. Deborah Hersman, chairwoman of the National Transportation Safety Board, linked cell phone use while driving to an addiction. "Addiction to those devices is a very good way to think about it. It's not unlike smoking. We have to get to a place where it's not in vogue anymore, where people recognize it's harmful and there's a risk and it's not worth it."[8]

The practice of texting on cell phones creates an even greater risk to drivers and others. Senator Charles Schumer of New York explained, "Studies show [texting while driving] is far more dangerous than talking on a phone while driving or driving while drunk, which is astounding." Christine Yager, a researcher at the Texas Transportation Institute, noted,"Our findings suggest that response times are even slower than what we originally thought. Texting while driving basically doubles a driver's reaction time and makes the driver less able to respond to sudden roadway dangers, if a vehicle were to make a sudden stop in front of them or if a child was to run across the road."[9]

Government bodies—legislatures, town councils, regulatory agencies—need to consider all relevant inputs in deciding whether or not to take action, and if so, what kind of action.

Public policy goals can be broad (e.g., full employment) and high-minded (equal opportunity for all) or narrow and self-serving. National values, such as freedom, democracy,

---

[8] "U.S. Safety Board Urges Cellphone Ban for Drivers," *The New York Times*, December 13, 2011, *www.nytimes.com;* and "Reframing the Debate over Using Phones behind the Wheel," *The New York Times*, December 17, 2011, *www.nytimes.com.* Also see "Traffic Safety Facts: Distracted Driving 2009," National Highway Traffic Safety Administration report, DOT HS 811379.

[9] "Texting while driving dangerous, study confirms: How dangerous?" *CBS News—Health Pop*, October 6, 2011, *www.cbsnews.com.*

and a fair chance for all citizens to share in economic prosperity, have led to the adoption of civil rights laws and economic assistance programs for those in need. Narrow goals that serve special interests are more apparent when nations decide how tax legislation will allocate the burden of taxes among various interests and income groups, or when public resources, such as oil exploration rights or timber cutting privileges, are given to one group or another. Whether the goals are broad or narrow, for the benefit of some or the benefit of all, most governments should ask, "What public goals are being served by this action?" For example, the rationale for a government policy to regulate cell phone usage while driving has to be based on some definition of public interest, such as preventing harm to others, including innocent drivers, passengers, and pedestrians.

> The goal of cell phone regulations is to prevent deaths and serious injuries resulting from calling or text messaging while driving. However, some members of the public have insisted on their right to use their phones in their vehicles. Traveling salespersons, for example, depend on their phones as an important tool of the job. Some regulations have addressed this by permitting drivers to use hands-free devices that enable them to keep their hands on the wheel. But some government safety experts have disagreed, saying, "When you are on a call, even if both hands are on the wheel, your head is in the call, and not your driving."

The issue of banning the use of cell phones, hand-held or hands-free, for the sake of making our roads a little safer for all, remains at the forefront. The goals of saving lives, reducing injuries, and eliminating health care costs might justify some form of cell phone regulation. The policy decision would depend, in part, on whether the benefits of the regulation are greater or less than the costs that would be imposed on the public.

Governments use different *public policy tools* to achieve policy goals. The tools of public policy involve combinations of incentives and penalties that government uses to prompt citizens, including businesses, to act in ways that achieve policy goals. Governmental regulatory powers are broad and constitute one of the most formidable instruments for accomplishing public purposes.

> As federal action limiting cell phone use in the United States continued to stall, the public looked to state and local governments to ban the use of cell phones by drivers while operating their vehicles. The state of New York passed the first law banning cell phone use while driving in 2001. By 2012, nine other states (California, Connecticut, Delaware, Maryland, Nevada, New Jersey, Oregon, Washington, and West Virginia) and the District of Columbia, Guam, and the Virgin Islands have completely banned the use of cell phones while driving without a hands-free device. The use of all cell phones by novice drivers was restricted in 31 states and the District of Columbia. Thirty-eight states, the District of Columbia, and Guam have banned text messaging for all drivers. And this is not just a public policy issue for Americans. More than 45 nations, including Australia, China, France, Germany, India, Israel, Japan, Russia, Spain, Taiwan, and the United Kingdom ban calling while driving.[10]

Public policy effects are the outcomes arising from government regulation. Some are intended; others are unintended. Because public policies affect many people, organizations, and other interests, it is almost inevitable that such actions will please some and displease others. Regulations may cause businesses to improve the way toxic substances

---

[10] For a complete listing of states and countries that have regulated cell phone use while driving, see *www.iihs.org/laws /cellphonelaws.aspx* and *cellular-news.com/car_bans*.

are used in the workplace, thus reducing health risks to employees. Yet other goals may be obstructed as an unintended effect of compliance with such regulations. For example, when health risks to pregnant women were associated with exposure to lead in the workplace, some companies removed women from those jobs. This action was seen as a form of discrimination against women that conflicted with the goal of equal employment opportunity. The unintended effect (discrimination) of one policy action (protecting employees) conflicted head-on with the public policy goal of equal opportunity.

The debate over cell phone legislation was filled with conflicting predicted effects. The proponents obviously argued that the ban on cell phone use reduced accidents and saved lives. Opponents of such legislation pointed to numerous other distractions that were not banned, such as drivers reading the newspaper, eating, putting on makeup, or shaving. In a four-state study conducted by the Highway Loss Data Institute, a nonprofit organization funded by the auto insurance industry, researchers found no difference in collision claims in the four states that had banned cell phones before and after the bans took effect. It also found no differences in collision claim rates between states with and without cell phone bans. The study concluded that the issue was distracted drivers, not cell phones. "People have been driving distracted since cars were invented. Focusing on mobile phones isn't the same as focusing on distracted driving. Distraction is what has always caused car crashes and mobile phones don't appear to be adding to that," said a spokesperson for the Insurance Institute for Highway Safety. A study funded by AT&T found that the cost of lives saved by banning cell phones while driving was estimated to be about $2 billion, compared with about $25 billion in benefits lost, meaning a cell phone ban would cost society about $23 billion.[11]

As the cell phone safety examples illustrate, managers must try to be aware of the public policy inputs, goals, tools, and effects relevant to regulation affecting their business.

Types of Public Policy

Public policies created by governments are of two major types: economic and social. Sometimes these types of regulation are distinct from each other and at other times they are intertwined.

Economic Policies

One important kind of public policy directly concerns the economy. The term **fiscal policy** refers to patterns of government collecting and spending funds that are intended to stimulate or support the economy. The recent actions by the U.S. government to provide loans and other financial assistance to troubled automobile, banking, and insurance companies—sometimes referred to as "bailouts"—are examples of fiscal policies. So were recent temporary reductions in Social Security payroll deductions, designed to stimulate the economy by putting more money in people's wallets. Governments spend money on many different activities. Local governments employ teachers, trash collectors, police, and firefighters. State governments typically spend large amounts of money on roads, social services, and parklands. National governments spend large sums on military defense, international relationships, and hundreds of public works projects such as road building. During the Great Depression of the 1930s, public works projects employed large numbers of people,

---

[11] "Hello? Cell Phones Cause Crashes," *Wired News,* December 2, 2002, www.wired.com/news/wireless; "Mobile Phone Use Doesn't Cause More Car Crashes: US Study," *Cnet Australia,* February 2, 2010, www.cnet.com.au; and "Study: No Evidence Cell Phone Bans Reduce Crashes," *Fox News,* July 7, 2011, www.foxnews.com.

put money in their hands, and stimulated consumption of goods and services. Today, fiscal policy remains a basic tool to achieve prosperity.

By contrast, the term **monetary policy** refers to policies that affect the supply, demand, and value of a nation's currency. The worth, or worthlessness, of a nation's currency has serious effects on business and society. It affects the buying power of money, the stability and value of savings, and the confidence of citizens and investors about the nation's future. This, in turn, affects the country's ability to borrow money from other nations and to attract private capital. In the United States, the Federal Reserve Bank—known as the Fed—plays the role of other nations' central banks. By raising and lowering the interest rates at which private banks borrow money from the government, the Fed influences the size of the nation's money supply and the value of the dollar. During the recent economic downturn, the Fed's action to lower interest rates nearly to zero—an example of a monetary policy—was intended to stimulate borrowing and help the economy get moving again.

Other forms of economic policy include *taxation policy* (raising or lowering taxes on business or individuals), *industrial policy* (directing economic resources toward the development of specific industries), and *trade policy* (encouraging or discouraging trade with other countries).

Social Assistance Policies

The last century produced many advances in the well-being of people across the globe. The advanced industrial nations have developed elaborate systems of social services for their citizens. Developing economies have improved key areas of social assistance (such as health care and education) and will continue to do so as their economies grow. International standards and best practices have supported these trends. Many of the **social assistance policies** that affect particular stakeholders are discussed in subsequent chapters of this book.

> One area often addressed by social assistance policies is housing. Many governments have programs that subsidize rent payments, guarantee home loans, or provide housing directly for low-income citizens or military veterans. For example, Brazil's *Minha Casa, Minha Vida* ("My House, My Life") program has built one million homes since 2009 for low-income families. Mortgages are provided by a government-affiliated bank. Many of the first units built by the program were intended to house families displaced by development for the World Cup and Olympic Games in Rio de Janeiro.[12]

One particularly important social assistance policy—health care—has been the focus for concern on the international front and for national and state lawmakers. As discussed later in this chapter, the U.S. government has wrestled with the need for better health care for its citizens and the challenge of how to pay for this care.

Government Regulation of Business

Societies rely on government to establish rules of conduct for citizens and organizations called *regulations.* **Regulation** is a primary way of accomplishing public policy, as described in the previous section. Because government operates at so many levels (federal, state, local), modern businesses face complex webs of regulations. Companies often require lawyers, public affairs specialists, and experts to monitor and manage the interaction with government. Why do societies turn to more regulation as a way to solve problems? Why not

---

[12] "Minha Casa, Minha Vida Development," *The Rio Times,* May 17, 2011, *riotimesonline.com.*

just let the free market allocate resources, set prices, and constrain socially irresponsible behavior by companies? There are a variety of reasons.

Market Failure

One reason is what economists call **market failure**, that is, the marketplace fails to adjust prices for the true costs of a firm's behavior. For example, a company normally has no incentive to spend money on pollution control equipment if customers do not demand it. The market fails to incorporate the cost of environmental harm into the business's economic equation, because the costs are borne by someone else. In this situation, government can use regulation to force all competitors in the industry to adopt a minimum antipollution standard. The companies will then incorporate the extra cost of compliance into the product price. Companies that want to act responsibly often welcome carefully crafted regulations because they force competitors to bear the same costs.

> The issue of global warming, caused in part by greenhouse gas emissions, is such a big issue that no single firm or industry can afford to take the first step and try to control it in order to minimize the harm to our planet and environment. World leaders have met periodically since 1995 under the auspices of the United Nations to negotiate and update a convention (treaty) to limit countries' greenhouse gas emissions. Many hope that this international agreement will create a path for businesses to follow to improve the health of our planet. While people may disagree on how to accomplish this important goal, the challenge is beyond what the marketplace can tackle and it requires some form of government intervention by many countries.

Negative Externalities

Governments also may act to regulate business to prevent unintended adverse effects on others. **Negative externalities**, or spillover effects, result when the manufacture or distribution of a product gives rise to unplanned or unintended costs (economic, physical, or psychological) borne by consumers, competitors, neighboring communities, or other business stakeholders. To control or reverse these costs, government may step in to regulate business action.

> As further described in a case study at the end of the book, patients taking Vioxx, a prescription pain medication made by Merck, became deeply concerned when evidence emerged of cardiovascular risk. The Drug Safety Oversight Board was established in 2005 to monitor Food and Drug Administration–approved medicines once they were on the market and to update physicians and patients with pertinent and emerging information on possible risks and benefits.[13]

Natural Monopolies

In some industries, **natural monopolies** occur. The electric utility industry provides an example. Once one company has built a system of poles and wires or laid miles of underground cable to supply local customers with electricity, it would be inefficient for a second company to build another system alongside the first. But once the first company has established its natural monopoly, it can then raise prices as much as it wishes because there is no competition. In such a situation, government often comes in and regulates prices and

---

[13] "FDA to Establish New Drug Oversight Board," *SFGate,* February 15, 2005, *www.sfgate.com.*

access. Other industries that sometimes develop natural monopolies include cable TV, broadband Internet service, software, and railroads.

Ethical Arguments

There is often an ethical rationale for regulation as well. As discussed in Chapter 4, for example, there is a utilitarian ethical argument in support of safe working conditions: It is costly to train and educate employees only to lose their services because of preventable accidents. There are also fairness and justice arguments for government to set standards and develop regulations to protect employees, consumers, and other stakeholders. In debates about regulation, advocates for and against regulatory proposals often use both economic and ethical arguments to support their views. Sometimes firms will agree to self-regulate their actions to head off more costly government-imposed regulatory reform, as shown in the following example.

> Consumer advocates took their battle directly to the food and beverage companies themselves since consumers were having great difficulty in determining which products were, in fact, healthy and which were not. The confusion occurred due to inconsistent labels and language used by the food and beverage companies to note the nutritional elements of their products. Responding to an antiobesity campaign led by First Lady Michelle Obama, business members of the Grocery Manufacturers Association and the Food Marketing Institute rolled out a voluntary food-package labeling program in 2011 to help consumers make healthier food choices. The new labels included both potentially harmful ingredients, such as sodium, calories, and fat, and beneficial nutrients—vitamins, minerals and protein. While controversy erupted whether the consumer would be able to make sense out of all this new information, the White House formally pronounced this effort "as a significant first step" to protect American consumers.[14]

Types of Regulation

Government regulations come in different forms. Some are directly imposed; others are more indirect. Some are aimed at a specific industry (e.g., banking); others, such as those dealing with job discrimination or pollution, apply to all industries. Some have been in existence for a long time—for example, the Food and Drug Act was passed in 1906— whereas others, such as the Wall Street Reform and Consumer Protection (or Dodd-Frank) Act of 2010, are of much more recent vintage. Just as public policy can be classified as either economic or social, so regulations can be classified in the same fashion.

Economic Regulations

The oldest form of regulation is primarily economic in nature. **Economic regulations** aim to modify the normal operation of the free market and the forces of supply and demand. Such modification may come about because the free market is distorted by the size or monopoly power of companies, or because the consequences of actions in the marketplace are thought to be undesirable. Economic regulations include those that control prices or wages, allocate public resources, establish service territories, set the number of participants, and ration resources. The decisions by the Federal Trade Commission (FTC) to prevent anticompetitive business practices, discussed later in this chapter, illustrate one kind of economic regulation. The U.S. Congress responded to the global recession, in part, by passing the **Dodd-Frank Act**, as discussed next.

---

[14] "Food Makers Devise Own Label Plan," *The New York Times*, January 24, 2011, *www.nytimes.com*.

The passage of the Dodd-Frank Act in 2010, heralded as the most comprehensive financial regulatory reform measure since the Great Depression, revolutionized many business activities. Among other things, the Dodd-Frank Act affected the oversight and supervision of financial institutions, provided for a new resolution procedure for large financial companies, created a new agency responsible for implementing and enforcing compliance with consumer financial laws, introduced more stringent regulatory capital requirements, effected significant changes in the regulation of over-the-counter derivatives, reformed the regulation of credit rating agencies, implemented changes to corporate governance and executive compensation practices, required registration of advisers to certain private funds, and effected significant changes in the securities markets.[15]

The role of the Dodd-Frank Act in regulating a complex financial product called derivatives is explored in the discussion case at the end of this chapter.

Antitrust: A Special Kind of Economic Regulation

One important kind of economic regulation occurs when government acts to preserve competition in the marketplace, thereby protecting consumers. **Antitrust laws** prohibit unfair, anticompetitive practices by business. (The term *antitrust law* is used in the United States; most other countries use the term *competition law*.) For example, if a group of companies agreed among themselves to set prices at a particular level, this would generally be an antitrust violation. In addition, a firm may not engage in **predatory pricing**, the practice of selling below cost to drive rivals out of business. If a company uses its market dominance to restrain commerce, compete unfairly, or hurt consumers, then it may be found guilty of violating antitrust laws.

For example, in 2009 Intel, the global leader in computer chip manufacturing, agreed to pay $1.25 billion to rival Advanced Micro Devices to settle antitrust and patent disputes originating in Europe. The European Union, which brought the charges against Intel, alleged that the firm paid computer makers and retailers to postpone, cancel, or avoid AMD products entirely, thus denying customers a choice for the chips they wanted in their computers. Intel's settlement also resolved a federal antitrust case pending in Delaware and two antitrust charges against Intel in Japan. AMD also agreed to withdraw all regulatory complaints worldwide against Intel. In a joint statement, the companies said, "While the relationship between the two companies has been difficult in the past, this agreement ends the legal disputes and enables the companies to focus all of our efforts on product innovation and development."[16]

The two main antitrust enforcement agencies are the Antitrust Division of the U.S. Department of Justice and the Federal Trade Commission. Both agencies may bring suits against companies they believe to be guilty of violating antitrust laws. They also may investigate possible violations, issue guidelines and advisory opinions for firms planning mergers or acquisitions, identify specific practices considered to be illegal, and negotiate informal settlements out of court. Antitrust regulators have been active in prosecuting price

[15] "The Dodd-Frank Act: A Cheat Sheet," Morrison & Foerster, n.d., *www.mofo.com*; "Dodd-Frank Law: Too Big to Succeed," *Chicago Sun Times*, May 15, 2012, *www.suntimes.com*; and "Dodd-Frank Fulfills a Century-Old Vision for Regulation," *American Banker*, May 24, 2012, *www.americanbanker.com*.

[16] "Europe Fines Intel a Record $1.45 Billion in Antitrust Case," *The New York Times*, May 14, 2009, *www.nytimes.com*; and "Intel Will Pay $1.25 Billion to Settle Disputes with Rival," *The New York Times*, November 13, 2009, *www.nytimes.com*.

fixing, blocking anticompetitive mergers, and dealing with foreign companies that have violated U.S. laws on fair competition.

> The Justice Department's head, Christine A. Varney, publicly stated in 2009 that she would restore an aggressive enforcement policy against corporations that use their market dominance to elbow out competitors or to keep them from gaining market share, a significant turnaround from the tone set during the Bush administration during the mid-2000s. In 2011, the U.S. Justice Department sued to block AT&T's proposed $39 billion takeover of T-Mobile USA, a move that jeopardized AT&T's goal of becoming the largest U.S. cell phone carrier. The case was scheduled for trial in 2012. The U.S. government argued that combining the second and fourth largest cell phone companies in the United States would harm competition and likely raise prices for consumers. The antitrust challenge came five months after AT&T announced its takeover plans of T-Mobile.[17]

If a company is found guilty of antitrust violations, what are the penalties? The government may levy a fine—sometimes a large one, such as the $100 million penalty paid by Archer Daniels Midland for fixing the price of lysine and citric acid. In the case of private lawsuits, companies may also be required to pay damages to firms or individuals they have harmed. In addition, regulators may impose other, nonmonetary remedies. A *structural remedy* may require the breakup of a monopolistic firm; this occurred when AT&T was broken up by government order in 1984. A *conduct remedy,* more commonly used, involves an agreement that the offending firm will change its conduct, often under government supervision, as was the case with Intel shown above. For example, a company might agree to stop certain anticompetitive practices. Finally, an *intellectual property remedy* is used in some kinds of high-technology businesses; it involves disclosure of information to competitors. All these are part of the regulator's arsenal.

Antitrust regulations cut across industry lines and apply generally to all enterprises. Other economic regulations, such as those governing stock exchanges, may be confined to specific industries and companies.

Social Regulations

Social regulations are aimed at such important social goals as protecting consumers and the environment and providing workers with safe and healthy working conditions. Equal employment opportunity, protection of pension benefits, and health care for citizens are other important areas of social regulation. Unlike the economic regulations mentioned above, social regulations are not limited to one type of business or industry. Laws concerning pollution, safety and health, health care, and job discrimination apply to all businesses; consumer protection laws apply to all relevant businesses producing and selling consumer goods.

> An example of a social regulation is federal rules for automobile emissions and mileage standards. Beginning in 2011, the federal government rolled out new standards to be applied to automobiles made between 2011 and 2025. By 2025, all new cars and trucks sold in the United States must have a performance equivalency of 54.5 miles per gallon while reducing greenhouse emission gases to 163 grams per mile. These new requirements could save families an estimated $8,200 in fuel costs over the lifetime of the vehicle, relative to a 2010 standard. In addition to

---

[17] "Administration Plans to Strengthen Antitrust Rules," *The New York Times*, May 11, 2009, *www.nytimes.com*; and "U.S. Sues to Stop AT&T Deal," *The Wall Street Journal*, September 1, 2011, *online.wsj.com*.

Exhibit 8.A

In 2010, led by President Obama, Congress passed the Affordable Care Act, often referred to as "Obamacare." The basic purpose of the law was to hold insurance companies accountable for their costs and services to their customers, lower the rising health care costs, provide Americans with greater freedom and control over their health care choices, and ultimately improve the quality of health care in America. Its provisions would be rolled out over 10 years. In 2010, the government began giving subsidies to small businesses that offered health coverage to employees, insurance companies were barred from denying coverage to children with pre-existing illnesses, and children were permitted to stay on their parents' insurance policies until age 26.

The health care reform law aroused strong passions on both sides. Proponents of the law argued that the more than 5.1 million people on Medicare would save over $3 billion in prescription drug costs, 105 million Americans would no longer have lifetime dollar limits on their health care coverage, and approximately 54 million Americans would receive greater preventative medical coverage. Health care fraud would decline by $4.1 billion annually due to new fraud detection measures, and 2.5 million young adults would retain health care coverage under their parents' plan. Most importantly, most Americans would now have health insurance coverage.

But, opponents challenged the new law as filled with myths, untruths, and harmful consequences. Some believed that the act would do nothing to bring down the cost of health care. Business leaders worried that the burden of providing their employees with health care insurance would result in bankruptcy or cause employers to reduce the level of health care coverage for their employees. Many worried that the mandate infringed on individual rights—including the right to go without health insurance if they chose. Several states sued, saying the law violated the constitution.

In 2012, the U.S. Supreme Court upheld the act as constitutional (only one small portion of the act was ruled unconstitutional). A majority of the justices ruled that it was within Congress's powers to impose a tax on those who failed to acquire health insurance as mandated by the act, allowing the Obama administration to move ahead with implementing other provisions of the Affordable Care Act.

Sources: "What's in the Bill," *The Wall Street Journal*, March 22, 2010, *online.wsj.com;* "Get the Facts Straight on Health Reform—A More Secure Future," *The White House*, n.d., *www.whitehouse.gov;* "Federal Judge Rules That Health Law Violates Constitution," *The New York Times*, January 31, 2011, *www.nytimes.com;* "Health Care Law's Day in Court," *Pittsburgh Post-Gazette*, March 25, 2012, *www.post-gazette.com;* and "Supreme Court Upholds Mandate as Tax," *The Wall Street Journal*, June 28, 2012, *online.wsj.com.*

cost-savings and environmental benefits, this social regulation also would help the country achieve its goal of less dependence on foreign oil.[18]

The most significant social regulation in the United States since the 1960s was the comprehensive reform of health care coverage passed by Congress in 2009. It is described in Exhibit 8.A.

Who regulates? Normally, for both economic and social regulation, specific rules are set by agencies of government and by the executive branch, and may be further interpreted by the courts. Many kinds of business behavior are also regulated at the state level. Government regulators and the courts have the challenging job of applying the broad mandates of public policy.

Figure 8.1 depicts these two types of regulation—economic and social—along with the major regulatory agencies responsible for enforcing the rules at the federal level in the United States. Only the most prominent federal agencies are included in the chart. Individual states, some cities, and other national governments have their own array of agencies to implement regulatory policy.

---

[18] "President Obama Announced New Fuel Economy Standards," *The White House Blog*, July 29, 2011, *www.whitehouse .gov/blog.*

FIGURE 8.1 Types of Regulation and Regulatory Agencies

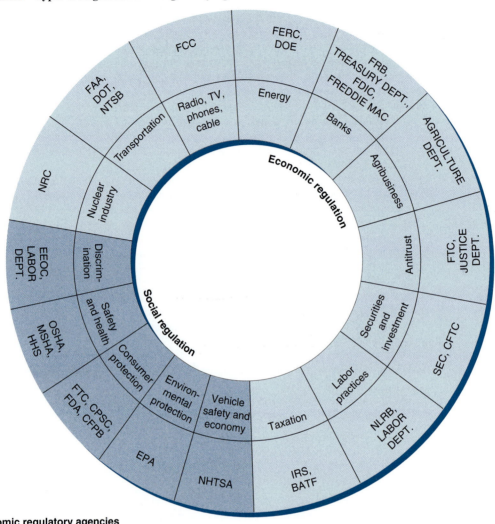

Economic regulatory agencies

NRC	Nuclear Regulatory Commission
FAA	Federal Aviation Administration
FCC	Federal Communications Commission
FERC	Federal Energy Regulatory Commission
FRB	Federal Reserve Board
CFTC	Commodity Futures Trading Commission
FREDDIE MAC	Federal Home Loan Mortgage Corporation
DOT	Department of Transportation

FTC	Federal Trade Commission
SEC	Securities and Exchange Commission
NLRB	National Labor Relations Board
IRS	Internal Revenue Service
BATF	Bureau of Alcohol, Tobacco, Firearms and Explosives
FDIC	Federal Deposit Insurance Corporation
DOE	Department of Energy
NTSB	National Transportation Safety Board

Social regulatory agencies

EEOC	Equal Employment Opportunity Commission
OSHA	Occupational Safety and Health Administration
MSHA	Mine Safety and Health Administration
FTC	Federal Trade Commission
HHS	Department of Health and Human Services

CPSC	Consumer Product Safety Commission
FDA	Food and Drug Administration
EPA	Environmental Protection Agency
NHTSA	National Highway Traffic Safety Administration
CFPB	Consumer Financial Protection Bureau

There is a legitimate need for government regulation in modern economies, but regulation also has problems. Businesses feel these problems firsthand, often because the regulations directly affect the cost of products and the freedom of managers to design their business operations. In the modern economy, the costs and effectiveness of regulation, as well as its unintended consequences, are serious issues that cannot be overlooked. Each is discussed below.

The Effects of Regulation

Regulation affects many societal stakeholders, including business. Sometimes the consequences are known and intended, but at other times unintended or accidental consequences emerge from regulatory actions. In general, government hopes that the benefits arising from regulation outweigh the costs.

The Costs and Benefits of Regulation

The call for regulation may seem irresistible to government leaders and officials given the benefits they seek, but there are always costs to regulation. An old economic adage says, "There is no free lunch." Eventually, someone has to pay for the benefits created.

An industrial society such as the United States can afford almost anything, including social regulations, if it is willing to pay the price. Sometimes the benefits are worth the costs; sometimes the costs exceed the benefits. The test of **cost-benefit analysis** helps the public understand what is at stake when new regulation is sought.

Figure 8.2 illustrates the increase in costs of federal regulation in the United States since the 1960s. Economic regulation has existed for many decades, and its cost has grown more slowly than social regulation. Social regulation spending reflects growth in such areas as environmental health, occupational safety, and consumer protection. The rapid growth of social regulation spending that occurred from 1970 until the late 1990s slowed considerably during the George W. Bush era of the first decade of the 21st century. As expected by many experts, with the significant increase in regulation under the Obama administration, the costs of regulation have risen since 2007.

FIGURE 8.2
Spending on U.S. Regulatory Activities

Source: Veronique de Rugy and Melinda Warren, "Expansion of Regulatory Budgets and Staffing Continues in the New Administration," *Regulatory Budget Report October 2009*, Table 1, Mercatus Center, *mercatus.org*.

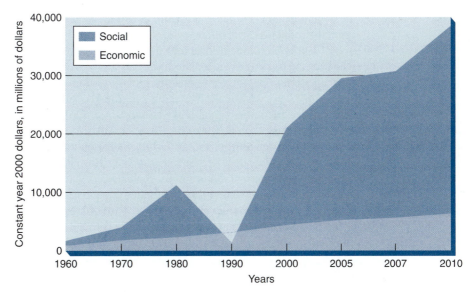

FIGURE 8.3

Staffing of U.S. Regulatory Activities

Source: de Rugy and Warren, Ibid., Table 2.

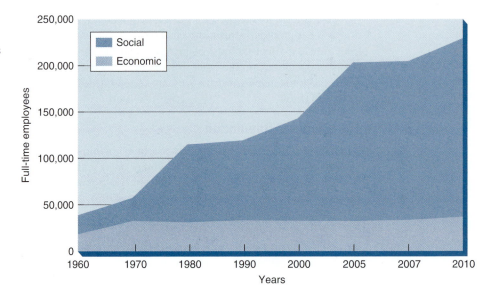

Economists Nicole Crain and Mark Crain issued a report sponsored by the Small Business Administration (SBA) in 2010 that calculated the cost to Americans of federal regulations—$1.75 trillion, about $15,000 per average American household. That was more than an average American paid in federal income taxes and almost double what the average family spent on housing, according to the report. The SBA also estimated that small businesses—those with fewer than 20 employees—paid an average of $10,585 per employee in regulatory costs or 35 percent more than paid by large businesses, those with more than 500 employees.[19]

Some economists felt that the high cost of regulation on business was worth it since the stakes were so high. Controlling environmental pollution and protecting worker and consumer safety, for example, benefit many citizens. How do the costs and benefits of regulation compare? The federal government's Office of Budget and Management reported that the annual benefits of major federal regulations from 2001 to 2011 ranged somewhere from $141 billion to $700 billion, while the estimated annual costs ranged from $43.3 billion to $67.3 billion. Although different methodologies produced different estimates, in all scenarios the benefits exceeded the costs.[20]

In addition to paying for regulatory programs, it takes people to administer, monitor, and enforce these regulations. Researchers at the Mercatus Center have documented staffing regulatory activities in the United States since the 1960s, as shown in Figure 8.3. In 1960, fewer than 40,000 federal employees monitored and enforced government regulations. Two decades later, in 1980, nearly 150,000 federal regulatory employees did so. In the early 1980s, President Reagan led a campaign to cut government regulation. This campaign continued during both of the Bush presidencies and the number of full-time federal employees dedicated to regulatory activities has modestly increased since the 1990s. As noted earlier, with the return to regulatory control and the addition of new funding and new agencies, the number of government employees at regulatory agencies increased between 2007 and 2010.

[19] "Red Tape Rises Again: Cost of Regulation Reaches $1.75 Trillion," *The Heritage Foundation Blog*, September 22, 2010, *blog.heritage.org;* and "The Cost of Doing Business in the U.S.," *The Wall Street Journal*, January 28, 2011, *online.wsj.com.*

[20] "Draft 2012 Report to Congress on the Benefits and Costs of Federal Regulations," *OIRA Report to Congress*, Office of Budget and Management, March 2012, *www.whitehouse.gov/omb.*

The United States has experimented with different forms of government regulation for more than 200 years, and experts have learned that not all government programs are effective in meeting their intended goals. With new regulations being added each year, redundancy is likely to occur. In 2011, President Obama ordered a massive investigation of overlapping and duplicative regulatory programs. He noted that there were 15 different agencies overseeing food-safety laws, more than 20 separate programs to help the homeless, and 80 programs for economic development. Senator Tom Coburn, who strongly supported this investigation, estimated that between $100 and $200 billion in duplicative spending would be uncovered.[21]

Although the Government Accountability Office, which undertook this exploration, did not release specific figures on spending overlap, it did report that there were 82 federal programs to improve teacher quality, 80 to help disadvantaged people with transportation, 47 for job training and employment, and 56 to help people understand finances. The GAO report outlined an extensive plan to overhaul the federal regulatory network to better serve society and to eliminate unnecessary spending.[22]

Continuous Regulatory Reform

The amount of regulatory activity often is cyclical—historically rising during some periods and declining during others. Businesses in the United States experienced a lessening of regulation in the early 2000s—*deregulation*—only to observe the return of regulatory activity around 2009 and continuing through the early 2010s—*reregulation*.

Deregulation is the removal or scaling down of regulatory authority and regulatory activities of government. Deregulation is often a politically popular idea. President Ronald Reagan strongly advocated deregulation in the early 1980s, when he campaigned on the promise to "get government off the back of the people." Major deregulatory laws were enacted beginning in 1975 when Gerald Ford was president and continued through the administrations of Jimmy Carter, Ronald Reagan, and George H.W. Bush, and returned during George W. Bush's administration. During these presidential administrations deregulation occurred in the commercial airlines, interstate trucking, railroads, and financial institutions industries. Some argued that when the 1933 Glass-Steagall Act was repealed in 1999 by the passage of the Financial Modernization Act, the lack of regulatory controls over the banking and securities industries led to the serious financial problems causing the economic recession that began circa 2007.

Deregulation has also occurred in Europe, especially in the arena of social regulation. In the United Kingdom, for example, the Approved Code of Practice (ACoP) governing various employee safety and health issues was downgraded to a "Guidance," a weaker form of regulatory control. In the Netherlands, the Ministry of Social Affairs proposed the deregulation of the Work Environment Act.[23]

Proponents of deregulation often challenge the public's desire to see government solve problems. This generates situations in which government is trying to deregulate in some areas while at the same time creating new regulation in others. **Reregulation** is the increase or expansion of government regulation, especially in areas where the regulatory activities had previously been reduced. The scandals that rocked corporate America in the early 2000s—and the failure or near-failure of a number of big commercial and investment banks

---

[21] For an interesting ethical analysis of this regulatory investigation, see Thomas Hemphill, "The Obama Administration's Regulatory Review Initiative: A 21st Century Federal Regulatory Initiative?" *Business and Society Review*, Summer 2012, pp. 185–95.

[22] "Billions in Bloat Uncovered in Beltway," *The Wall Street Journal*, March 1, 2011, *online.wsj.com*.

[23] From the Sixth European Work Hazards Conference, the Netherlands, *www.geocities.com/rainforest/8803/dereg1.html*.

in 2008—brought cries from many stakeholder groups for reregulation of the securities and financial services industries. As a result, the United States has seen much reregulation in the 2010s with the passage of laws and rules governing the financial services and health care industries, as discussed earlier. As in the United States, many governments around the world reasserted their regulatory authority over the banking industry in the aftermath of the global recession. The economic think tank McKinsey & Company described the worldwide return to regulation, or *reregulation,* in these words:

> Since September 2008, governments have assumed a dramatically expanded role in financial markets. Policymakers have gone to great lengths to stabilize them, to support individual companies whose failure might pose systemic risks, and to prevent a deep economic downturn. . . . In short, governments will have their hand in industry to an extent few imagined possible only recently.[24]

Regulation in a Global Context

International commerce unites people and businesses in new and complicated ways, as described in Chapter 6. U.S. consumers routinely buy food, automobiles, and clothing from companies located in Africa, Asia, Australia, Canada, Europe, and Latin America. Citizens of other nations do the same. As these patterns of international commerce grow more complicated, governments recognize the need to establish rules that protect the interests of their own citizens. No nation wants to accept dangerous products manufactured elsewhere that will injure its citizens, and no government wants to see its economy damaged by unfair competition from foreign competitors. These concerns provide the rationale for international regulatory agreements and cooperation.

In cases where businesses operate in multiple countries, regulations imposed in one jurisdiction can affect companies operating out of others.

> For example, in 2012, the European Union imposed a carbon emissions fee on all airlines flying in and out of EU airspace in an effort to limit greenhouse gas emissions, a serious environmental problem discussed in Chapter 10. The new rule went into effect on January 1, 2012, and within one month more than two dozen countries expressed their opposition to the EU's Emissions Trading System and the carbon-dioxide emissions fee. A spokesman for the Chinese Air Transport Association explained, "We and the Chinese government have repeatedly and clearly expressed our views on this policy, which are in line with those of the U.S." The Chinese Air Transport Association, which includes China's four largest airlines, issued a prohibition on its airline members from paying the EU emissions fee. A few months later, India joined the group of nations protesting the EU emission fee, which had grown to 26 nation members, and launched a threat toward the EU. "We will take retaliatory actions to counter steps taken by the EU. If Europe bans our carriers we will ban theirs as well." Nevertheless, the European Union "remains confident that Chinese [and other] airlines will comply with our legislation." Although the program was launched in January 2012, the payment of the fees was not due until 2013.[25]

---

[24] "Leading through Uncertainty," *McKinsey Quarterly*, December 2008, *www.mckinseyquarterly.com.*

[25] "China Bans Its Airlines from Paying EU Emissions Fee," *The Wall Street Journal*, February 6, 2012, *online.wsj.com;* and "India May Ban European Airlines on EU Emission Rule," *The Wall Street Journal*, May 25, 2012, *online.wsj.com.*

At other times, the issues themselves cut across national borders, so international regulation is needed. Sometimes, nations negotiate agreements directly with one another, and at other times they do so under the auspices of the United Nations or regional alliances. For example, the United Nations monitors international uses of nuclear power due to the great potential for harm to those living near nuclear power plants and based on the threat of converting this technology into nuclear weapons. The United Nations was called to Iran to investigate and determine if this country was developing enriched uranium that could be used for nuclear weaponry. While some enriched uranium was discovered, it was unclear if Iran was developing nuclear weapons. The U.N. investigation was ongoing in the hope that international pressure could be levied to deter Iran from creating a nuclear arsenal.[26]

Whether at the local, state, federal, or international levels, governments exert their control seeking to protect society through regulation. The significant challenge involves balancing the costs of this form of governance against the benefits received or the prevention of the harms that might occur if the regulation is not in place and enforced. Businesses have long understood that managing and, if possible, cooperating with the government regarding regulation generally leads to a more productive economic environment and financial health of the firm.

Summary

- Government's relationship with business ranges from collaborative to working at arm's length. This relationship often is tenuous, and managers must be vigilant to anticipate any change that may affect business and its operations.

- A public policy is an action undertaken by government to achieve a broad public purpose. The public policy process involves inputs, goals, tools or instruments, and effects.

- Regulation is needed to correct for market failure, overcome natural monopoly, and protect stakeholders who might otherwise be hurt by the unrestricted actions of business.

- Regulation can take the form of laws affecting an organization's economic operations (e.g., trade and labor practices, allocation of scarce resources, price controls) or focus on social good (e.g., consumer protection, employee health and safety, environmental protection).

- Antitrust laws seek to preserve competition in the marketplace, thereby protecting consumers. Remedies may involve imposing a fine, breaking up a firm, changing the firm's conduct, or requiring the disclosure of information to competitors.

- Although regulations are often very costly, many believe that these costs are worth the benefits they bring. The ongoing debate over the need for and effectiveness of regulation leads to alternating periods of deregulation and reregulation.

- The global regulation of business often occurs when commerce crosses national borders or the consequences of unregulated business activity by a national government are so large that global regulation is necessary.

[26] "New Global Regulations for Safer Vehicles," *United Nations Economic Commission for Europe,* press release, March 31, 2008, *www.unece.org;* and "U.N. Nuclear Agency Probes Iran Uranium Find," *World News,* May 25, 2012, *article.wn.com.*

Key Terms

antitrust laws, *171*
cost-benefit analysis, *175*
deregulation, *177*
Dodd-Frank Act, *170*
economic regulation, *170*
fiscal policy, *167*

market failure, *169*
monetary policy, *168*
natural monopolies, *169*
negative externalities, *169*
predatory pricing, *171*
public policy, *164*

regulation, *168*
reregulation, *177*
social assistance policies,
168
social regulation, *172*

Internet Resources

www.businesslink.gov.uk	Better Regulation
business.usa.gov	Business USA
www.cato.org	Cato Institute
www.consumerfinance.gov	U.S. Consumer Financial Protection Bureau
www.economywatch.com	Economy Watch
www.federalreserve.gov	Board of Governors of the Federal Reserve System
www.ftc.gov	U.S. Federal Trade Commission
mercatus.org	Mercatus Center, George Mason University
www.ncpa.org	National Center for Policy Analysis
www.reginfo.gov	U.S. Office of Information and Regulatory Affairs
www.regulations.gov	Regulations.gov
www.un.org/en/law	International Law, United Nations
www.usa.gov	Government Made Easy

Discussion Case: *Derivative Losses at JPMorgan Chase*

JPMorgan Chase (sometimes referred to by its short name, JPMorgan) was one of the largest banks in the United States and the only major bank to remain profitable during the 2008 financial crisis. In May 2012, the bank surprised the financial community and the American public when it announced that one of its derivative trading groups had lost an astonishing $2 billion of the bank's money. Derivatives were financial instruments that derived their value from changes in the price of commodities (such as wheat), the level of interest rates, or an underlying asset such as mortgages. They were bought and sold—usually by big institutions such as pension funds or sovereign wealth funds—which were essentially making a bet on whether the prices of the underlying assets would go up or down. The leading creators and brokers of derivatives were five large Wall Street banks—JPMorgan, Goldman Sachs, Morgan Stanley, Bank of America, and Citigroup. These banks also traded derivatives for their own investment portfolios, seeking to profit from their own insights into market movements. The derivative business produced about $20 billion in revenues for the five major banks in 2010.

Within minutes after JPMorgan's announcement of their losses, the company's stock lost almost 10 percent of its value, wiping out about $15 billion in market value. Fitch Ratings downgraded the bank's credit rating by one notch and Standard & Poor's cut its outlook of JPMorgan to "negative," indicating that a credit-rating downgrade would follow. Other banks were caught in the decline in confidence. Morgan Stanley, Citigroup, and Goldman Sachs stock all closed down about 4 percent. Critics of the banking community were quick to jump on the reported JPMorgan losses. "It just shows they can't manage risk—and if JPMorgan can't, no one can," said Simon Johnson, former chief economist for the International Monetary Fund.

When Congress had debated financial regulatory reform in 2010, it considered imposing government rules on the trading of derivatives. Trading in some kinds of derivatives (particularly those whose value was tied to mortgages), which were largely unregulated at the time, had profoundly destabilized the U.S. and world economies in 2008, and Congress sought to avoid a similar situation in the future. For this reason, it sought to extend government oversight. Unlike stocks and bonds, which were traded on public exchanges such as the New York Stock Exchange, most derivative deals were private agreements between two parties. Congress proposed instead that derivatives be traded in public "clearinghouses" run by intermediaries, where regulators could scrutinize these transactions. The big banks, including JPMorgan, had argued vigorously against this, saying that intermediaries could reveal sensitive pricing information or the structure of the deal, potentially benefiting rivals and reducing the banks' profits. But in 2010, Congress decided to extend government regulation over the derivatives market, despite the industry's opposition.

In addition to requiring regulated trading through clearinghouses, the Dodd-Frank Act also included a provision called the Volker Rule. This rule, named after a former head of the Federal Reserve, Paul Volker, who had suggested it, said that banks could not trade derivatives for their own accounts—something they had commonly done before Dodd-Frank. The purpose of the rule was to prevent banks from taking on excessive risk by making big bets—and leaving taxpayers on the hook to bail them out if something went seriously wrong, as it had in 2008. An exception was made for derivatives trading done to hedge risk in a bank's own portfolio. In 2012, the Securities and Exchange Commission was still trying to figure out exactly how to implement this part of the law—and what exactly a hedging trade was, as opposed to some other kind—so banks were still largely free to do what they wanted. Bank lobbyists were still busy arguing for a loose interpretation of the rule.

JPMorgan's huge losses startled both Congress and regulators, and again posed the question of what kinds of regulations were necessary. Many wondered if the bank's (and its shareholders') losses could have been avoided if a strict interpretation of the Volker Rule had already been in effect. "It is premature to conclude whether the Volker Rule in the Dodd-Frank Act would have prohibited these trades," said Bryan Hubbard, spokesperson for the U.S. Office of the Comptroller, referring to the fact that the specific rules had not yet been written. Representative Barney Frank, coauthor of the Dodd-Frank Act, commented, "When a supposedly responsible, well-run organization could make such an enormous mistake with derivatives, that really blows up the argument, 'Oh, leave us alone, we don't need you to regulate us.'" To Frank, the losses underscored the continuing need for strong government oversight.

Weeks later, after an internal investigation by the bank, JPMorgan chief executive officer Jamie Dimon announced that three high-ranking executives were leaving the company: Ina Drew, who ran the risk management unit that was responsible for the company's derivative losses; Achilles Macris, who was in charge of the London-based desk that placed the trades; and Javier Martin-Artajo, a trader and managing director of Macris's team. Dimon also said that the trading positions taken had produced losses that could go as high as $5 billion. Later, others estimated that the losses could be as high as $9 billion. Unlike the banking crisis a few years earlier, these losses would be absorbed by the bank—or its shareholders—and a bailout, which would have passed the costs along to the taxpayers, would not be needed. At the company's annual meeting a few days later, Dimon addressed the issue of increased regulation. While he continued to criticize the cost and complexity of added regulation, he said he supported most of the proposed regulatory rules, including some of the Volker Rule, but did not elaborate further.

Sources: "Banks Falter in Rules Fight," *The Wall Street Journal*, April 14, 2010, *online.wsj.com;* "Calls to Toughen Regulation Follow JPMorgan Loss," *Yahoo! Finance*, May 11, 2012, *finance.yahoo.com;* "JPMorgan Sought Loophole on Risky Trading," *The New York Times*, May 12, 2012, *www.nytimes.com;* "Three to Exit J.P. Morgan after Losses," *The Wall Street Journal*, May 13, 2012, *online.wsj.com;* "In Washington, Mixed Messages over Tighter Rules for Wall St.," *The New York Times Dealb%k*, May 14, 2012, *dealbook.nytimes.com;* "Inside J.P. Morgan's Blunder," *The Wall Street Journal*, May 18, 2012, *online.wsj.com;* "Bank Regulators Under Scrutiny in JPMorgan Loss," *The New York Times*, May 25, 2012, *www.nytimes.com;* and "JPMorgan Trading Loss May Reach $9 Billion," *The New York Times Dealb%k*, June 28, 2012, *dealbook.nytimes.com.*

Discussion Questions

1. Does this case indicate that JPMorgan and the federal government were in a collaborative partnership or working at arm's length? Why do you think so?
2. Which stakeholders benefited, and which were hurt, by JPMorgan's actions in this case? For those that were hurt, wasn't this a risk they were willing to take?
3. Were the regulations of derivatives trading legislated by Congress in 2010 an example of economic or social regulations? What were the arguments in favor of and opposed to these regulations?
4. Do you believe the government should have regulated the trading of derivatives further, and why or why not? If so, what kinds of regulations would you favor?

CHAPTER NINE

Influencing the Political Environment

Businesses face complicated issues in managing their relationships with politicians and government regulators. Managers must understand the political environment and be active and effective participants in the public policy process. They need to ensure that their company is seen as a relevant stakeholder when government officials make public policy decisions and must be familiar with the many ways that business can influence these decisions. The opportunities afforded businesses to participate in the public policy process differ from nation to nation. Sound business strategies depend on an understanding of these differences, enabling businesses to manage worldwide business–government relations effectively.

This Chapter Focuses on These Key Learning Objectives:

- Understanding the arguments for and against business participation in the political process.
- Knowing the types of corporate political strategies and the influences on an organization's development of a particular strategy.
- Assessing the tactics businesses can use to be involved in the political process.
- Examining the role of the public affairs department and its staff.
- Recognizing the challenges business faces in managing business–government relations in different countries.

Many businesses have utilized the services of the American Legislative Exchange Council (ALEC), well known for its role in shaping conservative legislation and lobbying influence. It has advocated against health care reform, to reduce state taxes on businesses, and to limit the political influence of labor unions. ALEC also was instrumental in many states in the creation of "stand your ground" laws, under which citizens were given the right to use guns or other weapons to protect themselves against assailants. After the public backlash in the Treyvon Martin case in 2012—in which a black teenager was shot to death in Florida and his assailant defended his actions by claiming protection under Florida's "stand your ground" law—many businesses began to distance themselves from ALEC. In 2012 Walmart joined other firms, such as Amazon.com, Coca-Cola, Kraft Foods, McDonald's, General Electric, Sprint Nextel, and a dozen more, bending to pressure from civil rights groups. Walmart was the largest seller of firearms in the country and the largest employer of black workers and thus particularly vulnerable to protests surrounding the Treyvon Martin case. Walmart's public affairs vice president explained the company's action by saying, "ALEC had strayed from its core mission to advance the Jeffersonian principles of free markets."

One industry that has been active in the political arena is solar power. Because solar energy has historically been more expensive to produce than fossil fuel energy, the industry has relied heavily on government incentives and subsidies to level the playing field. Although some major energy companies have entered the solar business, most of the 3,400 solar companies in the United States are small, such as Namasté Solar, a Boulder, Colorado, firm of 60 employees that installs solar energy systems for commercial and residential customers. The solar industry's trade association, the Solar Energy Industries Association, has been very active in government affairs and advocacy, winning a number of policy victories. The federal stimulus bills of 2008 and 2009 provided tax credits, grants, and loans for solar installations and companies that made solar equipment (one of which, Solyndra, later failed). States—such as Hawaii, which required all new construction to have solar water heaters by 2010—and cities—such as Berkeley, California, which loans money to residents to install solar panels—have also helped the industry with friendly policies.[1]

As the examples above demonstrate, many businesses—big and small—have become active participants in the political process to promote a variety of goals, from supporting organizations charged with developing legislation to support economic development and job growth to lobbying government regulators through a trade association to receive tax credits and grants. They are not always successful, however, as seen in the political partnership of businesses with ALEC, which took on a new and controversial agenda. Yet, at other times, political action can bolster the industry, as seen in the solar power industry's political efforts. Which alliances to join and political tactics to use may depend on the situation. In general, business recognizes the necessity of understanding the political environment and of addressing political issues as they arise. This is a constant challenge for business and managers entrusted with managing the political environment.

This chapter focuses on managing business–government relations and political issues. Businesses do not have an absolute right to exist and pursue profits. The right to conduct commerce depends on compliance with appropriate laws and public policy. As discussed in Chapter 8, public policies and government regulations are shaped by many actors, including

[1] "Wal-Mart Latest to Leave Conservative Advocacy Group ALEC," *Los Angeles Times,* May 31, 2012, *www.latimes.com;* "General Electric, Sprint Nextel Latest Companies to Leave ALEC," *Political Capital,* August 27, 2012, *go.bloomberg.com /political-capital;* "U.S. Solar Industry Year in Review 2008," *Solar Energy Industries Association, www.seia.org;* and "Namaste Solar Becomes Poster Child for Economic Recovery," *Greentech Innovations Report,* February 17, 2009, *www.greentechmedia.com.*

business, special interest groups, and government officials. The emergence of public issues often encourages companies to monitor public concerns, respond to government proposals, and participate in the political process. This chapter discusses how managers can ethically and practically meet the challenge of managing the business–government relationship.

Participants in the Political Environment

In many countries the political environment features numerous participants. These participants may have differing objectives and goals, varying access to political tools, and disparate levels of power or influence. The outcomes sought by businesses may be consistent, or at odds, with the results desired by interest groups. Participants may argue that their needs are greater than the needs of other political actors, or that one group or another group does not have the right to be involved in the public policy process. To better understand the dynamic nature of the political environment, it is important to explore who participates in the political process and their claims of legitimacy.

Business as a Political Participant

There is a serious debate between those who favor and those who oppose business involvement in governmental affairs. This debate involves the question of whether, and to what extent, business should legitimately participate in the political process. As shown in Figure 9.1, some people believe business should stay out of politics, while others argue that business has a right to be involved.

Proponents of business involvement in the political process often argue that since other affected groups (such as special interest groups) are permitted to be involved, it is only fair that business should be, too. This justice and fairness argument becomes even stronger when one considers the significant financial consequences that government actions may have on business.

> An Irishman walks into a bar. This may sound like the opening line of a joke but it actually is the beginning of a television advertisement about responsible drinking, developed by British beverage maker Diageo. The company-sponsored ads promoting moderation in drinking, the first of their kind in the United Kingdom, were aired during prime time to maximize their impact. A Diageo spokesperson admitted that while the company wanted to discourage binge drinking by young people, a growing concern, it also hoped its campaign would help Diageo avoid possible governmental regulation of their product and its advertisements.[2]

FIGURE 9.1
The Arguments for and against Political Involvement by Business

Why Business Should Be Involved	Why Business Should Not Be Involved
A pluralistic system invites many participants.	Managers are not qualified to engage in political debate.
Economic stakes are high for firms.	Business is too big, too powerful—an elephant dancing among chickens.
Business counterbalances other social interests.	Business is too selfish to care about the common good.
Business is a vital stakeholder of government.	Business risks its credibility by engaging in partisan politics.

[2] "Promoting Moderation," *Ethical Performance Best Practices*, Winter 2007/2008, p. 8.

Businesses see themselves as countervailing forces in the political arena and believe that their progress, and possibly survival, depends on influencing government policy and regulations. But others are not as confident that the presence of business enhances the political process. In this view, business has disproportionate influence, based on its great power and financial resources.

In a 2011 Harris poll, a large majority of those polled believed that big companies had too much political power (88 percent). Political action committees, a favorite political instrument for businesses, were seen as too powerful by 87 percent of the public, as were political lobbyists (by 84 percent). What is the group perceived as having the least amount of power in politics? The answer is small businesses; only 5 percent of those surveyed felt that they had too much political power. In the 18 years that the Harris Poll has been asking these questions, people have become increasingly concerned about big companies, lobbyists, and labor unions having too much political power.[3]

Although the debate over whether businesses should be involved in the political environment rages on, the facts are that in many countries businesses are permitted to engage in political discussions, influence political races, and introduce or contribute to the drafting of laws and regulations, as discussed later in this chapter. But businesses do not act alone in these activities. Other stakeholders also are active participants in the political environment.

Stakeholder Groups in Politics

Various stakeholder groups, representing many varied concerns and populations, have a voice in politics and the public policy process. These groups often use the same tactics as businesses to influence government officials, elections, and regulation.

Labor unions have been involved in U.S. politics for decades. The AFL-CIO (a federation of unions) and the Teamsters Union, for example, have formed political action committees to influence electoral races and legislation. The International Brotherhood of Electrical Workers, as shown later in Figure 9.4, is often one of the top three groups in terms of political contributions. One report that analyzed political contribution data found that 159 House members counted the labor sector as their top campaign supporters, the same number of House members that counted the finance, insurance, and real estate sector as their top backers.[4]

Coalition Political Activity

Business organizations and stakeholder groups do not always act alone in the political process; often two or more participants join together to act in concert. Such **ad hoc coalitions** bring diverse groups together to organize for or against particular legislation or regulation. Politics can create unusual alliances and curious conflicts, as the following example illustrates.

Daylight saving time involves setting clocks forward in specific areas of the country to increase the amount of daylight that falls later in the day. At various times, different industries have lobbied for or against extending these adjustments. For example, the barbecue industry has argued that an extra few weeks of daylight saving would

[3] "Big Companies, PACs, Banks, Financial Institutions and Lobbyists Seen by Strong Majorities as Having Too Much Power and Influence in DC," *HarrisInteractive*, June 1, 2011, *www.harrisinteractive.com.*

[4] "Labor Lobbying, Union PAC Contributions and More in Capital Eye Opener," *Open Secrets Blog*, September 5, 2011, *www.opensecrets.org.*

boost the sale of grills, charcoal, and utensils, which are usually used in the evening. The candy industry said that if daylight saving was not extended past Halloween, candy sales would decline as fewer children went out to trick-or-treat. The Air Transport Association, representing major U.S. airlines, argued that daylight saving time placed U.S. international flight schedules out of sync with European schedules. The National Parent Teacher Association also was opposed, claiming children would be going to school in the dark morning hours, increasing the potential for more accidents and abductions. In 2006, President Bush signed into law a National Energy Plan that, among other energy initiatives, extended daylight saving time four weeks. The major reason was to conserve electricity by having most work activity fall within daylight hours.[5]

Influencing the Business–Government Relationship

Most scholars and businesspeople agree: Business must participate in politics. Why? Quite simply, the stakes are too high for business not to be involved. Government must and will act upon many issues, and these issues affect the basic operations of business and its pursuit of economic stability and growth. Therefore, businesses must develop a corporate political strategy.

Corporate Political Strategy

A **corporate political strategy** involves the "activities taken by organizations to acquire, develop, and use power to obtain an advantage."[6] This advantage may involve, for example, changing or not changing a particular allocation of resources, such as government support for a project supported by business or the support of an industry, such as the solar power industry discussed at the beginning of this chapter. These strategies might be used to further a firm's economic survival or growth. Alternatively, a corporate political strategy might target limiting a competitor's progress or ability to compete. Strategies also may be developed to simply exercise the business's right to a voice in government affairs, such as businesses collaboration with ALEC, discussed earlier in this chapter. Organizations differ in how actively they are involved in politics on an ongoing basis. Some companies essentially wait for a public policy issue to emerge before building a strategy to address that issue. This is likely when they believe the threat posed by unexpected public issues is relatively small.

On the other hand, other companies develop an ongoing political strategy so that they are ready when various public issues arise. Firms are most likely to have a long-term political strategy if they believe the risks of harm from unexpected public issues are great, or when the firm is a frequent target of public attention. For example, firms in the chemical industry, which must contend with frequently changing environmental regulations and the risk of dangerous accidents, usually have a sophisticated political strategy. The same may be true for firms in the entertainment industry, which must often contend with policy issues

[5] "Daylight Savings Extension Draws Heat over Safety, Cost; PTA, Airlines Fight 4-Week Proposal," *USA Today*, July 22, 2005, p. A1; and "President Bush Signs into Law a National Energy Plan," White House Press Release, August 8, 2005, *www.whitehouse.gov*.

[6] The quotation is from John F. Mahon and Richard McGowan, *Industry as a Player in the Political and Social Arena* (Westport, CT: Quorum Press, 1996), p. 29. Also see Jean-Philippe Bonardi, Amy J. Hillman, and Gerald D. Keim, "The Attractiveness of Political Markets: Implications for Firm Strategy," *Academy of Management Review* 30 (2005), pp. 397–413, for a thorough discussion of this concept.

FIGURE 9.2
Business Strategies for Influencing Government

Source: Adapted from Amy J. Hillman and Michael A. Hitt, "Corporate Political Strategy Formulation: A Model of Approach, Participation, and Strategy Decisions," *Academy of Management Review* 24 (1999), Table 1, p. 835. Used by permission.

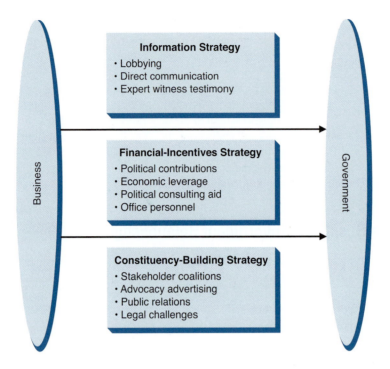

such as intellectual property rights, public standards of decency, and licensing rights to new technologies.

Political actions by businesses often take the form of one of the following three strategic types, also shown in Figure 9.2:

- *Information strategy* (where businesses seek to provide government policymakers with information to influence their actions, such as lobbying).
- *Financial-incentives strategy* (where businesses provide incentives to influence government policymakers to act in a certain way, such as making a contribution to a political action committee that supports the policymaker).
- *Constituency-building strategy* (where businesses seek to gain support from other affected organizations to better influence government policymakers to act in a way that helps them).[7]

The various tactics used by businesses when adopting each of these political strategies are discussed next in this chapter.

Political Action Tactics

The tactics or tools used by business to influence the public policy process are often similar to those available to other political participants. Sometimes business may have an advantage since it might have greater financial resources, but often it is how tactics are used—not the amount of money spent—that determines their effectiveness. This section will discuss tactics used by business in the three strategic areas of information, financial incentives, and constituency building.

[7] Amy J. Hillman and Michael A. Hitt, "Corporate Political Strategy Formulation: A Model of Approach, Participation, and Strategy Decisions," *Academy of Management Review* 24 (1999), pp. 825–42.

Promoting an Information Strategy

As shown in Figure 9.2, some firms pursue a political strategy that tries to provide government policymakers with information to influence their actions. Lobbying is the political action tool most often used by businesses when pursuing this type of political strategy, but some firms also use various forms of direct communication with policymakers. These various information-strategy approaches are discussed next.

Lobbying

An important tool of business involvement in politics is **lobbying**. Many companies hire full-time representatives in Washington, DC, state capitals, or local cities (or the national capital in other countries where they operate) to keep abreast of developments that may affect the company and, when necessary, to communicate with government officials. These individuals are called lobbyists. Their job is to represent the business before the people and agencies involved in determining legislative and regulatory outcomes. Lobbying involves direct contact with a government official to influence the thinking or actions of that person on an issue or public policy. Lobbyists communicate with and try to persuade others to support an organization's interest or stake as they consider a particular law, policy, or regulation.

Businesses, trade associations, and other groups spend a great deal on lobbying. Figure 9.3 shows the total number of lobbyists and the amount spent on lobbying activity from 1998 to 2011. As illustrated, the number of lobbyists peaked in 2007 and by 2011 the number was about the same as in the early 2000s. The amount spent on lobbying, however, has continued to rise to over $3 billion each year. The organizations spending the most on lobbying since 2000 were the U.S. Chamber of Commerce, the American Medical Association, General Electric, the Pharmaceutical Research and Manufacturers of America,

FIGURE 9.3
Total Federal Lobbying Spending and Number of Lobbyists, 1998–2011, by U.S. Business

Sources: Center for Responsive Politics at *www.opensecrets.org.* Used with permission.

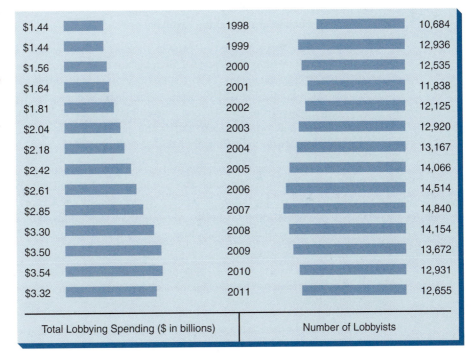

Total Lobbying Spending ($ in billions)	Year	Number of Lobbyists
$1.44	1998	10,684
$1.44	1999	12,936
$1.56	2000	12,535
$1.64	2001	11,838
$1.81	2002	12,125
$2.04	2003	12,920
$2.18	2004	13,167
$2.42	2005	14,066
$2.61	2006	14,514
$2.85	2007	14,840
$3.30	2008	14,154
$3.50	2009	13,672
$3.54	2010	12,931
$3.32	2011	12,655

the American Hospital Association, and the AARP (formerly the American Association of Retired People).[8]

Under U.S. law and EU directive (and in other nations as well), lobbying activities are severely limited and must be disclosed publicly.[9] Lobbying firms and organizations employing in-house lobbyists must register with the government. They must also file regular reports on their earnings (lobbyists) or expenses (organizations), and indicate the issues and legislation that were the focus of their efforts. Lobbyists have also historically provided politicians with various perks and gifts, creating the potential for inappropriately influencing policy. As the following story shows, instances of political corruption can occur anywhere in the world.

> In 2011, four European members of parliament were indicted for corruption involving allegations of wrongdoing with lobbyists. One member, Pablo Zalba of Spain, admitted that he amended two pieces of consumer protection legislation at the request of members of an undercover team of reporters posing as lobbyists but denied accepting any illegal payments for his actions. The investigators said it was clear that Zalba was told he would be paid for his services. Earlier, three other members of parliament, Slovenian Zoran Thaler, Austrian Ernst Strasser, and Romanian Adrian Severin, allegedly accepted offers of cash in exchange for influencing laws. Thaler and Strasser resigned from their political positions when these allegations appeared in the media. Severin was expelled from his political party but remained in parliament as an independent.[10]

In response to what some viewed as widespread ethical violations exhibited by lobbyists toward elected officials, Congress passed sweeping new legislation in 2007 directed at lobbyists and their interaction with politicians in an effort to bring ethics back into the political process, as described in Exhibit 9.A.

Businesses sometimes hire former government officials as lobbyists and political advisors. These individuals bring with them their personal connections and detailed knowledge of the public policy process. This circulation of individuals between business and government is often referred to as the **revolving door**.

> In 2012, Microsoft hired a former senior FTC attorney who led several of the agency's antitrust investigations of rival Google. Not to be outdone, Google hired a former top FTC patent expert. This type of "revolving door" hiring between a federal agency and the industry the agency scrutinizes is common. Apple hired a former top litigator from the FTC and Intel employed the FTC's former associate general counsel and former chief of staff while the FTC was conducting an investigation of Intel's possible antitrust activities.[11]

The 2010, congressional elections saw many members of Congress defeated in their bids for re-election, and some chose to leave office voluntarily. Where did these seasoned politicians go? According to a study undertaken by the Center for Responsive Politics, 52.6 percent of former members of Congress were employed by a lobbying firm or client, whereas only 20.5 percent found work in a federal agency or state government unit.

---

[8] For a complete listing of lobbyists and their expenses by organization and by industry, see *www.opensecrets.org/lobby.*

[9] For a detailed account of lobbying regulations in the United States, see Lobbying Disclosure Act Guidance at *lobbyingdisclosure.house.gov;* and for a description of the EU directive, see "New EU Lobbying Rules to Cover National Embassies," *EurActiv*, October 29, 2009, *www.euractiv.com.*

[10] "Fourth Euro MP Named in Lobbying Scandal," *BBC News*, March 28, 2011, *www.bbc.co.uk.*

[11] "FTC Attorney to Join Microsoft," *The Wall Street Journal*, February 29, 2012, *online.wsj.com.*

Under the "temptation rules," lawmakers and their aides are barred from accepting any gifts, meals, or trips from lobbyists, with penalties up to $200,000 and five years in prison for violating these new rules. "You are basically asking people to certify, with big penalties, that nobody has lied on their expense accounts," said one of the biggest lobbyists in Washington. Yet, the lobbyist also shared his skepticism about the impact of these rules since "these are people [lobbyists and government employees] who are sharing apartments together, playing on the same softball teams, dating each other—young people with active social lives."

In a 2009 *New York Times* report, 1,150 trips taken by members of Congress were investigated, such as a tour of a prince's vineyard and castle in Liechtenstein, an afternoon at a ski resort in the Alps, a flight to Inner Mongolia, and a trip that included a stay at the historic King David Hotel in Jerusalem and attendance at a gala party at the Western Wall. Each of these "junkets," as they are called, were paid for by private firms or groups, circumventing the prohibition of lobbyists paying for entertaining members of Congress. Yet, the report also indicated that in each of these trips, lobbying for some type of congressional action occurred—passage of a law, creating a congressional hearing or investigation, or approval of a government contract with a business firm.

Sources: "Tougher Rules Change Game for Lobbyists," *The New York Times*, August 7, 2007, *www.nytimes.com*; and "Rules for Congress Curb but Don't End Junkets," *The New York Times*, December 7, 2009, *www.nytimes.com*.

A Government Accountability Office report announced in 2011 that 37 percent of the more than 2,000 employees who left the Securities and Exchange Commission (SEC) between 2005 and 2010 were employed as "accountants, economists, attorneys, and other professions particularly relevant to SEC examinations and investigations."[12] It appears that as individuals leave their elected or appointed office there are ample opportunities to return to Congressional Hill or regulatory agencies as lobbyists, investigators, examiners, or in other roles.

While it is perfectly legal for government officials to seek employment in industry, and vice versa, the revolving door carries potential for abuse. Although it may be praised as an act of public service when a business executive leaves a corporate position to work for a regulatory agency, that executive may be inclined to act favorably toward his or her former employer. Such favoritism would not be fair to other firms also regulated by the agency. Businesses can also seek to influence public policy by offering jobs to regulators in exchange for favors, a practice that is considered highly unethical. In a survey of Americans, 51 percent thought that when a company offered a government regulator a job it was a form of a bribe. Fifty-nine percent of those surveyed believed that some companies routinely hired regulators to get favorable treatment from the government and nearly as many (53 percent) thought companies that regularly hired former regulators received that special treatment.[13]

Despite the public's strong concerns, lobbying—as well as hiring former government officials for positions in the corporate world—is normally legal, but great care must be exercised to act ethically.

Direct Communications

Businesses can also promote an information strategy through direct communication with policymakers, another kind of information strategy.

---

[12] *Opensecrets.org* pledged to follow the Center for Responsible Politics' long-term investigation into the revolving door issue. See *www.opensecrets.org*. Also see "SEC Urged to Adopt More Revolving Door Safeguards," *Reuters*, July 12, 2011, *www.reuters.com*.

[13] "51% Think It's Bribery When a Company Offers a Government Regulator a Job," *Financial*, May 25, 2011, *finchannel.com*.

Democracy requires citizen access and communication with political leaders. Businesses often invite government officials to visit local plant facilities, give speeches to employees, attend awards ceremonies, and participate in activities that will improve the officials' understanding of management and employee concerns. These activities help to humanize the distant relationship that can otherwise develop between government officials and the public.

One of the most effective organizations promoting direct communications between business and policymakers is **The Business Roundtable**. Founded in 1972, the Roundtable is an organization of chief executive officers (CEOs) of leading corporations representing $6 trillion in annual revenues and more than 14 million employees. The organization studies various public policy issues and advocates for laws that it believes "foster vigorous economic growth and a dynamic global economy." Some issues the Roundtable has taken a position on in recent years include corporate governance, job creation and training, sustainability, health care, international trade, and cybersecurity. One of the most distinctive aspects of the Roundtable's work is that CEOs are directly involved. Once the Roundtable has formulated a position on a matter of public policy, CEOs go to Washington, DC, to talk personally with lawmakers. The organization has found that this direct approach works very well.[14]

Expert Witness Testimony

A common method of providing information to legislators is for CEOs and other executives to give testimony in various public forums. Businesses may want to provide facts, anecdotes, or data to educate and influence government leaders. One way that government officials collect information in the United States is through public congressional hearings, where business leaders may be invited to speak. These hearings may influence whether legislation is introduced in Congress, or change the language or funding of a proposed piece of legislation, or shape how regulation is implemented. In some cases, the very future of the industry may be at stake.

Google's executive chairman, Eric Schmidt, testified before a Senate hearing in 2011 to answer questions and hopefully fend off possible antitrust actions against his company. In addition to Google hiring at least 25 lobbying and communication firms to address issues of online piracy (further explored in the discussion case at the end of this chapter) and antitrust, Schmidt wanted to personally calm any concerns that the senators might have about Google's dominance of the Internet search industry. Schmidt was reminded that a decade earlier Microsoft's chief executive, Bill Gates, appeared ill-prepared for his congressional testimony and soon after the government filed an antitrust suit against his firm. One lesson Schmidt learned from Gates's experience was: Don't appear arrogant. "We understand with success comes scrutiny, and we're looking forward to the hearing and answering any questions senators may have about our business," said a Google spokesperson.[15]

Promoting a Financial-Incentive Strategy

Businesses may wish to influence government policymakers by providing financial incentives in the hope that the legislator will be persuaded to act in a certain way or cast a vote favorable to the business's interests. Political action committees and economic leverage are the two most common political action tools when pursuing this strategy.

---

[14] More information about The Business Roundtable is available at *www.businessroundtable.org.*

[15] "Google Girds for a Grilling," *The Wall Street Journal*, September 19, 2011, *online.wsj.com.*

2002—The Bipartisan Campaign Reform Act (BCRA), also known as the McCain-Feingold Act, had two key provisions. BCRA prohibited political party committees from accepting corporate, union, or unlimited individual contributions to stem the growing role of **soft money** (unlimited contributions to the national political parties by individuals or organizations for party-building activities) given to candidates, and BCRA barred corporations, unions, and nonprofit groups from using their treasuries to fund television ads mentioning a federal candidate shortly before an election.

2003—Federal Election Commission v. Beaumont. The U.S. Supreme Court upheld the federal ban on corporate contributions to candidates, including those by incorporated nonprofit advocacy groups.

2003—McConnell v. Federal Election Commission. The U.S. Supreme Court upheld the constitutionality of the McCain-Feingold Act in a challenge brought by a diverse group, including the California Democratic Party and the National Rifle Association.

2007—Wisconsin Right to Life v. Federal Election Commission. The U.S. Supreme Court ruled that groups could run issue or advocacy advertisements close to an election without any restrictions, weakening the BCRA.

2010—Republican National Committee v. Federal Election Commission. The U.S. Supreme Court refused to overturn the core element of the McCain-Feingold Act, a ban on soft-money donations to national political parties.

2010—Citizens United v. Federal Election Commission (discussed more fully in Exhibit 9.D). The U.S. Supreme Court eliminated the ban on corporation and union activities used to urge voters to support or oppose specific candidates.

2011—Cao v. Federal Election Commission. The U.S. Supreme Court declined to hear a challenge to limit how much a political party could spend in coordination with the party's nominees.

2012—SpeechNow.org v. Federal Election Commission (discussed more fully later in the chapter). The U.S. Supreme Court ruled unconstitutional the ban on individual campaign contribution limits to 527 organizations, also discussed later in the chapter.

Sources: "The 2012 Election Will Cost $6 Billion," *Bloomberg Businessweek*, October 3–9, 2011, pp. 32–33; and "Speechnow.org v. FEC," Federal Election Commission website, n.d., *www.fec.gov.*

Political Action Committees

One of the most common political action tools used by business is to form and contribute to a political action committee. Since the mid-1970s, companies have been permitted to spend company funds to organize and administer **political action committees (PACs)**.

PACs are independently incorporated organizations that can solicit contributions and then channel those funds to candidates seeking political office. Since 2002, a number of laws and court decisions have significantly affected campaign financing, particularly the role of the corporation in election campaigns, as described in Exhibit 9.B.

Extensive fund-raising—whether from individual contributions, political action committee contributions, federal funding, or other sources—is essential for any politician seeking to be elected. Exhibit 9.C shows the amount of funding needed for candidates to compete for the United States presidency in 2008.

Individuals, political parties, and PACs can contribute to political campaigns. As shown in Figure 9.4, an individual can directly contribute up to $2,500 to any candidate per election and $117,000 in total. PACs, and national, state, district, or local political parties contributions are also restricted, as also shown in Figure 9.4.

In 2012, the Federal Election Commission (FEC) ruled that individuals could make modest contributions to the politician of their choice via mobile messaging. By acquiring the correct six-digit "short code," unique to each political candidate running for

Exhibit 9.C

The Cost of Running for the Presidency

In 2008, for the first time ever, candidates for the presidency of the United States raised more than $1 billion. Leading the way were Democrat Barack Obama and Republican John McCain, but even Bob Barr, the Libertarian Party candidate, and Independent Ralph Nader found that raising big money was necessary to gain recognition and to get their message out to the American people. Obama chose not to receive any funding from political action committees and declined any public (federal) funds, which would impose spending limits on his campaign. McCain, alternatively, did accept federal funding, and thus was limited to spending only $84 million on his campaign. Like Obama, Nader refused contributions from political action committees. Shown below are the amounts that each candidate raised and the sources of the funding.

For the 2012 presidential election, neither Barack Obama nor Mitt Romney elected to receive federal funds. Therefore, their ability to raise private campaign funds from individuals, PACs, and their national party was unlimited (unlike John McCain in 2008). Experts predicted that the campaign fund-raising totals for each presidential candidate would top the $1 billion plateau, with Romney slightly ahead of Obama in total funds raised for the campaign.

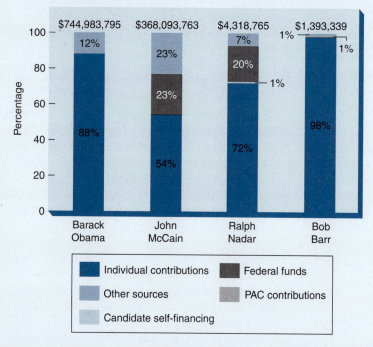

Sources: "Banking on Becoming President," Center for Responsive Politics, n.d., *www.opensecrets.org*; "Campaign 2012: Obama Fundraising Plea Says He Will Be Outspent," *Los Angeles Times*, June 26, 2012, *articles.latimes.com*; and, "Obama Close to Raising $1 Billion after Near-Record September Tally," *Washington Post*, October 6, 2012, *www.washingtonpost.com*.

an office, individuals could text that number with the amount of their donation and the contribution would appear on their cell phone bill. Those running the political campaign did not see the name of the contributor, only the telephone number, so contributions were limited to $50 a month per cell phone number since any larger amount would have to be filed with the FEC and a donor's name would be required. Donors had to attest that they were U.S. citizens, at least 18 years old, and were using their own funds (not those of a relative or an employer).[16]

[16] "Please Text $$$ To My Campaign ☺," *Bloomberg Businessweek*, June 18–24, 2012, p. 28.

FIGURE 9.4   **Campaign Contribution Limits for 2012**

	To each candidate per election	To national party per calendar year	To state, district, and local party per calendar year	To any other political committee per calendar year	Total contribution limits
Individuals may give	$2,500	$30,800	$10,000 (combined limit)	$5,000	$117,000 ($46,200 to candidates; $70,800 to PACs and parties)
National Party Committee may give	$5,000	No limit	No limit	$5,000	$43,100 to senate candidates per campaign
State, District, & Local Party Committee may give	$5,000 (combined limit)	No limit	No limit	$5,000 (combined limit)	No limit
PAC (more than 50 contributors) may give	$5,000	$15,000	$5,000 (combined limit)	$5,000	No limit
PAC (less than 50 contributors) may give	$2,500	$30,800	$10,000 (combined limit)	$5,000	No limit

Source: See *www.fec.gov/pages/brochures/contriblimits.shtml.*

While there are now many more options available for channeling funds to influence political campaigns, businesses have found PAC contributions to be one of the most effective political action tools. When an industry becomes the target of proposed regulations—as the financial services and health care industries recently did—firms within that industry often increase their political spending. Figure 9.5 lists the top political action committees by contribution, comparing data from 2001 through 2012, and shows that the labor unions and trade associations that dominated the top 10 PAC list in 2001–2002 have been replaced by a growing number of business organizations—Honeywell International, AT&T, Lockheed Martin, and Boeing. Figure 9.5 also illustrates the overall growth in the size of PAC contributions by the top 10 contributors from 2001–2002 to 2007–2008, with projections for record-breaking contributions for the 2012 election cycle.

But, sometimes a business discovers that there is a downside to making political contributions, as the next example shows.

In 2010, Target welcomed the opportunity afforded by recent changes in campaign finance laws to get more involved in politics. (The landmark *Citizens United* case that opened the doors for greater business involvement in politics is discussed later in the chapter.) The Minnesota retailer donated $150,000 to a political group, Minnesota Forward, an organization that supported pro-business candidates throughout the state. Minnesota Forward was backing a conservative candidate running for governor who, in addition to being pro-business, was against same-sex marriage. Hundreds of gay-rights supporters demonstrated outside Target stores across the nation, and more than 240,000 people signed a petition promising a boycott. A note was placed on the retailer's Facebook page that read, "Boycott Target until they cease funding anti-gay politics." Target chief executive Gregg Steinhafel apologized in a letter to his employees, saying, "The intent of our political contribution to [Minnesota] Forward was to support economic growth and job creation. While I firmly believe that a business climate conducive to growth is critical to our

FIGURE 9.5 Political Action Committee Activity

	PAC Name	2001–2002	PAC Name	2007–2008	PAC Name	2011–2012*
1.	National Association of Realtors	$3,648,526	National Association of Realtors	$4,020,900	Honeywell International	$1,768,562
2.	Laborers Union	$2,814,200	International Brotherhood of Electrical Workers	$3,344,650	National Beer Wholesalers Association	$1,491,500
3.	Association of Trial Lawyers of America	$2,813,753	AT&T, Inc.	$3,108,200	AT&T Inc.	$1,360,000
4.	National Auto Dealers Association	$2,578,750	American Bankers Association	$2,918,143	American Association for Justice	$1,298,500
5.	American Medical Association	$2,480,972	National Beer Wholesalers Association	$2,869,000	International Brotherhood of Electrical Workers	$1,293,150
6.	American Federation of State/County/ Municipal Employees	$2,423,500	National Auto Dealers Association	$2,864,000	Lockheed Martin	$1,271,500
7.	Teamsters Union	$2,390,003	International Association of Fire Fighters	$2,734,900	American Bankers Association	$1,182,750
8.	United Auto Workers	$2,339,000	Operating Engineers Union	$2,704,067	Credit Union National Association	$1,168,000
9.	International Brotherhood of Electrical Workers	$2,249,300	American Association for Justice	$2,700,500	Every Republican Is Crucial PAC	$1,101,000
10.	Carpenters & Joiners Union	$2,243,000	Laborers Union	$2,555,850	Boeing	$1,069,000

* 2011–2012 = incomplete election cycle; data as of June 2012.
Sources: "Top PACs" for 2001–2002, 2007–2008, and 2011–2012, Center for Responsive Politics, *www.opensecrets.org.*

future, I realize our decision affected many of you in a way I did not anticipate, and for that I am genuinely sorry." Target declined to comment on the suggestion that the firm withdraw its donation.[17]

Business organizations have been somewhat balanced in their support of Democrat versus Republican candidates through various PACs. For example, the following companies, through political action committee contributions, have generally supported Democratic candidates: American Crystal Sugar, ITT Industries, Lockheed Martin, Siemens, and Qwest Communications. Republican candidates could count on the following firms for financial support: AT&T, Boeing, Deloitte & Touche, Honeywell International, and United Parcel Service.[18]

As noted earlier, until 2010 corporations were not permitted by law to make *direct contributions* to political candidates for national and most state offices. That is, companies

[17] "Target Discovers Downside to Political Contributions," *The Wall Street Journal*, August 7, 2010, *online.wsj.com.*
[18] For a more comprehensive listing of business contributions by political party, see *www.opensecrets.org/pacs.*

In a 5-to-4 decision in 2010 the U.S. Supreme Court upheld the argument made by Citizens United, a conservative nonprofit political organization, that its First Amendment right to free speech was violated by the Federal Election Commission's restrictions on campaign contributions. At issue was Citizens United's attempt to air a 90-minute documentary entitled "Hillary: The Movie," during Hillary Rodham Clinton's campaign to become the Democratic Party nominee for the presidency in 2008. The controversial film was banned by a U.S. District Court because it violated the Bipartisan Campaign Reform Act's restriction of no electronic communications within 30 days of a primary. Citizens United argued that the documentary was fact-based and nonpartisan, but the lower court ruled that it had no other purpose than to discredit Clinton's candidacy for the presidency.

Justice Anthony Kennedy wrote for the majority opinion, "if the First Amendment has any force, it prohibits Congress from fining or jailing citizens, or associations of citizens, for simply engaging in political speech." Republican campaign consultant Ed Rollins stated that the decision added transparency to the election process and would make it more competitive.

The *Citizens United* decision sent shock waves through the world of campaign financing since it allowed corporations, and also labor unions, for the first time in the history of the United States, to directly contribute to political campaigns. Critics said it would "corrupt democracy" by allowing corporate funds to flow directly into campaigns. At the time of the decision, 80 percent of Americans surveyed opposed the *Citizens United* ruling, and 65 percent strongly opposed it. Nearly three out of four Americans supported an effort by Congress to reinstate limits on corporate and union spending on election campaigns.

Two years later, a Montana Supreme Court ruling upholding a 100-year-old state law challenged the *Citizens United* decision. The Montana law banned corporate political contributions based on a perceived risk from corporate power injected into state campaigns and elections. The U.S. Supreme Court declined to consider its *Citizens United* ruling in 2012, thus overturning the Montana decision.

Unexpectedly, an assessment of the super PAC contributions, allowed under the *Citizens United* ruling, revealed that the feared unlimited flow of cash from corporations and unions did not occur. Rather, a *Bloomberg Government* report showed that most of the contributions, from December 2011 through May 2012, were coming from wealthy individuals, not businesses.

Sources: "Summary *Citizens United v. Federal Election Commission* (Docket No. 08-205)," Cornell University School of Law, n.d., *topics.law.cornell.edu/supct/cert/08-205*; "Money Grubbers: The Supreme Court Kills Campaign Finance Reform," *Slate*, January 21, 2010, *www.slate.com*; "Justices, 5–4, Reject Corporate Spending Limit," *The New York Times*, January 21, 2010, *www.nytimes.com*; "How Much Has *Citizens United* Changed the Political Game?" *The New York Times*, July 17, 2012, *www.nytimes.com*; "*Citizens United v. Federal Election Commission*," IIT Chicago—Kent College of Law, June 1, 2012, *www.oyez.org*; "Supreme Court Faces Pressure to Reconsider *Citizens United* Ruling," *The Washington Post*, May 20, 2012, *www.washingtonpost.com*; "Court Rejects Corporate Campaign Spending Limits," *The Wall Street Journal*, June 25, 2012, *online.wsj.com*; and "The Cash Behind the Super PACs," *Bloomberg Businessweek*, July 23–29, 2012, p. 28.

could not simply write a check from their own corporate treasuries to support a candidate, say, for president. But that all changed with the Supreme Court ruling in *Citizens United v. the Federal Election Commission*, as explained in Exhibit 9.D.

In 2010, a federal district court ruling in a lawsuit filed by *SpeechNow.org* opened the door for the creation of so-called super PACs. The court ruled that as long as PACs did not contribute *directly* to candidates, parties, or other PACs, they could accept *unlimited* contributions from individuals, unions, or corporations. This decision led to the rise of **super PACs**, technically known as independent expenditure-only committees. Because contribution limits had been removed by the court, these organizations were able to raise and spend vast amounts of money, so long as they were not actually affiliated with any campaigns. Although super PACs were technically independent, they often worked to support particular candidates, as the following example illustrates.

In 2012, billionaire conservative casino mogul Sheldon Adelson pledged $10 million to the super PAC *Restore Our Future,* committed to support Mitt Romney's presidential campaign. This contribution followed the $21 million that Adelson and his family gave to another super PAC in support of Newt Gingrich when Gingrich was running for the Republican presidential nomination earlier in 2012. Adelson's net worth was estimated to be roughly $25 billion, and experts predicted that he might contribute as much as $100 million through various channels during the 2012 elections. The Democrats also had wealthy political contributors. Billionaire investor George Soros donated $1 million to the super PAC *American Bridge 21st Century,* a pro-Democratic group pledged to help Barack Obama and other Democrats, and another $1 million to *America Votes,* an organization run by Democrats. DreamWorks Animation SKG chief executive Jeffrey Katzenberg and his wife gave $2 million to the pro-Obama super PAC *Priorities USA Action* in 2011. Actor Morgan Freeman also contributed to the *Priorities USA Action* PAC, giving $1 million in support of Barack Obama.[19]

Super PACs can advocate a conservative viewpoint, such as *Restore Our Future*; *Red, White & Blue*; and *Endorse Liberty*; as well as a more liberal perspective, such as *Priorities USA Action*; *Majority PAC*; and *Women Vote!* As of June 2012, 576 groups had organized as super PACs and reported contributions of more than $220 million in the 2012 election cycle.

While politicians collect money for their own campaigns, many of them also raise funds to support other politicians' election races. Known as **leadership PACs**, these PACs allow politicians to make donations, typically to other members of their party, showing leadership and to gain more influence within their party, possibly to leverage opportunities for party leadership or committee positions. As of June 2012, leadership PACs had reportedly raised more than $14 million in contributions for the 2012 election cycle, with Republicans slightly ahead of Democrats 58 to 42 percent.[20]

As mentioned earlier in Exhibit 9.B, another important campaign financing effort was the Bipartisan Campaign Reform Act (BCRA) of 2002, which imposed a ban on soft money—unlimited contributions to the national political parties by individuals or organizations for party-building activities.

Although these restrictions were generally lifted by the *Citizens United* and the *SpeechNow.org* judicial decisions, BCRA did give rise to the creation of **527 organizations**, named after their provision in the tax code. These organizations often use various advocacy tactics, such as telephone calls, television or radio announcements, and social media messages to bring attention to a political issue. In the 2010 election cycle, 527 organizations raised more than $540 million and, as of June 2012, had acquired nearly $250 million for the 2012 election cycle. Examples of 527 organizations are *Citizens United,* discussed earlier; *College Republican National Committee,* representing the nation's oldest and largest youth political organization; and *Emily's List,* an organization committed to electing pro-choice Democratic women, recruiting and funding viable women candidates, helping them build and run effective campaign organizations, and mobilizing women voters to help elect progressive candidates across the nation.[21]

---

[19] "Adelson Gives $10 Million to Pro-Romney Super PAC," *WSJ Blogs*, June 13, 2012, *blogs.wsj.com;* "Campaign Aid Is Now Surging into 8 Figures," *The New York Times*, June 13, 2102, *www.nytimes.com;* "Soros Makes 2012 Splash with Big Donations," *The Wall Street Journal*, May 7, 2012, *blogs.wsj.com;* and "Morgan Freeman Donates $1M to Pro-Obama PAC," *ABC News*, July 19, 2012, *abcnews.go.com.*

[20] All PACs data is from Open Secrets at *www.opensecrets.org.*

[21] See *www.citizensunited.org, www.crnc.org,* and *emilyslist.org.*

Economic Leverage

Another political action tool often used by businesses when pursuing a financial incentive strategy is to use their economic leverage to influence public policymakers. **Economic leverage** occurs when a business uses its economic power to threaten to leave a city, state, or country unless a desired political action is taken. Economic leverage also can be used to persuade a government body to act in a certain way that would favor the business, as seen in the following story.

> When the state of Pennsylvania was considering legalizing slot machines at racetracks, the owners of a National Hockey League team located in the state, the Pittsburgh Penguins, were lobbying for a new ice hockey arena to be built with public funds. Government leaders were hesitant to use public funds for a new arena unless substantial private funds were also available. Ted Arneault, owner of the Mountaineer Racetrack and Gaming Resort and part owner of the Pittsburgh Penguins, offered a deal. He said his company would contribute $60 million to build the new ice hockey arena if the state would approve the use of slot machines at Pennsylvania racetracks, including his proposed racetrack facility near Pittsburgh. Legislators agreed.[22]

In this example, the business owner successfully used economic leverage. By committing his own private money to help support the construction of a new ice hockey arena, he was able to persuade politicians to vote in favor of legislation to approve the use of slot machines at racetracks in the state.

Promoting a Constituency-Building Strategy

The final strategy used by business to influence the political environment is to seek support from organizations or people who are also affected by the public policy or who are sympathetic to business's political position. This approach is sometimes called a *grassroots strategy,* because its objective is to shape policy by mobilizing the broad public in support of a business organization's position, or a *grasstops strategy,* because its objective is to influence local opinion leaders. Firms use several methods to build support among constituents. These include advocacy advertising, public relations, and building coalitions with other affected stakeholders. With the increase in the availability of technology, firms have turned to social media as a grassroots tool as the following example shows.

> Social media has dramatically changed how the public connects to the political environment. In 2012 Google launched a new election website, called Google Politics and Elections, the day before the Iowa caucuses formally began the presidential nomination campaigns. The site allowed users to compare candidates' rankings in searches, news stories, blogs, and YouTube videos and provided a "politics and election toolkit" and a 2012 political calendar to track the whereabouts of the candidates. Facebook provided a new app—"2012: What Matters Most"—to encourage its users to get involved in the 2012 political campaigns. This app allowed Facebook to poll its users for their opinions on a variety of issues ranging from immigration, energy, and the environment to national security, the economy, and the national debt. The results were broadcasted on *Reuters*' digital billboards in Times Square.[23]

---

[22] "Penguins, Arneault Make $107 Million Private Funding Proposal for New Arena Project," *Pittsburgh Post-Gazette*, June 24, 2003, p. A1.

[23] "Google Launches New Election Site," *Pittsburgh Business Times*, January 3, 2012, *www.bizjournals.com;* "Facebook Users to Put Political Views Up in Lights on Times Square," *The New York Times—Media Decoder*, January 29, 2012, *mediadecoder.blogs.nytimes.com;* and "Facebook to Display User's Political Beliefs on Times Square," *The Hollywood Reporter*, January 30, 2012, *www.hollywoodreporter.com.*

Stakeholder Coalitions

Businesses may try to influence politics by mobilizing various organizational stakeholders—employees, stockholders, customers, and the local community—to support their political agenda. If a political issue can negatively affect a business, it is likely that it also will negatively affect that business's stakeholders. If pending regulation will impose substantial costs on the business, these costs may result in employee layoffs, or a drop in the firm's stock value, or higher prices for the firm's customers. Often, businesses organize programs to get organizational stakeholders, acting as lobbyists or voters, to influence government officials to vote or act in a favorable way.

> In 2012, politicians and businesspeople from the state of Pennsylvania and the city of Pittsburgh wanted to convince Shell Oil Company to build its new petrochemical plant in southwestern Pennsylvania. Shell was looking for a convenient location for a plant to process the growing supply of natural gas extracted from the region by hydraulic fracturing (also called *fracking* and further discussed in Chapter 11). The southwestern Pennsylvania area had many attractive elements—access to railroad and water transportation systems, business-friendly politicians, a trained and available workforce, and plenty of natural gas. Pennsylvania governor Tom Corbett spent months hosting meetings where Shell's executives could meet with various political and business leaders. Then he learned that many of the Shell Oil executives were big Pittsburgh Steeler fans, the local professional football team. Corbett arranged for the Shell executives to tour Heinz Field, home of the Steelers, including a glimpse in the team's locker room, and to meet with Steelers executives. Soon after, Shell announced that it would build its new plant in Monaca, just 25 miles northwest of Pittsburgh. Shell Oil's spokesperson declined to confirm that the Heinz Field outing and meeting with Steeler officials had "clinched the deal," but he did say that "the governor is an excellent ambassador and salesman for his state and hometown of Pittsburgh, and he is a huge Steelers fan."[24]

Advocacy Advertising

A common method of influencing constituents is **advocacy advertising**. Advocacy ads focus not on a particular product or service, like most ads, but rather on an organization's or company's views on controversial political issues. Advocacy ads, also called *issue advertisements,* can appear in newspapers, on television, or in other media outlets. They have been legal in the United States since 1978, but greater involvement by businesses and other nonprofit (advocacy) organizations in the political process resulted in their use to dramatically increase after the 2010 *Citizens United v. FEC* U.S. Supreme Court decision, discussed earlier. A media expert reported that television and radio stations received more than $2.5 million in revenue each year from issue advertisements since the *Citizens United* decision, compared to less than $1 million each year previously. Many recent examples of advocacy advertisements are discussed in Chapter 19, including organizations seeking to promote their political position with regard to federal energy policy in the United States.

> As the U.S. presidential campaign heated up in 2012, advocacy advertisements populated some of television's highest rated shows. Ads appeared during the broadcasts of NBC's *Today* show and *Dateline NBC* in some states and focused on the nation's increasing debt burden, telling President Obama to "stop the spending." Other ads focused on the economy and advocated who was the best candidate to help the country recover from the recession, and were seen by viewers watching

---

[24] "Corbett Made Pass to Oil Execs with Steelers," *Pittsburgh Post-Gazette*, March 16, 2012, *www.post-gazette.com.*

the television network's evening newscasts. These ads "are trying to get opinion leaders, early donors and the press to focus on certain issues or events," said Joe Mercurio, a political media expert.[25]

Trade Associations

Many businesses work through **trade associations**—coalitions of companies in the same or related industries—to coordinate their grassroots mobilization campaigns, such as the American Legislative Exchange Council, discussed at the beginning of this chapter. Other examples of trade associations include the National Realtors Association (real estate brokers), National Federation of Independent Businesses (small businesses), the National Association of Manufacturers (manufacturers only), or the U.S. Chamber of Commerce (broad, diverse membership).[26]

The U.S. Chamber of Commerce represents more than 3 million businesses of all sizes, sectors, and regions. The chamber has a multimillion-dollar budget, publishes a widely circulated magazine, and operates a satellite television network to broadcast its political messages. The Chamber of Commerce takes positions on a wide range of political, economic, and regulatory questions and actively works to promote its members' views of what conditions are necessary for them to effectively compete in a free marketplace.

Activities of trade associations may include letters, telephone calls, tweets, blogs, e-mails, and other Internet communications to register approval or disapproval of a government official's position on an important issue.

Legal Challenges

A political tactic available to businesses (and other political participants) is the use of legal challenges. In this approach, business seeks to overturn a law after it has been passed or threatens to challenge the legal legitimacy of the new regulation in the courts. Such an approach is shown in the following example.

> The passage of the Family Smoking Prevention and Tobacco Act of 2009 sparked numerous legal challenges from marketing, advertising, and tobacco manufacturing firms. The ban on outdoor advertisement of any tobacco product within 1,000 feet of schools and playgrounds effectively outlawed legal advertising in many cities. In addition, according to the opponents of the bill, which included the Association of National Advertisers and the American Civil Liberties Union, the new rule was a violation of free speech, a right protected under the First Amendment of the U.S. Constitution. They also contended that restricting many forms of print advertising to black-and-white text interfered with legitimate communication to adults about the tobacco products. Nearly a decade earlier the U.S. Supreme Court struck down a Massachusetts ban on tobacco ads, including outdoor billboards and signs that could be seen within 1,000 feet of any public playground and elementary or secondary school, stating that the law was an unconstitutional limit of the First Amendment's right to free speech because it was too broad.[27]

---

[25] "Political Ads Target News Shows," *Huffington Post*, June 17, 2012, *www.huffingtonpost.com.*

[26] The classic discussion of corporate political action can be found in Edwin Epstein, *The Corporation in American Politics* (Englewood Cliffs, NJ: Prentice Hall, 1969). An up-to-date discussion of current trends in American political and civic life is in Robert D. Putnam, *Bowling Alone* (New York: Simon and Schuster, 2000), especially ch. 4.

[27] "Tobacco Firms Sue to Block Marketing Law," *The New York Times*, September 1, 2009, *www.nytimes.com;* and "Tobacco Regulation Is Expected to Face a Free-Speech Challenge," *The New York Times*, June 16, 2009, *www.nytimes.com.*

FIGURE 9.6
Levels of Business
Political Involvement

Level 3   Aggressive Organizational Involvement—direct and personal

- Executive participation
- Involvement with industry working groups and task forces
- Public policy development

Level 2   Moderate Organizational Involvement—indirect yet personal

- Organizational lobbyist
- Employee grassroots involvement
- Stockholders and customers encouraged to become involved

Level 1   Limited Organizational Involvement—indirect and impersonal

- Contribution to political action committee
- Support of a trade association or industry activities

Levels of Political Involvement

Business executives must decide on the appropriate level of political involvement for their company. As shown in Figure 9.6, there are multiple levels of involvement and many ways to participate. To be successful, a business must think strategically about objectives and how specific political issues and opportunities relate to those objectives.

Organizations often begin at the lowest level of political participation, *limited organizational involvement.* Here managers of the organization are not ready or willing to become politically involved by giving their own time or getting their stakeholders involved, but they want to do something to influence the political environment. Organizations at this level may show their political interest, for example, by writing out a check to a trade association to support an industry-backed political action, such as hiring a lobbyist on a specific issue.

When the organization is ready for *moderate political involvement,* managers might directly employ a lobbyist to represent the company's political strategy in Washington or the state capital to push the firm's political agenda. This is a more active form of political involvement since the lobbyist is an employee of the organization. Getting the organization's stakeholders involved is another way a firm can increase its political involvement. Employees can write letters or send e-mails or tweets to their congressperson or become involved in a political campaign. Senior executives might communicate with stockholders or customers on particular issues that might affect the firm and its stakeholders and encourage them to write letters, blog, or otherwise voice their concerns. Some firms have sent letters to their stockholders soliciting their political contributions for a particular candidate or group of candidates but have asked that the contributions be sent to the company. Then the company takes all of the contributions to the candidate or candidates, clearly indicating that the contributions are from the firm's stockholders. This technique is called **bundling**.

The most direct and personal involvement in the political environment is achieved at the third level—*aggressive organizational involvement*—where managers become personally involved in developing public policy. Some executives are asked to sit on important task forces charged with writing legislation that will affect the firm or the firm's industry. When state legislatures were writing laws limiting the opportunities for corporate raiders to acquire unwilling companies in their states, the legislators turned to corporate general counsels, the company attorneys, to help draft the laws. Another example of aggressive organizational involvement is provided by The Business Roundtable, described earlier in this chapter.

Activities Conducted within the Public Affairs Department	Percent of Companies, 2005	Percent of Companies, 2008	Percent of Companies, 2011
Federal government relations	95%	95	90
State government relations	85	91	85
Issues management	82	84	83
Local government relations	79	76	77
Business/trade association oversight	75	81	78
Political action committee	83	80	76
Coalitions	71	78	72
Grassroots/grasstops	75	74	70
Community relations	58	57	51

Source: Foundation for Public Affairs, *The State of Corporate Public Affairs, 2011–2012* (2012), based on a survey of 130 companies. Used by permission.

Managing the Political Environment

In many organizations, the task of managing political activity falls to the department of public affairs or government relations. The role of the **public affairs department** is to manage the firm's interactions with governments at all levels and to promote the firm's interests in the political process. (*Public relations,* discussed in Chapter 19, is a different business function.) The creation of public affairs units is a global trend, with many companies in Canada, Australia, and Europe developing sophisticated public affairs operations.[28] As shown in Exhibit 9.E, nearly all of the most frequently performed activities by public affairs officers or departments involve a political action tactic, and attention has remained relatively stable for most of these political activities since the 2000s.

Most companies have a senior manager or executive to lead the public affairs department. This manager is often a member of the company's senior management committee, providing expertise about the company's major strategy and policy decisions. The size of the department and the support staff varies widely among companies. Many companies assign employees from other parts of the business to work on public affairs issues and to help plan, coordinate, and execute public affairs activities. In this way, the formulation and implementation of the policies and programs developed by a company's public affairs unit are closely linked to the primary business activities of the firm.

The heads of most public affairs departments are senior vice president or vice president positions; some report directly to the CEO, while others are one level below this in the organizational hierarchy. Most work out of company headquarters; most of the rest—particularly those whose work focuses on government relations—work in Washington, DC. More than half of the senior public affairs executives, 55 percent, sit on the corporation's strategic planning committee. The typical public affairs executive spends most of the day direct

[28] The global patterns of public affairs practice are documented in *Journal of Public Affairs,* published by Henry Stewart Publishing beginning in 2001. For an excellent review of public affairs development around the world, see Craig S. Fleisher and Natasha Blair, "Surveying the Field: Status and Trends Affecting Public Affairs across Australia, Canada, EU and the U.S.," in *Assessing, Managing, and Maximizing Public Affairs Performance,* Management Handbook series, ed. Craig S. Fleisher (Washington, DC: Public Affairs Council, 1997).

lobbying with federal or state politicians, hosting visits by politicians to the company's locations, or attending fund-raising activities.[29]

Business Political Action: A Global Challenge

Most of the discussion so far in the chapter has focused on business political activity in the United States. As more companies conduct business abroad, it is critical that managers be aware of the opportunities for and restrictions on business involvement in the political processes in other countries. Other societies and governments also struggle with issues of participation in the political environment, campaign financing, and maintaining a fair ethical climate throughout the public policy process. One example is the issue of lobbying.

In 2010, the Chinese government ordered the closure of thousands of "regional liaison offices"—basically, lobbying firms—which local governments and companies operated in the country's capital of Beijing in order to receive favorable treatment from Chinese officials. The questionable actions by individuals employed at these liaison offices were featured in a government investigative report. Two local government lobbyists, for example, reportedly spent more than $96,000 to buy 777 bottles of expensive Chinese liquor to entertain high-ranking government officials. These liaison offices were often referred to as "*pao bu, qian jin,*" which means "run forward" but also can be translated as "go to the ministry and give money." But many objected to the Chinese government's action. An analyst of Chinese governmental affairs commented, "This is serious. These offices are strong symbols of provincial sovereignty, and by seeking to shut them down, the central government is trying to keep regional officials from lobbying too hard for local interests."[30]

In Japan, a more pluralistic political environment than China's characterizes the public policy process. The major actors are members of big business, agriculture, and labor. These special interest groups are quite powerful and influential. Some of the largest interest groups support more than a few hundred candidates in each important election and provide them with large financial contributions. The *Kiedanren,* or federation of economic organizations, is mostly concerned with Japanese big business, but other interest groups promote the concerns of small and medium-size businesses, such as barbers, cosmeticians, dry cleaners, innkeepers, and theater owners. Some political influence is in the hands of smaller groups such as the teachers union (*Nikkyoso*), Japan Medical Association, employers association (*Nikkeiren*), and a labor union (*Rengo*).[31]

Despite efforts to maintain an ethical political environment, political corruption is common in many countries around the world. Consider the case of Lebanon.

In the 2009 parliamentary elections, hundreds of millions of dollars streamed into the small nation from around the globe. Seen as a key player in the hotly contested Middle East, voters were given cash or in-kind services presumably paid for by political candidates. Candidates offered their competitors huge sums to withdraw from

[29] Foundation for Public Affairs, *The State of Corporate Public Affairs, 2008–2009* (Washington, DC: Foundation for Public Affairs, 2008), pp. 23–25.

[30] "China to Move against Local Lobbyists," *The New York Times*, January 26, 2010, *www.nytimes.com*.

[31] Ryan Beaupre and Patricia Malone, "Interest Groups and Politics in Japan," *alpha.fdu.edu/~woolley/JAPANpolitics /Beaupre.htm*.

the race. Thousands of Lebanese citizens flew back to their native country with the expectation they would vote for the candidate that paid for the trip. Surprisingly, Lebanon was the first Arab country to impose campaign-spending limits, although analysts admitted that the monitoring was very loose and applied only to the last two months before the election. The laws were laughably easy to circumvent, according to Lebanese election monitors.[32]

Although political corruption appears around the world, in varying degrees, there have been efforts to minimize political corruption, promote fairness in the electoral process, control the rapid rise in the costs of campaigning, enhance the role of political parties in elections, and encourage grassroots participation by various societal groups.

Since 1999, the Global Electoral Organization (GEO) Conference has been held every two to four years to bring together more than 300 of the world's top election officials and democracy advocates to celebrate "transparency in the election process." In 2011, the GEO met in Botswana, Africa, where delegates from western and eastern Europe, central Asia, the Middle East, North America, and Africa discussed the most critical issues in election administration, including how to resolve election disputes, the role of the media in elections, electoral reform, engaging electoral stakeholders, and tracking money in political campaigns. One conference delegate explained, "I think standards are changing and politicians will have to recognize this—that as we are now in the 21st century, public opinion is applying different standards to politics, to politicians, to political parties. They're not allowed to do things they were doing in the 19th and 20th centuries. People have high expectations, high demands, and they will keep politicians accountable."[33]

Political action by business—whether to influence government policy or the outcome of an election—is natural in a democratic, pluralistic society. In the United States, business has a legitimate right to participate in the political process, just as consumers, labor unions, environmentalists, and others do. One danger arising from corporate political activity is that corporations may wield too much power. As businesses operate in different communities and countries, it is important that ethical norms and standards guide managers as they deal with political issues. If corporate power tips the scales against other interests in society, both business and society may lose. Whether it is in the media-rich arena of electoral politics or the corridors of Congress where more traditional lobbying prevails, business leaders must address the issues of how to manage relationships with government and special interests in society in ethically sound ways. Ultimately, business has an important long-term stake in a healthy, honest political system.

Summary

- Some believe that businesses should be involved in politics because their economic stake in government decisions is great and they have a right to participate, just as do other stakeholders in a pluralistic political system. But others believe that businesses are too big, powerful, and selfish, and that they wield too much influence in the political arena.

---

[32] "Foreign Money Seeks to Buy Lebanese Votes," *The New York Times*, April 23, 2009, *www.nytimes.com.*

[33] "Credible Elections for Democracy—the GEO 2011," *Institute for Democracy and Electoral Assistance*, 2011, *www.idea.int /geo2011.*

- There are three political strategies: information, financial incentives, and constituency-building. Some firms implement strategies as needed, on an issue-by-issue basis, while other firms have a long-term, ongoing political strategy approach.

- Some of the political action tactics available for business include lobbying, direct communications, expert witness testimony, political action committee contributions, economic leverage, advocacy advertising, trade association involvement, legal challenges, and encouraging the involvement of other stakeholders.

- Businesses manage their government interactions through a public affairs department. Most public affairs officers report to the CEO or some high-level official, although how these departments are structured is widely varied.

- The differing national rules and practices governing political activity make business's political involvement complex in the global environment. Many governments, like the United States, are trying to restrict lobbying or political contributions or are trying to make the political process more transparent.

Key Terms

ad hoc coalitions, *186*
advocacy advertising, *200*
bundling, *202*
corporate political strategy, *187*
economic leverage, *199*
527 organizations, *198*

leadership PACs, *198*
lobbying, *189*
political action committees (PACs), *193*
public affairs departments, *203*
revolving door, *190*

soft money, *193*
super PACs, *197*
The Business Roundtable, *192*
trade associations, *201*

Internet Resources

www.businessroundtable.org   The Business Roundtable
www.commoncause.org   Common Cause
www.consumeraction.org   Consumer Action
explore.data.gov/ethics   Ethics.data.gov—government data center
lobbyingdisclosure.house.gov   Lobbying Disclosure, U.S. House of Representatives
www.ncpa.org   National Center for Policy Analysis
www.nfib.com   National Federation of Independent Businesses
www.opensecrets.org   Opensecrets.org
www.politicsonline.com   PoliticsOnline: News, Tools & Strategies
pac.org   Public Affairs Council
www.pdc.wa.gov   Public Disclosure Commission
www.fec.gov   U.S. Federal Election Commission

Discussion Case: *Stop Online Piracy Act—A Political Battle between Old and New Media*

The Stop Online Piracy Act (SOPA) was introduced in the U.S. House of Representatives in 2011, along with a companion bill in the U.S. Senate, the Protect Intellectual Property Act (PIPA). If passed, SOPA would give the owners of film, music, or other intellectual property new tools to protect themselves from online piracy or theft. They could sue to force Internet service providers, search engines, payment processors, and advertisement networks to block or stop doing business with websites linked to online piracy. Business was split on the proposed law. The Motion Picture Association of America, the Recording Industry Association of America, and the U.S. Chamber of Commerce—considered "old media"—supported SOPA. But online companies, such as AOL, Twitter, Google, Facebook, Yahoo!, eBay, and others—the "new media"—opposed it. As one blogger remarked, this could become "the biggest controversy in 2012."

Old media proponents argued that the SOPA legislation was needed since rogue websites steal America's innovative and creative products by attracting more than 53 million visits per year, leading to unauthorized downloads of music, films, and books and threatening more than 19 million American jobs in creative industries. More than 400 businesses and organizations, many from the entertainment or publishing industries, collectively contributed $91 million to congressional lobbying efforts in support of SOPA. This was the most the entertainment industry had ever spent on a lobbying effort. Other supporters turned to social media and sent out tweets advocating the necessity of SOPA.

Opponents of SOPA, by contrast, argued that "the bill, as drafted, would expose law-abiding U.S. Internet and technology companies to new uncertain liabilities, private rights of action, and technology mandates that would require monitoring of Web sites," according to a letter sent to members of the House and Senate Judiciary Committees by Goggle, Facebook, Yahoo!, and eBay. Several Internet companies proposed an alternative bill that would punish foreign websites that engaged in copyright infringement through international trade law. "We have a chance to reset the legislative table to find out what kind of legislation is needed," said Markham Erickson, executive director of NetCoalition, a trade group comprised mostly of Internet companies. "We have an opportunity to step back, recalibrate and understand what the problem is." Google's director of public policy added, "Like others, we believe Congress wants to get this right, and we know there are targeted and smart ways to shut down foreign rouge Web sites without asking U.S. companies to censor the Internet."

The new media organizations introduced novel political strategies to combat the act. Critics created a "Censorship US" day and its website encouraged political protest using social media tactics. In January 2012, Reddit.com, a social news site, was joined by other Internet sites, including the politically oriented MoveOn.org, the popular technology and culture blog BoingBoing, and the Internet humor site Cheezburger Network, for a day-long, sitewide blackout to protest SOPA. Wikipedia, the world's free online encyclopedia, was dark for a day except for a short paragraph urging users to protest SOPA on the ground it could "fatally damage the free and open Internet." (Google, Facebook, and Twitter declined to participate in the blackout, despite their public opposition to SOPA. Some criticized the companies, accusing them of being unwilling to sacrifice a day's worth of revenue.)

The critics of SOPA also undertook more traditional political efforts, such a letter writing campaign, sending of e-mails, and making telephone calls to various influential members of Congress. Facebook hired former a White House press secretary, Joe Lockhart, to push the company's opposition in Congress. Goggle reportedly spent $5 million in the first quarter of 2012 to combat SOPA (a 240 percent increase from Google's lobbying spending in the first quarter of 2011), with Microsoft spending $1.8 million, and Amazon and Apple $500,000 each during the same period.

The Stop Online Piracy Act "awakened the entire world," said a Harvard law professor. "They are realizing just how big this fight was becoming." In response, many in Congress reversed their initial position in support of SOPA. "Thanks for all the calls, e-mails and tweets. I will be opposing #SOPA and #PIPA," tweeted Senator Jeff Merkley. Later, Senator Grassley, a senior Republican on the Senate Judiciary Committee, withdrew his support for a bill he helped write.

Political analysts commented that the new media's protests seemed to have worked. Initially 81 members of Congress supported the bill, compared with only 25 legislators opposed (the rest were undecided), but crumbling support may have contributed to Senator Harry Reid's announcement in January 2012 that the Senate's vote on the SOPA counterpart, PIPA, would be delayed. The House quickly followed, announcing that the House Judiciary Committee would postpone consideration of the legislation "until there is wider agreement on a solution." The committee's chair, Lamar Smith, commented, "I have heard from the critics and I take seriously their concerns regarding proposed legislation to address the problem on online piracy."

Sources: "Google, Facebook Warn against New US Piracy Legislation," *BBC News: Technology*, November 16, 2011, *www.bbc.com/news/technology;* "Bills to Stop Web Piracy Invite a Protracted Battle," *The New York Times*, January 15, 2012, *www.nytimes.com;* "Stop Online Piracy Act (SOPA): 2012's Biggest Controversy-to-be?" *Toonari Post*, January 16, 2012, *www.toonaripost.com;* "In Fight over Piracy Bills, New Economy Rises against Old," *The New York Times*, January 18, 2012, *www.nytimes.com;* "Wikipedia Dark, Google Lobbies in Protest of Anti-piracy Bill," *Canada.com*, January 18, 2012, *www.canada.com;* "PIPA Vote and SOPA Hearing Pushed Off as Copyright Bills' Congressional Support Collapses," *Forbes*, January 20, 2012, *www.forbes.com;* and "Under Scrutiny, Google Spends Record Amount on Lobbying," *The New York Times—Bits*, April 23, 2012, *bits.blogs.nytimes.com.*

Discussion Questions

1. Which of the political tactics discussed in this chapter are evident in this case?
2. Why were the political tactics used by the "new media" so effective in this case?
3. Would the effectiveness of these tactics vary, depending on the political issue at stake?
4. What can traditional companies learn from the new forms of political activity described in this case?

PART FIVE

Business and the Natural Environment

CHAPTER TEN

Sustainable Development and Global Business

The world community faces unprecedented ecological challenges in the 21st century. Many political and business leaders have embraced the idea of sustainable development, calling for economic development without destroying the natural environment or depleting the resources on which future generations depend. A critical task in coming decades for government policymakers, civil society organizations, corporate leaders, and entrepreneurial innovators will be to find ways to meet simultaneously both economic and environmental goals.

This Chapter Focuses on These Key Learning Objectives:

- Understanding how business and society interact within the natural environment.
- Defining sustainable development.
- Assessing the major threats to the Earth's ecosystem.
- Recognizing the ways in which population growth, inequality, and economic development interact with the world's ecological crisis.
- Examining common environmental issues that are shared by all nations and businesses.
- Analyzing the steps both large and small businesses can take globally to reduce ecological damage and promote sustainable development.

In 2012, representatives of the world's nations gathered in Rio de Janeiro, Brazil, on the 20th anniversary of the first World Summit on Sustainable Development. The event, called Rio+20, took a hard look at how far the world had come in the previous two decades and what needed to be done, moving forward, to address the urgent need for sustainable development. Would it be possible, the delegates had asked in 1992, to foster economic growth sufficient to lift the majority of the world's people out of poverty without hurting the ability of future generations to meet their own needs? To do so, they reasoned, would require progress on many fronts, including tackling the daunting ecological challenges of accelerating climate change, loss of biodiversity, deforestation, and water scarcity.

Of the many remarkable changes that had occurred in the two decades between the two Earth Summits, one of the most striking was the involvement of businesses, both large and small, from all over the globe in the pursuit of sustainability. In 1992, a few visionary business organizations had met alongside world leaders to consider the implications, for them, of the conference proceedings. Now, two decades later, companies of all types had embraced the challenges of operating within the limits of the Earth's natural systems. Many had recognized the cost savings associated with operating more efficiently, the opportunities to serve consumer markets in emerging economies, the benefits of reducing regulatory risk, and the competitive advantages of innovation in "green" technology. Consider the following examples:

- In 2012, Nike introduced a remarkable new athletic shoe called the Flyknit. Constructed from synthetic yarn and fashioned by a high-tech knitting machine, the Flyknit's upper was made in a single continuous piece, rather than by stitching together dozens of odd-shaped cloth and leather pieces as in a conventionally made shoe. The shoe offered many advantages to athletes, including its light weight and superior comfort. But an important added benefit was that the product was much more sustainable. The new process eliminated vast quantities of wasted scraps. And, because the shoe could be manufactured mostly by machine, the company thought it might be cost-effective to produce in the United States, avoiding the emissions produced by transporting shoes across the Pacific.[1]

- Jetliners flying in and out of Paris, Amsterdam, Frankfurt, and other European airports routinely tracked their emissions of carbon dioxide and other global warming gases. Because airlines were required to buy carbon credits if they exceeded their quotas under international treaties, they had become highly creative in finding ways to reduce their use of jet fuel. They had purchased lighter, more efficient planes, worked with air traffic control to reduce time spent idling on runways, redesigned routes to get from one point to another more directly, and experimented with plant-based fuels. The result was lower carbon emissions, even as the skies were becoming ever more interconnected.

- In 2012, Sahz Holdings, a Malaysian company, invested $33 million in a new factory to make supercapacitors, storage devices used to extend the life span of batteries in electric vehicles, smartphones, and solar-powered devices. With support from the Malaysian government, the company had worked with researchers at a local university to develop a "green" technology to make activated carbon, a critical ingredient in supercapacitors. The company figured out how to use renewable local plants—such as bamboo, coconut shells, and durian fruit skins—as raw material for its activated carbon, providing work for local farmers and avoiding the use of nonrenewable coal. Said one of the Malaysian professors

---

[1] "Is Nike's Flyknit the Swoosh of the Future?" *Bloomberg Businessweek,* March 19, 2012.

who worked on the project, "This will help us maintain our conservation efforts and also use our natural resources to produce high quality and value-added products."[2]

These examples suggest some of the tremendous creativity that businesses, governments, and society were bringing to the ecological challenges addressed by Rio+20. Could all of these groups, working together, put the global economy on a more sustainable course? This chapter will describe the major sustainability challenges facing society and the opportunities these challenges present to businesses globally. The following chapter will focus on specific areas of government regulation and the ways in which businesses, in the United States and other countries, have sought to manage environmental issues.

Business and Society in the Natural Environment

Business and society operate within the natural environment. The extraordinary planet on which we live provides the abundant resources humans use to thrive, but it also imposes constraints. We have only one Earth, and its resources are finite. For human society to survive over time it must operate *sustainably,* in a way that does not destroy or deplete these natural resources for future generations. This fundamental truth confers on business leaders both great challenges and great opportunities.

Chapter 1 introduced the idea of systems theory and explained how businesses cannot be understood in isolation, but only in relationship to the broader society in which they operate. This idea can be extended to the relationship between business and society, on one hand, and the natural environment, on the other. In this view, business and society can be most fully understood in relationship to the broader *natural environment* in which they are embedded and with which they interact. This relationship is illustrated in Figure 10.1.

FIGURE 10.1
Business, Society, and the Natural Environment: An Interactive System

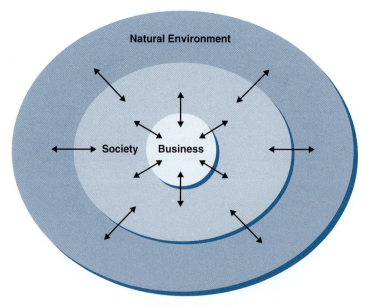

[2] "Sahz to Commercialize Production of Super-Capacitors," Malaysian Investment Development Authority, press release, February 25, 2012, at *www.mida.gov.my;* "Malaysian Scientists Use Tropical Fruits to Make Batteries," February 1, 2011, at *www.scidev.net;* and University of Nottingham, "Making Batteries Last Longer in Electric Vehicles," press release, January 7, 2011, at *www.nottingham.ac.uk.*

The well-known image of the Earth as seen from space—a blue-and-green globe, girdled by white clouds, floating in blackness—dramatically shows us that we share a single, unified natural system, or **ecosystem**. Preserving our common ecosystem and assuring its continued use is an urgent imperative for governments, business, and society. As KPMG International stated in its 2012 report, *Expect the Unexpected,* "The central challenge of our age must be to decouple human progress from resource use and environmental deterioration."[3]

Sustainable Development

The need for balance between economic progress and environmental protection is captured in the concept of **sustainable development**. This term refers to development that "meets the needs of the present without compromising the ability of future generations to meet their own needs" or, more simply, "ensuring a better quality of life for everyone, now and for generations to come."[4] The concept includes two core ideas:

- Protecting the environment will require economic development. Poverty is an underlying cause of environmental degradation. People who lack food, shelter, and basic amenities misuse resources just to survive. For this reason, environmental protection will require providing a decent standard of living for all the world's citizens.

- But economic development must be accomplished sustainably, that is, in a way that conserves the Earth's resources for future generations. It cannot occur at the expense of degrading the forests, farmland, water, and air that must continue to support life on this planet. We must leave the Earth in as good shape—or better shape—than we found it.

Meeting the goal of sustainability is like trying to solve an extraordinarily complex puzzle, in which businesses, governments, civil society, and individuals must work together to achieve common goals.

At its core, sustainable development is about fairness—a central tenet of ethics, as explained in Chapter 4. Fairness requires that the benefits and burdens of an action be distributed equitably, according to an accepted rule. Sustainable development requires an equitable distribution of the benefits gained from the use of natural resources for both current generations (the developing world countries should receive its fair share along with the countries in the developed world) and across generations (the present generation should not gain at the expense of future generations). This can only occur if governments and business leaders work to promote economic development that does not further degrade the environment. For this to happen, the very nature of consumption itself will need to change as people come to emphasize the quality of their lives over the quantity of goods they own, and innovation in a dynamic market economy will need to find new ways to meet human aspirations in a more resource-efficient manner.

What would a sustainable society look like? Of course, there are many paths to sustainability, and there is no way to know for sure what the future will hold. But, one vision of what might be possible is provided by Masdar, a new city in the Persian Gulf that is being designed from the ground up as a completely sustainable community. Masdar is described in Exhibit 10.A.

---

[3] *"Expect the Unexpected: Building Business Value in a Changing World,"* KPMG International, 2012.

[4] World Commission on Environment and Development, *Our Common Future* (Oxford: Oxford University Press, 1987), p. 8; "Sustainable Development: The UK Government's Approach," online at *http://sd.defra.gov.uk.*

Exhibit 10.A

Masdar: A Completely Sustainable Community

Masdar City is a planned development within the boundaries of Abu Dhabi, the capital of the Persian Gulf nation United Arab Emirates (UAE) and, by *Fortune magazine*'s estimate, the wealthiest city in the world. Separated from the rest of Abu Dhabi by a perimeter wall, Masdar has been conceived as the world's first completely sustainable community—and a preview of what a "greener" society might look like. In this futuristic city, no regular cars will be allowed. Rather, people will travel from place to place in a state-of-the-art light rail transit system or in personal rapid transit pods that will zip through underground tunnels. Buildings will be constructed of sustainably harvested wood and other environmentally friendly materials. The city's all-renewable energy will come from a solar power plant and a wind farm outside the perimeter walls. Eighty percent of the city's water, which will come from a desalinization plant, will be recycled; and waste will be incinerated or turned into fertilizer. The city will house both people and clean-tech enterprises, along with the postgradute Masdar Institute for Science and Technology. The entire project, which will cost the government and other investors around $20 billion, is slated for completion by 2025.

Why would a nation that is home to one of the largest oil companies in the world want to develop an urban model of clean technology and innovation? Recognizing that its oil reserves will eventually run out, the UAE has decided to position itself as a global leader in the transition to a non–carbon-based economy.

Source: *www.masdar.ae.*

Threats to the Earth's Ecosystem

Humankind is now altering the face of the planet, rivaling the forces of nature herself—glaciers, volcanoes, asteroids, and earthquakes—in impact. Human beings have literally rerouted rivers, moved mountains, and burned vast forests. By the early part of the 21st century, human society had transformed about half of the Earth's ice-free surface and made a major impact on most of the rest. In many areas, as much land was used by transportation systems as by agriculture. Although significant natural resources—fossil fuels, fresh water, fertile land, and forest—remained, exploding populations and rapid economic development had reached the point where, by some measures, the demands of human society had already exceeded the carrying capacity of the Earth's ecosystem.

These rapid changes pose severe threats to many businesses. They face limited supplies of critical resources, unpredictable weather changes, and increased political risk, among many other challenges. Yet the environmental problems faced by society also present business with great opportunities. Established firms and innovative entrepreneurs who can figure out, for example, how to build offices and houses that are more energy-efficient, produce energy without irreversibly altering the climate, or devise systems to recycle and reuse obsolete electronics, can both help society and enjoy great commercial success.

Human activity affects three major forms of natural resources: water, air, and land. Biologists distinguish between *renewable* resources, such as fresh water or wind, that can be naturally replenished and *nonrenewable* resources, such as fossil fuels (oil, gas, and coal), that once used are gone forever. Many natural resources, renewable and nonrenewable, are now being depleted or polluted at well above sustainable rates. Consider the following examples.

Water Resources

Only 3 percent of the water on the Earth is fresh, and most of this is underground or locked up in ice and snow. Only about one-tenth of 1 percent of the Earth's water is in lakes, rivers, and accessible underground supplies, and thus available for human use. Water is, of course, renewable: Moisture evaporates from the oceans and returns to earth as freshwater precipitation, replenishing used stocks. But in many areas, humans are using up or polluting water faster than it can be replaced or naturally purified, threatening people and businesses that depend on it. This has been especially true in developing countries.

> The Ganges River supports more than 400 million Indians, providing water for drinking, irrigation, fishing, transportation, and trade along its 1,500-mile course from high in the Himalayan mountains to the coastal city of Kolkata (Calcutta). Hindus believe the river to be holy, and it is the site of many religious observances. But the Ganges is increasingly polluted, choked with raw sewage, industrial waste, animal carcasses, and even human remains. "The [river] is the silken thread which binds this country together. What will happen if it breaks?" asked one Indian.

By one estimate, if society were able to eliminate all pollution, capture all available fresh water, and distribute it equitably—all of which are unlikely—demand would exceed the supply within a hundred years. By the early 2010s, water shortages had already caused the decline of local economies and in some cases had contributed to regional conflicts. In Africa, for example, water disputes had flared among Egypt, Ethiopia, and Sudan, the three countries traversed by the world's longest river, the Nile. In the Middle East, disagreement over access to water from the River Jordan had exacerbated conflict between Israel and Palestine. One-third of the world's population lives in countries experiencing moderate to high water stress.[5]

Fossil Fuels

Fossil fuels, unlike water, are nonrenewable. By the end of the 20th century, human society was using 60 times more energy as it did in 1860, when industrialization was in its early stages. Most of this came from the burning of fossil fuels; 83 percent of energy used in the United States, for example, comes from the combustion of coal, oil, and natural gas.[6] The amount of fossil fuel burned by the world economy in one year took about a million years to form, and only one barrel is discovered for every three or four consumed. No one knows how much longer it will be possible to produce oil economically. However, some estimates suggest that oil production will peak by 2020, or may even have already occurred.[7] Coal reserves are plentiful and could last three to four more centuries, although coal is more polluting than either oil or natural gas. Eventually, however, many fossil fuel reserves will be depleted, and the world economy will need to become much more energy efficient and switch to renewable energy sources, such as those based on water, wind, and sunshine.

Arable Land

Arable (fertile) land is necessary to grow crops to feed the world's people. Land, if properly cared for, is a renewable resource. Although the productivity of land increased through much of the 20th century, by the 2010s much of the world's arable land was threatened with decline from soil erosion, loss of nutrients, and water scarcity. Worldwide, a fifth of irrigated land required reclamation because of salinization (excess salt) or poor drainage.[8] In many areas, overly intensive farming practices and climate change have caused

---

[5] Information on world water resources may be found at *www.wri.org* and *www.enviroscope.iges.or.jp.*

[6] "Trends in Renewable Energy Consumption and Electricity 2009," March 31, 2011, available at *www.eia.doe.gov.*

[7] The website of the Association for the Study of Peak Oil and Gas may be found at *www.peakoil.net.* For one analysis that takes into consideration both proven and probable oil reserves, see R. W. Bentley et al., "Assessing the Data of the Global Oil Peak," *Energy Policy,* 35 (12), December 2007.

[8] The most recent statistics may be found at the website of the United Nations Environmental Program at *www.unep.org.*

previously arable land to turn into desert (this process is called *desertification*). In 2001, a massive dust storm caused by overgrazed grasslands in China blew all the way across the Pacific, darkening skies over North America.[9] The United Nations has estimated that 12 million hectares of arable land are lost every year to desertification (one hectare equals about two and a half acres).[10]

Forces of Change

Pressure on the Earth's resource base is becoming increasingly severe. Three critical factors have combined to accelerate the ecological crisis facing the world community and to make sustainable development more difficult: population growth, world income inequality, and the rapid industrialization of many developing nations.

The Population Explosion

A major driver of environmental degradation is the exponential growth of the world's population. A population that doubled every 50 years, for example, would be said to be growing exponentially. Many more people would be added during the second 50 years than during the first, even though the rate of growth would stay the same. Just 10,000 years ago, the Earth was home to no more than 10 million humans, scattered in small settlements. For many thousands of years, population growth was gradual. Around 1950, the world population reached 2.5 billion. World population crossed the 6 billion mark in 1999 and the 7 billion mark in late 2011. The United Nations estimates that the population will reach around 10 billion by 2100. To gain some perspective on these figures, consider that a person born in 1950 who lives to be 75 years old will have seen the world's population increase by more than 5 billion people.

Population growth in the coming decades will not be distributed equally. In the industrialized countries, especially in Europe, population growth has already slowed. Almost all of the world's population growth over the next century is predicted to be in less developed countries, especially in Africa, as shown in Figure 10.2.

The world's burgeoning population will put increasing strain on the Earth's resources. Each additional person uses raw materials and adds pollutants to the land, air, and water. The world's total industrial production would have to quintuple over the next 40 years just to maintain the same standard of living that people have now, if technology remains unchanged. Protecting the environment in the face of rapid population growth is very difficult. For example, in some parts of western Africa, population growth has put great pressure on available farmland, which is not allowed to lie fallow. Because much of the available firewood has already been cut, people use livestock dung for fuel instead of fertilizer. The result has been a deepening cycle of poverty, as more and more people try to live off less and less productive land.

World Income Inequality and Economic Development

A second important cause of environmental degradation is the inequality between rich and poor. Although economic development has raised living standards for many, large numbers of the world's people continue to live in severe poverty. According to the most recent estimates, around 2.5 billion people (about 37 percent of the world's population) had incomes below the international "moderate" poverty line of $2 a day. These people, most of them in sub-Saharan Africa, South Asia, East Asia, and the Pacific, lived very near the margin of

---

[9] This dust storm was tracked by NASA. See *http://science.nasa.gov.*

[10] The most recent statistics may be found at the website of the United Nations Convention to Combat Desertification, at *www.unccd.int/en.*

FIGURE 10.2
Population of the World and Major Areas, 1950–2100

Source: United Nations Population Division, "World Population Prospects: The 2010 Revision: Highlights and Advance Tables," 2011. The projections represent the medium-range scenario. Other estimates are higher and lower. All estimates are available at *www.un.org/esa/population*.

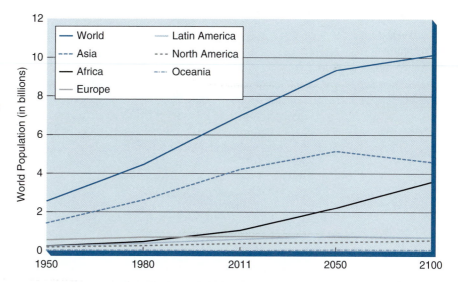

subsistence. They had only a tiny fraction of the goods and services enjoyed by those in the industrialized nations.[11]

> Some of the most extreme poverty is found on the outskirts of rapidly growing cities in developing countries. In many parts of the world, people have moved to urban areas in search of work. Often, they must live in slums, in makeshift dwellings without sanitation or running water. In Manila in the Philippines, a sprawling city of 12 million people, more than a third of the inhabitants live in such shantytowns. Hundreds died when a garbage dump nearby shifted, burying scores of people. Today, more than half of all humans live in cities—many recent migrants to so-called megacities of 10 million or more, such as Lagos, Jakarta, and Mumbai—that lack adequate housing or infrastructure to support them.[12]

The world's income is not distributed equally. The gap between people in the richest and poorest countries is large and getting larger. In 2011, the income of the average American, for example, was 39 times the income of the average Vietnamese and 90 times that of the average Tanzanian. Figure 10.3 illustrates the distribution of private consumption among the world's people, one measure of inequality. The 20 percent of people in the highest-income countries consumed 77 percent of the world's good and services, while the 20 percent in the poorest countries consumed just 1.5 percent. The 60 percent in the middle-income countries consumed 22 percent.

Inequality is an environmental problem because countries (and people) at either extreme of income tend to behave in more environmentally destructive ways than those in the middle. People in the richest countries consume far more fossil fuels, wood, and meat, for example. People in the poorest countries, for their part, often misuse natural resources just to survive, for example, cutting down trees for fuel to cook food and keep warm.

A final source of pressure on the Earth's resource base is the rapid industrialization of many countries. Many parts of Africa, Asia, and Latin America are developing at a rapid pace.

[11] "Dire Poverty Falls Despite Global Slump, Report Finds," *The New York Times,* March 6, 2012. Current data may be found at *www.worldbank.org*.

[12] Data on urban population trends are available at *www.unpa.org*.

FIGURE 10.3

Share of the World's Private Consumption by Income Fifths

Source: "Consumption and Consumerism," March 6, 2011, at *www.globalissues.org,* based on data from *World Bank Development Indicators 2008.*

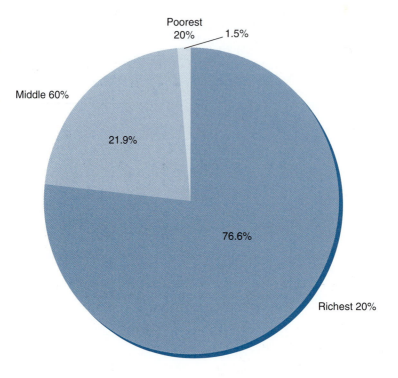

This is positive because it is reducing poverty and slowing population growth. But economic development has also contributed to the growing ecological crisis. Industry requires energy, much of which comes from burning fossil fuels, releasing pollutants. The agricultural "green" revolution, although greatly increasing crop yields in many parts of the world, has caused contamination by pesticides, herbicides, and chemical fertilizers. Development is often accompanied by rising incomes, bringing higher rates of both consumption and waste. In many instances, environmental regulations have lagged the pace of development.

China dramatically illustrates the tight connection between rapid economic development and environmental risk. China is one of the fastest-growing economies in the world, expanding at a rate approaching 10 percent annually on average over the past 30 years. The evidence of industrialization is everywhere, from skyscrapers under construction, to cars crowding the streets, to factories operating 24/7 to produce goods for export. Yet a major consequence has been increased pollution. Fifty-eight percent of China's main rivers are too dirty for human consumption. In Beijing, residents can rarely see nearby mountains because of bad air. The country has some of the world's worst acid rain; 30 percent of its agricultural land is acidified, according to the Worldwatch Institute. China and other fast-growing developing nations challenge business and society to "leapfrog" stages and move directly to cleaner technologies and methods of production. In 2012, Chinese authorities imposed tough new air pollution standards—apparently in response to an online campaign by citizen activists, a highly unusual development in the communist nation.[13]

[13] "China Combats Air Pollution with Tough Monitoring Rules," *The Guardian (U.K.),* March 1, 2012; and Worldwatch Institute, *State of the World 2006: Special Focus—China and India* (New York: W.W. Norton, 2006).

The Earth's Carrying Capacity

Some observers believe that the Earth's rapid population growth, people's rising expectations, and the industrialization of developing countries are on a collision course with a fixed barrier: the limited **carrying capacity** of the Earth's ecosystem. The world's resource base, the air, water, soil, minerals, and so forth, is essentially finite, or bounded. We have only one Earth; the ecosystem itself is not growing. If human societies use up resources faster than they can be replenished, and create waste faster than it can be dispersed, environmental devastation will be the inevitable result.[14] Many believe human society is already overshooting the carrying capacity of the Earth's ecosystem. Just as it is possible to eat or drink too much before your body sends you a signal to stop, so too are people and businesses using up resources and emitting pollution at an unsustainable rate. But because of delays in feedback, society will not understand the consequences of its actions until the damage has been done.

One method of measuring the Earth's carrying capacity, and how far human society has overshot it, is called the **ecological footprint**. This term refers to the amount of land and water a human population needs to produce the resources it consumes and to absorb its wastes, given prevailing technology.

A 2010 study showed that for each living human being, the Earth contained 4.5 acres of biologically productive area—farmland, forest, fresh water, and so forth. At the same time, each person had, on average, an ecological footprint of 6.7 acres. What that means is that human society was using resources and producing waste at a rate about one and a half times above what the Earth's ecosystem could sustainably support. (Overshooting the Earth's carrying capacity is possible in the short run because people can consume resources without allowing them to regenerate.) Historical data show that human society first exceeded world ecological capacity in the late 1980s, and the gap between the two has been widening steadily since then.

Not surprisingly, some nations and individuals have bigger ecological footprints than others. For example, in the United States the average citizen has an ecological footprint of 20 acres, more than four times their share of the world's resources. By comparison, in Panama the average citizen's ecological footprint is 7 acres, and in Bangladesh it is less than 2 acres.[15] These differences reflect the higher levels of consumption and less efficient use of resources in some countries, relative to others.

What can a person do to reduce his or her personal ecological footprint? A website and mobile device application called One Million Acts of Green (*www.onemillion-actsofgreen.com*) enables individuals or groups to select various "acts of green"—such as drinking tap rather than bottled water, carpooling to work, or turning down the air conditioner—and share their commitments on Facebook or other social media networks. Once users achieve a particular goal, the site—operated by GreenNexxus, founded by an environmental entrepreneur—aggregates the results to show how small actions by many people can add up to big environmental benefits. Companies can also sign up to track the actions of their own employees. By 2012, the website had documented enough "acts of green" to save 12 million kilowatt hours of electricity, avoid almost a billion pounds of carbon emissions, and conserve 81 million gallons of water. The site's slogan was, "When we all do one act, we act as one."[16]

---

[14] James Gustave Speth, *The Bridge at the Edge of the World* (New Haven: Yale University Press, 2008); Herman E. Daly, *Beyond Growth: The Economics of Sustainable Development* (Boston: Beacon Press, 1996); and Paul Hawken, Amory Lovins, and L. Hunter Lovins, *Natural Capitalism: Creating the Next Industrial Revolution* (Boston: Little, Brown, 1999).

[15] Data are drawn from the Global Footprint Network, *Ecological Footprint Atlas 2010*, at *www.footprintnetwork.org*. Individuals can estimate their own ecological footprint by taking a quiz available at *www.myfootprint.org*.

[16] Information courtesy of Peter Corbyn, CEO of *www.greennexxus.com*.

Acting together, how can human society bring the Earth's carrying capacity—and the demands placed on it—back into balance? This is without a doubt one of the great challenges now facing the world's people. Any solution will require change on many fronts.

- *Technological innovation.* One approach is to develop new technologies to produce energy, food, and other necessities of human life more efficiently and with less waste. Vast solar arrays in the desert, offshore wind turbines, or state-of-the-art utility plants that pump carbon dioxide deep into the earth could power homes and businesses. Genetic engineering could create more nutritious and productive crops. (Some concerns about genetic engineering are explored in Chapter 13.) Energy-efficient homes and commercial buildings could allow people to go about their lives while using fewer of the Earth's resources. A newly formed company that is harnessing new technologies to model environmental impacts for its corporate customers is described in Exhibit 10.B.

- *Changing patterns of consumption.* Individuals and organizations concerned about environmental impact could decide to consume less or choose less harmful products and services, or to buy from companies committed to sustainability in their own operations. Mobile applications, such as those developed by goodguide.com, allow individuals to scan a product's barcode in a store with their smartphones and receive instant information on its environmental impact. They can modify their purchasing decisions, based on this knowledge. In a consumer society, when many people decide to reduce their personal footprints, society's footprint becomes smaller. For example, homes, workplaces, and places of entertainment could be built closer to each other and to public transit, so people could get where they needed to go with less wasted energy.[17]

- *"Getting the prices right."* Some economists have called for public policies that impose taxes on environmentally harmful products or activities. For example, when an individual bought gasoline—or a utility burned coal to make electricity—they would be charged an added carbon tax. Because prices would reflect true environmental costs, individuals and firms would have an incentive to make less harmful choices. Along these lines, *New York Times* columnist Thomas Friedman has argued for "a fixed, durable, long-term price signal that raises the price of dirty fuels and thereby creates sustained consumer demand for, and sustained private sector investment in, renewables."[18]

Some contemporary thinkers have gone even further and suggested that what is needed is nothing less than a completely new set of values about what is truly important. In this view, society needs a new "sustainability consciousness" that views the quality of life—not the quantity of things—as the most worthy goal of human aspiration. David Korten has stated this view eloquently in his book, *The Great Turning:*

> The Great Turning begins with a cultural and spiritual awakening—a turning in cultural values from money and material excess to life and spiritual fulfillment, from a belief in our limitations to a belief in our possibilities, and from fearing our differences to rejoicing in our diversity. . . . The values shift of the cultural turning leads us to redefine wealth—to measure it by the health of our families, communities, and natural environment.[19]

Technological innovation, smart consumption, and accurate accounting all hold the promise of helping human society realize this vision of the future.

---

[17] A discussion of sustainable urban planning and design may be found in Jonathan Barnett et al., *Smart Growth in a Changing World* (Washington, DC: American Planning Association, 2007).

[18] "Is It Weird Enough Yet?" *The New York Times,* September 13, 2011.

[19] David Korten, *The Great Turning* (San Francisco: Berrett Kohler, 2006).

Exhibit 10.B

Using the Cloud to Model Environmental Benefits

GT Nexus, a fast-growing startup based in Oakland, California, monitors supply chain information for more than 100 companies in a remotely located, cloud-based system. The firm's corporate customers—among them, Hewlett-Packard, Home Depot, Procter & Gamble, and Fiat—submit information online about their orders, payments, and logistics. GT Nexus then tracks and models these data on its massive servers, allowing its customers to drive down costs in their supply chains. For example, Del Monte Foods paid off its investment in the cloud-based data system in just three years; among other improvements, it was able to cut its inbound transit time on average by four days for the many products it sourced from all over the world. But GT Nexus's data also offer the potential for reducing environmental impacts. The firm showed a reporter for *The New York Times* how a customer could, for example, model a proposed shipment of goods for different pollution outcomes, depending on various modes of transportation, ports of entry, and congestion on the routes. The result could be a collaborative use of information technology to move goods more efficiently through a global supply network.

Sources: "Better Economic Forecasts, from the Cloud," *The New York Times,* March 15, 2012; and "Is It Clear Sailing through the Cloud?" *Cargo Business,* April 2012. The company's website *is www.gtnexus.com.*

Global Environmental Issues

A **commons** is a shared resource, such as land, air, or water that a group of people use collectively. The *paradox of the commons* is that if all individuals attempt to maximize their own private advantage in the short term, the commons may be destroyed, and all users, present and future, lose. The only solution is restraint, either voluntary or through mutual agreement.[20] The *tragedy of the commons*—that freedom in a commons brings ruin to all—is illustrated by the following parable.

> There was once a village on the shore of a great ocean. Its people made a good living from the rich fishing grounds that lay offshore, the bounty of which seemed inexhaustible. Some of the cleverest fishermen began to experiment with new ways to catch more fish, borrowing money to buy bigger and better equipped boats. Since it was hard to argue with success, others copied their new techniques. Soon fish began to be harder to find, and their average size began to decline. Eventually, the fishery collapsed, bringing economic calamity to the village. A wise elder commented, "You see, the fish were not free after all. It was our folly to act as if they were."[21]

In a sense, we live today in a global commons, in which many natural resources, like the fishing grounds in this parable, are used collectively. Some environmental problems are inherently global in scope and require international cooperation. Typically these are issues pertaining to the *global commons,* that is, resources shared by all nations. Four global problems that will have major consequences for business and society are ozone depletion, climate change, decline of biodiversity, and threats to marine ecosystems.

Ozone Depletion

Ozone is a bluish gas, composed of three bonded oxygen atoms, that floats in a thin layer in the stratosphere between 9 and 28 miles above the planet. Although poisonous to humans in the lower atmosphere, ozone in the stratosphere is critical to life on Earth by

[20] Garrett Hardin, "Tragedy of the Commons," *Science* 162 (December 1968), pp. 1243–48.

[21] Abridgment of "The Story of a Fishing Village," from *1994 Information Please Environmental Almanac.* Copyright © 1993 by World Resources Institute. Reprinted by permission of Houghton Mifflin Co. All rights reserved.

absorbing dangerous ultraviolet light from the sun. Too much ultraviolet light can cause skin cancer and damage the eyes and immune systems of humans and other species.

Since the mid-1970s, scientists have understood that chlorofluorocarbons (CFCs), manufactured chemicals formerly widely used as refrigerants, insulation, solvents, and propellants in spray cans, could react with and destroy ozone in the upper atmosphere. This has caused a thin spot, or hole, in the Earth's ozone layer, particularly over Antarctica and in the northern latitudes over Europe and North America during the summer, when the sun's ultraviolet rays are the strongest and pose the greatest danger.

In 1987, world leaders negotiated the **Montreal Protocol**, agreeing to cut CFC production; the agreement was later amended to ban CFCs, along with several other ozone-depleting chemicals. Participating countries will have until 2030 to phase out hydrofluorocarbons (HFCs), related chemicals also damaging to the ozone layer. As of 2012, 197 countries, all but a tiny handful, had signed the protocol. Scientists believe that if the agreement is honored, the ozone layer will recover by 2050.[22]

> A number of companies have seen the shift from CFCs to less damaging chemicals as an opportunity for innovation and market growth. DuPont, Allied Signal, Elf-Altochem, and several other chemical companies have developed profitable substitutes for banned ozone-depleting chemicals. All the major appliance manufacturers, such as Electrolux in Sweden and Whirlpool in the United States, have brought out successful new lines of CFC-free refrigerators and freezers, and carmakers have developed air-conditioners that operate without the dangerous coolant.

The world community still faces the challenge of restricting the manufacture of other ozone-depleting substances not yet fully regulated by treaty. But overall, this is an example of world governments working together effectively to address a global environmental threat.

Climate Change

Another difficult problem facing the world community is **climate change**. This term refers to changes in the Earth's climate caused by increasing concentrations of carbon dioxide and other pollutants produced by human activity. These have caused the average surface temperature of the Earth to rise over time, a phenomenon known as **global warming**. But because these gases also have a variety of other complex effects on the climate, scientists often prefer the more general term *climate change.*

The Earth's atmosphere contains carbon dioxide and other trace gases that, like the glass panels in a greenhouse, prevent some of the heat reflected from the Earth's surface from escaping into space, as illustrated in Figure 10.4. Without this so-called greenhouse effect, the Earth would be too cold to support life. Since the Industrial Revolution, which began in the late 1700s, the amount of greenhouse gases in the atmosphere has increased by as much as 25 percent, largely due to the burning of fossil fuels such as oil and natural gas. According to the Intergovernmental Panel on Climate Change (IPCC), a group of the world's leading atmospheric scientists, the Earth has already warmed by between 0.6 and 0.9 degrees Celsius over the past century. (One degree Celsius equals 1.8 degrees Fahrenheit, the unit commonly used in the United States.) The IPCC found that most of the increase was "very likely" due to human-generated greenhouse gases. Depending on whether or not society curbs greenhouse gas emissions, the Earth could warm by as much as 6.4 degrees Celsius (11.5 degrees Fahrenheit) more by 2100.[23]

---

[22] The text of the Montreal Protocol and its various amendments and a list of signatories may be found at *http://ozone.unep.org.*

[23] These estimates are from "Climate Change 2007: Synthesis Report—Summary for Policymakers," November 2007. The next full IPCC report is due in 2014. A complete set of materials may be found at IPCC's website, *www.ipcc.ch.*

FIGURE 10.4
Global Warming

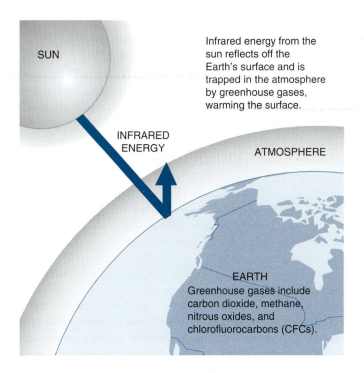

The possible causes of global warming are numerous. The burning of fossil fuels, which releases carbon dioxide, is the leading contributor. But consider the following additional causes.

- *Black carbon.* Recent scientific research has shown that black carbon—the sooty smoke that is created by the incomplete combustion of diesel engines, wildfires, and cookstoves fueled by dung, wood, and charcoal—is the second largest contributor to climate change, responsible for as much as 18 percent of global warming. Black carbon, which can travel thousands of miles in the atmosphere, absorbs heat and settles on glaciers, speeding up melting. A global alliance to reduce black carbon and simultaneously reduce global warming and advance economic development by promoting the use of clean cookstoves in developing nations is described in the discussion case at the end of this chapter.

- *Deforestation.* Trees and other plants absorb carbon dioxide, removing it from the atmosphere. Deforestation—cutting down and not replacing trees—thus contributes to higher levels of carbon dioxide. Scientists have estimated that about half of all original forests have already been cut. Burning forests to clear land for grazing or agriculture also releases carbon directly into the atmosphere as a component of smoke. And when trees are removed, their leaves do not shade the ground, leading to still more warming. Large-scale deforestation thus contributes in several ways to climate change.

- *Beef production.* Methane, a potent greenhouse gas, is produced as a by-product of the digestion of some animals, including cows. Cattle ranching therefore contributes to global warming. According to the Food and Agriculture Organization of the United Nations, livestock are responsible for 18 percent of greenhouse gas emissions, measured in carbon equivalents. As the world's economies develop, people tend to eat more meat; the world's meat consumption is projected to double between 2000 and 2050.[24]

[24] "Humans' Beef with Livestock: A Warmer Planet," *Christian Science Monitor,* February 20, 2007. The report cited is *Livestock's Long Shadow: Environmental Issues and Options* (Rome: United Nations Food and Agriculture Organization, 2006).

- *CFCs.* In addition to destroying the ozone, these are also greenhouse gases. The Montreal Protocol, discussed earlier in this chapter, will have the additional beneficial consequence of slowing global warming. An ongoing problem, however, is that the chemicals now used as substitutes for CFCs (including hydrofluorocarbons, or HFCs) are themselves powerful greenhouse gases. (In fact, one pound of HFC released into the atmosphere has more than 3,000 times the warming impact as the same amount of carbon dioxide.)[25]

If global warming continues, the world may experience extreme heat waves, air pollution crises, violent storms, damaging wildfires, and even epidemics of tropical diseases in the 21st century. The polar ice caps may partially melt, raising sea levels and causing flooding in low-lying coastal areas such as Florida, Bangladesh, and the Netherlands. It may become as difficult to grow wheat in Iowa as it is now in arid Utah. Such climate change could devastate many of the world's economies and destroy the habitats of many species.[26]

In 1997, representatives of many of the world's nations gathered in Kyoto, Japan, to consider amendments to the Convention on Climate Change, an international treaty on global warming. In difficult negotiations, the parties hammered out an agreement called the **Kyoto Protocol**, whose purpose was to stabilize the concentration of greenhouse gases in the atmosphere at a level that would prevent dangerous interference with the climate system. The Kyoto Protocol went into effect in 2005, after countries representing 55 percent of the world's carbon emissions had ratified it. The European Union took an immediate lead, restricting the amount of carbon that could be emitted by power, steel, paper, cement, and glass plants. An official there commented that although compliance with Kyoto would cost money in the short run, energy conservation would cause European firms to become "leaner and more efficient, and that could turn into a long-term business advantage."[27] By 2012, 193 nations had ratified the agreement; the United States, which was responsible for 18 percent of the world's carbon emissions, was not among them.[28] The United Nations hosts an annual meeting, called the Conference of the Parties, at which nations negotiate amendments to the treaty. Among the recent changes to the Kyoto Protocol are agreements to allow developed countries to meet their greenhouse gas reduction targets, in part, by buying carbon offsets through various trading mechanisms such as the European Climate Exchange.

Many companies—whether or not required by treaty to do so—have taken action to reduce their carbon emissions. A study showing the effects of carbon reduction on economic performance is described in Exhibit 10.C.

Decline of Biodiversity

Biodiversity refers to the number and variety of species and the range of their genetic makeup. To date, approximately 1.7 million species of plants and animals have been named and described. Many scientists believe these are but a fraction of the total. According to recent research, the total number may be closer to 9 million, but no one knows for sure.[29]

---

[25] Janos Mate, Kert Davies, and David Kanter, "The Risks of Other Greenhouse Gases," in *2009 State of the World: Into a Warming World* (New York: W.W. Norton, 2009).

[26] Photographs of observable evidence of global warming may be found on the website of *National Geographic,* at *http://environment.nationalgeographic.com/environment/global-warming.*

[27] "New Limits on Pollution Herald Change in Europe," *The New York Times,* January 1, 2005.

[28] The website of the U.N. Framework Convention on Climate Change and a list of countries that have ratified the protocol are at *http://unfccc.int.*

[29] "How Many Species? A Study Says 8.7 Million, but It's Tricky," *The New York Times,* August 30, 2011.

The Carbon Disclosure Project (CDP) conducts an annual survey of 500 leading global companies' carbon management practices on behalf of institutional investors. (Institutional investors are further discussed in Chapter 14.) In 2011, the organization reported that companies with a strategic focus on climate change—so-called carbon performance leaders—had enjoyed a total return to investors of 82 percent over the previous six years, compared with 43 percent for the group as a whole. These leaders had aggressively pursued opportunities to operate more efficiently—helping the environment and their investors at the same time. For example, CSX, the only railroad classified as a performance leader, had invested $1.5 billion over the previous decade to reduce its greenhouse gas emissions. The company had adopted new technology to provide auxiliary power to its locomotives, allowing their diesel engines to shut down while idling. It had also trained its engineers to use the most fuel-efficient throttle settings and had lubricated its rails to reduce friction. These steps, among others, had allowed CSX to move a ton of freight 500 miles on just one gallon of diesel fuel. Concluded the CDP's CEO, "Business must continue to forge ahead, innovate and seek out opportunities by doing more with less. The decisions that perpetuate a legitimate, low carbon and high growth economy will bring considerable value to those that have the foresight to make them."

Source: Carbon Disclosure Project, *CDP Global 500 Report 2011: Accelerating Low Carbon Growth,* available online at *www.cdproject.net.*

Scientists estimate that species extinction is now occurring at 100 to 1,000 times the normal, background rate, mainly because of pollution and the destruction of habitat by human society. Biological diversity is now at its lowest level since the disappearance of the dinosaurs some 65 million years ago. Genetic diversity is vital to each species' ability to adapt and survive and has many benefits for human society as well. By destroying this biological diversity, we are actually undermining our survivability as a species.

A major reason for the decline in the Earth's biodiversity is the destruction of rain forests, particularly in the tropics. Rain forests are woodlands that receive at least 100 inches of rain a year. They are the planet's richest areas in terms of biological diversity. Rain forests cover only about 7 percent of the Earth's surface but account for somewhere between 40 and 75 percent of the Earth's species. At the rate that the original tropical rain forests are currently being cut, all will be gone or severely depleted within 30 years. The reasons for destruction of rain forests include commercial logging, cattle ranching, and conversion of forest to plantations to produce cash crops for export. Overpopulation also plays a part, as landless people clear forest to grow crops, raise livestock, and cut trees for firewood.

The destruction is ironic because rain forests may have more economic value standing than cut. Rain forests are the source of many valuable products, including foods, medicines, and fibers. The pharmaceutical industry, for example, each year develops new medicines based on newly discovered plants from tropical areas. The U.S. National Cancer Institute has identified 1,400 tropical forest plants with cancer-fighting properties. As rain forests are destroyed, so too is this potential source of new medicines.

Some businesses have taken important steps to conserve tropical rain forests. Members of the Consumer Products Forum, an alliance of leading companies including Coca-Cola, Unilever, and Walmart, have agreed not to buy any raw materials—such as beef, soybeans, palm oil, timber, and paper—whose production requires the destruction of forest. For example, Unilever announced it would only buy Indonesian palm oil that came from sustainably operated plantations. The company's CEO stated, "We believed that this could be done without curtailing the expansion of production because there is sufficient unforested land available to meet even the most optimistic estimates of demand, and because yields would improve significantly if everyone adopted the principles of sustainable agriculture."[30]

The Convention on Biological Diversity, an international treaty first negotiated in 1992, addresses many of these issues. By 2012 it had been ratified by 193 countries. (The United States was not among them; it declined to ratify, citing concerns with provisions on intellectual property rights and financial assistance to developing countries.) The treaty commits these countries to draw up national strategies for conservation, to protect ecosystems and individual species, and to take steps to restore degraded areas. It also allows countries to share in the profits from sales of products derived from their biological resources.

Threats to Marine Ecosystems

A final issue of concern is threats to the world's **marine ecosystems**. This term refers broadly to oceans and the salt marshes, lagoons, and tidal zones that border them, as well as the diverse communities of life that they support. Salt water covers 70 percent of the Earth's surface and is home to a great variety of species, from tiny plankton to the giant blue whale, from kelp beds to mangrove forests. Marine ecosystems are important to human society in many ways. Fish, marine mammals, and sea plants provide food and other useful products such as fertilizer, animal feed, cooking and heating oil, medicines, clothing, and jewelry. Healthy coastal zones protect coastlines from erosion and filter runoff from the land. Many communities have survived for centuries off the bounty of the sea.

Today, the health of these ecosystems is increasingly threatened. Some of the key issues include the following:

Fish populations. Oceans provide 90 percent of the world's fish catch. The United Nations has estimated that of the world's marine fisheries, 87 percent are fully exploited or overexploited, and some fisheries—such as those for cod off the Grand Banks (eastern United States and Canada) and for anchovies off Peru—have probably been permanently destroyed by overfishing.[31] Active management, such as limiting the number of fishing boats, establishing fish quotas, or banning fishing for periods of time, has allowed fish to regenerate in some areas.

Coral reefs. Coral reefs are limestone structures that develop from the skeletons of aquatic life and are host to great biological diversity. Today, however, they are in decline from pollution, oceanic warming, damage from ships, and cyanide and dynamite fishing. The Nature Conservancy estimates that at their current rate of decline, 70 percent of coral reefs will be gone within 50 years.

Coastal development. Much of the world's population growth is now concentrated in coastal areas, often in ecologically fragile areas. In the United States, for example, 50 percent of the population lives in countries bordering the ocean—which comprise just 17 percent of the land. Inappropriate development can put pressure on ecologically fragile areas.[32]

Ocean acidity. One effect of increased concentrations of greenhouse gases in the atmosphere has been gradual acidification of the oceans, as seawater has absorbed excess

[30] "It's Happening, but Not in Rio," *The New York Times*, June 24, 2012; *www.unilever.com/sustainable-living;* and *www.theconsumergoodsforum.com.*

[31] "The State of World Fisheries and Acquaculture, 2012," at *www.fao.org.*

[32] Pew Charitable Trusts, "Coastal Sprawl: The Effects of Urban Development on Aquatic Ecosystems in the United States," *www.pewtrusts.org.*

carbon dioxide (which becomes carbonic acid). The result has been the destruction of aquatic life, which is often highly sensitive to acidity.[33]

One group of businesses whose actions directly affect the health of the oceans is the cruise ship industry.

> More than 200 cruise ships, many carrying 5,000 or more passengers and crew members, ply the world's seas, taking some 14 million people a year on a cruise vacation. Cruise ships are literally floating cities, producing on average 30,000 gallons of human waste and seven tons of garbage and solid waste a day. Under international agreements, beyond 12 miles from shore, cruise ships are permitted to discharge untreated sewage, gray water (from kitchens, baths, and laundries), and garbage (except plastic) directly into the ocean. Cruise ships also produce large amounts of oily bilge water, toxic chemicals, and pollution from burning heavy fuel oil, and carry invasive species in their ballast water.[34]

In an effort to address these issues, in 2003 the Cruise Line Industry Association developed a set of voluntary environmental standards, which exceeded the requirements of U.S. and international law. Since then, the industry has dramatically reduced its waste streams, improved fuel efficiency, and cut air pollution. Individual cruise operators have also taken action. Celebrity Cruises, for example, began outfitting its ships with smokeless gas engines. Carnival Cruises began an onboard recycling program, and Royal Caribbean decided not to discharge any waste water while cruising near Australia's Great Barrier Reef. Holland America Lines (a subsidiary of Carnival) partnered with the nonprofit Marine Conservation Institute to redesign onboard menus to feature only sustainably sourced seafood and developed educational programs on ocean conservation for its guests.[35]

Response of the International Business Community

Since so many ecological challenges cross national boundaries, the international business community has a critical role to play in addressing them. This section describes some of the important voluntary initiatives undertaken by companies around the world to put the principle of sustainable development into practice. Other actions by business to address environmental challenges will be explored in Chapter 11.

Life-cycle analysis (LCA), also called *life-cycle assessment,* involves collecting information on the lifelong environmental impact of a product, all the way from extraction of raw material to design, manufacturing, distribution, use, and ultimate disposal. The aim of life-cycle analysis is to minimize the adverse impact of a particular product at all stages, from *cradle to grave.* Having this information can permit companies to make informed choices about how to reduce a product's footprint. For example, a Procter & Gamble life-cycle analysis of its Tide detergent brand found that its greatest environmental impact occurred in the home—when customers washed their clothes in hot water. The company decided to reformulate

[33] "Ocean Acidity May Threaten Coral Reefs, Animals," *Associated Press,* July 9, 2012.

[34] "Cruise Ship Pollution: Background, Laws and Regulations, and Key Issues," CRS Report for Congress, February 6, 2008; The Ocean Conservancy, "Cruise Control: A Report on How Cruise Ships Affect the Marine Environment," *www .oceanconservancy.org;* and "Protect Our Oceans: Stop Cruise Ship Pollution," *www.oceana.org.*

[35] "In Time for Earth Day 2012 Holland America Line Debuts 'Our Marvelous Oceans' Video Series in Partnership with Marine Conservation Institute," press release, April 19, 2012; and Center for Environmental Leadership in Business, "A Shifting Tide: Environmental Challenges and Cruise Industry Responses," *www.celb.org.*

Tide as a cold water-only detergent.[36] Walmart, Dell, Alcoa, and other companies recently organized the Sustainability Consortium to advance LCA for thousands of products.[37]

Industrial ecology refers to designing factories and distribution systems as if they were self-contained ecosystems. For example, businesses can save materials through closed-loop recycling, use wastes from one process as raw material for others, and make use of energy generated as a by-product of production.

> An example of industrial ecology may be found in the town of Kalundborg, Denmark, where several companies have formed a cooperative relationship that produces both economic and environmental benefits. The local utility company sells excess process steam, which had previously been released into a local fjord (waterway), to a local pharmaceutical plant and oil refinery. Excess fly ash (fine particles produced when coal is burned) is sold to nearby businesses for use in cement making and road building. Meanwhile, the oil refinery removes sulfur in the natural gas it produces to make it cleaner burning and sells the sulfur to a sulfuric acid plant. Calcium sulfate, produced as a residue of a process to cut smoke emissions, is sold to a gypsum manufacturer for making wallboard. The entire cycle both saves money and reduces pollution.[38]

Extended product responsibility refers to the idea that companies have a continuing responsibility for the environmental impact of their products or services, even after they are sold. This implies, for example, that firms pay close attention to the energy efficiency of their products when used by the consumer. It also implies that companies design products for disassembly, that is, so that at the end of their useful life they can be disassembled and recycled. At Volkswagen, the German carmaker, engineers design cars for eventual disassembly and reuse. At the company's specialized auto recycling plant in Leer, old cars can be taken apart in just three minutes. Steel, precious metals, oil, acid, and glass are separated and processed. A new process enables even shredder residue—formerly unusable bits of plastic and upholstery fabric—to be diverted from landfill and reused.[39] This is sometimes called *cradle to cradle*, because materials that are used to create one product are later reused to create another.

Carbon neutrality is when an organization or individual produces net zero emissions of greenhouse gases. Since virtually all activity produces some atmospheric warming, this is usually accomplished by a combination of energy efficiencies (to reduce their own emissions) and carbon offsets (to reduce others' emissions). **Carbon offsets** (sometimes called *carbon credits*) are investments in projects that remove carbon dioxide (or its equivalent in other climate-warming pollutants, such as black carbon) from the atmosphere. This can be done, for example, by paying others to plant trees, produce clean energy, or sequester (bury underground) earth-warming gases. A number of organizations now broker carbon offsets to businesses and individuals wishing to reduce their climate impact.

> In 2012, the British retailer Marks & Spencer announced that it had met its commitment, made five years earlier, to become carbon neutral. To achieve this ambitious goal, the company had built an experimental "learning store" in the United Kingdom as well as an "eco-factory" in partnership with a supplier in

---

[36] "Life Cycle Analysis and Green Business Development," October 20, 2011, at *www.claritycommunicationsconsulting.com.*

[37] "The Renaissance of Lifecycle Thinking," August 9, 2009, at *www.greenbiz.com.* For more information on the Sustainability Consortium, see *www.sustainabilityconsortium.org.*

[38] This case is described in *Business and Sustainable Development: A Global Guide,* at *www.bsdglobal.com.*

[39] More information about this technology is available at *www.sicontechnology.com.*

Sri Lanka, to try out new approaches that could be diffused through its system. It had installed solar panels and radically cut energy use at its stores and warehouses, improved the fuel efficiency of its delivery fleet, and reduced the number of business flights taken by employees. It also introduced new products, such as the "first ever carbon neutral bra," part of its Autumn Leaves lingerie collection. Marks & Spencer offset the remainder of its carbon emission by investing in carbon reduction projects. The retailer called its initiative Plan A. As its chief executive explained, "Every business and individual needs to do their bit to tackle the enormous challenges of climate change and waste. We believe a responsible business can be a profitable business. We are calling this 'Plan A' because there is no 'Plan B.'"[40]

Other companies that have achieved—or pledged to achieve—carbon neutrality include salesforce.com, Nike, News Corporation, Timberland, and Van City.[41]

Sustainable development will require **technology cooperation** through long-term partnerships between companies in developed and developing countries to transfer environmental technologies, as shown in the following example.

In Vietnam, Schneider Electric, a global energy company based in France, entered into a partnership with an affiliated local company and a French NGO to provide electricity to villagers in the rural province of Quang Binh, which was not connected to the Vietnamese national power grid. In 2010, the partnership established a micro solar power plant to supply power to homes, schools, and government offices. Local residents, who paid for the electricity with interest-free microcredit, received training in the operation of the system—generating jobs and transferring technical knowledge to an isolated region.[42]

The idea of sustainable development is not only widely accepted in the business community, many firms are fully integrating the concept across many processes. A 2011 global survey of more than 3,000 business leaders, for example, reported that 57 percent said their companies had integrated sustainability into strategic planning, 54 percent into marketing, and 41 percent in supply chain management.[43]

Codes of Environmental Conduct

Earlier chapters of this text have discussed the emergence of standards and codes of conduct in the areas of ethics and global corporate citizenship. Similarly, a number of national and international organizations have developed *standards and codes of environmental conduct.* Some are designed to be universally applicable, while others are tailored to particular industries. All, however, share the characteristic that they are *voluntary:* corporations choose to comply with these codes to show customers, investors, regulators, and others that they have met certain environmental standards in their operations.

---

[40] "Marks & Spencer Operations Certified Carbon Neutral," at *www.environmental leader.com,* June 8, 2012; "Your Marks & Spencer: How We Do Business Report 2011," available at *http://plana.marksandspencer.com;* "Marks and Spencer Launches First Ever Carbon Neutral Bra," press release, April 13, 2011; and "M&S to Go Carbon Neutral in £200m Green Initiative," *The Independent,* January 15, 2007.

[41] A list of companies that have pledged or achieved carbon neutrality may be found in "Who's Going 'Carbon Neutral,'" at *www.bsr.org.*

[42] World Business Council for Sustainable Development, "Schneider Electric: Business Enabling Access to Energy," [case study], at *www.wbcsd.org.*

[43] "The Business of Sustainability: McKinsey Global Survey Results," *McKinsey Quarterly,* October, 2011.

Some of the leading universal codes and standards include the following:

✓ • The International Chamber of Commerce has developed the *Business Charter for Sustainable Development,* 16 principles that identify key elements of environmental leadership and call on companies to recognize environmental management as among their highest corporate priorities.[44]

✓ • The *CERES Principles,* 10 voluntary principles developed by the Coalition for Environmentally Responsible Economies (CERES), commit signatory firms to protection of the biosphere, sustainable use of natural resources, energy conservation, risk reduction, and other environmental goals.[45]

✓ • *ISO 14000* is a series of voluntary standards developed by the ISO, an international group based in Geneva, Switzerland, that permit companies to be certified as meeting global environmental performance standards.[46]

✓ • The *Greenhouse Gas Protocol* is a tool developed by the World Resources Institute and the World Business Council for Sustainable Development to help businesses meaure and manage their greenhouse gas emissions.[47]

Codes of environmental conduct have also been developed by and for specific industries.

A prominent example is the Equator Principles, a set of environmental standards for the financial services industry. Their focus is specific to banking: they commit signatories to determine, assess, and manage environmental risk in project financing. In other words, when a bank considers whether or not to lend money, for example, for the construction of an oil pipeline, it must examine the environmental impact of the project and whether or not its sponsors have systems in place to mitigate adverse impacts. Where borrowers are unable to comply, the bank will not loan them money. The Equator Principles, launched in 2003 and most recently reviewed in 2011, have spread widely in the financial industry. By 2012, 76 banks around the world had signed on, ranging from huge institutions such as Citigroup to regional banks such as Egypt's Arab African International Bank, China's Industrial Bank Company, and Uruguay's Banco de la Republica Oriental.[48]

Other industry-specific standards include the Forest Stewardship Council Principles in the forest products industry, the Marine Stewardship Council in the fishing industry, and the U.S. Green Building Code standards for the commercial and residential construction industry.

Protecting the environment and the well-being of future generations is not only a necessity, but also an opportunity for business. Environmental regulations are getting tougher, consumers want cleaner products, and employees want to work for environmentally conscious companies. Finding ways to reduce or recycle waste saves money. Many executives are championing the idea that corporations have moral obligations to future generations. The most successful global businesses in coming years may be those, like the ones profiled in this chapter, that recognize the imperative for sustainable development as an opportunity both for competitive advantage and ethical action.

---

[44] *www.iccwbo.org/policy/environment.*

[45] *www.ceres.org.*

[46] *www.iso.org.*

[47] *www.ghgprotocol.org.*

[48] The website of the Equator Principles is *www.equator-principles.com.*

Summary

- Business and society operate within a finite natural environment. This reality confers constraints but also provides opportunities.

- Many world leaders have supported the idea of sustainable development, that is, development that meets the needs of the present without hurting the ability of future generations to meet their own needs. Governments, businesses, and civil sector organizations are engaged in a range of innovations in an effort to reach this goal.

- Major threats to the Earth's ecosystem include depletion of nonrenewable resources such as oil and coal, air and water pollution, and the degradation of arable land.

- Population growth, income inequality, and rapid economic development in many parts of the world have contributed to these ecological problems. Human society is now using resources and producing waste at a rate well above what the Earth's ecosystem can sustainably support.

- Four environmental issues—climate change, ozone depletion, declining biodiversity, and threats to the marine ecosystem—are shared by all nations. International agreements are addressing these issues, although more remains to be done.

- Global businesses have begun to put the principles of sustainable development into action through such innovative actions as life-cycle analysis, industrial ecology, extended product responsibility, carbon neutrality, technology cooperation, and compliance with various voluntary codes.

Key Terms

biodiversity, *224*
carbon neutrality, *228*
carbon offset, *228*
carrying capacity, *219*
climate change, *222*
commons, *221*
ecological footprint, *219*

ecosystem, *213*
extended product responsibility, *228*
global warming, *222*
industrial ecology, *228*
Kyoto Protocol, *224*
life-cycle analysis, *227*

marine ecosystems, *226*
Montreal Protocol, *222*
ozone, *221*
sustainable development, *213*
technology cooperation, *229*

Internet Resources

www.ipcc.ch	Intergovernmental Panel on Climate Change
www.epa.gov/docs/ozone	Environmental Protection Agency ozone site
www.unep.org	United Nations Environmental Program
unfccc.int	United Nations Framework Convention on Climate Change
www.wbcsd.ch	World Business Council on Sustainable Development
www.iclei.org	International Council for Local Environmental Initiatives (ICLEI)
www.earthcharterinaction.org	The Earth Charter Initiative
www.worldwatch.org	The Worldwatch Institute
www.wri.org	World Resources Institute
www.earthtrends.wri.org	Earthtrends

Discussion Case: *Clean Cooking*

In a small village in rural Kenya, a woman bent over an open fire pit in the center of her hut cooking the evening meal. That morning, she had spent two hours collecting wood, animal dung, and scrap paper to use as fuel. Now, as she stirred the pot, the cook fire gave off a steady stream of sooty, acrid smoke, which filled the room despite a ventilation hole in the roof. The woman's young son played dangerously close to the open flame, while her daughter, coughing from the smoke, tried to read by the weak light of the fire.

In 2012, a similar scene was repeated in more than 600 million households every day across the developing world, with devastating effects on human health, the environment, and economic development.

Indoor air pollution from open cookstoves is a killer. The World Health Organization has estimated that soot, particles, and smoke from cooking is the fifth worst risk factor for health in developing countries, causing two million premature deaths a year from lung and heart disease—more than malaria and tuberculosis combined. Open cookstoves also lead to disfiguring burns, asthma, eye damage, and pregnancy complications. The effects are greatest on women and young children, who spend the most time near the hearth.

Women and girls also suffer from head and back injuries, animal attacks, and sexual violence while searching for and carrying heavy loads of fuel, often far from home. Time spent collecting fuel is time not spent attending school, working at a paid job, or running a small business.

Primitive cooking methods also harm the environment. Cutting trees to produce wood or charcoal leads to deforestation, loss of biodiversity, and watershed degradation. Moreover, the combustion of biomass in cooking produces more than a quarter of the world's black carbon, or soot. Scientists now believe that soot is second only to carbon dioxide in its overall contribution to global warming. Policymakers have been intrigued by the fact that while carbon dioxide stays in the atmosphere for decades, black carbon washes out within days or weeks. Reducing soot in the atmosphere would thus have a much more immediate effect on global warming than cutting carbon emissions.

In 2010, the United Nations Foundation, in collaboration with several governments (including the United States), launched the Global Alliance for Clean Cookstoves, with the ambitious goal of "100 by 20"—that 100 million households worldwide adopt clean and efficient cookstoves and fuels by 2020. The alliance recognized that reaching this goal would require more than money; it would require technical innovation in fuels and stove design, new mechanisms of financing, and on-the-ground campaigns to engage users from a wide range of cultures and cooking traditions. It would also require the support of businesses—large and small.

One company that saw an opportunity in the Global Alliance for Clean Cookstoves was Dow Corning. In 2011, the Midland, Michigan–based maker of silicon-based materials donated $5 million over five years to support the alliance. The firm had first become interested in the issue when its volunteer Citizen Service Corps participated in a clean cookstove project in Bangalore, India. Dow Corning believed that not only its money, but also its expertise in manufacturing and material science could be of value to the initiative.

At the same time, motivated by greater attention to the issue, social entrepreneurs across the globe began generating innovative ideas about how to design, manufacture, and finance more efficient and cleaner cookstoves—potentially a "win–win" for the environment and human health and well-being.

For example, in the west African country of Ghana, Suraj Wahab founded a small business, Toyola Energy Ltd., to produce a cookstove he invented called the *gyapa* ("good fire"). His company constructed the stove from locally sourced materials—scrap metal from construction sites and fired clay liners. Because it was designed to burn charcoal, a fuel used by 30 percent of Ghanaian households, twice as efficiently as in an open fire, each stove over the course of its life would prevent the release of global-warming emissions equivalent to the amount generated by a Honda Civic driven for one year.

Wahab had difficulty obtaining needed capital until he partnered with E+Co, a clean energy nonprofit that invested $270,000. E+Co helped Toyola calculate the carbon offset value of its cookstoves, which was then monetized and sold to the investment banking firm Goldman Sachs. By 2011, Toyola employed 150 people and had sold more than 150,000 cookstoves to eager Ghanaians, who welcomed the cost savings and health benefits they provided. More than a quarter of the company's revenue came from the sale of carbon offsets, helping keep the price to consumers as low as $7.

Similar stories of creative partnerships were occurring around the globe. In Bangladesh, Grameen Shakti—part of the Grameen family of microcredit organizations founded by Nobel Peace Prize laureate Mohammed Yunus—launched a program to spread improved cookstoves in rural areas. Grameen Shakti provided technical assistance and loans to entrepreneurs—many of them women—to set up small businesses to make, repair, and market cleaner-burning stoves.

The nonprofit Trees, Water, & People, based in Fort Collins, Colorado, built and distributed almost 50,000 cookstoves in Guatemala. Their stove was an insulated metal box topped by a removable cooking surface adapted to cooking tortillas and a chimney pipe to vent smoke through a roof hole. Increased fuel efficiency saved families about ten dollars a month, in a society in which 80 percent of the population lived on two dollars a day or less. Other organizations, such as Solar Cookers International, experimented with ways to harness the power of the sun—a completely renewable, clean, and free source of energy—to boil water and cook food.

Contributions like these moved the Alliance closer to its ambitious goal. "As we build a cookstoves market to the scale necessary to combat and defeat this silent killer," said its executive director in 2011, "the strong support and unique expertise of our partners and champions will be invaluable."

Sources: "Igniting Change," Global Alliance for Clean Cookstoves, November, 2011, at *www.cleancookstoves.org;* "Momentum Continues to Build for Global Alliance for Clean Cookstoves on First Anniversary," September 23, 2011, at *www.cleancookstoves.org;* World Bank, *One Goal, Two Paths: Achieving Universal Access to Modern Energy in East Asia and the Pacific,* 2011; "Forest Saving Stoves Program," at *www.treeswaterpeople.org;* "Climate Proposal Puts Practicality Ahead of Sacrifice," *The New York Times,* January 16, 2012; "Turning Carbon into Cash," *Newsweek,* December 14, 2009; "Black Carbon: The Dark Horse of Climate Change Drivers," *Environmental Health Perspectives,* April, 2011; "Black Carbon: An Overlooked Climate Factor," *TIME Magazine,* November 13, 2009; "Turning Carbon into Cash," *Newsweek,* December 14, 2009; "Clean Cookstoves: Dow Corning's Path to Public-Private Partnership," *http://dowcorningcitizenservicecorps .wordpress.com,* February 28, 2012; "A Quick (Partial) Fix for an Ailing Atmosphere," *Science,* January 13, 2012; and "Case Study: Toyola Energy Limited, Ghana," April 2011, at *www.ashdenawards.org.*

Discussion Questions

1. In what ways would the widespread adoption of clean cookstoves address the global environmental issues discussed in this chapter?

2. In what ways would the widespread adoption of clean cookstoves address the issues of economic development and poverty discussed in this chapter?

3. Which sectors (e.g., government, business, civil society) would need to be involved in a successful campaign to promote clean cookstoves in the developing world, and what would be the contributions of each?

4. What would be the benefit to multinational corporations, such as Dow Corning, of participating in this effort?

Managing Environmental Issues

Growing public concern about the health of the Earth's ecosystem has prompted political, corporate, and civil society leaders to become increasingly responsive to environmental issues. In the United States and other nations, government policymakers have moved toward greater reliance on economic incentives, rather than command and control regulations, to achieve environmental goals. At the same time, many businesses have become increasingly proactive and have pioneered new approaches to effective environmental management, sometimes in partnership with advocacy organizations. These actions have often given firms a competitive advantage by cutting costs, gaining public support, and spurring innovation.

This Chapter Focuses on These Key Learning Objectives:

- Knowing the main features of environmental laws in the United States and other nations.
- Understanding the advantages and disadvantages of different regulatory approaches.
- Assessing the costs and benefits of environmental regulation.
- Defining an ecologically sustainable organization and the stages through which firms progress as they become more sustainable.
- Understanding how businesses can best manage environmental issues.
- Analyzing how effective environmental management makes firms more competitive.

A sprawling factory just off Interstate 65 in Lafayette, Indiana, produces around 800 Subaru cars a day. The plant, which is owned by Fuji Industries of Japan, is one of the most environmentally responsible in the world. The factory sends no waste at all to landfills. "I put more on my curb every week than [the entire plant does]," commented the plant's head of environmental compliance. The company returns packaging materials—including the Styrofoam used to protect engines in transit—to suppliers, to be used again. Cafeteria scraps go to a nearby waste-to-energy power plant. The company processes and reuses solvent and oil. Dried paint sludge is shipped to other companies that use it to make railroad ties, parking lot bumpers, and bicycle helmets. Leftover metal slag goes to a company that extracts the copper it contains. These initiatives not only reduce the plant's environmental impact, they also save the company more than $2 million a year.[1]

New Zealand, following in the footsteps of the European Union, in 2008 adopted an innovative policy to curb global warming—a system of tradable permits for carbon dioxide emissions. Opting for a flexible, market-based approach, the New Zealand government allocated permits, or quotas, across broad sectors of its economy, including energy, manufacturing, and forestry. Companies that were able to cut their emissions of the greenhouse gases could sell their permits to others that had exceeded their quota, providing an incentive to reduce their pollution. Over time, the government ratcheted down the number of permits in circulation, driving down the overall carbon dioxide emissions. In 2011, an evaluation of the program's impact found a marked shift toward the use of renewable energy and a change from a net loss to a net gain of trees in the forest products industry. Sixty-three percent of business executives polled by the government said they supported the program, up from just 22 percent two years earlier.[2]

The Environmental Defense Fund (EDF), a leading environmental advocacy organization, has formed partnerships with a number of companies, including McDonald's, DuPont, Levi Strauss, and Starbucks, to improve their environmental performance. In one such partnership, it worked with FedEx, the world's largest express transportation company, to develop a more environmentally friendly delivery truck. The organization's scientists worked with FedEx and with Eaton, a truck manufacturer, to design a new hybrid vehicle, powered by both a conventional combustion engine and an electric motor that burned 50 percent less fuel and decreased emissions by more than 75 percent. By 2012, FedEx operated one of the largest fleets of commercial hybrid vehicles in North America. An important legacy of the partnership was that it had prompted the manufacturers to develop electric batteries for trucks, enabling greater fuel efficiency at other companies—such as Walmart, which began experimenting with hybrid tractor-trailers in its fleet.[3]

In the early years of the 21st century, many businesses, governments, and environmental advocacy organizations became increasingly concerned that old strategies for promoting environmental protection were failing and new approaches were necessary. Government policymakers moved toward greater reliance on economic incentives to achieve environmental goals. Environmentalists engaged in greater dialogue and cooperation with industry leaders. Many businesses pioneered new approaches to effective environmental management, such as using waste from one process as input for another.

---

[1] "Subaru Lessons: Environmental Savings Can Pay Off," *News-Sentinel* [Fort Wayne, Indiana], October 1, 2011; and "Greener and Cheaper: The Conventional Wisdom Is That a Company's Costs Rise as Its Environmental Impact Falls; Think Again," *The Wall Street Journal,* March 23, 2009. The website of Subaru Industries of America is at *www.subaru-sia.com.*

[2] "NZ Trading Scheme Slashes Carbon Emissions," *The Age* (Australia), August 2, 2011. New Zealand's *Emission Trading Scheme Review Report* is available at *www.climatechange.govt.nz.*

[3] "FedEx: Cleaner Air with Hybrid Trucks," at *www.edf.org;* and "Building the Most Fuel Efficient Truck," *Fleet Owner,* June 1, 2011. More information about EDF's corporate partnerships is available at *www.edf.org/approach/partnerships/corporate.*

The challenge facing government, industry, and environmental advocates alike, as they tried out new approaches and improved on old ones, was how to promote ecologically sound business practices in an increasingly integrated world economy.

Role of Government

In many nations, government is actively involved in regulating business activities in order to protect the environment. Business firms have few incentives to minimize pollution if their competitors do not. A single firm acting on its own to reduce discharges into a river, for example, would incur extra costs. If its competitors did not do the same, the firm might not be able to compete effectively and could go out of business. Government, by setting a common standard for all firms, can take the cost of pollution control out of competition. It can also provide economic incentives to encourage businesses, communities, and regions to reduce pollution, and offer legal and administrative systems for resolving disputes. Government cannot accomplish environmental goals by itself; its role, rather, is to make a critical contribution to a collective effort, together with business and civil society, to move toward sustainability.

In the United States, government has been involved in environmental regulation at least since the late 19th century, when the first federal laws were passed protecting navigable waterways. The government's role began to increase dramatically, however, around 1970. Figure 11.1 summarizes the major federal environmental laws enacted by the U.S. Congress in the modern environmental era. The nation's main pollution control agency is the **Environmental Protection Agency (EPA)**, which was created in 1970 to coordinate most of the government's efforts to protect the environment. Other government agencies involved in enforcing the nation's environmental laws include the Nuclear Regulatory Commission (NRC), the Occupational Safety and Health Administration (OSHA), and various regional, state, and local agencies.

Major Areas of Environmental Regulation

In the United States, the federal government regulates in three major areas of environmental protection: air pollution, water pollution, and land pollution (solid and hazardous waste). This section will review the major ecological issues and the U.S. laws pertaining to each, with comparative references to similar initiatives in other nations.

Air Pollution

Air pollution occurs when more pollutants are emitted into the atmosphere than can be safely absorbed and diluted by natural processes. Some pollution occurs naturally, such as smoke and ash from volcanoes and forest fires. But most air pollution today results from human activity, especially industrial processes and motor vehicle emissions. Air pollution degrades buildings, reduces crop yields, mars the beauty of natural landscapes, and harms people's health. The American Lung Association (ALA) estimated in 2011 that 154 million Americans, more than half of the population, were breathing unsafe air for at least part of each year. Fully 70 percent of the cancer risk from air pollution is due to diesel exhaust from trucks, farm and construction equipment, marine vessels, and electric generators. People living near busy highways and workers in occupations that use diesel equipment are particularly at risk.[4]

---

[4] American Lung Association, "State of the Air: 2011," at *www.lungusa.org*; and "Health Effects of Diesel Exhaust," at *http://ochha.ca.gov*.

FIGURE 11.1
Leading U.S.
Environmental
Protection Laws

Year	Law	Description
1969	National Environmental Policy Act	Created Council on Environmental Quality to oversee quality of the nation's environment.
1970	Clean Air Act	Established national air quality standards and timetables.
1972	Water Pollution Control Act	Established national goals and timetables for clean waterways.
1972	Pesticide Control Act	Required registration of and restrictions on pesticide use.
1973	Endangered Species Act	Conserved species of animals and plants whose survival was threatened or endangered.
1974 & 1996	Safe Drinking Water Act	Authorized national standards for drinking water.
1974	Hazardous Materials Transport Act	Regulated shipment of hazardous materials.
1976	Resource Conservation and Recovery Act	Regulated hazardous materials from production to disposal.
1976	Toxic Substances Control Act	Established national policy to regulate, restrict, and, if necessary, ban toxic chemicals.
1977	Clean Air Act amendments	Revised air standards.
1980	Comprehensive Environmental Response Compensation and Liability Act (Superfund)	Established Superfund and procedures to clean up hazardous waste sites.
1986	Superfund Amendments and Reauthorization Act (SARA)	Established toxics release inventory.
1987	Clean Water Act amendments	Authorized funds for sewage treatment plants and waterways cleanup.
1990	Clean Air Act amendments	Required cuts in urban smog, acid rain, and greenhouse gas emissions; promoted alternative fuels.
1990	Pollution Prevention Act	Provided guidelines, training, and incentives to prevent or reduce pollution at the source.
1990	Oil Pollution Act	Strengthened EPA's ability to prevent and respond to catastrophic oil spills.
1999	Chemical Safety Information, Site Security, and Fuels Regulatory Relief Act	Set standards for the storage of flammable chemicals and fuels.

One approach to reducing diesel pollution is a service called IdleAir, operated by Convoy Solutions of Knoxville, Tennessee. IdleAir provides an alternative for long-haul truck drivers who idle their engines at truck stops in order to provide power to the cab during rest breaks. An inexpensive window-mounted adapter allows drivers to hook up to a service module, so they can continue to enjoy heating, cooling, cable TV, and Internet access with their engines off. The solution is less expensive for truckers because it uses one-tenth the energy of idling, and reduces pollution by completely eliminating diesel emissions during rest breaks.[5]

The EPA has identified six criteria pollutants, relatively common harmful substances that serve as indicators of overall levels of air pollution. These are lead, carbon monoxide, particulate matter, sulfur dioxide, nitrogen dioxide, and ozone. (Ozone at ground level is a particularly unhealthy component of smog.) In addition, the agency also has identified a list of toxic air pollutants that are considered hazardous even in relatively small concentrations. These include asbestos, benzene (found in gasoline), dioxin, perchloroethylene (used in some dry-cleaning processes), methylene chloride (used in some paint strippers), and radioactive materials. Emissions of toxic pollutants are strictly controlled. In 2009, for the first time, the EPA classified carbon dioxide and several other greenhouse gases as pollutants, and thus subject to regulation, because of the potential hazards of global warming to human health.

A special problem of air pollution is **acid rain**. Acid rain is formed when emissions of sulfur dioxide and nitrogen oxides, by-products of the burning of fossil fuels by utilities, manufacturers, and motor vehicles, combine with natural water vapor in the air and fall to earth as rain or snow that is more acidic than normal. Acid rain can damage the ecosystems of lakes and rivers, reduce crop yields, and degrade forests. Structures, such as buildings and monuments, are also harmed. Within North America, acid rain is most prevalent in New England and eastern Canada, regions that are downwind of coal-burning utilities in the Midwestern states.[6] Acid rain is especially difficult to regulate because adverse consequences often occur far—often, hundreds of miles—from the source of the pollution, sometimes across international borders. The major law governing air pollution is the Clean Air Act, passed in 1970 and amended in 1990. The 1990 Clean Air Act toughened standards in a number of areas, including stricter restrictions on emissions of acid rain–causing chemicals.

The efforts of the U.S. government to reduce acid rain illustrate some of the difficult trade-offs involved in environmental policy. These are described in Exhibit 11.A.

Water Pollution

Water pollution, like air pollution, occurs when more wastes are dumped into waterways, lakes, or oceans than can be naturally diluted and carried away. Water can be polluted by organic wastes (untreated sewage or manure), by chemicals from industrial processes, and by the disposal of nonbiodegradable products (which do not naturally decay). Heavy metals and toxic chemicals, including some used as pesticides and herbicides, can be particularly persistent. Like poor air, poor water quality can harm ecosystems, decrease crop yields, threaten human health, and degrade the quality of life. Failure to comply with clean water laws can be very expensive for business, as the following example shows.

In 2010, a wellhead blowout at a deepwater drilling platform operated on behalf of BP (formerly British Petroleum) in the Gulf of Mexico caused the largest marine oil spill in U.S. history. For three months, as crews struggled to cap the well, as much as 5 million barrels of oil gushed into the waters of the Gulf of Mexico, causing extensive damage to marine life and devastating the coastal economies of adjacent states. Subsequent government investigations found that BP's relentless

---

[5] The company's website is *www.idleair.com.*

[6] More information about acid rain may be found at *www.epa.gov/acidrain.*

As part of its efforts to control acid rain, the U.S. government in 1990 initiated stricter new restrictions on the emission of sulfur dioxide by utilities. Many electric companies complied with the law by switching from high-sulfur coal, which produces more sulfur dioxide when burned, to low-sulfur coal, which produces less. This action had the beneficial effect of reducing acid rain.

But the law had some environmentally destructive results that had been unintended by regulators. Much of the highest-quality low-sulfur coal in the United States lies in horizontal layers near the tops of rugged mountains in Appalachia, including parts of West Virginia, Kentucky, Tennessee, and Virginia. Some coal companies discovered that the cheapest way to extract this coal was through what came to be known as mountaintop removal. Explosives were used to blast away up to 500 feet of mountaintop. Massive machines called draglines, 20 stories tall and costing $100 million each, were then used to remove the debris to get at buried seams of coal. A 2009 study using satellite images estimated that 1.2 million acres had been ravaged in this manner by surface mining.

Although coal operators were required to reclaim the land afterward—by filling in adjacent valleys with debris and planting grass and shrubs—many environmentalists believed the damage caused by mountaintop removal was severe. Many rivers and creeks were contaminated and habitat destroyed. Aquifers dried up, and the entire region became vulnerable to devastating floods. Many felt it was deeply ironic that a law that was designed to benefit the environment in one way had indirectly harmed it in another.

Source: "The High Cost of Cheap Coal: When Mountains Move," *National Geographic,* March 2006, pp. 105–23. Aerial maps showing the location and extent of surface mines may be found at *www.skytruth.org.* Studies on the extent of mountaintop removal mining and reclamation efforts are available at *http://ilovemountains.org.*

cost cutting and inadequate safety systems had contributed to the spill. In 2012, BP was negotiating civil fines and criminal penalties for violations of the Clean Water Act that could reach as high as $21 billion, in addition to payments of around $8 billion already made by the company to settle lawsuits with individuals and businesses harmed by the spill. Cases brought by shareholders, state governments, and the company's business partners were still pending. Much of the money from the government fines was slated to be returned to the Gulf states to aid in their recovery.[7]

In the United States, regulations address both the pollution of rivers, lakes, and other surface bodies of water and the quality of the drinking water. The main U.S. law governing water pollution is the Water Pollution Control Act, also known as the Clean Water Act. This law aims to restore or maintain the integrity of all surface water in the United States. It requires permits for most *point* sources of pollution, such as industrial emissions, and mandates that local and state governments develop plans for *nonpoint* sources, such as agricultural runoff or urban storm water. The Pesticide Control Act specifically restricts the use of dangerous pesticides, which can pollute groundwater.

The quality of drinking water is regulated by another law, the Safe Drinking Water Act of 1974, amended in 1996. This law sets minimum standards for various contaminants in both public water systems and aquifers that supply drinking water wells. The impacts of hydraulic fracturing, a method for extracting natural gas from underground shale formations, on the quality of drinking water—and how these impacts should be regulated—is explored in Exhibit 11.B.

[7] "BP Close to Spill Settlement," *The Wall Street Journal,* October 10, 2012.

Hydraulic fracturing—or *fracking,* as it is sometimes known—has been called the gold rush of the 21st century because so many companies and people are rushing to make their fortunes by extracting natural gas from underground shale formations. But, who will regulate its environmental impacts, especially on drinking water?

One of the largest reserves of natural gas in the world is the Marcellus Shale, a massive formation that underlies much of Pennsylvania, West Virginia, New York, Ohio, and Maryland. The Marcellus is estimated to contain 489 trillion cubic feet of recoverable gas (by comparison, the entire state of New York uses about 1 trillion cubic feet a year). Other shale formations lie under Illinois, Texas, Arkansas, Wyoming, and Colorado.

In recent years, technology has evolved to make possible the economic extraction of gas from the Marcellus and other shale formations. In hydraulic fracturing, a vertical well is drilled as deep as 7,000 feet before turning horizontally into the gas-bearing layer. Operators then pump in vast quantities of water, sand, and chemicals under high pressure to break up the shale and release the gas, which is brought back up the drill hole. By rotating the horizontal turns in successive passes, a single well can reach a large area underground.

Hydraulic fracturing has a number of benefits. The gas boom has reduced American dependence on foreign oil and created jobs and tax revenue. By 2015, for example, by some estimates gas drilling will add more than $4 billion to the economy of Pennsylvania annually. Natural gas burns cleaner than either coal or oil, producing less pollution and providing a possible bridge to a future economy based on renewable energy.

But fracking also carries serious environmental risks. Trucks and heavy equipment cause noise and air pollution in and around drilling sites. Chemicals injected underground in the fracking process include a host of toxins. Fluid that returns to the surface—called *flowback*—is often further contaminated by radioactive substances, heavy metals, and volatile organic compounds from deep in the earth. Flowback is often shipped to sewage treatment plants, where it is treated and discharged into lakes and rivers that supply drinking water for downstream communities. The problem is that sewage plants are designed to treat sewage, not contaminated industrial wastewater.

In 2005, Congress exempted hydraulic fracturing from the Safe Drinking Water Act. Critics called this exemption the "Halliburton loophole" because it was recommended by the Energy Task Force headed by former vice president Dick Cheney, who had earlier served as CEO of Halliburton, a company active in the fracking industry. Some states, counties, and cities moved to regulate hydraulic fracturing on their own. For example, several states passed laws requiring that companies disclose the chemicals in their fracking fluids, and others put all drilling permits on hold until they better understood the risks. Some cities—including Pittsburgh and Buffalo—banned fracking outright. But regional and local leaders faced great challenges in properly regulating gas extraction from a geological formation that did not respect political boundaries. In 2012, the White House established an interagency working group so that various federal agencies could better coordinate their oversight of the hydraulic fracturing industry.

Sources: "Obama Issues Order to Coordinate Fracking Oversight," *The Washington Times,* April 13, 2012; "Drilling Down" [series of articles], *The New York Times,* various dates (2011), at *www.nytimes.com/interactive/us/DRILLING _DOWN_SERIES;* "Hydraulic Fracturing Position Paper," Stark Development Board (Stark County, Ohio), June 30, 2011; "Halliburton Loophole," *www.earthworksaction.org;* and "Select State Laws Governing Hydraulic Fracturing in the Marcellus Shale" and "Environmental Impacts Associated with Hydraulic Fracturing," The Network for Public Health Law, at *www.networkforphl.org.*

Land Pollution

The third major focus of environmental regulation is the contamination of land by both solid and hazardous waste. The United States produces an astonishing amount of solid waste, adding up to more than four pounds per person per day. Of this, 46 percent is recycled, composted, or incinerated, and the rest ends up in municipal landfills.[8] Many businesses and communities have tried to reduce the solid waste stream by establishing recycling programs.

> Of all the world's nations, Germany has made probably the greatest progress in reducing its solid waste stream. In the 1990s, faced with overflowing landfills and not enough space for new ones, the German government passed a series of strict recycling laws. Manufacturers and retailers were required to take back almost all packaging waste, from aluminum cans, to plastic CD wrappers, to cardboard shipping boxes. Packaging material was labeled with a green dot, indicating that it could be disposed of in special containers, from which it would be whisked to processing centers for recycling and reuse, at the manufacturer's expense. The incentive was that Germans had to pay for trash pickup—but not for recycling. By 2011, Germany was recycling around two-thirds of its household waste and had become a model for the rest of Europe.

The safe disposal of hazardous waste is a special concern. Several U.S. laws address the problem of land contamination by hazardous waste. The Toxic Substances Control Act of 1976 requires the EPA to inventory the thousands of chemicals in commercial use, identify which are most dangerous, and, if necessary, ban them or restrict their use. For example, polychlorinated biphenyls (PCBs), dangerous chemicals formerly used in electrical transformers, were banned under this law. The Resource Conservation and Recovery Act of 1976 (amended in 1984) regulates hazardous materials from "cradle to grave." Toxic-waste generators must have permits, transporters must maintain careful records, and disposal facilities must conform to detailed regulations. All hazardous waste must be treated before disposal in landfills.

Some studies have suggested that hazardous waste sites are most often located near economically disadvantaged African-American, Hispanic, and Native American communities. Since 1994, the EPA has investigated whether state permits for hazardous waste sites violate civil rights laws and has blocked permits that appear to discriminate against minorities. The effort to prevent inequitable exposure to risk, such as from hazardous waste, is sometimes referred to as the movement for **environmental justice**.[9] For example, Native American tribes in Utah, Nevada, and New Mexico have organized to block the construction of nuclear waste disposal facilities on their land, saying the facilities would threaten their health, culture, and economic viability.[10]

A promising regulatory approach to waste management, sometimes called **source reduction**, was taken in the Pollution Prevention Act of 1990. This law aims to reduce pollution at the source, rather than treat and dispose of waste at the end of the pipe. Pollution can be prevented, for example, by using less chemically intensive manufacturing processes, recycling, and better housekeeping and maintenance. Source reduction often saves money, protects worker health, and requires less abatement and disposal technology. The law provides guidelines, training, and incentives for companies to reduce waste.

The major U.S. law governing the cleanup of existing hazardous waste sites is the Comprehensive Environmental Response, Compensation, and Liability Act, or

---

[8] Environmental Protection Agency, "Municipal Solid Waste in the United States: Facts and Figures for 2010," *www.epa.gov/epawaste.*

[9] Robert D. Bullard, "Environmental Justice in the 21st Century," Environmental Justice Resource Center, available at *www.ejrc.cau.edu/ejinthe21century.htm;* Christopher H. Foreman, Jr., *The Promise and Perils of Environmental Justice* (Washington, DC: Brookings Institution, 2000); and Bunyan Bryant, ed., *Environmental Justice: Issues, Policies, and Solutions* (Washington, DC: Island Press, 1995).

[10] Nuclear Information and Resource Service, "Environmental Racism, Tribal Sovereignty, and Nuclear Waste," at *www.nirs.org.*

CERCLA, popularly known as **Superfund**, passed in 1980. This law established a fund, supported primarily by a tax on petroleum and chemical companies that were presumed to have created a disproportionate share of toxic wastes. The EPA was charged with establishing a National Priority List of the most dangerous toxic sites. Where the original polluters could be identified, they would be required to pay for the cleanup; where they could not be identified or had gone out of business, the Superfund would pay.

> One of the largest hazardous waste sites on the Superfund list is an almost 200-mile long stretch of the Hudson River, extending from Hudson Falls, New York, to Manhattan. Over a period of three decades until the late 1970s, General Electric (GE) factories discharged an estimated 1.3 million pounds of PCBs, cancer-causing chemicals formerly used in electrical equipment, into the river. Since the company was responsible, it was required to supervise and pay for the cleanup. In 2011, GE began the second and final phase of the job, which required dredging the riverbed to remove PCB-contaminated sediment, removing and treating the water it contained, and trucking the residue to a permitted landfill. The cost to the company had already exceeded $1.3 billion.[11]

Remarkably, one in four U.S. residents now lives within four miles of a Superfund site. The 1,200 or so sites originally placed on the National Priority List may be just the tip of the iceberg. Congressional researchers have said that as many as 10,000 other sites may need to be cleaned up. Some analysts estimated that the entire cleanup could cost as much as $1 trillion and take half a century to complete.

Alternative Policy Approaches

Governments can use a variety of policy approaches to control air, water, and land pollution. The most widely used method of regulation historically has been to impose environmental standards. Increasingly, however, government policymakers have relied more on market-based and voluntary approaches, rather than command and control regulations, to achieve environmental goals. These different approaches are discussed next.

Environmental Standards

The traditional method of pollution control is through **environmental standards**. Standard allowable levels of various pollutants are established by legislation or regulatory action and applied by administrative agencies and courts. This approach is also called **command and control regulation**, because the government commands business firms to comply with certain standards and often directly controls their choice of technology.

One type of standard is an *environmental-quality standard*. In this approach a given geographical area is permitted to have no more than a certain amount or proportion of a pollutant, such as sulfur dioxide, in the air. Polluters are required to control their emissions to maintain the area's standard of air quality. A second type is an *emission standard*. For example, the law might specify that manufacturers could release into the air no more than 1 percent of the ash (a pollutant) they generated. Emission standards, with some exceptions, are usually set by state and local regulators who are familiar with local industry and special problems caused by local topography and weather conditions. Sometimes, the EPA mandates that companies use the *best available technology*, meaning a particular process

---

[11] "GE to Finish Cleanup Project," *The Wall Street Journal*, December 24, 2010. The EPA posts regular reports on the progress of the cleanup at *www.epa.gov/hudson*.

that the agency determines is the best economically achievable way to reduce negative impacts on the environment.

Market-Based Mechanisms

In recent years, regulators have begun to move away from command and control regulation, favoring increased use of **market-based mechanisms**. This approach is based on the idea that the market is a better control than extensive standards that specify precisely what companies must do.

One approach that has become more widely used is to allow businesses to buy and sell the right to pollute, in a process known as **cap-and-trade**. New Zealand's *tradable permit* program for carbon emissions, described in one of the opening examples of this chapter, illustrates this approach. The U.S. Clean Air Act of 1990 also incorporated the concept of tradable permits as part of its approach to pollution reduction. The law established emission levels (called "caps") and permitted companies with emissions *below* the cap to sell ("trade") their rights to the remaining permissible amount to firms that faced penalties because their emissions were above the cap. Over time, the government would reduce the cap, thus gradually reducing overall emissions, even though individual companies might continue to pollute above the cap. Companies could choose whether to reduce their emissions—for example, by installing pollution abatement equipment—or to buy allowances from others. One study showed that the tradable permit program for acid rain may have saved companies as much as $3 billion per year, by allowing them the flexibility to choose the most cost-effective methods of complying with the law.[12] Some have criticized cap-and-trade systems, because they allow richer companies in effect to buy the right to pollute.

Another market-based type of pollution control is establishment of *emissions charges* or *fees*. Each business is charged for the undesirable waste that it emits, with the fee varying according to the amount of waste released. The result is, "The more you pollute, the more you pay." In this approach, polluting is not illegal, but it is expensive, creating an incentive for companies to clean up. In recent years, both federal and state governments have experimented with a variety of so-called *green taxes* or *eco-taxes* that levy a fee on various kinds of environmentally destructive behavior. In addition to taxing bad behavior, the government may also offer various types of positive incentives to firms that improve their environmental performance. For example, the government may decide to purchase only from those firms that meet a certain pollution standard, or it may offer aid to those that install pollution control equipment. Tax incentives, such as faster depreciation for pollution control equipment, also may be used. Governments may also levy eco-taxes on individuals.

> Since 2008, for instance, auto registration fees in Ireland have been based on greenhouse gas emissions, with owners paying €104 to €2,100, depending how polluting their vehicle is. The eco-tax was designed to encourage people to buy cleaner cars. Other countries with similar programs include the Netherlands, Portugal, Canada, Spain, and Finland. Germany has enacted eco-taxes on gasoline and electricity, with the intention of promoting energy efficiency.[13]

In short, the trend has been for governments to use more flexible, market-oriented approaches—tradable allowances, pollution fees and taxes, and incentives—to achieve environmental objectives where possible.

---

[12] For more on the tradable permit system for acid rain, see *www.epa.gov/acidrain*.

[13] Ireland's auto registration system is explained at *www.motortax.ie*.

Information Disclosure

Another approach to reducing pollution is popularly known as *regulation by publicity,* or *regulation by embarrassment.* The government encourages companies to pollute less by publishing information about the amount of pollutants individual companies emit each year. In many cases, companies voluntarily reduce their emissions to avoid public embarrassment.

The major experiment in regulation by publicity has occurred in the area of toxic emissions to the air and water. The 1986 amendments to the Superfund law, called SARA, included a provision called the Community Right-to-Know Law, which required manufacturing firms to report, for a list of specified toxic chemicals, the amount on site, the number of pounds released, and how (if at all) these chemicals were treated or disposed of. The EPA makes this information available to the public in the *Toxics Release Inventory,* or *TRI,* published annually and posted on the Internet.

From 1998 to 2010, reporting manufacturers in the United States cut their releases and disposal of these chemicals to the air, water, and land overall by 41 percent, according to TRI data.[14] The improvements, in many instances, had been completely voluntary. Apparently, fear of negative publicity had compelled many companies to act. Recently, however, the TRI numbers have begun to trend up—mostly reflecting toxic emissions from the metal mining industry. The environmental impacts of gold mining are explored in the discussion case at the end of this chapter.

The advantages and disadvantages of alternative policy approaches to reducing pollution are summarized in Figure 11.2.

Civil and Criminal Enforcement

Companies that violate environmental laws are subject to stiff civil penalties and fines, and their managers can face prison if they knowingly or negligently endanger people or the environment. Proponents of this approach argue that the threat of fines and even imprisonment can be an effective deterrent to corporate outlaws who would otherwise degrade the air, water, or land. In 2011, the EPA brought criminal charges against 249 defendants; of those charged, 21 percent were corporations.[15]

> Massey Energy, one of the nation's largest coal companies, paid $20 million in 2008 to settle charges it had violated the Clean Water Act. Regulators found that for years Massey had illegally dumped metals, sediment, and acid mine drainage into nearby waterways, polluting hundreds of rivers and streams in West Virginia and Kentucky. Besides the fine, Massey was required to spend $10 million on new procedures and employee training, to set aside land for conservation, and to undertake water cleanup projects downstream from its mines.[16]

Massey is discussed further in a case at the end of this book.

European regulators and prosecutors have also actively pursued corporate environmental criminals. For example, the EU standardized its laws against marine pollution and raised maximum penalties after a series of oil tanker wrecks fouled the coasts of France, Spain, and Portugal. Europe is the world's largest importer of oil, and 90 percent is transported to the continent by seagoing ships.[17]

---

[14] TRI data are available at *www.epa.gov/TRI.* The Right-to-Know Network provides a searchable database with information on releases by specific companies at *www.rtk.net.*

[15] "FY2011 Enforcement & Compliance Annual Results: Criminal Enforcement," at *www.epa.gov/compliance.*

[16] "Massey Energy to Pay Largest Civil Penalty Ever for Water Permit Violations," EPA press release, January 17, 2008.

[17] "The Community Framework for Cooperation in the Field of Accidental or Deliberate Marine Pollution," at *http://ec.europa.eu/echo/civil_protection/civil/marin/mp01_en_introduction.htm.*

FIGURE 11.2

Advantages and Disadvantages of Alternative Policy Approaches to Reducing Pollution

Policy Approach	Advantages	Disadvantages
Environmental standards	• Enforceable in the courts. • Compliance mandatory.	• Across-the-board standards not equally relevant to all businesses. • Requires large regulatory apparatus. • Older, less efficient plants may be forced to close. • Can retard innovation. • Fines may be cheaper than compliance. • Does not improve compliance once compliance is achieved.
Market-based mechanisms		
Cap-and-trade systems	• Gives businesses more flexibility. • Achieves goals at lower overall cost. • Saves jobs by allowing some less efficient plants to stay open. • Permits the government and private organizations to buy allowances to take them off the market. • Encourages continued improvement.	• Gives business a license to pollute. • Permit levels are hard to set. • May cause regional imbalances in pollution levels. • Enforcement is difficult.
Emissions fees and taxes	• Taxes bad behavior (pollution) rather than good behavior (profits).	• Fees are hard to set. • Taxes may be too low to curb pollution.
Government incentives	• Rewards environmentally responsible behavior. • Encourages companies to exceed minimum standards.	• Incentives may not be strong enough to curb pollution.
Information disclosure	• Government spends little on enforcement. • Companies able to reduce pollution in the most cost-effective way.	• Does not motivate all companies.
Civil and criminal enforcement	• May deter wrongdoing by firms and individuals.	• May not deter wrongdoing if penalties and enforcement efforts are perceived as weak.

The U.S. Sentencing Commission, a government agency responsible for setting uniform penalties for violations of federal law, has established guidelines for sentencing environmental wrongdoers. Under these rules, penalties would reflect not only the severity of the offense but also a company's demonstrated environmental commitment. Businesses that have an active compliance program, cooperate with government investigators, and promptly assist any victims would receive lighter sentences than others with no environmental programs or that knowingly violate the law. These guidelines provide an incentive for businesses to develop active compliance programs to protect themselves and their officers from high fines or even prison if a violation should occur.[18]

[18] For a discussion of criminal liability in environmental law, and how to avoid it, see Frank B. Friedman, *Practical Guide to Environmental Management*, 11th ed. (Washington, DC: Environmental Law Institute, 2011).

Costs and Benefits of Environmental Regulation

One central issue of environmental protection is how costs are balanced by benefits. In the four decades or so since the modern environmental era began, the nation has spent a great deal to clean up the environment and keep it clean. Some have questioned the value choices underlying these expenditures, suggesting that the costs—lost jobs, reduced capital investment, and lowered productivity—exceeded the benefits. Others, in contrast, point to significant gains in the quality of life and to the economic payoff of a cleaner environment.

Businesses in the United States have invested heavily in environmental protection. According to the U.S. Census Bureau, in 2005, for example, manufacturing firms spent about $6 billion in capital expenditures (e.g., installing pollution controls) and about $21 billion in operating costs (e.g., paying for wages and supplies) to comply with environmental regulations.[19] The industries that spent the most were chemicals, oil, and coal. (This survey did not include the electric power industry; that industry's costs, already high, will increase when new rules governing the emission of mercury and other dangerous toxins go into effect.)[20] Business spending to comply with environmental regulation has diverted funds that might otherwise have been invested in new plants and equipment or in research and development, and strict rules have sometimes led to plant shutdowns and loss of jobs. Some regions and industries, in particular, have been hard hit by environmental regulation, especially those with high abatement costs, such as paper and wood products, chemicals, petroleum and coal, and primary metals. Economists often find it difficult, however, to sort out what proportion of job loss in an industry is attributable to environmental regulation and what proportion is attributable to other causes.

In many areas, the United States has made great progress in cleaning up the environment. The benefits of this progress have often been greater than the costs, as these figures show:

- Although problems remain, as noted earlier in this chapter, overall emissions of nearly all major air pollutants in the United States have dropped substantially since 1990, the date of the Clean Air Act amendments. By 2010, levels of volatile organic compounds had dropped by 52 percent, nitrous oxides by 48 percent, sulfur dioxide by 65 percent, and lead by 60 percent. A study done for the EPA showed that by the year 2020, the Clean Air Act amendments will have prevented 230,000 premature deaths from air pollution, averted more than 2 million asthma attacks, and prevented 17 million lost workdays, among other gains. The cost of clean air compliance was predicted to be $65 billion annually in 2020, about one-thirtieth of the predicted economic value of the act's benefits.[21]

- Water quality has also improved. Since the Water Pollution Control Act went into effect in 1972, many lakes and waterways have been restored to ecological health. The Cuyahoga River in Ohio, for example, which at one time was so badly polluted by industrial waste that it actually caught on fire, has been restored to the point where residents can fish and even swim in the river. By one estimate, 33,000 more miles of rivers and streams were swimmable in 2000 than would have been the case without the Clean Water Act.[22]

[19] U.S. Census Bureau, "Pollution Abatement Costs and Expenditures: 2005" (April 2008).

[20] "Benefits and Costs of Cleaning Up Toxic Air Pollution from Power Plants," at *www.epa.gov/mats*.

[21] "Air Quality Trends," *www.epa.gov/airtrends;* and "The Benefits and Costs of the Clean Air Act 1990 to 2020," pp. 3 and 13, *www.epa.gov/air.* The estimated cost of compliance includes the costs to both government and businesses.

[22] "A Benefits Assessment of Water Pollution Control Programs Since 1972," prepared for the U.S. Environmental Protection Agency, January 2000. This and other studies of the costs and benefits of environmental regulations are available from the National Center for Environmental Economics at *www.epa.gov/economics/*.

Environmental regulations also stimulate some sectors of the economy. While jobs are lost in industries such as forest products and high-sulfur coal mining, others are created in areas like recycling, environmental consulting, wind turbine and solar panel production and installation, waste management equipment, and air pollution control. For example, operators of coal-fired power plants predicted that big required cuts in mercury emissions, announced in 2011, would cost thousands of jobs. But trade groups said that the regulations could add 300,000 jobs a year through 2017 in companies that make equipment to reduce emissions.[23] Jobs are saved or created in industries such as fishing and tourism when natural areas are protected or restored. Moreover, environmental regulations can stimulate the economy by compelling businesses to become more efficient by conserving energy, and less money is spent on treating health problems caused by pollution.

Sectors of the economy that produce goods and services with an environmental benefit are known as the **clean economy**. In 2012, the U.S. government for the first time estimated the size of the clean economy, reporting that 3.1 million people (2.4 percent of the total number employed) were employed there. Three-quarters of these jobs were in the private sector. A similar study conducted by the Brookings Institution in 2011 found that most "green jobs" were in mature industries, such as wastewater treatment and mass transit. But the fastest-growing segment of the clean economy was in the newer alternative energy industries such as wind energy, solar power, and the so-called smart grid (which used technology to deliver electricity more efficiently).[24]

Because of the complexity of these issues, economists differ on the net costs and benefits of environmental regulation. In some respects, government controls hurt the economy, and in other ways they help, as summarized in Figure 11.3. An analysis of data from several studies found that, on balance, U.S. environmental regulations did not have a large overall effect on economic competitiveness because losses in one area tended to balance gains in another. What is clear is that choices in the area of environmental regulation reflect underlying values, expressed in a democratic society through an open political process. Just how much a society is prepared to pay and how "clean" it wants to be are political choices, reflecting the give and take of diverse interests in a pluralistic society.

FIGURE 11.3
Costs and Benefits of Environmental Regulations

Costs	Benefits
• Manufacturers spent $21 billion on operating costs and $6 billion on capital expenditures annually to comply with environmental regulations.	• Emissions of nearly all pollutants dropped since 1970.
• Some jobs were lost in particularly polluting industries.	• Air and water quality improved; some toxic-waste sites were cleaned up; health improved; natural beauty was preserved or enhanced.
• Competitiveness of some capital-intensive, "dirty" industries was impaired.	• Jobs were created in the clean economy sector, such as environmental products and services, alternative energy, and tourism.

[23] "Regulations Create Jobs, Too," *Bloomberg Businessweek,* February 9, 2012.

[24] "A Tally of Green Jobs," *New York Times,* March 22, 2012; "Measuring Green Jobs," at: *www.bls.gov/green;* and "Sizing the Clean Economy: A National and Regional Green Jobs Assessment," July 13, 2011, at: *www.brookings.edu.*

The Greening of Management

Environmental regulations, such as the laws governing clean air, water, and land described in this chapter, establish minimum legal standards that businesses must meet. Most companies try to comply with these regulations, if only to avoid litigation, fines, and, in the most extreme cases, criminal penalties. But many firms are now voluntarily moving beyond compliance to improve their environmental performance in all areas of their operations. Researchers have sometimes referred to the process of moving toward more proactive environmental management as the **greening of management**. This section describes the stages of the greening process and discusses what organizational approaches companies have used to manage environmental issues effectively. The following section explains why green management can improve a company's strategic competitiveness.

Stages of Corporate Environmental Responsibility

Although environmental issues are forcing all businesses to manage in new ways, not all companies are equally green, meaning proactive in their response to environmental issues. One widely used model identifies three main stages of corporate environmental responsibility.

According to this model, companies pass through three distinct stages in the development of green management practices.[25] The first stage is *pollution prevention*, which focuses on "minimizing or eliminating waste before it is created." Subaru Automotive of America's effort to minimize waste, mentioned earlier in this chapter, is an example of pollution prevention. The second stage is *product stewardship.* In this stage, managers focus on "all environmental impacts associated with the full life cycle of a product," from the design of a product to its eventual use and disposal. Hewlett-Packard, for example, has designed its laser printer ink cartridges so they can be refurbished and reused, and provides a mailing label for customers to return them free of charge. Finally, the third and most advanced stage is *clean technology,* in which businesses develop innovative new technologies that support sustainability—that actually provide environmental benefits, rather than simply prevent harm.

> General Electric, a company long associated with pollution, from building coal-fired power plants to dumping toxic chemicals in the Hudson River, took a dramatic turn in 2005. Jeffrey Immelt, the company's new CEO, announced a new strategy he dubbed "ecomagination." He pledged to double GE's investment in developing renewable energy, fuel cells, efficient lighting, water filtration systems, and cleaner jet engines. Immelt's reason was that clean technologies represented a huge commercial opportunity. "Increasingly for business," he said, "green is green." In 2010, the company reported that it had invested $5 billion in clean tech research and development and had earned $85 billion in revenues from its ecomagination portfolio of products and services.[26]

Where are most companies on this continuum of environmental responsibility? A 2011 worldwide survey of senior executives by KPMG and the Economist Intelligence Unit found that 62 percent of companies had a coherent strategy for sustainability for the entire business, and an additional 33 percent were in the process of developing one. Forty-four percent reported their intention to develop new products to reduce or prevent social or

[25] Stuart Hart, "Beyond Greening: Strategies for a Sustainable World," *Harvard Business Review,* January–February 1997. All quotes in this paragraph are taken from this article. An alternative stage model may be found in Dexter Dunphy, Suzanne Benn, and Andrew Griffiths, *Organisational Change for Corporate Sustainability* (New York: Routledge, 2003).

[26] "2010 Ecomagination Annual Report," at *www.ecomagination.com.*

environmental problems in the next five years (a possible indicator of the *clean technology* stage). Almost one in four saw sustainability as a source of new business opportunities. In short, most big companies are increasingly addressing sustainability issues—and seeing them as a source of innovation and growth.[27]

The Ecologically Sustainable Organization

An **ecologically sustainable organization (ESO)** is a business that operates in a way that is consistent with the principle of sustainable development, as presented in Chapter 10. In other words, an ESO could continue its activities indefinitely, without altering the carrying capacity of the Earth's ecosystem. Such businesses would not use up natural resources any faster than they could be replenished or substitutes found. They would make and transport products efficiently, with minimal use of energy. They would design products that would last a long time and that, when worn out, could be disassembled and recycled. They would not produce waste any faster than natural systems could absorb and disperse it. They would work with other businesses, governments, and organizations to meet these goals.[28]

Of course, no existing business completely fits the definition of an ecologically sustainable organization. The concept is what social scientists call an ideal type; that is, a kind of absolute standard against which real organizations can be measured. A few visionary businesses, however, have embraced the concept and begun to try to live up to this ideal.

One such business is Interface, a $1 billion company based in Atlanta, Georgia, that makes 40 percent of the world's commercial carpet tiles. In 1994, CEO Ray C. Anderson announced, to many people's surprise, that Interface would seek to become "the first sustainable corporation in the world." Anderson and his managers undertook hundreds of initiatives. For example, the company started a program by which customers could *lease,* rather than *purchase,* carpet tile. When tile wore out in high-traffic areas, Interface technicians would replace just the worn units, reducing waste. Old tiles would be recycled, creating a closed loop. In 2011, Interface reported that in 17 years it had saved $430 million by cutting waste, and had adopted a goal of "Mission Zero"—no negative impact on the environment—by 2020. Another initiative undertaken by the company was to tag all products with a special label called an *environmental product declaration (EPD).* Similar to a nutrition label on packaged food, the third-party verified EPD listed the raw materials, energy use, emissions, and waste generation associated with each product, allowing Interface customers to make environmentally informed decisions. The company charted its sustainability progress on its website on a graphic superimposed on an image of Mount Everest.[29]

No companies, including Interface, have yet become truly sustainable businesses, and it will probably be impossible for any single firm to become an ESO in the absence of supportive government policies and a widespread movement among many businesses and other social institutions.

[27] KPMG International, in cooperation with the Economist Intelligence Unit, "Corporate Sustainability: A Progress Report," 2011, available online at *www.kpmg.com.*

[28] Mark Starik and Gordon P. Rands, "Weaving an Integrated Web: Multilevel and Multisystem Perspectives of Ecologically Sustainable Organizations," *Academy of Management Review,* October 1995.

[29] "Giving You the Complete Picture: Interface's EPDs," at *www.interfaceflor.com;* "Interface Rolls Out Environmentally Friendly Carpet Solutions," April 19, 2011, at *www.chinanewsasia.com;* and Ray C. Anderson with Robin White, *Business Lessons from a Radical Industrialist* (New York: St. Martin's Press, 2011). Interface's sustainability initiatives are further described at *www.interfaceglobal.com/sustainability.*

Environmental Partnerships

Many businesses that are seeking to become more sustainable have formed voluntary, collaborative partnerships with environmental organizations and regulators to achieve specific objectives, as illustrated by the FedEx example at the beginning of this chapter. These collaborations, called **environmental partnerships**, draw on the unique strengths of the different partners to improve environmental quality or conserve resources.[30]

> Starbucks Corporation is the largest coffeehouse company in the world, with almost 20,000 stores in 58 countries. For more than a decade, the company has partnered with Conservation International (CI) to promote coffee farming methods that protect biodiversity, mitigate climate change, and reduce harm from pesticides and fertilizers. For example, in Chiapas, Mexico, and Sumatra, Indonesia, the partners have worked with local farmers to develop coffee varieties that thrive in the shade of native trees, conserving habitat and sequestering carbon. The company has also worked with CI to develop a set of purchasing guidelines based on sustainability and has committed to paying a premium price to suppliers who meet the standards. The two organizations renewed and extended their partnership in 2011. Conservation International noted on its website that it viewed Starbucks "as a natural partner to our work because of shared geographies: most of the world's key coffee-growing regions are the same areas where biological diversity is richest and most threatened."[31]

Environmental Management in Practice

Companies that have begun to move toward environmental sustainability have learned that new structures, processes, and incentives are often needed. Some of the organizational elements that many proactive green companies share are the following:

Top management with a commitment to sustainability. The most environmentally proactive companies almost all have CEOs and other top leaders with a strong espoused commitment to sustainability. An example is Bob McDonald, CEO of Procter & Gamble, who also holds the title of executive sponsor of sustainability. "We don't treat environmental sustainability as something separate from our base business," McDonald said. "When we operate sustainably, we earn gratitude, admiration, and trust that lead to opportunity, partnerships, and growth."[32] Most proactive companies give their environmental managers greater authority and access to top levels of the corporation. The role of top-level managers in setting the tone at the top for environmental excellence is illustrated in the case, "Kimpton Hotels' EarthCare Program," that appears at the end of this book.

Chief sustainability officer. An emerging role at some leading firms is the **chief sustainability officer (CSO)**. The first such officer was appointed in 2004 at DuPont; a 2011 survey found 29 such officers at large U.S. firms. Ninety percent of these CSOs

[30] Dennis A. Rondinelli and Ted London, "How Corporations and Environmental Groups Cooperate," *Academy of Management Executive* 17, no. 1 (2003); and Frederick J. Long and Matthew B. Arnold, *The Power of Environmental Partnerships* (Fort Worth, TX: Dryden Press, 1995).

[31] "Starbucks and Conservation International Extent Longstanding Partnership" [press release], September 8, 2011, at *www.conservation.org*. The progress of the partnership can be followed at *www.conservation/campaigns/starbucks* and *www.starbucks.com/responsibility*.

[32] "Behind Procter & Gamble's Sustainability Vision," September 27, 2010, at *www.greenbiz.com*.

reported directly to the CEO or to an individual who did. They often supervised extensive staffs of specialists and coordinated the work of managers in many areas, including research and development, marketing, and operations, whose work was related to a firm's sustainability mission.[33]

Employee engagement. The CSO of the software firm CA Technologies commented in a recent blog post, "Finding ways to engage employees in the process of improving corporate sustainability was a must or meaningful change would be limited. Our internal sustainability motto quickly became 'Driven from the top down, energized from the bottom up.'" The company gives "green star" awards to individuals and teams that go "above and beyond" to meet sustainability goals.[34] Environmental staff experts and specialized departments are most effective when they work closely with the people who carry out the company's daily operations. For this reason, many green companies involve line managers and employees directly in the process of change.

Cross-functional teams. Another organizational element is the use of ad hoc, cross-functional teams to solve environmental problems, including individuals from different departments. For example, when Siemens Building Technologies, a provider of fire safety, security, and control systems, undertook a comprehensive effort to green the organization, it created a cross-functional team drawn from marketing, product design, procurement, manufacturing, facilities, and human resources. Its goal was to pull together key players with the skills and resources to get the job done, wherever they were located in the corporate structure. Local sustainability champions in each of the company's 110 field offices worked to put the vision into practice.

Rewards and incentives. Businesspeople are most likely to consider the environmental impacts of their actions when their organizations acknowledge and reward this behavior. The greenest organizations tie the compensation of their managers, including line managers, to environmental achievement and take steps to recognize these achievements publicly. At Xcel Energy, a utility that is a leading supplier of wind power, one-third of the CEO's bonus is linked to meeting specific sustainability goals set annually by the board.[35] Since 2008, Intel has linked all employees' bonuses to meeting environmental goals, such as reducing the company's carbon emissions and designing energy-efficient new products. The company believes that doing so helps focus employees' attention on the importance of meeting sustainability goals.[36]

Environmental Audits

Green companies not only organize themselves to achieve environmental goals; they also closely track their progress toward meeting them. Chapter 7 introduced the concept of social performance auditing and presented recent evidence on what proportion of companies report results to their stakeholders. In the 1990s, in a parallel development, many companies began to audit their environmental performance. More recently, many firms have moved to integrate their social and environmental reporting into a single **sustainability report**. In 2011, 95 percent of the world's top 250 companies issued such an integrated report,

---

[33] *CSO Back Story: How Chief Sustainability Officers Reached the C-Suite* (Weinreb Group, September 2011).

[34] "Sustainability and Employee Engagement: A Win–Win for Business" [blog], March 15, 2012, at *http://community.ca.com /blogs;* and "Swag, Cash, or Kudos: The Best Rewards of Employee Engagement," May 22, 2012, at *greenbiz.com.*

[35] "Comp Committees Link Incentive Pay [to] Environmental Goals," *www.compensationresources.com,* n.d., appears to be 2007.

[36] R. G. Eccles et al., "The Impact of a Corporate Culture of Sustainability on Corporate Behavior and Performance," Harvard Business School Working Paper, May 9, 2012.

up from just 64 percent six years earlier. A much smaller proportion integrates social, environmental, *and* financial data in a single document. (This is called *triple bottom line* reporting and is discussed in Chapter 7.)[37]

> An example of a company that has undertaken a fully audited, integrated report is Novozymes, a Danish biotechnology firm. The company produced its first environmental report in 1993 and its first combined social and environmental report six years later. Since 2002, it has produced a single report to stakeholders that integrates its financial, social, and environmental results. The company acknowledges the challenge of preparing a single report "in accordance with more than one set of rules and guidelines," but says that the process improves transparency and accurately reflects its commitment to sustainability.[38]

As discussed earlier in Chapter 7, the movement to audit and report on social and environmental performance has gained momentum in recent years in many regions of the world.

Environmental Management as a Competitive Advantage

Some researchers believe that by moving toward ecological sustainability, business firms gain a competitive advantage. That is, relative to other firms in the same industry, companies that proactively manage environmental issues will tend to be more successful than those that do not. Effective environmental management confers a competitive advantage in five different ways, as follows.[39]

Cost Savings

Companies that reduce pollution and hazardous waste, reuse or recycle materials, and operate with greater energy efficiency can reap significant cost savings. An example is Herman Miller, the office furniture company, which has gone to great lengths to reduce waste in its manufacturing process.

> Herman Miller goes to great lengths to avoid wasting materials. The company sells fabric scraps to the auto industry for use as car linings; leather trim to luggage makers for attaché cases; and vinyl to the supplier to be re-extruded into new edging. Burnable solid waste is used as fuel for a specialized boiler that generates all the heating and cooling for the company's main complex in Zeeland, Michigan. The result is that the company actually makes money from materials that, in the past, it would have had to pay to have hauled away and dumped.[40]

---

[37] *KPMG International Survey of Corporate Responsibility Reporting 2011*, at *www.kpmg.com*. Toyota's social and environmental reports are available at *www.toyota.co.jp/en/csr*.

[38] Novozymes's website and integrated reports are at *http://novozymes.com/en*.

[39] For a collection of articles by leading scholars, see Sanjay Sharma and J. Alberto Aragon-Correa, eds., *Corporate Environmental Strategy and Competitive Advantage* (Northampton, MA: Edgar Elgar Academic Publishing, 2005). For a general statement of the argument that environmental management confers a competitive advantage, see Michael E. Porter and Claas van der Linde, "Green and Competitive: Beyond the Stalemate," *Harvard Business Review*, September–October 1995, pp. 120 ff; Stuart L. Hart, "Beyond Greening: Strategies for a Sustainable World," *Harvard Business Review*, January–February 1997, pp. 66–76; and Renato J. Orsato, "Competitive Environmental Strategies: When Does It Pay to Be Green?" *California Management Review* 48, no. 2 (Winter 2006), pp. 127–43.

[40] Herman Miller's sustainability initiatives are described at *www.hermanmiller.com*.

Exhibit 11.C

Greening the Built Environment

For most companies, their buildings—the offices, factories, stores, and warehouses where their employees work—account for a huge share of their overall environmental impact. The U.S. Energy Information Administration has estimated that commercial buildings and industrial facilities together account for almost half of the nation's energy consumption (the rest comes from transportation and residential use). Many companies have realized that improving operating efficiencies in their real estate holdings can yield tremendous savings, as well as reduce their environmental footprint.

One approach is to design buildings from the ground up to conserve resources both in their construction and use. The U.S. Green Building Council has developed a certification process called LEED (Leadership in Energy and Environmental Design) for both new and retrofitted buildings. Adopting these standards has brought companies many benefits. For example, Adobe, the maker of digital authoring tools, owns five LEED-certified buildings, including its corporate headquarters in San Jose, California, which was completely retrofitted. Adobe introduced scores of improvements—from motion sensors that turned off lights when people left their offices to landscape irrigation linked to weather satellites, so sprinklers did not operate when it was raining. The improvements cost a total of $1.4 million, but saved Adobe $1.2 million per year. "I was one of the naysayers saying, no, green costs money, it doesn't save money. [But] once I started seeing the cost savings, [I jumped] right up on that bandwagon . . . because it works," said the company's director of global facilities services.

Sources: Rocky Mountain Institute, "Adobe Systems Corporate Headquarters" [case study], at *http://bet.rmi.org/files/case-studies/adobe/adobe_systems.pdf;* "Green Building for a Profitable Future," *http://bet.rmi.org/rmi-news/green-building-for-a-profitable-future.html;* and U.S. Energy Information Administration, "Annual Energy Outlook 2012," at *www.eia.gov.* (Data are forecasts for 2012.) The website of the U.S. Green Building Council is at *www.usgbc.org.*

Many companies have found they are able to obtain significant cost savings by more efficiently managing their real estate portfolios. How some companies have managed the built environment to save money and improve their environmental performance is described in Exhibit 11.C. One company that has benefited from this trend is Autodesk, a maker of software for architects and other designers. The company has developed software called Ecotect® Analysis that enables architects to calculate the energy and water usage of proposed designs, and to make the most efficient use of daylight and shadows. "I think [sustainability] is one of the single biggest problems we face as a civilization," said Autodesk CEO Carl Bass. "We are trying to give people better tools to make better decisions."[41]

A 2011 survey by McKinsey found that the most common reason given by executives for addressing sustainability was to lower costs and improve operational efficiency; 33 percent cited this as their top reason.[42]

Product Differentiation

Companies that develop a reputation for environmental excellence and that produce and deliver sustainable products and services can attract environmentally aware customers. For example, shoppers might select cell phones with power-saving features, such as "unplug charger" reminders, or cleaning products formulated with ingredients that are not environmentally harmful. Creating "green" products and services—and pitching them to environmentally aware customers—is sometimes called **green marketing**.

[41] "Carl Bass: Environmentalist, Craftsman, CEO," February 9, 2012, at *www.greenbiz.com.* Autodesk's sustainable building design software is described at *http://usa.autodesk.com/ecotect-analysis.*

[42] "The Business of Sustainability: McKinsey Global Survey Results," October 2011, at *www.mckinseyquarterly.com.*

A growing trend is one marketing experts have termed *collaborative consumption.* The Internet and social networking have greatly facilitated the common use of products or services that people need on an occasional basis. Companies such as ZipCar (which provides cars), Netflix (movies), and Chegg (textbooks) all buy a stock of a particular product and then make it available to drivers, viewers, or students who wish to use it for a period of time and then return it. Because the net effect of collaborative consumption is to reduce wasted resources associated with individual ownership, it often attracts environmentally aware customers.[43]

Green marketing has had a mixed track record. Consumer survey data released in 2009 showed that 36 percent of Americans said they "almost always" or "regularly" bought green products. But *The New York Times* reported in 2011 that sales of many green products had fallen significantly since the financial crisis, as consumers cut spending.[44] Many consumers remain skeptical about whether or not environmental claims made by manufacturers are credible. Companies are said to be guilty of **greenwashing** (formed from the words "green" and "whitewash") when they mislead consumers regarding the environmental benefits of a product or service. According to TerraChoice, an environmental marketing firm, many green claims are suspect, particularly those for children's toys, baby products, cleaning supplies, and do-it-yourself building products. These run the gamut from ads that offer no proof for their claims, to ones that are simply vague ("all natural"), or irrelevant ("CFC-free," even though CFCs have been illegal for years).[45]

In short, green marketing can provide a competitive edge, but only if it is honest and meets a genuine need.

Environmental excellence may also attract business customers, a trend that has emerged in the gold mining industry, as illustrated in the discussion case at the end of this chapter.

Technological Innovation

Environmentally proactive companies are often technological leaders, as they seek imaginative new methods for reducing pollution and increasing efficiency. In many cases, they produce innovations that can win new customers, penetrate new markets, or even be marketed to other firms as new regulations spur their adoption.

> IBM's semiconductor chip-making plant in Burlington, Vermont, uses vast quantities of ultrapure water to clean its products. The water bill for this single facility has been as high as $10,000 *a day.* To reduce costs, IBM managers devised an elaborate system of electronic sensors to track the movement of water at every point and used the data to drive greater efficiencies—nearly doubling the "water productivity" of the plant over 10 years. "We did fifty different things," reported the plant's operation manager. "Angles of usage, treatment, energy capture, using less pump capacity, capturing internal pressure that comes with the water in the line—fifty different things." In the process, IBM had the startling revelation that it had done more than save money on water; it had created an entirely new business of consulting with other firms on how to do the same thing. The head of IBM's "Big Green Innovations" project told a reporter, "We think there is a big business opportunity around managing water."[46]

[43] "Collaborative Consumption: Doing More with Less . . . Together," *Stanford Social Innovation Review,* February 17, 2012; and "Beyond Zipcar: Collaborative Consumption," *Harvard Business Review,* October 1, 2010.

[44] "As Consumers Cut Spending, 'Green' Products Lose Allure," *The New York Times,* April 21, 2011.

[45] TerraChoice, "The Seven Sins of Greenwashing," 2010, *http://terrachoice.com.*

[46] Charles Fishman, *The Big Thirst: The Secret Life and Turbulent Future of Water* (New York: Free Press, 2011), Chapter 5, "Money in the Pipes."

Reduction of Regulatory Risk

Another benefit for companies that are proactive with respect to their environmental impacts is that they are often better positioned than their competitors to respond to new government mandates. For example, when new rules went into effect in Europe in 2006 that banned all electronics products that included six toxic substances, including lead, cadmium, and mercury, companies that had learned how to make their products free of these substances prior to the ban suddenly had a big advantage in winning European accounts. More recently, the United Kingdom announced that, starting in 2013, all large British companies would be required to report annually on their greenhouse gas emissions. "The biggest winners will be the companies that took the early steps to measure and report on carbon, and understand the risks better," commented a partner in the sustainabilty and climate change practice of a leading accounting firm.[47]

Strategic Planning

Companies that cultivate a vision of sustainability must adopt sophisticated strategic planning techniques to allow their top managers to assess the full range of the firm's effects on the environment. The complex auditing and forecasting techniques used by these firms help them anticipate a wide range of external influences on the firm, not just ecological influences. Wide-angle planning helps these companies foresee trends—new markets, materials, technologies, and products.

> In 2012, Toyota Motor Corporation was named to the "Global 100 Most Sustainable Corporations" list, announced annually at the World Economic Forum in Davos, Switzerland. It was the eighth year in a row the company had been so honored. The winners were selected based on their "exceptional capacity to address their sector-specific environmental, social, and governance risks and opportunities." Toyota, well known for its ability to anticipate market trends, had been among the first to produce a commercially successful hybrid vehicle, the Prius, and had pledged to adapt hybrid technology in all its vehicles by the mid-2020s. As U.S. carmakers struggled—and some went into bankruptcy—in the deep recession of the late 2000s, Toyota fared relatively well. The same sophisticated planning that enabled Toyota to weather the recession had also contributed to its ability to meet the public's increased interest in less polluting, more efficient transportation.[48]

The McKinsey survey mentioned earlier in this chapter found that 57 percent of executives said that their companies had integrated sustainability into their strategic planning process.[49]

A theme of this chapter is that achieving a sustainable economy and society will require a collaborative effort among government, business, and civil society. The U.S. government, like that of many other countries, has adopted many environmental laws and regulations constraining business behavior. These are critically important, as they assure that minimum standards are met by all. But many proactive companies are moving beyond compliance, recognizing that operating sustainably will help them become more competitive in the global marketplace by cutting costs, attracting environmentally aware customers, spurring innovation, reducing regulatory risk, and encouraging long-range strategic planning.

---

[47] "U.K. to Mandate CO2 Reporting for Largest Corporations," June 20, 2012, at *www.greenbiz.com*.

[48] A list of the Global 100 most sustainable corporations is available at *www.global100.org*. Information on Toyota's sustainability initiatives is at *www.toyota.co.jp/en/environment*.

[49] "The Business of Sustainability," op. cit.

Summary

- Government environmental laws and regulations focus on protecting the ecological health of the air, water, and land, and limiting the amount of pollution that companies may emit.

- Environmental laws have traditionally been of the command and control type, specifying standards and results. New laws, in both the United States and Europe, have added market incentives to induce environmentally sound behavior and have encouraged companies to reduce pollution at the source.

- Environmental laws have brought many benefits. Air, water, and land pollution levels are in many cases lower than in 1970. A continuing challenge is to find ways to promote a clean environment and sustainable business practices without impairing the competitiveness of the U.S. economy.

- Companies pass through three distinct stages in the development of green management practices. Many businesses are now moving from lower to higher stages. An ecologically sustainable organization is one that operates in a way that is consistent with the principle of sustainable development.

- Effective environmental management requires an integrated approach that involves all parts of the business organization, including top leadership, line managers, and production teams, as well as strong partnerships with stakeholders and effective auditing.

- Many companies have found that proactive environmental management can confer a competitive advantage by saving money, attracting green customers, promoting innovation, reducing regulatory risk, and developing skills in strategic planning.

Key Terms

acid rain, *238*
cap-and-trade, *243*
chief sustainability officer (CSO), *250*
clean economy, *247*
command and control regulation, *242*
ecologically sustainable organization (ESO), *249*

environmental justice, *241*
environmental partnerships, *250*
Environmental Protection Agency (EPA), *236*
environmental standards, *242*
greening of management, *248*

green marketing, *253*
greenwashing, *254*
market-based mechanisms, *243*
source reduction, *241*
Superfund (CERCLA), *242*
sustainability report, *251*

Internet Resources

www.epa.gov — Environmental Protection Agency
www.envirolink.org — Environmental organizations and news
www.GreenBiz.com — Green Business Network
www.sustainablebusiness.com — Network of sustainable small businesses
www.environmentalleader.com — Briefing for executives
www.sustainability.com — SustainAbility (consultancy)
www.sustainablog.org — Blogs on green and sustainable businesses
www.sustainablebusiness.com — Site for green businesses

Discussion Case: *Digging Gold*

Gold mining is one of the most environmentally destructive industries in the world. Most gold today is extracted using a technique called cyanide heap-leaching. Workers dig and blast the earth in open-pit mines so massive that astronauts can see them from space. Using huge earth-moving machines, they pile the gold-bearing ore into mounds the size of pyramids, then spray them with a solution of cyanide to leach out the gold. In a series of steps, gold is then removed from the drainage at the bottom of the heap and is further refined in smelters into pure bars of the precious metal.

Heap-leaching enables the economic extraction of gold from low-grade ores; some modern mines use as much as 30 tons of rock to produce a single ounce of precious metal. But this process can be highly damaging to the environment. Cyanide is one of the most potent poisons known; a pellet the size of a grain of rice can kill a person. Most spent cyanide solution is stored in reservoirs, where it gradually breaks down. But these reservoirs are prone to accidents. In 2000, at a gold mine in Romania operated by the Australian firm Esmeralda Exploration, 100,000 tons of wastewater laced with cyanide spilled into a tributary of the Danube River. The toxic plume washed all the way to the Black Sea, causing a massive kill of fish and birds and contaminating the drinking water of 2.5 million people.

After this incident, a Romanian citizen's group called Alburnus Maior organized to block construction of a new gold mine by the Canadian firm Gabriel Resources at Rosia Montana. "We have to decide whether we want [these] mountains to become a no-man's land," said Eugen David, a local farmer and activist.

Transportation of materials to and from mines, which are often located in remote areas, poses additional risks. A truck carrying containers of mercury (a by-product of gold extraction) from the Yanacocha Mine in Peru, owned by U.S.-based Newmont Mining, spilled its load on a rural road. Villagers from the area, not understanding the danger, collected the hazardous liquid metal. More than 1,000 people became ill, some permanently, a lawsuit later filed on their behalf charged.

In most developed nations, environmental laws prohibit the discharge of mining waste directly into waterways. But elsewhere in the world, laws are often weaker and regulations poorly enforced. In Indonesia, U.S.-based Freeport McMoran's Grasberg operation, the largest gold mine in the world, dumped its waste directly into local rivers, badly damaging downstream rain forests and wetlands. An official of the Environment Ministry said that the agency's regulatory tools were so weak that it was like "painting on clouds" to get the company even to follow the law.

Gold mining also pollutes the air. The entire process of metal extraction—from diesel-powered earth-moving equipment to oil- and coal-burning smelters—consumes large quantities of fuel, contributing to global warming. Smelters produce oxides of nitrogen and sulfur, components of acid rain, as well as traces of toxic metals such as lead, arsenic, and cadmium.

Another environmental hazard of gold extraction is acid mine drainage. Often, the rock that harbors gold also contains sulfide minerals. When this rock is crushed and exposed to air and water, these minerals form sulfuric acid. As this acid drains from mine debris, it picks up other metals, such as arsenic, mercury, and lead, creating a toxic brew that can drain into groundwater and waterways. This process can go on for decades, long after a mine has shut down.

In the United States, although mining companies have to follow environmental laws, no law specifically ensures that a mine will not create acid runoff. Sixty-three Superfund sites are abandoned mines; the EPA has estimated their cleanup cost at $7.8 billion. In a study for Congress in 2005, the General Accounting Office called for new rules to require mining companies to post adequate surety bonds (a kind of insurance) to cover the costs of remediation if they went out of business.

Pegasus Gold, a Canadian company, declared bankruptcy in 1998 and abruptly shut down its Zortman-Landusky mine in Montana, once the largest gold mine in the United States, sticking the state's taxpayers with a $33 million bill for ongoing water treatment and cleanup. The citizens of Montana subsequently voted to ban cyanide heap-leach mining completely anywhere in the state. After an effort to overturn this initiative failed, Canyon Resources, a company that held the rights to a valuable Montana deposit, said it was looking into other ways to extract gold, including an innovative new technology that used bacteria instead of cyanide.

In 2004, Earthworks, an environmental NGO based in the United States, launched a campaign called "No Dirty Gold," and called on jewelry retailers to support the Golden Rules, agreeing to source only from responsibly operated mines. Many retailers—from Tiffany & Co. and Cartier to Walmart and JCPenney—signed on. Two years later, Earthworks joined with mining companies, retailers, and jewelers in the Madison Dialogue, an ongoing conversation about how best to encourage best environmental practices in their industry. A manager from Cartier, the jewelry retailer, said, "It is our duty to provide our clients with creations that are beautiful, desirable . . . and responsibly made. As times change, so do society's expectations."

Sources: Earthworks and Mining Watch Canada, *Troubled Waters: How Mine Waste Dumping Is Poisoning Our Oceans, Rivers, and Lakes,* February 2012; "The New Gold Standard," *Time,* February 6, 2009; "Dirty Metals: Mining, Communities, and the Environment," a Report by Earthworks and Oxfam America, *www.nodirtygold.org;* "Beyond Gold's Glitter: Torn Lands and Pointed Questions," *The New York Times,* October 24, 2005, pp. A1, A10; "Tangled Strands in Fight over Peru Gold Mine," *The New York Times,* October 25, 2005, pp. A1, A14; "Hardrock Mining: BLM Needs to Better Manage Financial Assurances to Guarantee Reclamation Costs," GAO Report to the Ranking Minority Member, Committee on Homeland Security and Governmental Affairs, U.S. Senate, June 2005; Jared Diamond, *Collapse: How Societies Choose to Fail or Succeed* (New York: Viking, 2005), ch. 15, "Big Business and the Environment: Different Conditions, Different Outcomes"; Websites of Westerners for Responsible Mining, *www.bettermines.org,* and Alburnus Maior, *www.rosiamontana.org;* and additional articles in the Northwest Mining Association Bulletin, *High Country News,* and *Billings Gazette.* The website of the Madison Dialogue is at *www.madisondialogue.org.*

Discussion Questions

1. Using the classification system presented in the chapter section "Major Areas of Environmental Regulation," explain what type(s) of pollution is (are) generated by gold mining. Which of these do you think is (are) most damaging to the environment, and why?

2. Using the classification system presented in the chapter section "Alternative Policy Approaches," explain what type(s) of government regulation would most effectively address the concerns you identified in question 1.

3. In your view, what role should nongovernmental organizations (NGOs) and citizen movements play in reducing the adverse environmental impacts of gold mining?

4. Which of the gold mining companies mentioned in this case are more—or less—environmentally responsible? What factors, in your view, might cause these differences?

PART SIX

Business and Technology

Technology, Organizations, and Society

Technology is an unmistakable economic and social force in both business and the world where we live. Global and local communications, business exchanges, and the simple tasks that make up our daily lives are all significantly influenced by technology. Whether we are at home, in school, or in the workplace, emerging technological innovations have dramatically changed how we live, play, learn, work, and interact with others, raising important social and ethical questions.

This Chapter Focuses on These Key Learning Objectives:

- Defining technology and its characteristics.
- Recognizing the evolving phases of technology throughout history and what fuels technological innovation today.
- Examining how technological innovations have changed the way organizations operate and interact with their stakeholders around the world.
- Analyzing the emerging social networking phenomenon—texting, instant messaging, tweets, blogs, vlogs, spam, and phishing—and the challenges they create for businesses and government policymakers.
- Recognizing socially beneficial uses of technology in education and medicine.
- Evaluating recent efforts to address and narrow the digital divide.

Technology experts point to the early 1900s as a time of technological breakthroughs. Electrification, the creation of the telephone, the dawn of the automobile age, and the invention of stainless steel and the radio amplifier fueled exponential economic growth. These experts now are pointing to the 2010s and three grand technological transformations with the potential to rival the growth found in the past century: the ability to process enormous amounts of data, smart manufacturing, and the wireless revolution. Processing power and data storage are virtually free in the cloud, and a simple handheld iPhone has the same computing power as the room-sized IBM mainframe computer of the 1970s. Utilizing new materials—such as metal alloys, graphene (instead of silicon) transistors, and meta-metals that possess properties not found in nature—will enable engineers to design and build from the molecular level, radically improving quality and reducing waste. The wireless revolution will soon connect every person on the planet with everyone else. Billions more people will be able to communicate, socialize, and trade in real time than ever before. How we embrace and use technology are also changing dramatically.

In just a decade, from 2000 to 2010, active blogs grew from 12,000 to 141 million. Less than 300,000 books were published in 2000, yet more than a million were published in 2010, and most are electronically accessible. Daily text messaging rose from 400,000 to 4.5 billion and e-mails from 12 billion to 247 billion (while letters mailed each day declined from 208 billion to 176 billion). The cost of hard-drive storage decreased from $10 per gigabyte to $.06 per gigabyte. The average person spent 2.7 hours per week online in 2000, but nearly 20 hours per week by 2010. Not only were more people using technology, they were increasingly demanding more of technology.

By 2012, Google searches exceeded three billion per day. The company reported that if search results were slowed by just four-tenths of a second, it would reduce the number of searches by eight million per day. But the company also recognized that its users wanted information at an ever-faster pace. One in four people abandoned a web page that took more than four seconds to load. Fifty percent of mobile users abandoned a web page if it did not load in 10 seconds, and three out of five mobile users reported that they would not return to that site in the future. More users relied on their mobile technology in 2012. Seventy-nine percent of mobile web consumers used their phones for shopping, and 40 percent said they would abandon an e-commerce site that did not load in three seconds. Amazon.com, the global leader in e-commerce, registered about $67 million in sales each day. The company reported that a one-second web page delay could potentially result in a loss of $1.6 billion in sales to the company annually.[1]

Technology is a major factor in our lives, helping us communicate with others around the world and across town, providing new opportunities for business to promote its activities, and improving the quality of our lives. But what are the consequences of the extraordinarily rapid pace of technological change? Has technology replaced human contact and, if so, what are the consequences of this change in how we relate to others? Who decides what technology should emerge and dramatically affect our lives? Should businesses be allowed to use technology freely, or should there be some constraints on its use by business? Who should determine what these constraints are?

---

[1] "Enough Said: Facts That Speak for Themselves—Instant America," *Daily Infographic*, April 1, 2012, *dailyinfographic.com;* "Exactly How Much Are the Times A-Changing?" *Newsweek*, July 26, 2010, *newsweek.com;* and "The Coming Tech-Led Boom," *The Wall Street Journal*, January 30, 2012, *online.wsj.com.*

Technology Defined

Technology is a broad term referring to the practical applications of science and knowledge to commercial and organizational activities. The dominant feature of technology is *change and then more change.* As discussed at the beginning of this chapter, new technological breakthroughs are again changing our lives. Sometimes the pace of change is so fast and furious that it approaches the limits of human tolerance, and people lose their ability to cope with it successfully. Although technology is not the only cause of change in society, it is a primary cause. It is either directly or indirectly involved in most changes that occur in society.

Another feature of technology is that *its effects are widespread,* reaching far beyond the immediate point of technological impact in unpredictable ways. Technology ripples through society until every community is affected by it. An example of a technology with widespread effects is cloud computing—the use of publicly accessible servers to store users' text, photos, videos, and other data at remote sites, rather than on their own computers.[2]

> Cloud computing led to fundamental changes in several industries and markets. It helped create a market for netbooks, tablets, Kindles, and other small, less-expensive personal computers that had wireless connectivity but usually lacked the large amounts of local storage provided by a hard drive or optical drive. By 2009, consumers had fully embraced the tablet market and realized they did not need as much storage capability. This trend created profits for manufacturers and retailers of tablets, but created problems for others. Cable and satellite television providers, for example, began losing revenue as consumers realized they could watch programs and videos on their tablets instead of their televisions. And the storage of personal information on remote sites created the potential for a greater invasion of individual privacy and the use of personal information to target marketing, as shown later in Chapter 13.[3]

A final feature of technology is that it is *self-reinforcing.* As stated by Alvin Toffler, "Technology feeds on itself. Technology makes more technology possible."[4] This self-reinforcing feature means that technology acts as a multiplier to encourage its own faster development. It acts with other parts of society so that an invention in one place leads to a sequence of inventions in other places. Thus, invention of the microprocessor led rather quickly to successful generations of the modern computer, which led to new banking methods, electronic mail, bar-code systems, global tracking systems, and so on.

Phases of Technology in Society

Six broad phases of technology have developed, as shown in Figure 12.1. As shown, societies have tended to move sequentially through each phase, beginning with the lowest technology and moving higher with each step, so the six phases roughly represent the progress of civilization throughout history. The first phase was the nomadic-agrarian, in which people hunted wild animals for meat and gathered wild plants for food. The second was the

---

[2] For a different view of the explosion of technology in our society, see Michael Mandel, "Innovation Interrupted," *Business-Week,* June 15, 2009, pp. 34–40.

[3] "Asus T91 Netbook Battery Not Replaceable," *Boingboing blog,* May 17, 2009, *gadgets.boingboing.net;* and "$200 Laptops Break a Business Model," *The New York Times,* January 26, 2009, *www.nytimes.com.* Also see "Cloud Computing's Big Bang for Business," *BusinessWeek,* June 15, 2009, pp. 42–48, and "The Power of the Cloud," *Bloomberg BusinessWeek,* March 7–13, 2011, pp. 53–59.

[4] Alvin Toffler, *Future Shock* (New York: Bantam, 1971), p. 26.

FIGURE 12.1   **Phases in the Development of Technology**

Technology Level	Phases in the Development of Technology	Approximate Period	Activity	Primary Skill Used
1	Nomadic-agrarian	Until 1650	Harvesting	Manual
2	Agrarian	1650–1900	Planting and harvesting	Manual
3	Industrial	1900–1960	Building material goods	Manual and machine
4	Service	1960–1975	Providing services	Manual and intellectual
5	Information	1975–2000	Thinking and designing	Intellectual and electronic
6	Semantic	2000–today	Relevance and context	Intellectual and networking

agrarian, corresponding with the domestication of animals and plants. The first two used manual labor exclusively. The third was the industrial, characterized by the development of powered machinery, first in the textile industry and later in many other forms of manufacturing. The fourth was the service phase, marked by the rise of service industries and intellectual labor. The fifth was the **information phase**. This phase emphasized the use and transfer of knowledge and information rather than manual skill. Businesses of all sizes, including the smallest firms, explored the benefits of the information age through the availability of nanotechnology and similar inventions. These inventions catapulted societies into **cyberspace**, where information is stored, ideas are described, and communication takes place in and through an electronic network of linked systems. The technology developed in this age provided the mechanisms for more information to be produced in a decade than in the previous 1,000 years.

The **semantic phase**, which began around 2000, saw the development of processes and systems to enable organizations and people to navigate through the expanding amount of links and information available on the Internet. Networked services analyzed user requests and made assumptions based upon context, location, the user's history, and other factors. Search engines, such as Google, employed massive clusters of computers to analyze the *metadata* or descriptive information embedded within web pages, documents, and files. A Google search for a specific airline flight, for example, might return links to a flight tracking website, an estimated time of departure or arrival for that day's flight, weather forecasts, and airport maps. A blog article might be automatically linked to popular or recent articles in other blogs with similar keywords or tags. Social interaction is an important part of the semantic phase. Services such as Facebook, Twitter, and LinkedIn analyzed the transactions and metadata from each user's activity to suggest new contacts, entertainment, and links.[5]

Where will technology head next? Some observers have suggested that society is now at the beginning of a new phase dominated by *biotechnology*. As discussed in more detail in Chapter 13, **biotechnology** is a technological application that uses biological systems or living organisms to make or modify products or processes for specific use. Its applications are common in agriculture, food science, and medicine. This emerging phase of technology extends beyond the design and analysis of information to the manipulation of organisms that produce fabricated products or act as components within a computer network. Other technology experts, as discussed at the beginning of this chapter, see the next phase as defined by the creation of new meta-metals and smart manufacturing or by the impact of the wireless revolution.

[5] Tim Berners-Lee, James Hendler and Ora Lassila, "The Semantic Web," *Scientific America*, May 2001, *www.scientificamerican.com.*

Fueling Technological Growth

As Figure 12.1 demonstrates, in recent decades the pace of technological change has accelerated, and the time lapse between phases has dramatically shortened. Several factors have fueled these developments.

Government: Government investment has helped launch many new technologies, including the Internet, and these trends continue.

In 2012, President Obama unveiled his Big Data R&D Initiative and committed more than $200 million in new funding to "improve our ability to extract knowledge and insights from large and complex collections of digital data." Numerous government agencies were involved in this project, including the White House Office of Science and Technology, National Science Foundation, National Institute of Health, Department of Defense, and many others. The initiative's goals were to advance state-of-the-art core technologies needed to collect, store, preserve, manage, analyze, and share huge quantities of data, to harness these technologies to accelerate the pace of discovery in science and engineering, to strengthen the country's national security, and to expand the workforce needed to develop and use Big Data technologies.[6]

Private investment: Venture capitalists are investors who provide capital to start-up companies that do not have access to public funding. They have long targeted technological innovation, with the aim of making outsized returns. Venture capital–backed companies have generally performed well. For example, these companies experienced revenue growth of 1.6 percent between 2008 and 2010, while U.S. sales dropped 1.5 percent overall. Venture capital–backed companies also employed 11 percent of the U.S. workforce in 2010, with jobs increasing from 8.69 million in 2000 to 11.87 million in 2010 for venture capital–backed companies.[7]

When Google was first created, two venture capital firms invested $25 million in the fledgling search engine company. Fourteen years later, Google's revenue approached $38 billion annually, with assets of $72.5 billion. Facebook started with $500,000 from "super venture capitalist angel" Peter Thiel; after Facebook went public in 2012, the company was worth $15 billion. Similarly, Sequoia Capital took a chance on YouTube with a $3.5 million initial investment, and a year later Google acquired the online video service site for $1.65 billion in stock.[8]

Business investment: Business firms have also invested directly in technology through their research and development (R&D) operations. These investments have often benefited the business, as well as produced innovations that have moved their industries forward.

For example, Google relies heavily on data centers to provide search services and cloud-based applications to individual and corporate users. Its innovations in this area have given it a competitive edge over its rivals. Google has invested billions of

---

[6] "Obama Administration Unveils $200M Big Data R&D Initiative," *The Computing Community Consortium Blog*, March 29, 2012, *www.cccblog.org/2012/03/29*.

[7] For additional information, see *Venture Impact: The Importance of Venture-Backed Companies to the U.S. Economy*, Edition 6.0 (Arlington, VA: National Venture Capital Association, 2011).

[8] "These Angels Go Where Others Fear to Tread," *BusinessWeek*, June 1, 2009, pp. 44–48; and Google.com company website.

dollars in developing highly modular data centers that house the company's servers and networking equipment in shipping containers. These data centers were designed to use electricity, water, and other resources in a highly efficient manner. Google opened its data center in The Dalles, Oregon, in 2007, becoming a leading customer of the Grand Coulee Dam's inexpensive electric power. Computer equipment, especially hard disk drives, is highly sensitive to temperature, humidity, and airborne pollution. Data centers require massive heating and air conditioning facilities. Google's network is highly distributed and redundant, so a single Google search may require servers that are spread across a continent to deliver relevant results in less than a second.[9]

The combination of government, private investor, and business investment in technology has continued to drive innovation forward. But ultimately, technology continues to evolve because of people's insatiable desire for it. They forever seek to expand the use of technology in their lives, probably because of the excitement in having new things and their belief that these new things may help them better adapt to their environment. As Bill Joy, Sun Microsystems' chief scientist, explained,

> By 2030, we are likely to be able to build machines, in quantity, a million times as powerful as the personal computer of today. As this enormous computing power is combined with the manipulative advances of the physical sciences and the new, deep understanding in genetics, enormous transformative power is being unleashed. These combinations open up the opportunity to completely redesign the world, for better or worse: The replicating and evolving processes that have been confined to the natural world are about to become realms of human endeavor.[10]

Technology as a Powerful Force in Business

Technology and business have been intertwined since the Industrial Revolution. The connection between the two became even stronger in the information and semantic phases. Today, technology influences every aspect of the global marketplace—driving innovation, affecting partnerships, and changing business–stakeholder relationships. It has created great opportunities for business, but also serious ethical and social challenges. This section will explore some ways in which three technologies—the Internet, e-business, and m-commerce—have presented both opportunities and challenges for business.

The Internet

More people have more access to technology than ever before. Residents of developing countries increasingly enjoy energy-powered appliances, entertainment devices, and communications equipment. Individuals and businesses in developed countries in North America, Europe, and portions of Asia more than ever are dependent on electronic communication devices for access to information and for conducting business transactions. In today's workplace environment, nearly every North American manager has a desktop or laptop computer, fax machine, voice mail, mobile phone, PDA, and a host of other electronic devices to connect the manager to other employees, customers, suppliers, and information. These technology devices have become common tools.

---

[9] Bobbie Johnson, "Google's Power Hungry Data Centers," *The Guardian*, May 3, 2009, *www.guardian.co.uk.*

[10] Bill Joy, "Why the Future Doesn't Need Us," *Wired*, April 2000, *www.wired.com/wired/archive/8.04/joy.*

The Emergence of the Internet

One of the most visible and widely used technological innovations over the past decade has been the Internet. The **Internet** is a global network of interconnected computers, enabling users to share information along multiple channels linking individuals and organizations. Springing to life in 1994, this conduit of information revolutionized how business was conducted, students learned, and households operated.

Any estimate of the number of Internet users is clearly only an estimate. In 2008, China surpassed the United States with the most Internet users by country. Just four years later China had more than 500 million Internet users, compared to the United States' 245 million, as shown in Figure 12.2.

While opportunities to use the Internet are growing quickly, some limitations have appeared, such as in China when the government attempted to convert all identification records to its digital database systems.

Ma Cheng was told by the Chinese government that she had to change her given name from "Cheng" to an approved name that could be recorded in a modernized version of the country's identity database. The database would not accommodate handwritten characters as names, and "Cheng" was one of over 22,000 characters

FIGURE 12.2   **Top 20 Internet Users by Country, 2012**

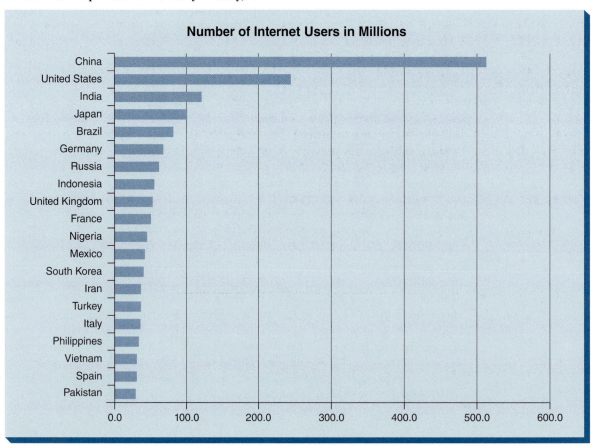

Source: Internet World Stats, 2012 Q1, *www.internetworldstats.com.*

that was not included in the system's 32,252 Chinese character set. Sixty million Chinese citizens were in a similar predicament as the government completed a long-delayed conversion from handwritten identity cards to computer readable cards with embedded microchips and digital color photographs. This change also affected Internet users in China, who often used pseudonyms, or fake names, to protect their identity when criticizing the government or its policies for fear of retaliation. From a systems perspective, the government's decision was logical and highly efficient. Eighty-five percent of China's population used one of a hundred common surnames; the remaining 15 percent were told that they had to conform to the new system. It also would allow the Chinese government to have more control over and stifle political dissidents.

The United Nations recognizes a personal name as a basic human right, but researcher Andrea DiMaio noted that "different identity credentials are being used for different government services, and emerging forms of personal identity, through mobile devices or social media, will challenge the status quo." While a minority of Chinese citizens fought to keep their names through temporary cards and political influence, many Chinese decided to conform to their government's wishes and selected new names from an approved list.[11]

New ways of going online are contributing to the growing use of the Internet. Digital music players and game consoles from Apple, Microsoft, Sony, and Nintendo now include web browsers, e-mail and messaging capability, and wireless Internet access. These small, handheld devices are popular among young adults and mobile professionals who have come to expect easy, pervasive Internet access wherever they go. Some smartphones, including BlackBerrys, Nokias, and Androids, among others, include WiFi connectivity to provide users with faster data transfer speeds than mobile phone carriers can provide. When device manufacturers add features such as digital cameras, video recording, and GPS, these portable devices become useful tools for collecting and distributing information.

Thousands of new Internet users each day demonstrate the power of this technology as a force in our lives. The Internet also has been adopted by businesses to create new opportunities for commerce, as described in the following sections.

E-Business

During the information and semantic phase of technological development, shown in Figure 12.1, electronic business exchanges between businesses and between businesses and their customers emerged. These electronic exchanges, generally referred to as **e-business**, consist of buying and selling goods and services between businesses, organizations, and individuals electronically—that is, via Internet-based systems. During the past few years, e-business revenue has increased at a faster pace than that of traditional, or nonelectronic, business and is predicted to continue to rise, as shown in Figure 12.3.

E-business has grown dramatically and become a way of life, from large companies and smaller start-up businesses to individuals interested in shopping online. As technology became more affordable and easier to use, small and medium-sized businesses committed investment dollars to e-business and technology systems. These businesses discovered that

---

[11] "Name Not On Our List? Change It," *The New York Times*, April 21, 2009, *www.nytimes.com;* "Even Chinese Struggle with Smart ID Cards," *The Gartner Blog Network*, April 21, 2009, *blog.gartner.com;* and "China to Force Internet Users to Register Real Names," *The Telegraph*, May 5, 2010, *www.telegraph.co.uk.*

FIGURE 12.3
Global E-Business
Sales Growing

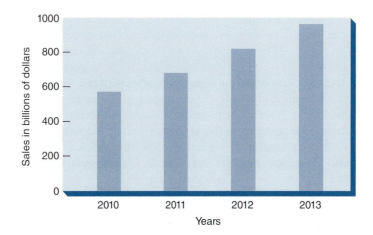

the adoption of technology was a money-saver rather than an expense in the long run and that it gave the businesses a competitive edge over rivals by enabling them to add new services and operate more efficiently.

> When a computer programmer offered to create a custom package for Top Dog Daycare, owners Joelle and Tom Hilfers were shocked but agreed to take the plunge, on a payment plan. Three years and nearly $30,000 in technology investments later, the Hilfers do not know how they ever survived without the company's K-9 Connect software, which allows dog owners to book appointments online, view their accounts, post photos of their pets, and look in on them during the day through a live webcam. K-9 Connect also stores the pets' vaccination records, meal plans, and special requirements and has pages on e-commerce, dog training, and dog grooming. Business at Top Dog Daycare tripled since adopting the computerized system.[12]

E-business is undoubtedly here to stay, and new applications appear inevitable. One controversial area where e-business has made a significant impact is online gambling. Some of the world's largest gaming companies opened up new business opportunities by developing mobile gaming systems that allowed guests in their hotels to place wagers on the casino floor without ever leaving their rooms. Using handheld PDA-type devices, individuals can make wagers on sporting or other events. This generated an even greater revenue pool for the gaming companies but raised an important ethical question—is it good that people can place their bets anywhere in the hotel-casino building? What if children of the hotel guests get a hold of these devices? On the casino floor, drunken guests can be spotted and steered away from the tables, but remote betting circumvents this control.

With each new innovation comes the important ethical question: *Should* we develop and offer the new application? At present, many inventors, computer programmers, and business managers appear only to be asking, *Can* we develop and offer the new application? Both questions are paramount as technology and e-business continue to influence individual, business, and society interactions in the world in which we live.

---

[12] "High Tech Isn't Just for the Big Guys," *The New York Times*, January 20, 2005, *www.nytimes.com;* and see the company's website at *topdogdaycare.net.*

The QR, or quick response, code was created in Japan in 2008 and quickly became an opportunity for mobile phone users worldwide to access information that could be stored in their phones. QR codes appear in magazine advertisements, on billboards, in web pages and even on someone's clothing. Once it is uploaded to a smartphone it provides businesses, especially retailers, with the means to send information ranging from the location of their nearest store to features about an item available for purchase or an event that is to take place. Retailers also use QR codes to provide potential users with discount coupons. QR codes are more useful than standard bar codes because they can store more data, including URL links, geo coordinates, and text. The other key feature of QR codes is that instead of a clumsy handheld scanner to scan the code, most mobile phones can scan for the information.

QR codes are also making their way into the classroom. Educators seeking to integrate technology into their teaching use QR codes to help students create resumes that can easily be sent to prospective employers and to show that the applicant is technologically able. QR codes can be displayed throughout the classroom to provide learning stations for students. Many educators like using QR codes because it is a more environmentally friendly way to provide information to students, rather than printing information on paper and distributing it in the classroom.

Sources: "What Is a QR Code and Why Do You Need One?" *Search Engine Land*, October 15, 2009, *searchengineland.com;* and "Twelve Ideas for Teaching with QR Codes," *Edutopia*, December 5, 2011, *www.edutopia.org.*

M-Commerce

Cellular telephones, or cell phones, use radio technology to enable users to place calls from a mobile device, with transmission over a service area divided into small "cells," each with its own low-power radio transmitter. The first generation of cell phones, introduced in the 1980s, were clumsy analog devices; today's digital "smartphones" provide a range of applications, including e-mail and Internet access, in addition to voice communications. Given the significant increase in smartphone users, businesses have looked for ways to reach out to these potential customers. One major breakthrough was the creation of the QR code. The **QR code**, an abbreviation for "quick response," consists of a square made up of black and white spaces that when read by a cell phone transmits information to the user. The QR code is described more fully in Exhibit 12.A.

In North America, cell phones were initially used mainly as a communications tool. But American cell phone users have joined many Europeans and Asians to embrace what they call a "mobile phone" in a different way—as a method of conducting commerce. **M-commerce**, commerce conducted via mobile or cell phones, provides consumers with an electronic wallet when using their mobile phones. People can trade stocks or make consumer purchases of everything from hot dogs to washing machines and countless other products. France Telecom has marketed a mobile phone with a built-in credit card slot for easy wireless payments. Walmart, Target, 7-Eleven, Google, Sunoco, and many other companies provided the option for customers to turn their smartphones into devices for making purchases.

Recognizing that one-third of Starbucks customers in the United States used smartphones, in 2011 the company introduced "mobile pay" to its customers. Accessed through an iPhone or Android application, users downloaded a free app, preloaded it with cash, and then quickly and securely paid for their drinks and other items with their smartphones just by waving the smartphone over a scanner during checkout. Within months Starbucks reported they had processed 42 million mobile payment transactions. "You are going to see us as a company that will push the

Robert Bornstein, a psychologist at Adelphia University, says, "The superconnected may develop a dual-dependency. They're not only counting on other people too much, they're also hooked on the devices themselves, sometimes to the point where they feel utterly disconnected, isolated, and detached without them." Exactly how bad is the dependency on technology, specifically wireless devices? Some experts have warned that handheld e-mailing devices are so addictive that soon compulsive users will need to be weaned off them using treatment programs like the ones used by drug addicts. This overreliance upon technology can also cause physical problems, such as

- BlackBerry thumb—a pain or numbness in the thumbs caused by constant e-mailing, messaging, or Internet surfing on handheld devices.
- Cell phone elbow—arthritic pain and swelling in the elbow from constantly holding a cell phone to the ear, which in some severe cases may cause nerve damage.
- PDA (personal data assistant) hunch—neck pain caused by looking straight down at your PDA mini-monitor.

It is common in the technological world for someone to view multiple screens, listen to music on an iPod, and send an e-mail or tweet all at the same time and for hours on end. The extensive interaction with many technological devices can be hazardous for the user. Loren Frank, a researcher at the University of California, San Francisco, concluded, "Almost certainly, downtime lets the brain go over experiences it's had, solidify them, and turn them into permanent long-term memories." When the brain is constantly stimulated, this learning process is prevented. "Instead of having long relaxing breaks [allowing time for the brain to process the information], like taking two hours for lunch, we have a lot of micro-moments," explained Marc Berman, a University of Michigan neuroscientist.

Source: "Wireless Dependency," *The New York Times,* February 17, 2007, *www.nytimes.com;* and "Digital Devices Deprive Brain of Needed Downtime," *The New York Times*, August 24, 2010, *www.nytimes.com.*

envelope around mobile pay," said Starbucks chief digital officer. "We want to innovate in that area before others catch up."[13]

Mobile phones also offer greater security and protection against theft. Moses Githua lives in Nairobi, Kenya, and is referred to as an "unbanked," someone who does not use the traditional banking system to save, invest, or take out a line of credit. It was not that Githua was too poor, but rather that he chose to avoid small banks because of their excessive fees. Githua found a different way to save his money—he opened an account with M-PESA, a service that allows people to transfer money with their mobile phones, but Githua used M-PESA in a different way. He simply would load up his account, let it sit there for days until he needed it, and then would use his "digital wallet" to pay for what he needed. Besides the convenience, this system protected Githua from thieves who preyed on the unbanked, who often carried their cash in their pockets, or hid it in a jar or under their bed. Researchers studying this practice predict that by 2012, 1.7 billion of the unbanked poor worldwide will use the mobile phone as their bank.[14]

But with the potential for greater m-commerce activity worldwide, some stakeholder groups warned that accompanying the increased usage would be increased frustration. Critics predicted more unwanted and unsolicited mobile text messages and incidents of malware and spyware. Some other undesirable consequences of mobile technology are described in Exhibit 12.B.

---

[13] "Starbucks Brews Up Major M-Commerce Success," *Daily Deal Media*, April 11, 2012, *www.dailydealmedia.com;* and "Payments Network Takes On Google," *The Wall Street Journal,* August 15, 2012, online.wsj.com.

[14] "In Kenya, Keeping Cash Safe On a Cell Phone," *Bloomberg Businessweek*, September 12–18, 2011, pp. 55–56.

Social Networking—Tools and Threats

Social networking, a system using technology to enable people to connect, explore interests, and share activities around the world, exploded on to the technology scene in the early 2000s, altering many social and human interactions. By 2011, 1.2 billion people worldwide used social networking sites at least once per month. eMarketer estimated double-digit annual growth in social networking usage; the number of social networking site users could top 1.85 billion by 2014. The largest number of social network users is in Asia, where it was predicted that by December 2012 more than 600 million Internet users would access social sites. About half of these users are in China, where social network users outnumber those in the United States nearly two to one.[15]

Facebook was the most popular networking site worldwide, even though Facebook was banned in China as of 2012. By May 2012, Facebook reportedly had 750 million monthly visitors, followed by Twitter (also banned in China), which attracted 250 million monthly visitors, LinkedIn had 110 million monthly visitors, MySpace had more than 70 million users (although the number of users of this site has declined steadily since 2009), and Google+ had 65 million monthly visitors. But many new social networking sites appeared almost daily, such as Dogster, PotSpace, and CafeMom. By 2012, there were more than 200 social networking sites with diverse topics and users' interests, ranging from Athlinks, focusing on running and swimming buffs, to Ravelry, a network for knitting and crocheting enthusiasts.[16]

Social networking has also ventured into the workplace. Some businesses initially questioned their employees' use of these services and tried to ban them from the workplace. But, recently, businesses have warmed up to social networking. In a study conducted by Robert Half Technology in 2011, companies surveyed reported that only 31 percent banned social networking sites completely, down from 54 percent in 2009, and slightly more than half of the firms permitted social networking usage for business purposes, up from only 19 percent in 2009.[17]

Many businesses use social media tools to reach out to their customers. McKinsey & Company, one of the world's largest consulting companies, recently found that 39 percent of companies surveyed already used social media services as their primary digital tool to reach customers and expected that percentage to rise to 47 percent by 2015. The greatest usage of social media tools was found in the telecommunications industry, where 86 percent of the companies surveyed said they extensively use social media to reach out to customers, followed by pharmaceuticals (74 percent), retailing (69 percent), transportation (69 percent) and health care (67 percent).[18] (The use of social networking tools is also discussed in Chapters 15 and 16.)

While many businesses saw the benefits of social networking, they also found that social networking provided an opportunity for stakeholders to bring issues to the public's view or challenge the company's decisions, as the following stories show.

[15] "Where in the World Are the Hottest Social Networking Countries?" *eMarketer*, February 29, 2012, *www.emarketer.com*.

[16] "Social Media Networking Explodes in Usage on Mobile Devices," *Examiner.com*, October 21, 2011, *www.examiner.com;* "With Friends Like This, Who Needs Facebook?" *Bloomberg Businessweek*, September 13–19, 2010, pp. 35–37; and "Top 15 Most Popular Social Networking Sites," *eBiz/MBA*, May 2012, *www.ebizmba.com*.

[17] "Social Work? More Companies Permit Social Networking on the Job," *Robert Half Technology*, May 26, 2011, *rht.mediaroom.com*.

[18] "Demystifying Social Media," *McKinsey Quarterly*, April 2012, *www.mckinseyquarterly.com* and "How Social Technologies Are Extending the Organization," *McKinsey Quarterly*, November 2011, *www.mckinseyquarterly.com*.

- In 2010, a group of parents who were upset that American Eagle Outfitters decided to withdraw the company's support for a day care center near its Pittsburgh headquarters started a Facebook page. Within days, the Facebook page had 40 friends enabling parents to share information and stories about finding a new day care option and to express their displeasure over American Eagle's decision.

- Local 23 of the United Food and Commercial Workers union created a Facebook page to rally membership during negotiations with a grocery store chain. Between 750 and 800 people accessed the page for information. Most were union workers, but some politicians also accessed the page to keep up with issues in the negotiation.

- Justin Kurtz was outraged that he had to pay $118 to get his car out of an impound lot after being towed from his apartment complex parking lot, despite having a permit to park there. He created a Facebook page called "Kalamazoo Residents against T&J Towing," and in only a few days 800 people had logged on to the site, posting comments about their own frustrating experiences with the towing company. T&J Towing Company claimed that Kurtz's permit was not clearly visible and they were justified in towing his car.[19]

Blogs and Vlogs

A **blog** is a web-based journal or log maintained by an individual with regular entries of commentary, descriptions, or accounts of events or other material such as graphics or video. The blogging revolution began in the early 2000s. Just a few years later, it was widely popular, and many believed already out of control. While difficult to count the total number of blogs, *BlogPlus* estimated in 2011 there were more than 156 million blogs and said that number would be out of date the moment it was published.

Technorati surveyed more than 7,000 bloggers and placed them into the following categories based on their use or purpose of their blogs:

- Hobbyist bloggers (60 percent) are the backbone of the blogging community. They blog "to have fun" and do not use their blog to generate income. Most spend less than three hours per week blogging, yet half faithfully respond individually to comments from readers.

- Professional bloggers (18 percent) are independent bloggers and use blogging either to supplement their income or as their full-time job. They do not rely on blogging for their primary source of income and primarily focus on personal musings or technology.

- Corporate bloggers (8 percent) blog as part of their full-time job or blog full-time for a company or organization they work for. Their focus is primarily technology or business. Seventy percent of these bloggers share their expertise, 61 percent seek greater professional recognition, and 52 percent seek to attract new customers.

- Entrepreneur bloggers (13 percent) blog about the company they own. Most (84 percent) focus on the industry they work in, with 46 percent blogging about business, and 40 percent about technology. Seventy-six percent blog to share their expertise, 70 percent blog to gain professional recognition, and 68 percent attempt to attract new customers for their business.[20]

[19] "Using Web to Change Corporate Behavior Isn't as Easy as Point and Click," *Pittsburgh Post-Gazette*, June 29, 2010, *www.post-gazette.com;* and "When Online Grievances Are Met with a Lawsuit," *The New York Times*, May 31, 2010, *www.nytimes.com.*

[20] "State of Blogosphere 2011," *Technorati*, November 4, 2011, *www.technorati.com.*

As blogging spread into all areas of our lives, ethical questions about blogs emerged. According to a *Los Angeles Times* report, thousands of bloggers, described above as "corporate bloggers," were being paid by companies or their marketing firms to promote or attack various products on the market. Critics argue that this blurred the ethical line between what was honest opinion or helpful information and what was an advertisement paid for by companies to influence individuals' purchasing decisions. (A case about this issue, "Carolina Pad and the Mommy Bloggers," appears at the end of this book.) In the United States, bloggers are required to disclose to the Federal Trade Commission any connection with the companies they blog about, including the receipt of free products from the companies or if they were paid by companies.[21] Medical professionals also weighed in on the blogging controversy, claiming that patients were posting unfounded and damaging reports on a doctor's performance. While some doctors admitted that blogs provided many patients with useful information, medical misinformation from uncensored blogs was far more harmful.[22]

A new generation of blogs appeared in the first decade of the 21st century, called **vlogs**, or video web logs. All that was needed was access to a digital camera that could capture moving images and high-speed Internet access.

> When the Baker family started Old Westminster Winery in Westminster, Maryland, Drew Baker, the vineyard manager, decided to create a vlog to educate potential customers about his family's new company. Using his iPhone and YouTube, Baker wanted to generate demand for the company's product so that they would have customers lined up ready to buy the wine when it was ready in 2013. Baker knew that if he followed his motto—"Be creative"—his vlog would achieve the success he sought. "If it's boring, no one is going to watch it," said Baker, who posted eight vlogs covering topics such as explaining the wine-making process to how to become a member of the company's Century Club to receive special benefits. Baker reported that these vlogs reached 700 viewers on YouTube almost immediately.[23]

The vlog medium has attracted thousands of aspiring video producers. The number of vlogs posted to the Internet continues to mushroom due to improved streaming video technology, faster Internet speeds, new websites that will host the video free of charge, and new cell phones and other devices designed to play videos. Videos produced by individuals and small companies found their way to on-demand services offered by cable companies and new networks that solicit user content. While most viewers stumbled across vlogs while web surfing, others found them on Apple's iTunes directory, which listed some vlogs, calling them video podcasts.

Spam and Unsolicited Commercial E-mail

The emergence of the Internet not only launched the blog and vlog avalanche but also the onslaught of *spam*. **Spam** refers to **unsolicited commercial e-mails** (also called UCE or junk e-mail) sent in bulk to valid e-mail accounts. These messages can vary from harmless advertisements for commercial products to offensive material and finance scams. Spam has created problems for e-mail users as it has caused extra network traffic and wasted time sorting through the irrelevant or unwanted e-mails to access desired messages. Spam also

---

[21] "Soon, Bloggers Must Give Full Disclosure," *The New York Times*, October 6, 2009, *www.nytimes.com.*

[22] "Questions about Blogging Chart New Ethical Territory in Cyberspace," Institute for Global Ethics, *Ethics Newsline*, March 19, 2007, *www.globalethics.org.*

[23] "Vlogging Takes Center Screen," *Baltimore Business Journal*, October 12, 2011, *www.bizjournals.com/baltimore.*

infiltrated cell phones. By 2012, U.S. cell phone users reported receiving nearly 4.5 million spam texts annually, more than double what was reported in 2009. Although these texts were spread across 250 million text message–enabled phones, so not as commonplace as e-mail spam, "unsolicited text messaging is a pervasive problem," explained a Federal Trade Commission attorney. "It is becoming very difficult to track down who is sending the spam."[24]

Spamming was big business and a big headache for business. Internet watchdogs reported that the number of malicious websites blocked for hosting malware, software designed to infiltrate and damage a computer, tripled by 2009, with nearly 3,000 potentially harmful websites being intercepted daily. That year, the percentage of e-mail-borne malware containing links to malicious sites reached its highest level, 20.3 percent. The global ratio of spam in e-mail traffic was 1 in every 1.32 e-mails.[25]

Yet, in general, businesses seem slow to combat the growing trend of spam e-mails at work. In a 2012 survey of information technology decision makers in the United States and the United Kingdom, 74 percent reported that they received too much spam, and more than 80 percent of the survey respondents reported that the volume of spam appearing in their workplaces was increasing at a rapid pace. What was most troublesome from the survey results was that 70 percent of the managers said that their company's spam solution was either marginally effective or not effective at all.[26]

Governments have stepped in to monitor, control, and prosecute spammers who use the Internet for illegal activity.

> The United Kingdom has passed anti-spam legislation in 2003 making it a crime to send unsolicited e-mail messages to people's private e-mail addresses or cell phones. The government believed that the threat of $8,000 for a conviction and limitless fines if the case made its way to a jury would deter the growing spam problem. Since 2003, very few cases were brought to court or a jury trial and, in most cases, the complainants received settlement payments under the protection of the law.[27]

The United States has a similar law—the CAN-SPAM Act of 2003—which established rules for commercial e-mails, gave recipients the right to be removed from e-mail lists, and spelled out penalties for violations (up to $16,000 per offense). Senders of e-mails are prohibited from using false or misleading header information or deceptive subject lines. The e-mail must identify that it is an advertisement and tell the recipient where the sender is located. Recipients also are to be told how they can opt out of receiving future e-mails, and these requests must be honored promptly.[28]

Phishing

Compounding the problem of spam or unsolicited commercial e-mail is **phishing**, the practice of stealing consumers' personal identity data and financial account credentials by using fake e-mails that appeared to be from legitimate businesses to trick users into divulging

---

[24] "Spam Invades a Last Refuge, the Cell Phone," *The New York Times*, April 7, 2012, *www.nytimes.com*.

[25] "Infected Websites Increase Three-Fold, and Email-borne Malicious Links Reaches Nine Month High," *MessageLabs Press Releases*, March 31, 2009, *www.messagelabs.co.uk*.

[26] *Small Businesses Heavily Reliant on Their Antivirus Security Suite for Protection Against Spam: Research Brief* (GFI Software, 2012), available at *www.gfi.com/documents/Research-brief-psam.pdf*.

[27] "Gordon Dick v. Transcom Internet Services Ltd.," *Scotch Spam!*, 2007, *www.scotchspam.co.uk*.

[28] For more information on the CAN-SPAM Act, see "The CAN-SPAM Act: A Compliance Guide for Business," *Federal Trade Commission BCP Business Center*, at *business.ftc.gov*.

identifying personal data such as usernames and passwords, or to open attachments that installed viruses or malware (malicious software). The Anti-Phishing Working Group (APWG), a U.S. industry association, reported in 2012 that 39 percent of the world's personal computers were infected with some type of malware. The APWG also reported that phishing attacks increased toward the end of the year, as the holiday season approached and more users engaged in online shopping or e-commerce activities.[29]

> Businesses have not sat idly by while con artists have gone phishing. Bromium, a technology start-up company, developed a system that allowed the virus into the computer but created a temporary, virtual compartment to house the virus. If the virus attempted to spread into the main areas of the computer, a program was activated that dissolved the virus before damage could be done to the rest of the computer. In 2012, 15 companies, including e-mail service providers (Google, Microsoft, and AOL) and financial service companies (Bank of America, Fidelity Investments, and PayPal), created DMARC.org (Domain-based Message Authentication, Reporting and Conformance) to promote a standard set of technologies intended to lead to more secure e-mail. If e-mails could be authenticated, customers would be more likely to trust that the messages were legitimate and feel freer to update a user account with sensitive information, rather than fearing that these e-mails were phishing attacks.[30]

Government Censorship of the Internet

Many people believe that information on the Internet should be universally accessible. Some believe that restrictions should be placed on some categories of information, such as sexually explicit material, gambling, or Nazi or racist propaganda. Some countries, however, have gone much further, imposing censorship on broad categories of online information. Government efforts at controlling the Internet significantly increased in the early 2010s based on political, security, or religious grounds.

- *China.* The Chinese government operates one of the most sophisticated systems of Internet censorship in the world. It requires all China-based websites and blogs to register with the government and blocks access to many kinds of information, including material critical of the government. In 2009, Chinese government officials censored a YouTube video, which it said was fabricated, that showed Chinese police brutally beating Tibetans after riots in Lhasa, the Tibetan capital. However, some people found ways to access banned sites, such as YouTube and Facebook, by "scaling the wall"—circumventing government efforts to restrict access to information on the Internet. The Chinese government countered with more severe measures, including requiring all mobile phone users to furnish identification when buying SIM cards, a portable memory chip used in mobile phones.[31]
- *United Arab Emirates and Saudi Arabia.* The U.A.E. and Saudi Arabia banned the use of BlackBerry technology in their countries in August 2010, citing national security

---

[29] "Phishing Activity Trends Report, 2nd Half 2011," *Anti-Phishing Working Group*, April 2012, *www.antiphishing.org/reports.*

[30] "A Computer Made of Tiny Prisons," *Bloomberg Businessweek*, June 25–July 1, 2012, pp. 37–38; and "Email Giants Move to Slash 'Phishing,'" *The Wall Street Journal*, January 30, 2012, *online.wsj.com.*

[31] "China Orders Web Sites, Blogs to Register with Government," *The Wall Street Journal*, June 7, 2005, *online.wsj.com;* "YouTube Blocked in China, Google Says," *The New York Times*, March 25, 2009, *www.nytimes.com;* "Scaling the Digital Wall in China," *The New York Times*, January 16, 2010, *www.nytimes.com;* and "China Requires ID for Mobile Phone Numbers," *The New York Times*, September 1, 2010, *www.nytimes.com.*

concerns because the devices operated beyond the government's ability to monitor their use. The decision prevented hundreds of thousands of users from accessing e-mail and the web on their handsets and constrained the commercial and tourism industries there. The key issue was whether the encrypted messaging system might be exploited by terrorists or other criminals who could not be monitored by the local authorities. Some believed that the government actions were an effort by the conservative nations' leaders to limit the growing influence of Western technology and values. In an agreement between local government leaders and Research In Motion (RIM), the manufacturer of BlackBerry, RIM consented to share encryption data from e-mails with government officials and install a local data server, enabling the national governments with greater access to information. The agreement avoided a serious backlash from businesses and citizens who were increasingly dependent upon BlackBerry technology.[32]

- *Pakistan*. In 2010, the Pakistani government, with the support of conservative Islamic groups, broadened an existing ban on social networking sites to include YouTube, some Flickr and Wikipedia sites, and about 450 individual web pages, because of what it described as "growing sacrilegious content." (The ban followed one day after a Pakistani court ruled that access to the Facebook site should be temporarily suspended for 12 days, citing offensive drawings of the Prophet Muhammad.) Despite the objections of many Pakistani citizens, who included nearly 25 million Internet users, the Pakistan Telecommunications Authority said in a statement that the ban was "in line with the Constitution of Pakistan, the wishes of the people of Pakistan." After YouTube removed the offensive material, the ban on this site was lifted.[33]

- *Syria*. The Syrian government, reacting to the role social media played in promoting a rebellion in the country, in 2011, demanded that citizens turn over their Facebook passwords and turn off their 3G mobile phones when directed. These efforts sharply limited the ability of dissidents to upload videos of protests to YouTube, according to several activists in Syria. With foreign journalists barred from the country, dissidents communicated with those exiled from the country through Facebook, YouTube, and Twitter to draw attention to the brutal military crackdown on protesters that allegedly killed more than 700 people and led to mass arrests. One year later, Internet users in Syria reported limited but increasing access to YouTube and Facebook, indicating that the government's ban on social network sites may be lifting.[34]

In 2012, Google reported that government requests to remove content from its site were rapidly increasing. Dorothy Chou, a Google senior policy analyst, commented, "It's alarming not only because free expression is at risk, but because some of these requests come from countries you might not expect—Western democracies not typically associated with censorship."[35] Some possible options available to companies in response to this growing trend are described in Exhibit 12.C.

---

[32] "Saudi Arabia to Block BlackBerry Messaging," *The New York Times*, August 1, 2010, *www.nytimes.com;* "Saudis Ease on BlackBerry," *The Wall Street Journal*, August 11, 2010, *online.wsj.com;* and "U.A.E. Halts Plan to Block BlackBerry," *The New York Times*, October 8, 2010, *www.nytimes.com.*

[33] "Pakistan Widens Online Ban to Include YouTube," *The New York Times*, May 20, 2012, *www.nytimes.com;* "Facebook Banned in Pakistan," *ABCNews*, May 19, 2010, *abcnews.go.com;* and "Pakistan Maintains Facebook Ban," *The Wall Street Journal*, May 20, 2010, *online.wsj.com.*

[34] "Seeking to Disrupt Protesters, Syria Cracks Down on Social Media," *The New York Times*, May 22, 2011, *www.nytimes.com;* and "Syria Facebook, YouTube Ban Lifted," *Huffington Post*, May 17, 2012, *www.huffingtonpost.com.*

[35] "Google Says Governments Are Making More Requests for Users' Data," *Los Angeles Times*, June 18, 2012, *www.latimes.com.*

Exhibit 12.C

Company Options When Government Censorship Occurs

What can an Internet provider do when asked by government officials to provide sensitive user information or to take down content from its site because it is offensive to the government? Here are some options:

- Accept all demands and comply with all government requests.
- Negotiate with government officials as to what is and is not permissible to be on the site or what user information is to be shared with the government.
- Voluntarily limit the type of information that is collected on individuals and organizations, avoiding information that could be considered private to the user or desired by the government.
- Partner with other technology firms to develop clear industry-wide procedures and guidelines that could be used to govern the collection and sharing of information, especially when operating in repressive countries.
- Partner with other technology firms to lobby the United States and other governments for legislation supporting Internet freedom and users' privacy, with the intent that this legislation could provide protection for technology firms.
- Provide technical and financial resources to human rights and other nonprofit organizations working against government censorship, and support the development of anonymizer, encryption, and proxy server technologies to protect sensitive information.
- Emphasize greater transparency and, when withdrawing content from its site, clearly post for viewers that the content was withdrawn by order of the government censors.
- Withdraw all service provided in countries in protest of the government censorship activities.
- Refuse to begin operations in countries with a repressive government or a history of Internet censorship.

Clearly, these options are not all compatible; choosing among them requires a company to make a careful assessment of its values and the particular situation it faces. Some of these actions could have significant economic consequences, so firms have to balance the potential for financial losses with their desire to support Internet freedom and protect users' safety and privacy.

Socially Beneficial Uses of Technology

Despite all the abuses of technology documented above—the challenges of social networking, the misuse of blogs and vlogs, the intrusions of spam and phishing, and censorship of the Internet—technology clearly can be used to improve the quality of our lives. How we communicate with others, conduct business, learn new things, and acquire information is enhanced by technology.

Technology and Education

Technology has democratized education by enabling students in some of the poorest and most remote communities to access the world's best libraries, instructors, and courses available through the Internet. (The status of the digital divide and the issue of who has access and who does not have access to technology are discussed later in the chapter.) A digital learning environment provides students with skills to rapidly discover and access information needed to solve complex problems.

After a decade of planning, the United States launched, in 2010, a dramatic new initiative to bring even more technology to the educational environment. The National Center for Research in Advanced Information and Digital Technologies received congressional approval through the Department of Education to provide grants so

Exhibit 12.D

Are Cell Phones and Laptops in the Classroom a Good Thing?

Cell phone manufacturers and service providers believe the key to improving the math skills of students is for them to spend more time on their cell phones in the classroom. At the Mobile Learning 09 conference in Washington, DC, CTIA, a wireless industry trade group, announced its campaign for more cell phones in schools. According to research funded by Qualcomm, a maker of cell phone chips, "smartphones can make students smarter." The trade industry responded to criticism that this was simply a self-promotional ploy by saying that smartphones would bring many of the capabilities of computers into the classroom—and they were smaller, cheaper, and more popular with students.

In trial projects in Chicago, San Diego, and Florida, students used cell phones to record themselves solving problems and posted the videos to a private social networking site where classmates could watch. The studies showed that students with the phones performed 25 percent better on an end-of-the-year algebra exam than did students without the devices in similar classes. After experimenting with cell phones in the classroom in North Carolina, one teacher said, "[the cell phones] took average-level kids and made them into honors-level kids."

But, when laptops were mandated in Idaho classrooms so that high school students could complete an online course required for graduation, a different reaction occurred. Since tens of millions of dollars were needed to purchase laptops, salaries for teachers and administrators were cut, causing an uproar from those negatively affected by the program. Teachers also objected to becoming more like computer aides in the classroom than instructors. "Teachers don't object to technology," said an executive at the American Institutes for Research, "they object to being given a resource with strings attached and without the needed support to use it effectively to improve student learning."

Sources: "Industry Makes Pitch That Smartphones Belong in Classroom," *The New York Times*, February 16, 2009, *www.nytimes.com;* and "Teachers Resist High-Tech Push in Idaho Schools," *The New York Times*, January 3, 2012, *www.nytimes.com.*

that schools, libraries, and museums could tap into digital technology research. "It's time that education had the equivalent of what the National Science Foundation does for science, Darpa [Defense Advanced Research Projects Agency] does for the national defense, and what N.I.H. [National Institutes for Health] does for health," said Lawrence Grossman, cochair of the nonprofit organization. To build support for the project, the organization created three prototypes: an educational video game for biology students called Immune Attack; a game for museums called Discovering Babylon; and a computer simulation to train firefighters in high-rise fires. The Center is supported by congressional allocation and private funding sources.[36]

Yet, some educators, parents, and technology advocates wonder if technology may be crossing over the line, as discussed in Exhibit 12.D.

Medical Information via the Internet

The explosion of medical information on the Internet has dramatically affected people's lives. How people are examined, diagnosed, and treated; how health-related information is collected and stored; and the time and costs associated with health care have all been changed by technological innovations. The merging of social media and medical records occurred when Facebook, the social media giant discussed earlier in the chapter, announced that it would encourage its millions of members to advertise their organ donor status on their pages. With thousands of people dying each year awaiting an organ transplant,

[36] "After 10 Years, Federal Money for Technology in Education," *The New York Times*, January 25, 2010, *www.nytimes.com.*

Dr. Andrew M. Cameron, surgical director of liver transplants at Johns Hopkins Hospital, reacted to Facebook's new effort by saying, "This is going to be a historic day in transplant. The math will radically change, and we may well eliminate the problem [of a lack of transplant donors]."[37]

While the abundance of medical information available on the Internet was welcomed by medical practitioners and the public in general, some warned that this easily available information might create a group of **cyberchondriacs**, a term referring to people who leap to the most dreadful conclusions while researching health matters online. In a study conducted by Microsoft researchers, they found that self-diagnosis, enabled by easy-to-use medical search engines, led web surfers to conclude the worst about what ailed them. People searching medical web sites often focused on the most sensational or worst possible diagnosis; for example, if suffering from a headache, the cyberchondriac might conclude the cause was a brain tumor, even though a much more likely reason might be something as benign as caffeine withdrawal.[38]

Another emerging issue within the arena of medical care and technology focused on **digital medical records**, or how a patient's medical records should be stored and linked to other health care providers. National and local regulations and practice, along with language issues and privacy concerns, were frequent obstacles to the implementation of these systems. Insurers, medical equipment companies, and pharmaceutical companies each have their own concerns regarding electronic records. In 2009, the U.S. government announced plans to spend $19 billion to spur the use of digital or electronic patient records, as part of a national effort to reduce medical costs. Included in this funding was more than $1 billion in grants to help hospitals transition to digital medical records.[39]

However, as appealing as the government's plan to bring technology to enhance patient medical record keeping might be, some medical personnel feared that the digitization of medical records could lead to incorrect information entered into medical records, with serious consequences.

Over a three-year period, from 2008 to 2011, the U.S. Food and Drug Administration received 370 reports of problems involving health information technology, many leading to serious injuries or death. Consider Genesis Burkett, a 40-day-old infant, who received an intravenous solution containing a massive overdose of sodium chloride—more than 60 times the amount ordered by Genesis's physician—because a pharmacy technician unwittingly typed the wrong information into a field on a screen, resulting in Genesis's death. According to FDA reports, another patient died after a computer network problem caused delays in transmitting a critically important diagnostic image. Vital signs from patient monitors disappeared from electronic medical records after being viewed by hospital staff risking the health of these patients until new information could be collected and stored. Another patient died after getting therapy meant for someone else after a wrong name was entered electronically on a scan performed by radiologists.

However, as serious as these problems are, most studies reported that there are fewer errors and tragic consequences from using digital medical records than the old, handwritten way of recording and storing patients' medical information. An investigation published in the *Archives of Internal Medicine* looked at malpractice

[37] "Facebook Is Urging Members to Add Organ Donor Status," *The New York Times*, May 1, 2012, *www.nytimes.com.*

[38] "Microsoft Examines Causes of 'Cyberchondria,'" *The New York Times*, November 25, 2008, *www.nytimes.com.*

[39] "Microsoft, Google in Healthy Competition," *Cnet*, May 18, 2009, *news.cnet.com;* and "On Talk Radio, Obama Stands by Health-Care Plan," *Pittsburgh Post-Gazette*, August 20, 2009, *www.post-gazette.com.*

claims before and after electronic medical record keeping at Massachusetts' medical institutions from 1995 through 2007. The rate of malpractice claims was 84 percent less after electronic medical record keeping was adopted.[40]

While generally seen as a good idea, the digitalization of patient health records and the sharing of that information to enhance medical care in the United States appear to require the same diligence and monitoring that was necessary with the old-fashioned medical record keeping system.

Special Issue: The Digital Divide in the United States and Worldwide

The gap between those who have access to technology and those who do not has been called the **digital divide**.[41] Some people have computers, cell phones, and Internet access; others do not. Access to technology is often lower among people in developing countries compared to those in developed countries; it is also often lower in developed countries among persons of color and the less affluent. The digital divide is a problem, because less advantaged individuals and societies may not enjoy the same benefits of technology as others.

In the United States, the digital divide persists—although it may be getting smaller over time. A 2012 study found that people with higher incomes had a 60 percent greater likelihood of home Internet access than those in the next lower income group. Internet access in African-American homes was 60 percent less than in Caucasian homes and rural residents had 40 percent less access than urban dwellers.[42] But efforts to narrow the gap have occurred.

The U.S. government has subsidized Internet upgrades for schools and libraries and has provided digital textbooks in poor and rural areas. The falling prices of laptops and the newest generation of cell phones and Internet-enabled handheld devices have made these devices more affordable to many. The government has also provided free cell phones and up to 250 free minutes for individuals that qualify, such as people seeking housing or job opportunities. The Federal Communications Commission (FCC) announced in 2011 the "Connect to Compete" program, designed to bring lower-income Americans online. In 2010, 31 percent of Americans lived in areas where broadband was available but were unable to pay for an Internet connection. Under the Connect to Compete program, households with at least one child and an annual income below $29,000 could buy broadband Internet access for $10 a month. The FCC estimated that the program could bring the Internet to 15 and 25 million Americans.[43]

Globally, progress in narrowing the digital divide has been slower, but is still evident. A 2012 study of 142 countries by the World Economic Forum concluded, "Despite all the efforts that we have seen in the past, the digital divide still exists between developing countries and developed countries." However, increasing numbers of people around the world

[40] "Baby's Death Spotlights Safety Risks Linked to Computerized Systems," *Chicago Tribune*, June 27, 2011, *articles .chicagotribune.com;* and "Electronic Records Tied to Fewer Malpractice Claims," *Tissue Pathology*, June 28, 2012, *www.tissuepathology.com/weblob.*

[41] For a different viewpoint, see Walter Block, "The 'Digital Divide' Is Not a Problem in Need of Rectifying," *Journal of Business Ethics* 53 (2004), pp. 393–406.

[42] "Digital Divide Widens, Research Finds," *University of Buffalo School of Management*, 2012, *mgt.buffalo.edu.*

[43] "Internet Service Upgrade Coming to Poor and Rural Schools," *The New York Times*, September 20, 2010, *www.nytimes.com;* "Wireless Riches from Serving the Poor," *Bloomberg Businessweek*, January 17–23, 2011, pp. 19–20; and "Finally, a Reason to Love the Cable Companies," *Bloomberg Businessweek*, November 21–27, 2011, p. 39.

were gaining access for the first time. Researchers found that the world was becoming more "hyper-connected," fostering greater global trade and interpersonal communications online. New companies, such as Cellbazaar, a service from Grameenphone, allowed individuals from the world's poorest countries to buy and sell goods over their mobile phones.[44]

But, in Latin America and the Caribbean, people "continue[d] to suffer from an important lag in adopting information and communication technology more broadly," according to the World Economic Forum study. These areas desperately needed to develop the technology infrastructure necessary to educate their citizens and provide information and communication tools to their businesses.

Christopher Vollmer, executive at Booz & Company, explained the vital importance of bridging the digital divide globally: "We found that economically, the more countries are able to move up the digitization index, it actually improves GDP [gross domestic product] performance, it's associated with positive job growth and it's very critical for innovation."[45] Yet, more work needed to be done as some countries, such as Sweden, Singapore, Finland, Denmark, Switzerland, Netherlands, Norway, the United States, Canada, and Britain, were at the high end of the digitization index, while poorer countries, such as Nepal, Syria, East Timor, and Haiti, were at the low end.

The unmistakable economic and social force of technology is evident in every part of the world, in every industry, and in every aspect of our lives. The technologically driven semantic phase has changed how businesses operate and the quality of our lives, regardless of where we live or what we do. These profound changes give rise to important, and possibly perplexing, questions about whether technology should be controlled or who should manage technology and its growth. These issues are discussed in the following chapter.

Summary

- Technology is the practical application of science and knowledge that is rapidly changing and spreading across societies.
- Six phases of technology represent the progress of civilization throughout history and is fueled by economic growth and research and development.
- Technology has changed how businesses offer, sell, and account for their goods and services in the global marketplace and their interactions with their stakeholders around the world through e-business and m-commerce. Individuals are investing and buying goods and services online at an astonishing rate.
- Technology has exponentially increased our ability to communicate with others around the world through e-mail and social networking, yet some technological innovations also provide significant threats to our privacy and safety. Some national governments have taken steps to censor the Internet.
- Socially beneficial uses of technology in education and medicine have opened up new learning opportunities, significantly changed medical record keeping, and offered new sources for acquiring medical information.
- A mixed picture emerged when attempting to see if the digital divide gap was closing or widening in the United States. There appeared to be a broad digital divide gap when comparing developed countries to developing countries.

---

[44] See *Grameenphone.com* and *cellbazaar.com* for additional information.

[45] "Digital Divide Splits Developed and Developing Nations," *Dawn.com*, April 5, 2012, *dawn.com*.

Key Terms

biotechnology, *263*
blog, *272*
cellular telephones, *269*
cyberchondriacs, *279*
cyberspace, *263*
digital divide, *280*
digital medical records, *279*

e-business, *267*
information phase, *263*
Internet, *266*
m-commerce, *269*
phishing, *274*
QR code, *269*
semantic phase, *263*

social networking, *271*
spam, *273*
technology, *262*
unsolicited commercial
e-mails, *273*
vlog, *273*

Internet Resources

www.antiphishing.org	Anti-Phishing Working Group
www.bio.org	Biotechnology Industry Organization
www.computerworld.com	Computer World
www.digitaldividenetwork.org	Digital Divide Network
www.ebizmba.com	eBiz/MBA
www.ecommercetimes.com	E-Commerce Times
www.foresight.org	Foresight Institute
www.internetsociety.org	Internet Society
www.networkworld.com	Network World
www.pewinternet.org	Pew Internet and American Life Project
socialmediatoday.com	Social Media Today
technorati.com	Technorati
www.whatissocialnetworking.com	Social Networking

Discussion Case: *How Protected Is Your Online Privacy?*

"Solitude and privacy have become more essential to the individual; but modern enterprise and invention have, through invasions upon [personal] privacy, subjected [individuals] to mental pain and distress. In this, as in other branches of commerce, the supply creates demand."

This quotation appeared in the *Harvard Law Review*. Besides the sobering sentiment expressed, the more startling fact is that it was written in 1890, more than 120 years ago! Technology, whether it is in the 1890s or 2010s, can violate our sense of privacy as individuals. Consider these examples:

• Malicious programs launched by hackers spread through Facebook and Twitter accounts in 2009, taking over people's accounts and sending out messages to the users' friends and followers. One user found out five days later that his account had been sending out lingerie ads to all of his professional acquaintances.

• When Google introduced *Buzz,* its answer to Facebook and Twitter, in 2010, users found themselves with an instant, and in many cases unwelcome, collection of "friends," automatically selected by Google from their e-mail contact lists. The users complained that their e-mail information contained names of personal physicians and illicit lovers, as well as the identities of whistle-blowers and antigovernment activists, most of whom would not want their identities made available to these "friends."

- In 2010, a *Wall Street Journal* investigation discovered that Facebook regularly transmitted identifying information—providing access to peoples' names and in some cases their friends' names—to dozens of advertising and Internet tracking companies. These firms used the information to build user profiles to market new apps or games. The use of apps was a growing source of revenue for Facebook since it sold virtual currency that could be used to pay for games. This activity affected tens of millions of Facebook users, including people who set their profiles to Facebook's strictest privacy settings.

- The *Wall Street Journal* probe revealed that MySpace also had been transmitting information to advertising companies that could be used to identify users. Users' information was sent, without their knowledge, once they clicked on ads on the MySpace website. At that time, MySpace had 58 million visitors monthly in the United States.

As this epidemic of privacy violations became public, many organizations, including the social network companies and the U.S. government, pledged to correct the situation. Some businesses, such as Microsoft and McAfee, saw this situation as an opportunity to offer online consumers software to protect them from online monitoring. Other companies offered users a commission every time their personal details were shared with marketing companies. "Data is a new form of currency," said a technology executive. The reasoning seemed to be that if the online advertising industry was bringing in $26 billion a year in sales from accessing this information, the consumers should share in the profits.

Apple, Facebook, and Google also took the offensive and created plans to better protect their customers. In 2011, Apple announced it would no longer automatically track an iPhone's location, but download a subset, or cache, of the database from each phone. This limited access to data prohibited Apple from locating the user who was using WiFi or a cell phone. While Apple needed to track its users to provide better service—for example, to identifying WiFi hotspots and cell towers—the new software would reduce the size of the database cached on the phone, cease backing up the cache, and delete the cache entirely when the location tracking feature was turned off.

Facebook acknowledged the security vulnerabilities found in the *Wall Street Journal* investigation and reported that they had addressed the problem in 2011. "We've conducted a thorough investigation, which revealed no evidence of this issue resulting in user's private information being shared with unauthorized third parties," the company stated. "[Facebook has a] strong policy enforcement and technical measures that allow us to quickly catch and take action against suspicious behavior on the platform."

Google also was caught up in the *Wall Street Journal* investigation. It had allegedly used a special computer code that tricked the Safari web-browsing software to allow Google to monitor users' activities. Safari was designed to block such tracking by default. Google reported in 2012 that it had disabled its code after being contacted by the *Wall Street Journal,* although the company maintained that "The [Wall Street] Journal [investigation] mischaracterize[d] what happened and why."

Finally, legislators also took action. Senators John Kerry and John McCain introduced a "privacy bill of rights," which included a "do not track" provision patterned after the "do not call" law that allowed people to block telemarketing calls to their phone. The proposed law would impose strict rules on companies that gather personal data, including requiring that people be given the right to access data collected about them and to block the information from being used or distributed. Although the Internet industry had resisted legislative controls for more than a year, a coalition of Internet giants joined the White House in support of the Kerry-McCain "do not track" provision. This provision allowed for a button to be embedded in most web browsers to give people greater control over the personal data collected about them.

Yet, some experts questioned whether these measures would be enough. They pointed to powerful new methods of tracking, such as ones found on MSN.com and Hulu.com, that were almost impossible for computer users to detect. These new techniques were called "supercookies." These supercookies were similar to a traditional cookie, a small file routinely installed on users' computers to track their activities online, but were capable of recreating users' profiles after people deleted regular cookies.

Sources: "Technology Outpaces Privacy (Yet Again)," *The New York Times*, December 11, 2010, *www.nytimes.com;* "Crooks Hijack Facebook Accounts, Injuring Dignity," *The New York Times*, December 14, 2009, *www.nytimes.com;* "Critics Say Google Invades Privacy with New Service," *The New York Times*, February 13, 2010, *www.nytimes.com;* "Facebook in Privacy Breach," *The Wall Street Journal*, October 18, 2010, *online.wsj.com;* "MySpace, Apps Leak User Data," *The Wall Street Journal*, October 22, 2010, *online.wsj.com;* "Internet Gets New Rules of the Road," *The Wall Street Journal*, December 22, 2010, *online.wsj.com;* "Web's Hot New Commodity: Privacy," *The Wall Street Journal*, February 28, 2011, *online.wsj.com;* "Apple Plans Fix for iPhone Location Data," *The Wall Street Journal*, April 27, 2011, *online.wsj.com;* "Facebook Security Flaw Exposed User Accounts," *The Wall Street Journal*, May 11, 2011, *online.wsj.com;* "Google's iPhone Tracking," *The Wall Street Journal*, February 17, 2012, *online.wsj.com;* "Web Firms to Adopt 'No Track' Button," *The Wall Street Journal*, February 23, 2012, *online.wsj.com;* "Senators Offer Privacy Bill to Protect Personal Data," *The Wall Street Journal*, April 13, 2011, *online.wsj.com;* "F.T.C. Backs Plan to Honor Privacy of Online Users," *The New York Times*, December 1, 2010, *www.nytimes.com;* and "Latest in Web Tracking: Stealthy 'Supercookies,'" *The Wall Street Journal*, August 18, 2011, *online.wsj.com.*

Discussion Questions

1. How much privacy should people expect when using a social networking site or going online for information, shopping, or other tasks?

2. Who should be responsible for protecting Internet users' personal information? In your response, please address the appropriate role of the government, business, and individuals.

3. Should consumers share in the revenue generated from sales created by accessing the personal information from social networking and other Internet sites?

4. Do you believe there is a conflict between the economic interests of companies such as Facebook, MySpace, or Google, and their obligation to protect the personal information of their users? If you were an executive of one of these companies, how would you resolve that conflict?

CHAPTER THIRTEEN

Managing Technology and Innovation

Technology through innovation fosters change and more change. Technological change has raised ethical and social questions of privacy, security, ownership, health, and safety. What are the implications of this fast-paced change and attention to innovation for our society and those who live in it? Moreover, who is responsible for determining how much technological change should occur or how fast things should change? Should technology be controlled, and if so, who should be in charge of managing technology and innovation and the challenges they pose for our global community?

This Chapter Focuses on These Key Learning Objectives:

- Evaluating the growth in breaches of personal information privacy.
- Understanding where these attacks come from and what their effects are.
- Evaluating initiatives taken by government and business to minimize invasions of privacy.
- Recognizing the emerging role and responsibilities of the organization's chief information officer.
- Examining violations of intellectual property through the piracy of software, music, movies, and books, and how business and government attempt to prevent these illegal actions.
- Recognizing the benefits, as well as the ethical and social challenges, that arise from technological breakthroughs in science and medicine.

Technology raises serious ethical questions, whether it involves a careless mistake made by a company employee that compromises sensitive information, efforts by journalists to acquire private information about politicians and their family members, or the mishandling of genetically modified crops that threatens farmers' livelihoods, as shown by the following examples.

Citibank mistakenly printed 600,000 customers' Social Security numbers on the envelopes containing their year-end tax statements, the company acknowledged in 2010. The letters were sent out through the U.S. Postal Service, and the numbers appeared at the lower edge of the envelopes. In a letter sent to all affected customers a month after the incident occurred, Citibank called the mistake a "processing error" and promised it would not happen again. "We believe there is little or no risk to you," said the Citibank letter, "however, we wanted to bring this to your attention, apologize, and confirm that changes have been made for all future mailings." The company did not say why the explanation was sent to its customers a month after the incident, but did offer to its customers a free 180-day credit monitoring service to ensure no fraudulent activity occurred due to the exposed personal information.

For more than 10 years, former British chancellor and prime minister Gordon Brown had his bank account information, legal documents, and family's medical records accessed by journalists looking for scandalous news or political information that could expose and embarrass Brown. *The Sun*, a British tabloid newspaper, reportedly acquired medical information about Brown's son, Fraser, who had cystic fibrosis. It was also discovered that Brown's tax records were stolen from his accountant's computer. The British police reported that Brown's private information was seized from Glenn Mulcaire, a private investigator who specialized in phone hacking for the *News of the World*, another British tabloid, which led to the eventual closure of the newspaper and the arrests of several prominent figures at the company.

In 2011, Bayer Cropscience agreed to pay $750 million to settle a lawsuit brought by U.S. rice farmers in Missouri and other midwestern states whose crops had been contaminated by genetically modified (GM) rice. Bayer Cropscience, a unit of the German company Bayer, had developed a strain of rice called "Liberty Link" that was genetically modified to tolerate a herbicide made by Bayer, so that farmers could spray their fields for weeds without killing their rice crops. Liberty Link had not yet been approved by the government for human consumption. But, somehow, Bayer's GM rice became comingled with ordinary rice. When customers around the world found out, they rejected imported U.S. rice, and prices tumbled. "I think [the settlement] sends a signal to those who develop genetically modified seeds that they need to keep those seeds very carefully contained until they're approved for human consumption," said one of the lawyers representing farmers in the lawsuit. He added, "We were very careful all along . . . not to say that these lawsuits are anti-GMO [genetically modified organisms] because many of our farmers use GM crops."[1] (Controversies surrounding genetically modified rice are also explored in a case on Ventria Bioscience at the end of this book.)

Are individuals' rights to privacy at the mercy of those with the technological ability to gain access to facts about individuals without their permission? How can customers, political figures, or individuals guard against the unauthorized access to personal information, as presented in the discussion case at the end of the chapter? How can farmers be assured that their crops will not be contaminated by unwanted genetic traits? Have those

---

[1] "Genetic Rice Lawsuit in St. Louis Settled for $750 Million," *St. Louis Post-Dispatch*, July 2, 2011, *www.stltoday.com.*

asking the technological question "Can it be done?" overwhelmed and silenced those asking the ethical question "Should it be done?" Issues of privacy, security, health, and safety abound in our age of innovation.

Bill Joy, Sun Microsystems' chief scientist, warned of the dangers of rapid advances in technology:

> The experiences of the atomic scientists clearly show the need to take personal responsibility, the danger that things will move too fast, and the way in which a process can take on a life of its own. We can, as they did, create insurmountable problems in almost no time flat. We must do more thinking up front if we are not to be similarly surprised and shocked by the consequences of our inventions.[2]

As this quotation implies, technology and innovation pose numerous challenges for society. If these important questions are not discussed and answered for the betterment of all members of society and in ways that protect our personal rights, what will be the ethical consequences?

Violations of Privacy: Causes and Costs

The potential for violations of privacy can come from many different sources. Some violations are caused by people inside the business organization, while others are brought on by strangers to the company. Some violations are simply careless actions, while others are intentional, as discussed at the beginning of the chapter. Next we discuss how common these breaches of privacy are, who is behind them, and what they have cost businesses and individuals. Then, the efforts taken by various organizations and businesses to combat these violations will be discussed.

According to a PricewaterhouseCoopers executive, "Cybercrime has emerged as a formidable threat, thanks to deeply determined, highly skilled, and well-organized cyber criminals from nation states to hacktivists, from criminal gangs to lone-wolf perpetrators. Organizations need to be aware and adjust to this changing landscape."[3] In a survey of 583 U.S. companies, 90 percent said their companies' computers were breached at least once by hackers over the past year. Nearly 60 percent reported two or more breaches and more than 50 percent said they had little confidence of being able to stave off future attacks. As shown in Figure 13.1, the number of instances of identity theft and the losses associated with these fraudulent activities are increasing.

FIGURE 13.1
Cases of Identity Theft and Fraud Losses in the U.S., 2006–2009

Source: John W. Moore, "From Phishing to Advanced Persistent Threats: The Application of Cybercrime Risk to the Enterprise Risk Management Model," *Review of Business Information Systems*, 2010, pp. 27–36.

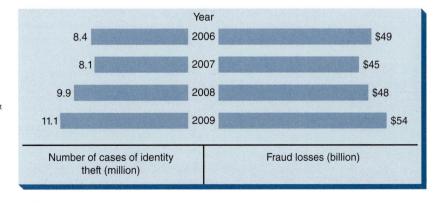

[2] Bill Joy, "Why the Future Doesn't Need Us," *Wired*, April 2000, *www.wired.com/wired/archive/8.04/joy.*
[3] "PwC Reports Increase in Fraud, Cyber Crime," *WebCPA*, November 29, 2011, *www.accountingtoday.com.*

Open Security Foundation reported that 262,812,546 records were exposed or stolen in 2011 from more than 800 separate cyberattack incidents. A server left open in the Texas Comptroller's office exposed Social Security numbers for 3.5 million teachers and other state employees in Texas. A stolen laptop from the Sutter Medical Foundation contained 3.3 million names and other identifying information, along with 943,000 patient diagnoses. A hacker acquired the names, user names, and passwords of 13.2 million players of the popular online game MapleStory. An attack on SK Communications, a global Internet company, caused the personal information of 35 million South Korean Internet users to be unprotected (the entire national population is 50 million). Hackers made off with 77 million names, e-mail addresses, and passwords after breaching Sony's PlayStation network. Tapes containing the medical records of more than 5 million military patients were stolen out of an employee's car who worked for SAIC, a defense contractor. In all, Open Security reported a 37.4 percent increase in the number of reported hacking incidents in 2011.[4]

Recent technological advances have increased the number of ways that privacy violations may occur. McKinsey & Company coined the term the "Internet of Things," to describe sensors and actuators that are embedded in physical objects—from roadways to pacemakers—and are linked through wired and wireless networks. These networks churn out huge volumes of data and help managers better understand and manage their businesses.[5] Yet, with these technological advances come potential for abuses. For example, companies welcomed Radio Frequency Identification (RFID) technology as a way to track packages and inventory. Yet, many experts have raised ethical questions about the ways RFID technology also enables businesses, governments, and criminals to gather information about presale, sales transaction, and postsale activities. The RFID tags, if they remain on the packages, could continue to record information long after the sale was made, possibly providing information on future purchases or personal travel.[6] The increase in the number of cell phones enabling users to take clearer pictures of what is happening around them has also raised concerns. Sometimes this technology has aided law enforcement in capturing criminals, who were caught breaking into an automobile or store. But in other cases, people felt that their privacy was violated when they were caught in a romantic or embarrassing situation.

Who is behind these attacks? In some cases, employees simply make inadvertent mistakes.

In 2012, the Kroll Advisory Solutions study of the health care industry found that 27 percent of the companies responding reported at least one security breach in the past 12 months, up from 19 percent in 2010 and 13 percent in 2008. Human error by employees was a major factor, according to the survey respondents, with 79 percent of respondents saying the security breaches were initiated by employees, and 56 percent saying that the breaches occurred because employees had unauthorized access to information.[7]

In other cases, criminals and their networks deliberately hack into company data. One of the most harmful forms of criminal activity involving computers is a zombie. A **zombie**

---

[4] See the DataLossDB project sponsored by the Open Security Foundation at *datalossdb.org.*

[5] "The Internet of Things," *McKinsey Quarterly,* March 2010, *www.mckinseyquarterly.com.*

[6] For an excellent discussion of the ethical issues surrounding RFID technology, see Alan R. Peslak, "An Ethical Exploration of Privacy and Radio Frequency Identification," *Journal of Business Ethics* 59 (2005), pp. 327–45.

[7] "Survey Finds Steady Increase in Healthcare Data Breaches," *Disuk,* April 18, 2012, *news.disuk.com.*

In 2005, about 150 business school applicants took advantage of a 10-hour security vulnerability on a site maintained by ApplyYourself, Inc., a Virginia-based company that manages admissions data for dozens of elite business schools. A hacker was able to post instructions to a bulletin board belonging to a *BusinessWeek* online forum enabling individuals to access their own admissions files. Since most of the schools had not made final admissions decisions on the applicants, the individuals saw only preliminary evaluations or data, and some accessed only blank screens.

Nonetheless, many of the universities affected took the breach of security very seriously. "This behavior is unethical at best—a serious breach of trust that cannot be countered by rationalization," said Kim Clark, dean of the Harvard Business School. Most schools—including Carnegie Mellon, Harvard, Duke, and MIT—decided to deny admission to the prospective students who had accessed the ApplyYourself site. Stanford officials decided to review each hacker's case individually before making a final decision, but added, "Our mission statement talks about principled, innovative leaders and we take the principled part seriously."

A few days after the incident occurred, Dartmouth broke ranks from the other universities and announced that it would admit some of the 17 business school applicants who had hacked into its computerized database. After lengthy discussions among Dartmouth faculty and staff, the university decided that the action should be a major strike against the prospective students but was not enough, by itself, to disqualify them. Dartmouth's dean, Paul Danos, said, "Their curiosity got the best of them. All of them expressed some remorse. Some were admitted. Some were rejected."

Sources: "Business Schools Bar Applicants Who Hacked Admissions Web Site," Institute for Global Ethics, *Ethics Newsline*, March 14, 2005, *www.globalethics.org;* and "Dartmouth Swims against Tide, Will Admit Some of Hackers," *Pittsburgh Post-Gazette,* March 18, 2005, p. B6.

is a hijacked computer that can be remote controlled by the attacker to respond to the attacker's commands. According to a study by the security firm McAfee, by 2008 18 percent of all computers in the United States were infected by malicious programs that tricked users into installing or running virus-laden programs and then continuously running the programs in the background, often without the user's knowledge, responding to signals sent out by zombie attackers.[8] More recently, zombies have attacked and controlled smartphones.

> In just a two-month span in 2010, experts estimated that one million smartphones used in China were contaminated with an infection called the Zombie Virus. The virus hid in antivirus applications and transmitted the users' SIM card information to the attacker. The attacker then remotely controlled the phone, sending URL links to all the user's contacts, over and over again. The virus sent out so many text messages that it created a cost estimated at 2 million yuan (or about $300,000) a day in message fees. This attack was similar to one that occurred earlier in 2010 in Russia.[9]

The corporate nemesis responsible for creating and spreading computer zombies, viruses, and other disruptions is called a computer hacker. **Computer hackers** are individuals, often with advanced technology training, who, for thrill or profit, breach a business's information security system. (The discussion case at the end of this chapter presents one example of a hacking incident at a large bank.) Businesses are not the only organizations vulnerable to the predatory practices of hackers, as some prestigious universities found out in 2005. This incident is described in Exhibit 13.A.

---

[8] "Computer Hijackings Increase by 50% in 2008," and "New Worm Targets Cell Phones, Turns Them to Zombies," *Switched*, May 29, 2009, *www.switched.com.*

[9] "Zombie Virus Attacks Millions of Smart Phones," *PC Pitstop Tech Talk*, November 23, 2010, *techtalk.pcpitstop.com.*

Although businesses are spending millions of dollars to protect the information they store from hackers and other criminals, they have had only limited success. "Comodohacker," a self-proclaimed super hacker, is a 21-year-old software engineering student in Tehran. He sneaked into the computer systems of a Dutch security firm in 2011, created fake credentials that allowed him to snoop on Internet connections that appeared to be secure, and accessed as many as 300,000 unsuspecting individuals' online communications. In addition, he created a hole in an online security mechanism that was trusted by millions of Internet users all over the world. Comodohacker's antics brought into question the security systems used at Google and Facebook, as well as shook users' confidence in the Internet globally.[10]

The overwhelming challenge to protect personal information stored in computer systems around the world seems impossible, and many believe that we are losing the war against hackers. The top cybercop at the Federal Bureau of Investigation said, as he was leaving the bureau, "fending off hackers is unstoppable. Computer criminals are simply too talented and defensive measures too weak to stop them."[11]

But, the war against cybercrime has enjoyed some successes. For example, in 2009 the U.S. Justice Department indicted eight Russian and eastern European computer hackers, alleging that they were part of a crime ring that broke into ATMs in hundreds of cities worldwide. The alleged hackers gained access to a computer system at RBS WorldPay, the U.S. payment division of Royal Bank of Scotland, and cloned prepaid ATM cards that were then used to withdraw cash from 2,100 ATMs from 280 cities around the world. The entire heist took only 12 hours and the robbers made off with $9 million.[12]

While hacking into large businesses' information systems tends to draw the headlines, small businesses are believed to be at greater risk from cyberattacks.

City Newsstand, Inc.'s owner, Joe Angelastri, discovered that cyber thieves had planted a software program in his company's cash registers at his two Chicago-area magazine shops and sent customers' credit card information to Russia. MasterCard demanded an investigation, at Angelastri's expense, and the attack cost him about $22,000. Many small businesses have become easy targets for cybercriminals. These organizations have little, if any, security and few or no technical experts on staff to guard against attacks on confidential customer information stored in their computer systems. Visa, Inc., reported that 95 percent of the credit card breaches it discovered were on its smallest business customers in 2009.[13]

A new threat emerged on the scene in the 2010s for security experts to confront— **hacktivists**. Hacktivists are individuals or groups who hack into government or corporate computer networks and then release information to try to embarrass those organizations or gain leverage against them. Security experts acknowledge that hacktivists were responsible for 58 percent of all known data thefts in 2011. This reflects a significant change in the motivation for hacking into computer systems.

In the past, hacking was most often a profit-making scheme undertaken by criminals, but now it is often based on political or cause-related issues. Anonymous is one of the most well-known hacktivist groups and claimed responsibility for attacks on websites in Tunisia, Algeria, and Zimbabwe. Other Anonymous targets included military contractors, law enforcement agencies, and corporations, including Sony, News Corporation, and Apple. Other hacktivists

---

[10] "Hacker Rattles Security Circles," *The New York Times,* September 11, 2011, *www.nytimes.com.*

[11] "U.S. Outgunned in Hacker War," *The Wall Street Journal,* March 27, 2012, *online.wsj.com.*

[12] "Hackers Indicted in Widespread ATM Heist," *The Wall Street Journal,* November 11, 2009, *online.wsj.com;* and "U.S. Indicts 8 in Worldwide Hacking Ring," *The New York Times,* November 12, 2009, *www.nytimes.com.*

[13] "Hackers Shift Attacks to Small Firms," *The Wall Street Journal,* July 21, 2011, *online.wsj.com.*

were less focused on the violent disruption of computer systems. The Chaos Computer Club, reportedly Europe's largest hacker group, explained that its main purpose was "teaching gifted young people how to use hacking skills to bring about political change."[14]

The Management of Information Security

What have governments done to slow down, if not stop, the wave of cyberattacks?

Given the global nature of the problem, some believed international government coordination was necessary. Since 2007, representatives from the United States and 27 European countries have gathered annually for Data Privacy Day. This event, which brings together privacy professionals, government leaders, academics and students, and business executives, was designed to raise awareness and generate discussion about data privacy practices and rights. Supporting events are held in Canada, Europe, and the United States throughout the year. In 2012, a Data Privacy Day conference was held on the campus of Indiana University to bring awareness to and educate people on FERPA, the Family Educational Rights and Privacy Act. Other events included making available recordings and PowerPoint slides focusing on privacy and security risks in higher education and privacy initiatives undertaken by the U.S. Department of Education.[15]

The United States has undertaken a number of projects to stem invasions of privacy on the Internet. Children are exceptionally vulnerable to invasions of privacy especially when accessing the Internet. The Children's Online Privacy Protection Act of 1998, also known as COPPA, requires commercial websites to collect a verifiable form of consent from the parent or guardian of any user below the age of 13.[16] Website operators must post user privacy policies and adhere to Federal marketing restrictions, even if the website is operated from outside the United States.

In 2010, the U.S. government also launched the "Perfect Citizen" program to detect cyber assaults on private U.S. companies and government agencies running critical infrastructures, such as the electricity grid and nuclear power plants. Monitored by the National Security Agency, sensors were deployed in computer networks that would be triggered by unusual activity suggesting an impending cyberattack. Although the results of this program are highly confidential, a Raytheon's company spokesperson, whose company was awarded a $100 million contract for the initial phase of this program, said, "Our government feels that they need to ensure the public sector is doing all they can to secure infrastructure critical to our national security."[17]

Nevertheless, it may be difficult for governments, acting alone, to control breaches of Internet information security. Businesses themselves—both Internet companies and any firm collecting and storing sensitive information—will also have to be involved.

Businesses' Responses to Invasions of Information Security

When faced with serious privacy challenges, many businesses have gone to great lengths to build strong defenses to protect information and ensure stakeholder privacy, as shown in these two examples from the financial community.

---

[14] "Activists Commit More Data Breaches Than Cybercriminals," *The Guardian,* March 22, 2012, *www.guardian.co.uk;* and, "Activists Turn 'Hacktivists' on the Web," *BBC News,* March 16, 2010, *news.bbc.co.uk.*

[15] See the Data Privacy Day 2012 website at *staysafeonline.org;* and the 2012 Data Privacy Day events held at Indiana University at *protect.iu.edu/privacy/dataprivacyday.*

[16] See the Children's Online Privacy Protection Act website at *www.coppa.org.*

[17] "U.S. Program to Detect Cyber Attacks on Infrastructure," *The Wall Street Journal,* July 7, 2010, *online.wsj.com.*

A number of top financial companies and banks, such as Wells Fargo and Bank of America, joined together in 2010 to develop and implement updates to fix security flaws found in wireless banking applications that allowed a computer hacker to obtain sensitive data like usernames, passwords, and financial information. Andrew Hoog, chief investigative officer for viaForensics, a computer and mobile security firm, explained, "You could trick the user with a fake email or text message, sending the user to a website that would infect the device and allow the hacker to steal this data." According to security experts, 12 million Americans actively used mobile-banking services in 2009 and were increasingly vulnerable to this sort of hacking. Experts expected the user base to increase dramatically in the next few years, as shown in this chapter's discussion case.[18]

In a separate occurrence, rising cybersecurity threats pushed big banks to begin to share information with one another, something that was rarely done in this highly competitive industry. Security officials from many Wall Street financial firms, including Morgan Stanley and Goldman Sachs, met to discuss the creation of a center that would sift through mountains of bank data to detect potential cyberattacks. Also, Bank of America engaged other banks in discussions at quarterly meetings to devise solutions to perceived cyberthreats. These initiatives encouraged banks to work together to better protect the bank's information from unauthorized access, which could shut down electronic operations, steal funds, or misuse personal information.[19]

Other protections against hackers have been created and used to thwart invasions of privacy. When a group of suspected hackers broke into a U.S.-based computer system, they thought they had successfully penetrated the security system guarding an important website. Rather, they had technologically walked into a *honeypot,* a system used by security professionals to lure hackers to a fabricated website where the hacker's every move can be tracked. Lance Spitzner, creator of numerous honeypot traps, posted his findings of hacker activities on the Internet for the security community to see and learn from these discoveries.[20] Another method some businesses have used to reduce criminal intrusion of their sites is to pay hackers for their proprietary methods—so others will not use them.

> Jarrad Sims and Tin Tam were college buddies who spent most of their days trying to hack into computer security systems belonging to the Boeing Company. They did not fear being arrested, though, since Boeing was paying them to do it. Sims and Tam were looking for "Trojan horses," which would enable hackers to gain access to computers when people clicked on dangerous links. They were also trying to squash "worms" that would replicate, spread, and corrupt computer files within the company's system and/or fight "logic bombs" that could hide in computers and then "go off" and delete files at a specific time.[21]

Many other companies, like Boeing, had hired professional hackers to locate security system weaknesses, so that "real hackers" could not as easily break in and create havoc in their computer systems.

The Chief Information, Security, Technology Officer

Businesses often entrust the responsibility for managing technology and its many privacy and security issues to the **chief information officer (CIO)** or individuals with similar titles

---

[18] "Banks Rush to Fix Security Flaws in Wireless Apps," *The Wall Street Journal,* November 5, 2010, *online.wsj.com.*

[19] "Banks Unite to Battle Online Theft," *The Wall Street Journal,* January 10, 2012, *online.wsj.com.*

[20] "Around the World, Hackers Get Stuck in 'Honeypots,'" *The Wall Street Journal,* December 19, 2000, p. A18; and see Spitzner's website at *http://project.honeynet.org.*

[21] "With So Much at Stake, Companies Turn to Hired Hackers," *Los Angeles Times,* April 15, 2012, *articles.latimes.com.*

In a study conducted by the Meta Group entitled *The CIO as Enterprise Change Agent,* almost half (47 percent) of the CIOs surveyed reported that they have broadened their responsibilities beyond the traditional CIO-only role. Some of these emerging responsibilities include:

- Establishing an innovative language to enable everyone throughout the organization to be clear about the objectives, processes, and timetables for any project that involves technology or information.
- Providing structure to welcome inventive thinking and creating protocols for testing and reviewing these novel ideas.
- Educating others in the organization to help open the eyes of organizational members to what is possible and what is not regarding technological initiatives or information.
- Applying marketing knowledge to ensure that innovative ideas reach the proper stakeholders inside and outside of the organization and have a meaningful impact.
- Acting as the lead security officer to protect information and data integrity by overseeing all functions of information technology in the organization.
- Participating in organizationwide committees and projects to maintain a clear emphasis on the value of information, as well as protect against threats to information.

In the past decade since the creation of the CIO position within most business organizations, the CIO role has evolved from primarily being focused only on the collection and protection of information to a senior executive role essential to all business functions and operations.

Sources: The Meta Group study of the role of the CIO can be found at "New Roles, New Responsibilities: Today's CIO," n.d., *www.cioupdate.com*. Additional information for this exhibit is from "What Are the Duties of a CIO?" *eHow,* n.d., *www.ehow.com;* and "The Duties of a CIO," *Ezine Articles,* n.d., *ezinearticles.com*.

such as *chief security officer* or *chief technology officer.* Many firms have elevated the role of their data processing managers by giving them the title of chief information officer. Recently this role has expanded even more to include broader responsibilities and greater influences on corporate policies and practices. In a study of CIOs from around the world, McKinsey & Company found that most CIOs reported to their chief executive officer rather than to the chief financial officer or chief operating officer.

> According to one security expert, "The CIO is a 'general.' Generals are not concerned with how the weapons function or how the rank-and-file are performing. This is the job of the lieutenants. The general focuses on the strategic application of resources on the battlefield. It is his/her duty to bring the plans of the sovereign (e.g. the CEO, the board of directors) to fruition."[22]

Along with reporting to the highest levels within the business came additional responsibilities. The CIO's role was changing dramatically, becoming more integrated into the overall strategic direction of the firm. "CIOs themselves are in the midst of a make-or-break personal change-management project: CIOs who can only take orders, who can't speak the language of the business, who can't step out of the proverbial back-office and into the front lines of customer service, social media or supply chain management will soon go the way of the ancient tech gear," warned Thomas Wailgum of *CIO Magazine.* Wayne Shurts, CIO of the grocery chain SuperValu concurred, "You're part of the strategic leadership team; you're on the inside of all the issues to help the company win today, tomorrow, and the next decade."[23] As shown in Exhibit 13.B, the duties assigned to a CIO are quite diverse.

[22] Steven Fox, "The Art of CIO Success," *CSO Security and Risk,* June 29, 2009, *blogs.csoonline.com.*
[23] "The New CIO Role: Big Changes Ahead," *CIO.com,* August 20, 2010, *www.cio.com.*

Protecting Intellectual Property

With advances in technology, protecting the ownership of intellectual property has become more challenging than ever. The ideas, concepts, and other symbolic creations of the human mind are often referred to as **intellectual property**. In the United States, intellectual property is protected through a number of special laws and public policies, including copyrights, patents, and trademark laws. Not all nations have policies similar to those in the United States.

With the ease of accessing information through technology, especially the Internet, have come serious questions regarding protecting intellectual property. From software and videogame piracy to downloading copyrighted music, movies, and books for free, many new means for using others' intellectual property have unlawfully emerged.

Business and Government Responses to Violations of Intellectual Property

Theft of intellectual property, artistic performance, or copyrighted material exploded with the entrance of the Internet and global connectivity. Whether it is computer-based software, musical recordings, video movie productions, or lately electronic versions of books, piracy is on the rise and victims are retaliating, turning to governments for enforcement and protection of their rights, or seeking collaborative solutions to this ethical challenge.

The illegal copying of copyrighted software, or **software piracy**, is a global problem. According to the Business Software Alliance (BSA), in 2011 more than half of the world's personal computer users—57 percent—admitted they acquired pirated software. The commercial value of this pirated software climbed to a record $63.5 billion in 2011. "If 57 percent of consumers admitted they shoplift, authorities would react by increasing police patrols and penalties. Software piracy demands a similarly forceful response—concerted public education and vigorous law enforcement," said BSA president Robert Holleyman. As shown in Figure 13.2, the frequency with which individuals pirate software differs greatly between mature and emerging economies.

Piracy was most severe in China, where the illegal software market was worth nearly $9 billion in 2011 compared with a legal software market of less than $3 million. Software

FIGURE 13.2
Self-Reported Piracy Habits by National Economies, 2011

Source: "Shadow Market: 2011 BSA Global Software Piracy Study," *Business Software Alliance,* May 2012, *portal.bsa .org/globalpiracy2011.*

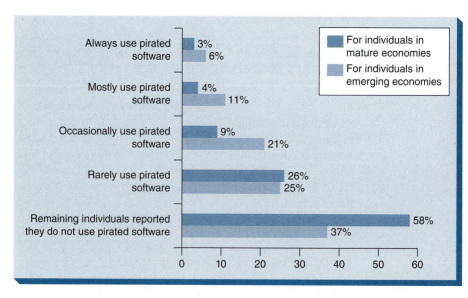

pirates were disproportionately young and male, and often lived in developing countries. They also tended to be the most insatiable software users, reporting that they installed 55 percent more software on their computers than did nonpirates.[24]

Companies have sought assistance on the issue of software piracy from governmental agencies and the courts both inside and outside the United States. For example, the Argentinean Supreme Court upheld a lower court ruling that the country's antiquated copyright laws did not cover software, thus denying software manufacturers any legal basis to attack those with pirated materials in Argentina. However, the outcry from U.S. software makers and vendors was so strong that within months the Argentinean Chamber of Deputies made software piracy a crime punishable by fines or imprisonment or both. In 1998, the United States passed the **Digital Millennium Copyright Act**, making it a crime to circumvent antipiracy measures built into most commercial software agreements between the manufacturers and their users. In China, where experts estimate that most software in use is unlicensed, government officials also took steps to curb piracy.

> The Chinese government announced that computer makers must ship all their products with licensed operating systems preinstalled and inspected all government computer systems for licensed software. "This is good news, marking a clear step in the right direction to reverse the serious problem of software piracy that frustrates the development in China for both foreign and domestic vendors," explained the president of the Beijing-based United States Industry Technology Office. In 2009, China sent 11 people to prison for manufacturing and distributing pirated Microsoft software throughout the world. Microsoft called the group part of "the biggest software counterfeiting organization we have ever seen, by far" and estimated its global sales at more than $2 billion.[25]

Laws attempting to stem software piracy and reinforce intellectual property rights exist in many other countries, including Saudi Arabia, the United Arab Emirates, Vietnam, and India.[26] FAST, the Federation Against Software Theft, applauded efforts by the British government, where potential offenders could face fines of up to £50,000, nearly $80,000, and/or a prison sentence of up to 10 years.[27] However, not all government efforts have been successful.

> The websites of the Ukrainian president and former interior minister were put out of action as disgruntled Internet users fought back against the government's efforts to shut down a popular file sharing site—*Ex.ua*. Millions of Ukrainians obtained movies, music, and software for free from this site despite allegations that the property was pirated. After the government took action, Ukrainians bombarded government websites with automated requests, which overloaded their system's capacity. With an average monthly wage of $330 in the Ukraine, most people could not afford to purchase movies, music, or software legally and they turned to sites like *Ex.ua* where content is "shared" by other users and available free of charge.[28]

[24] "Well over Half the World's Computer Users Admit Pirating Software, BSA Study Funds," *Business Software Alliance,* May 15, 2011, *www.bsa.org.*

[25] "China Begins Effort to Curb Piracy of Computer Software," *The New York Times,* May 30, 2006, *www.nytimes.com;* and "Chinese Court Jails 11 in Microsoft Piracy Ring," *The New York Times,* January 1, 2009, *www.nytimes.com.*

[26] For a description of India's 2010 Copyright Amendment Bill, see "India to Align Copyright Norms with Global Standards," *The Economic Times,* October 15, 2010, *economictimes.indiatimes.com.*

[27] "Anti-Piracy Group FAST Applauds Government Business Guide to Navigating UK IP Law," *ComputerWeekly.com,* n.d., *www.computerweekly.com.*

[28] "Ukraine Government Websites Attacked after Piracy Crackdown," *Reuters,* February 1, 2012, *www.reuters.com.*

Technology now enables individuals to download music from the Internet at a faster pace than ever before, and to store the music for repeated listening. Individuals have downloaded millions of songs onto their iPods or burned them onto CDs and had their favorite collections of songs available for their listening pleasure whenever they wanted—all without the cost of purchasing the music. This process denied legitimate compensation to the artists who created the music and to the companies that manufactured or distributed these artists' CDs.

> The International Federation of the Phonographic Industry (IFPI) reported that worldwide sales of recorded music fell by about 10 percent in 2009 and the organization used this data to renew its call for a tougher crackdown on the digital piracy of music. "We're all fed up with talking about piracy," said the IFPI chief executive. "It's boring talking about piracy, but it is a problem and we can't avoid it." While global sales via the Internet, mobile phones, and other digital methods rose 12 percent in 2009 to $4.2 billion, the IFPI pointed to estimates that 95 percent of the music downloaded via the Internet was pirated.[29]

Faced with a dramatic decline in music generated by French musicians, attributed mostly to the lack of financial incentives due to piracy, the French government approved its toughest crackdown on musical piracy in February 2012. The government imposed a "three-strikes system," and sent 822,000 warnings by e-mail to suspected piracy offenders by the end of 2012. Those were followed up by 68,000 second warnings, sent through registered mail. Of those, 165 cases progressed to the third stage, where the courts were authorized to impose fines of €1,500, or nearly $2,000, and to suspend Internet connections for a month.[30]

Much of the blame is leveled at college students and young adults. The Motion Picture Association of America claimed that 44 percent of the industry's domestic losses came from illegal downloading of movies by college students or recent graduates. Verifying these figures is difficult, since many people download from their homes or Internet cafes, not college dormitories or on-campus computer labs. Nonetheless, the U.S. motion picture industry reportedly lost $6.1 billion to piracy worldwide, with most of the losses outside the United States. And piracy was spreading to new forms of entertainment.[31] The government also targeted websites that provided users with access to unauthorized movies.

> In 2010, U.S. federal authorities seized the domain names of nine websites accused of letting users watch illegal on-demand versions of first-run movies. Since these sites had registered their domain names through U.S.-based registration services, authorities could take control of these sites even though only some of the sites were based in the United States, with others operating out of Germany, the Netherlands, the United Kingdom, and the Czech Republic. At a news conference announcing these actions, a government official reported that on June 15 alone 37,000 people watched an illegally obtained copy of *Sex in the City 2* at a single website. "I don't think we stopped Internet piracy in a day, but this is going to be a sustained effort," explained a government official.[32]

The printed word now faced the same test of intellectual property and copyright protection as music and movies have for more than a decade.

[29] "Music Industry Counts the Cost of Piracy," *The New York Times,* January 21, 2010, *www.nytimes.com.*

[30] "Copyright Cheats Face the Music in France," *The New York Times,* February 19, 2012, *www.nytimes.com.*

[31] "Piracy Figures Are Restated," *The Wall Street Journal,* January 23, 2008, *online.wsj.com.*

[32] "Nine Movie Sites Busted in Pirating Crackdown," *The Wall Street Journal,* July 1, 2010, *online.wsj.com.*

John Wiley & Sons, a textbook publisher, employed three full-time staff members to search for unauthorized copies of their books. In April 2009, the company uncovered 5,000 titles—five times more than a year ago—and sent notices to various site managers to take down the digital version of Wiley's books. "It's a game of Whac-a-Mole," said the president of the Science Fiction and Fantasy Writers of America. "You knock one down and five more pop up." Sites like Scribd and Wattpad, which invite users to upload documents such as college theses and self-published novels, were primary targets as illegal reproductions of popular titles have appeared on their sites. Both sites reportedly remove copyrighted material immediately upon notification by the publisher.[33]

Despite efforts at the international, national, and business levels, piracy continues to rise each year globally, as shown in Figure 13.3, and it does not appear that countermeasures are being successful in the attempt to control this growing issue.

FIGURE 13.3

Commercial Value of Pirated Software, by Region, 2007–2011

Source: "Shadow Market: 2011 BSA Global Software Piracy Study," *Business Software Alliance,* May 2012, *portal.bsa .org/globalpiracy2011.*

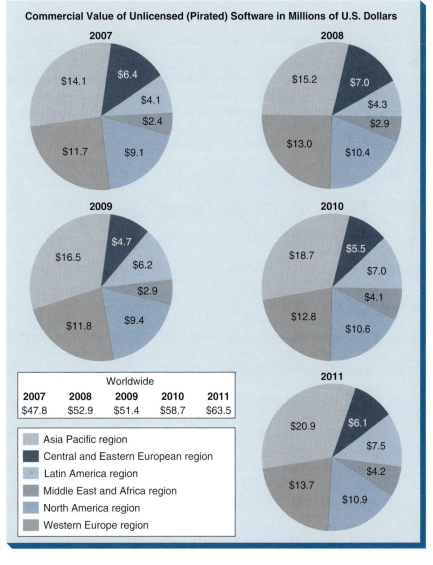

Commercial Value of Unlicensed (Pirated) Software in Millions of U.S. Dollars

	Worldwide			
2007	2008	2009	2010	2011
$47.8	$52.9	$51.4	$58.7	$63.5

- Asia Pacific region
- Central and Eastern European region
- Latin America region
- Middle East and Africa region
- North America region
- Western Europe region

Managing Scientific Breakthroughs

Dramatic advances in the biological sciences also have propelled the impact of technology on our lives and business practices. As explained in Chapter 12, biotechnology refers to a technological application that uses biological systems or living organisms to make or modify products or processes for specific use. Recent unprecedented applications of biological science to industry have made possible new, improved methods of health care and agriculture, but they have also posed numerous ethical challenges regarding safety and the quality of life.

> As Bill Joy of Sun Microsystems warns, speaking of biotechnology as well as other innovative applications of science, "21st century technologies . . . are so powerful that they can spawn whole new classes of accidents and abuses. Most dangerously, for the first time, these accidents and abuses are widely within the reach of individuals or small groups. They will not require large facilities or rare raw materials. Knowledge alone will enable the use of them."[34]

Nanotechnology

One of the most significant technology changes affecting business is the emergence of **nanotechnology**, the application of engineering to create materials on a molecular or atomic scale. Because these small particles, just a few billionths of a meter in size, have a relatively large surface area, nanomaterials exhibit physical properties that are markedly different from their normal scale equivalents. Applications of nanotechnology spread through the scientific and business communities like wildfire in the early 2000s, giving rise to some remarkable products, as illustrated by the following examples.

> Nanoscale silver particles can be mixed into molten plastic to create containers that retard food spoilage—or even purify contaminated water. Under Armour has added nanoparticles to athletic clothing to inhibit the growth of odor-causing bacteria. There are "nano-pants," stain-resistant chinos and jeans whose fabric contain nano-sized whiskers that repel dirt and oil. Nanocylces made from carbon nanotubes are stronger and lighter than standard steel bicycles. Nanoscale materials have also been used in consumer electronics. Apple's iPod Nano uses a flash storage system that includes nanomaterials.

In 2012, a professor at the University of Pennsylvania demonstrated an exciting application of nanotechnology: aerial robots that could swoop through the air from one corner of the room to another. Within a few days more than 200,000 people had viewed his video online at *ted.com*. These robots, called "flying quadrobots," were designed to move in formation and fill in a gap if one dropped out. They had built-in gyroscopes and other sensors that could relay information about their position and surroundings to an on-board processor, which allowed the quadrobots to react instantly to situations. What was most intriguing was that the flying quadrobots, which used nanotechnology, were only the size of a human hand.[35]

Yet, some warned about potential problems associated with nanotechnology. The Center for Responsible Nanotechnology created a list of 11 separate and severe risks, including the danger of criminal or terrorist use, environmental damage, and health risks

---

[34] Joy, "Why the Future Doesn't Need Us."

[35] "Swarm of Nanoquadrobots Sweep TED Audience," *Crazy Engineers*, March 4, 2012, *www.crazyengineers.com*.

from unregulated products.[36] Medical researchers have determined that nanoparticles can penetrate human skin and enter the bloodstream, but further research is needed to determine whether nanomaterials can be toxic to humans and other life forms. Dr. Adnan Nasir, a professor of dermatology at the University of North Carolina, explained, "The smaller the particle, the further it can travel through tissue, along airways or in blood vessels, especially if the nanoparticles are indestructible and accumulate and are not metabolized; if you accumulate them in the organs, the organs could fail."[37] So far, at least, the U.S. government has not regulated the use of nanomaterials and nanoparticles in consumer products.

Human Genome

When Celera Genomics Group announced that it had finished the first sequencing of a **human genome**, the achievement was hailed as the most significant scientific breakthrough since landing a man on the moon. Strands of human deoxyribonucleic acid, or DNA, are arrayed across 23 chromosomes in the nucleus of every human cell, forming a unique pattern for every human. These strands are composed of four chemical units, or letters, used over and over in varying sequences. These replicated letters total 3 billion and form the words, or genes—our unique human signature—that instruct cells to manufacture the proteins that carry out all of the functions of human life.[38] The identification of human genes is critical to the early diagnosis of life-threatening diseases, the invention of new ways to prevent illnesses, and the development of drug therapies to treat a person's unique genetic profile. Since this revolutionary discovery, the National Human Genome Research Institute has undertaken and promoted additional research. In 2012, 10 grants totaling $10.5 million were awarded to develop new technologies to help researchers identify millions of genomic elements that play a role in determining what genes are present and at what levels in different cells. In 2012, the European Medicines Agency recommended to the European Commission the approval of gene therapy to treat a variety of rare genetic diseases, creating new opportunities in Europe.[39]

However, while advances in understanding DNA were exalted as one of the humanity's greatest achievements, ethical challenges emerged in private and public research focusing on genetics.

> One family, afflicted by a rare genetic heart disease called Brugada syndrome, wondered how others might react if they learned of the family's medical condition. Would employers want to hire someone who might die prematurely or require an expensive implantable defibrillator? Would they be eligible for individual health care coverage or be able to afford life insurance if their condition were known? The underlying fear for this family and others with genetic conditions was whether they would be treated fairly if their genetic fingerprints became public.

The debate over whether advances in human genome sequencing and genetic research outweigh the risks or harms will continue for years. What is clear is that our scientific understanding of the human body and its makeup has changed, and significant technological

---

[36] For a complete listing of the risks, see Center for Responsible Nanotechnology at *www.crnano.org*.

[37] "New Products Bring Side Effect: Nanophobia," *The New York Times*, December 4, 2008, *www.nytimes.com;* and "The Smaller, the Better? Consumer Groups Sound the Alarm over Nanotechnology," *PalmBeachPost.com*, May 17, 2009, *www.palmbeachpost.com*.

[38] "Genetic Secrets of Malaria Bug Cracked at Last," *The Wall Street Journal*, January 18, 2002, pp. B1, B6.

[39] "European Agency Backs Approval of a Gene Therapy," *The New York Times*, July 20, 2012, *www.nytimes.com;* and "Bits of Mystery DNA, Far From 'Junk,' Play Crucial Role," *The New York Times*, September 5, 2012, *www.nytimes.com*.

Exhibit 13.C

Stem Cell Research under the Obama Administration

Coinciding with the inauguration of President Barack Obama, on January 23, 2009, the Food and Drug Administration approved the world's first test of a therapy from human embryonic stem cells on humans. Although federal regulators stated that political considerations had no role in the decision, it was clear to others that the new administration was taking a new approach to stem cell research.

Two months later, Obama reversed the Bush administration limits on federal funding for embryonic stem cell research, as part of a pledge to separate science and politics. By lifting funding restrictions, Obama avoided one of the most controversial issues surrounding stem cell research—whether taxpayer money should be used to experiment on embryos themselves. Yet, analysts agreed that Obama's executive order made it clear that "the government intends to support human embryonic stem cell research," said a science advisor to the president.

More than a year later, in August 2010, a federal district judge blocked Obama's presidential order and banned the use of federal money spent on "destroying embryos." The next day the federal government froze all grants for scientists and imposed other restrictions in the area of stem cell research. But, the seesaw battle took another turn in April 2011 when a federal appeals court, in a 2-to-1 vote, overturned the lower court's ruling and reinstated Obama's stem cell research agenda.

Sources: "F.D.A. Approves a Stem Cell Trial," *The New York Times,* January 23, 2009, *www.nytimes.com;* "Obama Set to Reverse Bush's Stem Cell Restrictions," *The New York Times,* March 7, 2009, *www.nytimes.com;* "Obama Is Leaving Some Stem Cell Issues to Congress," *The New York Times,* March 9, 2009, *www.nytimes.com;* "U.S. Judge Rules Against Obama's Stem Cell Policy," *The New York Times,* August 23, 2010, *www.nytimes.com;* and "Stem Cell Research Ban Overturned by U.S. Appeals Court," *The Huffington Post,* April 29, 2011, *www.huffingtonpost.com.*

innovations are on the horizon. What is not clear is who, if anyone, can manage these changes to better ensure the improvement of the quality of our lives and society.

Biotechnology and Stem Cell Research

Complementing the discovery of DNA sequencing were numerous medical breakthroughs in the area of regenerative medicine. **Tissue engineering**, the growth of tissue in a laboratory dish for experimental research, and **stem cell research**, research on nonspecialized cells that have the capacity to self-renew and to differentiate into more mature cells, were two such breakthroughs. Both offered the promise that failing human organs and aging cells could be rejuvenated or replaced with healthy cells or tissues grown anew. While the promise of immortality may be overstated, regenerative medicine provided a revolutionary technological breakthrough for the field of medicine.

Stem cell research spilled over from the laboratories into government arenas as politicians weighed in on the ethical controversy. In 2009, a majority of Americans, 52 percent, supported easing or removing entirely the restrictions on stem cell research imposed by former President Bush. (Exhibit 13.C explores the position of the Obama administration on stem cell research.) Support for stem cell research was evident in California, where nearly 60 percent of voters supported Proposition 71, which set aside $350 million annually for a decade or a total of more than $3 billion, dwarfing the $25 million the National Institutes of Health had allocated to embryonic stem cell research. However, the European Court of Justice banned in 2011 the issuing of patents for embryonic stem cell research on ethical grounds, citing a respect for human dignity as the basis for the ruling. Yet, the ruling did permit research "to correct a malformation and improve the chances of life."[40]

[40] "California Vote Brings Windfall for Stem Cells," *The Wall Street Journal,* November 4, 2004, pp. B1, B7; and "Stem Cell Patent Ban," *BBC News,* October 18, 2011, *www.bbc.co.uk.*

Supported by private and government funding, hundreds of biotechnology companies and university laboratories were actively pursuing new approaches to replace or regenerate failed body parts. Research included efforts to insert bone growth factors or stem cells into a porous material cut to a specific shape, creating new jaws or limbs. Genetically engineered proteins were successfully used to regrow blood vessels that might repair or replace heart valves, arteries, and veins. The process to regrow cartilage was used to grow a new chest for a boy, and a human ear was grown on a mouse. By 2012, stem cell research was moving out of the laboratory and clinical trials were being conducted as a possible treatment for age-related macular degeneration, a common disorder in the elderly that can cause blindness. "It's a big step forward for regenerative medicine," said a retina specialist. Initial results reported that two patients in the trial, who were legally blind, were acquiring some eyesight.[41]

Cloning

In 1986, a Danish scientist announced the first successful cloning of a sheep from fetal cells. Another significant breakthrough occurred in 1997, when Ian Wilmut of the Roslin Institute unveiled Dolly, the first mammal to be cloned from adult cells. In 2003 doctors in China reported they had become the first to make an infertile woman pregnant with an experimental technique devised in the United States for women who have healthy genes but defects in their eggs that prevent embryos from developing. Critics argued that this technique came perilously close to human cloning.[42]

As each new announcement of a more advanced and successful cloning experiment was announced to the public, more fears arose. Whether it was a vision of Jurassic Park dinosaurs running loose in a metropolitan downtown area or the eerie absurdity of cloning multiple Adolf Hitlers in the film *The Boys of Brazil,* fears of cloning living tissue invaded our lives.

In 1997, when Dolly appeared on the cloning scene, there were no laws on record that prevented scientists from attempting human cloning. Experts recognized that the technique used in Scotland to clone a sheep was so simple and required so little high-tech equipment that most biology laboratories with a budget of a few hundred thousand dollars could attempt it.

In response to a growing concern over unrestricted or unsupervised cloning on a global scale, in 2005 the United Nations approved (by a vote of 84 in favor, 34 against and 37 abstentions) a declaration that prohibited all forms of human cloning "inasmuch as cloning is incompatible with human dignity and the protection of human life." Proponents of the declaration saw this as a first step toward the promotion of human rights and a complete ban on all human cloning. Although difficult to enforce, this action was intended to discourage cloning efforts.[43]

Cloning of animals was beyond the focus of the United Nations ban and continued to thrive. Although a fraction of the total number of cows, cattle, or pigs in the United States, the presence of cloned dairy animals increased at a fast pace and received positive support from the FDA. In 2008 the FDA declared that food from cloned animals and their offspring was safe to eat, but imposed a voluntary ban on the sale of cloned animals.

[41] "Stem-Cell Clinical Trials Move Debate Beyond Labs," *The Wall Street Journal,* October 10, 2011, *online.wsj.com;* and "Stem Cell Study May Show Advance," *The New York Times,* January 23, 2012, *www.nytimes.com.*

[42] "Pregnancy Created Using Infertile Woman's Egg Nucleus," *The New York Times,* October 14, 2003, *www.nytimes.com.*

[43] "General Assembly Adopts United Nations Declaration on Human Cloning by Vote of 84–34–37," *United Nations press release GA/10333,* August 3, 2005, *www.un.org.*

Only their by-products, such as milk from cloned cows or the cloned animals' offspring, were permitted to be sold.[44]

At Edinburgh's Centre for Regenerative Medicine (the same scientists that first cloned Dolly in 1979), researchers created cloned brain tissue from patients suffering from schizophrenia, bipolar depression, and other mental illnesses in the hope to better understand the neurological properties of these conditions.[45] These and many other emerging scientific breakthroughs perched on the horizon for stem cell research. Yet, specific and binding ethical guidelines for scientists engaging in this volatile field are clearly needed. The debate over how to govern this scientific community and its work inevitably will continue for years.

Genetically Engineered Foods

The biotechnological revolution targeting improvements in health care was also adapted for use by the agricultural industry. Technological advances in genetics and biology led to an unprecedented number of innovations. **Genetic engineering**, altering the natural makeup of a living organism, allowed scientists to insert virtually any gene into a plant and create a new crop or a new species. The economic force of this technological revolution was immediately apparent. Venture capitalists injected $750 million into the agricultural industry in the early 2000s, an area generally ignored by venture capitalists for decades.

In Europe, a severe backlash emerged to **genetically modified foods**, or GM foods, that is, food processed from genetically engineered crops. Protesters there called GM foods "Frankenstein foods."

> In 2008, both France and Germany passed national bans on the use of various kinds of genetically modified seeds. Despite French and German farmers' protests that the ban would inflict great economic harm on them and the countries' economy, the German agriculture minister said, "The decision is not a political decision, it's a decision based on the facts." He affirmed the government's commitment to protect the safety of consumers and the environment. In 2009, Austria and Hungary passed their own national bans on growing genetically modified crops. While Europe continued to allow each nation to decide whether to allow the planting or sale of genetically modified foods, the European Union has had a GM food labeling law in place since the 1990s, so that all European consumers can make their own decisions to purchase this type of food or not.[46]

By contrast with Europe, genetically modified foods are quite common in grocery stores in the United States. Although most GM corn grown in the United States is made into animal feed or ethanol, it is also processed into food industry staples such as corn syrup or tortilla chips. Monsanto breeds a soybean seed that yields oil commonly used as a substitute for trans-fat oils at many fast-food restaurants. Biotech cotton ends up in the food chain as cottonseed oil used to make mayonnaise and margarine. But problems with using

[44] "Animal Clones' Offspring Are in Food Supply," *The Wall Street Journal,* September 2, 2008, *online.wsj.com;* "F.D.A. Says Food from Cloned Animals Is Safe," *The New York Times,* January 16, 2008, *www.nytimes.com;* and "Cloning Animals for Food: Is It Safe?" *Bright Hub,* February 28, 2010, *www.brighthub.com.*

[45] "Cloning Scientists Create Human Brain Cells," *The Guardian,* January 29, 2012, *www.guardian.co.uk.*

[46] "French Court Says Ban on Gene-Altered Corn Seed Will Remain, Pending Study," *The New York Times,* March 20, 2008, *www.nytimes.com;* "Germany Bars Genetically Modified Corn," *The New York Times,* April 15, 2009, *www.nytimes.com;* "Europe to Allow Two Bans on Genetically Altered Crops," *The New York Times,* March 3, 2009, *www.nytimes.com;* and "Europe Has GM Food Label Law," *Health Impact News Daily,* May 22, 2012, *healthimpactnews.com.*

GM seed appeared to be on the horizon. In 2011 Monsanto reported that some of its genetically modified seed, grown to resist attacks by bugs that could ruin crops, was losing its bug resistance possibly due to the way that farmers were using biotech crops. This could cause some farmers to switch to a different strain of GM seed produced by one of Monsanto's competitors. "These are isolated cases, and it isn't clear how widespread the problem will become. But it is an early warning that management practices need to change," said an Iowa State University entomologist.[47]

In some economically developed countries and most developing countries around the world, genetically modified food was welcomed as a way to increase crop yields. By 2007, the number of developing countries planting genetically modified seeds outnumbered developed countries, according to a report from the International Service for the Acquisition of Agri-biotech Applications (ISAAA). Four years later, in 2011, total global planting of genetically modified seeds grew 8 percent from 2010. Roughly 160 million hectares, or 395.2 million acres, were planted with biotech crops, according to the ISAAA. These crops were planted by 16.7 million farmers in 29 countries. This biotechnology was increasingly significant in Brazil, Argentina, China, India, and South Africa, said an ISAAA spokesperson. But, with this growth also came resistance.[48]

> When Monsanto attempted to partner with the United States to develop a biotech aid package in Nepal, conflicts arose. Monsanto offered to provide Nepali farmers with hybrid genetically modified seeds. But, the Nepali government envisioned a program in which it would assist its farmers in developing their own hybrid seeds from the abundance of seeds already available. The government preferred this approach to training 20,000 farmers to use Monsanto's seeds, which would make them financially dependent upon Monsanto. The government had to choose between helping the farmers immediately by providing them with Monsanto hybrid seeds and developing a long-term agricultural process that could benefit many people living in Nepal.[49]

Despite some concerns and objections raised over genetically modified crops, another application of biotechnology—genetically engineering plants to grow medicines—is explored in the case, "Ventria Bioscience and the Controversy over Plant-Made Medicines," at the end of this book.

The controversies over genetic engineering, stem cell research, cloning, and genetically modified food production raise serious ethical and social issues. The questions concerning the role of businesses, social activist groups, or governments in overseeing these technological developments must continue to be addressed, as new innovations appear on the horizon.

Summary

- Many organizations, including small businesses, are vulnerable to breaches of personal information privacy and the frequency of these violations is increasing.
- Cyberattacks come from within the organization, by employees, as well as outside the organization, by hackers and hacktivists, threatening companies' control of information and imposing significant costs on businesses.

[47] "Monsanto Corn Plant Losing Bug Resistance," *The Wall Street Journal,* August 29, 2011, *online.wsj.com.*

[48] "Planting of Biotech Crops Grow Globally in 2011," *Dawn.com,* February 8, 2012, *dawn.com.*

[49] "Monsanto and Genetically Modified Food Insecurity," *Future Challenges,* March 30, 2012, *futurechallenges.com.*

- Governments have taken steps to better protect individual privacy. Many businesses have developed elaborate information security systems to more quickly detect hacking efforts and to patch corrupted systems, and have even hired internal hackers.
- Businesses have entrusted the management of technology to their chief information officers. These managers often report to the company's CEO and are being entrusted with greater strategic responsibilities within the company.
- Threats of software, music, movie, and book piracy challenge businesses' ownership of their property, prompting governmental responses to these ethical violations with the imposition of penalties through fines and imprisonment.
- Nanotechnology, human genetic research, stem cell research, human cloning, and genetically modified foods carry great promise for society, but have also raised serious concerns. Businesses and governments have attempted to address the objections of activists, while promoting the benefits of these scientific technological breakthroughs.

Key Terms

chief information officer (CIO), *292*
computer hackers, *289*
Digital Millennium Copyright Act, *295*

genetic engineering, *302*
genetically modified foods, *302*
hacktivists, *290*
human genome, *299*
intellectual property, *294*

nanotechnology, *298*
software piracy, *294*
stem cell research, *300*
tissue engineering, *300*
zombie, *288*

Internet Resources

www.bioportfolio.com	Bioterrorism Biodefense
www.bsa.org	Business Software Alliance
www.crnano.org	Center for Responsible Nanotechnology
www.cio.com	Chief Information Officer professional website
www.coppa.org	Children's Online Privacy Protection Act
genomics.energy.gov	Genome Projects of the U.S. Department of Energy, Office of Science
www.improveagriculture.com	A Place to Learn about Sustainable Agriculture
www.iipa.com	International Intellectual Property Alliance
isscr.org	International Society for Stem Cell Research
www.nano.gov	National Nanotechnology Initiative
www.opensecurityfoundation.org	Open Security Foundation
www.projecthoneypot.org	Project Honey Pot
www.ftc.gov/infosecurity	Bureau of Consumer Protection, Data Security

Discussion Case: *Cardholders' Information at Citigroup Hacked*

On May 10, 2011, Citigroup, a 200-year-old U.S. financial services institution with more than 200 million customer accounts in 160 countries, discovered a breach in their credit card information systems. Bank officials believed that about 200,000 credit cardholders, or 1 percent of its customers, were affected. Within 24 hours the company launched an internal investigation to determine the cause of the breach and to assess the significance of the damages. The investigation took 12 days to complete.

The investigation concluded that names, account numbers, and e-mail addresses were exposed, but more sensitive data, such as Social Security numbers, credit card expiration dates, and the three-digit security code located on the back of the cards, were not accessed. It also discovered that more than 360,000 cardholder accounts, more than three times the originally estimated 100,000, had been breached. The bank alerted law enforcement agencies and customers. In a notification letter, mailed on or shortly after June 3, Citigroup reassured customers that they would not be held liable for fraudulent charges. The company also offered customers free identity theft protection assistance if they believed that they were a victim of improper use of their card or of identity theft. The bank also provided replacement cards, with new numbers. Public notification of the security breach occurred on June 9.

Citigroup customers were outraged; not only at the security breach, but that it took the bank three weeks to notify them of the risk that criminals might be able to access their credit card information. Consumer advocates accused Citigroup of dragging its feet before notifying customers that some of the data had been compromised. "Every minute that passes after a hacker gains access to customers' confidential information means a greater risk of both monetary and identity theft," said Mandeep Khera, an executive at an online security firm. Khera said that Citigroup "had done a disservice to customers because of the delay."

In response, the bank reported that it had taken appropriate measures to protect certain customers by sending out an internal fraud alert to all those customers deemed at risk. The company did not disclose the criteria used to determine which customers were perceived as being at risk. A Citigroup spokesperson also explained that the figures provided were always rough estimates and the discrepancy regarding how many accounts were exposed could be attributed to an increase in the number of its credit card accounts and other factors. It was later reported that customers lost $2.7 million due to the cyberattack. The bank reimbursed customers for these losses.

Once the breach was made public, Citigroup security experts joined federal authorities, including the Secret Service and the FBI, in continuing investigations into how the bank was attacked. They discovered that hackers had infiltrated a "garden variety" security hole in the company's website for credit card users that was so common it was listed as one of the top 10 risks compiled by the Open Web Application Security Project. The *New York Times* reported that hackers had used a technique that allowed them to leapfrog from account to account on the Citi website by changing the numbers in the URLs that appeared after customers had entered valid usernames and passwords. The hackers wrote a script that automatically repeated the exercise tens of thousands of times. "That's an easy attack to detect and they just didn't do it," said the chief executive officer of Aspect Security. "It's really a common flaw." Citi reported that it had implemented additional enhanced procedures to prevent similar incidents from happening in the future.

Some security experts suggested that Citigroup's response was reasonable. By discovering and investigating the breach internally and before making a public statement, the bank was able to report verified information to calm customers' fears, especially for those whose data were not compromised.

The Senate banking committee announced that it would hold hearings on data security prompted by Citigroup's experience since this security breach followed other attacks, such as at Sony, RSA Security, and Lockheed Martin. A few days before the Citigroup attack, the International Monetary Fund reported that it had been hit by "a cybersecurity incident." These attacks were fueling concerns among financial regulators and security experts that banks and other organizations were not doing enough to protect themselves and their customers and other stakeholders. In addition, the Federal Deposit Insurance Corporation, which regulates the nation's banks, announced that it was pushing for stronger account security measures at those institutions. The agency also reported that it was "developing additional guidance to enhance authentication procedures when customers access their online accounts."

Unfortunately, three months later, Citigroup announced another security breach involving 92,400 customers at its Japanese unit. The cardholders' names, account numbers, phone numbers, and birthdates were illegally sold to a third party.

Sources: "FDIC Calls for Stricter Security Efforts after Citigroup Hacking," *USA Today,* June 9, 2011, *www.usatoday.com;* "Citi Defends Delay in Disclosing Hacking," *The Wall Street Journal,* June 13, 2011, *online.wsj.com;* "Citigroup Hack Exploited Easy-to-Detect Web Flaw," *The Register,* June 14, 2011, *www.theregister.co.uk;* "Citi Says Many More Customers Had Data Stolen by Hackers," *The New York Times,* June 16, 2011, *www.nytimes.com;* "Citigroup: $2.7 Million Stolen from Customers As Result of Hacking," *The Huffington Post,* June 27, 2011, *www.huffingtonpost.com;* and "Citigroup Hacked Again—92,000 Customers' Info Exposed from Japan," *The Hacker News,* August 8, 2011, *thehackernews.com.*

Discussion Questions

1. Did Citigroup act quickly enough to inform customers of potential vulnerabilities to customers' funds and identities, or should the bank have waited, as it did, until the internal investigation was completed?

2. If you were a credit card customer, would you feel secure that banks, such as Citi, are adequately protecting your personal information and guarding against criminals accessing your money or stealing your identity?

3. What role should government play in protecting individuals against hackers acquiring sensitive personal information, or should this remain the responsibility of the companys storing the information?

4. Are hacking incidents simply a way of life in the information age or should our sensitive, personal information be better protected?

PART SEVEN

Business and Its Stakeholders

CHAPTER FOURTEEN

Stockholder Rights and Corporate Governance

Stockholders occupy a position of central importance in the corporation because they are the company's owners. As owners, they pursue both financial and nonfinancial goals. How can stockholders' rights best be protected? What are the appropriate roles of top managers and boards of directors in the governance of the corporation? How can their incentives be aligned with the interests of the company's stockholders? And how can government regulators best protect the rights of investors? As investors struggled with the aftermath of the financial crisis, these questions seemed more urgent than ever.

This Chapter Focuses on These Key Learning Objectives:

- Identifying different kinds of stockholders and understanding their objectives and legal rights.
- Knowing how corporations are governed and explaining the role of the board of directors in protecting the interests of owners.
- Analyzing the function of executive compensation and debating if top managers are paid too much.
- Evaluating various ways stockholders can promote their economic and social objectives.
- Understanding how the government protects against stock market abuses, such as fraudulent accounting and insider trading.

AIG International was one of the largest insurance companies in the world—an organization that for decades had insured individuals and organizations against all manner of hazards. In late 2008, investors—and those holdings its policies—were shocked to learn that the firm was on the verge of collapse. It turned out that the company had written large numbers of insurance contracts (called "credit default swaps") on complex financial instruments, including mortgage-backed securities. For a time, these contracts had been big moneymakers for AIG. But as housing prices fell and the value of securities backed by their mortgages plunged, the insurance company was forced to put up collateral—money it did not have. Alarmed at the effect AIG's collapse might have on the financial system, the U.S. government stepped in with a $182 *billion* bailout—the largest of a private firm in history—becoming, in the process, AIG's majority shareholder. In 2012, although the government had begun to sell off its shares, the U.S. Treasury still owned 70 percent of the company.[1]

The near-collapse of AIG was, without a doubt, a disaster for the company's stockholders; in a single year, the share price fell from around $50 to mere pennies. Why did the board of directors and top executives fail to manage the apparently excessive risk taken on by the firm? Why didn't government regulators do a better job of protecting stockholders' interests? What role did compensation and reward systems play in the firm's behavior? Why didn't stockholders themselves figure out what was going on and sell their shares before it was too late? And once the government held a majority stake, how could it best use its new ownership role?

Stockholders are the legal owners of corporations. But as the debacle at AIG so vividly illustrates, their rights are not always protected. In the late 2000s and early 2010s, in the wake of major losses by stockholders at AIG and other firms, many groups took steps to improve the overall system of corporate governance. This chapter will address the important legal rights of stockholders and how corporate boards, government regulators, managers, and activist shareholders can protect them. It will also discuss changes in corporate practice and government oversight designed to better guard stockholder interests, in both the United States and other nations, and how recently enacted legislation has strengthened regulation of the financial markets.

 Stockholders

Stockholders (or shareholders, as they also are called) are the legal owners of business corporations. By purchasing shares of a company's stock, they become part owners. For this reason, stockholders have a big stake in how well their company performs. They are considered one of the market stakeholders of the firm, as explained in Chapter 1.[2]

Stock ownership today is increasingly global. In 2010, the total value of stocks in the world was $54 trillion, down from $65 trillion before the stock market collapse of 2008–2009. The market capitalization (total value) of stocks in the United States is by far larger than that of any other country, but stock ownership has grown in many other parts of the world.[3] One way to compare the extent of stock ownership among countries is to examine their

---

[1] "U.S. Government Sells $6B in AIG Shares," March 8, 2012, at *http://abcnews.go.com.*

[2] The following discussion refers to publicly held corporations; that is, ones whose shares of stock are owned by the public and traded on the various stock exchanges. U.S. laws permit a number of other ownership forms, including sole proprietorships, partnerships, and mutual companies. The term *private equity* refers to shares in companies that are not publicly traded.

[3] Comprehensive data on stock market capitalization by countries is available in "Market Capitalization of Listed Companies," at *http://data.worldbank.org.*

FIGURE 14.1

Stock Market Capitalization Relative to Gross Domestic Product, for Selected Countries and Regions, 2010

Source: McKinsey Global Institute, *Mapping Global Capital Markets 2011,* August 2011, p. 4. Used by permission.

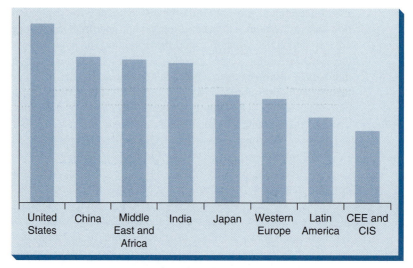

Note: CEE and CIS refers to central and eastern Europe and the Commonwealth of Independent States, respectively.

market capitalization relative to their GDP (gross domestic product, a measure of the size of their economies). By this yardstick, the United States leads, but many other countries and regions are not far behind, as shown in Figure 14.1. Not only are domestic stock markets growing in many nations, but investors are crossing borders in their search for well-diversified portfolios. Extensive cross-border investing has occurred among the United States, Europe, and Japan—and increasingly among these regions and the emerging markets of China, Latin America, central and eastern Europe, and other parts of Asia.

Who Are Stockholders?

Whether in the United States or other countries, two types of stockholders own shares of stock in corporations: individual and institutional.

- *Individual stockholders* are people who directly own shares of stock issued by companies. These shares are usually purchased through a stockbroker and are held in brokerage accounts. For example, a person might buy 100 shares of Intel Corporation for his or her portfolio. Such stockholders are sometimes called "Main Street" investors, because they come from all walks of life.

- *Institutions,* such as pensions, mutual funds, insurance companies, and university endowments, also own stock. For example, mutual funds such as Fidelity Contrafund and pensions such as the California Public Employees Retirement System (CalPERS) buy stock on behalf of their investors or members. These institutions are sometimes called "Wall Street" investors. For obvious reasons, institutions usually have more money to invest and buy more shares than individual investors.

Since the 1960s, growth in the numbers of such **institutional investors** has been phenomenal. In 2010, institutions accounted for 63 percent of the value of all equities (stocks) owned in the United States, worth a total of about $15 *trillion*—about eight times the value of institutional holdings two decades earlier.[4] In an unprecedented twist, the U.S. government itself became

[4] U.S. Census Bureau, *Statistical Abstract of the United States 2012,* "Equities, Corporate Bonds, and Treasury Securities—Holdings and Net Purchases by Type of Investor: 2000 to 2012," Table 1201. These data are based on the Federal Reserve Bank's flow of funds accounts.

a major institutional shareholder in 2008 and 2009 as it acquired ownership in a number of firms, including AIG, Citigroup, and General Motors, which it bailed out with taxpayers' money (by 2012, the government had sold its shares in the two latter organizations).

Slightly over half of all U.S. households own stocks, either directly or indirectly through holdings in mutual funds. Stockholders are a diverse group. People from practically every occupational group own stock. Although middle-aged people are more likely to own stock, slightly less than 40 percent of young households (with a decision maker under the age of 35) do so. At all ages, equity ownership is higher as income and education rises.[5]

Do racial groups have different rates of stock ownership? According to Federal Reserve data, around 58 percent of white households own stock, compared with 30 percent of African-American households and 24 percent of Hispanic households. One possible explanation for these disparities, one study concluded, was different attitudes toward risk. Fifty-three percent of African-Americans, for example, said they were "unwilling to take risks with their investments," compared with 38 percent of whites. (Stocks are riskier, but also have a higher potential for gain than many other kinds of investments.) Another factor, said the researchers, was that "white investors are more experienced with the stock market, so that they are prepared for the inevitable drops."[6]

Figure 14.2 shows the relative stock holdings of individual and institutional investors from 1965 through 2010 in the United States. It shows the growing influence of the institutional sector of the market over the past four decades, with an apparent reversal of the overall trend following the financial crisis.

FIGURE 14.2
Household versus Institutional Equity Ownership in the United States, 1965–2010, by Market Value

Source: U.S. Census Bureau, *Statistical Abstract of the United States, 2012,* Table 1201; and Securities Industry Association, *Securities Industry Fact Book* (New York: Securities Industry Association, 2008). Household sector includes nonprofit organizations. Based on Federal Reserve Flow of Funds Accounts (revised). Used by permission.

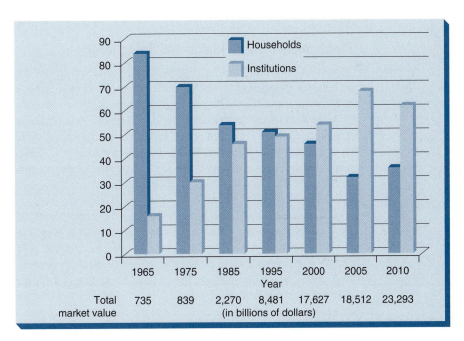

[5] U.S. Census Bureau, *Statistical Abstract of the United States 2012,* "Stock Ownership by Age of Head of Family and Family Income 2001 to 2007," Table 2011; and "Equity and Bond Ownership in America, 2008," Investment Company Institute and the Securities Industry Association, 2008. It should be noted that these figures precede the stock market downturn that began in 2008.

[6] Sherman D. Hanna and Suzanne Lindamood, "The Decrease in Stock Ownership by Minority Households," *Financial Counseling and Planning* 19, no. 2 (2008), pp. 46–58; and private correspondence with Sherman Hanna. Data are for 2007.

Objectives of Stock Ownership

Individuals and institutions own corporate stock for a number of reasons. Foremost among them is to make money. People buy stocks because they believe stocks will produce a return greater than they could receive from alternative investments. Stockholders make money when the price of the stock rises (this is called *capital appreciation*) and when they receive their share of the company's earnings (called *dividends*). Most companies pay dividends, but some—particularly new companies with good prospects for rapid growth—do not. In this case, investors buy the stock with the goal of capital appreciation only.

Stock prices rise and fall over time, affected by both the performance of the company and by the overall movement of the stock market. For example, in 2008 and early 2009 share values declined sharply as the global economy fell into a severe recession, in what is called a *bear market.* This was followed by a period in which markets rose again in a *bull market,* which produced gains for many investors. Typically, bull and bear markets alternate, driven by the health of the economy, interest rates, world events, and other factors that are often difficult to predict. Although stock prices are sometimes volatile, stocks historically have produced a higher return over the long run than investments in bonds, bank certificates of deposit, or money markets.

Although the primary motivation of most stockholders is to make money from their investments, some have other motivations as well. Some investors use stock ownership to achieve social or ethical objectives, a trend that is discussed later in this chapter in the section on social investment. Investors may also buy stock in order to take control of a company in a hostile takeover bid. Some investors have mixed objectives; for example, they wish to make a reasonable return on their investment but also to advance social or ethical goals.

Stockholders' Legal Rights and Safeguards

As explained in Chapter 1, managers have a duty to all stakeholders, not just to those who own shares in their company. Nevertheless, in the United States and most other countries, stockholders have legal rights that are often more extensive than those of other stakeholders.

To protect their financial stake in the companies whose stocks they hold, stockholders have specific legal rights. Stockholders have the right to share in the profits of the enterprise if directors declare dividends. They have the right to receive annual reports of company earnings and company activities and to inspect the corporate books, provided they have a legitimate business purpose for doing so and that it will not be disruptive of business operations. They have the right to elect members of the board of directors, usually on a "one share equals one vote" basis. They have the right to hold the directors and officers of the corporation responsible for their acts, by lawsuit if they want to go that far. Furthermore, they usually have the right to vote on mergers, some acquisitions, and changes in the charter and bylaws, and to bring other business-related proposals before the stockholders. And finally, they have the right to sell their stock. Figure 14.3 summarizes the major legal rights of stockholders.

Many of these rights are exercised at the annual stockholders' meeting, where directors and managers present an annual report and shareholders have an opportunity to approve or disapprove management's plans. Because most corporations today are large, typically only a small portion of stockholders vote in person. Those not attending are given an opportunity to vote by absentee ballot, called a **proxy**. The use of proxy elections by stockholders to influence corporate policy is discussed later in this chapter.

How are these rights of stockholders best protected? Within a publicly held company, the board of directors bears a major share of the responsibility for making sure that the firm

FIGURE 14.3
Major Legal Rights of Stockholders

- To receive dividends, if declared
- To vote on
    Members of board of directors
    Major mergers and acquisitions
    Charter and bylaw changes
    Proposals by stockholders
- To receive annual reports on the company's financial condition
- To bring shareholder suits against the company and officers
- To sell their own shares of stock to others

is run with the shareholders' interests in mind. We turn next, therefore, to a consideration of the role of the board in the system of corporate governance.

Corporate Governance

The term **corporate governance** refers to the process by which a company is controlled, or governed. Just as nations have governments that respond to the needs of citizens and establish policy, so do corporations have systems of internal governance that determine overall strategic direction and balance sometimes divergent interests. The collapse of Lehman Brothers and other investment banks and mortgage lenders during the financial crisis of 2008–2009 has focused renewed attention on corporate governance, because at times the control systems in place have not effectively protected stockholders and others with a stake in the company's performance.

The Board of Directors

The **board of directors** plays a central role in corporate governance. The board of directors is an elected group of individuals who have a legal duty to establish corporate objectives, develop broad policies, and select top-level personnel to carry out these objectives and policies. The board also reviews management's performance to be sure the company is well run and stockholders' interests are protected. Boards typically meet in full session around six times a year.

Corporate boards vary in size, composition, and structure to best serve the interests of the corporation and the shareholders. A number of patterns do exist, however. According to a survey of governance practices in 100 market-leading firms, corporate boards average 12 members. Typically, 10 or 11 of these are *outside* directors (not managers of the company, who are known as *inside* directors when they serve on the board). (The New York Stock Exchange requires listed companies to have boards with a majority of outsiders.) Board members may include chief executives of other companies, major shareholders, bankers, former government officials, academics, representatives of the community, or retired executives from other firms. Nearly all companies have at least one woman on the board; the average number is two. Members of ethnic minorities make up about one out of six directors.[7]

---

[7] Korn/Ferry International, *KFMC100: New Directors and New Directions at America's Most Valuable Public Companies* (2011). Data based on boards of directors at the 100 most valuable U.S.-based firms, by market capitalization as of May 1, 2011.

Board structure in Europe is quite different from its counterpart in the United States. Many European boards use what is called a *two-tier system*. This means that instead of one board, as is common in the United States, these companies have two boards. One, which is called the *executive board,* is made up of the CEO and other insiders. The other, which is called the *supervisory board,* is made up of outsiders and has an independent chairperson. These boards operate autonomously, but of course also coordinate their work. This system is used in all firms in Germany and Austria and in many firms in Denmark, Finland, the Netherlands, Norway, Poland, and Switzerland. Other European nations often use a hybrid system, which has elements of both the unitary and two-tiered systems.[8]

Corporate directors are typically well paid. Compensation for board members is composed of a complex mix of retainer fees, meeting fees, grants of stock and stock options, pensions, and various perks. In 2010, median compensation for directors at the largest U.S. corporations was $212,512, an increase of 6 percent from the prior year, and analysts expected gains of about 10 percent in 2011. (Of this compensation, 46 percent was paid in cash and 54 percent in stock or stock options.)[9] By comparison, in Europe in 2011 the average cash compensation of a public company director was about $95,000.[10]

Director pay does not necessarily correlate with performance. According to a study by compensation specialists Pearl Meyers and Associates, the highest-paid directors in 2007, right before the financial crisis, were in the securities industry—that is, Wall Street's leading investment banks. They were paid, on average, $341,500. Ironically, by the end of 2008 all five of the securities industry firms surveyed by Meyers—Lehman Brothers, Bear Stearns, Merrill Lynch, Morgan Stanley, and Goldman Sachs—had either collapsed, been acquired, or been converted into a commercial bank.[11]

Some critics believe that board compensation is excessive, and that high pay contributes to complacency by some directors who do not want to jeopardize their positions by challenging the policies of management. (Compensation of executives is discussed later in this chapter.)

Most corporate boards perform their work through committees as well as in general sessions. The compensation committee (present in 100 percent of corporate boards), normally staffed by outside directors, administers and approves salaries and other benefits of high-level managers in the company. The nominating committee (97 percent) is charged with finding and recommending candidates for officers and directors, especially those to be elected at the annual stockholders' meeting. The executive committee (42 percent) works closely with top managers on important business matters. A significant minority of corporations (17 percent) now have a special committee devoted to issues of corporate responsibility. Often, these committees work closely with the firm's department of corporate citizenship, as discussed in Chapter 7.[12]

[8] Heidrick & Struggles, "European Corporate Governance Report 2011: Challenging Board Performance," at *www.heidrick.com,* pp. 10–11.

[9] "Compensation for Corporate Directors Increased Moderately in 2010, Towers Watson Analysis Finds," at *www.towerswatson.com;* and "Company Directors See Pay Skyrocket," *USA Today,* October 26, 2011.

[10] Heidrick & Struggles, op. cit., p. 47.

[11] Pearl Meyer & Partners, *2007 Director Compensation,* at *www.execpay.com.*

[12] Korn/Ferry International, *34th Annual Board of Directors Study.* Data are for 2007.

One of the most important committees of the board is the audit committee. Present in virtually all boards, the audit committee is required by U.S. law to be composed entirely of outside directors and to be "financially literate." It reviews the company's financial reports, recommends the appointment of outside auditors (accountants), and oversees the integrity of internal financial controls. Their role is often critical; at Enron, for example, lax oversight by the audit committee was a major contributor to the firm's collapse in 2001. Directors who fail to detect and stop accounting fraud, as occurred at Enron, may be liable for damages. At WorldCom—a leading telecommunications company that collapsed in 2002 in the wake of a major accounting fraud—investors successfully sued former members of the board of directors for $55 million.[13] Because of tighter regulations and increased risk, audit committees now meet more frequently than they used to, on average nine times a year. The National Association of Corporate Directors reported that board members devoted on average around four hours a week to their duties.[14]

How are directors selected? Board members are elected by shareholders at the annual meeting, where absent owners may vote by proxy, as explained earlier. Thus, the system is formally democratic. However, as a practical matter, shareholders often have little choice. Typically, the nominating committee, working with the CEO and chairman, develops a list of possible candidates and presents these to the board for consideration. When a final selection is made, the names of these individuals are placed on the proxy ballot. Shareholders may vote to approve or disapprove the nominees, but because alternative candidates are often not presented, the vote has little significance. The selection process therefore tends to produce a kind of self-perpetuating system. This has begun to change, however, as institutional shareholders may now nominate candidates under some conditions, and some have shown willingness to withhold support from management-nominated candidates.

Because boards typically meet behind closed doors, scholars know less about the kinds of *processes* that lead to effective decision making by directors than they do about board composition and structure.

In their book *Back to the Drawing Board,* Colin Carter and Jay Lorsch observe, based on their extensive consulting experience, that boards develop their own norms that define what is—and is not—appropriate behavior. For example, *pilot boards* see their role as actively guiding the company's strategic direction. *Watchdog* boards, by contrast, see their role as assuring compliance with the law—and intervening in management decisions only if something is clearly wrong. These norms are often powerfully influenced by the chairman. Boards that share a consensus on behavioral norms tend to function more effectively as a group than those that do not.[15]

Principles of Good Governance

In the wake of the corporate scandals of the early 2000s and the financial crisis later in the decade, many sought to define the core principles of good corporate governance. What kinds of boards were most effective? By the 2010s, a broad consensus had emerged among public agencies, investor groups, and stock exchanges about some key features of effective boards. These included the following:

---

[13] "Judge Approves $3.65 Billion Settlement for WorldCom Investors," *The New York Times,* September 22, 2005.

[14] "Company Directors See Pay Skyrocket," op cit.

[15] Colin B. Carter and Jay W. Lorsch, *Back to the Drawing Board: Designing Corporate Boards for a Complex World* (Boston: Harvard Business School Press, 2003).

- *Select outside directors to fill most positions.* Normally, no more than two or three members of the board should be current managers. Moreover, the outside members should be truly independent; that is, should have no connection to the corporation other than serving as a director. This would exclude, for example, directors who themselves performed consulting services for the company on whose board they served, or who were officers of other firms that had a business relationship with it. The audit, compensation, and nominating committees should be comprised *solely* of outsiders. By the 2010s, virtually all major companies were following these practices.

- *Hold open elections for members of the board.* Since 2010, the government has permitted dissident shareholders, under certain conditions, to put their own candidates for the board on the proxy ballot. Some shareholders have argued that candidates should have to get at least 50 percent of votes to be elected (most companies required only a plurality).[16] Some thought that directors should stand for election every year (a practice called *board declassification*); others thought that staggered terms were a better idea (for example, on a nine-person board, three individuals would stand for election each year for a three-year term). In any event, the idea was to give shareholders more control over the selection of directors.

- *Appoint an independent lead director (also called a nonexecutive chairman of the board).* Many experts in corporate governance also believed that boards should separate the duties of the chief executive and the board chairman, rather than combining the two in one person as done in many corporations, especially in the United States. The independent lead director can hold meetings without management present, improving the board's chances of having completely candid discussions about a company's affairs. For example, in 2011 Arthur Levinson was named nonexecutive chairman at Apple after the death of Steve Jobs, who had briefly served in this role.[17] Of the 100 largest U.S. companies, by 2010 only 31 had separated the positions of CEO and board chairman, and only 11 had an independent lead director.[18]

- *Align director compensation with corporate performance.* Like top executives, directors should be paid based, at least in part, on how well the company does. For example, Coca-Cola announced in 2007 that it would change the way its directors were compensated. Members of the board would be paid only if the company met its earnings-per-share target of at least 8 percent annual compound growth over a three-year period. If the company did not, directors would get nothing.[19] In Japan, directors' compensation has traditionally been seniority-based, but in recent years some companies have introduced performance-based pay.[20]

- *Evaluate the board's own performance on a regular basis.* Directors themselves should be assessed on how competent they were and how diligently they performed their duties. Normally, this would be the responsibility of the governance committee of the board. In the wake of the corporate scandals of the early 2000s, many companies made dramatic improvements in this area, and almost all companies now evaluate director performance. For example, the board of directors of Becton, Dickinson, a medical technology company, sponsors an annual evaluation of its own performance and effectiveness, examining

[16] Testimony of Anne Simpson [representing CalPERS] before the U.S. Senate Committee on Banking, Housing, and Urban Affairs, July 12, 2011.

[17] "Apple Appoints New Chairman and Elects Disney's Chief to Board," *The New York Times,* November 15, 2011.

[18] Korn-Ferry International, *KFMC100,* op. cit.

[19] "Coke Directors Agree to Give Up Pay If Company Misses Earnings Goals," *The Wall Street Journal,* April 6, 2006.

[20] ISS, "Increase in Director Compensation Ceiling Proposals," at *www.issgovernance.com.*

its role, organization, and meetings. In Europe, three-quarters of public companies now conduct regular board evaluations.[21]

The movement to improve corporate governance has been active in other nations and regions, as well as the United States, as some of these examples show. The Organization for Economic Cooperation and Development (OECD), representing 34 nations, issued a revised set of principles of corporate governance in 2004 to serve as a benchmark for companies and policymakers worldwide. In 2009, OECD issued a report that concluded that the financial crisis affecting many of its member states had been caused, to an important extent, by failures of corporate governance.[22] For its part, the European Union has worked hard to modernize corporate governance practices and harmonize them across its member states. Corporate governance reforms have also taken hold in South Africa, India, and many other nations. But progress had been slow in many emerging market countries.

> According to Governance Metrics International (GMI), governance practices in emerging market (EM) companies are very different from those in the United States, Canada, the United Kingdom, and Australia. Only 35 percent of boards in EM countries have a majority of independent directors (compared with 93 percent in the latter group of countries). In Japan, for example, almost all companies have a majority of inside directors. Only 50 percent have a compensation committee (compared with 98 percent). As an example of poor governance, GMI cited a Brazilian steel company where one man served as chairman, CEO, and chief financial officer, and a bank he controlled managed transactions for the firm.[23]

In short, by the 2010s the movement to make boards more responsive to shareholders was an international one, although much work remained to be done, especially in emerging market countries.

Special Issue: Executive Compensation

Setting **executive compensation** is one of the most important functions of the board of directors. The emergence of the modern, publicly held corporation in the late 1800s effectively separated ownership and control. That is, owners of the firm no longer managed it on a day-to-day basis; this task fell to hired professionals. This development gave rise to what theorists call the *agency problem*. If managers are merely hired agents, what will guarantee that they act in the interests of shareholders rather than simply helping themselves? The problem is a serious one, because shareholders are often geographically dispersed, and government rules make it difficult for them to contact each other and to organize on behalf of their collective interests. Boards meet just a few times a year. Who, then, is watching the managers?

An important mechanism for aligning the interests of the corporation and its stockholders with those of its top managers is executive compensation. But recent events suggest the system is not always doing its job.

---

[21] Heidrick & Struggles, op. cit, p. 29.

[22] Grant Kirkpatrick, "The Corporate Governance Lessons from the Financial Crisis," OECD, February 2009. For the complete principles, see *www.oecd.org.* Information about recent changes in corporate governance practices in Europe is available at the website of the European Corporate Governance Institute, *www.ecgi.org.*

[23] "GMI Announces New Country Ratings for Corporate Governance," September 23, 2009, at *www.csrwire.com;* and "Governance Metrics International Releases Ratings on 3800 Global Companies," press release, February 28, 2006.

In the years leading up to the financial crisis, a number of top executives made out handsomely, even as their companies were spiraling toward collapse. At Merrill Lynch, Stanley O'Neal earned $70 million in compensation over his four years as CEO—and then an additional $161 million in severance pay when the board fired him in 2007. Just a year later, Merrill went under. Angelo Mozilo, the CEO of the disgraced subprime mortgage lender Countrywide, was paid $125 million in the year before his company collapsed and was taken over by the Bank of America. In response to these and other similar cases, some legislators and shareholders called for "clawback"—a process by which executives of failed firms would have to pay back some of their earnings. By 2011, fully 84 percent of large U.S. firms had adopted such policies, according to the research firm Equilar, and all financial services firms were required to have them.

Many critics feel that executive pay has become excessive—not just at companies accused of fraud but in fact at most companies—reflecting aggressive self-dealing by managers without regard for the interests of others.

Executive compensation in the United States, by international standards, is very high. In 2011, the median total compensation of chief executives of the largest corporations in the United States was $9.6 million, including salaries, bonuses, and the present value of retirement benefits, incentive plans, and stock options, according to the compensation firm Equilar. This amount represented a gain of around 6 percent over the prior year. (The all-time peak median pay, about $13 million, occurred in 2000, at the height of the stock market boom of the late 1990s.) The highest paid executive in 2011 was Timothy D. Cook, the new CEO of Apple, who took home an eye-popping $378 million, almost all in the form of a one-time grant of stock.[24] Because the Equilar survey included only public companies, it did not capture the often outsized pay of hedge fund and private equity fund executives.

Many companies, like Apple, compensate their senior executives in part with grants of stock or **stock options**. The latter represent the right (but not obligation) to buy a company's stock at a set price (called the strike price) for a certain period. The option becomes valuable when, and if, the stock price rises above this amount. Grants of stock and stock options are often seen as a way to align executives' interests with those of shareholders. The idea is that executives will work hard to improve the company's performance, because this would lift the stock and increase the value of their compensation. But critics have highlighted a danger of equity-based compensation: that unscrupulous executives may become so fixated on the value of their options that they will do anything to increase the stock price, even if this involves unethical accounting practices.

By contrast, top managers in other countries earn much less. Although the pay of top executives elsewhere is catching up, it is still generally well below what comparable managers in the United States earn. Figure 14.4 represents graphically the gap between executive pay in the United States and Europe; it shows that median CEO pay in Europe is about half what it is in the United States. Chief executives in Japan make even less, in general, than their European counterparts, earning about half a million dollars annually on average.[25]

These disparities caused friction in some international mergers. For instance, shareholders at GlaxoSmithKline, a pharmaceutical company formed through a merger of British and American firms, complained loudly when the board proposed a $28 million benefits

---

[24] "Typical CEO Made $9.6 Million Last Year, Study Finds," *Associated Press,* May 25, 2012; "For CEOs, Pay Lags Behind Results," *The Wall Street Journal,* March 26, 2012; and "In Executive Pay, A Rich Game of Thrones," *The New York Times,* April 7, 2012.

[25] "In Japan, Underpaid—and Loving It," *Bloomberg Businessweek,* July 1, 2010. Data are for 2009.

FIGURE 14.4   Relative Median Executive Compensation in the United States and Selected
European Nations

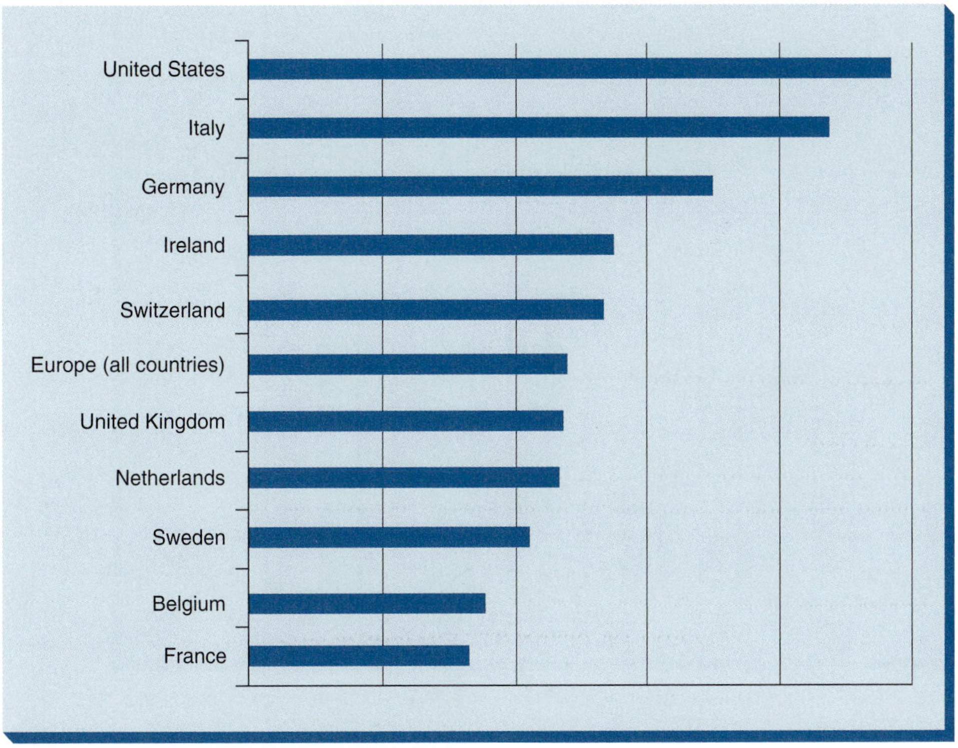

Source: Martin J. Conyon et al., "The Executive Compensation Controversy: A Transatlantic Analysis," February 13, 2011, available at
http://digitalcommons.ilr.cornell.edu. Data are for 2008.

package for CEO Jean-Pierre Garnier. Garnier, who was born in France but had moved to
the United States to head the merged company, said he needed more pay to "stay motivated." But this level of compensation seemed out of line to many European shareholders,
and it was later reduced.[26]

Another way to look at executive compensation is to compare the pay of top managers
with that of average employees. In the United States, CEOs in 2010 made 325 times what the
average worker did. Figure 14.5 shows that since 1990 the ratio of average executive to
average worker pay has increased markedly during periods of economic expansion, but fallen
back during periods of economic contraction, such as the Great Recession of 2008–2009.
The ratio, which has started to rise again, is now three times greater than it was in 1990.

A provision of the 2010 Dodd-Frank Act (introduced in Chapter 8) required major U.S.
firms for the first time to disclose the ratio of their CEO's compensation to the median
compensation of all their employees. Business groups lobbied intensely to repeal or
weaken this rule, calling it unnecessarily burdensome.

Why are American executives paid so much? Corporate politics play an important role.
In their book, *Pay without Performance: The Unfulfilled Promise of Executive Compensation*, Lucian A. Bebchuk and Jesse M. Fried argue that one reason salaries are so high is
that top managers have so much influence over the pay-setting process. Compensation

[26] "Mad about Money: The Outrage over CEO Pay Isn't Only a U.S. Phenomenon; Just Ask Shareholders in Europe," *The Wall
Street Journal,* April 14, 2003.

FIGURE 14.5 **Ratio of Average CEO Pay to Average Production Worker Pay, 1990–2010**

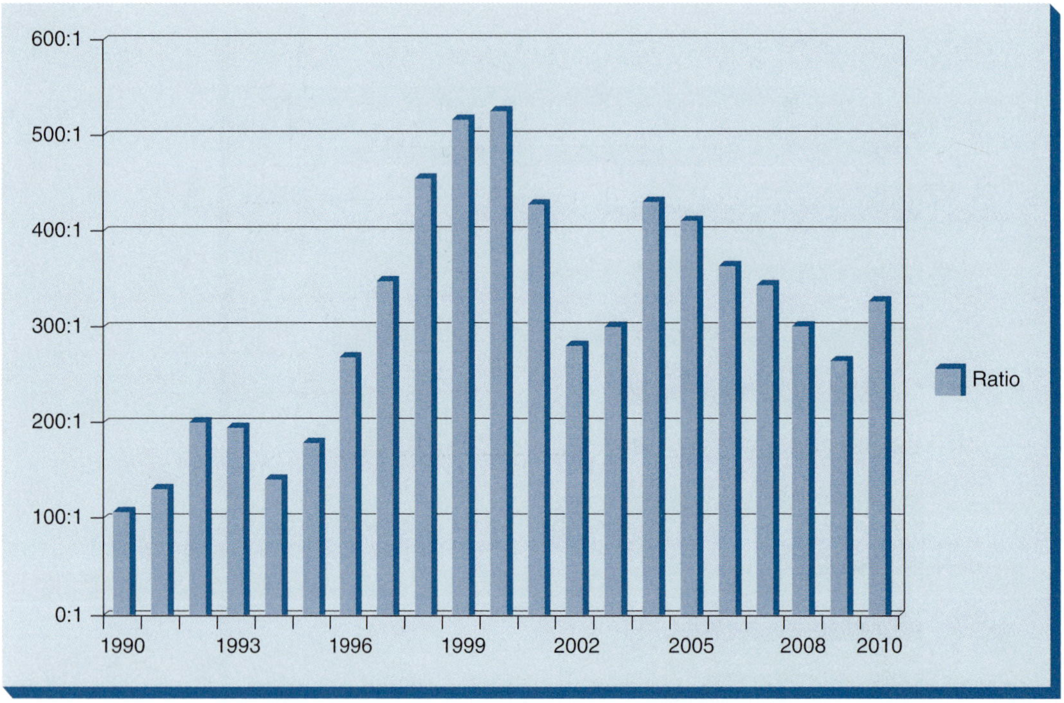

Source: Institute for Policy Studies, "Executive Excess 2011: 18th Annual Executive Compensation Survey," August 31, 2011, at *www.ips-dc.org*. Surveys from earlier years were published jointly with United for a Fair Economy at *www.faireconomy.org*. Used by permission.

committees are made up of individuals who are selected for board membership by the CEO, and they are often linked by ties of friendship and personal loyalty. Many are CEOs themselves and sensitive to the indirect impact of their decisions on their own salaries. Moreover, compensation committees rely on surveys of similar firms and usually want to pay their own executives above the industry average, over time ratcheting up pay for all.[27]

Some observers say that the comparatively high compensation of top executives is justified. In this view, well-paid managers are simply being rewarded for outstanding performance.

For example, Fabrizio Freda, the CEO of the beauty products company Estée Lauder, earned $21 million in 2011, up more than 50 percent from the previous year. But the company, which he joined in 2008, had been stunningly successful: in 2010, the total return to shareholders (change in the share price plus dividends paid) jumped 90 percent. To at least some investors, his generous compensation was clearly worth it.[28]

Supporters also argue that high salaries provide an incentive for innovation and risk taking. In an era of intense global competition, restructuring, and financial crisis, the job of CEO of large corporations has never been more challenging, and the tenure in the top job has become shorter. Another argument for high compensation is a shortage of labor. In this

[27] Lucian A. Bebchuk and Jesse M. Fried, *Pay without Performance: The Unfulfilled Promise of Executive Compensation* (Cambridge, MA: Harvard University Press, 2004).
[28] "In Executive Pay, a Rich Game of Thrones," op. cit.

view, not many individuals are capable of running today's large, complex organizations, so the few that have the necessary skills and experience can command a premium. Today's high salaries are necessary for companies to attract or retain top talent. Why shouldn't the most successful business executives make as much as top athletes and entertainers?

On the other hand, critics argue that inflated executive pay hurts the ability of U.S. firms to compete with foreign rivals. High executive compensation diverts financial resources that could be used to invest in the business, increase stockholder dividends, or pay average workers more. Multimillion-dollar salaries cause resentment and sap the commitment—and sometimes lead to the exodus of—hard-working lower and mid-level employees who feel they are not receiving their fair share. As for the performance issue, critics suggest that as many extravagantly compensated executives preside over failure as they do over success. Many executives get outsized salaries despite their companies' dismal performance—a reality that sometimes prompts shareholder activism.

Executive compensation has also been the subject of government regulations. Under U.S. government rules, companies must clearly disclose what their five top executives are paid, and lay out a rationale for their compensation. Companies must also report the value of various perks, from the personal use of corporate aircraft to free tickets to sporting events, which had previously escaped investor scrutiny. Under the so-called **say-on-pay** provisions of the Dodd-Frank Act, which went into effect in 2011, public companies must hold shareholder votes on executive compensation at least once every three years. Many voluntarily now do so annually. (The governments of the United Kingdom, Australia, and Norway also require such votes.) Although such say-on-pay referendums are not binding on management, they provide a mechanism for shareholders to voice displeasure over excessive compensation. One such election in 2012, in which shareholders voted against a proposed executive compensation package at Citigroup, is profiled in the discussion case at the end of this chapter.

For their part, many companies have responded to stakeholder pressure by changing the process by which they set executive pay. Most boards now staff their compensation committees exclusively with outside directors and permit them to hire their own consultants. Many firms have sought to restructure compensation to tie top executives' pay more closely to performance. A few top managers have even taken pay cuts—such as AIG's CEO Edward Liddy, who worked for an annual salary of $1 in 2008, as the company received billions of dollars of government bailout money.[29] A tiny handful of companies have said that top executives cannot earn more than a certain multiple of others' pay. Whole Foods Market, for example, has a rule that no executive's salary and bonus can be more than 14 times what the average worker makes. "We have a philosophy of shared fate, that we're in this together," said John Mackey, the company's cofounder and CEO.[30]

How to structure executive compensation to best align managers' interests with those of stockholders and other stakeholders will remain a core challenge of corporate governance.

Shareholder Activism

Shareholders do not have to rely exclusively on the board of directors. Many owners, both individual and institutional, have also taken action directly to protect their own interests, as they define them. This section will describe the increased activism of three shareholder groups: large institutions, social investors, and owners seeking redress through the courts.

---

[29] "AIG Says Liddy Took a $1 Salary," *The Wall Street Journal*, May 1, 2009.

[30] "Putting a Ceiling on Pay," *The Wall Street Journal*, April 12, 2004. Whole Foods' measure of executive pay does not include the value of stock options.

The Rise of Institutional Investors

As shown earlier, institutional investors—pensions, mutual funds, endowment funds, and the like—have enlarged their stockholdings significantly over the past two decades and have become more assertive in promoting the interests of their members.

One reason institutions have become more active is that it is more difficult for them to sell their holdings if they become dissatisfied with management performance. Large institutions have less flexibility than individual shareholders, because selling a large block of stock could seriously depress its price, and therefore the value of the institution's holdings. Accordingly, institutional investors have a strong incentive to hold their shares and organize to change management policy.

The Council of Institutional Investors (CII) is an organization that represents institutions and pension funds with investments collectively exceeding $3 trillion. The council has developed a Shareholder Bill of Rights and has urged its members to view their proxies as assets, voting them on behalf of shareholders rather than automatically with management. The activism of institutional shareholders has often improved company performance. One study showed that in the five years before and after a major pension fund became actively involved in the governance of companies whose shares it owned, stock performance improved dramatically, relative to the overall market.[31]

The activism of institutional investors has begun to spread to other countries. In many cases, U.S.-based pension and mutual funds that have acquired large stakes in foreign companies have spearheaded these efforts. In 2012, U.S. investors owned more than $5 trillion worth of foreign securities.[32] To protect their globalized investments, fund managers have become active in proxy battles in Japan, Britain, Hong Kong, and many other countries. In addition, sovereign wealth funds operated by the governments of Singapore, Abu Dhabi, and China have recently become more active as institutional investors.

Activism by institutional shareholders has historically been uncommon in Canada, where many companies are owned by families or a small number of investors. This has begun to change, however. In 2011, Pershing Square Capital Management, a hedge fund that actively intervenes in many companies it invests in, bought $1 billion worth of shares of Canadian Pacific, a railroad (about one-eighth of its total value), and quickly gained support from other investors for a bold plan to shake up the leadership of the company. The following year, it succeeded, deposing the CEO and putting its own candidates on the board. "Mr. Ackman's victory," *The Wall Street Journal* wrote, "serves as a wake-up call for Canada's clubby boardroom culture."[33]

In short, the movement for the rights of shareholders—like the investments they hold—is becoming increasingly globalized.

Social Investment

Another movement of growing importance among activist shareholders is **social investment**, sometimes also called *social responsibility investment.* This refers to the use of stock ownership as a strategy for promoting social objectives. This can be done in two ways:

[31] "The 'CalPERS Effect' on Targeted Company Share Price," July 31, 2009, at *www.calpers-governance.org.*

[32] Board of Governors of the Federal Reserve System, "U.S. International Equity Investment," March 2012, at *www.federalreserve.gov.*

[33] "Canadian Pacific Capitulates," *The Wall Street Journal,* May 18, 2012; and "America's Export to Canada: Shareholder Activism," *The New York Times,* February 14, 2012.

through selecting stocks according to various social criteria, and by using the corporate governance process to raise issues of concern.

Stock Screening

Shareholders wishing to choose stocks based on social, environmental, or governance criteria often turn to screened funds. A growing number of mutual funds and pension funds use *social screens* to select companies in which to invest, weeding out ones that pollute the environment, overpay their executives, discriminate against employees, make dangerous products like tobacco or weapons, or do business in countries with poor human rights records. In 2010, according to the Social Investment Forum Foundation, $3.1 trillion in the United States was invested in mutual funds or pensions using social responsibility as an investment criterion, accounting for about one in every eight investment dollars. Between 2005 and 2010, socially responsible investment grew more than 34 percent, while all assets under professional management grew only 3 percent.[34]

In recent years, socially responsible investing has also grown rapidly in Europe and beyond. In Europe, $7.2 trillion—almost double the amount just two years earlier—were invested using social criteria, according to the European Social Investment Forum.[35] Growth has been driven, in part, by government rules requiring pension funds to disclose the extent to which they use social, environmental, or ethical criteria in selecting investments. It has also been influenced by growing demand by investors who want to align their investment choices with their values. Most evidence shows that socially screened portfolios provide returns that are competitive with the broad market.[36]

Social criteria may also be used when selling stocks. For example, some have at various times called for divestment (sale of stock) from companies that had operations in China, where some products were made by forced labor, and in Nigeria, Myanmar (Burma), and Sudan, where repressive regimes had been accused of human rights abuses.

Social Responsibility Shareholder Resolutions

Another important way in which shareholders have been active is by sponsoring **social responsibility shareholder resolutions**. This is a resolution on an issue of corporate social responsibility placed before stockholders for a vote at the company's annual meeting.

The Securities and Exchange Commission (SEC), a government regulatory agency that is further described later in this chapter, allows stockholders to place resolutions concerning appropriate social issues, such as environmental responsibility or alcohol and tobacco advertising, in proxy statements sent out by companies. The SEC has tried to minimize harassment by requiring a resolution to receive minimum support to be resubmitted— 3 percent of votes cast the first time, 6 percent the second time, and 10 percent the third time it is submitted within a five-year period. Resolutions cannot deal with a company's ordinary business, such as employee wages or the content of advertising, since that would constitute unjustified interference with management's decisions.[37]

In 2011, shareholder activists sponsored around 400 resolutions dealing with major social issues. Backers included church groups, individual shareholders, unions, environmental

---

[34] Social Investment Forum Foundation, "2010 Report on Socially Responsible Investing Trends in the United States," at *www.socialinvest.org.*

[35] Data are as of December 31, 2009. Annual surveys of socially responsible investment in Europe are available on the website of the European Social Investment Forum at *www.eurosif.org.*

[36] A compilation of studies on the performance of socially responsible investments, relative to the broader market, may be found at *www.sristudies.org* and *http://fsinsight.org.*

[37] Current SEC rules on shareholder proposals may be found at *www.sec.gov/rules/final.*

groups, socially responsible mutual funds, and public pension funds. Many of these groups were members of a coalition, the Interfaith Center on Corporate Responsibility (ICCR), which coordinated the activities of the social responsibility shareholder movement. In the 2012 proxy season, some of the issues most commonly raised in these resolutions included disclosure of political spending, energy extraction practices, sustainability reporting, anti-bias policies, and worker safety.

> For example, in 2012 several large pension funds supported proposals at Walmart that would require more complete disclosure of the company's political contributions and how it structured executive compensation. The pension funds said greater transparency would benefit shareholders. The pension funds also withheld support for the re-election of some directors, citing allegations of bribery at the company's Mexican subsidiary. Despite support from some institutional investors, none of the proposals passed.[38]

Although most social responsibility shareholder resolutions fail, as they did at Walmart, they have become more influential over time. In 2011, such resolutions garnered, on average, 21 percent of votes cast, an all-time high. Almost one-third were supported by 30 percent or more, the threshold at which many boards pay serious attention.[39] Moreover, these figures do not capture the full influence of these proposals. In recent years, managers have often entered into a dialogue with shareholder activists and acted on an issue before the election so the resolution would be withdrawn. For example, Chesapeake Energy eliminated some of the toxic additives in its hydraulic fracturing fluids after discussing the issue with concerned investors.[40] According to one study, 20 percent of companies always work with shareholders to resolve their concerns, and 59 percent sometimes do so. Companies that rank high on various measures of corporate social responsibility, not surprisingly, are more likely to try to address shareholder concerns than those that do not.[41]

Stockholder Lawsuits

Another way in which stockholders can seek to advance their interests is by suing the company. If owners think that they or their company have been damaged by actions of company officers or directors, they have the right to bring lawsuits in the courts, either on behalf of themselves or on behalf of the company (the latter is called a *derivative* lawsuit). **Shareholder lawsuits** may be initiated to check many abuses, including insider trading, an inadequate price obtained for the company's stock in a buyout (or a good price rejected), or failure to disclose material information in a timely manner. The outcome can be very expensive for companies, as illustrated by the following example.

> Several institutional shareholders sued Bank of America, saying that the bank and its top executives had failed to disclose what they knew about billions of dollars in losses suffered by Merrill Lynch in the weeks leading up to its acquisition by the

[38] "Once-Reticent Investors Join Shareholder Revolts," *The New York Times,* June 7, 2012; "At Annual Meeting, Wal-Mart to Confront Shareholder Unrest," *The New York Times,* May 31, 2012; and "Walmart Announces 2012 Annual Shareholders' Meeting Voting Results," press release, June 4, 2012.

[39] Data in these two paragraphs are drawn from Ernst & Young, *Leading Corporate Sustainability Issues in the 2012 Proxy Season: Is Your Board Prepared?* (2012), and *2011 Proxy Season Review: Highlights and Leading Implications* (July 2011). These and other studies of shareholder resolutions are available at *www.ey.com/US/en/Issues/Governance-and-reporting.*

[40] CERES, "Proxy Power: Shareholder Successes on Climate, Energy, and Sustainability," February 2012, at *www.ceres.org.*

[41] Kathleen Rehbein, Stephen Brammer, Jeanne Logsdon, and Harry J. Van Buren III, "Understanding Corporate Responses to Shareholder Activists: Uniform or Heterogeneous?" *International Association for Business and Society Proceedings,* 2009.

bank in early 2009. Shareholders had voted to approve the buyout, only to learn of Merrill's huge losses two weeks later. When the news broke, Bank of America's stock promptly fell by 60 percent. The shareholder suit demanded $50 billion—the approximate market losses experienced by investors at that time. The lawsuit was settled in 2012 before going to trial, reportedly for around $20 million, far short of what shareholders had demanded. Some plaintiffs said the settlement was unfair and vowed to continue fighting in the courts.[42]

In many ways—whether through their collective organization, the selection of stocks, the shareholder resolution process, or the courts—shareholder activists can and do protect their economic and social rights.

Government Protection of Stockholder Interests

The government also plays an important role in protecting stockholder interests. This role has expanded, as legislators have responded to the corporate scandals of the early 2000s and the business failures later in the decade.

Securities and Exchange Commission

The major government agency protecting stockholders' interests is the **Securities and Exchange Commission (SEC)**. Established in 1934 in the wake of the stock market crash and the Great Depression, its mission is to protect stockholders' rights by making sure that stock markets are run fairly and that investment information is fully disclosed. The agency, unlike most in government, generates revenue to pay for its own operations. (The revenue comes from fees paid by companies listed on the major stock exchanges.)

Government regulation is needed because stockholders can be damaged by abusive practices. Two areas calling for regulatory attention are protecting stockholders from fraudulent financial accounting and from unfair trading by insiders.

Information Transparency and Disclosure

Giving stockholders more and better company information is one of the best ways to safeguard their interests, and this is a primary mission of the SEC. The stockholder should be as fully informed as possible in order to make sound investments. By law, stockholders have a right to know about the affairs of the corporations in which they hold ownership shares. Those who attend annual meetings learn about past performance and future goals through speeches made by corporate officers and documents such as the company's annual report. Those who do not attend meetings must depend primarily on annual reports issued by the company and the opinions of independent financial analysts.

In recent years, management has tended to disclose more information than ever before to stockholders and other interested people. Prompted by the SEC, professional accounting groups, and individual investors, companies now disclose a great deal about their financial affairs, with much information readily available on investor relations sections of company web pages. Stockholders can learn about sales and earnings, assets, capital expenditures and depreciation by line of business, details of foreign operations, and many other financial matters. Corporations also are required to disclose detailed information about directors and

---

[42] "Bank of America Accord in Lawsuit Is Challenged," *The New York Times,* April 20, 2012; "Bank of America Settles Shareholder Lawsuit for $20 Million," June 21, 2012, at *www.investorplace.com;* and "A $50 Billion Claim of Havoc Looms for Bank of America," *The New York Times,* September 27, 2011.

top executives and their compensation. In addition, many companies have begun reporting detailed information about social and environmental, as well as financial, performance, as discussed in Chapter 7.

Although the overall trend has been toward greater transparency, some observers felt that a lack of disclosure about complex financial instruments, such as mortgage-backed securities, that became common in the mid-2000s, may have led investors to underestimate their risk.

> In early 2008, Bear Stearns, an investment banking firm that had been a fixture on Wall Street for almost a century, abruptly collapsed and was sold to JP Morgan Chase. Bear Stearns was a pioneer in the business of securities backed by subprime mortgages and other risky collateral. When investors began to suspect that the firm's assets were worth much less than they had thought, and that it might not be able to meet its obligations, the Federal Reserve and Treasury stepped in and forced a quick sale to JP Morgan Chase. The firm's sale price was just $10 a share, a shocking drop from a share value of $172 just over a year earlier. In 2012, former Bear Stearns employees won a $10 million settlement to compensate them for losses in the value of company stock held in their retirement accounts.[43]

The Dodd-Frank Act has tightened regulation on issuers of complex securities, such as those backed by subprime mortgages. The role of credit rating agencies in evaluating risk is explored in the case, "Moody's Credit Ratings and the Subprime Mortgage Meltdown," at the end of this book.

Information is useful to investors only if it is accurate. Fraudulent financial statements filed by WorldCom, Enron, and Adelphia in the early 2000s misled investors and led to billions of dollars of losses in the stock market. The reasons for these accounting scandals were complex. They included lax oversight by audit committees, self-dealing by managers, and shareholders who were not sufficiently vigilant. Another problem was that some accounting firms had begun to make more money from consulting and other services than they did from providing routine financial audits. Often, accounting firms provided both consulting and audit services to the same company, creating a potential conflict of interest. Arguably, some accountants were afraid to blow the whistle on questionable financial transactions, out of fear of losing a valuable consulting client.

In 2002, in response to concerns about the lack of transparency in financial accounting, Congress passed an important new law that greatly expanded the powers of the SEC to regulate information disclosure in the financial markets. The law, called the Sarbanes-Oxley Act (for its congressional sponsors), had strong bipartisan support and was signed into law by President George W. Bush. The major provisions of the Sarbanes-Oxley Act are summarized in Chapter 5.

Insider Trading

Another area the SEC regulates is stock trading by insiders. **Insider trading** occurs when a person gains access to confidential information about a company's financial condition and then uses that information, before it becomes public knowledge, to buy or sell the company's stock. Since others do not know what an inside trader does, the insider has an unfair advantage.

---

[43] "Bear Stearns Employee Suit Wins Early Approval," April 5, 2012, at *www.bloomberg.com*. The story of the collapse of Bear Stearns is told in William D. Cohan, *House of Cards: A Tale of Hubris and Wretched Excess on Wall Street* (New York: Doubleday, 2009).

In 2011, Raj Rajaratnam, founder and former manager of the prominent hedge fund Galleon Group, was sentenced to 11 years in prison for 14 counts of illegal insider trading, the longest-ever sentence for this crime. He was also ordered to pay $157 million in fines and forfeitures. Federal prosecutors built their case from wiretap evidence. Over several months, they listened as Rajaratnam—as *The New York Times* put it—"brazenly and matter-of-factly swapped inside stock tips with corporate insiders and fellow traders." In one particularly shocking example, a member of the board of directors of Goldman Sachs called Rajaratnam seconds after a board meeting to share earnings information. The government said that Galleon Group had made $63 million in all from illegal trades. Dozens of other people in Rajaratnam's network were also implicated, and some were convicted. "The defendant knew the rules, but he did not care," said one of the government prosecutors. "Cheating became part of his business model."[44]

Insider trading is illegal under the Securities and Exchange Act of 1934, which outlaws "any manipulative or deceptive device." The courts have generally interpreted this to mean that it is against the law to:

- Misappropriate (steal) nonpublic information and use it to trade a stock.
- Trade a stock based on a tip from someone who had an obligation to keep quiet (for example, a man would be guilty of insider trading if he bought stock after his sister, who was on the board of directors, told him of a pending offer to buy the company).
- Pass information to others with an expectation of direct or indirect gain, even if the individual did not trade the stock for his or her own account.

In an important legal case, *U.S. vs. O'Hagen*, the Supreme Court clarified insider trading law. The court ruled that someone who traded on the basis of inside information when he or she *knew* the information was supposed to remain confidential was guilty of misappropriation, whether or not the trader was directly connected to the company whose shares were purchased. Under the new court interpretation, insider trading rules would cover a wide range of people—from lawyers, to secretaries, to printers—who learned of and traded on information they knew was confidential. They would not, however, cover people who came across information by chance, for example, by overhearing a conversation in a bar.

The best-known kind of insider trading occurs when people improperly acquire confidential information about forthcoming mergers of large corporations in order to buy and sell stocks before the mergers are announced to the public. More recently, another kind of insider trading, called *front-running,* has become more common. Front-runners place buy and sell orders for stock in advance of the moves of big institutional investors, such as mutual funds, based on tips from informants. This form of insider trading is often harder for regulators to detect and prosecute. In 2012, Congress passed a law that extended insider trading rules to its own members (who had previously been exempt), so they could not profit from confidential information obtained as lawmakers.[45]

Insider trading is contrary to the logic underlying the stock markets: All stockholders ought to have access to the same information about companies. In the Galleon Group case described above, Rajaratnam had insider information that ordinary investors did not—information that he used to give his fund and its investors an unfair advantage over others. If ordinary investors think that insiders can use what they know for personal gain, the system

---

[44] "Hedge Fund Billionaire Is Guilty of Insider Trading" and "A Circle of Tipsters Who Shared Illegal Secrets," *The New York Times,* May 11, 2011; and "Rajaratnam Ordered to Pay $92.8 Million Penalty," *The New York Times,* November 8, 2011.

[45] "Obama Signs Bill Banning Insider Trading by Federal Lawmakers," *The New York Times,* April 4, 2012.

of stock trading could break down from lack of trust. Insider trading laws are important in order for investors to have full confidence in the fundamental fairness of the stock markets.

Another responsibility of the SEC is to protect investors against fraud. One situation where they apparently failed to guard against a massive scheme to cheat investors was the fraud perpetrated by Bernard Madoff.

> The victims of Madoff's fraud—including prominent universities, charities, and cultural institutions, as well as individual investors—lost as much as $65 *billion.* Where were the government regulators in all of this? In congressional hearings, SEC chairman Christopher Cox admitted that his agency had missed repeated warnings, dating back to 1999, that things might be amiss at Madoff's firm. "I am gravely concerned by the apparent multiple failures over at least a decade to thoroughly investigate these allegations or at any point to seek formal authority to pursue them," said Cox. *The New York Times* wrote in a harsh editorial that the agency's failure to uncover the Madoff fraud "exemplifies its lackadaisical approach to enforcing the law on Wall Street."[46]

Evidence suggests that the SEC has become much more assertive since 2009, when Madoff was sentenced. In a 2012 review of the agency's performance, *Bloomberg Businessweek* wrote, "In four years the SEC has gone from inept and inattentive to winning record penalties. It has fined big banks, busted hedge funds, and nabbed traders by the dozens." Among the main reasons for the agency's renewed vigor were better funding and greater regulatory authority granted the SEC under the Dodd-Frank Act.[47]

Stockholders and the Corporation

Stockholders have become an increasingly powerful and vocal stakeholder group in corporations. Boards of directors, under intense scrutiny after the recent wave of corporate scandals and business failures, are giving close attention to their duty to protect owners' interests. Reforms in the corporate governance process are under way that will make it easier for them to do so. Owners themselves, especially institutional investors, are pressing directors and management more forcefully to serve stockholder interests. The government, through the Securities and Exchange Commission, has taken important new steps to protect investors and promote fairness and transparency in the financial marketplace.

Clearly, stockholders are a critically important stakeholder group. By providing capital, monitoring corporate performance, assuring the effective operation of stock markets, and bringing new issues to the attention of management, stockholders play a very important role in making the business system work. A major theme of this book is that the relationship between the modern corporation and *all* stakeholders is changing. Corporate leaders have an obligation to manage their companies in ways that attempt to align stockholder interests with those of employees, customers, communities, and others. Balancing these various interests is a prime requirement of modern management. While stockholders are no longer considered the only important stakeholder group, their interests and needs remain central to the successful operation of corporate business.

[46] "Standing Accused: A Pillar of Finance and Charity," *The New York Times*, December 13, 2008; "SEC Issues Mea Culpa on Madoff," *The New York Times*, December 17, 2008; "SEC Knew Him as a Friend and Foe," *The New York Times*, December 18, 2008; and "You Mean That Bernie Madoff?" *The New York Times* [editorial], December 19, 2008.

[47] "Outmanned, Outgunned, and on a Roll," *Bloomberg Businessweek*, April 23–April 29, 2012.

Summary

- Individuals and institutions own shares of corporations primarily to earn dividends and receive capital gains, although some have social objectives as well. Shareholders are entitled to vote, receive information, select directors, and attempt to shape corporate policies and action.

- In the modern system of corporate governance, boards of directors are responsible for setting overall objectives, selecting and supervising top management, and assuring the integrity of financial accounting. The job of corporate boards has become increasingly difficult and challenging, as directors seek to balance the interests of shareholders, managers, and other stakeholders. Reforms have been proposed to make boards more responsive to shareholders and more independent of management.

- Some observers argue that the compensation of top U.S. executives is justified by performance, and that high salaries provide a necessary incentive for innovation and risk taking in a demanding position. Critics, however, believe that it is too high. In this view, high pay hurts firm competitiveness and undermines employee commitment.

- Shareholders have influenced corporate actions by forming organizations to promote their interests and by filing lawsuits when they feel they have been wronged. They have also organized under the banner of social investment. These efforts have included screening stocks according to social and ethical criteria, and using the voting process to promote shareholder proposals focused on issues of social responsibility.

- Recent enforcement efforts by the Securities and Exchange Commission have focused on improving the accuracy and transparency of financial information provided to investors. They have also focused on curbing insider trading, which undermines fairness in the marketplace by benefiting those with illicitly acquired information at the expense of those who do not have it. Some believed that the SEC had not acted vigorously enough to prevent the financial crisis, however, and said that new regulations were needed.

Key Terms

board of directors, *313*
corporate governance, *313*
executive compensation, *317*
insider trading, *326*
institutional investors, *310*

proxy, *312*
say-on-pay, *321*
Securities and Exchange Commission (SEC), *325*
shareholder lawsuits, *324*
social investing, *322*

social responsibility shareholder resolutions, *323*
stockholders, *309*
stock option, *318*

Internet Resources

www.nyse.com	New York Stock Exchange
www.irrc.org	Investor Responsibility Research Center
www.cii.org	Council of Institutional Investors
www.socialinvest.org	Social Investment Forum
www.socialfunds.com	Site for socially responsible individual investors
www.ecgi.org	European Corporate Governance Institute
www.issgovernance.com	Institutional Shareholder Services (ISS)
www.calpers-governance.org	California Public Employees Retirement System
www.sec.gov	U.S. Securities and Exchange Commission

Discussion Case: *Citigroup Shareholders Say No on Pay*

In 2012, Citigroup's shareholders shocked the bank's managers by voting "no" on a proposed $15 million pay package for CEO Vikrim Pandit. In a so-called say-on-pay referendum, mandated by the new Dodd-Frank Act, a solid majority—55 percent—of shareholders withheld approval of the compensation package. Although the vote was not binding, it clearly signaled to Citigroup's board and CEO that shareholders were unhappy. "Here we have the majority of shareholders indicating frustration with the overall level of compensation for executives," said a representative of the labor federation AFL-CIO. "If it can happen at Citigroup, it can happen anywhere."

The target of this rebuke, Citigroup Inc., often called simply Citi, was a leading global bank. Citi had been formed from a series of financial megamergers, culminating with one with Travelers Group in 1998. At its core was a bank that served retail customers at 4,600 branches in the United States and around the world. Citigroup also served businesses and other institutional clients, providing investment banking, brokerage, and lending services. A separate unit called Citi Holdings, established after the financial crisis, included various unwanted assets that Citi was trying to divest. The bank was known worldwide by its logo: the word "citi" in blue lower-case type against a white background, with a red eyebrow connecting the two i's.

During the financial crisis, Citi had had a near-death experience. Like many other banks at the time, Citi had purchased mortgages and other consumer loans and repackaged them into securities called collateralized debt obligations, or CDOs. It both sold these to investors and traded them for its own accounts—eventually acquiring over $40 billion worth of the risky instruments. Initially, the strategy was highly successful. But the game began to unravel in 2007, as the value of the CDOs on Citi's books began to fall, and the firm was forced to announce billions of dollars of write-downs on bad assets. As the crisis deepened in late 2008 and 2009, the U.S. government provided Citi with a series of multimillion-dollar cash infusions in an effort to stave off total collapse of the bank. Since then, Citi had struggled to recover, gradually divesting itself of its risky assets and paying back its government loans.

Under Section 951 of the Dodd-Frank Act—passed by lawmakers in response to the financial crisis—public companies were required to give shareholders an opportunity to cast advisory votes at least once every three years on the compensation of top executives. (Companies with a market capitalization below $75 million were exempt until 2013.) The Council of Institutional Investors strongly supported this provision, saying that say-on-pay votes provided boards with useful shareholder feedback and could serve as a "starting point for dialog on excessive or poorly structured executive pay." In 2011, the first year Section 951 was in effect, shareholders approved most compensation packages; say-on-pay resolutions won, on average, 92 percent support, and were rejected outright in only about 2 percent of elections.

The executive pay package shareholders were asked to vote on at Citi was complex. For 2011, Pandit was awarded a base salary of $1.7 million and a cash bonus of $5.3 million. At the time of the vote, Pandit had already received these payments. The remainder of the $15 million package was to be paid over the following four years, partly in stock and partly in cash. Neither his deferred compensation nor his job was guaranteed.

In its proxy statement, the board defended its proposal by noting that Pandit, who had taken over as CEO in late 2007, had "led Citi's return to profitability and . . . positioned the company for future growth." It pointed out that the bank's net income in 2011 was $11 billion, an increase of 4 percent over the prior year, and that the bank had enjoyed eight consecutive quarters of profitability. Citi had repaid its government loans. Moreover, the board noted, much of the compensation was deferred and subject to meeting performance targets. Although they did not mention it in the proxy statement, directors were certainly well aware that Pandit had drawn a salary of just $1 a year in 2009 and 2010, reflecting Citi's precarious state.

But many shareholders—including several large institutional investors—disputed the board's logic. Two proxy advisory firms, Institutional Shareholders Services (ISS) and Glass, Lewis and Co., recommended that their clients vote "no" on Citi's pay proposals, citing the misalignment of pay with shareholder returns. Several big public pension funds and institutional asset management firms agreed and cast their votes accordingly. Their main complaint, said a representative of CalPERS, the California public pension fund, was that "the bank has not anchored rewards to performance." The bank's shares had declined more than 90 percent since 2006, and Citi had recently failed a "stress test" by the Federal Reserve to see if the bank had sufficient reserves to withstand a severe downturn. An analysis by *Forbes* ranked Citi's performance in the bottom three of 17 U.S. banks.

After the vote, the bank's chairman called the shareholder rejection "a serious matter" and said the board would listen to the shareholders' concerns. The directors' options were limited, however. They could either ignore the vote or change the CEO's compensation package. The latter course was complicated, however, because about $7 million had already been paid out, and most observers thought Pandit was unlikely to give back his earnings voluntarily. The board also faced a risk of litigation. At several other firms, no-on-pay votes had been followed by shareholder lawsuits charging that the board had wasted their money on excessive compensation. Because the Dodd-Frank Act was so new, legal precedents were few, and the outcome of such lawsuits difficult to predict.

"It's time to roll up your sleeves, go back to the drawing board and come back to shareholders with long-term performance targets, risk-adjusted, that really make sense," declared a representative of CalPERS.

Sources: "Citigroup's CEO Rebuffed on Pay by Shareholders," *The New York Times,* April 17, 2012; "Citigroup Has Few Options After Pay Vote," *The New York Times,* April 18, 2012; "Citi Cleans Out Closet," *The Wall Street Journal,* October 4, 2011; "Citigroup Investors Reject Pay Plan," *The Wall Street Journal,* April 17, 2012; "Citigroup Shareholders' Vote on Exec Pay Sends a Message," *Los Angeles Times,* April 18, 2012; PBS NewsHour, "Citigroup Shareholders Assert Say Over CEO's Pay," April 18, 2012, at *www.pbs.org/newshour;* "Enhanced Investor Protection after the Financial Crisis," testimony of Anne Simpson, Senior Portfolio Manager Global Equities, CalPERS, before the U.S. Senate Committee on Banking, Housing, and Urban Affairs, July 12, 2011; and Institutional Shareholder Services, "2011 U.S. Postseason Report," September 29, 2011. Citigroup's website is at *www.citigroup.com;* its proxy statements are available in the investor relations portion of the site.

Discussion Questions

1. Do you agree with the provision of the Dodd-Frank Act that mandates advisory shareholder votes on executive compensation? Why or why not?

2. What are the arguments for and against the proposed executive compensation package at Citigroup? Do you agree or disagree with the proposed package, and why or why not?

3. What were the interests of institutional shareholders in this matter, and why did so many of them vote against the proposed package? If you were an individual shareholder, how would you have voted?

4. What do you think the board of directors should do now that a majority of shareholders have rejected the proposed pay package?

Consumer Protection

Safeguarding consumers while continuing to supply them with the goods and services they want, at the prices they want, is a prime social responsibility of business. Many companies recognize that providing customers with excellent service and product quality is an effective, as well as ethical, business strategy. Consumers, through their organizations, have advocated for their rights to safety, to be informed, to choose, to be heard, and to privacy. Government agencies serve as watchdogs for consumers, supplementing the actions taken by consumers to protect themselves and the actions of socially responsible corporations.

This Chapter Focuses on These Key Learning Objectives:

- Analyzing the reasons for consumer advocacy and the methods consumer organizations use to advance their interests.
- Knowing the five major rights of consumers.
- Assessing the ways in which government regulatory agencies protect consumers and what kinds of products are most likely to be regulated.
- Determining how consumer privacy online can best be protected.
- Examining how the courts protect consumers and efforts by businesses to change product liability laws.
- Evaluating how socially responsible corporations can proactively respond to consumer needs.

In the summer of 2011, a frightening outbreak of food-borne illness gripped Europe, as a dangerous strain of the bacterium E. coli sickened more than 4,000 people in 10 nations. Scrambling to identify the source, government health officials at first suspected tomatoes, cucumbers, peppers, or lettuce, and warned people not to eat them. Eventually, though, the outbreak was traced to raw sprouts grown on a farm in northern Germany, apparently from contaminated seeds imported from the Middle East. The seeds had been sprouted in warm water—a perfect medium for bacteria. By the time the outbreak had run its course, 50 people had died, making it the deadliest in European history. The farm at the epicenter was shut down, and European governments paid more than $300 million to compensate farmers for losses they had sustained. The fast-moving outbreak highlighted how widely food-borne illnesses could spread from their point of origin, as seeds, fresh produce, and people flowed across national boundaries. "We are eating off a global plate," said the former chief of the European Food Safety Authority.[1]

Google paid $500 million to the U.S. government in 2011 to settle charges that it had knowingly run illegal "sponsored links" on its search engine. At issue were paid advertisements placed by Canadian pharmacies seeking mail-order customers in the United States. Because drug prices were strictly controlled in Canada, medicines were often cheaper there. Customers in the United States seeking to fill a prescription for, say, blood pressure or cholesterol medication, found that they could save money by ordering online from a Canadian pharmacy. The U.S. Food and Drug Administration (FDA) banned such cross-border sales, however, saying that the practice put Americans' health at risk. Online Canadian pharmacies were not subject to the FDA's jurisdiction, the government said, and drugs they sold might be tainted or misbranded—or might not even come from Canada at all but from criminal imposters. Investigators found that Google executives up to the highest levels had been aware of the ads. Although the company had not itself imported drugs, the government felt that it had, in effect, acted as an accomplice by allowing the online pharmacies to advertise on its site.[2]

What would happen if businesses could literally read your mind to determine why you choose to buy some products or services, but not others? A new field, called *neuromarketing,* does just that. Scientists working for one of some 150 neuromarketing firms worldwide scan the brains of volunteers, using functional magnetic resonance imaging (fMRI) machines, while asking questions, showing them images and videos, and allowing them to examine products. As the volunteers respond, the fMRI records how the parts of their brains associated with pleasurable feelings, memory, and comprehension react. One such study showed, for example, that product placements integrated into a television program were more effective than stand-alone ads, because viewers were paying more attention at the time. Another showed that people responded more positively to perfume ads showing the source of the fragrance—say, roses—than ones showing a couple in a passionate embrace. Many leading companies—including Facebook, McDonald's, Disney, Citigroup, and Unilever—already use this technology to understand better how to boost the effectiveness of advertising. But some consumer activists sounded a warning. "It's having an effect on individuals that individuals are not informed about," said the director of the Center for Digital Democracy.[3]

---

[1] "Germany Says Bean Sprouts Are Likely E. Coli Source," *The New York Times,* June 10, 2011; "E. Coli Fallout: My Salad, My Health," *The New York Times,* June 11, 2011; and "Germany's E. Coli Outbreak: A Global Lesson," *Food Safety News,* June 18, 2011. Data on infections and deaths are from the World Health Organization, at *www.who.int.*

[2] "Google Forks Over Settlement on Rx Ads," *The Wall Street Journal,* August 25, 2011; "New Heat for Google CEO," *The Wall Street Journal,* August 27, 2011; and "Behind Google's $500 Million Settlement with the U.S.," *The New York Times,* August 27, 2011. The government's press release announcing the settlement is at *www.justice.gov/opa.*

[3] "How the Ad Man Can Get Inside Your Head," *The Observer* (United Kingdom), January 15, 2012; "Marketing on the Brain," *Marketing,* November 2, 2011; and "Making Ads That Whisper to the Brain," *The New York Times,* November 13, 2010.

These three examples demonstrate some of the complexities of serving consumers today. Companies face challenging—and often conflicting—demands to produce a safe and high-quality product or service, keep prices down, protect privacy, prevent fraud and manipulation, and meet the changing expectations of diverse customers around the world. This chapter examines these issues and the various ways that consumers and their advocates, government regulators, the courts, and proactive business firms have dealt with them.

Advocacy for Consumer Interests

As long as business has existed—since the ancient beginnings of commerce and trade—consumers have tried to protect their interests when they buy goods and services. They have haggled over prices, taken a careful look at the goods they were buying, compared the quality and prices of products offered by other sellers, and complained loudly when they felt cheated by shoddy products. So, consumer self-reliance—best summed up by the Latin phrase *caveat emptor,* meaning "let the buyer beware"—has always been one form of consumer protection and is still practiced today.

However, the increasing complexity of economic life has led to organized, collective efforts by consumers to safeguard their own rights in many nations. These organized activities are usually called *consumerism* or the **consumer movement**.

Today, many organized groups actively promote and speak for the interests of millions of consumers. In the United States, one organization alone, the Consumer Federation of America, brings together 300 nonprofit groups to espouse the consumer viewpoint; they represent more than 50 million Americans. Other active U.S. consumer advocacy organizations include Public Citizen, the National Consumers League, the Public Interest Research Group (PIRG), and the consumer protection unit of the American Association for Retired People (AARP).

Many other nations have also experienced movements for consumer rights. Consumers International is an international nongovernmental organization that represents more than 220 consumer groups in 115 nations. Headquartered in London, it has offices in Asia, Latin America, and Africa. Its growth since 1960 has paralleled the expansion of global trade and the integration of many developing nations into the world economy, as discussed in Chapter 6. In Europe, the consumer movement has also been active, as illustrated by the following example.

> In 2012, consumer rights organizations in 11 European countries organized to force Apple to provide a free two-year warranty, as required by European Union law. The company had been providing a one-year warranty and requiring consumers to pay more for an AppleCare Protection Plan extended warranty. "Consumers should not be misled or confused as to fundamental EU consumer rights," said the director general of the European Consumer Organization, a consortium of 42 independent consumer advocacy organizations. She said the case was particularly important, because Apple's products were market leaders, and the company's practices had a wide impact.[4]

The most effective consumer advocacy organizations today harness a wide range of technologies to get the word out to their constituents. One such organization is Consumer Reports (CR, formerly called Consumers Union), which conducts extensive tests on

---

[4] "Apple Warranty Practices Criticized by European Consumer Groups," *Bloomberg,* March 19, 2012, at *www.bloomberg.com.*

selected consumer products and services. CR publishes the results of its tests, with ratings on a brand-name basis, online at *www.consumerreports.org,* which is supported through subscriptions. In addition, the organization's extensive website provides a great deal of free information. Consumers Union also hosts online chats on a range of consumer rights topics and sponsors a site called *HearUsNow.org* to aggregate consumer appeals to companies. A recent petition on the site, for example, called on Facebook to strengthen users' privacy controls, saying, "Let me see all my data and control it!" CR also offers RSS feeds on various topics and a service that alerts supporters by e-mail so they can make their voices heard electronically on various legislative issues relevant to consumer rights.[5]

Reasons for the Consumer Movement

The consumer movement exists because consumers want to be treated fairly and honestly in the marketplace. Some business practices do not meet this standard. Consumers may be harmed by abuses such as unfairly high prices, unreliable and unsafe products, excessive or deceptive advertising claims, violations of privacy, and the sale of products that may be harmful to human health.

Additional reasons for the existence of the consumer movement are the following:

- *Complex products have enormously complicated the choices consumers need to make when they shop.* For this reason, consumers today are more dependent on business for product quality than ever before. Because many products, from smartphones to hybrid automobiles, are so complex, most consumers have no way to judge at the time of purchase whether their quality is satisfactory. In these circumstances, unscrupulous business firms can take advantage of customers.

- *Services, as well as products, have become more specialized and difficult to judge.* When choosing health plans, Internet service providers, credit cards, or colleges, most consumers do not have adequate guides for evaluating whether they are good or bad. They can rely on word-of-mouth experiences of others, but this information may not be entirely reliable. Or the consumer may not be told that service will be expensive or hard to obtain.

- *When businesses try to sell either products or services through advertising, claims may be inflated or they may appeal to emotions.* For example, Samsung's print and video ads for its SF notebook computer showed a naked woman, with her long hair strategically covering her breasts, under the slogan "true beauty is curved." One blogger, a woman, found the ad "distasteful"; she commented that a computer and the female form were "certainly two things that I thought would never have anything in common."[6] In the process, consumers do not always receive reliable and relevant information about products and services.

- *Technology has permitted businesses to learn more than ever about their customers—potentially violating their privacy.* As more and more people go online to browse, compare products and services, and purchase items, companies are able to learn a great deal about their preferences, desires, and habits. New businesses, such as Acxion, described later in this chapter, have emerged that track and aggregate consumer data for others. Such tracking poses threats to individual privacy.

- *Some businesses have ignored product safety.* Business has not always given sufficient attention to product safety. Certain products, such as automobiles, pharmaceutical

[5] See *www.consumersunion.org* and *http://hearusnow.org.*

[6] *http://christine-gazette.blogspot.com.*

drugs, medical devices, processed foods, and children's toys, may be particularly susceptible to causing harm. The case of tainted sprouts, mentioned in the opening example of this chapter, is just one of the latest incidents of unsafe food.

The Rights of Consumers

The central purpose of the consumer movement around the world is to protect the rights of consumers in the marketplace. It aims to make consumer power an effective counterbalance to the power of business firms that sell goods and services.

Consumer advocates argue that consumers are entitled to five core rights. These are:

1. *The right to be informed:* to be protected against fraudulent, deceitful, or grossly misleading information, advertising, and labeling, and to be given the facts to make an informed purchasing decision.

2. *The right to safety:* to be protected against the marketing of goods that are hazardous to health or life.

3. *The right to choose:* to be assured, wherever possible, access to a variety of products and services at competitive prices; and in those industries in which competition is not workable and government regulation is substituted, to be assured satisfactory quality and service at fair prices.

4. *The right to be heard:* to be assured that consumer interests will receive full and sympathetic consideration in the formulation of government policy and fair and expeditious treatment in the courts.

5. *The right to privacy:* to be assured that information disclosed in the course of a commercial transaction, such as health conditions, financial status, or identity, is not shared with others unless authorized.

Consumers' efforts to protect their own rights, through direct advocacy, are complemented by the actions of government regulators, the courts, and businesses themselves.

How Government Protects Consumers

The role of government in protecting consumers is extensive in many nations. This section will describe legal protections afforded consumers in the United States and offer some comparisons with other countries.

Goals of Consumer Laws

Figure 15.1 lists some of the safeguards provided by U.S. **consumer protection laws**. Taken together, these safeguards reflect the goals of government policymakers and regulators in the context of the five rights of consumers outlined above. Many of these safeguards are also embedded in the laws of other nations.

First, some laws are intended to provide consumers with better information when making purchases. Consumers can make more rational choices when they have accurate information about the product. For example, the laws requiring health warnings on cigarettes and alcoholic beverages broaden the information consumers have about these items. Manufacturers, retailers, and importers must spell out warranties (a guarantee or assurance by the seller) in clear language and give consumers the right to sue if they are not honored. The Truth in Lending Act requires lenders to inform borrowers of the annual rate of interest to be charged, plus related fees and service charges. A recent case in

FIGURE 15.1

Major Consumer Protections Specified by Consumer Laws

Information protections

Hazardous home appliances must carry a warning label.

Home products must carry a label detailing contents.

Automobiles must carry a label showing detailed breakdown of price and all related costs.

Lenders must provide timely and understandable information about mortgages and other consumer loans.

Tobacco advertisements and products must carry a health warning label.

Alcoholic beverages must carry a health warning label.

All costs related to real estate transactions must be disclosed.

Warranties must specify the terms of the guarantee and the buyer's rights.

False and deceptive advertising are prohibited.

Food and beverage labels must show complete nutritional information.

Food advertising must not make false claims about nutrition.

Direct hazard protections

Hazardous toys and games for children are banned from sale.

Safety standards for motor vehicles are required.

National and state speed limits are specified.

Hazardous, defective, and ineffective products can be recalled under pressure from the EPA, CPSC, NHTSA, and FDA.

Pesticide residue in food is allowed only if it poses a negligible risk.

Pricing protections

Unfair pricing, monopolistic practices, and noncompetitive acts are regulated by the FTC and Justice Department and by states.

Liability protections

When injured by a product, consumers can seek legal redress.

Privacy protections

Limited collection of information online from and about children is allowed.

Other protections

No discrimination in the extension of credit is allowed.

which mortgage lenders were found to have violated truth in lending rules is presented in Exhibit 15.A.

Deceptive advertising is illegal in most countries. Manufacturers may not make false or misleading claims about their own product or a competitor's product, withhold relevant information, or create unreasonable expectations. In the United States, the Federal Trade Commission (FTC) enforces the laws prohibiting deceptive advertising.

For example, in 2011 Reebok International paid around $25 million in refunds and attorneys' fees to settle charges brought by the FTC. The government said that the athletic gear maker had deceptively advertised its "toning shoes," marketed under the names EasyTone and RunTone. Reebok had claimed in an ad campaign that the shoes, which had pockets of moving air in their soles, created instability that helped tone leg muscles as the wearer walked or ran. But the FTC's bureau of consumer protection found that the company's claims were unsupported by scientific

Exhibit 15.A

Predatory Lending at Countrywide

Did Countrywide—the largest mortgage lender in the United States until its collapse in 2008—defraud and deceive its customers during the housing bubble of the mid-2000s?

The attorneys general of 11 states later settled with Countrywide in the largest predatory lending case in U.S. history. Predatory lending—which is prohibited under federal and many state laws—occurs when a lender, such as a bank or mortgage company, uses unfair, deceptive, or fraudulent practices when making a loan. The states' lawsuit charged that Countrywide had misled its customers about the terms of their home loans, pushing them into loans they could not afford. For example, it had used "bait and switch" tactics to put borrowers who thought they were getting fixed-rate loans into riskier payment-optional loans (in which the amount owed could increase over time) or ones with initially low "teaser" rates that later jumped much higher.

As part of the settlement, Countrywide—which had been acquired by Bank of America—was required to modify the terms of many of the loans it made between 2004 and 2007, at a cost of over $8 billion. Nearly 400,000 mortgage holders were expected to benefit. "Countrywide must now bail out homeowners it recklessly misled into mortgages doomed to fail," said one of the state attorneys general who had brought the suit.

Sources: "Countrywide Settles Fraud Cases for $8.4 Billion," *Bloomberg.com,* October 6, 2008; and "Bank of America in Settlement Worth over $8 Billion: Up to 390,000 Borrowers Covered in Deal with State Attorneys General over Risky Loans Originated by Countrywide Financial," *The Wall Street Journal,* October 6, 2008.

evidence.[7] Deceptive advertising is also illegal in Europe, where U.K. regulators recently warned British athletes preparing for the 2012 summer Olympics not to use their Twitter feeds to promote their sponsors' brands without disclosing that they had been paid for their endorsements.[8]

U.S. law also requires food manufacturers to adopt a uniform nutrition label, specifying the amount of calories, fat, salt, and other nutrients contained in packaged, canned, and bottled foods. Labels must list the amount of trans fat—partially hydrogenated vegetable oils believed to contribute to heart disease—in cakes, cookies, and snack foods. Nutritional information about fresh fruits and vegetables, as well as fish, must be posted in supermarkets. Strict rules also define what can properly be labeled "organic." An emerging issue is the use of the "organic" label on personal care products, such as shampoos, toothpaste, and skin lotions, for which labeling rules are much weaker. "The [personal care products] industry is still rife with unsubstantiated organic claims," said the executive director of the Center of Environmental Health, which brought a suit against 26 companies under a California state labeling law.[9]

A second aim of consumer legislation is to protect consumers against possible hazards. As the opening example about contaminated sprouts showed, consumers can be injured—and even killed—by dangerous products. U.S. laws seek to safeguard consumers in many ways, such as requiring warnings about possible side effects of pharmaceutical drugs, placing limits on flammable fabrics, restricting pesticide residues in fresh and processed foods, banning lead-based paints, and requiring regular inspections to eliminate contaminated meats. In 2008, following a major recall of toys contaminated with lead paint, Congress

[7] "Reebok to Pay $25 Million in Customer Refunds to Settle FTC Charges of Deceptive Advertising in EasyTone and RunTone Shoes," press release, September 28, 2011, at *www.ftc.gov.*

[8] "Olympic Stars Warned over Twitter Plugs for Sponsors as Fair Trading Watchdog Cracks Down on 'Deceptive' Advertising," *Daily Mail* [United Kingdom], April 9, 2012.

[9] "Environmental Group Sues 26 Companies for False Organic Labeling of Personal Care Products," June 22, 2011, at *www.naturalnews.com.*

passed the Consumer Product Safety Improvement Act, which required that toys and infant products be tested before sale and gave regulators more resources to work with. The law was viewed as controversial, because it impacted many small businesses that were not implicated in the toy recall.

The third and fourth goals of consumer laws are to promote competitive pricing and consumer choice. When competitors secretly agree to divide up markets among themselves, or when a single company dominates a market, this artificially raises prices and limits consumer choice. Both federal and state antitrust laws forbid these practices, as discussed in Chapter 8. Competitive pricing also was promoted by the deregulation of the railroad, airline, trucking, telecommunications, banking, and other industries in the 1970s and 1980s and of the telecommunications, ocean shipping, and parts of the financial services industries in the late 1990s. Before deregulation, government agencies frequently held prices artificially high and, by limiting the number of new competitors, shielded existing businesses from competition.

A fifth and final goal of consumer laws is to protect privacy. This issue has recently received heightened regulatory attention, as discussed later in this chapter. The Children's Online Privacy Protection Act, which took effect in 2000, limits the collection of information online from and about children under the age of 13. The Federal Trade Commission has established a "do not call" list to protect individuals from unwanted telemarketing calls at home, and some have called for similar "do not track" rules to protect Internet users. Unwanted calls to a person's mobile phone are also illegal. Other threats to privacy caused by the emergence of new technologies are discussed later in this chapter and in Chapters 12 and 13.

Major Consumer Protection Agencies

Figure 15.2 depicts the principal consumer protection agencies that operate at the federal level of the U.S. government, along with their major areas of responsibility. The oldest of the seven is the Department of Justice, whose Antitrust Division dates to the end of the 19th century. The Food and Drug Administration was founded in the first decade of the 20th century. The Federal Trade Commission was established in 1914 and has been given additional powers to protect consumers over the years, including in the area of online privacy. Three of the agencies—the Consumer Product Safety Commission, the National Highway Traffic Safety Administration, and the National Transportation Safety Board— were created during the great wave of consumer regulations in the 1960s and early 1970s. The most recent is the Consumer Financial Protection Bureau, which is further described later in this chapter. Not included in Figure 15.2 are the Department of Agriculture, which has specific responsibility for the inspection of meat and poultry, and the Environmental Protection Agency, which has authority over genetically modified food and some chemicals that may affect consumers.

The Civil Rights Division of the Department of Justice enforces the provisions of the Civil Rights Act that prohibit discrimination against consumers. For example, in 2011 Countrywide paid $335 million to settle a lawsuit brought by the Justice Department saying that the mortgage lender had charged African-Americans and Hispanics more for their home loans than white borrowers with similar credit histories.[10] (Countrywide is also discussed in Exhibit 15.A.)

The National Highway Traffic Safety Administration (NHTSA), which is part of the Department of Transportation, affects many consumers directly through its authority over automobile safety. For example, the agency develops regulations for car air bags, devices

---

[10] "Countrywide Will Settle a Bias Suit," *The New York Times,* December 21, 2011.

FIGURE 15.2
Major Federal Consumer Protection Agencies and Their Main Responsibilities

Agency	Main Responsibilities
Federal Trade Commission	Competitive pricing Deceptive trade practices Packaging and labeling Consumer credit disclosure and reporting Online privacy
Food and Drug Administration	Safety, effectiveness, and labeling of drugs, foods, food additives, cosmetics, and medical devices Standards for radiation exposure Toxic chemicals research
Consumer Product Safety Commission	Safety standards for consumer products Flammable fabrics, hazardous substances, poison prevention packaging
National Highway Traffic Safety Administration (Transportation Department)	Motor vehicle safety standards Automobile fuel economy standards National uniform speed limit Consumer safeguards for altered odometers
Department of Justice	Fair competition Consumer civil rights
National Transportation Safety Board	Airline safety
Consumer Financial Protection Bureau	Fairness and transparency in consumer financial products and services

that inflate rapidly during a collision, preventing the occupant from striking the steering wheel or dashboard. Driver and passenger-side air bags have long been required as standard equipment on most cars. In 2011, the agency adopted new rules requiring all passenger vehicles to have safety equipment, such as side air bags, that would prevent occupants— even those not wearing seat belts—from being thrown out of the car in a rollover accident.

The rules would be phased in from 2013 to 2018.[11] Another issue the NHTSA is involved in is distracted driving.[12]

> According to the Centers for Disease Control, 5,000 people die and nearly half a million are injured every year in the United States in crashes caused by drivers who are distracted by another activity, such as texting, talking on a handheld phone, or eating and drinking. More than a quarter of American drivers aged 18 to 29 reported texting or e-mailing "regularly" or "fairly often" while driving. In response, several states passed laws banning drivers' use of handheld devices. In 2012, the NHTSA proposed a set of guidelines for carmakers, to encourage them to design vehicles that allowed drivers to interact safely with communications, navigation, entertainment, and other tools. "Distracted driving is a dangerous and deadly habit on America's roadways—that's why I've made it a priority to encourage people to stay focused behind the wheel," said the U.S. transportation secretary.[13]

One consumer protection agency with particularly significant impact on the business community is the Food and Drug Administration (FDA). The FDA's mission is to assure the safety and effectiveness of a wide range of consumer products, including pharmaceutical drugs, medical devices, foods, and cosmetics. The agency has authority over *$1 trillion* of products, about a quarter of all consumer dollars spent each year.

One of the FDA's main jobs is to review many new products prior to their introduction. This job requires regulators to walk a thin line as they attempt to protect consumers. On one hand, the agency must not approve products that are ineffective or harmful. On the other hand, the agency must also not delay beneficial new products unnecessarily. The FDA can also pull existing products off the market or put restrictions on their use, if they are found to harm consumers. Historically, the FDA has had a reputation as a cautious agency that has advocated tough and thorough review before approval. This policy has stood in contrast to those of its counterparts in Europe and some other nations, which have tended to favor quick approval followed by careful field monitoring to spot problems.

> One group of products that is *not* fully regulated by the FDA is dietary supplements, such as the vitamins, minerals, and herbal remedies often sold at health food stores. In 1994, the supplement industry successfully lobbied Congress for a law that exempted their products from most government regulation. As a result, unlike pharmaceutical drugs, supplements do not have to be approved by the FDA before being sold, although the manufacturer itself is supposed to ensure that that the product is safe—and the government can take action after a supplement is on the market. For example, the FDA banned ephedra, an herbal stimulant, after several users, including a professional athlete, died. Recently, the agency warned the makers of body-building supplements containing a substance known as DMAA, sold under names like Napalm, Code Red, and Jack3D, that they had not shown them to be safe.[14]

---

[11] "Automakers Face Tough New Rollover-Crash Rule," *CNN Money*, January 13, 2011, at *http://money.cnn.com.*

[12] The most recent rules concerning air bags are available at *www.nhtsa.dot.gov.*

[13] "U.S. Department of Transportation Proposes 'Distraction' Guidelines for Automakers," press release, February 16, 2012, at *www.nhtsa.gov.*

[14] "FDA Challenges Marketing of DMAA Products for Lack of Safety Evidence," press release, April 27, 2012, at *www.fda.gov/NewsEvents.* Information on the FDA's regulation of dietary supplements is at *www.fda.gov/food/dietarysupplements.*

Exhibit 15.B

The Consumer Financial Protection Bureau

In 2010, as part of the Dodd-Frank Act, Congress created a new agency called the Consumer Finan-cial Protection Bureau (CFPB). Its purpose was "to make markets for consumer financial products and services work in a fair, transparent, and competitive manner." The CFPB consolidated under one roof various consumer financial protection activities, which had previously been spread across seven different federal agencies. Among its mandates were to ensure that consumers had timely and understandable information about loans, to protect them from unfair and deceptive practices and discrimination, and to promote healthy innovation in the financial services industry.

One of the bureau's first initiatives was "Know Before You Owe," a campaign to help consumers clearly understand the costs and risks of various financial products, such as student loans. In 2011, the amount owed on student loans—estimated at $865 billion—was second only to mortgages as a portion of household debt. But students and their families had difficulty comparing aid packages, because colleges often failed to distinguish clearly between loans and scholarships or to disclose the total debt a student would accumulate during their education. The bureau worked with the Depart-ment of Education to develop a standardized disclosure form that would allow students to make side-by-side comparisons of financial aid offers from several colleges; for example, by seeing how much their monthly payments would be after graduation.

The law also allowed the CFPB to oversee previously unregulated nonbank financial institutions, such as so-called payday lenders, which regularly provided short-term, emergency loans at high in-terest rates to nearly 20 million Americans. "This is an important step forward for protecting consum-ers," said CFPB's director. "Holding both banks and nonbanks accountable to consumer financial laws will help create a fairer, more transparent market for consumers."

Sources: "Consumer Financial Protection Bureau Launches Nonbank Supervision Program," press release, January 5, 2012; *Building the CFPB: A Progress Report,* July 18, 2011; and *Semi-Annual Report of the Consumer Financial Protection Bureau: July 21–December 31, 2011,* all at *www.consumerfinance.gov.*

The FDA's role in the approval and subsequent review of Vioxx, a pain medication with-drawn from the market by its manufacturer after it was associated with heart attacks and strokes, is discussed in a case at the end of this textbook.

In 2010, Congress established, as part of the Dodd-Frank Act (also discussed in Chapters 8 and 14), a new consumer regulatory body, called the Consumer Financial Pro-tection Bureau. The purposes and actions of this agency are described in Exhibit 15.B. The debate over whether government should become involved in protecting consumer privacy is discussed in the next section of this chapter.

All seven government regulatory agencies shown in Figure 15.2 are authorized by law to intervene directly into the very center of free market activities, if that is considered nec-essary to protect consumers. In other words, consumer protection laws and agencies substi-tute government-mandated standards and the decisions of government officials for decision making by private buyers and sellers.

Consumer Privacy in the Digital Age

In the early 21st century, rapidly evolving information technologies have given new ur-gency to the broad issue of **consumer privacy**. Shoppers have always been concerned that information they reveal in the course of a sales transaction—for example, their credit card or driver's license numbers—might be misused. But in recent years, fast-changing tech-nologies have increasingly enabled businesses to collect, buy, sell, and use vast amounts of personal data about their customers and potential customers. The danger is not only that this information might rarely be used fraudulently, but also that its collection represents a violation of privacy and might lead to unanticipated harms.

Individuals are often unaware of how much information about themselves they reveal to others as they shop, interact with friends, play games, or look for information online. A variety of technologies make this possible. Many websites place *cookies*—or more powerful *Flash cookies*—on a computer hard drive, to identify the user during each subsequent visit and to build profiles of their behavior over time. *Web beacons* embedded in e-mails and websites retrieve information about the viewer. In *deep packet inspection,* third parties access and analyze digital packets of information sent over the Internet, such as pieces of e-mails or Skype calls, to infer characteristics of the sender. Not just retailers, but also Internet service providers such as Comcast, search engine operators such as Google, and informational services such as Dictionary.com, also track their users. So-called *data aggregators* purchase and combine data about individuals collected from various sources and compile them into highly detailed portraits to be sold to retailers, service providers, and advertisers.[15]

> An example of a data aggregator is Acxiom Corporation, based in Conway, Arkansas. Acxiom, called the "quiet giant" of the industry, has built the largest consumer database in the world, with an average of 1,500 data points on each of 500 million people. It not only collects information from multiple sources, but also analyzes it, placing individuals into categories such as "savvy singles," "flush families," and "downtown dwellers." Acxiom's customers include 47 of the Fortune 100 and such well-known companies as Wells Fargo, Toyota, and Macy's, which pay for "360-degree views" of customers and prospective customers.[16]

"It's a digital vacuum cleaner," said the executive director of the Center for Digital Democracy, speaking of the data aggregation industry. "They're tracking where your mouse is on the page, what you put in your shopping cart, and what you don't buy. A very sophisticated commercial surveillance system has been put in place."[17]

The main reason for all this tracking is to tailor commercial messages to individuals. The term **behavioral advertising** refers to advertising that is targeted to particular customers, based on their observed online behavior. For example, a shopper might view a dress while browsing online for an outfit for an upcoming event, and then later when checking a news site might see an advertisement for the same dress pop up on her screen. According to AudienceScience, a digital marketing technology company, behavioral advertising was used by 85 percent of ad agencies in 2011, and these agencies planned to increase their spending on it significantly going forward. The reason most often cited by survey respondents was that targeted ads were simply "more effective."[18]

Advertisements tailored to a user's interests and preferences have many advantages for both buyer and seller. The buyer is more likely to receive messages that are relevant, and the seller is more likely to reach prospective customers. For example, Amazon tracks its customers' preferences, so on subsequent visits to the website it can recommend books, electronics, and other products that a person might like—a potential benefit to shoppers.

---

[15] This discussion of the use of technology to collect information about customers draws on Lori Andrews, *I Know Who You Are and I Saw What You Did: Social Networks and the Death of Privacy* (New York: Free Press), Chapter 2.

[16] "Consumer Data, But Not for Consumers," *The New York Times,* July 21, 2012; and "You for Sale: Mapping, and Sharing, the Consumer Genome," *The New York Times,* June 16, 2012.

[17] "FTC to Review Online Ads and Privacy," *The New York Times,* November 1, 2007.

[18] "Audience Targeting—Key Indicator of Online Advertising Success," press release, May 5, 2011, at *www.audiencescience.com.*

But the vast collection of information that makes behavioral advertising possible also carries risks. For example, in a practice called *weblining,* individuals may be denied opportunities, such as credit, based on their online profiles. Some people are simply worried that information collected for the purpose of advertising might fall into the wrong hands, without their knowledge or consent. *Consumer Reports* found in a 2012 survey that 71 percent of respondents were "very concerned" about companies sharing information about them without their permission.[19]

The dilemma of how best to protect consumer privacy in the digital age, while still fostering legitimate commerce, has generated a wide-ranging debate. Three major solutions have been proposed: consumer self-help, industry self-regulation, and privacy legislation.

- *Consumer self-help.* In this view, the best solution is for users to employ technologies that enable them to protect their own privacy. For example, special software can help manage cookies, encryption can protect e-mail messages, and surfing through intermediary sites can provide user anonymity. Individuals can learn about and use privacy settings on websites they access. Specialized services, such as one called Privacy-Choice, score various sites on how they handle personal data, offering consumers tools for choosing which to do business with. "We have to develop mechanisms that allow consumers to control information about themselves," commented a representative of the Center for Democracy and Technology, a civil liberties group.[20] Critics of this approach argue that many unsophisticated web surfers are unaware of these mechanisms, or even of the need for them. A recent survey of Facebook users, for example, estimated that 28 percent of them shared all or almost all of their "wall" posts with the general public—not just their "friends."[21]

- *Industry self-regulation.* Many Internet-related businesses have argued that they should be allowed to regulate themselves. In their view, the best approach would be for companies to adopt voluntary policies for protecting the privacy of individuals' information disclosed during electronic transactions. For example, the Digital Advertising Alliance, a marketing trade group, developed an icon—a turquoise triangle placed in the upper right-hand corner of some online ads—that users could click to shield their behavior from tracking.[22] One advantage of the self-regulation approach is that companies, presumably sophisticated about their own technology, might do the best job of defining technical standards. Critics of this approach feel, however, that industry rules would inevitably be too weak. After all, companies often made money from selling personal information to advertisers, giving them a disincentive to protect it.

- *Privacy legislation.* Some favor new government regulations protecting consumer privacy online. In 2012, the Federal Trade Commission issued a comprehensive report on protecting consumer privacy. The commission recommended that businesses adopt a number of best practices, including greater disclosure of how they collected and used consumers' information, simple "opt out" tools, improved security, and time limits on the retention of data. The FTC also recommended that Congress consider enacting new

---

[19] "Consumers Worried about Companies Sharing Their Online Data," April 4, 2012, at *http://news.consumerreports.org.* A summary of polling data on online privacy may be found at the website of the Electronic Privacy Information Center, *http://epic.org/privacy/survey.*

[20] "A New Tool in Protecting Online Privacy," *The New York Times,* February 12, 2012. More information about privacy protection for consumers is available at *www.cdt.org* (Center for Democracy and Technology), *www.epic.org/privacy* (Electronic Privacy Information Center), and *www.privacyrights.org* (Privacy Rights Clearinghouse).

[21] "Facebook and Your Privacy," *Consumer Reports,* June 2012.

[22] "For Online Privacy, Click Here," *The New York Times,* January 19, 2012.

legislation addressing these issues.[23] Consumer privacy protections are generally stronger in the European Union than in the United States. Under European data protection laws, people must be notified when information is collected about them and be given a chance to review and correct it if necessary. An Austrian law student recently used these rules to force Facebook to give him thousands of pages of data about him it had collected, and then used this information to press the company publicly for stronger privacy protections.[24]

Any approach to online privacy would face the challenge of how best to balance the legitimate interests of consumers—to protect their privacy—and of business—to deliver increasingly customized products and services in the digital age. The issue of online privacy is also explored in the discussion case that appears in Chapter 12.

Special Issue: Product Liability

Who is at fault when a consumer is harmed by a product or service? This is a complex legal and ethical issue. The term **product liability** refers to the legal responsibility of a firm for injuries caused by something it made or sold. Under laws in the United States and some other countries, consumers have the right to sue and to collect damages if harmed by an unsafe product. Consumer advocates and trial attorneys have generally supported these legal protections, saying they are necessary both to compensate injured victims and to deter irresponsible behavior by companies in the first place. Some in the business community, by contrast, have argued that courts and juries have unfairly favored plaintiffs, and they have called for reforms of product liability laws. This section describes this debate and recent changes in relevant U.S. law. The special issue of whether or not food companies and restaurants should be held liable for obesity is profiled in the discussion case at the end of this chapter.

Strict Liability

In the United States, the legal system has generally looked favorably on consumer claims. Under the doctrine of **strict liability**, courts have held that manufacturers are responsible for injuries resulting from use of their products, whether or not the manufacturers were negligent or breached a warranty. That is, they may be found to be liable, whether or not they knowingly did anything wrong. Consumers can also prevail in court even if they were partly at fault for their injuries. The following well-publicized case illustrates the extent to which businesses can be held responsible under this strict standard.

> An 81-year-old woman was awarded $2.9 million by a jury in Albuquerque, New Mexico, for burns suffered when she spilled a cup of hot coffee in her lap. The woman, who had purchased the coffee at a McDonald's drive-through window, was burned when she tried to open the lid as she sat in her car. In the 1994 case, McDonald's argued that customers like their coffee steaming, that their cups warned drinkers that the contents are hot, and that the woman was to blame for spilling the coffee herself. But jurors disagreed, convinced by arguments that the woman's burns were severe—requiring skin grafts and a seven-day hospital stay— and by evidence that McDonald's had not cooled down its coffee even after receiving

---

[23] "FTC and White House Push for Online Privacy Laws," *The New York Times,* May 9, 2012; "FTC Issues Final Commission Report on Protecting Consumer Privacy," press release, March 26, 2012, at *www.ftc.gov/opa;* and Federal Trade Commission, *Protecting Consumer Privacy in an Era of Rapid Change* (2012).

[24] "Facebook and the Future: The Battle Heats Up Between Business and Privacy Interests," *Irish Times,* February 23, 2012.

many earlier complaints. McDonald's appealed the jury's verdict and later settled the case with the woman for an undisclosed amount.[25]

In this case, McDonald's was held liable for damages even though it provided a warning and the customer's actions contributed to her burns.

Huge product liability settlements, like the McDonald's case, are well publicized, but they remain the exception. According to the U.S. Department of Justice, one in five non-criminal cases was a tort (liability) case, and plaintiffs (the people suing companies) won 34 percent of product liability cases filed. The average settlement in all tort cases was $201,000, although a few settlements were much higher.[26]

The product liability systems of other nations differ significantly from that of the United States. In Europe, for example, judges, not juries, hear cases. Awards are usually smaller, partly because the medical expenses of victims are already covered under national health insurance, and partly because punitive damages are not allowed. In a few cases, however, companies have faced tough penalties. Baxter International, the health care company, was forced to pay over $250,000 each to the families of 10 kidney patients in Spain. They had died after receiving dialysis on machines equipped with Baxter filters that caused lethal gas bubbles to form in their blood.[27]

Historically, product liability cases have been exceedingly rare in China. But that began to change in 2009, in the wake of China's tainted-milk scandal. The previous year, almost 300,000 children became ill—and at least six died—after drinking baby formula contaminated by the industrial chemical melamine. Milk producers had apparently knowingly added the hazardous chemical to boost the formula's protein content. More than 200 families brought suit against the formula companies, even though the government sought to keep the case out of the courts. Eventually, two people were executed for their roles in the scandal, and the company most responsible was fined and declared bankruptcy.[28]

Should guns be subject to product liability laws, or are they a special case? This issue is profiled in Exhibit 15.C.

Product Liability Reform and Alternative Dispute Resolution

Many businesses have argued that the evolution of strict liability has unfairly burdened them with excess costs. Liability insurance rates have gone up significantly, especially for small businesses, as have the costs of defending against liability lawsuits and paying large settlements to injured parties. Moreover, businesses argue that it is unfair to hold them financially responsible in situations where they were not negligent.

Businesses have also argued that concerns about liability exposure sometimes slow research and innovation. For example, many pharmaceutical companies halted work on new contraceptive methods because of the risk of being sued. Despite the need for new contraceptives that would be more effective and also provide protection against viral

[25] "How a Jury Decided That a Coffee Spill Is Worth $2.9 Million," *The Wall Street Journal,* September 1, 1994; and "McDonald's Settles Lawsuit over Burn from Coffee," *The Wall Street Journal,* December 2, 1994.

[26] U.S. Department of Justice, Office of Justice Programs, Bureau of Justice Statistics, "Federal Tort Trials and Verdicts, 2002–03," August 2005, *www.ojp.gov/bjs.*

[27] "Baxter Will Settle with Families of 10 Dialysis Patients Who Died," *The Wall Street Journal,* November 29, 2001.

[28] "Two Executed in China over Tainted Milk," *CNN World,* at: *http://articles.cnn.com;* "Tainted-Milk Victims File Lawsuit in China's Highest Court," *The Wall Street Journal,* January 20, 2009; and "Chinese Parents File Milk Lawsuit," *The Wall Street Journal,* October 1, 2008.

Two hundred million guns are in circulation in the United States, and a third of all households own at least one. In 2009, more than 31,000 Americans died, and many more were injured, from gun violence.

In the late 1990s, a number of cities and counties brought suit against the firearms industry, demanding compensation for the medical and law enforcement costs of gun violence. The governments argued that gun manufacturers were liable because they had failed to apply commonsense consumer product safety standards to firearms. So-called Saturday night specials—cheap, easily hidden handguns—for example, lacked locks or other protective devices and sometimes misfired, causing unintentional injury. Some guns, such as automatic assault rifles, seemed to have been customized for killing. Moreover, gun makers knowingly made large shipments to regions that had lax gun laws, looking the other way while weapons fell into the hands of criminals.

Most manufacturers, however, disputed these arguments. They pointed out that guns are legal; in fact, they are the only consumer products that the U.S. Constitution (in the Second Amendment) guarantees the right to own. No one, least of all gun manufacturers, has ever claimed that guns do not kill. Guns have a legitimate, even beneficial, purpose in hunting, self-defense, and law enforcement.

The gun liability lawsuits did not fare well in the courts. In a series of decisions in favor of manufacturers, judges and juries seemed to be saying that criminals, not gun makers, were the real killers. In 2005, Congress passed the Protection of Lawful Commerce in Arms Act, which barred lawsuits against gun makers and dealers. Manufacturers could still be held liable, however, if a defect in design or construction caused a gun to malfunction, causing an injury.

Source: Statistics on deaths due to firearms are from the Centers for Disease Control and are reported by the Legal Community Against Violence at *www.lcav.org.*

diseases, such as herpes and AIDS, research had virtually come to a halt by the late 1990s, according to some public health groups.[29]

In 2005, Congress passed the Class Action Fairness Act, the first significant reform of product liability laws in many years. The two key elements of this legislation were:

- *Most large class-action lawsuits were moved from state to federal courts.* This provision applied to cases involving $5 million or more and that included plaintiffs from more than one state. Supporters of the law said this would prevent lawyers from shopping for friendly local venues in which to try interstate cases.

- *Attorneys in some kinds of cases were paid based on how much plaintiffs actually received, or on how much time the attorney spent on the case.* Under the old system, attorneys were often paid a percentage of the settlement amount. This sometimes led to excessive compensation for the lawyers.

Although most businesses welcomed these changes, some called for further reforms, such as shifting the burden of proof to consumers and limiting punitive damages.

Product liability reforms such as those included in the Class Action Fairness Act have faced vigorous opposition from consumers' organizations and from the American Trial Lawyers Association, representing plaintiffs' attorneys. These groups have defended the existing product liability system, saying it puts needed pressure on companies to make and keep products safe.

Plaintiffs scored a legal victory in 2009 when the U.S. Supreme Court decided an important case called *Wyeth v. Levine.* Diana Levine, a musician, was injected with an anti-nausea drug made by Wyeth after complaining of migraines. The drug's

[29] "Birth Control: Scared to a Standstill," *BusinessWeek,* June 16, 1997.

label said that "extreme care" should be used to avoid hitting an artery, which could lead to "gangrene requiring amputation." Unfortunately, this happened to the musician, whose right arm had to be amputated. In the ensuing lawsuit, Wyeth defended itself on the grounds that because the FDA had approved the warning label, the company was shielded from the lawsuit. The Supreme Court disagreed and said the suit could go forward—federal regulatory approval had not preempted the company's liability under state laws.[30]

One approach to settling disagreements between companies and consumers, other than going to court, is **alternative dispute resolution** (ADR). ADR can take the form of *mediation,* a voluntary process to settle disputes using a neutral third party, or *arbitration,* the use of an impartial individual to hear and decide a case outside of the judicial system. The American Arbitration Association (AAA), for example, offers mediation of mortgage foreclosure claims and disputes over insurance claims arising from natural disasters. AAA also offers due process guidelines for companies that want to utilize arbitration to resolve disputes over products or services. Proponents of ADR argue that it is a faster and less expensive way to resolve company–consumer disputes and does not tie up the judicial system with minor issues.

A controversial aspect of consumer ADR is the use of mandatory arbitration clauses. These are clauses in a purchase agreement—for example, for cell phone service, a credit card, or moving services—that require customers to agree to take any future disputes to arbitration rather than to court. In 2012, the U.S. Supreme Court upheld two such mandatory arbitration clauses. Consumer rights organizations have worked to pass a bill called the Arbitration Fairness Act that would limit the use of mandatory arbitration, on the grounds that it limits consumers' rights to use the courts when they have been harmed. Some corporations, such as Bank of America, have voluntarily responded to consumer complaints by discontinuing the use of mandatory arbitration clauses in their service contracts.[31]

Positive Business Responses to Consumerism

The consumer movement has demonstrated that business is expected to perform at high levels of efficiency, reliability, and fairness in order to satisfy the consuming public. Because business has not always responded quickly or fully enough, consumer advocates have turned to the government for protection. On the other hand, much effort has been devoted by individual business firms and by entire industries to encourage voluntary responses to consumer demands. Some of the more prominent positive responses are discussed next.

Managing for Quality

One way that many businesses address consumer interests is to manage quality in a highly proactive way. Quality has been defined by the International Organization for Standardization (ISO) as "a composite of all the characteristics, including performance, of an item, product, or service that bear on its ability to satisfy stated or implied needs." **Quality management**, by extension, refers to "all the measures an organization takes to assure quality." These might include, for example, defining the customer's needs, monitoring whether or not a product or service consistently meets these needs, analyzing the

---

[30] "High Court Eases Way to Liability Lawsuits," *The Wall Street Journal,* March 5, 2009.
[31] "Consumers May See New Limits on Mandatory Arbitration," *Bloomberg Businessweek,* May 21, 2012. For more information on efforts to limit mandatory arbitration, see *www.fairarbitrationnow.org.*

quality of finished products to assure they are free of defects, and continually improving processes to eliminate quality problems. Taking steps at all stages of the production process to ensure consistently high quality has many benefits. Responsible businesses know that building products right the first time reduces the risk of liability lawsuits and builds brand loyalty.

Chrysler Corporation, the U.S. car company, worked hard to boost its products' quality as it emerged from bankruptcy in the early 2010s. Understanding the crucial role of mechanical reliability and consistent fit-and-finish, the company invested $20 million in upgrading the Illinois factory where it planned to build its Dart, Jeep Compass, and Jeep Patriot models, and trained workers to audit vehicles randomly for problems. Chrysler's CEO empowered its quality chief to shut down production or delay a model launch if he needed to—as he did when inspectors found that the rear taillight on the new Chrysler 300 was not completely flush with the body. "Chrysler has made good strides in the products that are in the showrooms now, but it will take time," said the director of *Consumer Reports'* automotive test center.[32]

Managing for product and service quality is an attempt by business to address its customers' needs. It is an example of the interactive strategy discussed in Chapter 2, where companies try to anticipate and respond to emerging stakeholder expectations.

The Malcolm Baldrige National Quality Award, named for a former U.S. Secretary of Commerce, is given annually to organizations that demonstrate quality and performance excellence. A 2011 recipient was the Henry Ford Health System, a system of seven hospitals and care facilities in Michigan. The health system was cited for its high customer satisfaction scores, commitment to patient safety, and best-in-class innovations in health care delivery. For example, the health system designed a new hospital from the ground up with community involvement, incorporating a "Main Street" element to help patients feel at home.[33]

The challenging issue of business's responsibility for products that are safe and of high quality—but used by others in illegal or dangerous ways—is profiled in Exhibit 15.D.

Voluntary Industry Codes of Conduct

In another positive response, businesses in some industries have banded together to agree on voluntary codes of conduct, spelling out how they will treat their customers. Often, this action is taken to forestall even stricter regulation by the government. One such voluntary code is described in the following example.

The Western Growers Association, a trade association of farmers, adopted voluntary guidelines for growers and handlers of leafy green vegetables. The move followed a 2007 outbreak of E. coli poisoning, in which three people died and hundreds were sickened. Public health investigators traced the rash of illnesses to spinach grown on a California farm that had become contaminated with infected wild pig feces. Over 100 farm companies subsequently signed on to the new standards in an effort to alleviate customer concerns—and to reduce pressure for mandatory government rules.[34]

[32] "New Chrysler Battling Old Defects," *The Wall Street Journal,* May 10, 2012; and "Chrysler Invests to Boost Quality," *The Wall Street Journal,* April 3, 2012.
[33] "Malcolm Baldrige National Quality Award 2011 Award Recipient, Health Care Category: Henry Ford Health System," at *http://www.nist.gov/baldrige/award_recipients/ford_profile.cfm.*
[34] "Government Hails Produce Handling Rules," *San Francisco Chronicle,* March 24, 2007; and "E. Coli Outbreak from Fresh Spinach Has USDA Mulling New Leafy Green Regulations," *NEWSInferno.com,* November 30, 2007.

What should a company do when customers use a legitimate product for an illegal or unethical purpose? This problem confronted General Electric (GE), the diversified global technology firm, in Asia. Among GE's many health care products was a line of lightweight, portable ultrasound scanners used for diagnostic imaging. These devices were less expensive and easier to transport than earlier models, making their use in developing nations and rural areas more practical—and popular. For example, by the early 21st century, sales of ultrasound devices in India, where GE was the market leader, had reached $77 million annually.

But GE's portable ultrasound machines were, in some settings, used in a shocking and unexpected way: to identify the gender of female fetuses, which were then aborted. In some cultures, including parts of India and China, many families had a strong preference for sons over daughters. Sometimes, this preference reflected a belief that sons were responsible for caring for their parents in old age, or for carrying on the family name or traditions. At other times, poor families felt they could not afford the high cost of a dowry when a daughter married. Whatever the reason, some unscrupulous medical practitioners used GE's ultrasound devices to facilitate the selective abortion of female fetuses. In 2011, the ratio of boys to girls in India was 112 to 100; in China it was 121 to 100. (In nature, the ratio is 105 to 100.) Millions of girls were simply never born.

As it became aware of the scope of the problem, General Electric moved proactively to prevent the unethical use of its products. In both India and China, laws prohibited the use of ultrasound for sex selection. GE worked closely with regulators responsible for enforcing these laws to assure that its products were only sold to (and serviced for) properly licensed practitioners, and it trained its sales representatives not to deal with anyone suspected of participating in selective abortions. It followed up with audits. The company also promoted positive images of women, for example, by sponsoring female athletes. GE wrote in a blog posted to its website that its experience had shown that "a manufacturer can take [steps] to reduce the risk that its products will be misused in ways that violate human rights."

Sources: Mara Mvistendahl, *Unnatural Selection: Choosing Boys over Girls and the Consequences of a World Full of Men* (New York: PublicAffairs, 2011); "The War Against Girls," *The Wall Street Journal,* June 24, 2011; "Medical Quandary: India's Skewed Sex Ratio Puts GE Sales in Spotlight," *The Wall Street Journal,* April 18, 2007; and "Promoting Ethical Product Use," at *http://citizenship.geblogs.com.*

Consumer Affairs Departments

Many large corporations operate consumer affairs departments, often placing a vice president in charge. The **consumer affairs officer** typically manages a complex network of contacts with customers. The contact infrastructure usually includes a website with a self-service component; many sites are interactive, allowing customers to post comments or questions that are answered electronically by customer relations staff. Most companies also host a call center, using an interactive voice response system that leads callers to an appropriately trained customer service representative. Increasingly, they use sophisticated software that pulls customer feedback from multiple channels, including surveys, social media, and unsolicited feedback, to analyze and respond to issues in real time.[35]

Cutting-edge consumer affairs offices also proactively monitor customer reactions to their products and advertising, using a wide range of social media. Doing so can help companies avoid costly gaffes.

Johnson & Johnson posted a promotion for its pain reliever, Motrin, on its website. The ad showed a mother who was suffering from back and neck pain from wearing a baby carrier, and referred to mothers who "wear their babies." Many mothers who

[35] "Listening to the Voice of the Customer," *Customer Relationship Management,* July 1, 2012.

saw the ad were annoyed, and they started messaging, blogging, and twittering. "A baby will never be a fashion statement," said one. Fortunately, Johnson & Johnson actively monitored its brand in the social media, and within 24 hours had taken down the ads and issued an apology to its customers. What could have been a public relations nightmare was quickly averted.[36]

Experienced companies are aware that consumer complaints and concerns can be handled more quickly, at lower cost, and with less risk of losing goodwill by a consumer affairs department than if customers take a legal route or if their complaints receive widespread publicity.

Product Recalls

Companies also deal with consumer dissatisfaction by recalling faulty products. A **product recall** occurs when a company, either voluntarily or under an agreement with a government agency, takes back all items found to be dangerously defective. Sometimes these products are in the hands of consumers; at other times they may be in the factory, in wholesale warehouses, or on the shelves of retail stores. Wherever they are in the chain of distribution or use, the manufacturer tries to notify consumers or potential users about the defect. For example, in 2012 Black & Decker voluntarily recalled an under-counter-mounted coffeemaker, after numerous reports that the handle had broken off, causing burns and cuts.[37] The case "Mattel and Toy Safety," which appears at the end of this book, describes a recall carried out by Mattel after discovering that some of its toys had been contaminated by dangerous lead paint.

One problem with recalls is that the public may not be aware of them, so dangerous products continue to be used. For example, several babies were killed when Playskool Travel-Lite portable cribs unexpectedly collapsed, strangling them. Although the Consumer Product Safety Commission (CPSC) ordered an immediate recall, not all parents and child care providers heard about it, and additional deaths occurred.[38] Some consumer organizations advocated a system that would require manufacturers of certain products—such as cribs—to include purchaser identification cards so users could be quickly traced in the event of a recall.[39]

The four major government agencies responsible for most mandatory recalls are the Food and Drug Administration, the National Highway Traffic Safety Administration, the Environmental Protection Agency (which can recall polluting motor vehicles), and the Consumer Product Safety Commission.

Consumerism's Achievements

The leaders of the consumer movement can point to important gains in both the United States and other nations. Consumers today are better informed about the goods and services they purchase, are more aware of their rights when something goes wrong, and are better protected against inflated advertising claims, hazardous or ineffective products, and unfair pricing. Several consumer organizations serve as watchdogs of buyers' interests, and a network of government regulatory agencies act for the consuming public.

---

[36] "Strategy and Social Media: Everything's Social Now," *Customer Relationship Management*, June 2009.

[37] "Black & Decker Coffeemakers Recalled by Applica Consumer Products Due to Injury Hazard," press release, June 1, 2012, at *www.cpsc.gov.*

[38] David Zivan, "The Playskool Travel-Lite Crib (A), (B), and (C)," Center for Decision Research, University of Chicago, November 5, 2002.

[39] For information on initiatives to protect children from dangerous products, see *www.kidsindanger.org.*

Some businesses, too, have heard the consumer message and have reacted positively. They have learned to assign high priority to the things consumers expect: high-quality goods and services, reliable and effective products, safety in the items they buy, fair prices, and marketing practices that do not threaten important human and social values.

All of these achievements, in spite of negative episodes that occasionally occur, bring the consuming public closer to realizing the key consumer rights: to be safe, to be informed, to have choices, and to be heard—as well as the newer right to privacy.

Summary

- The consumer movement represents an attempt to promote the interests of consumers by balancing the amount of market power held by sellers and buyers.
- The five key consumer rights are the rights to safety, to be informed, to choose, to be heard, and to privacy.
- Consumer protection laws and regulatory agencies attempt to assure that consumers are treated fairly, receive adequate information, are protected against potential hazards, have free choices in the market, and have legal recourse when problems develop.
- Rapidly evolving information technologies have given new urgency to the issue of consumer privacy. Three approaches to safeguarding online privacy are consumer self-help, industry self-regulation, and protective legislation.
- Business has complained about the number of product liability lawsuits and the high cost of insuring against them. Although consumer groups and trial attorneys have opposed efforts to change product liability laws, modest tort reforms have been legislated.
- Socially responsible companies have responded to the consumer movement by giving serious consideration to consumer problems, increasing channels of communication with customers, instituting arbitration procedures to resolve complaints, and recalling defective products. They have also pursued voluntary codes of conduct and quality management in an effort to meet, and even anticipate, consumers' needs.

Key Terms

alternative dispute resolution, *348*
behavioral advertising, *343*
consumer affairs officer, *350*

consumer movement, *334*
consumer privacy, *342*
consumer protection laws, *336*
deceptive advertising, *337*

product liability, *345*
product recalls, *351*
quality management, *348*
strict liability, *345*

Internet Resources

www.consumersinternational.org — Consumers International
www.cpsc.gov — U.S. Consumer Product Safety Commission
www.ftc.gov — U.S. Federal Trade Commission
www.bbb.org — Better Business Bureau
www.consumerfed.org — Consumer Federation of America
www.consumeraffairs.com — Consumer news and resource center
www.consumeraction.gov — Consumer action website (federal government)
www.socap.org — Society of Consumer Affairs Professionals
www.beuc.org — The European Consumer Organization
www.consumerreports.org — Consumer Reports

Discussion Case: *Big Fat Liability*

In 2012, the Institute of Medicine, an independent group that advises the government, reported that the annual cost of treating obesity-related chronic disease and disability had reached a staggering $190 billion annually in the United States. "Left unchecked," the Institute concluded, "obesity's effects on health, health care costs, and our productivity as a nation could become catastrophic." Said the chairman of the panel that authored the report, "If you believe this is a massive national problem, you have to deal with it in a systems way."

The problem of obesity, and its serious medical and economic effects, just kept getting bigger. According to the most recent government statistics:

- Almost 7 out of 10 American adults were overweight or obese, that is, with a body mass index (BMI) of 25 or more.[40] Seventeen percent of children and adolescents were obese, and almost a third were overweight or considered at risk of becoming so. Only 3 percent of Americans met the government's dietary recommendations, and less than a fifth exercised enough. One study estimated that by 2030, 42 percent of Americans would be obese, if current trends continued.

- Obesity in the United States among adults had doubled, and among adolescents had tripled, since 1980. Although these increases cut across all ages, genders, ethnic groups, and social classes, obesity was a particular problem for people from lower-income families and ethnic minorities.

- Obesity was a major cause of breathing problems, type 2 diabetes, heart disease, arthritis, infertility, and some kinds of cancer. In the United States, around 300,000 premature deaths a year were associated with being overweight—approaching the 400,000 deaths associated with cigarettes.

The immediate cause for this epidemic of obesity was that people were simply eating too much. Americans consumed, on average, around 2,600 calories a day, well above the healthy amount for most people. The critical question, of course, was to what extent, if at all, the food industry could be held responsible for the fattening of America. Many felt that food and lifestyle choices were an individual responsibility. Unlike cigarettes, food products were not normally addictive. Moreover, the rising level of obesity had many causes, and the exact role of particular companies was unclear. How could one know whether a person's obesity was caused by eating particular foods, overeating generally, a sedentary lifestyle, or genetic predisposition?

In an earlier case, the courts had already ruled that fast-food companies were not liable. In 2003, a judge in New York dismissed a lawsuit filed on behalf of two obese teenage girls against McDonald's. The lawsuit alleged that the fast-food giant had "negligently, recklessly, carelessly, and/or intentionally" marketed products to children—such as burgers, chicken nuggets, fries, and sodas—that were "high in fat, salt, sugar, and cholesterol." In his decision, the judge noted that the plaintiffs had failed to show that the girls had no way of knowing the risks of fast food. Moreover, the judge pointed out, "Nobody is forced to eat at McDonald's."

---

[40] Body mass index is calculated as a person's weight in pounds divided by the square of that person's height in inches, multiplied by 703. For example, a person who was 66 inches tall and weighed 140 pounds would have a BMI of 22.59 (140 divided by 66 times 66, times 703). "Overweight" is defined as a BMI of 25–29.9 and "obese" as a BMI of 30 or higher. A chart showing BMIs for various weights and heights is available online at *www.nhlbisupport.com/bmi.*

Others, however, thought the food industry was at least partially at fault. Fast food had become a big part of Americans' diets. In 1970, they spent $6 billion a year on it; four decades later, they spent nearly $140 billion. This trend seemed to parallel the obesity epidemic. The problem was not just the relatively high fat and sugar content of fast foods, but the super-sizing of portions. When fast-food restaurants increasingly began to compete on the basis of value—more for less—customers simply ate more.

For their part, food companies had concentrated on developing processed products, such as candy, gum, snacks, and bakery goods, which carried high profit margins along with excessive calories. They had introduced many more new products in these categories than entrées, fruits, and vegetables since the early 1980s, data showed. Moreover, both restaurants and food processors, in their critics' view, had failed to communicate adequately the health risks of some foods and had inappropriately marketed their products to children.

In response to growing public concern, some food companies and restaurant chains took voluntary steps to make their offerings healthier. Between 2005 and 2011, Kraft, the second-largest food company in the world, reformulated or introduced 5,500 products with reduced calories, fat, sugar, and salt, and it provided "healthy living" recipes on its website. In 2012, McDonald's rolled out new children's Happy Meals, containing apple slices and half the amount of fries. It also offered a smartphone app that permitted customers to access nutritional information. Some smaller chains—like Chipotle Mexican Grill, Jason's Deli, and Panera Bread—built business models around offering fresh, healthy fare. A number of major food companies, including General Mills, Campbell's Soup, and Unilever, joined a new foundation, the Partnership for a Healthy America, which pledged support for a campaign to remove 1.5 trillion calories from the food supply by 2015.

Sources: The Institute of Medicine, "Accelerating Progress in Obesity Prevention: Solving the Weight of the Nation" (2012) at *www.iom.edu;* "The ABCs of Beating Obesity," *The Wall Street Journal,* May 8, 2012; "Rates of Obesity and Severe Obesity to Climb by 2030—Study," *The Wall Street Journal,* May 7, 2012; "McDonald's Trims Its Happy Meal," *The New York Times,* July 26, 2011; and "Best Corporate Steward Finalist, Kraft Foods" (2011), at *http://bclc.uschamber.com.* Overweight and obesity statistics are from the Center for Disease Control's National Center for Health Statistics (*www.cdc .gov/nchs*) and the office of the U.S. Surgeon General (*www.surgeongeneral.gov*). Data on fast-food industry sales are from *www.fastfoodmarketing.org.*

Discussion Questions

1. To what extent do you believe that individuals are responsible for their own weight (or in the case of children, parents or guardians)?

2. In your opinion, should the food and restaurant industries be held liable for the rise of obesity, or not?

3. If you were a manager for a fast-food chain or food company, what actions would you take with respect to obesity, if any?

4. What do you think is the best solution to the obesity epidemic? What role can the food and restaurant industries, trial attorneys, government policymakers and regulators, and individual consumers play in a solution, if any?

CHAPTER SIXTEEN

Employees and the Corporation

Employees and employers are engaged in a critical relationship affecting the corporation's performance. There is a basic economic aspect to their association: Employees provide labor for the firm, and employers compensate workers for their contributions of skill and productivity. Yet, also present in the employee–employer exchange are numerous social, ethical, legal, and public policy issues. Attention to the rights and duties of both parties in this relationship can benefit the firm, its workers, and society.

This Chapter Focuses on These Key Learning Objectives:

- Understanding workers' rights to organize unions and bargain collectively.
- Knowing how government regulations assure occupational safety and health and what business must do to protect workers.
- Evaluating the limits of employers' duty to provide job security to their workers.
- Appraising the extent of employees' right to privacy, when businesses monitor employee communications, police romance in the office, test for drugs or alcohol, or subject employees to honesty tests.
- Debating if employees have a duty to blow the whistle on corporate misconduct, or if employees should always be loyal to their employer.
- Assessing the obligations of transnational corporations to their employees around the world.

Applying for a position as a correctional officer, a man was startled when the interviewer asked him for his Facebook login information, saying it was needed to check for possible gang affiliations. The man did as he was asked but later complained, calling the demand "invasive" and a "violation of [my] personal privacy." Increasingly, employers are conducting background checks on prospective hires by reviewing their social media history, and some use specialized services that "scrape" the web for anything applicants might have done or said online. A representative of the Electronic Privacy Information Center commented that employers were justified in investigating job-related expertise, but "should not be judging what people . . . do away from the workplace."[1]

Should employers, like the correctional services department in this example, have a right to review job applicants' social media pages? What information should be considered private, and what should be considered public? What if the job was not in the correction services field but in some other line of work, would the employer have the right to review an applicant's Facebook page then? Who should be responsible for protecting applicant and employee privacy?

Fourteen people died and dozens more were seriously injured in a fiery explosion at Imperial Sugar's refinery in Port Wentworth, Georgia, in 2008. Government investigators found that dangerous levels of highly combustible sugar dust had built up in the plant and had been ignited by a spark thrown off by metal machinery. A company manager later told Congress that he had warned his bosses that conditions at the plant were "shocking" and "disgraceful" and that a fatal disaster was likely—but was told to back off. But company representatives said that the government did not have specific standards for combustible dust to guide their actions.[2]

Who is responsible for the deaths and injuries of these refinery workers? What roles should government regulators, managers, and workers and their unions play in assuring the safety and health of people on the job?

In 2012, an Indonesian factory that made shoes for Nike Corporation agreed to pay $1 million to its 4,500 workers for hundreds of thousands of hours of uncompensated overtime. A union that had negotiated on behalf of the workers said that they had been required to work seven days a week without overtime pay or benefits. "This has the potential to send shockwaves through the Indonesian labor movement," said the union representing the workers. Human rights activists had long criticized Indonesian footwear and apparel suppliers for paying low wages, fighting efforts to unionize, and requiring long hours. Nike praised the factory managers' action, saying it would "continue to monitor and support their efforts."[3]

Who should be responsible for wages and working conditions in overseas supplier factories—the brand, the supplier, the local government, human rights activists, or workers and their representatives? What wages and conditions of work are fair?

All of these difficult questions will be addressed later in this chapter. As the situations giving rise to them suggest, the rights and duties of employers and employees in the

[1] "Some U.S. Employers Asking for Applicants' Facebook Login Info," *Associated Press,* March 21, 2012; and "Social Media History Becomes a New Job Hurdle," *The New York Times,* July 20, 2011.

[2] "Explosion Injures Dozens at Georgia Sugar Refinery," *The New York Times,* February 8, 2008; "Death Toll Rises from Explosion," *The New York Times,* April 24, 2008; "OSHA Seeks $8.7 Million Fine Against Sugar Company," *The New York Times,* July 26, 2008; and "Executive Said He Warned of Conditions at Refinery," *The New York Times,* July 30, 2008.

[3] "Nike Factory to Pay $1 Million to Indonesian Workers for Overtime," *The Guardian (U.K.),* January 12, 2012; and "Just Pay It: Wage Compensation for Indonesian Nike Workers," at *www.cleanclothes.org.*

modern workplace are incredibly complex—and have become more so as business has become increasingly global.

The Employment Relationship

As noted in Chapter 1, employees are a market stakeholder of business—and a critically important one. Businesses cannot operate without employees to make products, provide services, market to customers, run the organization internally, and plan for the future. At the same time, employees are dependent on their employers for their livelihood—and often much more, including friendship networks, recreational opportunities, health care, retirement savings, even their very sense of self. Because of the importance of the relationship to both parties, it must be carefully managed, with consideration for both legal and ethical obligations.

The employment relationship confers rights and duties on both sides. (As further explained in Chapter 4, a *right* means someone is entitled to be treated a certain way; rights often confer *duties* on others.) Some of these responsibilities are legal or contractual; others are social or ethical in nature. For their part, employers have an obligation to provide some measure of job security, a safe and healthy workplace, and equal opportunity for all. They must pay a decent wage and respect workers' rights to organize and bargain collectively, as guaranteed by U.S. law (and the laws of many other nations). Employers are also obliged to respect employees' rights to privacy and—to some extent at least—their rights to free speech and to do what they want outside the workplace.

But employees also have a duty to behave in acceptable ways. For example, most would agree that employees should not abuse drugs or alcohol in a way that impairs their work performance, use company e-mail to send offensive messages, or take the employer's property for their own personal use. Employees should deal with customers and coworkers in an honest, fair, and nondiscriminatory way. They should not reveal proprietary information to others outside the company, unless there is compelling reason to do so—such as an imminent threat to the public's safety. Some main rights and duties of employers and employees are summarized in Figure 16.1. How to balance these sometimes conflicting obligations poses an ongoing, and frequently perplexing, challenge to business.

This chapter considers the rights and duties—both legal and ethical—of both parties in the employment relationship. The following chapter explores the related issue of workforce diversity and discusses the specific legal and ethical obligations of employers with respect to equal employment opportunity.

FIGURE 16.1
Rights and Duties of Employees and Employers

Employee Rights/Employer Duties	Employee Duties/Employer Rights
• Right to organize and bargain	• No drug or alcohol abuse
• Right to a safe and healthy workplace	• No actions that would endanger others
• Right to privacy	• Treat others with respect and without harassment of any kind
• Duty to discipline fairly and justly	• Honesty; appropriate disclosure
• Right to blow the whistle	• Loyalty and commitment
• Right to equal employment opportunity	• Respect for employer's property and intellectual capital
• Right to be treated with respect for fundamental human rights	

Workplace Rights

Employees in the United States enjoy several important legal guarantees. They have the right to *organize and bargain collectively,* to have a *safe and healthy workplace,* and, to some degree, to have *job security.* This section will explore these three rights, emphasizing U.S. laws and regulation, but with comparative references to policies in other nations.

The Right to Organize and Bargain Collectively

In the United States, and in most other nations, employees have a fundamental legal right to organize **labor unions** and to bargain collectively with their employers. The exceptions are some communist countries (such as China, Vietnam, Cuba, and the People's Democratic Republic of Korea) and some military dictatorships (such as Eritrea), where workers are not permitted to form independent unions. Labor unions are organizations, such as the Service Employees International Union or the Teamsters, that represent workers on the job. Under U.S. laws, most private and public workers have the right to hold an election to choose what union they want to represent them, if any. Unions negotiate with employers over wages, working conditions, and other terms of employment. Employers are not required by law to agree to the union's demands, but they are required to bargain in good faith. Sometimes, if the two sides cannot reach agreement, a strike occurs, or employees apply pressure in other ways, such as appealing to politicians or refusing to work overtime.

The influence of labor unions in the United States has waxed and waned over the years. During the New Deal period in the 1930s, many workers, particularly in manufacturing industries such as automobiles and steel, joined unions, and the ranks of organized labor grew rapidly. Unions negotiated with employers for better wages, benefits such as pensions and health insurance, and improved job safety—significantly improving the lot of many workers. In 2011, the median weekly pay of full-time workers who were members of unions ($938) was 29 percent higher than that of nonunion workers ($729). (All workers, whether or not they are members of unions, are protected by wage and hour laws that require employers to pay at least a minimum wage and extra pay for certain kinds of overtime work.) Since the mid-1950s, the proportion of American workers represented by unions has declined. In 2011, only about 12 percent of all employees were union members. The percentage was higher—37 percent—in government employment than in the private sector, where just 7 percent were unionized.[4] In the wake of the Great Recession, elected officials in several states sought to weaken unions by limiting the rights of public sector workers. For example, the Wisconsin legislature in 2011 passed a law that took away the right of public sector unions (except those representing public safety officers) to bargain over pensions and health care benefits. It also limited future wage increases and ended automatic paycheck dues deductions.

Although unions overall remained weak, some groups of workers continued to organize.

In 2011, for example, the International Association of Machinists and Aerospace Workers succeeded in organizing workers at a factory in Virginia that made bookcases and coffee tables for sale at IKEA's big box furniture stores. Workers there had complained about low wages, long hours, and an intense pace of work. The company sometimes told workers on Friday that they would have to work a weekend shift. "In a rural, family oriented small community with strong religious values, this treatment [was] unacceptable," said the union's organizing director. Workers

---

[4] U.S. Bureau of Labor Statistics, "Union Members in 2011," January 27, 2012, at *www.bls.gov.*

were motivated to unionize, in part, because they were aware that IKEA paid its workers in Sweden (many of whom were union members) at least $19 an hour, compared with a starting salary of $8 at the Virginia plant. "The knowledge that the company [was] capable of meeting a different business model enabled them to seek an alternative," the union organizing director added.[5]

Other significant recent union organizing wins occurred at Smithfield Pork in North Carolina, the world's largest pork slaughterhouse, and Delta Pride, a catfish processor in Mississippi that employed mainly African-American women.[6]

Labor unions sought to exercise influence in other ways, as well. Unions organized in the political arena, using political action committees (PACs) and other methods (discussed in Chapter 9), and voted shares of stock in which their pension funds were invested (discussed in Chapter 14) to pursue their institutional objectives. A major legislative goal of unions was labor law reform; they sought legislation that would make it easier for workers to organize, for example, by shortening the time before an election and stiffening penalties for employers who intervened unfairly in the process.

Some labor unions departed from their traditional adversarial approach to work cooperatively with employers for their mutual benefit. At Kaiser Permanente (a large health maintenance organization), for example, management and unions forged a collaborative partnership aimed both at giving workers a greater say in the business and improving quality and productivity.[7] However, in some industries, old-line labor–management conflict predominated. Walmart, the world's largest private employer, has aggressively opposed efforts to organize its workers—going so far as to shut down one store in Quebec, Canada, where employees had voted to join a union.[8]

One issue that unions and others have been concerned with is job safety and health. It is discussed next.

The Right to a Safe and Healthy Workplace

Many jobs are potentially hazardous and a threat to worker health and safety. In some industries, the use of high-speed and noisy machinery, high-voltage electricity, extreme temperatures, or hazardous gases or chemicals poses risks. Careful precautions, extensive training, strict regulations, and tough enforcement are necessary to avoid accidents, injuries, illnesses, and even deaths on the job.

A Verizon technician working from a bucket truck in Brooklyn, New York, was electrocuted when he touched a high-voltage line without the necessary protective gear. Horrified onlookers watched from the street as the worker's body caught fire. OSHA investigators found that the company had not provided adequate training and had not ensured that gloves and helmets were worn during dangerous operations. "Verizon's culture of indifference puts profits over workers' safety," said a representative of the union.[9]

[5] "Ikea's Factory Workers Vote to Join Union," July 27, 2011, at *www.bloomberg.com*.

[6] "Victory at Smithfield: Union Scores Big Win in North Carolina," *Facing South*, Institute of Southern Studies, December 12, 2008; and Phil M. Dine, *State of the Unions* (New York: McGraw-Hill, 2008), Ch. 2.

[7] Thomas A. Kochan, Adrienne E. Eaton, and Robert B. McKersie, *Healing Together: The Labor–Management Partnership at Kaiser Permanente* (Ithaca: Cornell University Press, 2009).

[8] "Wal-Mart to Close Store in Canada with a Union," *The New York Times*, February 10, 2005.

[9] "Verizon Fined $140,000 after Electrocution Death," *The New York Times*, March 19, 2012; and "Verizon Worker Killed," *The Wall Street Journal*, September 15, 2011.

Exhibit 16.A

Violence in the Workplace

Stories of angry or distraught employees, ex-employees, or associates of employees attacking workers, coworkers, or superiors at work are disturbingly common. In some cases, workers who have lost their jobs—or who face some other financial threat—seek vengeance, often in calculated and cold-blooded fashion. In other cases, seemingly trivial events can provoke an assault. In one recent incident, a truck driver for a distribution warehouse in Manchester, Connecticut, was told by his managers at a disciplinary hearing that surveillance video showed him stealing beer from the company. They gave him a choice: either resign or be fired. Instead, the driver drew a handgun and walked through the warehouse, shooting and killing eight people and wounding two others before turning the gun on himself.[11]

Homicide is the fourth leading cause of death on the job (only vehicle accidents, contact with objects or equipment, and falls kill more). Every year, around 500 workers are murdered, and as many as 2 million are assaulted at work in the United States. Police officers, prison guards, taxi drivers, and people who handle money are most at risk. Although workplace violence is often considered an American problem, a survey by the International Labor Organization found that workplace assaults were actually more common in several other industrial nations, including France, England, and Argentina, than in the United States. Four percent of workers in the European Union said they had been subjected to physical violence in the past year.

OSHA has developed recommendations to help employers reduce the risk of violence. Employers should try to reduce high-risk situations, for example, by installing alarm systems, convex mirrors, and pass-through windows. They should train employees in what to do in an emergency situation. Unfortunately, many companies are poorly prepared to deal with these situations. Only 24 percent of employers offer any type of formal training to their employees in coping with workplace violence.

Sources: "Census of Fatal Occupational Injuries, 2010," April 25, 2012, at *www.bls.org;* and International Labor Organization, *Violence at Work,* 3rd ed., 2006. Current statistics are available at *www.cdc.gov/niosh/topics/violence.*

Over the past few decades, new categories of accidents or illnesses have emerged, including the fast-growing job safety problem of repetitive motion disorders, such as the wrist pain sometimes experienced by supermarket checkers, meat cutters, or keyboard operators. Some workers have even complained of "BlackBerry thumb," hand strain caused by using their thumbs to tap out messages on the small keyboards of their smartphones when working away from the office. In response, many businesses have given greater attention to **ergonomics**, adapting the job to the worker, rather than forcing the worker to adapt to the job. For example, ergonomically designed office chairs that conform to the shape of the worker's spine may help prevent low productivity and lost time due to back injuries.

Annually, nearly 3.1 million workers in private industry are injured or become ill while on the job, according to the U.S. Department of Labor. This amounts to more than three hurt or sick workers out of every hundred. Some of the highest rates are found in the primary and fabricated metals; lumber; warehousing; and food, beverage, and tobacco processing industries. In general, manufacturing and construction jobs are riskier than service jobs—although couriers and workers in nursing homes and hospitals suffer relatively high rates of injury.[10] Almost 5,000 workers die on the job annually. The reasons range from vehicle accidents, to contact with dangerous equipment, to explosion and fire. For example, a massive explosion at the Upper Big Branch coal mine in West Virginia in 2010 killed 29 workers in the worst coal mining disaster in the United States in 40 years. The causes of this disaster are explored in a case study at the end of this book.

Workplace violence—a particular threat to employee safety—is profiled in Exhibit 16.A.

[10] U.S. Bureau of Labor Statistics data, *www.bls.gov.* These data are for 2010.

[11] "Troubles Preceded Connecticut Workplace Killing," *The New York Times,* August 3, 2010.

In the United States, the Occupational Safety and Health Act, passed in 1970 during the great wave of social legislation discussed in Chapter 8, gives workers the right to a job "free from recognized hazards that are causing or likely to cause death or serious physical harm." This law is administered by the **Occupational Safety and Health Administration (OSHA)**. Congress gave OSHA important powers to set and enforce safety and health standards. Employers found in violation can be fined and, in the case of willful violation causing the death of an employee, jailed as well. In 2009, for example, the agency fined BP $87 million—on top of $21 million the company had already paid—for safety violations linked to an explosion of a refinery in Texas that killed 15 workers and injured 170.[12]

OSHA has had considerable success in improving worker safety and health. Although workers—such as the victims of the Upper Big Branch coal mine and BP refinery explosions—continue to die on the job, since OSHA's creation in 1970 the number of workplace deaths has fallen by more than two-thirds, even as the workforce has almost doubled. Very serious occupational illnesses, such as brown lung (caused when textile workers inhale cotton dust) and black lung (caused when coal miners inhale coal dust), have been significantly reduced. The rate of lead poisoning suffered by workers in smelters and battery plants, among other workplaces, has also fallen dramatically.

Although many businesses have credited OSHA with helping reduce lost workdays and worker compensation costs, others have criticized the agency's rules as being too costly to implement and administer. In 2011, for example, OSHA withdrew a proposed noise exposure standard, intended to prevent hearing loss, after employers complained it would be too expensive.[13] Some studies showed that the burdens of complying with regulations fell hardest on small businesses.[14] In part in response to employer criticisms, OSHA has entered into cooperative partnerships with employers, aimed at improving occupational safety and health for the benefit of both companies and their workers.

Although problems remain, three decades of occupational safety and health regulation in the United States and efforts by businesses and unions have significantly lowered deaths and injuries on the job. In many developing nations, however, conditions remain brutally dangerous.

In Bangladesh, a fast-growing garment and textile industry—mostly sourcing apparel to Western companies—has been the site of numerous tragedies. In 2012, a horrific fire at the Tazreen Fashions factory in the outskirts of Dhaka killed 112 workers. The factory did not have ceiling sprinklers or an outdoor fire escape, and flammable fabric had been illegally stored near electrical equipment on the first floor of the eight-story building. This was only the most recent in a series of fires and building collapses that had killed or seriously injured hundreds of Bangladeshi workers. Earlier that year, PVH Corporation—the parent of such brands as Tommy Hilfiger, Calvin Klein, and DKNY—had partnered with a group of NGOs and trade unions to provide worker training and push for stronger government enforcement of safety laws. In the wake of the Tazreen Fashions fire, many pushed for more urgent action to protect workers.[15]

[12] "U.S. Department of Labor's OSHA Issues Record Breaking Fines to BP," press release, October 30, 2009, at *www.osha.gov.*

[13] "OSHA Withdraws Proposed Interpretation Involving Occupational Noise Exposure Standard," *Washington DC Employment Law Update,* January 19, 2011, at *www.dcemploymentlawupdate.com.*

[14] U.S. House of Representatives Committee on Oversight and Government Reform, *Assessing Regulatory Impediments to Job Creation,* February 9, 2011, at *http://oversight.house.gov.*

[15] "Horrific Fire Revealed a Gap in Safety for Global Brands," *The New York Times,* December 6, 2012; and "PVH Corp. Announces Landmark Agreement with Coalition of NGOs and Bangladesh Labor Unions on Fire and Building Safety," press release, March 21, 2012, at *www.pvh.com.* More information on efforts to improve conditions in the Bangladeshi garment and textile industry is available online at *www.cleanclothes.org.*

Efforts by governments, businesses, and unions to improve conditions of workers in overseas factories are further discussed later in this chapter.

The special problem of smoking in the workplace—a safety and health threat to both smokers and nonsmokers—is addressed in the discussion case at the end of this chapter.

The Right to a Secure Job

Do employers have an obligation to provide their workers with job security? Once someone is hired, under what circumstances is it legal—or fair—to let him or her go? In recent years, the expectations underlying this most basic aspect of the employment relationship have changed, both in the United States and in other countries around the globe.

In the United States, since the late 1800s, the legal basis for the employment relationship has been **employment-at-will**. Employment-at-will is a legal doctrine that means that employees are hired and retain their jobs "at the will of"—that is, at the sole discretion of—the employer. However, over time, laws and court decisions have changed this. Today, employers' freedom to terminate workers has been dramatically curtailed. Some of the restrictions include the following:

- An employer may not fire a worker because of race, gender, religion, national origin, age, or disability. The equal employment and other laws that prevent such discriminatory terminations are further described in Chapter 17.

- An employer may not fire a worker if this would constitute a violation of public policy, as determined by the courts. For example, if a company fired an employee just because he or she cooperated with authorities in the investigation of a crime, this would be illegal.

- An employer may not fire a worker if, in doing so, it would violate the Worker Adjustment Retraining Notification Act (WARN). This law, passed in 1988, requires most big employers to provide 60 days' advance notice whenever they lay off a third or more (or 500 or more, whichever is less) of their workers at a work site. If they do not, they must pay workers for any days of advance notice that were missed.

   In 2008, workers at Republic Window and Doors in Chicago occupied their factory after the owner shut it down with only three days' notice. The workers, who were represented by the United Electrical Workers union, said that the abrupt plant closure violated the terms of WARN. After five days of tense negotiations, the sit-in ended when Bank of America agreed to lend the owner enough money to meet his financial obligations to the employees. Serious Materials, a California-based maker of energy-efficient windows, later bought the plant and pledged to rehire the laid-off workers.[16]

- An employer may not fire a worker simply because the individual was involved in a union organizing drive or other union activity.

- An employer may not fire a worker if this would violate an implied contract, such as a verbal promise, or basic rules of "fair dealing." For example, an employer could not legally fire a salesperson just because he or she had earned a bigger bonus under an incentive program than the employer wanted to pay.

Of course, if workers are covered by a collective bargaining agreement, it may impose additional restrictions on an employer's right to terminate. Many union contracts say

---

[16] "In Factory Sit-In, An Anger Spread Wide," *The New York Times,* December 8, 2008; and "New Owners to Reopen Window Plant, Site of a Sit-In in Chicago," *The New York Times,* February 27, 2009. The full provisions of the Worker Adjustment Retraining Notification Act are available at *www.doleta.gov/programs.*

employees can be fired only "for just cause," and workers have a right to appeal the employer's decision through the union grievance procedure. Many European countries and Japan have laws that extend "just cause" protections to all workers, whether or not they are covered by a union contract.

The commitments that employers and employees make to each other go beyond mere legal obligations, however. Cultural values, traditions, and norms of behavior also play important roles. Some have used the term **social contract** to refer to the *implied understanding* (not a legal contract, but rather a set of shared expectations) between an organization and its stakeholders. This concept includes, perhaps most significantly, the understanding between businesses and their employees.

Research suggests that the social contract governing the employment relationship has varied across cultures, and also across time. For example, in Europe, employers have historically given workers and their unions a greater role in determining company policy than do most U.S. employers. Employee representatives are often included on boards of directors, in a practice sometimes called *codetermination.* For many years, big Japanese companies offered a core group of senior workers lifelong employment; in exchange, these workers felt great loyalty to the company. This practice declined in the 1990s and early 2000s, as the Japanese economy stagnated.

> When the global recession hit Japan in 2008–2009, many employees found themselves without job security or a social safety net. By then, more than a third of the nation's workers were so-called nonregulars, hired on short-term contracts with fewer benefits and no protections against layoffs. In Japan, where workers must be employed for at least a year to get jobless benefits, many nonregulars who lost their jobs in the recession had nothing to fall back on. One worker who had been laid off from a Canon digital camera factory said, "We did our best, so Canon should have taken care of us. That is the Japanese way. But this isn't Japan anymore."[17]

In the former Soviet Union, many enterprises felt an obligation to provide social benefits, such as housing and child care, to their workers. These benefits declined with the advent of privatization in these formerly state-run economies.

Fierce global competition and greater attention to improving the bottom line have resulted in significant corporate restructuring and downsizing (termination) of employees in many countries. This trend has led some researchers to describe a *new social contract*. Increasingly, bonds between employers and employees have weakened. Companies aim to attract and retain employees not by offering long-term job security, but rather by emphasizing interesting and challenging work, performance-based compensation, and ongoing professional training. For their part, employees are expected to contribute by making a strong commitment to the job task and work team and to assume a share of responsibility for the company's success. But they cannot count on a guaranteed job.[18]

> The social contract between employers and workers was further weakened when several prominent companies cut or eliminated long-standing pension benefits. In 2008, for example, IBM froze its pension plan for current U.S. employees, meaning workers would no longer build up benefits with additional years of service, and shifted instead to a 401(k) plan. Other companies cutting defined benefit pensions, or eliminating them altogether, included such major firms as Verizon, Lockheed

[17] "In Japan, New Jobless May Lack Safety Net," *The New York Times,* February 8, 2009.

[18] James E. Post, "The New Social Contract," in Oliver Williams and John Houck, eds., *The Global Challenge to Corporate Social Responsibility* (New York: Oxford University Press, 1995).

Martin, Motorola, and General Motors. (Defined benefit pensions provide a predictable payout each month, usually based on a combination of an employee's age at retirement, years of service, and average pay.) "People just have to deal with a lot more risk in their lives, because all of these things that used to be more or less assured—a job, health care, a pension—are now variable," said one expert.[19]

According to a 2010 survey, only 17 percent of Fortune 100 companies still offered defined benefit pensions; the rest had switched to 401(k) or hybrid plans.[20]

Should companies have strong or weak bonds with their employees? When businesses invest in their employees by providing a well-structured career, job security, and benefits including pensions, they reap the rewards of enhanced loyalty, productivity, and commitment. But such investments are expensive, and long-term commitments make it hard for companies to adjust to the ups and downs of the business cycle. Some firms resolve this dilemma by employing two classes of employees: permanent workers, who enjoy stable employment and full benefits, and temporary workers and independent contractors, who do not. The U.S. Labor Department estimates that about 10 million Americans on the job, about 1 in every 14, are independent contractors. About 6 million, or 1 in every 24, are contingent workers who do not expect their jobs to last. On university campuses, to cite one example, many faculty members are part-timers who are not on a tenure (career) track and are often paid much less per course and receive fewer, if any, benefits.

Sara Horowitz, a labor lawyer, founded the Freelancers Union to serve the needs of independent workers—freelancers, consultants, temps, contingent workers, and the self-employed. This unusual labor organization grew very rapidly in the latter half of this century's first decade, attracting members by offering group health and disability insurance and other services to workers who would otherwise be on their own. "I started Freelancers Union because I believe in the radical notion of fairness," said Horowitz. "We should all have access to the social safety net, regardless of how we work."[21]

In general, during periods of economic expansion, employers are usually more willing to offer long-term commitments to workers and during periods of economic downturn are less likely to do so. In the severe recession that began in 2008, for instance, many workers were laid off, severing sometimes long-term employment relationships. However, this is not always the case. Exhibit 16.B describes a medical center that worked hard to avoid layoffs, even during a severe economic downturn. In any case, finding the right balance in the employment relationship between commitment and flexibility—within a basic context of fair dealing—remains a challenge to socially responsible companies.

Privacy in the Workplace

An important right in the workplace, as elsewhere, is privacy. Privacy can be most simply understood as the right to be left alone. In the business context, **privacy rights** refer primarily to protecting an individual's personal life from unwarranted intrusion by the employer. Many people believe, for example, that their religious and political views, their health conditions, their credit history, and what they do and say off the job are private matters and

---

[19] "More Companies Ending Promises for Retirement," *The New York Times,* January 9, 2006; "IBM to Freeze Pension Plans to Trim Costs," *The New York Times,* January 6, 2006; and "GM to Freeze Pension Plans of White-Collar Workers," *The New York Times,* March 8, 2006.

[20] Towers Watson, "2010 Defined Contribution Survey," June 2010, at *www.towerswatson.com.*

[21] *www.freelancersunion.org.*

In 2009, CEO Paul Levy of the Beth Israel Deaconess Medical Center in Boston faced a grim situation. Beth Israel, a major medical center, served three-quarters of a million people annually and employed 6,200 people in a wide range of professional and support roles. Like many businesses in the worst economic slump since the Great Depression, Beth Israel faced hard times. Reductions in government reimbursements, decisions by families to defer medical care, and a slowdown in research funding had combined to produce a $20 million budget shortfall for the fiscal year. The medical center faced the imminent prospect of laying off as many as 600 workers—adding yet another notch to the nation's unemployment rate, then 8.5 percent, the highest in a quarter-century.

Levy wanted to try a different approach. He called a series of town meetings, in which he asked for employees' support for an unusual initiative. "I'd like to do what we can to protect the low-wage earners—the transporters, the housekeepers, the food service people," he told his staff. "A lot of these people work really hard, and I don't want to put an additional burden on them. Now, if we protect these people, it means the rest of us will have to make a bigger sacrifice." He asked for their ideas.

Over the following days, Levy received thousands of e-mails, with suggestions for how the medical center could avoid layoffs. A week later, thanking the staff for their "generosity of spirit," Levy announced a series of steps—including pay cuts for top administrators, wage freezes for mid-level employees, and temporary elimination of the employer match for retirement savings plans. In addition, the heads of 13 medical departments voluntarily donated $350,000 and invited their colleagues to give more. The result was that the layoffs were pared to just 150, saving the jobs of 450 workers. Said a nurse coordinator, "Most people are willing to make a sacrifice so that our colleagues won't have to lose their jobs . . . [It] makes me glad to work here."

Sources: "How a Hospital Braces for a $20 Million Operating Loss," *The Wall Street Journal,* March 6, 2009; "A Head with a Heart," *Boston Globe,* March 12, 2009; "Sparing 450 Jobs at Beth Israel," *Boston Globe,* March 19, 2009; and "Beth Israel Finds Cure for Layoffs," *Boston Globe,* March 20, 2009. Paul Levy's reflections are available on his blog, *http://www.runningahospital.blogspot.com.* Unemployment statistics are available at *www.bls.gov.*

should be safe from snooping by the boss. Exceptions are permissible only when the employer's interests are clearly affected. For example, it may be appropriate for the boss to know that an employee is discussing with a competitor, through e-mail messages, the specifications of a newly developed product not yet on the market.

But other areas are not so clear-cut. For example, should a job applicant who is experiencing severe financial problems be denied employment out of fear that he may be more inclined to steal from the company? Should an employee be terminated after the firm discovers that she has a serious medical problem, although it does not affect her job performance, since the company's health insurance premiums may dramatically increase? At what point do company interests weigh more heavily than an employee's right to privacy? This section will address several key workplace issues where these privacy dilemmas often emerge: electronic monitoring, office romance, drug and alcohol abuse, and honesty testing.

Electronic Monitoring

As discussed in Chapters 12 and 13, changing technologies have brought many ethical issues to the forefront. One such issue is employee **electronic monitoring**. A wide range of technologies—e-mail and messaging, social media sites, voice mail, cell phones, GPS tracking, Internet browsing, and digitally stored video—enable companies to gather, store, and monitor information about employees' activities. A company's need for information, particularly about its workers, may be at odds with an employee's right to privacy.

A police officer in Ontario, California, sued his employer, saying his Fourth Amendment rights against unreasonable search and seizure had been violated. The police department had reviewed transcripts of text messages the officer had sent on an employer-issued device, including highly personal ones sent to his wife and mistress. But the Supreme Court disagreed, saying that as a government employee, the officer should not have expected that messages sent using government equipment would be private.[22]

Employee monitoring has grown in recent years, reflecting technological advances that make surveillance of employees easier and more affordable. According to a survey by the American Management Association, two-thirds of U.S. firms monitored workers' Internet usage and used software to block their access to inappropriate sites, such as ones used for social networking, shopping, or entertainment. About half stored and reviewed employees' e-mail messages and computer files. Smaller proportions used GPS technology to track company vehicles (8 percent) and cell phones (3 percent). "Workers' e-mail and other electronically stored information create written business records that are the electronic equivalent of DNA evidence," said the executive director of the ePolicy Institute.[23] These programs can be customized to the industry; for example, a hospital might scan for "patient info"; a high-tech company with proprietary technology might scan for a competitor's name or phone number.

Management justifies the increase in employee monitoring for a number of reasons. Employers have an interest in efficiency. When employees log on to the Internet at work to trade stocks, plan their vacations, chat with friends—or text-message their wives or mistresses, as in the Ontario example—this is not a productive use of their time. Employers also fear lawsuits if employees act in inappropriate ways. An employee who views pornographic pictures on a computer at work, for example, might leave the company open to a charge of sexual harassment—if other workers observed this behavior and were offended by it. (Sexual harassment is further discussed in the following chapter.) The employer also needs to make sure that employees do not disclose confidential information to competitors or make statements that would publicly embarrass the company or its officers. And monitoring is often used for training and quality control purposes.

Is electronic monitoring by employers legal? For the most part, yes. The Electronic Communications Privacy Act (1986) exempts employers. In general, the courts have found that privacy rights apply to personal, but not business, information, and that employers have a right to monitor job-related communication. In an important 1996 case, an employee sued his employer after he was fired for deriding the sales team in an internal e-mail, referring to them as "back-stabbing bastards." The court sided with the company, saying it owned the e-mail system and had a right to examine its contents. Yet, some have criticized recent court decisions like this one, saying public policy should do a better job of protecting employees from unwarranted secret surveillance.[24]

In seeking to balance their employees' concerns about privacy with their own concerns about productivity, liability, and security, businesses face a difficult challenge. One approach is to monitor employee communication only when there is a specific reason to do so, such as poor productivity or suspicion of theft. For example, the chipmaker Intel Corporation chose not to check its employees' e-mail routinely, feeling this would undermine

---

[22] "Privacy in the Cellular Age," *The New York Times,* June 18, 2010.

[23] American Management Association, "2007 Electronic Monitoring & Surveillance Survey," *www.amanet.org.*

[24] A summary of the law with respect to employee monitoring may be found in "Fact Sheet 7: Workplace Privacy and Employee Monitoring," at the website of the Privacy Rights Clearinghouse at *www.privacyrights.org.*

trust. Most management experts recommend that employers, at the very least, clearly define their monitoring policies, let employees know what behavior is expected, and apply any sanctions in a fair and evenhanded way.

Romance in the Workplace

Another issue that requires careful balancing between legitimate employer concerns and employee privacy is romance in the workplace. People have always dated others at work. In fact, a 2011 survey showed that 38 percent of workers said they had dated a coworker at least once during their careers, and of these relationships almost a third had led to marriage.[25] In fact, workplace dating has probably become more common as the average age of marriage has risen. (For women, that age is now around 26; for men, around 28.) Said one human resources director, "It's a reality that work is where people meet these days. When you don't meet at college, that's a pool of people that's taken away from you."[26] Yet office romance poses problems for employers. If the relationship goes sour, one of the people may sue, charging sexual harassment—that is, that he or she was coerced into the relationship. When one person in a relationship is in a position of authority, he or she may be biased in an evaluation of the other's work, or others may perceive it to be so.

For many years, most businesses had a strict policy of forbidding relationships in the workplace, especially those between managers and those reporting to them. They assumed that if romance blossomed, one person—usually the subordinate—would have to find another job. Today, however, most companies try to manage office relationships, rather than ban them outright. Southwest Airlines, for example, does not allow workers to report directly to someone with whom they are romantically involved. If a relationship develops, it is up to the people involved to come forward and to change assignments if necessary. A few companies require their managers to sign a document, sometimes called a *consensual relationship agreement,* stipulating that an office relationship is welcome and voluntary— to protect against possible harassment lawsuits if the people involved later break up.

Employee Drug Use and Testing

Abuse of drugs, both illegal drugs such as heroin and methamphetamine and legal drugs such as Oxycontin or Xanax when used inappropriately, can be a serious problem for employers. Only a small fraction of employees abuse illegal or prescription drugs. But those who do can cause serious harm. They are much more likely than others to produce poor-quality work, have accidents that hurt themselves and others, and steal from their employers. Some break the law by selling drugs at work to support their habits. Drug abuse costs U.S. industry and taxpayers an estimated $181 billion a year. This figure includes the cost of lost productivity, medical claims, rehabilitation services, and crime and accidents caused by drugs.[27]

One way business has protected itself from these risks is through **drug testing**. About two-thirds of companies test employees or job applicants for illegal substances, according to a 2011 study.[28] Significant drug testing first began in the United States following passage of the Drug-Free Workplace Act of 1988, which required federal contractors to establish and maintain a workplace free of drugs. At that time, many companies and public agencies initiated drug testing to comply with government rules. The use of drug tests has fallen somewhat in the past decade, as fewer people have tested positive. (The one class of drugs whose

[25] "Nearly One-Third of Workers Who Had Office Romance Married Their Co-Worker, Finds Annual CareerBuilder Valentine's Day Survey," press release, February 9, 2012, at *www.careerbuilder.com.*

[26] "Love on the Job: Breaking the Taboo at Bay Area Companies," *San Francisco Chronicle,* November 11, 2007.

[27] "Consequences of Illicit Drug Use in America," December 2010, at *www.whitehousedrugpolicy.gov.*

[28] "2011 HireRight Employment Screening Benchmark Report," at *http://hireright.com/benchmarking.*

use has recently risen is prescription opiates—medicines such as hydrocodone that are used to treat pain.)[29]

Typically, drug testing is used on three different occasions.

- *Preemployment screening.* Some companies test all job applicants or selected applicants before hiring, usually as part of a physical examination, often informing the applicant ahead of time that there will be a drug screening.
- *Random testing of employees.* This type of screening may occur at various times throughout the year. In many companies, workers in particular job categories (e.g., operators of heavy machinery) or levels (e.g., supervisors) are eligible for screening at any time.
- *Testing for cause.* This test occurs when an employee is believed to be impaired by drugs and unfit for work. It is commonly used after a work-related accident or some observable change in behavior.

An emerging issue is whether or not employers may terminate workers for testing positive for marijuana in states that permit its medical use. In 2011, a court in Washington upheld the decision of TeleTech Customer Care, a firm that handles customer service for Sprint, to fire an employee who failed a drug test, even though she had a valid prescription for medical marijuana. Some states, including Arizona and Montana, have passed "safe harbor" laws that shield employers from liability if they discipline workers who were impaired during work hours because of legal medical marijuana use.[30]

Employee drug testing is controversial. Although businesses have an interest in not hiring, or getting rid of, people who abuse drugs, many job applicants and employees who have never used drugs feel that testing is unnecessary and violates their privacy and due process rights. The debate over employee drug testing is summarized in Figure 16.2. In general, proponents of testing emphasize the need to reduce potential harm to other people and the cost to business and society of drug use on the job. Opponents challenge the benefits of drug testing and emphasize its intrusion on individual privacy.

Alcohol Abuse at Work

Another form of employee substance abuse—which causes twice the problems of all illegal drugs combined—is alcohol use and addiction. About 9 percent of full-time employees are heavy drinkers—that is, they had five or more drinks on five or more occasions in the past month. Like drug abusers, they can be dangerous to themselves and others. Studies show that up to 40 percent of all industrial fatalities and 47 percent of industrial injuries are linked to alcohol. The problem is not just hard-core alcoholics, however. Most alcohol-related problems in the workplace, one study found, were caused by people who occasionally drank too much after work and came in the next day with a hangover, or who went out for a drink on their lunch break. U.S. businesses lose an estimated $88 billion per year in reduced productivity directly related to alcohol abuse.[31]

---

[29] "Drug Testing Poses Quandary for Employers," *The New York Times,* October 24, 2010.

[30] "You Can Be Fired for Using Medical Marijuana, Justices Rule," *Seattle Times,* June 9, 2011; and "Current Practices and Issues in Workplace Drug Testing," *IOFM Security Director's Report,* November 2011, at *www.iofm.com/security.*

[31] The statistics reported in this paragraph are from the U.S. Substance Abuse and Mental Health Services Administration (SAMHSA), "Worker Substance Use and Workplace Policies and Programs," June 2007, and "Issue Brief for Employers: Save Money By Addressing Employee Alcohol Problems," both at *www.samhsa.gov;* 10th Annual Report to the U.S. Congress on Alcohol and Health, at *http://pubs.niaaa.nih.gov/publications/10report/intro.pdf;* and the website of the National Drug-Free Workplace Alliance at *www.ndwa.org.*

FIGURE 16.2

Pros and Cons of Employee Drug Testing

Arguments Favoring Employee Drug Testing	Arguments Opposing Employee Drug Testing
• Supports U.S. policy to reduce illegal drug use and availability • Improves employee productivity • Promotes safety in the workplace • Decreases employee theft and absenteeism • Reduces health and insurance costs	• Invades an employee's privacy • Violates an employee's right to due process • May be unrelated to job performance • May be used as a method of employee discrimination • Lowers employee morale • Conflicts with company values of honesty and trust • May yield unreliable test results • Ignores effects of prescription drugs, alcohol, and over-the-counter drugs • Drug use an insignificant problem for some companies

Company programs for drug abusers and alcohol abusers are often combined. Many firms recognize that they have a role to play in helping alcoholic employees. As with drug rehabilitation programs, most alcoholism programs work through **employee assistance programs (EAPs)** that offer counseling and follow-up. Almost all U.S. companies employing 5,000 or more workers provide EAPs for alcohol and drug abusers. Even small companies (employing 50 to 99) are involved; two-thirds now offer assistance, often by contracting with outside vendors.[32]

Employee Theft and Honesty Testing

Employees can irresponsibly damage themselves, their coworkers, and their employer by stealing from the company. Employee theft has emerged as a significant economic, social, and ethical problem in the workplace. A 2010 survey of large retail stores in the United States showed that 44 percent of all inventory losses were due to employee theft (shoplifting, administrative error, and vendor fraud accounted for the rest). The value of goods stolen by employees was more than $16 billion.[33]

Employee theft is also a problem in other parts of the world, as well. According to the 2011 Global Retail Theft Barometer, so-called retail crime (employee theft, shoplifting, and customer, supplier, and vendor fraud) costs European, North American, and Asian-Pacific businesses around $119 billion annually, or about 1.5 percent of sales. Of this, 35 percent was due to employee theft. The items most commonly stolen were clothing, accessories, groceries, and health and beauty products.[34]

Many companies in the past used polygraph testing (lie detectors) as a preemployment screening procedure or on discovery of employee theft. In 1988, the Employee Polygraph Protection Act became law. This law severely limited polygraph testing by employers and

---

[32] Families and Work Institute, "2012 National Study of Employers," at *http://familiesandwork.org.*

[33] Richard C. Hollinger and Amanda Adams, *2010 National Retail Security Survey* (Gainesville, FL: University of Florida, 2010).

[34] These data are for the 12-month period ending June 2011. The Global Retail Theft Barometer is available at *http://globalretailtheftbarometer.com.*

prohibited approximately 85 percent of all such tests previously administered in the United States. In response to the federal ban on polygraphs, many corporations have switched to written psychological tests that seek to predict employee honesty on the job by asking questions designed to identify desirable or undesirable qualities. When a British chain of home improvement centers used such tests to screen more than 4,000 applicants, theft dropped from 4 percent to 2.5 percent, and actual losses from theft were reduced from £3.75 million to £2.62 million.

The use of **honesty tests**, however, like polygraphs, is controversial. The American Psychological Association noted there is a significant potential for these tests to generate false positives, indicating the employee probably would or did steal from the company even though this is not true. Critics also argue that the tests intrude on a person's privacy and discriminate disproportionately against minorities.

In all these areas—monitoring employees electronically, policing office romance, testing for drugs, and conducting psychological tests—businesses must balance their needs to operate safely, ethically, and efficiently with their employees' right to privacy.

Whistle-Blowing and Free Speech in the Workplace

Another area where employer and employee rights and duties frequently conflict involves free speech. Do employees have the right to openly express their opinions about their company and its actions? If so, under what conditions do they have this right?

The U.S. Constitution protects the right to free speech. This means the government cannot take away this right. For example, the legislature cannot shut down a newspaper that editorializes against its actions or those of its members. However, the Constitution does not explicitly protect freedom of expression in the workplace. Generally, employees are not free to speak out against their employers, since companies have a legitimate interest in operating without harassment from insiders. Company information is generally considered to be proprietary and private. If employees, based on their personal points of view, were freely allowed to expose issues to the public and allege misconduct, a company might be thrown into turmoil and be unable to operate effectively.

On the other hand, there may be situations in which society's interests override those of the company, so an employee may feel an obligation to speak out. When an employee believes his or her employer has done something that is wrong or harmful to the public, and he or she reports alleged organizational misconduct to the media, government, or high-level company officials, **whistle-blowing** has occurred.

> A recent example of a whistle-blower was Michael Winston, a former executive at Countrywide Financial Corporation with responsibility for leadership development. Countrywide, which was later acquired by Bank of America, was a leading subprime lender during the housing boom of the first decade of this century. Winston had complained vigorously to the chief production officer about the company's strategy of funding almost all loans, whether or not the borrower was qualified. "I told him that you need to focus on customer satisfaction, on the quality of the loan portfolio, and on building leaders who would focus their people on that," Winston recalled. "I wrote him a very comprehensive memo." Soon afterwards, Winston's budget was cut, he was excluded from meetings, and his office was relocated. Eventually, he was fired. In 2011, he won a lawsuit against his former employer. "It [was] the littlest of Davids beating the biggest of Goliaths," said Winston.[35]

Other whistle-blowers are described in Exhibit 16.C.

[35] "How a Whistle-Blower Conquered Countrywide," *The New York Times,* February 19, 2011.

In 2009, Eli Lilly, a leading pharmaceutical company, paid $1.4 billion to settle charges that it had illegally marketed its drug Zyprexa—one of the biggest amounts ever in a case arising from allegations made by company whistle-blowers.

Zyprexa was one of a class of drugs known as atypical antipsychotics. The Food and Drug Administration (FDA) first approved Zyprexa in 1996 for the treatment of psychosis and later for schizophrenia and bipolar disorder—all serious psychiatric illnesses—in adults. Government scientists also found that the drug had potentially dangerous side effects, including weight gain, metabolic disorders, and heart failure. Under U.S. law, doctors may prescribe a medication in any way they choose, but drug makers are explicitly prohibited from marketing their products for any uses that have not been approved by the FDA.

In the early 2000s, several Lilly sales representatives came forward, charging that the company had organized an illegal nationwide campaign to convince doctors to prescribe Zyprexa for unapproved uses, particularly for the elderly in long-term care facilities. Under the slogan "5 at 5," the marketing campaign suggested that 5 mg of the drug (which was known to have a sedating effect) be given at 5 p.m. to control agitation, anxiety, and insomnia in older patients, particularly those with Alzheimer's or other forms of dementia. Explained the whistle-blowers' lawyer, "this potent antipsychotic was essentially used as a 'chemical restraint' for the elderly for whom [it] had no other health benefit." The company also promoted the drug for treating disruptive children.

Lilly's strategy was very effective. Since the drug's introduction, the company had sold $39 billion worth of Zyprexa, which cost as much as $25 for a daily pill. Forty percent of these sales were for off-label uses, investigators found. The company's illegal marketing, the government concluded, had generated hundreds of millions of dollars in profit, much of it paid for by taxpayers in the form of Medicare and Medicaid reimbursements. The government did not estimate the number of children, elders, and others who were harmed by dangerous or inappropriate medication. Nine whistle-blowers—several of whom had been fired by Lilly after complaining—shared $79 million of the settlement.

Sources: "Eli Lilly Pays a Record $1.4 Billion to Settle Federal and State Fraud Investigations into Illegal Zyprexa Off-Label Marketing Practices," *Biotech Business Week,* January 26, 2009; "Settlement Called Near on Zyprexa," *The New York Times,* January 15, 2009; and "Justice Department Beats Chest over Zyprexa Settlement," *The Wall Street Journal Health Blog,* January 15, 2009. Many of the legal documents from the case are available at *www.usdoj.gov/usao/pae/eli_lilly.html.*

Speaking out against an employer can be risky; many whistle-blowers find their charges ignored—or worse, find themselves ostracized, demoted, or even fired for daring to go public with their criticisms. Whistle-blowers in the United States have some legal protection against retaliation by their employers, though. As noted earlier in this chapter, most workers are employed *at will,* meaning they can be fired for any reason. However, most states now recognize a public policy exception to this rule. Employees who are discharged in retaliation for blowing the whistle, in a situation that affects public welfare, may sue for reinstatement and in some cases may even be entitled to punitive damages. The federal Sarbanes-Oxley Act, passed in 2002 (and described more fully in Chapters 4 and 14), makes it illegal for employers to retaliate in any way against whistle-blowers who report information that could have an impact on the value of a company's shares. More recently, the Dodd-Frank Act of 2010 (described more fully in Chapters 8 and 14) requires the government to pay a reward to whistle-blowers who voluntarily provide information that leads to successful prosecutions for violations of federal securities laws. Dodd-Frank also prohibits retaliation against employees who do so.[36]

[36] "SEC Approves New Rewards for Whistleblowers," *Washington Post,* May 25, 2011; and Securities and Exchange Commission, "Implementation of the Whistleblower Provisions of Section 21F of the Securities Exchange Act of 1934," August 12, 2011, at *www.sec.gov.*

Moreover, whistle-blowers sometimes benefit from their actions. The U.S. False Claims Act (also known as the Lincoln Law), as amended in 1986, allows individuals who sue federal contractors for fraud to receive up to 30 percent of any amount recovered by the government. In the past decade, the number of whistle-blower lawsuits—perhaps spurred by this incentive—increased significantly, exposing fraud in the country's defense, health care, municipal bond, and pharmaceutical industries. A case in which whistle-blowers and their attorneys used this law to launch a major case against Eli Lilly for illegal drug marketing is described in Exhibit 16.C.

Whistle-blowing has both defenders and detractors. Defenders point to the successful detection of fraudulent activities and prosecution of wrongdoers. Under the False Claims Act, through 2012 $34 billion had been recovered that would otherwise have been lost to fraud.[37] Situations dangerous to the public or the environment have been exposed and corrected because insiders have spoken out. Yet opponents cite hundreds of unsubstantiated cases, often involving disgruntled workers seeking to blackmail or discredit their employers.

When is an employee morally justified in blowing the whistle on his or her employer? According to one expert, four main conditions must be satisfied to justify informing the media or government officials about a corporation's actions. These are:

- The organization is doing (or will do) something that seriously harms others.
- The employee has tried and failed to resolve the problem internally.
- Reporting the problem publicly will probably stop or prevent the harm.
- The harm is serious enough to justify the probable costs of disclosure to the whistle-blower and others.[38]

Only after each of these conditions has been met should the whistle-blower go public.

Working Conditions around the World

Much of this chapter has focused on the employment relationship, and the legal and ethical norms governing it, in the United States. Workplace institutions differ dramatically around the world. Laws and practices that establish fair wages, acceptable working conditions, and employee rights vary greatly from region to region. As illustrated in an earlier example in this chapter that described a Nike contract factory in Indonesia, these differences pose a challenge to multinational corporations. By whose standards should these companies operate?

Recent headlines have turned the public's attention to the problem of **sweatshops**, factories where employees, sometimes including children, are forced to work long hours at low wages, often under unsafe working conditions. Several well-known companies in addition to Nike, including Walmart, Disney, and McDonald's, have been criticized for tolerating abhorrent working conditions in their overseas factories or those of their contractors. In recent years, student groups have pressured companies by rallying to prevent their colleges and universities from buying school-logo athletic gear, clothing, and other products made under sweatshop conditions.

Fair Labor Standards

The term *labor standards* refers to the conditions under which a company's employees—or the employees of its suppliers, subcontractors, or others in its commercial chain—work. Some believe that labor standards should be universal; that is, companies should conform to

---

[37] U.S. Department of Justice statistics, summarized at the website of Taxpayers against Fraud, *www.taf.org.*

[38] Manuel G. Velasquez, *Business Ethics: Concepts and Cases,* 7th ed. (Upper Saddle River, NJ: Pearson, 2012), p. 430.

common norms across all their operations worldwide. Such universal rules are sometimes called **fair labor standards**. For example, such standards might include a ban on all child labor, establishment of maximum work hours per week, or a commitment to pay a wage above a certain level. Others think that what is fair varies across cultures and economies, and it is often difficult to set standards that are workable in all settings. For example, in some cultures child labor is more acceptable (or economically necessary) than in others. A wage that would be utterly inadequate in one economic setting might seem princely in another. In some countries, unions are legal and common; in others, they are illegal or actively discouraged.

In the face of growing concerns over working conditions overseas, a debate has developed over how best to establish fair labor standards for multinational corporations. Several approaches have emerged.

Voluntary *corporate codes of conduct,* described in detail in Chapter 5, can include labor standards that companies expect their own plants and those of their contractors to follow. One of the first companies to develop such standards was Levi Strauss, a U.S. apparel maker. After the company was accused of using an unethical contractor in Saipan, the company reviewed its procedures and adopted a wide-ranging set of guidelines for its overseas manufacturing. Reebok, Boeing, Mattel, and other companies have followed suit.

Nongovernmental organizations (NGOs) labor codes have also been attempted. For example, the Council on Economic Priorities has developed a set of workplace rules called Social Accountability 8000, or SA 8000. Modeled after the quality initiative of the International Organization for Standardization, ISO 9000, SA 8000 establishes criteria for companies to meet in order to receive a "good working condition" certification. Other groups, including the International Labour Organization, the Caux Roundtable, and the United Nations, have also worked to define common standards to which companies can voluntarily subscribe. Some of these efforts are further described in Chapter 7.

Yet a third approach is *industrywide labor codes.* Groups of companies, sometimes with participation of government officials, NGOs, and worker and consumer representatives, define industrywide standards that they can all agree to. For example, many leading high-tech companies, including HP, Dell, Cisco, and Microsoft, have joined forces as the Electronic Industry Citizenship Coalition to establish a code of conduct that provides a uniform set of labor, health and safety, and environmental standards for their global supply chains.[39] Supporters said a common code would likely improve supplier compliance and lower the costs of training and monitoring.

Whatever the approach, certain common questions emerge in any attempt to define and enforce fair labor standards. These questions include the following.

- *What wage level is fair?* Some argue that market forces should set wages, as long as they do not fall below the level established by local minimum wage laws. Others feel that they should pay workers a fair share of the sale price of the product or of the company's profit. Still others argue that companies have a moral obligation to pay workers enough to achieve a decent family standard of living; this is called a **living wage**.

Exhibit 16.D further explains this concept and profiles several businesses that share a commitment to paying their employees a living wage.

- *Should standards apply just to the firm's own employees, or to all workers who have a hand in making its products?* Some say that while the responsibility of a firm to its own employees is clear, its responsibility to the employees of its subcontractors is indirect and therefore of lower importance. Other firms have embraced their responsibility for

---

[39] The code is available at *www.eicc.info/documents/EICCCodeofConductEnglish.pdf.*

Exhibit 16.D

Paying a Living Wage

The Ethical Trading Initiative (ETI), an alliance of companies, nongovernmental organizations, and unions, has defined a living wage as "a wage that allows a worker to provide for him or herself and family, to buy essential medicines, to send children to school, and to save for the future." ETI has called on companies around the world, big and small, to commit to paying all employees a living wage. The following are among those that have done so.

When *Novartis,* a major multinational pharmaceutical firm, committed to pay a living wage to all its employees around the world, it faced the daunting task of figuring out what exactly that would mean. The company brought in outside NGOs to help it estimate a "basic needs basket" of goods and services in the many nations where it operated. By 2006, it had met its goal of paying living wages to all 93,000 employees. "No other companies are doing this locally," said a company manager in Pakistan. "I can proudly say . . . that we are not just a profit-making business."

New Look, a fashion retailer based in the United Kingdom, partnered with its suppliers in Bangladesh to raise wages as part of a project sponsored by the ETI. In the first year, wages for machine operators increased 24 percent. This made a huge difference in the lives of the Bangladeshi workers, many of whom had had to pay up to 70 percent of their pay for rice and other basic foodstuffs. The company also worked to improve its forecasts, reducing last-minute changes in orders that had wreaked havoc on the factory's ability to schedule workers' hours.

By 2012, more than 100 cities and counties in the United States—including Detroit, Los Angeles, Denver, and Boston—had adopted laws that required public employers (and ones supported by taxpayer money) to pay a living wage, even if this was higher than the prevailing minimum wage.

Sources: Ethical Trading Initiative, "Living Wage: Make It a Reality," and "New Look and Echo Sourcing Work on Wages," June 23, 2009, at *www.ethicaltrade.org;* "Implementing a Living Wage Globally—The Novartis Approach," at *www.novartis.com/downloads/corporate-responsibility/responsible-business-practices/living-wage.pdf;* and "Interview with Mark Brenner: Living Wage Laws in Practice: The Boston, New Haven, and Hartford Experiences," at *www.peri.umass.edu.*

standards through the supply chain. The Gap, for example, requires factories that produce its branded apparel to pledge in writing to follow labor standards outlined in the company's code of vendor conduct.

- *How should fair labor standards best be enforced?* Adherence to fair labor standards, unlike national labor laws, for example, is strictly voluntary. Companies can adopt their own code, or agree to one of the NGO or industry codes. But who is to say that they, and their contractors, are actually living up to these rules? In response to this concern, a debate has emerged over how best to monitor and enforce fair labor standards. Some have advocated hiring outside accounting firms, academic experts, or advocacy organizations to conduct independent audits to determine if a code's standards are being met.

As businesses have become more and more global, as shown in Chapter 6, companies have faced the challenge of operating simultaneously in many countries that differ widely in their working conditions. For these companies, abiding by government regulations and local cultural traditions in their overseas manufacturing may not be enough. Many business leaders have realized that subscribing to fair labor standards that commit to common norms of fairness, respect, and dignity for all their workers is an effective strategy for enhancing their corporate reputations, as well as meeting the complex global challenges of corporate social responsibility.

Employees as Corporate Stakeholders

The issues discussed in this chapter illustrate forcefully that today's business corporation is open to a wide range of social forces. Its borders are very porous, letting in a constant flow of external influences. Many are brought inside by employees, whose personal values, lifestyles, and social attitudes become a vital part of the workplace.

Managers and other business professionals need to be aware of these employee-imported features of today's workforce. The employment relationship is central both to getting a corporation's work done and to helping satisfy the aspirations of those who contribute their skills and talents to the company.

Summary

- U.S. labor laws give most workers the right to organize unions and to bargain collectively with their employers. Although unions have weakened over time, they continue to represent workers in some parts of the economy, particularly in the public sector.

- Job safety and health concerns have increased as a result of rapidly changing technology in the workplace. U.S. employers must comply with expanding OSHA regulations and respond to the threat of violence at work.

- Employers' right to discharge "at will" has been limited, and employees now have a number of bases for suing for wrongful discharge. The expectations of both sides in the employment relationship have been altered over time by globalization, business cycles, and other factors.

- Employees' privacy rights are frequently challenged by employers' needs to have information about their health, their work activities, and even their off-the-job lifestyles. When these issues arise, management has a responsibility to act ethically toward employees while continuing to work for a high level of economic performance.

- Blowing the whistle on one's employer is often a last resort to protest company actions considered harmful to others. In recent years, U.S. legislation has extended new protections to whistle-blowers.

- The growing globalization of business has challenged companies to adopt fair labor standards to ensure that their products are not manufactured under substandard, sweatshop conditions.

Key Terms

drug testing, *367*
electronic monitoring, *365*
employee assistance programs (EAPs), *369*
employment-at-will, *362*
ergonomics, *360*
fair labor standards, *373*

honesty tests, *370*
labor union, *358*
living wage, *373*
Occupational Safety and Health Administration (OSHA), *361*

privacy rights, *364*
social contract, *363*
sweatshops, *372*
whistle-blowing, *370*

Internet Resources

www.ilo.org	International Labour Organization (ILO)
www.drugfreeworkplace.org	Institute for a Drug-Free Workplace
www.osha.gov	Occupational Safety and Health Administration
www.whistleblowers.org	National Whistleblowers Center
www.aclu.org	American Civil Liberties Union
www.afl-cio.org	American Federation of Labor-Congress of Industrial Organizations
www.workrights.org	National Workrights Institute
www.business.com/human-resources	Business.com (human resources topics)
http://www.state.gov/j/drl/	U.S. State Department, Bureau of Democracy, Human Rights, and Labor
www.ethicaltrade.org	Ethical Trading Initiative

Discussion Case: *No Smoking Allowed—On the Job or Off*

In 2012, Pennsylvania's Geisinger Health System adopted a new policy: it would no longer hire smokers. The hospital system had already banned smoking on the job, but this policy went further by saying it would not employ anyone who used tobacco products, even if they indulged their habit only off the job and on their own time. Applicants who had been offered a position would have to take a urine test to screen for nicotine. If they failed, they would be allowed to apply again in six months. Smokers who already worked for Geisinger would not lose their jobs.

"We're trying to promote a culture of wellness," said a representative of Geisinger, explaining the hospital system's change of policy. "We're not denying smokers their right to tobacco products. We're just choosing not to hire them."

Geisinger was just the most recent of a large number of health care institutions and insurers—including the Cleveland Clinic in Ohio, Baylor Health Care System in Texas, Humana Inc. in Arizona, and Anna Jacques Hospital in Massachusetts—to ban not just smoking, but smokers. "This is quite a trend. Hospital systems throughout the country are doing this increasingly," said a public health expert.

Other employers, while not refusing to hire smokers, had begun charging them more for health insurance. For example, in 2011 Macy's began charging employees who used tobacco products an extra $420 a year. A 2011 survey found than 19 percent of major U.S. employers—including such well-known names as PepsiCo, Safeway, Home Depot, and General Mills—imposed financial penalties on smokers. Some thought this trend would accelerate, since under the health care reform legislation passed in 2010, employers with particularly expensive health plans would be penalized with extra federal taxes.

By 2012, most U.S. employers—either acting voluntarily or because they were forced to by local and state antismoking laws—had banned smoking on the job or restricted it to a few separate areas. The health reasons for doing so were compelling. Secondhand smoke—smoke emitted from a lit cigarette, cigar, or pipe, or exhaled by a smoker—caused more than 50,000 nonsmoker deaths in the United States each year, according to medical research. Nonsmoking employees could be sickened, or even killed, by exposure to others' tobacco smoke at work, particularly in workplaces where smoking was common, such as hotels, bars, and restaurants.

Advocates offered several reasons for going further and banning or actively discouraging smoking off the job. Employees who used tobacco products were more expensive. Smokers, on average, cost their employers $1,800 more per year in health care costs, and lost twice as much production time, as nonsmokers. Some employers also gave a noneconomic argument: that they wanted their workers to set a good example. The CEO of the Cleveland Clinic, for example, explained his organization's policy not to hire smokers this way: "If we are to be advocates of healthy living and disease prevention, we need to be role models for our patients, our communities, and each other. In other words, if we are going to talk the talk, we need to walk the walk."

For their part, employees who smoked were divided in their reaction to tobacco restrictions or bans. Some smokers welcomed the pressure to quit. A study by researchers at the University of California found that employees who were covered by strong workplace smoking policies were more likely to quit the habit than other smokers. But others disagreed, calling employment restrictions and higher insurance charges discriminatory and unfair. Some were incensed at what they perceived as a violation of personal rights and freedoms. Some even argued that smoking was, in effect, an addiction to nicotine, and so their right to smoke should be protected under the Americans with Disabilities Act (further described in the following chapter).

The National Workrights Institute, a group promoting civil liberties, expressed concern that refusing to hire smokers could lead to other forms of discrimination. The institute's president pointed out, "There is nothing unique about smoking. The number of things we all do privately that have a negative effect on our health is endless. If it's not smoking, it's beer. If it's not beer, it's cheeseburgers."

Lawmakers weighed in on both sides of the issue. Many towns and cities, 23 states, the District of Columbia, Puerto Rico, and the Virgin Islands passed antismoking ordinances or laws that banned smoking in enclosed workplaces. But 29 states (sometimes the same ones) also passed laws making job discrimination against smokers illegal. Although these laws did not affect smoking bans or restrictions in the workplace, they did prohibit companies from refusing to hire smokers or from firing employees who continued to smoke. (Pennsylvania, where Geisinger was located, did not have such a law.)

Many other countries had historically been more tolerant of smoking, both in the workplace and elsewhere, than the United States. This had begun to change, however. By 2012, 168 countries had signed the World Health Organization's Framework Convention on Tobacco Control. Among other things, the convention called on governments to protect people from workplace exposure to secondhand smoke.

Sources: "Workplaces Ban Not Only Smoking, But Smokers," *USA Today,* January 6, 2012; "The Smokers' Surcharge," *The New York Times,* November 16, 2011; "Companies Get Tougher with Employees Who Smoke," *Bloomberg Businessweek,* June 30, 2011; "Hospitals Shift Smoking Bans to Smoker Ban," *The New York Times,* February 10, 2011; "A Message about Smoking," *http://myclevelandclinic.org/tobacco;* "Effect of Smoking Status on Productivity Loss," *Journal of Occupational and Environmental Medicine,* October 2006; and "UC Study Says Workplace Smoking Ordinances Help Employees Quit," *Cal-OSHA Reporter,* May 5, 2000. The website of the Framework Convention on Tobacco Control is at *www.who.int/tobacco/framework.* Other statistics are available at *www.cdc.gov/tobacco; http://no-smoke.org;* and *www.tobaccofreekids.org.*

Discussion Questions

1. Should employers have the right to ban or restrict smoking by their employees at the workplace? Why do you think so?

2. Should employers have the right to restrict or ban smoking by their employees off the job, or charge smoking employees more for health insurance? Why do you think so?

3. Should the government regulate smoking at work? If so, what would be the best public policy? Why do you think so?

4. Should multinational firms have a single corporate policy on smoking in the workplace, or vary their policies depending on local laws and norms of behavior in various countries where they do business?

Managing a Diverse Workforce

The workforce in the United States is more diverse than it has ever been, reflecting the entry of women into the workforce, immigration from other countries, the aging of the population, and shifting patterns of work and retirement. Equal opportunity laws and changing societal expectations have challenged corporations to manage workforce diversity effectively. Full workplace parity for women and persons of color has not yet been reached. However, businesses have made great strides in reforming policies and practices in order to draw on the skills and contributions of their increasingly varied employees.

This Chapter Focuses on These Key Learning Objectives:

- Knowing in what ways the workforce of the United States is diverse, and evaluating how it might change in the future.
- Understanding where women and persons of color work, how much they are paid, and the roles they play as managers and business owners.
- Identifying the role government plays in securing equal employment opportunity for historically disadvantaged groups, and debating whether or not affirmative action is an effective strategy for promoting equal opportunity.
- Assessing the ways diversity confers a competitive advantage.
- Formulating how companies can best manage workforce diversity, making the workplace welcoming, fair, and accommodating to all employees.
- Understanding what policies and practices are most effective in helping today's employees manage the complex, multiple demands of work and family obligations.

Marriott International, the global hospitality chain, employs 151,000 workers in 73 countries, doing jobs ranging from managing vacation resorts, to flipping burgers, to cleaning bathrooms and changing sheets. Their employees speak more than 50 different languages and represent dozens of distinct cultures. Many of Marriott's employees in the United States are immigrants, some are in welfare-to-work programs, and many are single parents. A large proportion work nights or odd hours. In an effort to address its employees' needs, Marriott established a Committee of Excellence—an external board of experts—to set diversity objectives and monitor progress. Among other initiatives, the company provided consultations on a wide range of personal issues, offered child care services, and operated *Sed de Saber* (thirst for knowledge) to teach life skills to Spanish-speaking employees. Marriott credited its innovative programs with helping it attract and retain committed employees from many backgrounds. "We strive to create an inclusive environment," said senior diversity executive David Rodriguez. "When our associates feel respected and valued, we know that they'll make our guests, suppliers, owners, and franchisees feel the same way too."[1]

The example of Marriott Corporation demonstrates both the promise and the perils of a workforce that encompasses tremendous diversity on every imaginable dimension. Having many different kinds of workers can be a great benefit to businesses, as it gives them a wider pool from which to recruit talent, many points of view and experiences, and an ability to reach out effectively to a diverse, global customer base. Yet, it also poses great challenges, as business must meet the mandates of equal employment laws and help people who differ greatly in their backgrounds, values, and expectations get along—and succeed—in the workplace.

The Changing Face of the Workforce

Human beings differ from each other in many ways. Each person is unique, as is each employee within an organization. Individuals are also similar in many ways, some of which are more readily visible than others. The term **diversity** refers to variation in the important human characteristics that distinguish people from one another. The *primary* dimensions of diversity are age, ethnicity, gender, mental or physical abilities, race, and sexual orientation. The *secondary* dimensions of diversity are many; they include such characteristics as communication style, family status, and first language.[2] Individuals' distinguishing characteristics clearly impact their values, opportunities, and perceptions of themselves and others at work. **Workforce diversity**—diversity among employees—thus represents both a challenge and an opportunity for businesses.

Today, the U.S. workforce is as diverse as it has ever been, and it is becoming even more so. Consider the following major trends:[3]

- *More women are working than ever before.* Married women, those with young children, and older women, in particular, have greatly increased their participation in the workforce. By 2020, the Bureau of Labor Statistics estimates that 47 percent of all workers will be women, nearly equal to their share of the population. One effect of this trend is that more employed men have wives who also work—changing the nature of their responsibilities within the family. Since the recession of 2008–2009, fewer women have

[1] More information about Marriott's diversity programs is available at *www.marriott.com/diversity.*

[2] This definition is based on Marilyn Loden, *Implementing Diversity* (New York: McGraw-Hill, 1995), ch. 2.

[3] Except as noted, the figures in the following paragraphs are drawn from "Labor Force Projections to 2020: A More Slowly Growing Workforce," *Monthly Labor Review,* January 2012, and *Statistical Abstract of the United States 2012* (Washington, DC: U.S. Census Bureau).

taken time off from work for child care or other reasons, as their income has become increasingly important to family budgets.[4]

- *Immigration has profoundly reshaped the workplace.* Between 2000 and 2010, nearly 14 million immigrants entered the United States, making it the highest decade of immigration in U.S. history—despite a net decline in jobs over this period. The leading countries of origin are now Mexico, China (including Hong Kong and Taiwan), India, the Philippines, Vietnam, El Salvador, Cuba, and Korea. In a recent shift, Asians have surpassed Hispanics as the largest group of immigrants overall. Immigrants now make up about 16 percent of U.S. workers, increasing linguistic and cultural diversity in many workplaces.[5] The discussion case at the end of this chapter focuses on how businesses and government have addressed the special issue of **undocumented immigrant workers** (noncitizens working without the legally required documents)—who now make up 5 percent of the U.S. workforce.

- *Ethnic and racial diversity is increasing.* Hispanics (defined by the Census as persons of Spanish or Latin American ancestry), now about 15 percent of U.S. workers, are expected to comprise almost 19 percent by 2020. Although less numerous than Hispanics overall, Asians are now the fastest-growing segment of the labor force. The proportion of African-Americans is expected to hold steady at around 12 percent. By 2020, the U.S. workforce is projected to be about 38 percent nonwhite (this category includes persons of Hispanic origin). In some states, such as California, these trends will be much more pronounced.

- *The workforce will continue to get older.* As the baby boom generation matures, birth rates drop, and people live longer and healthier lives, the population will age. Many of these older people will continue to work, whether out of choice or necessity. After the Great Recession, many older workers postponed retirement—or even re-entered the workforce—to recoup losses in their savings and home values. Said one 67-year-old utility company employee, "I felt that I was in a good position to retire until the market kept going down and down . . . [But] there's no point in retiring in this time of uncertainty until I have a better feel for where the economy is going." Employers will have to find new ways to accommodate older workers.[6]

- *Millennials are entering the workforce.* Even as many baby boomers extend their working years, so-called *millennials*—young people born after 1980 or so—are entering the workforce in large numbers, bringing fresh perspectives and practices. The observations of the senior diversity executive at Hewitt Associates on what the influx of millennials will mean for the workplace are presented in Exhibit 17.A.

Workforce diversity creates many new employee issues and problems. This chapter will consider the changing face of today's workplace, and its implications for management. Laws and regulations clearly require that businesses provide equal opportunity, and avoid discrimination and harassment. How to meet—and exceed—these mandates presents an ongoing challenge to businesses seeking to reap the benefits of a well-integrated, yet culturally diverse work population. We turn first to two important dimensions of workforce diversity: gender and race.

---

[4] "Time Outs Take an Increasing Toll on Women's Careers," July 20, 2010, at *www.amanet.org.*

[5] "In a Shift, Biggest Wave of Migrants Is Now Asian," *The New York Times,* June 18, 2012; "A Record-Setting Decade of Immigration: 2000–2010," Center for Immigration Studies, October 2011, *www.cis.org;* and U.S. Bureau of Labor Statistics, "Labor Force Characteristics of Foreign-Born Workers Summary," May 24, 2012, at *www.bls.gov.*

[6] Towers Watson, "The Economic Recession: Impact on Employment Trends and Retirement Patterns," August 2011, at *www.towerswatson.com;* and "Older Workers, Hurt By Recession, Seek New Jobs," *Associated Press,* March 31, 2009.

Andrés Tapia, chief diversity officer for the Hewitt Associates, a human resources consulting and benefits administration firm, has written compellingly about the ways in which generational identity is itself a dimension of diversity. "As a diversity leader," Tapia writes, "I've seen that a telltale sign of inclusion breakdown is when judgments pop up unchallenged and groupthink sets in about the new-comer. When behaviors by others are different from behaviors we all believe is right, it elicits one of two reactions about the other: They either are incompetent or a bad person. This is now happening in response to the millennials. As in other forms of diversity, this kind of stance not only is exclusion-ary, it is not helpful in addressing the real issues. Today, generational diversity is as much an issue as gender and racial diversity . . . . Just by the nature of who they are, millennials will transform the workplace."

Millennials, Tapia says, tend to be idealistic, technologically savvy, environmentally conscious, globally networked, and collaborative. In the workplace, they tend to challenge traditional planning, being told what to do, and rigidity in career paths. Corporations will need to change, he argues, to accommodate the talents of these young workers—who bring yet another dimension of diversity into an increasingly diverse workplace.

Source: Andrés Tapia, "The Millennials: Why This Generation Will Challenge the Workplace Like No Other," Hewitt Associates, 2008, *www.hewitt.com.*

Gender and Race in the Workplace

Gender and race are both important primary dimensions of workforce diversity. Women and persons of color have always worked, contributing both paid and unpaid labor to the economy. Yet, the nature of their participation in the labor force has changed, posing new challenges to business.

Women and Minorities at Work

One of the most significant changes in the past half-century has been the growing labor force participation of women. During the period following World War II, the proportion of women working outside the home rose dramatically. In 1950, about a third of adult women were employed. This proportion rose steadily for several decades, leveling off at around 59 percent in the mid-2000s. Participation rates (the proportion of women in the workforce) have risen for all groups of women, but the most dramatic increases have been among mar-ried women, mothers of young children, and middle-class women, those who had earlier been most likely to stay at home. Men's participation rates declined during this period; between 1950 and 2010, the proportion of adult men who worked fell from 86 percent to 71 percent, with a particularly sharp drop as a result of the recession of 2008–2009. Figure 17.1 shows the convergence of the labor force participation rates for men and women over the past 60 years.

Women have entered the labor force for many of the same reasons men do. They need income to support themselves and their families. Having a job with pay also gives a woman psychological independence and security. The high cost of living puts financial pressure on families, frequently pushing women into the labor force just to sustain an accustomed standard of living or to put children through college or care for aging parents. The inade-quacies and uncertainties of retirement plans and health care programs frequently mean that women, as well as men, need to save, invest, and plan for the future. When women divorce, they often can no longer rely on a partner's earnings for support.

FIGURE 17.1
**Proportion of Women
and Men in the
Labor Force,
1950–2010**

Source: U.S. Bureau of Labor
Statistics.

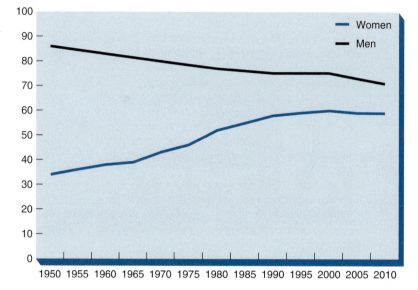

The rapid rise of female labor force participation in the postwar years also reflects the expansion of segments of the economy that were major employers of women. In 1940, about one-third of all U.S. jobs were white-collar (not requiring manual labor); today, more than 60 percent are white-collar. Professional, technical, and service jobs also grew relative to the economy. The creation of many new positions in fields traditionally staffed by women produced what economists call a demand-side pull of women into the labor force. More "women's jobs" meant more women working.

Labor force participation rates for minorities, unlike those of women, have always been high. For example, in 1970 about 62 percent of all African-Americans (men and women combined) worked; the proportion is the same today. Participation rates have also been consistently high for most other minority groups; for Asians, it is 65 percent; for Hispanics, 68 percent. The key change here has been the move of persons of color, in recent decades, into a wider range of jobs as barriers of discrimination and segregation have fallen; minorities have become better represented in the ranks of managers, professionals, and the skilled trades. These trends will be further discussed later in this chapter.

> The face of success in the United States is diverse, just as the workforce is. Consider Indra Nooyi, chairman and CEO of PepsiCo. Nooyi was born in Madras, India, and was educated at the Indian Institute of Management in Calcutta. In India, she held management positions in the pharmaceutical and textile industries before immigrating to the United States to attend the Yale School of Management. She joined PepsiCo in 1994, where she moved up quickly and became president and CEO in 2001. *Fortune Magazine* named Nooyi the most powerful woman in business in 2010. Speaking of the talents women bring to the executive suite, Nooyi joked in an interview, "If the Three Wise Men had happened to be women, they would have stopped and asked for directions, arrived at the stable on time, helped deliver the baby, cleaned up the stable after, made a casserole, brought practical gifts and there would have been peace on Earth."[7]

[7] "Indra Nooyi on How to Find Your Voice," *Good Housekeeping* (2011), at *www.goodhousekeeping.com*.

FIGURE 17.2 The Gender and Race Pay Gap, 1990–2010 (median weekly earnings of full-time workers, as a percentage of those of white men)

Source: U.S. Bureau of Labor Statistics, *Labor Force Characteristics by Race and Ethnicity, 2010,* August 2011, Table 14; U.S. Census Bureau, *Statistical Abstract of the United States 2009,* Table 626; and *Statistical Abstract of the United States 2000,* Table 696.

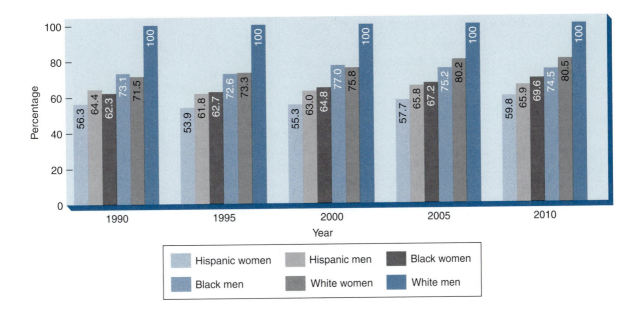

The Gender and Racial Pay Gap

One persistent feature of the working world is that women and persons of color on average receive lower pay than white men do. This disparity, called the **pay gap**, narrowed over the past three decades, as Figure 17.2 shows. But in 2010 black men still earned only slightly more than three-quarters of white men's pay; black women earned about 70 percent, and white women 81 percent. (These data are based on full-time workers only.) The pay gap for Hispanic women declined by about 5 percent since 2000; and the pay gap for Hispanic men, about 3 percent. The one group that tops white men in median weekly earnings is Asian-American men; they make about 10 percent more, on average. (Asian-American women make 91 percent of what white men earn.) An important reason is education; almost half of Asian-Americans hold a bachelor's degree or above, more schooling than any other ethnic group.[8]

Experts disagree about the cause of the pay gap between women and men. Some believe the continuing gender disparity in pay is evidence of sex discrimination by employers; others believe the gap reflects women's choices to pursue lower-paying jobs or slower advancement because of time off for family responsibilities. Many observers agree, however, that the pay gap persists, in part, because of what is called **occupational segregation**. This term refers to the inequitable concentration of a group, such a minorities or women, in particular job categories. The large pay gap for Hispanic workers, for example, partly reflects their concentration in several low-paid occupations. Fifty-nine percent of drywall installers, 44 percent of grounds maintenance workers, 42 percent of farmworkers, and 41 percent of private household cleaners are of Hispanic origin, according to the Census

[8] Asian American Center for Advancing Justice, "A Community of Contrasts: Asian Americans in the United States: 2011," at *www.advancingjustice.org.*

Bureau, although Hispanics make up only 14 percent of the workforce as a whole. Although women, for their part, have made great strides in entering occupations where they were formerly underrepresented, many remain concentrated in a few sex-typed jobs that some have called the "pink-collar ghetto." Women still make up 97 percent of pre-school and kindergarten teachers, 91 percent of bookkeepers, 98 percent of dental hygienists, and 96 percent of secretaries, for example. Eliminating the pay gap will require, therefore, business programs and government policies that create opportunity for women and people of color to move out of more segregated jobs into ones where the pay and chances for upward mobility are greater.[9]

> Occupational segregation is common in other societies, as well. In the United Kingdom, the government's Equality and Human Rights Commission found continuing high levels of labor market segmentation. In its triennial report, "How Fair Is Britain?" the Commission reported that a quarter of all Pakistani men in Britain worked as taxi drivers, and women made up 77 percent of secretaries but just 6 percent of engineers. Persons of Indian and Chinese descent were twice as likely to work as professionals as whites in Britain, the study found.[10]

One study found that even after taking into consideration differences in education, experience, race, industry, and occupation, women still earned just 91 cents for every dollar earned by men—presumably the remaining effect of discrimination.[11]

The most prestigious and highest-paying jobs in a corporation are in top management. Because most corporations are organized hierarchically, management jobs—particularly those at the top—are few. For that reason, only a small fraction of workers, of whatever gender or race, can hope to reach the upper levels in the business world. White men have traditionally filled most of these desirable spots. Business's mandate now is to broaden these high-level leadership opportunities for women and persons of color, a topic to which we turn next.

Where Women and Persons of Color Manage

Slightly more than 9 million U.S. women were working as managers by the early 2010s. As Figure 17.3 reveals, in 2010 more than 4 out of 10 managers—and a majority of managers in some categories—were women. Clearly, women have broken into management ranks. Women are more likely to be managers, though, in occupational areas where women are more numerous at lower levels, such as health care and education. Grouped by industry, women tend to be concentrated in service industries and in finance, insurance, real estate, and retail businesses. Women managers have also made gains in newer industries, such as biotechnology, where growth has created opportunity.

Where do persons of color manage? As is shown in Figure 17.3, African-Americans and Hispanics are underrepresented in management ranks in the United States, making up just 8.4 and 7.3 percent of managers, respectively. But they have approached or exceeded parity in a few areas. Blacks make up 12.4 percent of health care managers (more than their 11 percent of the workforce), for example. Hispanics are best represented in food service management. By contrast, Asians are somewhat overrepresented in management ranks, particularly in the fields of information systems, finance, and lodging. Figure 17.3 shows the patterns of diversity by gender, race, and ethnicity in various management categories.

---

[9] The data in this paragraph are drawn from Table 616, "Employed Civilians by Occupation, Sex, Race, and Hispanic Origin: 2010," in the U.S. Census Bureau, *Statistical Abstract of the United States 2012.*

[10] U.K. Equality and Human Rights Commission, "How Fair Is Britain? The First Triennial Review 2010," *www.equalityhumanrights.com.*

[11] "Shortchanged: Why Women Get Paid Less Than Men," *Bloomberg Businessweek,* June 21, 2012.

FIGURE 17.3
Extent of Diversity in Selected Management Occupations

Source: U.S. Census Bureau, *Statistical Abstract of the United States 2012*, Table 616.

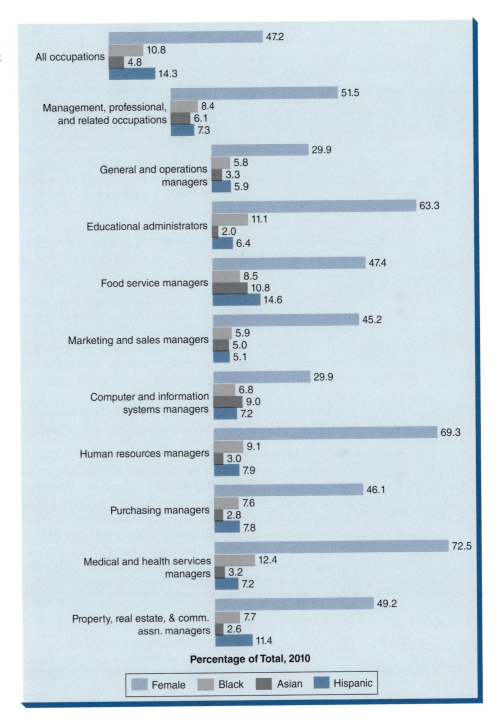

Percentage of Total, 2010

Female   Black   Asian   Hispanic

Breaking the Glass Ceiling

A few exceptional women and persons of color—and some women of color—have reached the pinnacles of power in corporate America.

In 2012, the CEO of Xerox Corporation was Ursula Burns, the first African-American woman to lead a major U.S. company. (She was also the first woman CEO to succeed another woman, Anne Mulcahy, who stepped down to become the chairman of the board in 2009.) Burns, who had been raised in a New York City housing project by a single mother, had gone on to earn a graduate degree in mechanical engineering at Columbia. She was recognized early in her career for extraordinary potential, and had worked her way up at Xerox through a series of increasingly responsible positions. When appointed CEO, Burns commented, "I'm in this job because I believe I earned it through hard work and high performance."[12]

High achievers such as Ursula Burns and Indra Nooyi remain unusual, however. Although women and minorities are as competent as white men in managing people and organizations, they rarely attain the highest positions in corporations. Their ascent seems to be blocked by an invisible barrier, sometimes called a **glass ceiling**. According to Catalyst, an advocacy organization for female executives, in 2011 only 14 percent of chief executive officers of the *Fortune* 500 companies were women.[13] Only 19 (4 percent) of these companies had a person of color as CEO. The latter group included Kenneth Chenault of American Express, Antonio Perez of Eastman Kodak, and Vikram Pandit of Citigroup.[14] In Europe, diversity in the top ranks is also rare.

> Failure to promote women to top-level positions may be hurting companies' financial performance. Studies by faculty members at Pepperdine University showed that "companies identified as being the best at promoting women outperformed the industry median" on three different measures of profitability (profit as a percentage of revenue, assets, and equity). The researchers concluded, "Firms exhibit higher profitability when their top executives make smart decisions. One of the smart decisions those executives have consistently made at successful *Fortune* 500 firms is to include women in the executive suite—so that regardless of gender, the best brains are available to continue making smart, and profitable, decisions."[15]

Women and minorities are also scarce on corporate boards. A 2011 study reported that only 16 percent of board members of *Fortune* 500 firms were women; only 3 percent were women of color.[16] Thirteen percent were minorities.[17] Worldwide, a survey of more than 4,000 companies found that only about 10 percent of directors were women.[18] Some have cited the lack of board diversity as a contributing factor in the financial crisis that began in 2008. A researcher from the International Centre for Women Business Leaders in the United Kingdom, for example, wryly noted that, "had there been a few more Lehman Sisters, it [Lehman Brothers, the investment banking firm that collapsed in 2008] would not have been in the state that it was in."[19] A study by Catalyst found that companies with three or more female directors had significantly higher returns on equity than those with no female directors.[20]

[12] "An Historic Succession at Xerox," *BusinessWeek*, June 8, 2009.

[13] "Catalyst 2011 Census: *Fortune* 500 Women Executives and Top Earners," *www.catalyst.org*.

[14] "*Fortune* 500 Black, Latino, and Asian CEOs," *DiversityINC*, posted February 19, 2012.

[15] Roy Douglas Adler, "Profit: Thy Name Is . . . Woman?" *Miller-McCune.com*, February 27, 2009.

[16] "2011 Catalyst Census: *Fortune* 500 Women Board Directors," *www.catalyst.org*.

[17] The Alliance for Board Diversity, "Missing Pieces: Women and Minorities on *Fortune* 100 Boards," 2011, *www.elcinfo.com*. Data on minority board membership are for 2010.

[18] "GMI Ratings' 2012 Women on Boards Report Shows Women Hold More Than One in Ten Seats Globally," press release, March 8, 2012, at *www.gmiratings.com*.

[19] "In a Male Recession, Women Are the First to Quit," *The Times (London)*, April 15, 2009.

[20] Catalyst, "The Bottom Line: Corporate Performance and Women's Representation on Boards (2004–2008), 2011," at *www.catalyst.org*.

In 2012, the European Union considered legislating quotas for women on boards of directors. In this, it was following the lead of several of its member states, including Norway, Spain, France, Italy, and Belgium, which had already done so. "Personally, I don't like quotas," said Viviane Reding, vice president of the European Commission, who nonetheless supported the effort. "But I like what quotas do. Quotas open the way for equality and they break through the glass ceiling." In 2012, only 14 percent of board seats in large European companies were held by women and 65 percent of boards included no women at all. Polls showed that three-quarters of Europeans supported mandating gender balance on company boards.[21]

Failure to attain the topmost jobs in some cases is due to lack of experience or inadequate education. Because gender and racial bias has kept women and minorities out of management until recent years, few have had time to acquire the years of experience that are typical of most high-ranking executives. Also, in earlier years women and minorities were discouraged from entering graduate schools of engineering, science, business, and law, the traditional pathways to top corporate management. Even as those barriers have been lowered, though, these groups remain underrepresented at executive levels.

What continues to hold women and minorities back? A study in the *Harvard Business Review* reported that the primary obstacle is **glass walls**: fewer opportunities to move sideways into jobs that lead to the top. Female and minority managers are often found in staff positions, such as public relations or human resources, rather than in line positions in such core areas as marketing, sales, or production where they can acquire the broad management skills necessary for promotion.[22] Another problem is that in filling top positions, recruiters rely on word-of-mouth—the old boys' network from which women and persons of color are often excluded. Sometimes women voluntarily choose to step off the career track to care for children or elderly relatives.[23] Other causes include a company's lack of commitment to diversity and too little accountability at the top management level for equal employment opportunity. However, recent advances by both women and minorities in the executive suite suggest that the glass ceiling may finally be cracking.[24]

Women and Minority Business Ownership

Some women and minorities have evaded the glass ceiling and risen to the top by founding or taking over their own businesses.

By the late 2010s, over 10 million businesses—40 percent of all privately held firms in the United States—were owned or controlled by women, according to the Center for Women's Business Research. Of these, about one in five was owned by a woman of color.

An example of a successful female entrepreneur is Tina Wells, who founded the Buzz Marketing Group in 1996 when she was still a teenager to help companies market successfully to young people. Today, the company uses social media and trend-spotting on behalf of many companies, including Nike, Steve Madden,

---

[21] "Quotas for Women on EU Boards: Good or Bad?" *The Wall Street Journal,* May 17, 2012; "E.U. Considers Quotas for Women in Boardrooms," *The New York Times,* March 4, 2012; and "Hard-Wiring Diversity into Your Business," *Boston Consulting Group Perspectives,* June 8, 2011, at *www.bcgperspectives.com.*

[22] "What's Holding Women Back?" *Harvard Business Review,* June 1, 2003. The reports of the Glass Ceiling Commission of the U.S. Department of Labor may be accessed at *www.dol.gov/oasam/programs/history/reich/reports/ceiling.pdf.*

[23] "How Women Are Redefining Work and Success," *BusinessWeek,* May 21, 2009.

[24] A comprehensive examination of the status of women is available in a report by the U.S. Department of Commerce, the Executive Office of the President, and the White House Council on Women and Girls, *Women in America: Indicators of Social and Economic Well-Being,* March 2011.

SonyBMG, Procter & Gamble, and American Eagle Outfitters. Wells, who is black, is also the author of several children's books and *Chasing Youth Culture and Getting It Right* and blogs for the Huffington Post. She told an interviewer that technology had been critical to the success of her business. "I have the world at the touch of my smartphone," Wells explained. "I can talk to thousands of millennials in our buzzSpotter network where they are the most: online!"[25]

Although most female-headed firms are small, collectively they employ over 13 million people in the United States and generate $1.9 trillion in sales.[26]

Persons of color have also used business ownership as a path to success. According to the U.S. Census Bureau, there were around 5.8 million minority-owned businesses in the United States in 2007. Within this group, Hispanic-owned businesses were the most numerous, followed by African-American and Asian-owned businesses.[27] Immigrants were responsible for a good share of the entrepreneurial spirit in the minority community; immigrants are nearly 30 percent more likely to start a business than are nonimmigrants.[28]

Government's Role in Securing Equal Employment Opportunity

Eliminating workplace discrimination and ensuring equal job opportunity have been major goals of public policy in the United States for four decades. This section reviews the major laws that govern business practices with respect to equal opportunity, affirmative action, and sexual and racial harassment.

Equal Employment Opportunity

Beginning on a major scale in the 1960s, U.S. presidents issued executive orders and Congress enacted laws intended to promote equal treatment of employees—that is, **equal employment opportunity**. These government rules apply to most businesses in the following ways:

- Discrimination based on race, color, religion, sex, national origin, physical or mental disability, or age is prohibited in all employment practices. This includes hiring, promotion, job classification and assignment, compensation, and other conditions of work.

- Government contractors must have written affirmative action plans detailing how they are working positively to overcome past and present effects of discrimination in their workforce. However, affirmative action plans must be temporary and flexible, designed to correct past discrimination, and cannot result in reverse discrimination against whites or men.

- Women and men must receive equal pay for performing equal work, and employers may not discriminate on the basis of pregnancy.

[25] "25 Inspiring Black Women Entrepreneurs," *Essence,* March 5, 2012, and "Tina Wells, Founder & CEO, Buzz Marketing Group: Technology Enables Me to Keep in Touch with Thousands of Teens Across the Globe," *The Next Women Business Magazine,* January 5, 2012.

[26] The Center for Women's Business Research, "Key Facts about Women-Owned Businesses," at *www.cfwbr.org.* These data include privately held businesses in which women own a controlling interest, privately held businesses owned equally by women and men (for example, by a married couple), and publicly traded companies with majority or substantial women's ownership.

[27] U.S. Census Bureau, "Survey of Business Owners: Company Summary: 2007," *www.census.gov.*

[28] Small Business Administration, "Estimating the Contribution of Immigrant Business Owners to the U.S. Economy," November 2008, at *www.sba.gov.*

FIGURE 17.4

Major Federal Laws and Executive Orders Prohibiting Job Discrimination

Equal Pay Act (1963)—Mandates equal pay for substantially equal work by men and women.

Civil Rights Act (1964; amended 1972, 1991, 2009)—Prohibits discrimination in employment based on race, color, religion, sex, or national origin.

Executive Order 11246 (1965)—Mandates affirmative action for all federal contractors and subcontractors.

Age Discrimination in Employment Act (1967)—Protects individuals who are 40 years of age or older.

Equal Employment Opportunity Act (1972)—Increases power of the Equal Employment Opportunity Commission to combat discrimination.

Pregnancy Discrimination Act (1978)—Forbids employers to discharge, fail to hire, or otherwise discriminate against pregnant women.

Americans with Disabilities Act (1990)—Prohibits discrimination against individuals with disabilities.

Family and Medical Leave Act (1993)—Requires companies with 50 or more employees to provide up to 12 weeks unpaid leave for illness, care of a sick family member, or the birth or adoption of a child.

Genetic Information Nondiscrimination Act (2008)—prohibits the use of genetic information in employment decisions.

In 2009, President Barack Obama signed into law the Lilly Ledbetter Fair Pay Act. Ledbetter, a supervisor at a Goodyear tire factory in Alabama, had filed a lawsuit shortly before her retirement in 1998, claiming that Goodyear had violated the equal pay laws. Ledbetter said that she had recently learned that for many years the company had been paying her less than men doing the same job. Her case eventually came before the Supreme Court, which ruled against Ledbetter, saying that because the discrimination had started more than 180 days before she filed suit, she had exceeded the time limits. Under the Ledbetter Act, the 180-day time limit would start fresh every time a worker received a discriminatory paycheck. "I will never receive a cent," said Ledbetter. (The law named after her was not retroactive.) "But with the president's signature today I have an even richer reward."[29]

Figure 17.4 outlines the major laws and one executive order that are intended to promote equal opportunity in the workplace. The provisions of one of these, the Americans with Disabilities Act, are further described in Exhibit 17.B. The major agency charged with enforcing equal employment opportunity laws and executive orders in the United States is the **Equal Employment Opportunity Commission (EEOC)**. The EEOC was created in 1964 and given added enforcement powers in 1972 and 1990. In 2011, bias complaints filed with the EEOC hit an all-time high.[30]

Companies that fail to follow the laws shown in Figure 17.4 often find themselves facing expensive lawsuits. One that threatened an enormous payout was recently dismissed by the nation's high court.

In 2011, the Supreme Court ruled in a 5–4 vote against the plaintiffs in a huge class action sex discrimination lawsuit against Walmart—the largest ever brought in the United States. The women who brought the suit claimed that female employees at Walmart were paid less than men in comparable positions, in spite of having

[29] "Obama Signs Equal-Pay Legislation," *The New York Times,* January 30, 2009.

[30] EEOC, "Private Sector Bias Changes Hit All-Time High," January 25, 2012, at *www1.eeoc.gov.*

Exhibit 17.B

Accommodating Persons with Disabilities

The Americans with Disabilities Act (ADA) of 1990 requires employers to make accommodations for disabled workers and job applicants and prohibits employers from discriminating on the basis of a person's disability. A disabled worker is defined by the law as one who can perform the essential functions of a job, with or without reasonable accommodations. (The law was amended in 2008 to make it easier for someone to establish that he or she has a disability under the ADA.) The law prohibits employers from asking in a job interview, for example, about a person's medical history or past treatment for mental illness or alcoholism. And it requires employers to make reasonable accommodations, for example, by modifying work equipment, adjusting work schedules, or making facilities accessible. The courts have interpreted the ADA to cover persons with acquired immunodeficiency syndrome (AIDS). This means that discrimination against persons with AIDS, or who are infected with HIV (the virus that causes AIDS), is prohibited, so long as the person can perform the essential elements of the job. Some businesses have complained about the law, citing its vagueness, the high cost of compliance, and the expense of defending against lawsuits. Although the ADA has benefited the nation's disabled, they are still less likely to be employed (34 percent of working-age adults with a disability have jobs) than are those with no disability (77 percent).

Source: Bureau of Labor Statistics, "Persons with a Disability: Labor Force Characteristics—2010," June 24, 2011, at *www.bls.gov.* Information about the law is available online at *www.eeoc.gov.*

greater seniority and equal or better qualifications. They also charged that women received fewer promotions to store management positions and waited longer to move up than men did. The court did not decide whether or not Walmart had discriminated against the specific plaintiffs. Rather, it ruled that the case could not move forward as a class action, because Walmart had not "operated under a general policy of discrimination." If the class action suit had prevailed, Walmart could have been required to pay hundreds of millions of dollars to current and past female employees.[31]

Potentially costly lawsuits can involve other forms of discrimination as well, such as those based on age, race, or disability.

Affirmative Action

One way to promote equal opportunity and remedy past discrimination is through **affirmative action**. Since the mid-1960s, major government contractors have been required by presidential executive order to adopt written affirmative action plans specifying goals, actions, and timetables for promoting greater on-the-job equality. Their purpose is to reduce job discrimination by encouraging companies to take positive (that is, affirmative) steps to overcome past employment practices and traditions that may have been discriminatory.

Affirmative action became increasingly controversial in the 1990s and early 2000s. In some states, new laws (such as Proposition 209 in California) were passed banning or limiting affirmative action programs in public hiring and university admissions, and the issue was debated in Congress and in the courts. Backers of affirmative action argued that these programs provided an important tool for achieving equal opportunity. In this view, women and minorities continued to face discriminatory barriers and affirmative action was necessary to level the playing field. Some large corporations backed affirmative action programs, finding them helpful in monitoring their progress in providing equal job opportunity. General

[31] "Justices Rule for Wal-Mart in Class-Action Bias Case," *The New York Times,* June 20, 2011.

Electric, AT&T, and IBM, for example, have said that they would continue to use affirmative action goals and timetables even if they were not required by law.

Critics, however, argued that affirmative action was inconsistent with the principles of fairness and equality. Some pointed to instances of so-called reverse discrimination, which occurs when one group is unintentionally discriminated against in an effort to help another group. For example, if a more qualified white man were passed over for a job as a police officer in favor of a less qualified Hispanic man to remedy past discrimination in a police department, this might be unfair to the white candidate.

In 2009, the Supreme Court heard a case brought by Frank Ricci, a white firefighter in New Haven, Connecticut. Earlier, Ricci had taken an exam for promotion to lieutenant and had scored sixth among 77 candidates. But the city decided to discard the results, because none of the 19 African-Americans who took the test qualified for promotion. Ricci and 19 other firefighters (one of whom was Hispanic) then sued the city, saying they had been the victims of reverse discrimination. The city defended its action, saying the test was flawed. The Supreme Court ruled in favor of the firefighter plaintiffs, saying they had been subjected to race discrimination "solely because the higher-scoring candidates were white."[32]

Critics of affirmative action also argued that these programs could actually stigmatize or demoralize the very groups they were designed to help. For example, if a company hired a woman for a top management post, other people might think she got the job just because of affirmative action preferences, even if she were truly the best qualified. This might undermine her effectiveness on the job or even cause her to question her own abilities. For this reason, some women and persons of color called for *less* emphasis on affirmative action, preferring to achieve personal success without preferential treatment.[33]

Sexual and Racial Harassment

Government regulations ban both sexual and racial harassment. Of the two kinds, sexual harassment cases are more prevalent, and the law covering them is better defined. But racial harassment cases are a growing concern to employers.

Sexual harassment at work occurs when any employee, woman or man, experiences repeated, unwanted sexual attention or when on-the-job conditions are hostile or threatening in a sexual way. It includes both physical conduct—for example, suggestive touching—as well as verbal harassment, such as sexual innuendoes, jokes, or propositions. Sexual harassment is not limited to overt acts of individual coworkers or supervisors; it can also occur if a company's work climate is blatantly and offensively sexual or intimidating to employees. Women are the targets of most sexual harassment. Sexual harassment is illegal, and the U.S. Equal Employment Opportunity Commission (EEOC) is empowered to sue on behalf of victims. Such suits can be very costly to employers who tolerate a hostile work environment, as the following example shows.

In 2011, a jury awarded a woman $95 million, believed to be the largest settlement ever for an individual in a sexual harassment suit. The plaintiff, in her mid-20s, worked for Aaron's Inc., a rent-to-own company, in St. Louis, Missouri. Her general manager had subjected her to months of escalating harassment, culminating in a shocking incident in which he threw her to the ground and sexually assaulted her.

---

[32] "Justices to Hear White Firefighters Bias Claims," *The New York Times,* April 10, 2009; and "Supreme Court Finds Bias against White Firefighters," *The New York Times,* June 30, 2009.

[33] See, for example, Ward Connerly, *Creating Equal: My Fight against Race Preferences* (San Francisco: Encounter Books, 2000).

The woman testified she had called a company hotline for help without results—and instead was denied a promotion after complaining about the assault. A judge later reduced the amount to $6 million.[34]

Increasingly, sexual harassment cases are settled in arbitration hearings, so the amounts paid are not made public.[35]

Women employees regularly report that sexual harassment is common. From 40 to 70 percent of working women (and from 10 to 20 percent of working men) have told researchers they have been sexually harassed on the job. In almost two-thirds of the cases, the individual who was the target did not report the incident.[36] This kind of conduct is most likely to occur where jobs and occupations are (or have been) sex-segregated and where most supervisors and managers are men. It is also common where women workers have low power relative to their supervisors. A recent study found, for example, that female farmworkers were commonly sexually harassed and assaulted. About 60 percent were illegal immigrants, the study found, and many were afraid of deportation if they complained. "It's easiest for abusers to get away with sexual harassment where there's an imbalance of power, and the imbalance of power is particularly stark on farms," said the study's author.[37]

In 2002, the European Union recognized sexual harassment as a form of gender discrimination and required its member states to bring their laws into compliance by 2005. Evolving norms about appropriate interactions at the workplace came as a shock to many, particularly in eastern and central Europe, where obscene jokes, suggestive remarks, and unwelcome advances at work were commonplace. One study found, for example, that 45 percent of Czech women had been sexually harassed, although most did not identify the behavior by this term. "Sexual harassment is something like folklore in the Czech Republic," said one researcher.[38]

Harassment can occur whether or not the targeted employee cooperates. It need not result in the victim's firing, or cause severe psychological distress; the presence of a hostile or abusive workplace can itself be the basis for a successful suit. Moreover, a company can be found guilty as a result of actions by a supervisor, even if the incident is never reported to top management.

Racial harassment is also illegal, under Title VII of the Civil Rights Act. Under EEOC guidelines, ethnic slurs, derogatory comments, or other verbal or physical harassment based on race are against the law, if they create an intimidating, hostile, or offensive working environment or interfere with an individual's work performance. Although fewer racial than sexual harassment charges are filed, their numbers have more than doubled since the early 1990s (to about 9,000 a year in 2011), and employers have been liable for expensive settlements. For example, YRC/Roadway Express, the nation's largest less-than-truckload freight hauling company, had to pay $10 million to settle charges of racial harassment at two Illinois facilities. African-American workers there charged that they had been subjected to multiple incidents of racist graffiti, comments, and cartoons—and even a hangman's noose,

[34] "Jury Awards $95 Million in Fairview Heights Sex Harassment Suit," June 10, 2011, at *www.stltoday.com;* and "Aaron's Settles Sexual Harassment Lawsuit for $6 Million," *Associated Press,* March 27, 2012.

[35] "The Silencing of Sexual Harassment," *Bloomberg Businessweek,* November 12, 2011.

[36] "Sexual Harassment Statistics in the Workplace," *www.sexualharassmentlawfirms.com.*

[37] "Report: Sexual Abuse of Female Farmworkers Common," *Washington Post,* May 16, 2012.

[38] "Sexual Harassment in the European Union: The Dawning of a New Era," *SAM Advanced Management Journal* 69, no. 1 (Winter 2004); and "Sexual Harassment at Work Widespread in Central Europe," *Plain Dealer (Cleveland),* January 9, 2000.

long a symbol of violence against blacks. Despite their complaints, the company had failed to take corrective action.[39]

What can companies do to combat sexual and racial harassment—and protect themselves from expensive lawsuits? The Supreme Court has ruled that companies can deflect lawsuits by taking two steps. First, they should develop a zero-tolerance policy on harassment and communicate it clearly to employees. Then they should establish a complaint procedure—including ways to report incidents without retaliation—and act quickly to resolve any problems. Companies that take such steps, the court said, would be protected from suits by employees who claim harassment but have failed to use the complaint procedure.

Developing mechanisms for preventing sexual and racial harassment is just one important action companies can take. Others positive steps by business are discussed in the following section.

What Business Can Do: Diversity Policies and Practices

All businesses, of course, are required to obey the laws mandating equal employment opportunity and prohibiting sexual and racial harassment; those that fail to do so risk expensive lawsuits and public disapproval. But it is not enough simply to follow the law. The best-managed companies go beyond compliance; they implement a range of policies and practices to make the workplace welcoming, fair, and accommodating to all employees.

Companies that manage diversity effectively take a number of related actions, in addition to obeying all relevant laws. Research shows that these actions include the following.

Articulate clear diversity goals, set quantitative objectives, and hold managers accountable. An important trend in diversity management is metrics—setting specific goals and offering incentives for meeting them.

> An example of a company that has done this is the German carmaker BMW. Historically, BMW has had difficulty attracting and retaining female executives, even though women make up a large share of its customers. Believing that "what gets measured is what gets done," the company set numerical goals for the proportion of women at all levels—including doubling the number of women managers by 2020. To assure that the job got done, BMW included specific targets in the annual performance reviews of its top executives. Their success in meeting them would impact their annual bonuses. Beginning in 2012, these targets were cascaded down to lower management levels as well. "You need to hold people accountable," declared the company's human resource and industrial relations director.[40]

Spread a wide net in recruitment, to find the most diverse possible pool of qualified candidates. Those in charge of both hiring and promotion need to seek all workers who may be qualified—both inside and outside the company. This often involves moving beyond word-of-mouth networks, which may produce a pool of applicants who are similar to people already working for the company or in particular jobs. One company's efforts to promote diversity in its hiring using a range of techniques are described in the following example.

[39] Equal Employment Opportunity Commission, "$10 Million Consent Decree Ends Racial Harassment Case Against YRC/Roadway Express," press release, September 15, 2010, at *www1.eeoc.gov.* Information on the latest government policies on racial and sexual harassment may be found at the EEOC website at *www1.eeoc.gov//eeoc/statistics/enforcement/race_harassment.*

[40] "Hard-Wiring Diversity into Your Business," *Boston Consulting Group Perspectives,* June 8, 2011, at *www.bcgperspectives.com.*

The accounting firm KPMG works hard to build a diverse workforce. The firm actively recruits at historically black colleges and universities and is a member of INROADS, a program that places minorities in internships with the company. It sponsors the PhD Project, which supports persons of color in doctoral programs that lead to faculty positions in colleges of business—where they can serve as role models for many students. In recent years, KPMG has embraced the use of technology to cast a wider net in hiring. For example, the company created a 48-hour "virtual" recruiting fair that recently drew 20,000 registrants who were able to interact with company recruiters online, view three-dimensional renderings of exhibits, learn about job opportunities, and upload their résumés. The fair generated more than 9,000 applications for openings in 40 countries.[41]

Identify promising women and persons of color, and provide them with mentors and other kinds of support. What techniques work to shatter the glass ceiling? One study of a group of highly successful women executives found that most had been helped by top-level supporters and by multiple chances to gain critical skills. Some companies have promoted mobility by assigning mentors—more senior counselors—to promising female and minority managers and by providing opportunities that include wide-ranging line management experience. For example, at the 2011 partners meeting of PricewaterhouseCoopers, a provider of tax and audit services, the CEO asked each of the firm's 2,500 partners to identify three to five women and Black, Latino, Asian, or Native Americans to mentor. At the end of the year, the CEO told them, each partner would be evaluated on how successfully they had advocated for their mentees. "Active sponsorship makes all the difference when it comes to advancing diverse professionals," said Maria Castañón Moats, the company's chief diversity officer.[42]

Set up diversity councils to monitor the company's goals and progress toward them. A **diversity council** is a group of managers and employees responsible for developing and implementing specific action plans to meet an organization's diversity goals. Sometimes, a diversity council will be established for a corporation as a whole; sometimes, it will be established within particular business units. An example of a company that has used diversity councils effectively is Pitney Bowes, a company whose business is mail-stream technology. It operates an international diversity and inclusion council, based in Europe, that includes representatives from all businesses and regions, who work together to support diversity through training, leadership example, recognition, and communications. Pitney Bowes has repeatedly been named to lists of the best employers of women and persons of color.[43]

Businesses that manage diversity effectively enjoy a strategic advantage. While fundamental ethical principles, discussed in Chapters 4 and 5, dictate that all employees should be treated fairly and with respect for their basic human rights, there are also bottom-line benefits to doing so.

- Having a widely diverse workforce boosts innovation, many executives believe. In a 2011 study by *Forbes,* 85 percent of executives of large global enterprises agreed with the proposition that "a diverse and inclusive workforce is crucial to encouraging different perspectives and ideas that drive innovation." "We have a vast amount of diversity [within the company] that comes into work every day to build technology that plays out

---

[41] "Virtually Speaking: Career Fairs Go Online," January 26, 2011, at *www.monsterww.com*. More information on KPMG's diversity initiatives is available at *www.kpmgcareers.com*.

[42] "No. 1: PricewaterhouseCoopers," *DiversityInc,* June 2012, at *www.diversityinc.com;* and "Our Commitment to Diversity," at *www.pwc.com*.

[43] Information about Pitney Bowes' diversity programs is available at *www.pb.com*.

around the world. You can't be successful on a global stage without it," commented the director of global diversity and inclusion at Intel.[44] Businesses with employees from varied backgrounds can often more effectively serve customers who are themselves diverse and can provide valuable insights into changing tastes and preferences. Explained the vice president of human resources, worldwide operations, for the toy maker Mattel, "Our Employee Resource Groups (ERGs) . . . help us define products that work for their regions or demographics. We have to make sure we are culturally sensitive. There have been some big near misses that we might not have avoided without the ERGs."[45]

- The global marketplace demands a workforce with language skills, cultural sensitivity, and awareness of national and other differences across markets. For example, Dr. Sally Saba, executive director of national supplier diversity for the Kaiser Foundation Health Plan, was born into a Muslim family in Egypt and later came to the United States, where she successfully ran a small business. Her own experiences as a minority business owner have given her deep insight into the suppliers she works with. "All of my life experiences contribute to the complexity of how I view the world and how I view people," Dr. Saba explained.[46]

Finally, companies with effective diversity programs can avoid costly lawsuits and damage to their corporate reputations from charges of discrimination or cultural insensitivity.

Another important step businesses can take to manage diversity effectively is to accommodate the wide range of family and other obligations employees have in their lives outside work. This subject is discussed in the next section.

Balancing Work and Life

The nature of families and family life has changed, both in the United States and in many other countries. The primary groups in which people live are just as diverse as the workforce itself. One of the most prominent of these changes is that dual-income families have become much more common. According to the latest U.S. Census data, in two-thirds of married couples with children at home (66 percent), both parents worked at least part-time. This was up from just a third of such families in 1976. (To round out the picture, in 29 percent of married couples with children, just the father worked; in 4 percent, just the mother worked. In the remainder, both parents were unemployed.)[47] Families have adopted a wide range of strategies for combining full- and part-time work with the care of children, elderly relatives, and other dependents. Commented the president of the Work and Family Institute, speaking of dual-career families, "It's time to move beyond, is it good, is it bad, and get to: how do we make it work?"[48] How to help "make it work" for employees trying to balance the complex, multiple demands of work and family life has became a major challenge for business.

Child Care and Elder Care

One critical issue for business is supporting workers with responsibilities for children and elderly relatives.

---

[44] "Global Diversity and Inclusion: Fostering Innovation through a Diverse Workforce," *Forbes Insights,* July 2011, at *www.forbes.com.*

[45] Ibid.

[46] "Diversity Management at Kaiser Permanente: This Female Muslim Entrepreneur Brings Sensitivity to Suppliers," May 25, 2012, at *http://diversity.inc.com.*

[47] The data in this paragraph are drawn from Table 601, "Married Couples by Labor Force Status of Spouse," in the U.S. Census Bureau, *Statistical Abstract of the United States 2012.*

[48] "Dual-Income Families Now Most Common," *San Francisco Chronicle,* October 24, 2000.

The demand for **child care** is enormous. Millions of children need daily care, especially the nearly 7 out of every 10 children whose mothers hold jobs. A major source of workplace stress for working parents is concern about their children; and problems with child care are a leading reason why employees fail to show up for work.

Business has found that child care programs, in addition to reducing absenteeism and tardiness, also improve productivity and aid recruiting by improving the company's image and helping to retain talented employees. Most large U.S. companies provide some type of child care assistance, including dependent care accounts (84 percent) and referral services (61 percent). About one in five large companies subsidizes on-site or near-site child care services.[49] An example is S.C. Johnson, a consumer products firm that cares for 500 children in a state-of-the-art center at its Racine, Wisconsin, headquarters. "This isn't a benefit," explained a company spokesperson. "It's a good business decision because we want to attract the best."[50]

In addition to caring for children, many of today's families have responsibilities for **elder care**. Employees' responsibilities for aging parents and other older relatives will become increasingly important to businesses in the coming decade as baby boomers pass through their forties and fifties, the prime years for caring for elderly family members. Forty-two million adults in the United States now care for an older person. More than half (58 percent) of family caregivers are currently employed. This is a concern for employers because caregivers often have to go to work late or leave early to attend to these duties, or are distracted or stressed at work by their responsibilities.[51] More than half of large corporations offer assistance to workers caring for older relatives, as illustrated by the following examples.

> IBM, where 36 percent of employees are affected by elder care issues, offers a website and professional counseling for the 36 percent of its employees who are affected by elder care issues. "I was able to read about it and talk to someone," said an IBM business analyst who had been caring for her mother, who had Alzheimer's. Ernst & Young, the accounting firm, provides consultations on available resources, backup emergency adult care services, and seminars on elder care.

Also available at many firms are referral services, dependent care accounts, long-term care insurance, and time off to deal with the often unpredictable crises that occur in families caring for elders.

When a mother or father is granted time off when children are born or adopted and during the important early months of a child's development, this is called a **parental leave**; when the care of elderly relatives is involved, this is called a **family leave**. Under the Family and Medical Leave Act (FMLA), passed in 1993, companies that employ 50 or more people must grant unpaid, job-protected leaves of up to 12 weeks to employees faced with serious family needs, including the birth or adoption of a baby. Smaller companies, not covered by the FMLA, usually do less for expectant and new parents and for those with ill family members.

Work Flexibility

Companies have also accommodated the changing roles of women and men by offering workers more flexibility through such options as flextime, part-time employment, job sharing, and working from home (sometimes called telecommuting because the employee keeps in

---

[49] Families and Work Institute, "2012 National Study of Employers," at *www.familiesandwork.org.* An open-source website for research on work and family is the Sloan Work and Family Research Network at *www.wfnetwork.bc.edu.*

[50] Information about S.C. Johnson's child care center is available at *www.scjohnson.com.*

[51] AARP Public Policy Institute, "Valuing the Invaluable: The Economic Value of Family Caregiving," 2011, *www.aarp.org;* and "Caring for Elderly Parents Catches Many Unprepared," *USA Today,* March 29, 2012.

touch with coworkers, customers, and others by phone or over the Internet). Abbott Laboratories, a global health care company that was named one of the "best companies" in 2011 by *Working Mother* magazine, demonstrates the benefits of the many kinds of work flexibility for both business and employees.

> Many of Abbott's employees, men and women, work flextime schedules, beginning and quitting at different times of the day. Others share jobs, with each working half a week. Many jobs are held on a part-time basis, leaving the worker time to be at home with children or elderly parents. Other Abbott employees telecommute from their homes. "After my son got sick, I needed to . . . drop down to part-time and work from home a few days a week," said one manager. "Abbott gave me the flexibility I needed to take care of my family." The company, whose work/life programs have been widely honored, says that its employees return the investment through their increased productivity, innovative thinking, and loyalty.[52]

Abbott is not the only corporation using these practices. A 2012 study found that 77 percent offered some kind of flexible work schedules, such as changing starting or quitting times, working from home, or compressed workweek schedules.[53] These arrangements can benefit employers by attracting and retaining valuable employees, reducing absences, and improving job satisfaction. "Organizations are realizing the value in giving employees more autonomy to produce their best work," commented a representative of the Society for Human Resource Management, which participated in the study. "At the same time," she noted, "organizations still struggling in a recovering economy are dependent on their workforce and less able to provide employees extended time away from work."[54]

However, many observers believe that most careers are still structured for people who are prepared to put in 40 hours a week at the office—or 50 or 60—giving their full and undivided commitment to the organization. Many women and men have been reluctant to take advantage of various flexible work options, fearing that this would put them on a slower track, sometimes disparagingly called the *Mommy track* or *Daddy track*. In this view, businesses will need to undergo a cultural shift, to value the contributions of people who are prepared to make a serious, but less than full-time, commitment to their careers.

What would such a cultural shift look like? Some have used the term **family-friendly corporation** to describe firms that would fully support both men and women in their efforts to balance work and family responsibilities. Job advantages would not be granted or denied on the basis of gender. People would be hired, paid, evaluated, promoted, and extended benefits on the basis of their qualifications and ability to do the tasks assigned. The route to the top, or to satisfaction in any occupational category, would be open to anyone with the talent to take it. The company's stakeholders, regardless of their gender, would be treated in a bias-free manner. All laws forbidding sex discrimination would be fully obeyed. Programs to provide leaves or financial support for child care, elder care, and other family responsibilities would support both men and women employees and help promote an equitable division of domestic work. And persons could seek, and achieve, career advancement without committing to a full-time schedule, year after year.[55] An example of a family-friendly

---

[52] "Abbott Named to *Working Mother* Magazine's 'Best Companies' for the Eleventh Consecutive Year," press release, September 15, 2011. The quote is from a press release dated September 23, 2008. Both are available at *www.abbott.com*.

[53] Families and Work Institute, "2012 National Study of Employers," at *www.familiesandwork.org*.

[54] "2012 National Study of Employers Reveals Increased Workplace Flexibility," Society for Human Resource Management, press release, April 30, 2012, at *www.shrm.org*.

[55] *Working Mother* magazine publishes an annual list of the "100 Best Companies for Working Mothers." The current year's list may be viewed at *www.workingmother.com*.

Exhibit 17.C

Domestic Partner Benefits

Many corporations in the United States now acknowledge differences in employee sexual orientation and gender identity. Lesbian, gay, bisexual, and transgender (LGBT) employees have become a vocal minority, winning important victories in the workplace. A 2012 report by the Human Rights Campaign Foundation found that 86 percent of the *Fortune* 500 companies included sexual orientation in their nondiscrimination policy, and 60 percent provided health benefits to domestic partners and same-sex spouses. Lotus Development was the first major employer to offer spousal benefits to same-sex partners; it was followed by many others, including AT&T, Wells Fargo, Microsoft, United Airlines, and the Big Three automakers. Other steps companies have taken to support their LGBT employees have included management training on sexual diversity issues, visible gay and lesbian advertising, and transgender-inclusive health coverage.

Source: Human Rights Campaign Foundation, *Corporate Equality Index 2012: Rating American Workplaces on Lesbian, Gay, Bisexual and Transgender Equality* at *www.hrc.org/cei.*

corporation is General Mills, long admired for its support of working parents. More than 40 percent of managers and executives are women, and 57 percent of all employees have flexible work schedules. The company has a special program to allow women to ramp up their hours gradually when they return to work after the birth or adoption of a child.[56]

An important step businesses can take is to recognize, and provide benefits to, nontraditional families. Some firms now offer domestic partner benefits to their gay and lesbian employees, extending health insurance and other benefits to the same-sex partners of employees. Although U.S. law does not explicitly bar discrimination based on sexual orientation, some local laws do; and many firms have found that extending health insurance and other benefits to the same-sex partners of employees is an effective strategy for recruiting and retaining valuable contributors. Domestic partner benefits are further described in Exhibit 17.C.

No other area of business illustrates the basic theme of this book better than the close connection between work and life. Our basic theme is that business and society are closely and unavoidably intertwined, so that what affects one also has an impact on the other. As the workforce has become more diverse, business has been challenged to accommodate their employees' differences. When people go to work, they do not shed their identities at the office or factory door. When employees come from families where there are young children at home, or where elderly parents require care, companies must learn to support these roles. Businesses that help their employees achieve a balance between work and life and meet their obligations to their families and communities often reap rewards in greater productivity, loyalty, and commitment.

Summary

- The U.S. workforce is as diverse as it has ever been and is becoming more so. More women are working than ever before, many immigrants have entered the labor force, ethnic and racial diversity is increasing, the workforce is aging, and millennials are entering the workplace.

- Women and persons of color have made great strides in entering all occupations, but they continue to be underrepresented in many business management roles, especially at

[56] "2011 *Working Mother* Best Companies," at *www.workingmother.com.*

top levels. Both groups face a continuing pay gap. The number of women-owned businesses has increased sharply, and many minorities, especially immigrants, also own their own businesses.

- Under U.S. law, businesses are required to provide equal opportunity to all, without regard to race, color, religion, sex, national origin, disability, or age. Sexual and racial harassment are illegal. Affirmative action plans remain legal, but only if they are temporary and flexible, designed to correct past discrimination, and do not result in reverse discrimination.

- Companies that manage diversity effectively have a strategic advantage because they are able to foster innovation, serve a diverse customer base, and avoid expensive lawsuits and public embarrassment.

- Successful diversity management includes articulating goals and measuring progress, recruiting widely, mentoring promising women and persons of color, and establishing mechanisms for assessing progress.

- Many businesses have helped employees balance the complex demands of work and family obligations by providing support programs such as child and elder care, flexible work schedules, domestic partner benefits, and telecommuting options.

Key Terms

affirmative action, *390*
child care, *396*
diversity, *379*
diversity council, *394*
elder care, *396*
equal employment opportunity, *388*
Equal Employment Opportunity Commission (EEOC), *389*

family-friendly corporation, *397*
family leave, *396*
glass ceiling, *386*
glass walls, *387*
occupational segregation, *383*
parental leave, *396*
pay gap, *383*

racial harassment, *392*
reverse discrimination, *391*
sexual harassment, *391*
undocumented immigrant worker, *380*
workforce diversity, *379*

Internet Resources

www.eeoc.gov	U.S. Equal Employment Opportunity Commission
www.familiesandwork.org	Families and Work Institute
www.abcdependentcare.com	American Business Collaboration for Quality Dependent Care
www.sba.gov	U.S. Small Business Administration
www.catalyst.org	Catalyst—"expanding opportunities for women and business"
www.multiculturaladvantage.com	Resources for diversity officers and professionals of diverse backgrounds
www.diversityinc.com	*Diversity Inc.* magazine and other resources
www.workingmother.com	*Working Mother* magazine and other resources

Discussion Case: *Unauthorized Immigrant Workers at Chipotle Mexican Grill Restaurants*

In May 2011, federal immigration agents descended on dozens of Chipotle Mexican Grill restaurants around the country, from Los Angeles to Atlanta, interviewing employees and managers. Their purpose was to determine whether—and to what extent—the fast-food chain was hiring unauthorized immigrant workers in violation of U.S. law. It was just the latest salvo in an ongoing government investigation of employment practices at the burrito chain. "We've got nothing to hide," said the company's attorney. "We're absolutely convinced that nobody did anything wrong."

Chipotle was a fast-growing chain of restaurants specializing in burritos, tacos, and salads made on premises from fresh ingredients. Founded in Colorado in 1993 by chef Steve Ells, in 2011 the company owned more than 1,200 restaurants in 41 states, Ontario, London, and Paris. Chipotle employed 31,000 people, 92 percent of whom were hourly employees. Operating under the slogan "Food with Integrity," the chain reported $2.27 billion in revenue and 11 percent sales growth in 2011, despite the struggling economy. Some analysts believed that one of the reasons for Chipotle's strong performance was, as the news service Reuters put it, its "uncanny ability to hold down labor costs."

Under government rules, foreign-born individuals are permitted to work legally in the United States under some conditions. They can obtain a green card, a work permit issued to permanent residents (most of whom are close relatives of U.S. citizens). Highly skilled workers in short supply can apply for an H-1 visa. Low-skilled workers can apply for an H-2 visa for temporary, seasonal work; however, these are available to only about 1 percent of the unauthorized population. When hiring, employers are required to fill out and keep on file an I-9 form, documenting a person's eligibility to work, and present it to government investigators if asked.

About half a million undocumented immigrants entered the United States every year during the past decade, two-thirds by crossing the Mexican–U.S. border and the rest by overstaying temporary visas. The Pew Research Center estimates there are 8.3 undocumented immigrants in the U.S. workforce, about 5 percent of the total. Three-quarters of them are Hispanic, mostly from Mexico but also from Central and South America. The main reason they immigrate is for economic opportunity; studies show, for example, that a Mexican man with a high school education can make two and a half times as much in the United States as in his home country, even after taking into account differences in the cost of living.

Most take low-skilled jobs in a small number of occupations and industries. Fully a quarter of farmworkers in the United States—and about a fifth of building and grounds maintenance workers—are undocumented immigrants. In the restaurant industry, they make up 12 percent of food-preparation workers and servers nationally—and much more in some regions, such as southern California. A recent study by the Food Chain Workers' Alliance found that undocumented workers earned a median hourly wage of $7.60 (compared with about $10 for other workers in the food industry) and were more than twice as likely to experience some kind of wage theft, such as unpaid hours. Forty-four percent of undocumented workers in the food industry were actually earning less than minimum wage.

Over the past decade, government policy toward people working in the United States illegally has undergone a sharp about-face. Under President George W. Bush, Immigration and Customs Enforcement (ICE), a division of the Department of Homeland Security, conducted a series of high-profile raids of factories, targeting foreign workers who were unable to produce authentic work papers. For example, in 2008, ICE agents arrested and deported hundreds of workers at a meatpacking plant in Iowa.

The Obama administration took a different approach, focusing its enforcement efforts on employers. ICE began conducting I-9 audits, checking businesses to make sure their employees' papers were in order. The Social Security Administration also began investigating situations where Social Security numbers provided by employees did not match their records (in the case of illegal workers, these numbers were often fictitious). If the agents found evidence of problems, they ordered that employers comply with the law—and in some cases imposed fines or even brought criminal charges against managers.

Chipotle was not the only employer targeted by these more recent investigations. For example, American Apparel, a garment company based in Los Angeles, terminated 1,800 undocumented workers in 2009 after an ICE audit found widespread irregularities. At L.E. Cooke Company, a family-owned nursery in California's Central Valley, the owner was forced to fire 26 of his 99 employees who had entered the country illegally. Many had worked for the nursery for many years and had specialized skills. "Telling them was probably the worst day of my life," the owner said. "I don't just sit at a desk here, I'm actually out in the fields harvesting with them."

At Chipotle, after an earlier probe in 2010 in Minnesota, the burrito chain dismissed around 450 workers who could not confirm their eligibility to work. The departures forced the company to hire new workers and supervisors to keep operations running. As the audits spread to other Chipotle locations, many workers quit, apparently leaving before they could be fired. In addition to dismissing illegal workers, the company also took steps to improve its document review procedures and started using e-Verify, a web-based system that helped employers confirm an individual's eligibility to work, even in states where it was not mandatory.

Even so, Chipotle's managers were clearly concerned about the possible repercussions of the government's actions. In a section in its 2011 annual report to shareholders describing future risks, the company noted: "Although we require all workers to provide us with government-specified documentation evidencing their employment eligibility, some of our employees may, without our knowledge, be unauthorized workers. This may subject us to fines or penalties, and we could experience adverse publicity that negatively impacts our brand and may make it more difficult to hire and keep qualified employees."

Sources: Food Chain Workers' Alliance, *The Hands That Feed Us: Challenges and Opportunities for Workers along the Food Chain,* June 6, 2012, at *www.foodchainworkers.org;* Restaurant Opportunities Centers United (ROC), *Behind the Kitchen Door: A Multi-Site Study of the Restaurant Industry,* February 14, 2011, at *http://rocunited.org;* "Chipotle's Undocumented Worker Problem Resurges," *Bloomberg Businessweek,* May 24, 2012; "Chipotle Faces US Criminal Probe for Hiring Illegals," April 20, 2011, at *www.reuters.com;* "Federal Agents Widen Chipotle Immigration Probe," May 2, 2011, at *www.reuters .com;* "Chipotle Workers Quit Ahead of Immigration Audits," March 8, 2011, *www.reuters.com;* "Chipotle Says 'Lost' 40 Illegal Workers in Capital," March 11, 2011, *www.reuters.com;* "Chipotle: Probes Regarding Immigrant Workers Could Last 2 Years," *The Wall Street Journal,* May 23, 2012; "A Crackdown on Employing Illegal Workers," *The New York Times,* May 29, 2011; "As Immigration Audits Increase, Some Employers Pay a High Price," *The New York Times,* July 13, 2011; Gordon H. Hanson, "The Economics and Policy of Illegal Immigration in the United States," Migration Policy Institute, December 2009; Jeffrey S. Passel and D'Vera Cohn, "A Portrait of Unauthorized Immigrants in the United States," Pew Research Center, 2009; and Chipotle Mexican Grill annual reports at *www.chipotle.com.*

Discussion Questions

1. Do you consider being an unauthorized immigrant a form of workplace diversity? How is it similar to and different from other kinds of workplace diversity discussed in this chapter?

2. What are the benefits and risks to employers, such as Chipotle and others mentioned in this case, of hiring unauthorized immigrants—whether or not they do so knowingly?

3. Other than employers, which stakeholders are helped and which are hurt when a business hires unauthorized immigrants?

4. Do you agree with the public policies and enforcement strategies described in this case? If not, what changes in both would you recommend?

5. Do you agree with Chipotle's response to the government's enforcement effort? What else should Chipotle's managers do now, and why?

CHAPTER EIGHTEEN

The Community and the Corporation

A strong relationship benefits both business and its community. Communities look to businesses for civic leadership and for help in coping with local problems, while businesses expect to be treated in fair and supportive ways by the community. As companies expand their operations, they develop a wider set of community relationships. Community relations programs, including corporate giving, are an important way for a business to express its commitment to corporate citizenship.

This Chapter Focuses on These Key Learning Objectives:

- Defining a community, and understanding the interdependencies between companies and the communities in which they operate.
- Analyzing why it is in the interest of business to respond to community problems and needs.
- Knowing the major responsibilities of community relations managers.
- Examining how different forms of corporate giving contribute to building strong relationships between businesses and communities.
- Evaluating how companies can direct their giving strategically, to further their own business objectives.
- Analyzing how collaborative partnerships between businesses and communities can address today's pressing social problems.

Whole Foods Market is a natural foods retailer with stores in many communities in North America and the United Kingdom. Founded in 1980 in Austin, Texas, the company believes that its business "is intimately tied to the neighborhood and larger community that we serve and in which we live." Whole Foods donates 5 percent of its net profit to charitable causes and operates a foundation that supports rural economic development, as well as projects that support animal welfare, organic production, and healthy nutrition. Each of the company's 310 stores hosts a community giving day three times a year, with 5 percent of the day's total sales revenue contributed to a worthy local nonprofit organization. Whole Foods also encourages its employees to volunteer their time and expertise to the community. Employees have been involved in a wide range of service projects, including organizing blood donation drives, raising money for breast cancer research, developing community gardens, renovating housing, and delivering "meals on wheels."[1]

When a powerful earthquake and tsunami devastated much of northeastern Japan in 2011, the supply of Japanese-made auto parts to assembly plants all over the world was disrupted. Honda Motor Company, a Japanese-based car company with manufacturing facilities in Ohio, Alabama, and Indiana, was forced to shut down its U.S. plants two days a week because of the parts shortage. Rather than simply sending its workers home, the company had a better idea: it gave them the option of reporting to work, with pay, to volunteer in their local communities. Many workers jumped at the chance, providing services to clients, taking care of overdue maintenance, and cleaning up storm damage. At the Furniture Bank of Central Ohio, where Honda employees were hard at work assembling tables, chairs, and other furnishings for needy families, the manager of community relations commented, "It's a little easier to assemble furniture than putting together a well-manufactured car."[2]

One of the leading financial institutions in the world, ING has operations in more than 50 countries. Based in the Netherlands, the company provides insurance, banking, and asset management services throughout Europe, with a growing presence in the Americas and Asia. Recognizing that the needs of the many communities where it does business differ, the company has delegated responsibility for corporate citizenship programs to business unit managers, provided their decisions are consistent with the firm's core values. The result has been a remarkable diversity of community initiatives. In India, ING trained secondary school heads; in the United States, it ran financial literacy classes for teens; in Malaysia, it worked on the conservation of rain forests. Across the globe, ING employees participated in a worldwide fund-raising effort for Chances for Children, the company's partnership with UNICEF, with a goal of positively impacting one million children by 2015.[3]

Why do businesses as diverse as Whole Foods Market, Honda, and ING invest in community organizations, projects, and charities? Why do they contribute their money, resources, and time to help others? What benefits do they gain from such activities? This chapter explains why many companies believe that being an involved citizen is part of their basic business mission. The chapter also looks at how companies participate in community life and how they build partnerships with other businesses, government, and community organizations. The core questions that we consider in this chapter are: What does it mean to be a good corporate neighbor? What is the business case for doing so?

---

[1] See *www.wholefoodsmarket.com/company/giving*.

[2] "Honda Pays Employees to Volunteer: Workers Helping Out Nonprofits During Company Downtime," *The Columbus Dispatch*, June 17, 2011; and "Honda Helps Employees Make Down Time Productive for Community," in *Focus on Results: The Community Involvement Index*, Center for Corporate Citizenship, 2011.

[3] Information on ING's community initiatives is available at *www.ingforsomethingbetter.com*.

The Business–Community Relationship

The term **community**, as used in this chapter, refers to a company's area of business influence. Traditionally, the term applied to the city, town, or rural area in which a business's operations, offices, or assets were located. With the rise of large, complex business organizations, the meaning of the term has expanded to include multiple localities. A local merchant's community relationships may involve just the people who live within driving distance of its store. A bank in a large metropolitan area, by contrast, may define its community as both the central city and the suburbs where it does business. And at the far extreme, a large transnational firm such as ING, ExxonMobil, or Nokia has relationships with numerous communities in many countries around the world.

Today the term *community* may also refer not only to a geographical area or areas but to a range of groups that are affected by an organization's actions, whether or not they are in the immediate vicinity. In this broader view, as shown in Figure 18.1, the *geographical* (sometimes called the *site*) community is just one of several different kinds of communities.

Whether a business is small or large, local or global, its relationship with the community or communities with which it interacts is one of mutual interdependence. As shown in Figure 18.2, business and the community each need something from the other. Business depends on the community for education, public services such as police and

FIGURE 18.1
The Firm and Its Communities

Source: Adapted from a discussion in Edmund M. Burke, *Corporate Community Relations: The Principle of Neighbor of Choice* (Westport, CT: Praeger, 1999), ch. 6.

Community	Interest
Site community	Geographical location of a company's operations, offices, or assets
Fence-line community	Immediate neighbors
Virtual communities	People who buy from or follow the company online
Communities of interest	Groups that share a common interest with the company
Employee community	People who work near the company

FIGURE 18.2
What the Community and Business Want from Each Other

Business Participation Desired by Community	Community Services Desired by Business
• Pays taxes	Schools—a quality educational system
• Provides jobs and training	Recreational opportunities
• Follows laws	Libraries, museums, theaters, and other cultural services and organizations
• Supports schools	Adequate infrastructure, e.g., sewer, water, and electric services
• Supports the arts and cultural activities	Adequate transportation systems, e.g., roads, rail, airport, harbor
• Supports local health care programs	Effective public safety services, e.g., police and fire protection
• Supports parks and recreation	Fair and equitable taxation
• Assists less advantaged people	Streamlined permitting services
• Contributes to public safety	Quality health care services
• Participates in economic development	Cooperative problem-solving approach

The professional sports franchise is one kind of business that has historically been particularly dependent on support from the community. Cities often compete vigorously in bidding wars to attract or keep football, basketball, baseball, hockey, and soccer teams. Communities subsidize professional sports in many ways. Government agencies build stadiums and arenas, sell municipal bonds to pay for construction, give tax breaks to owners, and allow teams to keep revenues from parking, luxury boxes, and food concessions. Some say that public support is warranted, because high-profile teams and sports facilities spur local economic development, offer wholesome entertainment, and build civic pride. But critics argue that subsidies simply enrich affluent team owners and players at taxpayer expense and shift spending away from other more deserving areas, such as schools, police and fire protection, social services, and the arts. In this view, this is a case in which the relationship between business and the community is deeply out of balance.

One of the most outrageous examples of this was the Paul Brown Stadium, built at an estimated cost to the public of $555 million to house the National Football League's Cincinnati Bengals after the team threatened to move to Baltimore. Hamilton County, where the stadium was located, issued bonds and raised its sales tax to pay for the new stadium, the most costly ever built at taxpayer expense. That was just the beginning, because the county had also agreed to pay for most operating expenses and capital improvements going forward. The Bengals got to keep the revenue from naming rights, advertising, tickets, suites, and most parking. In 2010, the annual cost to the county was $35 million, about 16 percent of its budget, a huge strain as the region struggled under the weight of a weak economy. "It's the monster that ate the public sector," said the administrator of the juvenile courts, speaking of the stadium. The juvenile courts had just seen their funding slashed, and had been forced to cut its programs for troubled youth.

Sources: "As Super Bowl Shows, Build Stadiums for Love and Not Money," *Bloomberg Businessweek,* February 3, 2012; "A Stadium's Costly Legacy Throws Taxpayers for a Loss," *The Wall Street Journal,* July 12, 2011; and "Stadium Boom Deepens Municipal Woes," *The New York Times,* December 25, 2009. A website critical of public subsidies to sports facilities is *www.fieldofschemes.com.*

fire protection, recreational facilities, and transportation systems, among other things. The community depends on business for support of the arts, schools, health care, and the disadvantaged, and other urgent civic needs, both through taxes and donations of money, goods, and time.

Ideally, community support of business and business support of the community are roughly in balance, so that both parties feel that they have benefited in the relationship. Sometimes, however, a business will invest more in the community than the community seems to provide in return. Conversely, a community sometimes provides more support to a business than the firm contributes to the community. Exhibit 18.A discusses subsidies by communities to professional sports franchises, an instance in which the relationship between business and the community is sometimes perceived as out of balance.

The Business Case for Community Involvement

The term **civic engagement** describes the active involvement of businesses and individuals in changing and improving communities. *Civic* means pertaining to cities or communities, and *engagement* means being committed to or involved with something. Why should businesses be involved with the community? What is the *business case* for civic engagement?

The ideas of corporate social responsibility and global citizenship, introduced in earlier chapters, refer broadly to businesses acting as citizens of society by behaving responsibly toward all their stakeholders. Civic engagement is a major way in which companies carry out their corporate citizenship mission. As explained in Chapters 3 and 7, business organizations that act in a socially responsible way reap many benefits. These include an enhanced reputation and ability to respond quickly to changing stakeholder demands. By acting responsibly, companies can also avoid or correct problems caused by their operations—a basic duty that comes with their significant power and influence. They can win the loyalty of employees, customers, and neighbors. And by doing the right thing, businesses can often avoid, or at least correctly anticipate, government regulations. All these reasons for social responsibility operate at the level of the community as well, via civic engagement.

Another specific reason for community involvement is to win local support for business activity. Communities do not have to accept a business. They sometimes object to the presence of companies that will create too much traffic, pollute the air or water, or engage in activities that are viewed as offensive or inappropriate. A company must earn its informal **license to operate**—or right to do business—from society. In communities where democratic principles apply, citizens have the right to exercise their voice in determining whether a company will or will not be welcome, and the result is not always positive for business.

> Walmart has encountered serious local objection to its plans to build superstores and distribution centers in a number of local communities. Walmart's founder, Sam Walton, now deceased, was fond of saying he would never try to force a community to accept a Walmart store. "Better to go where we are wanted," he is reported to have said. In recent years, however, Walmart management less often endorses that view. In a series of high-profile local conflicts, Walmart sparked intense local opposition when it tried to move into town. For example, in 2012 local activists organized to block construction of a Walmart neighborhood market in Los Angeles's Chinatown, saying it would destroy the "cultural fabric" of the community and the viability of its many family-owned small grocery stores. The problem of community opposition seems likely to grow more complex for Walmart as it continues its expansion into international markets.[4]

Through positive interactions with the communities in which its stores are located, Walmart is more likely to avoid this kind of local opposition.

Community involvement by business also helps build social capital. **Social capital** has been defined as the norms and networks that enable collective action. Scholars have also described it as "the goodwill that is engendered by the fabric of social relations."[5] When companies such as Whole Foods Market, described at the beginning of this chapter, work to address community problems such as blood shortages, hunger, and dilapidated housing, their actions help build social capital. The company and groups in the community develop closer relationships, and their people become more committed to each other's welfare. Many experts believe that high levels of social capital enhance a community's quality of life. Dense social networks increase productivity by reducing the costs of

---

[4] "Chinatown Walmart Opponents Plan 10,000-Strong March," *NBC Southern California*, at *www.nbclosangeles.com*. For the company's perspective on its community relationships, see *www.walmart.com*.

[5] Paul S. Adler and S. W. Kwon, "Social Capital: Prospects for a New Concept," *Academy of Management Review* 27, no. 1 (January/February 2002), pp. 17–40. For a more general discussion, see Robert D. Putnam, *Bowling Alone: The Collapse and Revival of American Community* (New York: Simon and Schuster, 2000).

doing business, because firms and people are more likely to trust one another. The development of social capital produces a win–win outcome because it enables everyone to be better off.[6]

Community Relations

The organized involvement of business with the community is called **community relations**. The importance of community relations has increased markedly in recent years,[7] as shown by the following statistics, drawn from a 2011 survey conducted by the Center for Corporate Citizenship:[8]

- 86 percent of companies have a specific community involvement strategy. (The study defined community involvement as "mobilizing the company's assets to address social issues and support social well-being beyond creating jobs and paying taxes.")
- Of these, two-thirds link their community involvement efforts to a broader corporate citizenship strategy.
- 80 percent of companies factor community involvement into their overall strategic plan.
- 59 percent of companies set their community involvement strategy centrally and execute locally.
- 71 percent reported information about their community involvement activities on their corporate website.

In support of this commitment, some corporations have established specialized community relations departments; others house this function in a department of public affairs or corporate citizenship. The job of the **community relations manager** (sometimes called the community involvement manager) is to interact with local citizens, develop community programs, manage donations of goods and services, work with local governments, and encourage employee volunteerism. These actions are, in effect, business investments intended to produce more social capital—to build relationships and networks with important groups in the community. Community relations departments typically work closely with other departments that link the company to the outside world, such as public relations (discussed in Chapter 19), as well as internal departments such as human resources. All these roles form important bridges between the corporation and the community.

An example of an executive with broad responsibility for building community relationships is Ann Wilson Cramer, whose title is director of corporate citizenship and corporate affairs for the Americas at IBM Corporation. (Her title had previously been community relations manager.) Based in Atlanta, Georgia, Cramer interacts with the community in a wide range of areas, including K–12 education, literacy, economic development, and support for the disadvantaged. The governor of Georgia commented of Cramer, "There are few people as full of energy, commitment, and heart." In an interview, Cramer said, "What it means to be a good corporate citizen isn't just doing good in the local community. It's lifting that up a notch, taking a strategic approach to making a difference, going from spare change to real change."[9]

---

[6] Some benefits of social capital are described on the World Bank website at: *www.worldbank.org.*

[7] Center for Corporate Citizenship, *Focus on Results: Community Involvement Index* (Boston, MA: Boston College, 2011). For related data, see *www.bcccc.net.*

[8] Ibid.

[9] "Heroes, Saints, and Legends," *Atlanta Business Chronicle,* May 18, 2012, at *www.bizjournals.com/atlanta;* and "Volunteer's Volunteer, Leader's Leader," December 2005, at *www.georgiatrends.com.*

Community relations departments are typically involved with a range of diverse issues. According to a survey of community involvement managers, education was viewed as the most important issue. Many companies had developed a specific focus on science, technology, engineering, and math (STEM) literacy among young people. Other critical issues included hunger, economic development, and environmental issues. Further down the list of issues, although still important, were health care, housing, disaster relief, and the arts.[10] (Figure 18.5, which appears later in this chapter, shows the issues to which companies donate the most money.) Although not exhaustive, this list suggests the range of needs that a corporation's community relations professionals are asked to address. These community concerns challenge managers to apply talent, imagination, and resources to develop creative ways to strengthen the community while still managing their businesses as profitable enterprises.

Several specific ways in which businesses and their community relations departments have addressed some critical concerns facing communities are discussed below. The all-important issue of business involvement in education reform is addressed later, in the section on collaborative partnerships and in the discussion case at the end of the chapter, which describes an innovative partnership between Fidelity Investments and a nonprofit organization committed to after-school programs for middle-school children.

Economic Development

Business leaders and their companies are frequently involved in local or regional economic development that is intended to bring new businesses into an area or to develop workforce skills. The Great Recession has made it even more imperative that businesses do so.

> In 2009, Microsoft Corporation launched a program called Elevate America to provide job training at a time when many were looking for work or seeking to improve their skills as the economy struggled to recover from a severe downturn. The company provided one million free vouchers for its online technology skills courses and certification exams in partnership with participating state governments. The following year, Microsoft extended the initiative by offering grants to nonprofits offering employment services, skills training, and job placement in technology-related fields. It also added a special program for veterans, addressing the specific challenges they faced in transitioning to civilian life. "The economy made it important to get out there and not to wait," said Akhtar Badshah, Microsoft's senior director of global community affairs.[11]

Housing

Another community issue in which many firms have become involved is housing. Life and health insurance companies, among others, have taken the lead in programs to revitalize neighborhood housing through organizations such as Neighborhood Housing Services (NHS) of America. NHS, which is locally controlled, locally funded, nonprofit, and tax-exempt, offers housing rehabilitation and financial services to neighborhood residents. Similar efforts are being made to house the homeless. New York City's Coalition for the Homeless includes corporate, nonprofit, and community members. Corporations also often work with nongovernmental organizations (NGOs) such as Habitat for Humanity to build

---

[10] Ibid., p. 2. Based on an opinion survey of 490 community involvement managers in 2011.

[11] "Microsoft Announces Elevate America Community Initiative Grants," Microsoft Corporate Citizenship Blog, February 3, 2011; *Together for the Recovery: Business Is Part of the Solution* (Business Civic Leadership Center Report, December 2009); and "Microsoft Hopes to Train 2 Million in IT by 2012," at *www.beyondsandiego.com* (n.d.).

or repair housing. Globally, businesses have also been active in housing issues, as illustrated by the following example.

> CEMEX, a global leader in the building materials industry that is based in Mexico, in 2010 launched an affordable housing initiative with the aim of creating "an integrated and collaborative approach to ensuring the future of housing and infrastructure in developing countries," according to the company. Worldwide, 1.1 billion people are estimated to live in urban areas without adequate housing. CEMEX brought its expertise to partnerships with governments, nonprofits, and financial institutions to develop housing solutions for a wide range of different settings. For example, the company developed an innovative concrete home that could be built for less than $10,000, including finishes and fixtures. As of 2012, the company had built almost 5,000 homes in Costa Rica, Guatemala, Mexico, Nicaragua, and Panama, including replacing homes destroyed by Hurricane Alex.[12]

Aid to Minority, Women, and Disabled Veteran-Owned Enterprises

Private enterprise has also extended assistance to minority, women, and disabled veteran-owned small businesses. These businesses often operate at an economic disadvantage. In some cases, they do business in economic locations where high crime rates, poor transportation, low-quality public services, and a low-income clientele combine to produce a high rate of business failure. In others, they face competition from more established suppliers. Many large corporations now have supplier diversity programs that seek out partnerships with such enterprises.

> AT&T has operated supplier diversity programs for more than 40 years. In 2011, the company spent $12 billion procuring products and services from minority, women, and disabled veteran-owned businesses—almost a quarter of its procurement spending. An example of such a supplier is Group O Direct, an Illinois–based firm that provides fulfillment services for customer promotions. Group O Direct, which is owned by Mexican-Americans, now has several other high-profile clients in addition to AT&T, including Caterpillar, PepsiCo, and Microsoft, and annual revenues of $515 million.[13]

Disaster, Terrorism, and War Relief

One common form of corporate involvement in the community is disaster relief. Throughout the world, companies, like individuals, provide assistance to local citizens and communities when disaster strikes. When floods, fires, earthquakes, ice storms, hurricanes, or terrorist attacks devastate communities, funds pour into affected communities from companies.

> Businesses from all over the world responded with great generosity to the communities impacted by the massive earthquake and tsunami that struck Japan in 2011. Many companies gave cash either directly or through the Red Cross. Others drew on their own special expertise to lend a hand. The Japanese airline ANA donated planes and crewmembers to fly relief supplies into the stricken region. Both Verizon and

---

[12] "CEMEX Lays Solid Foundation to Address Need for Affordable Housing," April 25, 2012, at *http://blogs.bcccc.net;* and "CEMEX Announces Progress on Its Affordable Housing Initiative," press release, October 13, 2011, at *www.cemex.com.*

[13] "NMSDC Honors Top Regional Minority Suppliers," National Minority Supplier Development Council, press release, October 24, 2011. AT&T's supplier diversity programs are described at *www.attsuppliers.com/sd.*

AT&T offered its customers free unlimited calls and text message service between the United States and Japan in the first weeks after the disaster, so family members and friends could reconnect. Health care companies Bayer, GlaxoSmithKline, and Novartis sent medicines and supplies; OshKosh B'Gosh sent clothing; IKEA sent blankets; and Shiseido sent disinfectant lotions. After the crisis at the Fukushima nuclear plant, CBI Polymers donated a quarter million dollars' worth of radiological decontamination products, and General Atomic donated its entire stock of dosimeters—devices worn by workers to measure their radiation exposure—to the Tokyo Electric Power Company, the operator of the crippled facility.[14]

International relief efforts are becoming more important, as communications improve and people around the world are able to witness the horrors of natural disasters, terrorism, and war. Corporate involvement in such efforts is an extension of the natural tendency of people to help one another when tragedy strikes. It is also a way for companies to build brand loyalty, as people often develop lasting gratitude to those who helped them in times of great need.

In all these areas of community need—economic development, housing, aid to minority enterprise, and disaster relief—as well as many others, businesses around the world have made and continue to make significant contributions.

Corporate Giving

An important aspect of the business–community relationship is **corporate philanthropy**, or **corporate giving**. Every year, businesses around the world give generously to their communities through various kinds of philanthropic contributions to nonprofit organizations.

America has historically been a generous society. In 2011, individuals, bequests (individual estates), foundations, and corporations collectively gave more than $298 billion to churches, charities, and other nonprofit organizations, as shown in Figure 18.3. Businesses are a small, but important, part of this broad cultural tradition of giving. In 2011, corporate contributions totaled $14.6 billion, or about 5 percent of all charitable giving. This amount included in-kind gifts claimed as tax deductions and giving by corporate foundations.

FIGURE 18.3
Philanthropy in the United States, by Source of Contributions, 2011 (in $ billions)

Source: Giving USA Foundation™, *Giving USA 2012* (Chicago, IL, 2012), pp. 3 and 8. Used by permission.

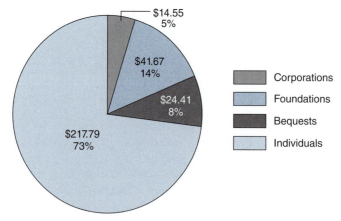

Corporations — $14.55 / 5%
Foundations — $41.67 / 14%
Bequests — $24.41 / 8%
Individuals — $217.79 / 73%

Total value of contributions was $298.42 billion.

[14] Business Civic Leadership Center, "Corporate Aid Tracker: Japanese Earthquake and Tsunami, March 2011," at *http://bclic.uschamber.com*.

As U.S. firms have become increasingly globalized, as shown in Chapter 6, their international charitable contributions have also grown. A 2011 survey by the Conference Board found that international giving comprised about 7 percent of all donations that were made the prior year by the 139 companies in the sample. The major factors driving international gifts were the size of the company's workforce in the receiving region and perceived humanitarian need. The Latin America–Caribbean region received the most (35 percent of international donations), probably reflecting the outpouring of aid to victims of the 2010 Haiti earthquake. It was followed by Europe (22 percent), Africa (21 percent), and Asia-Pacific excluding China (11 percent). Other regions received less.[15] To cite just one example, the Coca-Cola Foundation has donated millions of dollars to support education around the world. Its contributions have, among other projects, helped build schools in Chile, Egypt, and the Philippines.[16]

In the United States, tax rules have encouraged corporate giving for educational, charitable, scientific, and religious purposes since 1936.[17] Current rules permit corporations to deduct from their taxable income all such gifts that do not exceed 10 percent of the company's before-tax income. In other words, a company with a before-tax income of $1 million might contribute up to $100,000 to nonprofit community organizations devoted to education, charity, science, or religion. The $100,000 in contributions would then reduce the income to be taxed from $1 million to $900,000, thus saving the company money on its tax bill while providing a source of income to community agencies. Of course, nothing prevents a corporation from giving more than 10 percent of its income for philanthropic purposes, but it would not be given a tax break above the 10 percent level.

As shown in Figure 18.4, average corporate giving in the United States is far below the 10 percent deduction now permitted. Though it varies from year to year, corporate giving has generally ranged between one-half of 1 percent and 2 percent of pretax profits

FIGURE 18.4

Corporate Contributions in the United States, as a Percentage of Pretax Corporate Profits, 1972–2010

Source: Giving USA Foundation™, *Giving USA 2012* (Chicago, IL, 2012), p. 272. Used by permission.

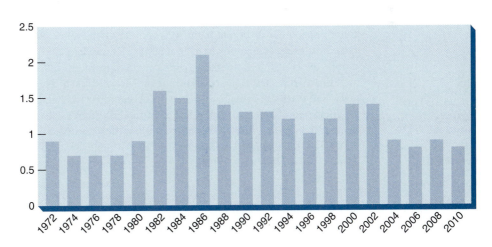

[15] "International Contributions," pages 28–39 in The Conference Board, *2011 Corporate Contributions Report.*

[16] More information about Coca-Cola's contributions to education is available at *www.thecoca-colacompany.com/citizenship/education.*

[17] The evolution of corporate philanthropy is summarized in Mark Sharfman, "Changing Institutional Rules: The Evolution of Corporate Philanthropy, 1883–1953," *Business and Society* 33, no. 3 (December 1994).

Exhibit 18.B

**Thanks for the Gift,
But Are Strings Attached?**

Many organizations, including schools and universities, social agencies, arts organizations, and other nonprofits, depend on—and gratefully receive—gifts from corporations, foundations, and individual philanthropists. Without this generosity, many of these organizations would be hard-pressed to survive economically. Yet, what if a gift comes with "strings attached"? Are there circumstances under which an organization should reject a gift, or its conditions?

Bayerische Motoren Werke, the auto company commonly known as BMW, donated $10 million to Clemson University. A major BMW plant is located in Greer, South Carolina, just 50 miles away from the university. In return for the largest gift ever received by the university at that time, BMW management asked for input in creating the curriculum for the automotive and motor sports graduate engineering program. The company also provided Clemson with what they thought was a profile of "the ideal student" and provided the university with a list of engineering professors and specialists to interview to staff the school's program. BMW even asked for approval rights over the school's architectural plans for a new building. The university expressed profound gratitude for the gift, which helped build a major Center for Automotive Research. But some critics expressed concern that the university had given BMW too much control. Said one researcher, "It looks like you've got a profit-making corporation calling the shots in a university setting."

Source: "BMW's Custom-Made University," *The New York Times*, August 29, 2006.

since the early 1960s, with a rise that reached a peak at 2.1 percent in 1986. Corporate giving was 0.8 percent of pretax profits in 2010. A few companies, including a cluster in the Minneapolis–St. Paul area that has pledged to donate 5 percent annually, give much more than this. The top givers in 2010, relative to pretax profits, were Macy's, Dow Chemical, Safeway, and Morgan Stanley.[18] One company, Newman's Own, the philanthropic corporation established by the late film star Paul Newman, gives *all* of its earnings to charity.

How has the Great Recession and its aftermath affected corporate giving? A 2011 analysis of this question by the Committee Encouraging Corporate Philanthropy (CECP) found "strikingly divergent paths in corporate giving since 2007." The financial crisis affected different companies in different ways. Some had cut back quite markedly. For example, the Housing Partnership Alliance, a nonprofit affordable housing group in Boston, said that it expected to lose funding from Merrill Lynch, Freddie Mac, Fannie Mae, and AIG—all financial firms hard-hit by the economic crisis. On the other hand, about a quarter of the companies surveyed had significantly increased their contributions since the start of the recession, often to meet communities' basic needs. Tyson Foods and Kroger Company, for example, had increased their donations of food to antihunger charities. Most observers expected business philanthropy overall to bounce back as the economy recovered.[19]

Exhibit 18.B asks how nonprofit organizations should respond when corporate donors attach conditions to their gifts.

In Europe, corporate philanthropy has lagged behind that in the United States, in part because tax breaks are less generous and differences in the law across countries make cross-border giving difficult. Greater spending on social welfare by governments had also

[18] *Giving USA 2012,* op. cit., 112.

[19] Committee Encouraging Corporate Philanthropy, "Companies Report Increased 2010 Contributions, but Show Divergent Paths since the Economic Downturn in 2007," press release, October 27, 2011, at: *www.corporatephilanthropy.org*, and "Nonprofits Gird for Loss of Funding: Fallout from Collapse of Wall Street Firms," *Boston Globe*, September 22, 2008.

reduced the need for private-sector donations, although Europe's persistent financial crisis may change this. Europe-based multinational corporations remain active, however, as illustrated by the following example.

> The motto of Nokia, the cellular phone company based in Finland, is "connecting people." In partnership with the International Youth Foundation, the company launched a program called "Make A Connection" to help develop life skills among young people in more than 20 countries. Over a nine-year period, the program had directly benefited 43,000 young people. In the Philippines, for example, the program's "text2teach" initiative used mobile technology to bring interactive, multimedia learning materials to 80 schools. Said Nokia's vice president for corporate social responsibility, "It's about developing the social glue within a peer group or community."[20]

Although most companies give directly, some large corporations have established nonprofit **corporate foundations** to handle their charitable programs. This permits them to administer contribution programs more uniformly and provides a central group of professionals that handles all grant requests. Eighty-one percent of large U.S.-based corporations have such foundations; collectively, corporate foundations gave about $42 billion in 2011.[21] Foreign-owned corporations use foundations less frequently, although firms such as Matsushita (Panasonic) and Hitachi use sophisticated corporate foundations to conduct their charitable activities in the United States. As corporations expand to more foreign locations, pressures will grow to expand international corporate giving. Foundations, with their defined mission to benefit the community, can be a useful mechanism to help companies implement philanthropic programs that meet this corporate social responsibility.

Forms of Corporate Giving

Typically, gifts by corporations and their foundations take one of three forms: charitable donations (gifts of money), in-kind contributions (gifts of products or services), and volunteer employee service (gifts of time). Many companies give in all three categories.

> An example of a particularly generous cash gift was one made by Intel, the computer chip maker. Intel, together with its foundation, in 2008 pledged $120 million over the next 10 years to the Society for Science & the Public Interest. The purpose of the gift was to support this organization's Science Talent Search, a prestigious science competition for high school seniors. The gift also included funds for outreach to young people and mentoring for program alumni. As part of the competition, every year 40 finalists traveled to Washington, DC, to present their research to members of the scientific community. Awards included college scholarships and computers. Many former winners had gone on to distinguished careers in science and entrepreneurship. "I can't think of a more critical time to invest in math and science education," said Intel's vice president for corporate affairs.[22]

[20] "Nokia & International Youth Foundation, Program Profile: Making a Connection," in *Alliances for Youth: What Works in CSR Partnerships* (2006), at *www.iyfnet.org.* "Making a Connection to Boost Life Skills," *Financial Times (London),* January 26, 2006; and *Corporate Social Responsibility Review 2008,* at *http://i.nokia.com.*

[21] *Giving in Numbers,* 2011 ed., op. cit., p. 33; and *Giving USA 2012,* op. cit., p. 3.

[22] "Intel Encourages More Youth to Participate in Math and Science," press release, October 20, 2008, *www.intel.com /pressroom.* The website of the Intel Science Talent Search is at *www.societyforscience.org.*

The share of all giving comprising **in-kind contributions** of products or services has been rising steadily for the past decade or so and has now surpassed cash contributions. Of U.S. corporate contributions in 2010, 38 percent were in-kind (noncash), 35 percent were cash, and the balance came in the form of contributions from affiliated foundations.[23] For example, high-technology companies have donated computer hardware and software to schools, universities, and public libraries. Grocery retailers have donated food, and Internet service providers have donated time online. Publishers have given books. The most generous industry, in terms of in-kind contributions, is pharmaceuticals, as illustrated by the following example.[24]

> In 2010, Pfizer contributed an extraordinary $3 *billion* to charity; 98 percent of this was in the form of medicines and other products and services. Many of these donations were directed to the poorest nations and communities in the world, where the company gave away drugs to treat malaria, HIV/AIDS, trachoma, and many other illnesses. In 2009, Pfizer announced it would give access to its "library" of 200,000 novel chemical compounds to Medicines for Malaria Venture, a nonprofit created to develop safe and effective drugs to treat malaria—a dreadful scourge that killed 881,000 people annually, most of them African children. "People are suffering in developing countries and we want to help by sharing resources and boosting research against tropical diseases," said a Pfizer executive.[25]

In-kind contributions can be creative—and they need not cost a lot. Frito-Lay, for example, donated publicity to Do Something—a nonprofit whose mission is to encourage young people to improve the world—by featuring photos of the organization's work on 500 million bags of Doritos chips. "It drove fabulous recognition for our organization and helped our Web traffic," said the grateful director.[26] The contribution was a low-cost one for Frito-Lay, which would have had to print its bags anyway.

Under U.S. tax laws, if companies donate new goods, they may deduct their fair-market value within the relevant limits. For example, if a computer company donated $10,000 worth of new laptops to a local school, it could take a deduction for this amount on its corporate tax return, provided this amount was less than 10 percent of its pretax income.

Business leaders and employees also regularly donate their own time—another form of corporate giving. **Volunteerism** involves the efforts of people to assist others in the community through unpaid work. According to a report by the Department of Labor, about 27 percent of Americans ages 16 and older volunteered during the prior year, donating on average 51 hours of their time.[27] Many companies encourage their employees to volunteer by publicizing opportunities, sponsoring specific projects, and offering recognition for service. Some companies partner with a specific agency to provide volunteer support over time, as illustrated by the following example.

---

[23] The Conference Board, "The 2011 Corporate Contributions Report," p. 23.

[24] Committee to Encourage Corporate Philanthropy, *Adding It Up 2004: The Corporate Giving Standard* (Boston, MA: Center for Corporate Citizenship at Boston College, 2006).

[25] *Giving USA*, p. 112, and "Pfizer and Medicines for Malaria Venture Advancing International Research Efforts in the Fight against Malaria," press release, April 22, 2009, *http://mediaroom.pfizer.com.* Pfizer's philanthropic initiatives are reported at *www.pfizer.com/responsibility.*

[26] "Philanthropy: A Special Report: Firm Decisions: As Companies Become More Involved in Giving, Charities Are Glad to Get Aid Faster and with Less Red Tape," *The Wall Street Journal,* December 10, 2007.

[27] "Volunteering in the United States, 2011," U.S. Department of Labor, press release, February 22, 2012.

KaBOOM! is a nonprofit organization that builds playgrounds. The group's goal is "to help develop a country in which all children have, within their communities, access to equitable, fun, and healthy play opportunities." Since it was founded in 1996, the organization has maintained a strong partnership with Home Depot, the building supply firm. Home Depot employees in many communities have volunteered their building skills, along with materials, to build KaBOOM! playgrounds in underserved neighborhoods. "Team Depot" volunteers, working alongside people from the community, can build a state-of-the-art playground in a single day. In 2008, Home Depot reached a milestone of 1,000 play spaces built in collaboration with KaBOOM![28]

An important trend is what is known as *skills-based volunteerism,* in which employee skills are matched to specialized needs. For example, Target, the Minneapolis–based retailer, has set up a pilot program under which employees with architectural design and construction skills can volunteer to help renovate public libraries.

Another approach is for companies to provide employees with *paid* time off for volunteer service in the community. For example, Wells Fargo offers a volunteer leave program, under which employees can apply for a fully paid sabbatical of up to four months to work in a nonprofit organization of their choice. In recent years, Wells Fargo employees on paid leave have trained teachers in Afghanistan; built homes in Oaxaca, Mexico; and helped renovate a facility for the mentally ill.[29] A 2012 survey found that 20 percent of employers allowed their employees to volunteer during regular work hours. Of these, more than half paid employees for up to 19 hours a year spent volunteering, and 31 percent paid them for 20 or more hours.[30]

Evidence shows that companies with robust volunteer programs reap benefits, even as communities gain from their workers' contributions of time and skill. For example, Green Mountain Coffee Roasters, a purveyor of specialty coffees and single-cup brewing systems based in Vermont, has an active volunteer program called Community Action for Employees (CAFÉ). Green Mountain employees can spend up to 52 hours per year of paid work time volunteering for nonprofits in their communities. The company's Dollars-for-Doers program provides a $250 grant to any organization to which an employee donates 25 hours or more in a year. Their 5,600 employees volunteer on average one day a year—and some much more. An academic study of the company's volunteer program found that employees who valued the program were more likely to be proud of their company and want to continue to work there. Moreover, their supervisors reported separately that these employees ranked higher than their peers in organizational citizenship. The researcher concluded the program had benefited Green Mountain directly through its impact on employees, quite apart from any impact it may have had on branding and consumer loyalty.[31]

[28] "The Home Depot and KaBOOM! Celebrate 1,000th Play Space," press release, April, 10, 2008. The website for KaBOOM! is at *www.kaboom.org.*

[29] Boston College Center for Corporate Citizenship, "Company Example: Wells Fargo," June 2007.

[30] "2012 National Study of Employers," at *http://familiesandwork.org.*

[31] David A. Jones, "Does Serving the Community Also Serve the Company? Using Organizational Identification and Social Exchange Theories to Understand Employee Responses to a Volunteerism Programme," *Journal of Occupational and Organizational Psychology* 83, (2010); and "Employee Volunteerism," at *www.gmcr.com.*

Exhibit 18.C

Many companies have turned to technology to improve the amount and effectiveness of employee volunteerism. "Technology is transforming the landscape," commented the executive director of the Mitsubishi Electric America Foundation. "The speed of communications enables us to quickly get information to and from our employees." Horizon Bank, for example, has linked Volunteer Match, a web-based service that enables nonprofits to post volunteer opportunities online, to its company intranet. The bank uses the service to track employee volunteer hours and makes a contribution to charities based on the number of hours its employees commit to them. Other providers of volunteer software include AmeriGives, AngelPoints, and JK Group. Some firms—among them, Oracle and IBM—have developed their own computerized systems to oversee their employees' volunteerism. Bank of America has developed a custom-designed website to measure and recognize employee volunteerism. BofA gives workers two hours a week of paid time to volunteer, and for every 50 hours contributed gives the organization a $250 contribution on the volunteer's behalf. Whether provided by outside vendors or in-house, software enables companies to better monitor the impact of their employees' work in the community. Commented the national director of community involvement for Deloitte, a large consulting firm, "We can be more strategic and more focused on social outcomes [and can more easily] answer questions about when and how we as a company [become] engaged."

Sources: "Corporate Philanthropy: Striving to Give in Good Times and Bad," *New Jersey Business,* September 2008; "Employee Volunteering/Giving Technology Vendor Survey," 2008, *www.bccc.net;* "Philanthropy: A Special Report: Firm Decisions: As Companies Become More Involved in Giving, Charities Are Glad to Get Aid Faster and with Less Red Tape," *The Wall Street Journal,* December 10, 2007; and "Corporate Volunteerism in the Internet Age," *The CRO,* December 14, 2006, *www.thecro.com.*

The increasing use of technology to help organize and promote employee volunteering is profiled in Exhibit 18.C.

Priorities in Corporate Giving

Overall, what kinds of organizations receive the most corporate philanthropy? The distribution of contributions reflects how businesses view overall community needs, and how this perception has changed over time. As shown in Figure 18.5, the corporate giving "pie" is divided into several main segments. The largest share of corporate philanthropy goes to health and human services; the next largest share goes to education. Civic

FIGURE 18.5

Priorities in Corporate Giving (percentage of corporate cash and in-kind contributions to various sectors)

Source: *2011 Corporate Contributions Report* (New York: The Conference Board, 2011), Tables 19–25. All data are for 2010. Used by permission of the Conference Board, a global business membership and research organization.

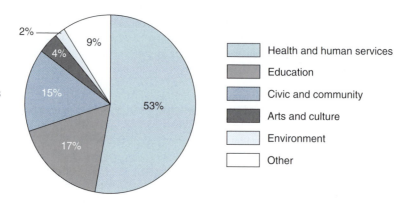

- Health and human services
- Education
- Civic and community
- Arts and culture
- Environment
- Other

and community organizations and culture and the arts also receive large shares of business philanthropy. Of course, these percentages are not identical among different companies and industries; some companies tend to favor support for education, for example, whereas others give relatively greater amounts to cultural organizations or community groups.

Corporate Giving in a Strategic Context

Communities have social needs requiring far more resources than are normally available, and businesses often face more demands than they can realistically meet. This is particularly true in hard economic times, when funds may be less plentiful. Companies must establish priorities to determine which worthy projects will be funded or supported with the company's in-kind or volunteer contributions and which ones will not. What criteria should community relations departments apply in determining who will receive corporate gifts? These are often difficult choices, both because businesses may want to support more charities than they can afford, and because saying no often produces dissatisfaction among those who do not get as much help as they want.

One increasingly popular approach is to target corporate contributions *strategically* to meet the needs of the donor as well as the recipient. **Strategic philanthropy** refers to corporate giving that is linked directly or indirectly to business goals and objectives. In this approach, both the company and society benefit from the gift.

> For example, Cisco Systems, a manufacturer of hardware for the Internet, has established a Networking Academy to train computer network administrators. From a modest start in 1997 in a high school near the company's headquarters in San Jose, California, by 2012 the program had expanded to include more than 10,000 sites in all 50 states and 165 countries, and had trained more than a million students. The academy initiative benefits communities throughout the world by providing job training for young people, many of whom go on to successful careers in systems administration. But it also benefits the company, by assuring a supply of information technology professionals who can operate Cisco's complex equipment. Companies and governments are more likely to buy from Cisco if they are confident skilled technicians are available.[32]

A study in the *Harvard Business Review* identified four areas in which corporate contributions were most likely to enhance a company's competitiveness, as well as the welfare of the community.[33] Strategic contributions focus on:

- *Factor conditions,* such as the supply of trained workers, physical infrastructure, and natural resources. Cisco's Networking Academy is an example of philanthropy that helps the donor by providing skilled employees both for Cisco and for its corporate customers.

- *Demand conditions,* those that affect demand for a product or service. When Microsoft provides free software to libraries and universities, new generations of young people learn to use these programs and are more likely later to buy computers equipped with the company's products.

---

[32] More information about the Networking Academy is available at *http://cisco.netacad.net.*

[33] Michael E. Porter and Mark R. Kramer, "The Competitive Advantage of Corporate Philanthropy," *Harvard Business Review,* December 2002.

- *Context for strategy and rivalry.* Company donations sometimes can be designed to support policies that create a more productive environment for competition. For example, contributions to an organization such as Transparency International that opposes corruption may help a company gain access to previously unreachable markets.
- *Related and supporting industries.* Finally, charitable contributions that strengthen related sectors of the economy may also help companies, as shown in the following example.

> The Marriott Resort and Beach Club on the island of Kauai in Hawaii had a problem. The luxury resort wanted to offer its guests native cuisine prepared with locally grown produce. But the island, which had long been dominated by sugar cane plantations, then in decline, did not have a diversified farming sector. The resort partnered with a local food bank to create a successful program to teach underemployed local residents to grow fruits and vegetables on their own land and to market their produce cooperatively. Today, the Hui meai'ai ("club of things to eat") provides employment for 56 local growers and supplies 25 businesses, including the Marriott.[34]

Of course, not all corporate contributions benefit their donors directly, nor should they. But most, if handled correctly, at least build goodwill and help cement the loyalty of employees, customers, and suppliers who value association with a good corporate citizen.

Specialists in corporate philanthropy recommend several other strategies to help companies get the most benefit from their contributions.[35]

- *Draw on the unique assets and competencies of the business.* Companies often have special skills or resources that enable them to make a contribution that others could not. For example, Google, Inc., provides free advertising on its search engine to nonprofit organizations in many countries. Donations to Direct Relief International, just one of many charities supported in this way, increased more than tenfold after it joined Google's program.[36]
- *Align priorities with employee interests.* Another successful strategy is to give employees a say in deciding who will receive contributions. An advantage of this approach is that it strengthens ties between the company and its workers, who feel that their values are being expressed through the organization's choices. For example, State Street Corporation, a global financial services firm based in Boston, has established community support program (CSP) committees made up of employees in its 36 offices in 25 countries. Each site is given a budget, and the local CSP committees manage grants, sponsor community events, and organize volunteer programs, with guidance from headquarters.[37]
- *Align priorities with core values of the firm.* McDonald's Corporation, the fast-food giant, focuses its philanthropic contributions on children's programs. One of the company's major recipients is the Ronald McDonald House Charities, which operates facilities where families can stay in a homelike setting while their child receives

---

[34] "A Productive Partnership: The Kauai Marriott Resort and Beach Club and the Kauai Food Bank," *In Practice* (Boston: The Center for Corporate Citizenship at Boston College, 2002).

[35] See, for example, David Hess, Nikolai Rogovsky, and Thomas W. Dunfee, "The Next Wave in Corporate Community Involvement: Corporate Social Initiatives," *California Management Review* 44, no. 2 (Winter 2002).

[36] "Google Grants Success Profile," *www.google.com/support/grants;* and "Google Starts Up Philanthropy Campaign," *The Washington Post*, October 12, 2005.

[37] Center for Corporate Citizenship, *Focus on Results: The Community Involvement Index* (2011), op. cit.

treatment at a nearby hospital. The program operates 309 houses in 52 countries, including new programs in Thailand, Indonesia, and Uruguay. Since 2002, the company has raised $170 million at its McHappy Day events for the RMHC and related charities. McDonald's believes that this initiative is consistent with its mission to "make a difference in the lives of children."[38]

In short, businesses today are taking a more strategic approach to all kinds of corporate giving. They want to make sure that gifts are not simply made randomly, but rather are targeted in such a way that they are consistent with the firm's values, core competencies, and strategic goals.

Measuring the Return on Social Investment

A final important trend in corporate philanthropy is assessment of impact. Increasingly, companies are using standard business tools to measure the outcomes of their investments in the community, just as they would any other investment. The benefits that accrue to business and society are sometimes called **return on social investment**. Return on social investment is often more difficult to measure than other kinds of return. For example, return to shareholders may be readily gauged by changes in share price and dividends paid. Return on investment in new machinery may be readily gauged by increases in productivity. By contrast, the results of corporate donations and employee volunteerism may occur over longer periods of time and be less amenable to measurement. Nevertheless, community relations and corporate giving professionals have made significant advances in developing appropriate metrics. Figure 18.6 shows the four elements that are often measured in assessing the return on social investment.

Inputs are the resources companies provide. They may include cash contributions, employee time, products and services, or logistics support. For example, a pharmaceutical company that has committed to help address the HIV-AIDS epidemic in sub-Saharan Africa might measure the value of medicines donated, employee time to administer the program, and cash donated to partner nongovernmental organizations in receiving countries.

Outputs are measures of the activities that took place—usually numerical counts of people and communities served. In the same example, outputs might be the number of persons who received antiretroviral medications and doses provided, the number of clinics provisioned, or the number of medical professionals trained.

Impacts represent the difference the program made; that is, the actual benefits that accrued to the people and communities served. It is similar to outputs, except that it tries to capture the actual results of the gift. How many cases of mother-to-child transmission of infection were prevented? What were the impacts on the ability of HIV-positive individuals to continue to work and contribute to the economic and social health of their communities? Since most firms partner with nonprofit agencies and governments, measuring impacts of their gifts generally requires close collaboration with these organizations.

An example of a company that has worked hard to measure the impact of its social investments is Intel. The chipmaker's "Intel Teach" program has trained more than 10 million teachers in 70 countries. Its purpose is to help teachers use technology to promote students' problem solving, critical thinking, and collaboration skills. The company does more than simply count the number of teachers trained (outputs); it works with research organizations to measure how they actually use technology in their own classrooms and the impact of these efforts on student learning (impacts).

[38] "Worldwide Corporate Social Responsibility 2010 Report," *www.mcdonalds.com,* and "Our History" [Ronald McDonald House Charities] at: *http://rmhc.org.*

FIGURE 18.6
**Measuring the
Return on Social
Investment**

Sources: Adapted from
"Effective Community
Engagement," *BCG
Perspectives,* May 22, 2012, at
www.bcgperspectives.com; and
*Measuring the Value of
Corporate Philanthropy: Social
Impact, Business Benefits, and
Investor Returns,* Committee
Encouraging Corporate
Philanthropy, 2010.

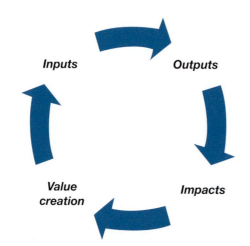

> "Intel is rigorously numerical," commented Wendy Hawkins, executive director of the Intel Foundation. "Measurement makes it more likely that our leaders will support and fund the philanthropy."[39]

Value creation represents the benefits to the business of the program. This is similar to the concept of enlightened self-interest, as presented in Chapter 3. Often this is the most difficult element to measure. In the same example used earlier, was the reputation of the pharmaceutical company enhanced? Did the firm develop new relationships and opportunities in developing countries? Did the program help it attract and retain the brightest scientists? Increasingly, companies are moving away from reliance on anecdotal evidence and trying to measure the business benefits quantitatively. As shown in Figure 8.6, when businesses benefit from their gifts (*value creation*), this enhances their ability to make further gifts (*inputs*), thus creating a kind of virtuous circle.

Recent research shows that 31 percent of companies measure the outputs of their community involvement efforts, and 23 percent measure the impacts. (This study did not examine the percentage that measured value creation.)[40]

Building Collaborative Partnerships

The term *partnership,* introduced in Chapter 6, refers to a voluntary collaboration among business, government, and civil society organizations to achieve specific objectives. The need for such **collaborative partnerships** is very apparent when dealing with community problems.

One arena in which collaborative partnerships among business, government, and communities have been particularly effective is education. As mentioned earlier in this chapter, community relations managers count education as the most critical challenge they face. Many school districts and colleges in the United States face an influx of new students from the so-called echo boom generation, increasing class sizes and making it more difficult to give students the individual attention they need. Many schools are challenged to educate new Americans, immigrants from other parts of the world who often do not speak English as their native language. More children are living in poverty, and many come from single-parent homes. A fast-changing economy demands that the technological tools accessible to

---

[39] "Intel® Teach Program Worldwide" and "The Positive Impact of eLearning—2012 Update," at *www.intel.com;* and "Three Cases of Better Corporate Philanthropy," December 22, 2010, at *http://blogs.hbr.org.*

[40] "Focus on Results: The Community Involvement Index" (2011), op. cit.

students be greatly expanded. All these challenges must be met in many states under conditions of extreme fiscal constraint, as tax revenues fall and budget crises loom. The difficulties faced by schools are of immediate concern to many companies, which rely on educational systems to provide them with well-trained employees equipped for today's high-technology workplace.

Business has been deeply involved with education reform in the United States for over two decades. A series of studies by The Conference Board identified four waves, or distinct periods, in corporate involvement in education reform from the 1980s to the present.[41] The first wave was characterized by *direct involvement* with specific schools. For example, a company might "adopt" a school, providing it with cash, equipment, and volunteer assistance, and promising job interviews for qualified graduates. The second wave focused on the *application of management principles* to school administration. Business leaders assisted schools by advising administrators and government officials who needed training in management methods, such as strategic planning and performance appraisal. The third wave emphasized advocacy for *public policy initiatives* in education, such as ones calling for school choice and adoption of national testing standards. The fourth wave, which is ongoing, focuses on *collaboration for systemic reform.* This involves collaborative partnerships among business organizations, schools, and government agencies. In such collaborations, all partners bring unique capabilities and resources to the challenge of educational reform. The result is often outcomes that are better than any of them could have achieved acting alone.[42]

> An example of a corporation involved in collaborative partnerships to improve education is IBM. Through its "Reinventing Education" initiative, IBM has partnered with schools in many states and eight countries, including Brazil, Vietnam, Mexico, and Ireland, to apply technology to improve student achievement and performance. Since the program's launch in 1994, IBM has donated more than $75 million in cash and high-tech equipment. But the program goes far beyond traditional philanthropy. According to an independent evaluation by the Center for Children and Technology, Reinventing Education "engages researchers, corporate managers, and educators in a long-term partnership, committed to serious sustained collaboration to improve schools." Successful experiments are spread, through the program, to many other schools. The Center for Children and Technology evaluation found that the partnership had produced "significant performance gains" for students in affiliated schools.[43]

The success of IBM's initiative illustrates the potential of collaborative partnerships that allow business to contribute its unique assets and skills to a broader effort to solve significant community problems.

Communities need jobs, specialized skills, executive talent, and other resources that business can provide. Business needs cooperative attitudes in local government, basic public services, and a feeling that it is a welcome member of the community. Under these circumstances much can be accomplished to upgrade the quality of community life. The range

[41] Susan Otterbourg, *Innovative Public–Private Partnerships: Educational Initiatives* (New York: The Conference Board, 1998); and Sandra Waddock, *Business and Education Reform: The Fourth Wave* (New York: The Conference Board, 1994).

[42] For a discussion of the benefits of collaborative partnerships, see Bradley K. Googins and Steven A. Rochlin, "Creating the Partnership Society: Understanding the Rhetoric and Reality of Cross-Sectoral Partnerships," *Business and Society Review* 105, no. 1 (2000), pp. 127–44.

[43] "Reinventing Education: IBM's Award-Winning Model School Reform Program" (2008) and Center for Children and Technology, "The Reinventing Education Initiative from an Evaluation Perspective" (2004), both at *www.ibm.com/ibm /ibmgives.*

of business–community collaborations is extensive, giving businesses many opportunities to be socially responsible.

Like education, other community challenges are, at their core, people problems, involving hopes, attitudes, sentiments, and expectations for better human conditions. Neither government nor business can simply impose solutions or be expected to find quick and easy answers to problems so long in the making and so vast in their implications. Moreover, neither government nor business has the financial resources on their own to solve these issues. Grassroots involvement is needed, where people are willing and able to confront their own needs, imagine solutions, and work to fulfill them through cooperative efforts and intelligent planning. In that community-oriented effort, government, nonprofit organizations, and businesses can be partners, contributing aid and assistance where feasible and being socially responsive to legitimately expressed human needs.

Summary

- The *community* refers to an organization's area of local influence, as well as more broadly to other groups that are impacted by its actions. Businesses and their communities are mutually dependent. Business relies on the community for services and infrastructure, and the community relies on business for support of various civic activities.

- Addressing a community's needs in a positive way helps business by enhancing its reputation, building trust, and winning support for company actions. Like other forms of corporate social responsibility, community involvement helps cement the loyalty of employees, customers, and the public.

- Many corporations have established community relations departments that respond to local needs and community groups, coordinate corporate giving, and develop strategies for creating win–win approaches to solving civic problems.

- Corporate giving comprises gifts of cash, property, and employee time. Donations currently average about 0.8 percent of pretax profits. Philanthropic contributions both improve a company's reputation and sustain vital community institutions.

- Many companies have adopted a strategic approach to philanthropy, linking their giving to business goals. Corporate giving is most effective when it draws on the unique competencies of the business and is aligned with the core values of the firm and with employee interests. Increasingly, companies are measuring the return on their social investment for both recipients and themselves.

- The development of collaborative partnerships has proven to be effective in addressing problems in education and other civic concerns. Partnerships offer an effective model of shared responsibility in which businesses and the public and nonprofit sectors can draw on their unique skills to address complex social problems.

Key Terms

civic engagement, *405*
collaborative partnerships, *420*
community, *404*
community relations, *407*

community relations manager, *407*
corporate foundations, *413*
corporate philanthropy (corporate giving), *410*
in-kind contributions, *414*

license to operate, *406*
return on social investment, *419*
social capital, *406*
strategic philanthropy, *417*
volunteerism, *414*

Discussion Case: *Fidelity Investments' Partnership with Citizen Schools*

Roy Fralin stood in front of a roomful of active sixth and seventh graders in an inner-city public school in Roxbury, Massachusetts. The classroom walls were covered with flip chart paper, which were packed with diagrams, numbers, and terms like "savings," "budget," and "investment." A student stood at the front of the classroom. Fralin handed him a Red Sox cap to illustrate a loan with interest. "OK, when you give it back, you'll owe me how much?" Another student shouted out the answer. "Great!" exclaimed Fralin. They exchanged high fives. "Now, how much are we putting away for your 401(k)?" The students punched their handheld calculators.

Fralin was not a public school teacher, and teaching personal finance to middle schoolers was not his regular job. He was a vice president and investment advisor at Fidelity Investments, where he worked mostly with high net-worth clients. But here he was, every Wednesday afternoon for 10 weeks, teaching a curriculum that Fidelity employees had developed called "How to Invest Like a Millionaire." The program was part of a partnership between an innovative nonprofit called Citizen Schools and Fidelity Investments, one of its corporate partners. "I just don't see any downside," Fralin later reflected in a clip posted to YouTube about his experience as a citizen teacher. "I think this is going to be a success."

In June 2012, Fidelity Investments was one of the leading providers of financial services in the world, administering $3.6 trillion in assets for 20 million individual and institutional clients. The company, which was privately owned, offered investment management, retirement planning, portfolio guidance, brokerage, and benefits outsourcing services. It also operated its own family of mutual funds. Fidelity maintained its headquarters in Boston, but had 10 regional operating centers and 170 retail locations. In 2011, the firm had more than 39,000 employees and revenues of around $13 billion.

In 2009, Fidelity set about rethinking its approach to community relations. For many years, the firm had been philanthropically active, giving to a wide range of charities in its home community and elsewhere. But the company had come to believe that it could have a greater impact by focusing on partnerships with a small number of what it called "best in class" nonprofit organizations. An issue of particular concern to Fidelity was education, especially the shocking dropout rates in many of the communities it served; nationally, 1.2 million students dropped out of high school every year, many of them as early as ninth grade. In researching various options for making a difference, the company learned that the middle school years were critical in determining whether or not students would go on to graduate from high school.

To focus its resources on this issue, Fidelity chose to partner with Citizen Schools (CS). Social entrepreneur Eric Schwarz had founded CS in 1995 in Boston to operate after-school programs for middle school students, aged 11 to 14, in disadvantaged communities. The nonprofit recruited volunteer professionals—"citizen teachers"—to offer after-school apprenticeships in subjects they were passionate about in schools in the CS network. As a culminating experience, students would present what they had learned to friends, family, and teachers at what CS called "WOW!" events. In 2012, Citizen Schools had active partnerships with 31 schools in low-income communities in seven states, serving more than 4,000 students.

Fidelity had contributed money to Citizen Schools since 1998, but in 2009 it significantly stepped up its commitment, becoming the nonprofit's lead national partner for its 8th Grade Academy (8GA), an initiative that helped students with academic and life decision making. In addition to its financial commitment, the company went beyond charity, encouraging its employees, like Roy Fralin, to teach in Citizen School programs. By 2012, Fidelity volunteers had taught more than 70 apprenticeships in such wide-ranging topics as robotics, law, and financial literacy in 22 middle schools. Several executives had served on various advisory boards. The company also donated meeting space and equipment. For example, students who had learned about web design from a Fidelity employee were invited to use the company's Center for Applied Technology for their WOW! event, presenting their work in a state-of-the-art facility.

An external evaluation commissioned by Citizen Schools showed that its programs had "successfully moved a group of low-income, educationally at-risk students toward high school graduation and advancement to college, and [had] set them up for full participation in the civic and economic life of their communities." Seventy-one percent of CS alumni completed high school in four years, compared with 59 percent of matched peers. Sixty-three percent of students who had participated in 8GA five or more years earlier had enrolled in college, compared with 41 percent of low-income students nationally.

Fidelity indicated that in an internal survey, 95 percent of the company's employees who had participated in the Citizen Schools partnership reported improved team-building skills, and three-quarters reported feeling more connected to their colleagues and having improved communication, public speaking, and presentation skills. Eighty-three percent said the program had provided an opportunity to teach skills directly related to their jobs. Betsey Brew Boyd, Fidelity's vice president for community relations, noted: "Fidelity's multi-dimensional partnership with Citizen Schools has yielded skills-based volunteering opportunities for employees, leadership experiences for high-performers, board memberships for executives, and a remarkably effective strategy for meaningful intervention in the lives of at-risk students."

Sources: Corporate Voices for Working Families, "Fidelity Investments" (case study), 2012, at *www.newoptionsproject.org;* "Fidelity Investments," at *www.citizenschools.org/investors/current-investors/fidelity-investments;* "Teaching Kids to Invest Like Millionaires" [Roy Fralin], at *www.youtube.com;* "Guest Blog: At Citizen Schools, Volunteers Make STEM Relevant through Web design," at *www.educationnation.com;* and private correspondence with representatives of Fidelity Investments and Citizen Schools. The website of Citizen Schools is at *www.citizenschools.org.* The website of Fidelity Investments is at *www.fidelity.com.*

Discussion Questions

1. What evidence do you see in this case of the three kinds of corporate philanthropy discussed in this chapter: contributions of cash, in-kind products or services, and employee time?

2. What are the benefits and risks to Fidelity Investments of its partnership with Citizen Schools?

3. Do you consider Fidelity Investment's partnership with Citizen Schools to be an example of strategic philanthropy, as defined in this chapter? Why or why not?

4. If you were a community relations manager for Fidelity Investments, how would you evaluate the impact of this partnership? What kinds of impacts would you attempt to measure, and why?

CHAPTER NINETEEN

Managing Public Relations

How the general public perceives a business firm can have a major effect on its performance. Therefore, building a positive relationship with the public through the management of the firm's public relations is of great importance. Most companies maintain a public relations office, whose job is to formulate public relations strategy, interact with the media and with the public directly, and respond to unanticipated crises. When a business attends to this important stakeholder relationship with the public, it helps both its reputation and its bottom line.

This Chapter Focuses on These Key Learning Objectives:

- Examining the structure and activities of a public relations department, both domestically and globally.
- Understanding how technology can enhance a public relations strategy for both small and large businesses.
- Evaluating strategies used by business organizations to influence public opinion.
- Identifying government regulatory agencies charged with protecting the public from illegal business practices.
- Assessing effective crisis management plans.
- Evaluating techniques used by business to assist employees who interact with the media.

In 2010, a Deepwater Horizon drilling rig at a British Petroleum well in the Gulf of Mexico exploded, killing 11 crew members. Crude oil continued to flow from the damaged well for 12 weeks after the explosion and spewed 200 million gallons of oil into the Gulf of Mexico, the worst environmental disaster in U.S. history. At the time, BP estimated that 5,000 barrels of oil were flowing to the surface per day. Two years later a BP engineer was arrested for obstruction of justice for deleting 300 text messages from his iPhone that he exchanged with his coworkers following the explosion. When finally retrieved, these messages reported that the oil flow rate was actually closer to 15,000 barrels per day and described how the company's "Top Kill" program to stop the flow was failing. When news of this cover-up was released to the public, a New Orleans–based environmental executive involved in the investigation of the oil spill said, "It was clear to anyone who knew flow rates that those [BP] estimates didn't make sense. We certainly feel vindicated."[1]

When online news services reported that United Airlines was filing for a second bankruptcy, in less than an hour more than 54 million shares of United Airlines stock were traded, causing the company's stock to fall from $12 per share to $3 before trading was halted. This stock plunge wiped out more than $1 billion in United Airlines' stock value. The problem was—the report was false! United Airlines blamed a *Chicago Tribune* article that was nearly a decade old—dating back to when United Airlines did file for bankruptcy protection but emerged four years later financially healthy. The newspaper article was posted on the website of a south Florida newspaper, where it was picked up by a research firm that posted a link to *Bloomberg News,* which in turn sent out a news alert based on information in the old article. An airline spokesperson said that this should remind people how negative news, rumors, and even outdated information can travel at lightning speed and influence investors' actions before they pause to check the facts.[2]

The importance of open and accurate communication flowing from both sides of the business–public stakeholder relationship is illustrated in these examples. As is often the case, BP's cover-up of important information was eventually discovered and made public. For United Airlines, inaccurate and dated information caused undeserved harm to the company when the public heard and acted on false rumors. The importance of a firm fostering good communications and public relations with its stakeholders is paramount in today's society where information travels through both conventional channels—television, radio, and newspapers—as well as social media outlets—blogs, websites, Twitter, e-mails, and others—reaching thousands, if not millions, of people in an instant. While businesses seek publicity and spend millions of dollars annually to improve their image among the public, there are minefields for public relations officers and company executives to navigate as they compete for the public's attention and dollars.

The General Public

The **general public** is broadly defined as an organizational stakeholder composed of individuals and groups found in society. As described in Chapter 1, the general public does not deal with business organizations through an economic exchange with the firm, but does affect the firm through its opinions of the firm's activities or performance, which in turn help shape the firm's public image or reputation, as discussed in Chapter 3.

[1] "Former BP Engineer Charged in Gulf Spill," *The Wall Street Journal*, April 24, 2012, *online.wsj.com;* and "Ex-BP Engineer Charged in Oil Spill Probe," *USA Today*, April 25, 2012, *www.usatoday.com.*

[2] "A Mistaken News Report Hurts United," *The New York Times*, September 9, 2008, *www.nytimes.com.*

The public may utilize its own stakeholder networks—consumer advocacy groups, employee labor unions, or local community action groups—and engage with government agencies, special interest groups, or the media to demand a certain level of performance or to condemn or praise a firm.

> After a series of privacy breaches and exposure of personal information for thousands of consumers in the EU, public outcry in the United Kingdom called for legislation to better protect consumers and the public citizenry in general. According to a survey conducted by the information security firm Symantec, 96 percent of the public wanted to be notified by businesses or the government if their personal information was stolen or lost. The public and the company apparently held different views on this issue. The same poll revealed that 9 of 10 U.K. information technology managers believed that the general public should *not* be informed if a data breach occurred.[3]

Companies should be aware of its public's position on important issues, especially since the public may not always share the same views as the firm.

Similarly, the firm can affect the general public's values, attitudes, and actions through various communication channels, such as television, billboards, the Internet, blogs, and other such vehicles, as will be discussed later. Just as the firm's responsible actions can enhance the quality of life for members of the public, so too can its hazardous behavior place the public at risk.

Public Relations in an Emerging Digital World

Given the importance of the general public to business and the potential for business to significantly benefit or harm the public, firms often create public relations departments, appoint public relations officers, and develop public affairs strategies to manage their relationship with the public. Bill Nielsen, former corporate vice president of public affairs at Johnson & Johnson, clearly articulated the importance of an effective public relations approach for businesses:

> In today's increasingly global world of business, there is a clear and, I believe, pressing agenda for public relations and corporate communications. . . . The agenda is all about the critical components of reputation that have to do with values and trust—trustworthiness being the ultimate condition of public approval that we seek for our companies, our clients, and our profession—on a global scale and wherever in the world we operate.[4]

An effective public relations program is fundamental to any organization's relationship with the public. A good **public relations** program sends a constant stream of information from the company to the public and opens the door to dialogue with stakeholders whose lives are affected by the company's operations. As one group of scholars has written, the essential role of the public relations program "appears to be that of a *window out* of the corporation through which management can perceive, monitor, and understand external change, and simultaneously, a *window in* through which society can influence corporate

---

[3] "Public Demand Data Breach Legislation," *Incisive Media Limited*, June 6, 2008, *www.v3.co.uk*. Similar protections are afforded consumers in the United States, as discussed in Chapter 15.

[4] Bill Nielsen, "The Singular Character of Public Relations in a Global Economy," International Distinguished Lecture at the Institute for Public Relations, October 11, 2006, p. 1. Entire address is available at *www.instituteforpr.com*.

policy and practice. This boundary-spanning role primarily involves the flow of information to and from the organization."[5]

A public relations program should be proactive, not reactive. Channels of communication with the media should be established on a continuing basis, not just after a problem has arisen. Specific techniques on how to best train employees to communicate using the media are discussed later in this chapter.

Public Relations Department

The role of the **public relations department** is to manage the firm's public image and, more generally, its relationship with the public. This department may also be called *media relations,* since much of its work involves interacting with the media. It does so through direct communications with the public (for example, through its website) and indirect communications with them through various media outlets, such as newspapers, television, radio, and magazines. The first public relations department was created by the inventor and industrialist George Westinghouse in 1889 when he hired two men to publicize his pet project, alternating current (AC) electricity. James Grunig, a professor at the University of Maryland, has described public relations as "building good relationships with strategic publics," requiring public relations managers to be "strategic communication managers rather than communication technicians."[6] Figure 19.1 shows the major activities carried out by public relations managers.

Most public relations officers have close links with top managers. According to a recent study by the Foundation for Public Affairs, nearly half of the public affairs executives surveyed report directly to the CEO, chairman of the board of directors, or company president, and another 30 percent report to the company's general counsel. According to the report, because of this access, public affairs executives have been able to persuade CEOs to become increasingly involved in corporate public affairs activities.[7]

FIGURE 19.1
Public Relations Activities
When asked, "Which of the following are you ultimately responsible for?" a group of public relations managers responded:

Source: "Corporate Survey: Beyond a Seat at the Table," *PRWeek,* October 2010, pp. 30–35.

Public Relations Activity	Percentage of Respondents Indicating the Activity Is Their Responsibility
Media relations	97 %
Crisis management	96
Executive communications	93
Social networks and applications	89
Online tracking	85
Blogger relations	84
Community relations	84
Employee communications	82
Public affairs / government relations	69
Issues advertising	54

[5] Boston University Public Affairs Research Group, *Public Affairs Offices and Their Functions: A Summary of Survey Results* (Boston: Boston University School of Management, 1981), p. 1.

[6] James Grunig (ed.), *Excellence in Public Relations and Communications Management* (Hillsdale, NJ: Lawrence Erlbaum Associates, 1992).

[7] "Public Affairs Goes Mainstream," *2011–2012 State of Corporate Public Affairs Report,* Foundation for Public Affairs.

Exhibit 19.A Public Relations Professional Associations

The *Public Relations Society of America* (PRSA) is the largest American professional association of public relations officers and communication professionals. It is committed to "the fundamental values of individual dignity and free exercise of human rights" and believes that "the freedom of speech, assembly, and the press are essential to the practice of public relations." In serving its clients' interests, the PRSA is dedicated to "the goals of better communication, understanding, and cooperation among diverse individuals, groups, and institutions of society." To this end, the PRSA adopted a Member Code of Ethics in 2000, replacing previous standards and codes for the industry in place since 1950. The new code presented six professional core values for its members and the public relations profession: advocacy, honesty, expertise, independence, loyalty, and fairness.

Founded in 1970, the *International Association of Business Communicators* (IABC) provides a professional network of about 15,000 business communication professionals in over 80 countries. IABC's professional network serves as a resource for its members to have a greater impact in their public relations job, assist in locating opportunities in the job market, enhance the members' public relations skills through various training programs, and enable members to identify new clients and make new friends.

The *International Public Relations Association* (IPRA), founded in 1955, proclaims as its mission "to promote the development of public relations practice internationally." IPRA is an active virtual global network of public relations practitioners communicating online and coming together to exchange knowledge, experience and expertise in regional and national conferences and workshops, including the World Public Relations Congress.[8]

Assisting the public relations officer are numerous professional organizations, as described in Exhibit 19.A.

New Technology-Enhanced Channels for Public Relations

Historically, public relations officers worked mostly through contact with traditional media outlets. An organization worked to enhance its public image by seeking positive coverage in news reports and feature stories, or by paid advertisements via television, radio, magazines, newspapers, or billboards. Public relations still involves these interactions, but as new technologies have emerged, the variety of available channels of communication has grown dramatically. Many of these new media outlets utilize social media technology, as described next.

A 2011 Pew Research Center and Knight Foundation report confirmed that television remained the major source of weather, traffic, and breaking news for consumers, with 71 percent of people watching the local television news for local information at least once a week. Yet for 11 other topics, such as government updates, job openings, restaurant reviews, and crime reports, people turned mainly to newspapers, the Internet, and websites.

The report also found social media outlets were widely used. Text messaging and the use of Twitter were the second most common means of news distribution on the local level. "There really is a nuanced ecosystem here with very old and very new sources blending," said Tom Rosenstiel, director of the Project for Excellence in Journalism, who collaborated with the Pew Research Center in the study.

[8] This information is from the following professional associations' websites: Public Relations Society of America, *www.prsa.org;* International Association of Business Communicators, *www.iabc.com;* and International Public Relations Association, *www.ipra.org.*

Younger adults relied on local television less and the Internet more for information, as the researchers expected. Yet, the emphasis on obtaining news from traditional sources, such as a newspaper, appeared to be waning for all population groups. A majority of those surveyed said that the "death of their local newspaper" would have at most a minor impact on their news diet. "There's a feeling that in the digital age, information is a commodity that's just available—and there's not always a sense of how it's generated or produced," commented Rosenstiel.[9]

More and more people are finding their news, marketing, or other public relations information through Internet-related vehicles, such as blogs, moblogs, vlogs, e-mails, social networking, podcasts, cell phones, personal digital assistants, and other technology-based communication sources. CEOs and other senior executives are some of the key participants in a new form of business communication—blogging. There is an unofficial "CEO Bloggers Club" that lists nearly 300 names of senior executives from 28 countries.[10]

Yet even blogging may be old school. Former Sun Microsystems CEO Jonathan Schwartz proclaimed, "Blogging was a silly diversion." He and many other CEOs found it easier to use Twitter, rather than blogs, to quickly send out their thoughts, questions, or comments. In 2012, Mario Sundar, a social media activist, reported that former General Electric CEO Jack Welch had 1.2 million Twitter followers and focused his tweets mostly on sports talk. Zappos' CEO Tony Hsieh claimed 1.6 million followers and posted mostly "pithy, inspirational quotes," according to Sundar. But there is business going on in tweets coming from senior executives. The chief marketing officer at clothing retailer Express, Lisa Gavales, has thousands of followers and the conversations often focused on fashion, new trends, and the company's latest product line. Whatever the social media outlet of choice, senior executives are finding these new communication channels to be important ways to send and acquire information from various stakeholder groups.[11]

The Internet-based communication revolution has significantly benefited smaller businesses as well.

According to comScore, a provider of digital intelligence, 1 billion individuals, aged 15 and older, accessed the Internet from their home or work computers in December 2008. By 2011, Internet users between the ages of 12 and 24 made up nearly 23 percent of the total U.S. online population and spent more than a quarter of their time on social networking sites. Teens between the ages of 12 and 17 spent even more time on social networking sites—nearly 30 percent. Companies who see these population groups as their target for various types of information can talk to this new audience in "real time," that is, instantaneously rather than waiting for the next edition of the newspaper or when their television or radio spot is aired. Small businesses can reach as many potential customers, job applicants, new suppliers, or the general public as easily and quickly as the largest business organizations by using the Internet.[12]

---

[9] "Pew Media Study Shows Reliance on Many Outlets," *The New York Times*, September 26, 2011, *www.nytimes.com*. For full report, see "72% of Americans Follow Local News Closely," *Pew Research Center*, April, 12, 2012, *pewinternet.org/Reports/2012/Local-news-enthusiasts.aspx*.

[10] See *www.thenewpr.com/wiki* for an updated list of senior executive bloggers from around the world.

[11] Check out *mariosandar.com* for a lively discussion about blogging, the use of Twitter, and the role of senior executives in social media.

[12] See "Check Your Trust Barometer: How Social Networking Sites Can Enhance Your Public Image," *hrtools*, 2008, *www.hrtools.com*; and "How the Next Generation Consumes Online Health," *comScore.com*, February 9, 2012, *blog.comscore.com/2012*.

Large organizations, too, are finding new public relations opportunities through use of the Internet. Many firms in diverse industries are using social networking to connect with their past or potential customers, prospective employees, and others in the communities where they operate as shown in these examples.

- Absolut Vodka had nearly 100 different videos posted to their website for viewers to watch. Some explained how to create a memorable party, of course aided by serving Absolut vodka, while others informed them what restaurants to visit with their friends—again, featuring ones that served Absolut vodka. The company also contacted people through its Facebook page entitled "top bartender," informing viewers about the company-sponsored bartender reality series on NBC following *Saturday Night Live.*

- AT&T participated in microblogging on Twitter—ATTNews, ATTDeals, ATTCustomerCare, and ATTblueroom. The company also had 30 commercial videos available on YouTube video—called Share AT&T. AT&T posted pictures showing the company's recovery vehicle ready to assist those in need after a disaster, and had a "fan page" on Facebook with more than 2 million likes by 2012.

- For its part, Starbucks utilized social media to participate in crowd-sourcing at My Starbucks Idea, where people could suggest, comment, or see an idea in action. These ideas ranged from a new product to how the company could be more socially responsible or environmentally friendly. Starbucks also participated in microblogging at its Twitter account, with nearly 2.5 million followers.[13]

Global Public Relations

Public relations strategies increasingly assume a global focus, since business interactions with the public through media channels frequently transcend national boundaries. Therefore, global businesses have extended their public relations strategies globally, as shown in the following example.

> P&G (formerly Procter & Gamble), based in Cincinnati, Ohio, is the largest consumer packaged goods company in the world. P&G created a comprehensive, yet unified network of public affairs departments to address the flow of information from the company to and from its stakeholders around the world. At P&G, public affairs is broken down into functions (corporate communications, global marketing and consumer and marketing knowledge, corporate digital communications, and global business services), product lines (male grooming, female beauty and grooming, cosmetics, fine fragrances, oral care, feminine care, baby care, general health care, pet care and snacks), and geographical regions (North America contacts, Ohio government relations, multicultural marketing public relations). Each contact point has its own set of contact information directing you to a person, location, office telephone number, mobile telephone number, and e-mail address.[14]

When public relations strategies take on a global perspective, new challenges emerge. For example, public relations managers must be sensitive to cultural disparities, as well as similarities, in crafting press releases and interactions with the media. The impact of the organization's public relations program could vary country to country given the culture,

---

[13] A more complete list of companies and their social networking activities was compiled by Resource Nation at *www.resourcenation.com/blog/companies-using-social-networking-to-boost-sales.*

[14] See P&G's website at *news.pg.com/media_contacts.*

social mores, political system, or history. A public relations manager must be able to communicate with local media and other stakeholder groups in their native language and avoid embarrassing or misleading communication due to poor translations. All of the basic public relations tasks are more complex in an international business environment.[15]

Businesses must also ensure that sufficient funding is allocated globally for a positive and effective public affairs impact. Some U.S.-based firms allocate a percentage of their public relations budget equivalent to the percentage of revenue generated from their overseas operations to global PR operations. But they sometimes fail to understand that *more* effort, thus additional resources, may be necessary to combat anti-American sentiment or to build a public relations presence where there has never been one.

Some businesses decentralize their global public relations programs and establish officers in each of the locations where they have operations. This helps to ensure that the local public relations strategy is in tune with local customs and emerging issues.[16] "Forward thinking companies will become more decentralized in their . . . communications. They will increasingly put tools out there to arm influencers, peers, enthusiasts, customers, and prospects, as well as employees—and then get out of the way and let the magic happen," explained Bob Geller, senior vice president at Fusion Public Relations.[17]

Influencing Public Opinion

Business organizations or industry associations may choose to influence or change public opinion on a variety of social or political issues that might affect an organization or industry. Using the powerful outreach of the media, messages are crafted to enlighten or educate the public regarding businesses' viewpoint or how the issue might affect the public.

Public Service Announcements

Since 1942, the Ad Council has been the leading producer of **public service announcements** (PSAs), addressing critical social issues for generations of Americans and global citizens. The Ad Council has created some of the most memorable slogans, such as its inaugural campaign of "Loose Lips Sink Ships," promoting secrecy of military operations during World War II to the more recent "Friends Don't Let Friends Drive Drunk" and "A Mind Is a Terrible Thing to Waste." More recently, PSA campaigns have ranged from disaster relief and energy efficiency to arts education and the prevention of childhood obesity. The longest running PSA in American history, introduced in 1944 and continuing today, features Smokey the Bear and his famous warning: "Only You Can Prevent Forest Fires." The forest fire prevention campaign has reduced the number of acres lost annually from 22 million to less than 10 million.[18]

Modeled after the actions taken by the Ad Council, businesses have discovered that public service announcement–like advertisements are an effective means for promoting various social issues or topics that resonate with the public, as demonstrated by Facebook and Time Warner when they combined to launch a campaign against bullying.

---

[15] For a thorough discussion of these issues see Craig S. Fleisher, "The Development of Competencies in International Public Affairs," *Journal of Public Affairs* 3, no. 3 (March 2003), pp. 76–82.

[16] For an excellent and thorough presentation of effective global public relations strategies, see Lou Hoffman, "Ten Pitfalls of International PR," *The Firm Voice*, June 11, 2008, *www.firmvoice.com.*

[17] "From 'Command and Control' to a Decentralized Marketing Tool," *Flack's Revenge* blog, February 23, 2009, *www.flacksrevenge.com.*

[18] See the Ad Council's website, *www.adcouncil.org.*

In 2011, Facebook and Time Warner announced that they were bringing together and expanding their individual efforts against bullying. The jointly sponsored program was called *Stop Bullying: Speak Up*. The program integrated broadcast, print, online, and social media to ignite a conversation and to educate parents, teachers, and young people about the actions that will help protect the youth from the impact of bullying. "For the past two years, we've been working closely with Facebook to expand the bullying prevention campaign that was started by our own Cartoon Network," said Jeff Bewkes, CEO of Time Warner. "In partnering with Facebook for the next phase of our effort, we will now be able to communicate this important message to an even broader audience. I'm confident that through our multiplatform approach and combined resources we can inspire even more people to take action against bullying." Facebook also unveiled its newly designed Family Safety Center and a "Social Report Tool" that enabled people to report bullying or harassment to parents, teachers, or trusted friends. "We deeply care about the safety of our nation's children and are proud to be partnering with Time Warner to raise awareness of bullying," said Sheryl Sandberg, COO at Facebook. "We believe that by working together with parents and teachers, we can teach young people to speak up and stop bullying."[19]

Image Advertisements

Image advertisements are used by business organizations to enhance their public image, create goodwill, or announce a major change such as a merger, acquisition, or new product line. These ads are different from issue advertisements, as discussed in Chapter 9, that focus on a public policy issue or piece of legislation. Image ads promote the image, or general perception, of a product or service, rather than promoting its functional attributes. They target the public's emotions and seek to influence the consumers' imaginations.

- As gas prices at the pump continued to rise across the United States in 2012 and the image of many oil-producing companies began to tarnish, Chevron introduced its "we agree" campaign. The company paid for two-page advertisements to appear in newspapers in major U.S. cities. The mega-headline read: "Big oil should support local schools," with a red-lettered stamp at the bottom: "WE AGREE." Chevron explained in its ads that students go on to become employees, which is why the company supports education in America by investing $100 million in the past three years alone.

- When stock prices fell and consumers began to question the financial stability of some American businesses, Fisk Johnson, CEO of S.C. Johnson, whose company has been run by five generations of members of the Johnson family, chose to talk to the American people in a full-page newspaper image advertisement. He began by saying: "Family is everything." He explained what it meant to the public that S.C. Johnson was a family company—"we do not report to Wall Street . . . decisions we make come down to caring for you and the world we share . . . [and] when I go to bed at night, I know what we're trying to do is right."

- Following the tragedy of the Gulf of Mexico oil explosion and spill, the American Petroleum Institute, the trade association for oil and natural gas companies, used advertisements in American newspapers to try to rebuild its image. "The people of America's oil and natural gas industry are working to help BP and the authorities respond to the spill. Clearly, there will be lessons to be learned, and we are fully committed to doing

---

[19] "Facebook and Time Warner Inc. Team Up to Expand Bullying Prevention Campaign," *Facebook*, July 14, 2011, *www.facebook.com;* and "Facebook and Time Warner Inc. Team to Expand Bullying Prevention Campaign," *Time Warner,* July 12, 2011, *www.timewarner.com.*

Exhibit 19.B

Going from Bad to Worse at Highmark

In 2011, the University of Pittsburgh Medical Center (UPMC), the largest hospital and medical care network in western Pennsylvania, and Highmark Blue Cross Blue Shield, western Pennsylvania's premier insurance carrier, announced that they would end their multiyear agreement in 2013. (This separation was later extended to 2014.) This change caused panic among western Pennsylvania residents, a region with one of the nation's highest elderly populations. For years, individuals covered by Highmark insurance could by treated at the many facilities in the UPMC network, at a significantly lower cost to the patient. Now, UPMC announced that it would no longer honor Highmark insurance and was instead creating its own insurance system. While most blamed UPMC for this situation, Highmark was also criticized for failing to renegotiate its contract.

But Highmark could not have predicted how its image would take another blow when in 2012 Highmark's CEO Kenneth Melani was accused of simple assault and defiant trespass. The incident revealed that Melani was having an affair with a Highmark employee and had reportedly confronted and attacked his mistress's husband. A few days later, Highmark fired Melani for "willful and gross misconduct."

In response to this escalating scandal, Highmark published a full-page announcement in the region's major western Pennsylvania newspapers. The announcement was a letter from Bob Baum, the chairman of Highmark's board of directors. Baum explained, "We, the 20,000 employees of Highmark, take very seriously what the 'Highmark' name and mission stands for. They have been synonymous with integrity and maintaining the highest standards in all aspects of our company. We've worked hard to live up to that. As we move forward, we will continue to keep our focus where it has always been and always belonged—on you. . . . We'll continue our 75-year mission of caring for the health and well-being of the cities, suburbs, and small towns that we, too, call home." Two months later, when William Winkenwerder was selected as the new CEO of Highmark, he said, "I think it's our job to repair that trust, to re-earn that trust and that's what we intend to do."

Baum, Winkenwerder, and the entire Highmark organization, from the board of directors to the thousands of company employees, knew that restoring confidence in the Highmark brand among the people of western Pennsylvania was essential, as many in the region remained uncertain about their health coverage.

Sources: "Highmark Issues Statement on CEO's Ouster," *Pittsburgh Post-Gazette*, April 5, 2012, *www.post-gazette.com*; and "New CEO Winkenwerder Targets Trust in Highmark," *Pittsburgh Post-Gazette*, June 5, 2012, *www.post-gazette .com*. The full-page announcement appeared in the *Pittsburgh Post-Gazette*, April 15, 2012, p. A-11. Also see the discussion over the insurance coverage conflict at *upmcvshighmark.blogspot.com*.

everything humanly possible to understand what happened and prevent it from ever happening again. . . . Oil and natural gas are vital domestic resources that power our way of life. We are committed to ensuring this energy is available—safely and with care for our environments—to all Americans today and into the future." The institute also provided its website—EnergyTomorrow.org—for the readers to access.[20]

An even more dramatic example of the use of image advertisements appeared in 2012 by Highmark as shown in Exhibit 19.B.

Protecting the Public through Government Regulation

Government regulation seeks to protect the public by controlling business's use of the media, although policymakers have been careful to not infringe upon the U.S. Constitution First Amendment's right to free speech, which applies to business organizations as well as

[20] The advertisements appeared in the *Pittsburgh Post-Gazette*, among other newspapers, sponsored by Chevron on February 2, 2012, pp. A6 and A-7; S.C. Johnson on November 8, 2009, p. A-15; and the American Petroleum Institute, June 17, 2010, p. C-6.

private citizens. Yet, the right to free speech is not an unrestricted right, and this activity does come with the obligation of acting in the best interest of the public and adhering to ethical principles. As discussed elsewhere, businesses must communicate *honestly* with various stakeholders, such as stockholders (Chapter 14), consumers (Chapter 15), and the community (Chapter 18).

Advertising used to promote the organization and its products must meet both ethical expectations and legal requirements. Thomas Jefferson, the author of the U.S. Constitution, warned, "Advertisements contain the only truth to be relied on in a newspaper." The Federal Trade Commission (FTC) is entrusted with ensuring that honesty and fairness are found in company advertising. The FTC attempts to ensure that the public is protected and guards against the following unethical business practices: the use of deception to distort the truth, the lack of fairness in information, and the use of fraud to manipulate. (The issue of deceptive advertising is further discussed in Chapter 15.)[21]

The FTC jurisdiction applies to advertising in any medium, including online advertisements. In a 1998 FTC report to Congress, the government agency noted that over 85 percent of all websites collected personal consumer information, yet only 14 percent of these sites provided any information to the consumer as to how this information would be used or protected. This report led to public concern over consumer privacy and later an increase in company privacy policies, as discussed in Chapter 15. The FTC has been vigilant in ensuring that consumers' rights to privacy are protected. In 2000, the Children's Online Privacy Protection Act (COPPA), discussed in Chapters 13 and 15, gave the FTC new powers to ensure privacy protection for children.

Another government agency with responsibility for regulating corporations' public relations activities is the **Federal Communications Commission (FCC)**. This agency was created in 1934 and charged with regulating interstate and international communications by radio, television, wire, satellite, and cable. The FCC regulates business advertisements, for example, by prohibiting all television stations from airing obscene programming at any time and indecent programming or profane language except after 10 p.m. The FCC also promotes open competition in the communications industry. The 1996 Telecommunications Act was passed to allow virtually any business to enter the telecommunications industry. Businesses were encouraged to become involved in providing telephone service, including local and long distance, cable programming and other video services, broadcast services, and services provided to schools. Thus, the FCC believed its role was not only to guard against inappropriate business activity that might harm the public, but also to foster a more competitive business environment.[22]

The government also monitors the dissemination of information to stockholders. The Securities and Exchange Commission (SEC), as discussed in Chapter 14, attempts to ensure that information distributed to all potential and current investors is timely and accurate. It operates under the belief that all investors, whether large institutions or private individuals, should have access to basic certain facts about an investment prior to buying it and as long as they hold it. Recently, greater transparency regarding company performance was mandated by the SEC for all publicly traded firms, increasing the public's knowledge of the financial risks faced by businesses. Some of the important issues focusing on how one company's CEO communicated with the public are covered in the discussion case at the end of the chapter.

Other government regulatory areas that affect the public include consumer product information, such as fuel mileage efficiency or the safety of pharmaceuticals or food, or environmental issues, such as air quality or the safety of nuclear power plants. Many of

---

[21] See FTC Commissioner Mary L. Azcuenaga's presentation before the Turkish Association of Advertising Agencies, April 8, 1997, for a thorough analysis of the FTC's role and the ethical principles it uses to guard against business's misuse of advertising at *www.ftc.gov/speeches/azcuenaga/turkey97.shtm.*

[22] For more information on the FCC's regulatory role, see *www.fcc.gov.*

these issues, and the regulatory agencies charged with enforcing these regulations, are discussed in other chapters.

Almost all countries regulate how products can be marketed to the public. In 2012, the Australian government enacted strict regulations as to how tobacco companies could package and market cigarettes. Companies were forced to use plain, logo-free packaging to make them less attractive to smokers, the first such move globally. Promotional text or colorful images were also banned under the Australian law. Graphic government health warnings were prominently displayed, with the brand name relegated to tiny, generic type shown at the bottom of the package. Cigarettes must be sold behind closed doors in retail outlets and advertising and sponsorships were banned. According to Australian Prime Minister Kevin Rudd, "The new branding for cigarettes will be the most hard-line regime in the world and cigarette companies will hate it."

An Imperial Tobacco Company of Australia spokesperson explained, "Introducing plain packaging just takes away the ability of a consumer to identify our brand from another brand," and the spokesperson said that the company planned to take legal action to block the regulation. Other tobacco companies threatened to slash prices and make the product more available to consumers to counter the government's efforts to decrease tobacco sales. In April 2012, British American Tobacco, Philip Morris, Imperial Tobacco, and Japan Tobacco filed a lawsuit claiming that the new law was unconstitutional. A prominent Australian barrister (attorney) said he thought that the government would win the case and this was "a brilliant Australian idea." Discussions were also ongoing in Britain to examine whether British tobacco companies would be required to follow suit with the plain packaging idea in the United Kingdom.[23]

Crisis Management

A critical function of the public relations manager is *crisis management*. Every organization is likely at some time to face a crisis that forces management and its employees to act quickly and without perfect information. A **corporate crisis** is a significant business disruption that stimulates extensive news media or social networking coverage. The resulting public scrutiny can affect the organization's normal operations and also can have a political, legal, financial, and governmental impact on its business. A crisis is any event with the potential to negatively affect the health, reputation, or credibility of the organization.[24] The Institute for Crisis Management breaks down corporate crises into four groups:

- "Acts of God"—earthquakes, tornados, violent storms, volcanic eruptions.
- Mechanical problems—breakdowns of or faulty equipment, metal fatigue.
- Human errors—through miscommunication, improper employee behavior.
- Management decision or indecision—often involving a cover-up or lack of urgency.[25]

---

[23] Quotations are from "Australia on Cigarette Labels: PM Vows 'Most Hard-line Regime in the World,'" *New York Daily News*, April 29, 2010, *www.nydailynews.com*. Other information from "Australia Wants Plain Boxes for Cigarettes," *The New York Times*, April 29, 2010, *www.nytimes.com*; "Tobacco Companies Prepare to Fight New Australian Regulations," *Marketplace Business*, May 19, 2011, *www.marketplace.com*; and "Plain-Packaging Cigarette Challenge in Australia's High Court," *The Guardian*, April 16, 2012, *www.guardian.com*.

[24] For a thorough guide on how to minimize the impact of a crisis, see Catherine H. Tinsley, Robin L. Dillon, and Peter M. Madsen, "How to Avoid Catastrophe," *Harvard Business Review*, April 2011, pp. 90–97; and for suggestions on what to avoid doing during a crisis, see Peter S. Goodman, "In Case of Emergency: What Not to Do," *The New York Times*, August 21, 2010, *www.nytimes.com*.

[25] From the Institute for Crisis Management's website, *www.crisisexperts.com*.

Exhibit 19.C

Excuse Me, There Is a Finger in My Chili!

On March 22, 2005, Denny Lynch, senior vice president for communications at Wendy's, one of the country's largest fast-food restaurant chains, received a shocking and unexpected call. A customer, Anna Ayala, claimed she had bitten down on a severed finger while eating a cup of chili purchased at a Wendy's restaurant in San Jose, California. Lynch knew that he had to act quickly, since this incident would certainly be the top story on the evening news and in the headlines of every major newspaper the next day.

Wendy's immediately assembled its crisis management team in its regional headquarters in Sacramento, California. Lynch prepared a statement for the press, instructed the company's website to be frequently updated, and began coordinating with the San Jose police department, which was already involved in the case. According to Lynch, "It went nonstop the next two or three days. Even when the Pope passed away, it still got coverage."

In the wake of the immediate crisis, Wendy's focused on trying to discover what had really happened. Through an internal investigation, Lynch learned that a 10-year veteran and trusted employee had prepared the chili for Ayala; he assured Lynch there was nothing improper in the food preparation.

While Lynch and his team worked furiously around the clock to discover the truth, Ayala, the woman who had made the accusation, was a guest on numerous morning and late night television shows. Yet, it was soon discovered that Ayala had a litigious history that included a settlement for medical expenses for her daughter, who had claimed she became sick at an El Pollo Loco restaurant in Las Vegas.

The public relations break Lynch and Wendy's needed occurred exactly one month after the initial incident, when Anna Ayala was arrested in her Las Vegas home for attempted grand larceny, accused of trying to extort $2.5 million from Wendy's. The finger in her chili was all a hoax. "The true victims are Wendy's owners and operators," said San Jose chief of police Rob Davis. Forensic evidence proved that the finger was not cooked at 170 degrees for three hours—the typical preparation of Wendy's chili. It was later discovered that Ayala acquired the finger through her husband's workplace, where a fellow worker had lost part of his finger in an industrial accident.

In September 2005, Ayala and her husband, Jaime Plascencia, pleaded guilty to attempted grand larceny and conspiring to file a false claim. Ayala was sentenced to 9 years in prison and her husband, who supplied the finger, was sentenced to 12 years and 4 months in prison.

Sources: "At CSI: Wendy's, Tracking a Gruesome Discovery," *The New York Times,* April 22, 2005, *www.nytimes.com;* "Finger in Chili Is Called Hoax; Las Vegas Woman Is Charged," *The New York Times,* April 23, 2005, *www.nytimes.com;* and "Stiff Sentences for Wendy's Chili-Finger Couple," *Bay City News,* January 18, 2006, *www.SFGate.com.*

A corporate crisis can take many different forms. It might be a terrorist attack, poor financial results, the death of a key executive or government official, employee layoffs, a charge of sexual harassment, or the filing of class-action lawsuits brought by injured customers. Or it might be something bizarre and unique, such as the crisis that confronted Wendy's, described in Exhibit 19.C. But crises, by definition, are often unique. To prepare for these unexpected events and sometimes tragedies, an organization must develop a crisis management plan before the crisis hits.

Crisis management is the process organizations use to respond to short-term and immediate corporate crises. Some businesses or industries are more prone to corporate crises than others. According to the Institute for Crisis Management, medical and surgical manufacturers, pharmaceutical companies, and software manufacturers (because of the sophisticated technology found in their products and the potential for disruptive impact on consumers' lives) are at the top of a recent list of crisis-prone industries.

While a majority of companies develop extensive crisis plans, only 29 percent of the corporate executives surveyed in 2011 said they were confident that their organization would respond effectively if a crisis occurred. "Part of that uncertainty may stem from the fact that even among those companies which have developed a crisis plan, 63 percent report that their company does not conduct annual training drills or exercises to test the effectiveness of their plan and ensure that all company employees know what to do if a crisis does occur," said Tom Campbell, a crisis management consultant. "Even more strikingly," explained Campbell, "fully one-third of those companies which do have a crisis plan could not recall the last time they actually reviewed or revised it, which clearly indicates an out-of-sight/out-of-mind approach to crisis management that may prove a company's undoing."[26]

Often the corporate crisis quickly escalates, producing intense pressures and many suggestions about what the company should do or not do from outside experts, politicians, and observers. Sometimes, as shown in the following example, allowing the wrong or incorrect message to be sent out can have devastating negative consequences.

An explosion in a Sago, West Virginia, coal mine trapped 13 miners. As is often the case when a mine collapses, little was known right away to tell the trapped miners' families and throngs of news reporters desperately seeking information. The International Coal Group (ICG), owner of the Sago Mine, wanted to avoid raising false hopes, while attempting to satisfy the hundreds of community residents and dozens of news crews' quest for updates. But after hours of no news, a report spread like wildfire: rescuers had found 12 miners alive. Relatives of the trapped miners, understandably, rejoiced, management at ICG breathed a sigh of relief, and the news media had its story—which was immediately broadcast globally. Then, minutes later, the real news emerged: only one miner had survived, and the others were dead. The joy and celebration turned to grief, anguish and, of course, anger. The foremost crisis management blunder had occurred: false information was disseminated, and the worst kind, false information regarding who is alive. Weeks of investigation after the disaster revealed that ICG was simply unable to control all rumors that were circulating during the disaster. But, more importantly, ICG's management did not step up when the rumor spread to say that they had no corroborating evidence to confirm this report. Clearly, a critical element of the crisis management strategy—controlling rumors and verifying all information—had failed.[27]

Unfortunately it is very costly to develop a strategic response once a crisis is upon an organization. Most experts recommend that organizations develop a crisis management plan ahead of time, citing the biblical wisdom: Noah built his ark *before* it began to rain. Since the first 24 hours during a crisis are the most crucial, having a plan ready for implementation when a crisis occurs is imperative.

According to experts, an effective crisis management plan must include these steps:

- *Get ready before the crisis hits* by creating an internal communication system that can be activated the moment a crisis occurs. Key employees must be identified in advance so that they are ready to address the issue. Scenario-based press releases, key discussion points, and procedures to activate the organization's website (to use the Internet to announce any news, product recalls, etc.) should be at the ready. Many organizations create a **dark site**, a website that is fully developed and uploaded with critical information,

---

[26] "Just 29% of Corporate Executives Confident of Weathering a Crisis Says Survey," *Business Wire*, August 11, 2011, *www.businesswire.com*.

[27] For a complete account of the crisis management effort by the International Coal Group during the Sago Mine disaster, see "Sago Mine: A Hard Lesson in Crisis Communication," *American Thinker*, January 6, 2006, *www.americanthinker.com*.

contacts for the media, and other useful details, ready to be activated at the moment it is needed. Wendy's, for example (see Exhibit 19.C), already had plans to scramble their crisis management team into action well before the crisis emerged and had key talking points ready for their conversations with the media.

- *Communicate quickly, but accurately.* Firms facing a crisis must communicate with the media and others promptly. Communications must always be honest and disclose fully what the company knows—even if it does not know the full story. Wendy's, for example, effectively communicated with the public even when it did not yet know how the finger got in the chili; the managers at Sago Mine, by contrast, at first failed to communicate and then allowed false information to circulate. The media have excellent resources and will find the truth whether the organization speaks it or not. It is often best to take the offensive and be the first to comment on a situation affecting the organization, thus placing the organization in greater control.

- *Use the Internet* to convey the public affairs message to minimize the public's fears and provide assistance. In addition to face-to-face press releases, Wendy's frequently updated its company website to communicate to the public and others what the company was doing about the crisis situation.

- *Do the right thing.* Often the true test of an organization is how it reacts in a time of crisis. Public relations managers should not try to minimize the seriousness of a problem or make excuses. It is possible for the organization to accept responsibility without accepting liability. It also is important that the organization be sympathetic. For example, Wendy's clearly expressed regret over its customers' fears and advised the public that it was doing everything possible to investigate.

- *Follow up* and, where appropriate, make amends to those affected. Seek to restore the organization's reputation. Wendy's relentless pursuit of the truth resulted in vindication for the company and assisted law enforcement in the prosecution of those making the false claims. With proper planning and effective implementation of a crisis management program, an organization may emerge from a crisis in a stronger condition.[28]

From multinational corporations to small businesses, organizations of any size at any location can face crisis situations, some more devastating and affecting more lives than others, and they all need a plan for what to do when handling any crisis as it unexpectedly occurs. A *crisis management guide* describing a series of critical crisis management checkpoints is shown in Exhibit 19.D.

Media Training of Employees

An important public relations step organizations can take is to provide **media training** to executives and employees who are likely to have contact with the media. Media training is necessary because communicating with the media is not the same as talking with friends or coworkers. By the late 2000s, engaging with "the media" took on a new dimension with the inclusion of social media. As many organizations and individuals have discovered, interacting with the public through social media tools allow for information to be disseminated faster and farther than ever before and preparation seems to be the key, as seen at Telstra.

---

[28] Adapted from Ronald J. Levine, "Weathering the Storm: Crisis Management Tips," *Metropolitan Corporate Counsel,* March 2002, pp. 3–4; and Mark Herford, "Crisis Make or Break—The First 24 Hours," *International Public Relations Association,* April 2009, *www.ipra.org.* Also see John F. Savarese, "Handling a Corporate Crisis: The Ten Commandments of Crisis Management," *Banking and Financial Services* 27 (2011), pp. 71–89.

1. Create and document policies and procedures and circulate them widely.

2. Know the policies and procedures and follow them.

3. Be prepared with a continuity plan to provide for continuing operations during crisis management phase.

4. Work as a team with assigned responsibilities and a clear leader and practice, practice, practice in mock drills.

5. Identify and understand the organization's vulnerabilities; most importantly, correct shortcomings.

6. Let your conscience be your guide, follow good ethical practice and remember the "front-page test." (Or, better yet, consider: What would Grandma say?)

7. Beware of dangerous and distorted minds and protect coworkers and facilities.

8. Put all phases of the event under a microscope and track and record activities.

9. Handle all records, samples, information, materials, and evidence with care.

10. Know the media and how to handle it. NEVER lie, cover up, or obfuscate.

11. Keep your eyes on the law and contact legal counsel; don't make decisions simply to avoid lawsuits.

12. Provide timely updates to coworkers and provide follow-up meetings and counseling.

Source: FosterHyland, Inc., *www.fosterhyland.com*. Used with permission, 2009. For a focus on the importance of the role of ethics and values during a crisis response and a series of steps to be taken during a crisis, see The Ethics Resource Center's *Accepting Responsibility Responsibly: Corporate Responses in Times of Crisis* (Washington, DC: Ethics Resource Center, 2011).

Telstra, Australia's leading telecommunications and information services company, launched a mandatory social media training program for its 40,000 employees in 2009. Grounded in the company's "Policy of 3Rs—responsibility, respect and representation" and taking the notion of transparency seriously, David Quilty, former Group Managing Director of Public Policy and Communication at Telstra, said, "Telstra sees social media as an opportunity to engage in conversations with our colleagues, customers and others with shared interests. . . . Telstra's a technology company so we want our people to use these new technologies. We don't purport to be social media experts, but we're genuinely looking at ways to use social media, both to communicate interactively with our customers and to have an open dialogue on issues that relate to Telstra and technology.[29]

More commonly, media training focuses on helping one interact with the public and media during a crisis situation for the company. As an organization's representative, an employee is normally assumed to be speaking for the organization or is expected to have special knowledge of its activities during this tense time. Under these circumstances, the words one speaks take on a special, official meaning. In addition, news reporters sometimes challenge an executive or spokesperson, asking penetrating or potentially embarrassing questions and expecting instant answers. Even in more deliberate news interviews, the time available for responding to questions is limited to a few seconds. Moreover, facial expressions, the tone of one's voice, and body language can convey both positive and negative impressions.

Many large business organizations routinely send a broad range of their employees to specific courses to improve their media skills—public relations experts, consumer service

---

[29] "Telstra Launches Interactive 3Rs Social Media Learning Module," *Telstra Exchange—TelstraNews*, December 17, 2009, *exchange.telstra.com.au*. Telstra's social media training guide is also available online to the public at *http://exchange.telstra.com.au/training/flip.html*.

representatives, communications specialists, government liaison officers, and others that typically interact with external organizational stakeholders. Media communication experts generally give their clients the following advice.

- *Be honest.* Always tell the truth and explain why you cannot discuss a particular subject.
- *Be current.* The media wants to speak with you because of your up-to-date knowledge. If you do not have current information, promise to find out and get back to the media.
- *Be accessible.* A spokesperson is expected to be on-call and promptly respond to demands made by the media, as long as the demands are reasonable.
- *Be helpful.* If you do not know the answer to a question, say so and offer to find out. Try to make the media's job easier; they will print or broadcast anyway, so if you are helping them there is a better chance of your message being heard.
- *Be understanding.* Understand the needs of the media, their pending deadline, or the importance of their acquiring background information.
- *Be cool, courteous, and professional.* You are representing your organization in the eyes of the media and the public. Remember, nothing is really ever "off the record."

Employees trained to interact with the media should know the basic message points that the organization wants communicated. These key points need to be reinforced with facts (for example, statistics) when possible, and elaborated upon in an interview or press conference. Many times the audience is not aware or knowledgeable of the organization's operations or product or whatever is the focus of the press conference. Therefore, it is important to be clear and avoid jargon or technical language. Finally, the spokesperson should close the interview by reiterating the organization's key message.

While the organization's spokesperson likely knows a lot of information about an issue, it is important to remember the final audience for the message. Typically the news media is looking for a **sound bite**, a short (often 30 seconds or less) clip of information that can be broadcast to the public. Sometimes the media does not print or broadcast what the spokesperson wants but rather what is controversial or sensational. The spokesperson needs to remember to keep on point and keep it short.

When the media asks a particularly tough question, the organization's spokesperson needs to shift the focus to the key message or use the question as a platform to return to the organization's agenda for the press conference. Some of the best techniques to assist a spokesperson to stay on point when challenged by a reporter with a tough question are the following:

- *Hooking.* Grab the reporter's attention by making a statement that influences the next question. For example, "We are undertaking a program to correct the situation." Typically the reporter will follow up by asking about the organization's new program.
- *Bridging.* Answer the challenging question but quickly move on to the key message. For example, "Yes, but . . . " or "What I can tell you is . . . " or "While that is true, what is important to know is . . . "
- *Flagging.* Emphasize key points and guide the reporter to them. For example, "Your listeners may not know that . . . " or "This is important news because . . . "

No matter how prepared a person is to handle the media, during a crisis situation it is often very difficult to clearly and calmly convey the organization's message. Some businesses practice with mock press conferences, as they do with their crisis management plans, so that the spokesperson can experience what it is like to answer the media's tough questions under pressure, better preparing them for the real thing.

Summary

- A well-crafted public relations department can open up a dialogue between the organization and the public, providing a window out from the organization to the public and a window in for the organization from the public. The public relations function must have both a domestic and global focus and activities for a global business organization.

- An effective public relations strategy should incorporate the use of new technological innovations, such as blogs, e-mails, social networking, cell phones, PDAs, and other technology-based communications sources. Both small and large businesses are realizing how important new technology is as an integral element of their public relations strategy.

- Business organizations can influence or change public opinion through public service announcements, image advertisements, and issue advertisements.

- Numerous regulatory agencies are charged with protecting the public, including the Federal Trade Commission, Federal Communications Commission, and Securities and Exchange Commission. These agencies govern the timely and accurate flow of information from business through their advertisements or company reports to various stakeholder groups.

- An effective crisis management plan is one that is ready to be implemented before the crisis occurs, enables the organization to quickly and accurately communicate to the media, utilizes the Internet to convey critical information to the public, and always remains focused on the organization's ethical responsibilities to its stakeholders.

- A business organization needs to conduct media training for employees likely to interact with the media so that the organization's message is heard and image is maintained, especially during a crisis.

Key Terms

corporate crisis, *437*
crisis management, *438*
dark site, *439*
Federal Communications Commission (FCC), *436*
general public, *427*

image advertisements, *434*
media training, *440*
public relations, *428*
public relations department, *429*

public service announcements, *433*
sound bite, *442*

Internet Resources

www.cprs.ca	Canadian Public Relations Society
www.prwatch.org	Center for Media and Democracy—PR Watch
asian-mall.de	The European Public Relations Federation
www.fcc.gov	U.S. Federal Communications Commission
www.instituteforpr.org	Institute for Public Relations (IPR)
www.iabc.com	International Association of Business Communications (IABC)
www.ipra.org	International Public Relations Association (IPRA)
www.prsa.org	Public Relations Society of America (PRSA)
www.sourcewatch.org	Source Watch
www.spinwatch.org	Spinwatch—Monitoring PR and Spin

Discussion Case: *"Pink Sliming" the Processed Beef Industry*

"Pink slime" certainly does not sound appetizing. This term was first coined by a microbiologist working for the U.S. Department of Agriculture (USDA) Food Safety and Inspection Service. It refers to lean finely textured beef (LFTB), a food product created by a process that recovers useful bits of meat from carcass trimmings. These bits are warmed, centrifuged to remove the fat, treated with ammonium hydroxide gas to kill germs, and then compressed into blocks that are frozen for later use. Although LFTB has never been sold directly to the public, it has been widely added to hamburgers and other prepared foods, and has been used in school lunches.

In 2012, after a number of news outlets ran stories raising an alarm about "pink slime," many nutritionists and chefs—among them the TV celebrity Jamie Oliver—led a campaign to ban lean finely textured beef. School food advocate Bettina Siegel collected 230,000 signatures on a letter to the USDA to ban LFTB. She wrote, "It is simply wrong to feed our children connective tissues and beef scraps that were, in the past, destined for use in pet food and rendering, and were not considered fit for human consumption. The idea that children are passively sitting in a lunchroom eating what the government sees fit to feed them and McDonald's has chosen not to use it, but the government is still feeding it to them. That really got my ire." Marion Nestle, a professor of nutrition at New York University said, "It sounds disgusting. A lot of people have been writing about it. Therefore, more people know about it, therefore more people are queasy about it."

In response to the uproar, McDonald's announced (as Siegel noted in her letter) that it was dropping LFTB from its hamburgers. Several national supermarkets, including Kroger and Safeway, also banned LFTB from their processed foods. Dropping demand for LFTB soon caused plant closures and layoffs of employees in the industry that produced this product. Beef Products Inc. (BPI), which had developed the process to create LFTB, closed three of its four LFTB facilities. AFA Foods filed for bankruptcy, citing financial damage caused by the "pink slime" media campaign, and Cargill, an international producer and marketer of food products, significantly scaled back production at its four beef processing facilities. These developments alarmed some food safety advocates, who feared that if LFTB were eliminated, bacteria-laden beef trimmings might be reintroduced into hamburgers, just as they used to be, and the meat would be less safe for human consumption.

The founder of BPI, 69-year-old Eldon Roth, was heartbroken over the campaign against "pink slime." Roth had come up with the idea for LFTB in 1993 after four children died of E. coli poisoning from eating hamburgers purchased at a *Jack in the Box* fast-food restaurant. He received government approval to treat meat with a puff of ammonium hydroxide after the fat was spun out. Ammonia occurs naturally in beef and other foods and has long been approved as an additive in many products, from cheese to pudding. Every carton of BPI beef was tested for E. coli and other dangerous microorganisms before being shipped to BPI customers. The editor of *Cattle Buyers Weekly* commented, "BPI has been in the forefront of food safety in the beef industry for a decade or more." Roth showed the same commitment to his employees as he did to product quality and vowed to keep paying his laid-off employees. But he faced the real possibility that he would be forced to let them go permanently. In 2012 BPI filed a defamation lawsuit against ABC News seeking at least $1.2 billion in damages. BPI claimed that the broadcaster unfairly disparaged its beef additive by labeling it "pink slime."

There are many benefits to using LFTB in the beef preparation process. It allows beef producers to maximize the use of beef from cattle and minimize waste. According to industry sources, LFTB recovers "10 to 12 pounds of edible lean beef from every animal, and saves another 1.5 million animals from slaughter. It is a more sustainable way to provide safe, quality, nutritious, abundant and affordable ground beef to Americans, who have made ground beef a dietary staple throughout the nation," explained Cargill's director of communications.

Cargill developed a video showing that LFTB is beef that is separated from fat, just as milk is separated from cream. Their webpage also tells the public, "[LFTB is] not scraps from the floor. It's not cartilage, tendons or other parts of the animal. It's not dog food. It's not filler. It's meat." The director of food safety and quality assurance at BPI explained, "We don't produce 'pink slime.' We produce 100 percent quality lean beef. That's it. That whole thing [the campaign against pink slime] is a farce. There's no substance to it." A professor of dairy and animal science at the Pennsylvania State University also came to the defense of BPI. "This is a company with a long-standing reputation of doing things right, working with regulatory agencies and food safety people. From a technical or logical standpoint, these are the folks you'd hold up and say this is the way you do it."

The USDA found itself in the crosshairs of a contentious debate. Some members of Congress wrote to the agency, "If fast-food chains won't serve pink slime, why should school cafeterias?" But other members disagreed, writing to the Agriculture Secretary to state their view that the attacks against the quality of LFTB were coming from "a few over-zealous individuals in the media. LFTB is 100 percent beef, safe and cost effective . . . and should be promoted as such." The USDA announced that although it would not ban LFTD, it would allow school districts to opt out of purchasing products that contained "pink slime."

Sources: "Pink Slime: Ammonia Treated Ground Beef Becoming a Rallying Cry," *Huffington Post*, March 14, 2012, *www.huffingtonpost.com;* "Pink Slime in Ground Beef: What's the Big Deal?" *CBS News*, March 14, 2012, *www.cbsnews.com;* "USDA Announces Additional Choices for Beef Products in the Upcoming School Year," *USDA News Release No. 0094.12*, March 15, 2012, *www.usda.gov;* "Backlash to the 'Pink Slime' Backlash," *Time Moneyland*, March 29, 2012, *moneyland.time.com;* "The Dilemma of Pink Slime: Cost of Culture?" *SFGate.com*, April 1, 2012, *www.sfgate.com;* "The Sliming of Punk Slime's Creator," *Bloomberg Businessweek*, April 12, 2012, *www.businessweek.com;* "Cargill: Decision by Retailers to Drop 'Pink Slime' Was 'Disappointing but Understandable,'" *Food Navigator-USA*, April 24, 2012, *www.foodnavigator-usa.com"*; Congressman Want USDA Chief to Campaign in Support of 'Pink Slime,'" *Food Poisoning Bulletin*, April 24, 2012, *foodpoisoningbulletin.com;* and, "ABC Sued for 'Pink Slime' Defamation," *The Wall Street Journal*, September 13, 2012, *online.wsj.com.*

Discussion Questions

1. After reading this case, should "pink slime" be banned as a hazardous food product or are the claims unfounded?

2. Develop a public relations strategy that BPI and other firms that manufacture LFTB could use to combat the bad publicity and efforts to ban the use of the product.

3. If BPI's founder were to conduct a press conference, what points should he emphasize to the media and convey to the public?

4. Besides a press conference, what other tools might BPI or other firms use to improve the public's opinion of their products?

Cases in Business and Society

The Upper Big Branch Mine Disaster

On Monday, April 5, 2010, just before 3:00 in the afternoon, miners at Massey Energy Corporation's Upper Big Branch coal mine in southern West Virginia were in the process of a routine shift change. Workers on the evening shift were climbing aboard "mantrips," low-slung electric railcars that would carry them into the sprawling, three-mile-wide drift mine, cut horizontally into the side of a mountain. Many day shift workers inside the mine had begun packing up and were preparing to leave, and some were already on their way to the portals. At one of the mine's main "longwalls," one thousand feet below the surface, a team of four highly experienced miners was operating a shearer, a massive machine that cut coal from the face with huge rotating blades. The shearer had been shut down for part of the day because of mechanical difficulties, and the miners were making one last pass before the evening shift arrived to take their places.

Suddenly, a spark thrown off as the shearer's blades cut into hard sandstone ignited a small pocket of flammable methane gas. One of the operators immediately switched off the high-voltage power to the machine. Seconds later, the flame reached a larger pocket of methane, creating a small fireball. Apparently recognizing the danger, the four miners on the longwall crew began running for the exit opposite the fire. They had traveled no more than 400 feet when coal dust on the ground and in the air ignited violently, setting off a wave of powerful explosions that raced through the mine's seven miles of underground tunnels. When it was over three minutes later, 29 miners (including all four members of the longwall crew) were dead, and two were seriously injured. Some had died from injuries caused by the blast itself, others from carbon monoxide suffocation as the explosion sucked the oxygen out of the mine. It was the worse mining disaster in the United States in almost forty years.

An evening shift miner who had just entered the mine and boarded a mantrip for the ride to the coal face later told investigators what he had experienced:

> All of a sudden you heard this big roar, and that's when the air picked up. I'd say it was probably 60-some miles per hour. Instantly black. It took my hardhat and ripped it off my head, it was so powerful.

This miner and the rest of his group abandoned the mantrip and ran for the entrance, clutching each other in the darkness. On the outside, stunned and shaken, they turned to the most senior member of their crew for an explanation. "Boys . . . , I've been in the mines a long time," the veteran miner said. "That [was] no [roof] fall. . . . The place blew up."[1]

By Anne T. Lawrence. Copyright © 2012 by the author. All rights reserved. This case was presented at the 2012 annual meeting of the Western Casewriters Association Annual Meeting.

[1] Governor's Independent Investigation Panel, *Report to the Governor*, p. 26. This account of the disaster is based on a reconstruction of the events of April 5, 2010, by federal and state investigators and by the United Mine Workers Union.

Massey Energy Corporation

At the time of the explosion, Massey Energy Corporation, the owner and operator of the Upper Big Branch mine, was one of the leading coal producers in the United States. The company, which specialized in the production of high-grade metallurgical coal, described itself as "the most enduring and successful coal company in central Appalachia," where it owned one-third of the known coal reserves. Massey extracted 37 million tons of coal a year, ranking it sixth among U.S. producers in tonnage. The company sold its coal to more than a hundred utility, metallurgical, and industrial customers (mostly on long-term contracts) and exported to 13 countries. In 2009, Massey earned $227 million on revenue of $2.7 billion. The company and its subsidiaries employed 5,800 people in 42 underground and 14 surface mines and several coal processing facilities in West Virginia, Kentucky, and Virginia.

Massey maintained that it brought many benefits to the nation as a whole and to the Appalachian region. The coal industry in the United States, of which Massey was an important part, provided the fuel for about half of the electricity generated in the United States, lessening the country's reliance on imported oil. The company provided thousands of relatively well-paying jobs in a region that had long been marked by poverty and unemployment. Economists estimated that for every job in the coal industry, around three and a half jobs were created elsewhere. The company donated to scholarship programs, partnered with local schools, and provided emergency support during natural disasters, such as severe flooding in West Virginia in May 2009. "We recognize that it takes healthy and viable communities for our company to continue to grow and succeed," Massey declared in its 2009 report to shareholders.

But critics saw a darker side of Massey. The company was one of the leading practitioners of mountaintop removal mining, in which explosives were used to blast away the tops of mountains to expose valuable seams of coal. The resulting waste was frequently dumped into adjacent valleys, polluting streams, harming wildlife, and contaminating drinking water. In 2008, Massey paid $20 million to resolve violations of the Clean Water Act, the largest-ever settlement under that law. In an earlier incident, toxic mine sludge spilled from an impoundment operated by the company in Martin County, Kentucky, contaminating hundreds of miles of the Big Sandy and Ohio rivers, necessitating a $50 million cleanup. Worker safety was also a concern. An independent study found that Massey had the worst fatality rate of any coal company in the United States. For example, in the decade leading up to the Upper Big Branch disaster, Peabody Coal (the industry leader in tons produced) had one fatality for every 296 million tons of coal mined; Massey's rate was one fatality per 18 million tons—more than 16 times as high.

Donald L. Blankenship

At the time of the Upper Big Branch mine disaster, the chief executive officer and undisputed boss of Massey Energy was Don Blankenship. A descendant of the McCoy family of the famous warring clans the Hatfields and the McCoys, Blankenship was raised by a single mother in a trailer in Delorme, a railroad depot in the coalfields of West Virginia. His mother supported the family by working 6 days a week, 16 hours a day, running a convenience store and gas station. Michael Shnayerson, who wrote about Blankenship in his book, *Coal River,* reported that the executive had absorbed from his mother the value of hard work—as well as contempt for others who might be less fortunate. "Anyone who didn't work as hard as she did deserved to fail," Shnayerson wrote. "Sympathy appeared to play no part in her reckonings."[2]

Blankenship graduated from Marshall University in Huntington, West Virginia, with a degree in accounting. As a college student, he worked briefly in a coal mine to earn money for tuition. In 1982, at age 32, he returned to the coalfields to join Massey Energy, taking a job as an office manager for a subsidiary called Rawls. Soon after, Massey announced it intended to spin off its subsidiaries as separate companies and re-open them as nonunion operations. The United Mine Workers, the union that then represented many Massey workers, struck the company. Jeff Goodell, a journalist who profiled Blankenship in *Rolling Stone,* described the young manager's technique for defeating the union at Rawls:

> Blankenship erected two miles of chain link fence around the facility, brought in dogs and armed guards, and ferried nonunion workers through the union's block-ades. The strike, which lasted more than a year, grew increasingly violent—strikers took up baseball bats against the workers trying to take their jobs, and a few even fired shots at the scabs. A volley of bullets zinged into Blankenship's office and smashed into an old TV. . . . For years afterward, Blankenship kept the TV with a bullet hole through it in his office as a souvenir.[3]

The union's defeat at Massey (by 2010, only about 1 percent of Massey's workers were union members, all of them in coal preparation plants rather than mines) contributed to the overall decline of the United Mine Workers in the coalfields. In the 1960s, unions represented nearly 90 percent of the nation's mine workers; by 2010, they represented just 19 percent.

Blankenship quickly moved through the management ranks. In 1990, only eight years after he joined the company, he became president and chief operating officer of the Massey Coal Company and in 1992 was promoted to CEO and chairman. (The company was renamed Massey Energy in 2000 when it separated from its parent, Fluor Corp.) By some measures, he was a successful CEO. Between 2001, the first full year of Massey's independent operation, and 2009, annual revenue increased from $1.2 billion to $2.7 billion. During this period, employment rose from around 3,700 to 5,800. Blankenship more than doubled the company's coal reserves, mainly through acquisitions of smaller firms. Massey shareholders, like all investors, were buffeted by the extreme volatility of the stock market during the 2000s. Nevertheless, an investor who purchased $10,000 worth of Massey stock in December 2004 would have a holding valued at $12,800 in December 2010—a rate of return close to that of the coal industry as a whole during this period.[4]

As CEO, Blankenship developed a reputation as a hands-on, detail-oriented manager. He lived in the coalfields and ran the company out of a double-wide trailer in Belfry, Kentucky, just over the West Virginia line. He signed off on all hires, all the way down to janitors. One manager expressed amazement when he learned that the CEO would have to approve a tankful of gasoline for his truck. Managers were required to fax production figures to Blankenship every half hour. Red phones connected mine managers directly to the CEO. "If the report was late or the numbers weren't good, or the mine was shut down for any reason," Shnayerson reported, "the red phone would ring. The terrified manager would pick it up to hear Mr. B demanding to know why the numbers

[2] Michael Shnayerson, *Coal River: How a Few Brave Americans Took on a Powerful Company—and the Federal Government—to Save the Land They Love* (New York: Farrar, Straus, and Giroux, 2008), p. 155.

[3] Jeff Goodell, "The Dark Lord of Coal Country," *Rolling Stone,* December 9, 2010.

[4] Massey, 2009 Annual Report, "Shareholder Information," p. 23.

weren't right."[5] Blankenship told an interviewer, "People talk about character being what you do when no one else is looking. But the truth of the matter is character is doing that which is unpopular if it's right, even if it causes you to be vilified."[6]

As CEO, Blankenship maintained a laser focus on productivity. In 2005, he sent a memo titled "RUNNING COAL" to all Massey underground mine superintendents that stated:

> If any of you have been asked by your group presidents, your supervisors, engineers, or anyone else to do anything other than run coal (i.e., build overcasts, do construction jobs, or whatever) you need to ignore them and run coal. This memo is necessary only because we seem not to understand that coal pays the bills.

A week later, after this memo had been widely circulated, he followed up with another one which referred to the company's S-1, P-2 (safety first, production second) program. He wrote: "By now each of you should know that safety and S-1 is our first responsibility. Productivity and P-2 are second."

Executive Compensation

Blankenship was well compensated for running Massey. As shown in Exhibit A, his total compensation in 2009 was almost $18 million; this was up from $11 million in 2008 and $9 million in 2007. Blankenship's base salary in all three years was close to $1 million. By far the greatest proportion of his total pay came from a performance-based incentive system established by Massey's board of directors. In its filings with the SEC, the board described its philosophy of compensation this way:[7]

> We compensate our named executive officers in a manner that is meant to attract and retain highly qualified and gifted individuals and to appropriately incentivize and motivate the named executive officers to achieve continuous improvements in company-wide performance for the benefit of our stockholders.[8]

Accordingly, the compensation committee of the board established an incentive plan for Massey's CEO. (Similar plans were in place for other senior executives as well.) The plan set specific performance measures for "areas over which Mr. Blankenship was responsible and positioned to directly influence outcome." These areas, and the proportion of his incentive compensation based on them, are shown in Exhibit B.

By one estimate, in the 10 years leading up to the disaster Blankenship received a total of $129 million in compensation from Massey.[9] "I don't care what people think," he once said during a talk to a gathering of Republican Party leaders in West Virginia, speaking of

---

[5] Michael Shnayerson, quoted in United Mine Workers of America, *Industrial Homicide: Report on the Upper Big Branch Mine Disaster*, p. 80.

[6] Jim Snyder, "Q&A with Don Blankenship," November 16, 2009, *http://thehill.com.*

[7] At the time of the UBB disaster, Massey was governed by a nine-person board of directors chaired by Blankenship. The other members were Baxter Phillips, Jr., Massey's president; Stanley Suboleski, formerly Massey's chief operating officer and later commissioner of the Federal Mine Safety and Health Review Commission under President George W. Bush; Lady Judge, an attorney and former commissioner of the Securities and Exchange Commission; Bobby R. Inman, a retired naval admiral and former director of the National Security Agency; James Crawford, a former coal industry executive; Robert Fogelsong, president and executive director of the Appalachian Leadership and Education Foundation; Richard Gabrys, formerly vice chairman of Deloitte and Touche; and Dan Moore, a retired banker. In 2009, directors earned $39,600 in cash and $90,000 in stock, plus $2,000 for each meeting attended, plus extra compensation for special duties (e.g., lead director). (Massey, Form 8-K, November 2009).

[8] Massey Energy, 2010 Proxy, p. 25.

[9] David Roberts, "Grist" [blog], April 9, 2010, *www.grist.org.*

Year	Salary	Bonus	Stock Awards	Option Awards	Incentive Plan	Change in Pension Value	Other(*)	Total Compensation
2009	933,369	300,000	3,869,819	—	11,549,156	573,618	609,875	17,835,837
2008	1,000,000	300,000	390,000	2,160,000	6,022,447	691,415	357,129	11,020,991
2007	1,000,000	300,000	604,800	1,700,000	5,257,576	111,794	386,480	9,361,000

Source: Massey Energy 2010 Proxy, "Compensation Discussion and Analysis" and "Compensation of Named Executive Officers."

Note: "Other" includes personal use of company cars, aircraft (Challenger 601 corporate jet), housing, and related costs and services.

himself in the third person. "At the end of the day, Don Blankenship is going to die with more money than he needs."[10]

Government Regulation of Mining Safety and Health

Coal mining had always been a hazardous occupation. Methane gas, an odorless and colorless by-product of decomposing organic matter that was often present alongside coal, was highly flammable. Methane explosions had contributed to the deaths of more than 10,000 miners in the United States since 1920. To mine safely, methane levels had to be constantly monitored, and ventilation systems had to be effective enough to remove it from the mine. Coal dust itself—whether on the floor or other surfaces, or suspended in the air—was also highly flammable. The standard practice was to apply layers of rock dust (crushed limestone) over the coal dust to render it inert. In addition to the ever-present danger of fire, miners had long contended with the threat of collapsing roofs and walls, dangerous mechanical equipment, and suffocation. Miners often developed coal workers' pneumoconiosis, commonly called black lung, a chronic, irreversible disease caused by breathing coal dust. (Black lung was preventable with proper coal dust control.)

Health and safety in the mining industry had long been regulated at both the federal and state levels. Over the years, lawmakers had periodically strengthened government regulatory control, mostly in response to mining disasters.

- In 1910, following an explosion at the Monongah mine in West Virginia in which 362 men died, Congress established the *U.S. Bureau of Mines* to conduct research on the safety and health of miners.

- The Federal Coal Mine Health and Safety Act, known as the *Coal Act*—which passed in 1969 after the death of 78 miners at the Consol Number 9 mine in Farmington, West Virginia—greatly increased federal enforcement powers. This law established fines for violations and criminal penalties for "knowing and willful" violations. It also provided compensation for miners disabled by black lung disease.

- The 1977 *Mine Act* further strengthened the rights of miners and established the Mine Safety and Health Administration, MSHA (pronounced "Em-shah") to carry out its

[10] Goodell, op. cit.

The calculation of incentive plan compensation was based on achievement of specific targets in these areas:

EBIT (earnings before interest and taxes)	15%
Produced tons	15%
Continuous miner productivity (feet/shift)	5%
Surface mining productivity (tons/man-hour)	5%
Environmental violations (% reduction)	10%
Fulfillment of contracts	15%
Nonfatal days lost due to injury and accident (% reduction)	10%
Identification of successors	5%
Employee retention	15%
Diversity of members	5%

Source: Massey Energy 2010 Proxy.

Note: A "continuous miner" is a large machine that extracts coal underground.

regulatory mandates. The law required at least four full inspections of underground mines annually.

- Then in 2006, after yet another string of mine tragedies focused public attention on the dangers of mining, Congress passed the Mine Improvement and New Emergency Response Act, known at the *MINER Act.* This law created new rules to help miners survive underground explosions and accidents.[11]

States like West Virginia that had significant mining industries also had their own regulatory rules and agencies.

Although MSHA was empowered to inspect mines unannounced and to fine operators for violations, the agency had limited authority to shut down a mine if a serious problem was present or if the operator refused to pay its fines. Criminal violations of mine safety laws were normally considered misdemeanors rather than felonies.

Over time, fatalities in the industry had declined. At the turn of the 20th century, around 300 to 400 miners died every year in the nation's coal mines; by the 1980s, this number had dropped to less than 50. Injuries and illnesses had also dropped. In part, these declines reflected tougher government regulations. They also reflected the rise of surface mining (mostly in the western United States), which tended to be safer, and the emergence of new technologies that mechanized the process of underground mining. The unionization of the mining industry had also given workers a greater voice and the right to elect safety representatives in many workplaces.

The Upper Big Branch Mine

Massey had bought the Upper Big Branch mine in 1993 from Peabody Coal. It was a particularly valuable property because its thick coal seam produced the high-grade metallurgic coal favored by utilities and the steel industry. Two hundred employees worked there on three, round-the-clock shifts. In 2009, Upper Big Branch produced

---

[11] "History of Mine Safety and Health Legislation," Mine Safety and Health Administration, *www.msha.gov.*

1.2 million tons of coal, about 3 percent of Massey's total. The mine, like all of those operated by Massey, was nonunion.

The regulatory record revealed a widespread pattern of safety violations at the Upper Big Branch mine and an increasingly contentious relationship between its managers and government regulators. As shown in Exhibit C, government inspectors had issued an increasing number of violations over time, with a sharp spike upward the year before the disaster. These data also showed that around 2006, management had begun to contest regulatory penalties rather than pay them. The state investigation reported the story that at one point Massey's vice president for safety—an attorney—"took a violation written by an inspector, looked at her people, and said, 'Don't worry, we'll litigate it away.'" Appealing the citations not only allowed the company to delay or avoid paying; it also blocked tougher sanctions, such as shutting down the mine.

Miners testified that they were intimidated or disciplined if they complained about safety. When one foreman told his men not to run coal until a ventilation problem was fixed, he was suspended for three days for "poor work performance." Another miner, who was killed in the blast, had told his wife that a manager had told him when he complained about conditions, "If you can't go up there and run coal, just bring your [lunch] bucket outside and go home." The father of a young miner who was still a trainee when he was killed at Upper Big Branch related his son's experience to investigators. The young man had told his father that when he had expressed concerns about safety to his supervisor, he was told, "If you're going to be that scared of your job here, you need to rethink your career."[12] Miners who were hurt on the job were told not to report their injuries, so an NFDL (non-fatal day lost) would not be recorded. A former Massey miner who testified before a Senate committee explained, "If you got hurt, you were told not to fill out the lost-time accident paperwork. The company would just pay guys to sit in the bathhouse or to stay at home if they got hurt."[13]

Investigators found that the company had kept two sets of books at UBB, one for its own record keeping and the other to show inspectors. "If a coal mine wants to keep two sets of books, that's their business," the administrator for MSHA later commented. "They can keep five sets of books if they want. But they're required to record the hazards in the official set of books."[14] Conditions that were recorded in the company's own books—but not the official set—included sudden methane spikes, inoperative safety equipment, and other dangers.

The mine also had a system in place, set up by its chief of security, to warn underground managers that an inspector was on the way—a clear violation of the law. A miner who survived the explosion later told Congress, "The code word would go out we've got a man [government inspector] on the property. . . . When the word goes out, all effort is made to correct the deficiencies."[15] A surviving miner testified:

> Nobody shuts one of Don Blankenship's mines down. It has never happened. Everyone knows when mine inspectors are coming, you clean things up for a few minutes, make it look good, then you go back to the business of running coal. That's how things work at Massey. When inspectors write a violation, the company lawyers challenge it in court. It's just all a game. Don Blankenship does what he wants.[16]

---

[12] UMW, op. cit., p. 81.

[13] UMW, op. cit., p. 78.

[14] "Mine Owners Misled Inspectors, Investigators Say," *The New York Times*, June 29, 2011.

[15] UMW, op. cit., p. 77.

[16] Jeff Goodell, op. cit.

Exhibit C

Year	Number of Citations	Assessed Penalty ($)	Amount Paid ($)
2000	240	55,325	55,325
2001	398	48,761	48,761
2002	221	64,726	64,726
2003	175	41,934	41,405
2004	238	48,371	48,371
2005	143	32,577	32,576
2006	173	191,249	84,411
2007	271	253,984	61,745
2008	197	239,566	105,965
2009	515	897,325	292,953

Source: MSHA data, reported in the appendices of *Industrial Homicide: Report on the Upper Big Branch Mine Disaster.*

After the disaster, Blankenship stated, "Violations are unfortunately a normal part of the mining process. There are violations in every coal mine in America, and UBB was a mine that had violations."

Causes of the Disaster

In the months following the tragedy at Upper Big Branch, three separate investigations—conducted by the federal MSHA, a commission established by the governor of West Virginia, and the United Mine Workers—examined the causes of the fatal explosion. All came to the same conclusion: that a spark from the longwall shearer had ignited a pocket of methane, which had then set off a series of explosions of volatile coal dust that had raced through the mine. Such events could only have happened in the presence of serious, systematic safety violations. Among the problems cited by the investigators were these:

- *Rock Dust.* Investigators found that the company had failed to meet government standards for the application of rock dust. As a result, explosive coal dust had built up on surfaces and in the air throughout the mine.

The state commission reported that the Upper Big Branch mine had only two workers assigned to rock dusting, and they typically worked at the task only three days a week and were frequently called away to do other jobs. Moreover, their task was often impossible because the mine's single dusting machine, which was about 30 years old, was broken most of the time. Federal investigators later determined that more than 90 percent of the area of the mine where the explosion occurred was inadequately rock dusted at the time of the explosion. They also found that the area of the longwall where the explosion began had not been rock dusted a single time since production started there in September 2009. The presence of large amounts of floating coal dust in the mine was also suggested by medical evidence. Seventy-one percent of the autopsied victims showed clinical signs of black lung disease, caused by breathing airborne coal dust. Nationally, the rate of black lung disease in underground coal miners was around 3 percent.

- *Ventilation.* Investigators found that the Upper Big Branch Mine did not have sufficient ventilation to provide the miners with fresh, breathable air, and to remove coal dust as well as methane and other dangerous gases.

Upper Big Branch, like many mines, used a so-called push-pull system in which large fans at the portal blew fresh air into the mine, and a fan on the other end pulled air out. The state investigation found that this system did not work very well at Upper Big Branch. The fans were powerful enough, but the plan was not properly engineered.

> The push-pull ventilation system at Upper Big Branch . . . had a design flaw: its fans were configured so that air was directed in a straight line even though miners worked in areas away from the horizontal path. As a result, air had to be diverted from its natural flow pattern into the working sections. . . . Because these sections were located on different sides of the natural flow pattern, multiple diversionary controls had to be constructed and frequently were in competition with one another.[17]

Poor ventilation had likely caused methane to build up near the longwall shearer, providing the fuel for the initial fireball, investigators found.

- *Equipment Maintenance.* Investigators concluded that water sprays on the longwall shearer were not functioning properly, and as a result were unable to extinguish the initial spark.

After the disaster, investigators closely studied the longwall shearer where the initial fire had started. They found that several of the cutting teeth on the rotating blades (called "bits") had worn flat and lost their carbide tips, so they were likely to create sparks when hitting sandstone. The investigators also examined the water nozzles on the shearer, which normally sprayed water onto the coal face during operation to cool the cutting bits, extinguish sparks, and push away any methane that might have leaked into the area. They found that seven of the nozzles were either missing or clogged. Tests found that the longwall shearer did not have adequate water pressure to keep the surface wet and cool. As a result, any small sparks thrown off during the mining process could not be extinguished.

In short, a series of interrelated safety violations had combined to produce a preventable tragedy. The United Mine Workers called the disaster "industrial homicide" and called for the criminal prosecution of Massey's managers.

For its part, Massey had a completely different interpretation of the causes of the events of April 5. An investigation commissioned by the company and headed by Bobby R. Inman, its lead independent director, said that the explosion was caused by a sudden, massive inundation of natural gas through a crack in the mine's floor—an Act of God that the company could not have anticipated or prevented. The company report stated:

> . . . the scientific data that [Massey] has painstakingly assembled over the last year with the assistance of a team of nationally renowned experts so far compels at least five conclusions. *First,* a massive inundation of natural gas caused the UBB explosion and coal dust did not contribute materially to the magnitude or severity of the blast; *second,* although an ignition source may never be determined, the explosion likely originated in the Tailgate 21 entries, but certainly not as a result of faulty shearer maintenance; *third,* [the company] adequately rock dusted the mine prior to the explosion such that coal dust could not have played a causal role in the accident; *fourth,* the mine's underground ventilation system provided significantly more fresh air than required by law and there is no evidence that ventilation contributed to the explosion; and *fifth,* MSHA has conducted a deeply flawed accident investigation that has been predicated, in part, upon secrecy, protecting its own self-interest,

---

[17] Governor's Independent Investigation Panel, op. cit., p. 61.

witness intimidation, obstruction of [company] investigators, and retaliatory citations.[18]

In a conversation with stock analysts six months after the disaster, Blankenship stated that he had a "totally clear conscience" and that he did not believe Massey had "contributed in any way to the accident."[19]

Discussion Questions

1. What were the costs and benefits to stakeholders of the actions taken by Massey Energy and its managers?

2. Applying the four methods of ethical reasoning (utilitarianism, rights, justice, and virtue), do you believe Massey Energy behaved in an ethical manner? Why or why not?

3. Who or what caused the Upper Big Branch mine disaster, and why do you think so?

4. What steps could be taken now to reduce the chances of a similar tragedy occurring in the future? In your answer, please address the appropriate roles of mining companies (and their directors and managers), government regulators and policymakers, and the workers and their union in assuring mine safety.

---

[18] *http://www.usmra.com/download/MasseyUBBReport.pdf,*

[19] "CEO says Massey has 'Clear Conscience' over Upper Big Branch," *Charleston Gazette,* October 27, 2010.

The Carlson Company and Protecting Children in the Global Tourism Industry

Marilyn Carlson Nelson, in her seventh year as chief executive officer (CEO) of the Carlson Company, a global marketing, travel, and hospitality company, faced a major dilemma. In 2006, the company was considering a proposal to expand its luxury Regency accommodations and services to Costa Rica. The venture gave many indications of being strategically sound and highly profitable, and it would also provide a basis for future expansion throughout Latin America. However, during the feasibility study of a promising property located in Papagayo, a popular tourist destination along Costa Rica's northern coast, company executives learned that the surrounding area was notorious for child trafficking and prostitution. This was of particular concern to Carlson Nelson, because under her leadership Carlson had, in 2004, signed the *Code of Conduct for the Protection of Children from Sexual Exploitation in Travel and Tourism* (the Code). This global project brought together the travel and tourism industry and nongovernmental organizations to prevent sexual exploitation of children at tourist destinations.

As part of its obligations under the Code, Carlson had adopted a corporate ethics policy designed to eliminate any organizational association with sex trafficking. Carlson Nelson was confronted with the need to assess whether the proposed Regent resort could ensure compliance with the Code in an environment where sexual exploitation of children was often an integral part of doing business. Should Carlson Companies decide to abandon the

By Robyn Linde and H. Richard Eisenbeis. Copyright © 2011 by the *Case Research Journal* and the authors. Used by permission. All rights reserved. This case study was generously funded by the *United Front for Children Conference: Global Efforts to Combat Sexual Trafficking in Travel and Tourism*, held at the University of Minnesota in Minneapolis in April 2006. The Curtis L. Carlson Foundation was one source of funding for the conference. Interviews for the case study were conducted between 2006 and 2008 with Carlson Companies executives, including Marilyn Carlson Nelson, then president and chief executive officer of Carlson Companies; Deb Cundy, assistant dean of external relations at the Carlson School of Management at the University of Minnesota; Doug Cody, corporate vice president of public relations and communications; Kim Olson, vice president, chief communications officer; Tom Polski, vice president of global communications and external relations; Bill Van Brunt, executive vice president, Carlson Companies; and Jay Witzel, president and CEO of Carlson Hotels Worldwide. Carol Smolenski of *End Child Prostitution Child Pornography and Trafficking of Children for Sexual Purposes* (ECPAT) was an especially valuable resource during the many drafts of this case. Robyn Linde would additionally like to thank Sally Kenney, Holiday Shapiro, Kathryn Sikkink, fellow case writers in Professor Kenney's seminar on *Case Studies on Women and Public Policy* at the University of Minnesota, and the anonymous reviewers for their helpful comments on earlier drafts.

project, it would certainly lose a viable opportunity to become a major player in the high-end Central American tourism market.

Carlson Companies, Marilyn Carlson Nelson, and the Code

Carlson's history was one of the classic business success stories in the American free enterprise system. Starting in 1938 with an idea and a $55 loan, entrepreneur Curtis L. Carlson founded the Gold Bond Stamp Company in his home town of Minneapolis. He knew that grocery stores, drug stores, gas stations, and other independent merchants could use stamps to drive customer loyalty and to distinguish themselves from their competitors. During the 1950s and 1960s, Gold Bond and its sister company, Top Value Stamps, helped revolutionize the way retail goods were marketed. Trading stamps proved to be right for the times and swept the nation in a wave of dramatic growth.[1]

In the late 1960s, when the trading stamp market reached its peak, the Gold Bond Stamp Company expanded into the hospitality industry. In the 1970s, the company acquired dozens of additional businesses, including T.G.I. Friday's and Radisson. To reflect its diversification, Gold Bond changed its name to Carlson Companies in 1973. Based in Minneapolis, Minnesota, Carlson brands generated more than $31.4 billion in gross sales system-wide and employed about 188,000 people in more than 140 countries by 1999. In 2006, to demonstrate that they were one company serving a variety of needs, the firm became known as the Carlson Company.[2]

The company had long been involved in philanthropy through its Curtis L. Carlson Family Foundation. Established in 1959, the foundation was one of many avenues Carlson Companies chose to carry out its charitable work. Curtis Carlson, the son of Swedish immigrants, became widely recognized in Sweden for his success in business as well as for his charitable endeavors. His ancestral ties to Sweden eventually led to a lasting friendship between the Carlson family and the royal family of Sweden.

Marilyn Carlson Nelson, Curtis Carlson's eldest daughter, graduated with honors from Smith College with a degree in international economics and a minor in theater. She also attended the Sorbonne in Paris and the Institute Des Hautes Etudes Economiques Politiques in Geneva, Switzerland, where she studied political science and international economics. Carlson Nelson succeeded her father as president and CEO of Carlson Companies in 1998. In this role, she was responsible for the day-to-day operations of one of the largest privately held companies in the world. Carlson Nelson led the management of a global business portfolio encompassing Carlson's major operating groups, specializing in corporate solutions and consumer services: Carlson Hospitality Worldwide (hotels, restaurants, and cruise ships); Carlson Wagonlit Travel (business travel and leisure travel brand); Carlson Leisure Group (leisure travel agencies and tour operators); and Carlson Marketing Group (incentive and loyalty marketing). By 2006, under Carlson Nelson's leadership, Carlson's annual sales exceeded $37 billion and it employed over 150,000 people worldwide. She was widely recognized as one of the world's most influential women.[3]

---

[1] Based on "Company History," *www.carlson.com.*

[2] Based on "Our Founder and History," *www.clcfamilyfoundation.com.*

[3] Beverly Kopf and Bobbie Birleffi, "Not Her Father's Chief Executive," *U.S. News and World Report,* October 2006, *http://www.usnews.com/usnews/news/articles/061022/30nelson.htm,* last accessed February 24, 2011; Maggie Rauch, "Leading the Field: Marilyn Carlson-Nelson," *Incentive Magazine,* May 1, 2006, *http://www.incentivemag.com/News/Industry/Articles/Leading-the-Field—Marilyn-Carlson-Nelson/,* last accessed February 24, 2011; "Carlson Chair and CEO Named 'Businesswoman of the Year,'" *Travel Daily News,* April 2005; "Marilyn Carlson Nelson (Chairman & CEO, Carlson Companies)" *Ethisphere,* December 2007, *http://ethisphere.com/marilyn-carlson-nelson/,* last accessed February 24, 2011; "The Word's Most Powerful Women," *Forbes,* 2005, *http://www.forbes.com/lists/2005/11/PV8L.html,* last accessed February 24, 2011.

Carlson Nelson defined her role as president and CEO of Carlson as follows:

A CEO has to train and operate like a jet pilot. Once the company's talented executive team is flying in formation, I'm usually raising peripheral vision issues—how a decision is going to impact other pieces of the business, how it's going to impact our shareholder relationships and our banking relationships. I really go through the various stakeholders in my mind. And I might try to impact the final outcome so that it will bring people the broadest possible ownership of the decision.

Carlson Nelson's general management style was described by other executives in the organization as being "collective." Kim Olson, vice president and chief communication officer, described Carlson Nelson as:

. . . having a participative leadership style. When making decisions at the corporate level, we hear and discuss all points of view before arriving at a decision. We believe these collective decisions enhance our sense of global corporate citizenship.

Tourism and the Commercial Sexual Exploitation of Children

Although the commercial sexual exploitation of children occurred in countries worldwide, the growing popularity and declining cost of travel and the rise of new communications technologies had changed the nature of child exploitation by facilitating the rise of global sex tourism. The World Tourism Organization defined organized sex tourism as:

Trips organized from within the tourism sector, or from outside this sector but using its structures and networks, with the primary purpose of effecting a commercial sexual relationship by the tourist with residents at the destination.

Prostitution, child prostitution, and sexual exploitation of children have existed throughout history. However, prior to the last quarter of the 20th century, the child segment had been confined largely to the poorer, more destitute countries of the world where selling female children for sex was often seen as an accepted means of family survival. By the 1990s, the survival dimension had changed dramatically. Trafficking children for sex had become a formidable international business and part of a multi-billion-dollar industry in which approximately two million children were exploited annually.

Basically, sex trafficking was a type of commercial trade in people, either across borders or within countries, whereby individuals were forced into sexual slavery. Children under the age of 18 made up a large portion of this trade and were trafficked for multiple reasons, including forced labor, criminal activity, and sexual exploitation. The travel and tourism industry facilitated the trafficking of children in two ways: (1) hotels, airlines, trains, and buses provided the means by which children were trafficked; and (2) more commonly, the industry transported the sex tourist to his/her destination and provided accommodations once there.

A few travel companies actually targeted sex tourists and actively sought their business. For example, an advertisement by Lauda Air, an Austrian airline, consisted of a picture of a partially clothed girl and captions reading, "From Thailand with Love," and "the tarts in the Bangkok Baby Club are waiting for us." Generally, however, companies in the travel and tourism industry downplayed their role in the sex trade and the sexual exploitation of children by turning a blind eye toward tourist industry practices that inadvertently exposed children around the world to sexual abuse and violence.

International and U.S. Law Regarding Sex Trafficking

International legal efforts to protect women and children from trafficking were first made at the beginning of the 20th century, when many conventions were established to end what was then referred to as "white slave traffic." Both international and U.S. enforcement officials had been unwavering in their condemnation of the trafficking of children. In addition, the International Criminal Court had declared it a crime against humanity, and a number of other international treaties and declarations had condemned the practice and called on states to prevent it. The most important and widely cited international agreement for the protection of children is the 1990 *Convention on the Rights of the Child,* which had been ratified by nearly every state in the international system. Article 35 of this convention provided that "States shall take all appropriate national, bilateral, and multilateral measures to prevent the abduction, sale, or traffic of children for any purpose or in any form."

Children's advocates had also targeted the demand side of child sex trafficking in hopes of curtailing the number of tourists who sexually exploited children while traveling. In 1994, the Child Sexual Abuse Prevention Act made it illegal for U.S. citizens and permanent-resident aliens to travel abroad to commit sexual acts with minors. As a result, the U.S. government was able to prosecute Americans for sexual acts with children even if those acts took place outside U.S. borders. Moreover, efforts to prosecute travel agencies that catered to sex tourists continued to increase.

Sex Trafficking and Child Sexual Exploitation in Costa Rica

By the late 1980s, Costa Rica had become one of the principal tourist destinations in Central America, and the expanding industry became the country's primary source of foreign capital. According to the U.S. Department of State, the boom in tourism had also resulted in Costa Rica becoming a "source, transit, and destination country" for sex trafficking.[4] Women and girls were trafficked into Costa Rica from Nicaragua, the Dominican Republic, Colombia, Guatemala, Russia, and Eastern Europe for sexual exploitation. Costa Rican women and girls were trafficked within the country as well as to other Central American countries, Mexico, and Japan. The problem of child prostitution in Costa Rica was so serious that one NGO, the National Institute for Children (PANI), put the number of child prostitutes at 3,000 in the capital, San Jose, alone. This group, along with other NGOs, had continued to fight against sex tourism and had condemned the practice in the West.

Nongovernmental organizations began to raise concerns about Costa Rica's problem with sex tourists and child exploitation in the late 1990s, but the Costa Rican government did not make concerted efforts to address the issue until 2006.[5] Not until 2009 did the

---

[4] Casa Alianza and ECPAT International, "Creating a Database as a Tool For Campaigning," San Jose (2002); ECPAT International, "Five Years after Stockholm," The Fifth Report on the Implementation of the Agenda for Action Adopted at the World Congress against Commercial Sexual Exploitation of Children, Sweden (2001); ECPAT International, "Informe Global de Monitoreo de las acciones en contra de la explotacion sexual comercial de ninos, ninas y adolescentes: Costa Rica" (2006); Michael B. Farrell, "Global Campaign to Police Child Sex Tourism," *The Christian Science Monitor,* April 22, 2004; Julia O'Connell Davidson and Jacqueline Sanchez Taylor, "Child Prostitution and Sex Tourism: Costa Rica," ECPAT International (1995); Susan Song, "Children as Tourist Attractions," Youth Advocate Program International Resources Paper, Washington, D.C. (2004); U.S. Department of State, "Trafficking in Persons Report" (2002); U.S. Department of State, "Trafficking in Persons Report" (2006); U.S. Department of State, "Trafficking in Persons Report" (2007); U.S. Department of State, "Trafficking in Persons Report" (2009); U.S. Department of State, "Trafficking in Persons Report" (2010); U.S. Department of State, Bureau of Democracy, Human Rights and Labor, Country Reports on Human Rights Practices, "Costa Rica" (2005).

[5] See U.S. Department of State "Trafficking in Persons Report" from 2002 to 2010 to see the evolution of Costan Rican efforts to curb child trafficking.

country make all forms of trafficking illegal: trafficking became punishable by prison terms of 6 to 10 years, which could be increased to 16 years if a minor was involved.[6] Despite these penalties, the U.S. Department of State determined that the government of Costa Rica did not meet the "minimum standards" for eliminating trafficking as endorsed by the United States.

The Marriott Incident

In 2002, a Marriott Resort Hotel employee in Papagayo, Costa Rica, was indicted for the aggravated pimping of minors in a case that involved a number of its hotel employees. The fallout for Marriott was next to catastrophic. The Interfaith Center on Corporate Responsibility, a coalition of faith-based investors that files shareholder actions against corporations in the name of social responsibility, organized a widespread shareholder campaign against Marriott. The First Swedish National Pension Fund (Första AP-fonde) also played a key role in drafting a shareholder resolution condemning Marriott for failing to adopt policies that would prevent similar exploitation from happening in the future. Marriott failed to respond. In 2005, immediately preceding its annual stockholder meeting, the resolution became public knowledge. Marriott was immediately subjected to severe and damaging criticism throughout the world. Although Marriott had been pressured prior to the litigation to adopt a strong policy against sexual exploitation of children, it had failed to do so. However, as a result of the international outrage stemming from the shareholder resolution, the firm undertook an internal review of its policies that eventually produced a human rights policy to combat child sex trafficking, somewhat placating its critics.[7]

Queen Sylvia, the Code, and Carlson Company's Response

In 1998, in response to concerns about the ways in which the travel and tourism industry facilitated child trafficking and at the initiative of Queen Silvia of Sweden, an influential NGO (ECPAT—End Child Prostitution, Child Pornography, and Trafficking of Children for Sexual Purposes), the Scandinavian Tourism Industry, and the World Tourism Organization combined forces to create a Code of Conduct for companies in the industry. The Code was a voluntary commitment for travel and tourism companies to pledge their aid in combating child trafficking. Key elements of the code included:

1. Establishing an ethical policy regarding commercial sexual exploitation of children.
2. Training personnel in the country of origin and travel destinations.
3. Introducing a clause in contracts with suppliers, stating a common repudiation of commercial sexual exploitation of children.
4. Providing information to travelers by means of catalogs, brochures, in-flight films, ticket slips, home pages, etc.

---

[6] Although 268 Costa Rican companies and organizations have become members to the code. See *www.thecode.org* for more information.

[7] Forsta AP-fonden, "Första AP-fonden Influences Marriott to Combat Child Sex Tourism," *http://www.ap1.se/en /Asset-management/Ethical-and-environmental-consideration-in-our-investments/Long-term-commitment-pays-off /Forsta-AP-fonden-influences-Marriott-to-combat-child-sex-tourism/*, last accessed February 24, 2011; Interfaith Centre on Corporate Responsibility, "Selling Innocence: Child Sex Tourisim," *http://www.docstoc.com/docs/66828019 /Accor-Hospitality-Asset-Management*, last accessed February 24, 2011; "Marriott Hotel Chain Combats Child Sexual Exploitation" (December 2006), *http://www.humantrafficking.org/updates/494*, last accessed February 24, 2011.

5. Providing information to local "key persons" at the destinations.
6. Filing annual reports to various monitoring bodies.

Companies that adopted the Code were required to submit annual reports on their corporate practices to international, transnational, and national monitoring bodies to demonstrate compliance with the Code, share information, build know-how about best practices, and identify problems. Companies that adopted the Code were also encouraged to monitor their employees and the practices of their contractors through documented spot checks.

As of November 2009, more than 947 companies in 37 countries had signed the Code, affecting millions of tourists who employed the services of these companies. However, only two U.S. companies had signed. The absence of signatories among U.S. companies presented a serious problem given that an estimated 25 percent of sex tourists outside of the United States were Americans who presumably utilized U.S. travel and tourism services. The majority of U.S. hoteliers, travel agencies, airlines, and tour companies had not signed the Code for fear of such consequences as:

1. Negative publicity that their adoption of the Code might generate.
2. The burden the Code imposed on companies to police their employees and contractors.
3. Litigation from trafficked children themselves.
4. Litigation initiated by guests who might witness trafficking while utilizing a company's travel and tourist services.
5. Absence of other corporate signatories.

Carlson Nelson and Queen Silvia of Sweden shared a long-held concern for at-risk children, which led to numerous collective projects over the years. Foremost among them was the establishment of the World Childhood Foundation, founded in 1999 by Queen Silvia along with 14 cofounders, including the Carlson Family Foundation. When asked by the Queen to become a signatory to the Code in 2004, Carlson Nelson enthusiastically committed. Carlson Companies thus became the first major North American travel and tourism company to sign, committing to the Code for all of Carlson's brands.[8] In signing the code, Carlson Nelson assured the tourism industry that all future decisions made by Carlson's executive team would take into consideration the next generation—"thinking about children and teens and the impact of the company's actions upon their welfare and development."

When asked about Carlson Companies' early adoption of the Code, Carlson Nelson remarked:

> We like to think that we play a leadership role on this particular issue. Sometimes I wish we weren't as far out in front as a leader because we had hoped that more travel and hotel companies would sign on to the Code.

However, initially there was not full agreement among executives within Carlson Companies that signing the Code was a good idea.[9] Concerns identified by Carlson executives essentially mirrored the concerns of other executives in the travel and tourism

---

[8] The other North American signatories at the time were the American Society of Travel Agents and Amazon Tours. Since then, three more companies have signed the Code: Millennium Hotel St. Louis, Delta Airlines, and Hilton Hotels.

[9] However, each Carlson executive interviewed made it clear to the researcher that signing the Code was Carlson Nelson's decision and that it was adopted as policy because she advocated for it. No different or alternative views were expressed during the course of the interviews.

industry. Doug Cody, corporate vice president of public relations and communications, further questioned:

> Why should Carlson get involved in something so ugly when there are so many other worthwhile causes that we could be involved with? . . . Do we really want to associate our name with such an ugly thing? No other major travel and tourism company has signed the Code in North America, and the issue of child trafficking is not widely discussed in the media. My primary concern is associating with it. Even though we are fighting against it, it could backfire and hurt you. People could misunderstand it or believe that somehow we were connected with it. There were a lot of reasons to say "no."

Cody's opinion about the public relations liability of the Code abruptly changed when Carlson Nelson invited him along to witness the signing of the Code at the United Nations with Queen Silvia. Upon seeing dozens of television cameras from around the world present to witness the signing, it occurred to Cody that the media exposure would prove very beneficial to the company—indeed "the eyes of the world were watching." Even so, Cody argued that other companies in the travel and tourism industry would be "steered away from the Code because of the legal ramifications if the Code is not followed once signed."

In retrospect, Tom Polski, vice president of global communications and external relations, said:

> The shift in thinking at Carlson Companies about the Code resulted from increased awareness of the whole issue through activities at the World Childhood Foundation. Carlson Companies and the travel and tourism industry are in the "happiness" business, and child trafficking is not very pleasant and people sometimes don't want to hear unpleasant things. I supported the Code because child exploitation is a reality in the travel and tourism business.

By many accounts, Carlson's corporate culture was noticeably affected by its newfound commitment to curtailing child trafficking. Jay Witzel, president and CEO of Carlson Hotels Worldwide, said:

> Once Carlson Companies signed the Code, the level of commitment to end child trafficking throughout the entire Carlson system rose to an unbelievable level where people actually started to say, "That is not going to happen here." Once you get to that position . . . the people on the staff have come to the conclusion that they can do something about it . . . it is not a hopeless situation. Signing the Code raised our diligence. It certainly raised our commitment and it raised the involvement of the greater community of Carlson hotels, their owners, operators, and employees to do something about it.

The Dilemma

Within a few years after signing the Code, Carlson Companies began planning for development of a Regent Hotel and Resort in the Papagayo region of Costa Rica. Regent, Carlson's luxury brand, provided higher-end accommodations to its patrons than its Radisson brand, which was already established in the capital of San Jose. The venture would be Carlson's first luxury hotel and resort in Central America. It offered Carlson the opportunity to expand its luxury chain into Costa Rica's lucrative and rapidly growing high-end tourist market, as well as the potential for further expansion into Central and South America. Initially, the proposed project was well received by Carlson executives, as its Radisson Hotel in San Jose was doing well.

It was Jay Witzel, president and CEO of Carlson Hotels Worldwide, who learned during the course of his research of the extensive problem of child sex trafficking in Costa Rica and immediately brought it to Carlson Nelson's attention. Witzel's concerns were well-founded. Between the opening of the first Radisson Hotel in San Jose in 1996 and the new opportunity in Papagayo, two important events had occurred that had a major impact on whether the project should be given the go ahead. First, Carlson had signed the Code of Conduct, creating new obligations within its companies in the fight against child sex trafficking. Concerns were raised about whether management would be able to fully enforce the Code once the resort became operational. If Carlson could not fully guarantee the protection of children within the resort complex, could or should this be considered a viable business opportunity? The second concern stemmed from the Marriott child sex trafficking case and its implications for Carlson's Regent resort. The fact that Carlson would face a similar environment in Costa Rica as Marriott was cause for alarm. Any plans to introduce the Regent brand to Costa Rica would have to be reassessed, especially in light of the proliferation of child sex trafficking in Costa Rica and new concerns over trafficking litigation.

However, the potential advantages of developing the hotel in Costa Rica were many. First, Carlson executives believed that it presented a lucrative business opportunity, one that they were hard-pressed to abandon. Additionally, the executives saw the opportunity to serve as a positive force and role model in the travel and tourism business, a prospect that was especially attractive to Carlson Nelson given her commitment to children. Witzel described his conversations about the Costa Rica project with Carlson Nelson as "robust." If they could succeed in meeting the challenges of socially responsible hotel management in a country rife with child sex trafficking, they could demonstrate the project's feasibility to others in the industry and the world.

But changes to the policies and practices of other travel and tourism companies were not the only positive externality that Carlson Nelson and her executives hoped for. They also believed that by empowering hotel employees to monitor and act against the exploitation of children in Carlson hotels, this vigilance would have a spillover effect, benefiting the communities to which the employees belonged. Carlson Nelson argued that:

> The more we train our employees, the better the potential that they will use their judgment and in a way, it becomes like a social anthropology and there is a higher likelihood that a culture will reject or self-correct around somebody who is acting inconsistently with our policy.

The goal was that the employees themselves would serve as agents of social change, improving the larger community of which they were a part.

Although the promises of both social change and increased revenue were certainly tempting, the project's disadvantages also caused Carlson management several concerns. The first arose as Carlson Nelson and the executive team watched the Marriott litigation. As the case unfolded, they became more and more aware of the impact the case would have on Carlson's future Costa Rica operations. They took special note of the Swedish National Pension Fund's blacklisting of the company and the very public international shaming of Marriott over the trafficking issue. It was disturbing that the actions of just a handful of Marriott employees brought that company international rebuke and a shareholder resolution against it. Second, there was the risk that the international community would associate Carlson's Regent Hotel with child sex trafficking simply because it was located in Costa Rica. A third concern was that the resort would fail to meet its obligations under the

Code and Carlson would risk public censure from the Code's monitoring body. Indeed, a variety of powerful stakeholders, including local politicians, corrupt law enforcement officers, travel agents, and others, would benefit substantially from child sex trafficking and could pressure employees to violate the Code.

Additionally, for the Code's implementation to be successful there had to be commitment from franchise owners—no easy task. Enforcement would require employees and contractors to monitor guests, business transactions, and one another in a way that might not be possible or even advisable. Was it worth the risk to place the reputation of Carlson, a highly respected international company, in the hands of franchise owners and untested local employees, some of whom might have multiple and conflicting loyalties? And, there was some doubt whether it would be possible for a hotel resort to create an environment intolerant of child sex trafficking without losing a significant portion of its high-end tourist trade. Was it possible that sex tourism constituted such a large share of tourism in Papagayo that by rejecting it in its hotel, Carlson would be unable to earn an acceptable return on its investment?

Yet, Carlson executives agreed that the biggest disincentive to developing the hotel was the fear of litigation, both from tourists who might witness child exploitation—despite efforts on Carlson's part to deter the practice—and from those who might be victimized by traffickers utilizing Carlson's services. If Carlson continued with the project, would it risk compromising its commitment to the Code and to eliminating the sexual exploitation of children? On the other hand, if Carlson abandoned the project, the company would forfeit a potentially lucrative business opportunity. Time was drawing near for the final decision. Should Carlson Nelson push forward with the project? Then again, were there other possible alternatives?

Discussion Questions

1. Why did the Carlson Company sign the Code of Conduct for the Protection of Children from Sexual Exploitation in Travel and Tourism? Do you agree with the company's decision, and why or why not?

2. What are the advantages and disadvantages to the Carlson Company of developing the hotel complex in Costa Rica?

3. What stakeholders would be affected by a decision to develop the hotel complex in Costa Rica, and how would they be affected? What are their interests and sources of power in this situation?

4. Would developing the hotel complex in Costa Rica be ethical, or not? Why do you think so?

5. If the Carlson Company decides to proceed with the hotel development, what steps can it take to assure that the company remains in compliance with the code of conduct it has signed?

Carolina Pad and the Bloggers

A few weeks before the start of the September 2009 Type-A Mom Conference in Asheville, North Carolina, April Whitlock received yet another pay-for-blog request. Whitlock had only been with Carolina Pad, a maker and distributor of school supplies, for nine months. As the company's first director of brand management, she had been hired for her knowledge of social media and innovative uses of the Internet. A major part of her Internet strategy was the creative use of blogs and bloggers, especially mommy bloggers.

Mommy bloggers were typically stay-at-home mothers who wrote about their lives and the products they used. Providing these individuals with products to review or occasionally to give away in contests on their blogs seemed like a reasonable way to release information to the public about new Carolina Pad designs and products. Mommy bloggers had traditionally disclosed on their blogs when they had received free samples for review. Their reviews then ranged from very positive to very negative.

With Carolina Pad's limited promotional budget (no money was budgeted for traditional media), Whitlock believed that blogs offered a tool for increasing exposure for Carolina Pad's product designs at a relatively low cost compared to advertising in traditional media. Carolina Pad was able to provide product samples to select bloggers for a few hundred dollars while the expenditure for many advertising options was cost prohibitive.

April received several requests from mommy bloggers for financial support to cover their travel expenses to attend the Type-A Mom Conference. These requests also contained specific commitments to promote Carolina Pad's products at the conference and to write blogs about Carolina Pad products. "What are the ethics of fulfilling such requests?" April wondered. She wondered if she should request additional funding to pay the bloggers or if she should refuse the requests. She believed bloggers' writings about Carolina Pad's products were effective, and she felt certain that competitors had received similar requests.

Carolina Pad

In 1945, Joseph (Joe) K. Hall Jr. and several business associates managed to scrape up enough money and equipment to start a school supply manufacturing company in Charlotte, North Carolina. Joe, a former teacher, principal, and coach, owned and operated Hall & Morris,

By Steven M. Cox, Bradley W. Brooks, S. Cathy Anderson, and J. Norris Frederick. Copyright © 2011 by the *Case Research Journal* and the authors. Used by permission. All rights reserved.

The authors of this case express sincere gratitude to two anonymous reviewers of the *Case Research Journal* and to Anne Lawrence, the editor of this special issue, for their particularly insightful and valuable comments and suggestions.

a school supply wholesale business in nearby Belmont, North Carolina. Hall & Morris transformed into a new company, Carolina Pad, that both manufactured and distributed school supplies.

As a manufacturer, Carolina Pad offered composition books, notebook paper, primary tablets, pencils, crayons, and other school supplies. To gain an edge over larger, more established counterparts, Joe sold products directly to schools in the Carolinas and Virginia—often out of the back of his truck.

When Clay Presley joined Carolina Pad as president in 2000, he quickly realized that business as usual was not an option. In the 1980s and 1990s, Carolina Pad, like many other paper product manufacturers, faced the twin challenges of declining profit margins and stiff competition from overseas. During Presley's first back-to-school season, sales had been very disappointing, revenues had declined, and margins had shrunk. In a pivotal staff meeting, Presley asked everyone, "What would the company look like if it started today?" The team decided it needed to move toward designing fashionable products and away from manufacturing traditional pads of paper. They decided to target high school–age girls. For the next back-to-school season, Carolina Pad added a plaid designer notebook to its traditional lineup. Retailers loved it. That season the new designs became the top seller at Wal-Mart Stores, Inc.

In 2003, Carolina Pad began outsourcing its manufacturing to locations in other countries at significantly lower costs. The resulting savings allowed Carolina Pad to invest more money in creative designs, branding, and marketing. That same year, Carolina Pad hired designer Jacqueline McFee to lead its creative design efforts. With a focus on the latest fads, the company developed new lines of stationery that included popular text messaging phrases to publicize environmentally friendly messages. A buyer at Family Dollar Stores, Inc., said Carolina Pad's designs had become a perennial bestseller. "Carolina Pad and Paper is the fashion and trend leader for this category," the buyer noted.[1]

Carolina Pad was widely credited with making fashion and design a key ingredient in the industry by creating a series of designs for its notebooks and binders intended to appeal to teenage girls. The company displayed the design name on the front of each notebook or binder and the Carolina Pad name on the back and/or the inside cover. (See Exhibit A for a description of the 2009 fashions and designs found on Carolina Pad's notebooks and pads.) Company sales grew from $30 million in 2000 to $104 million in 2008. By 2009, Carolina Pad products were sold in retail stores across North America and in parts of Europe and Asia.

April Whitlock

A Duke University graduate, April Whitlock was a marketing veteran with a variety of experiences. Prior to accepting a position with Carolina Pad, April had been responsible for developing the national brand and marketing strategy for Mom Corps, a company that recruited talented moms who had outstanding professional experience (especially lawyers, CPAs, MBAs, etc.) and had opted to stay at home as their children's primary caregiver. Mom Corps worked with companies to identify flexible contract or part-time opportunities for these women. Prior to Mom Corps, April had spent seven and a half years with

---

[1] Adam O'Daniel, "Carolina Pad's Strategy Takes It to the Head of the Class," *Charlotte Business Journal*, August 7, 2009. Retrieved from *http://charlotte.bizjournals.com/charlotte/stories/2009/08/10/story16.html?b= 1249876800^1895 411.*

What better way to express yourself than with products that reflect your personality? Our 2009 designs are in the stores now and you'll be seeing fabulous updates of some of our most popular designs, as well as a few new ones. Whether you want trendy or timeless elegance, there's something for you in one of our collections.

WHAT'S YOUR STYLE?

Feeling Chic-y?

You might want to try Pearl Stripe, designs with subtle color palettes and simple elegance. Simply Chic offers classic houndstooth, pinstripe, and scroll designs paired with bold color.

INSPIRED BY NATURE'S BEAUTY?

We've updated Carolina Pad classics Whimsical Flower and Graphic in Nature with new color palettes and designs.

WANT TO LIVE OUT LOUD?

Want to be noticed? The hip and fun Hot Chocolate and Eye Candy might be the right designs to get that second look!

The Kendall Kollection gives you great eye-catching design and lets you give back. Each product sold benefits The Leukemia & Lymphoma Society's efforts to fight Leukemia.

ARE YOU ECO-LOGICAL?

Our new Sasquatch Brand's eco-friendly products are in stores now. Get product and where-to-shop information at the Sasquatch website.

THE BASIC

Do you just want great functionality and durability? Notebound Colours and MX keep it simple.

LendingTree, where she had led key business-to-business marketing efforts. In her new role with Carolina Pad, April worked directly with its marketing, sales, and creative teams to shape the brand identities for all products.

In her thirties, April belonged to the first generation to be considered Internet natives rather than immigrants. As a member of the Public Relations Society of America (PRSA), she understood the power of Internet-based publicity. Websites such as Facebook® and Twitter® were reporting huge numbers of users. Facebook recently had reported over 400 million active users (users who had returned to the site within the last 30 days). In addition, online product reviews posted by online product evaluators and users on sites such as Epinions, cnet, consumer search, and Amazon were playing a more important role in the information search and decision process of consumers. Knowing that Carolina Pad's target market, teen girls, were heavy users of Internet social media, an Internet-based promotional strategy seemed a natural choice.

Within weeks of April's arrival, Carolina Pad had a presence on several major social media sites, including Facebook and YouTube. In addition, Carolina Pad became actively discussed on several blog sites such as Auntie Thesis, Eighty MPH Mom, A Bookish Mom, and Classy Mom Blog. April had been key in the development of product packages for bloggers to review, and several blog sites had sponsored contests where the prizes were Carolina Pad products that April had supplied.

History of Blogging

Modern blogging began in the mid-1990s as nothing more than individuals keeping online diaries of their personal lives. The term "blog" is a contraction of "web log" or "weblog." In the late 1990s, a number of online tools paved the way for modern blog sites. By 2001, blogging had become popular enough that researchers began identifying the differences between blogging and journalism. Bloggers began reporting on current events. Unfettered by traditional journalists' needs for multiple sources and accuracy, bloggers were free to address topics and events more quickly than the mainstream media could. A classic example occurred in 2002 when bloggers first broke the story of Senator Trent Lott honoring Senator Strom Thurmond by suggesting that the United States would have been better off if Thurmond had been elected president in 1948. The history of Thurmond's racial views created a flurry of comments, which eventually forced Lott to resign as majority leader.[2]

Recognizing the effect of blogs on public opinion, by 2004 many politicians, pundits, and opinion leaders were active bloggers. More recently, tweets (micro blogs in the form of text-based posts of up to 140 characters) from Iran were the first to break the story that the election of Mahmoud Ahmadinejad might have been rigged.[3] By 2008, the United States had an estimated 26.4 million blog sites accessed by 77.7 million unique visitors, and 77 percent of Internet users were reading blogs.[4]

Blogging and Business

This new word-of-mouth (WOM) method to share one's personal life and opinions caught the attention of marketers. Businesses increasingly embraced social media as many bloggers began reaching large audiences. Blog sites sold advertisements at rates that were often more attractive than traditional print media. *Forbes* magazine provided an example rate comparison in 2007:

> And while blog networks are quickly gaining scale, even their most coveted offerings are cost-competitive. To make a back-of-the-napkin comparison based on rate cards: A start-up looking to get attention will grab a third-of-a-page color ad in a magazine with a rate base of 600,000 and might pay $27,300; or it can pay $21,000 for 600,000 impressions for its ads on TechCrunch—a site covering start-ups represented by Battelle's Federated Media—assuming they take the priciest ad slot on one of tech's hottest sites.[5]

[2] Mark Glaser, "Trent Lott Gets Bloggered; Free Finance Sites Spoofed by WSJ.com Ads." Retrieved from *http://www.ojr.org/ojr/glaser/1040145065.php.*

[3] Lev Grossman, "Iran Protests: Twitter, the Medium of the Movement," *Time,* June 17, 2009. Retrieved from *http://www.time.com/time/world/article/0,8599,1905125,00.html.*

[4] Technorati.com, "State of the Blogosphere 2008" (2008). Retrieved from *http://technorati.com/blogging/feature/state-of-the-blogosphere-2008/.*

[5] Brian Caulfield, "Tech Boom, Media Bust," *Forbes,* July 17, 2009. Retrieved from *http://www.forbes.com/2007/07/16/redherring-print-blogs-tech-media-cx_bc_0716techmedia.html%20accessed%209-3-09.*

In addition to advertising, blog sites provided valuable publicity for consumer products. Bloggers reviewed products and made free products available to their readers for comments. Consumer product companies routinely provided sample products for blog site review, offered products for blog site contests, and provided advance information about new products and models.

Several sites had begun advertising their pay-for-blogging opportunities. ReviewMe.com, CreamAid.com, Bloggerwave.com, Smorty.com, Blogitive.com, and PayPerPost.com all were willing to compensate bloggers for comments on specific products. Two of these—ReviewMe.com and PayPerPost.com—provided the following information on their websites:

ReviewMe.com

1. Submit your site for inclusion into our ReviewMe publisher network. Begin by creating a free account using the link below.
2. If approved, your site will enter our ReviewMe marketplace and clients will purchase reviews from you.
3. You decide to accept the review or not.
4. You will be paid $20.00 to $200.00 for each completed review that you post on your site.

PayPerPost.com

> Get paid for blogging. You've been writing about Web sites, products, services and companies you love for years and you have yet to benefit from all the sales and traffic you have helped generate. That's about to change. With PayPerPost advertisers are willing to pay you for your opinion on various topics. Search through a list of Opportunities, make a blog posting, get your content approved, and get paid. It's that simple.

In addition, manufacturers went directly to bloggers to offer products and monetary compensation. Microsoft, for example, sent several bloggers a Ferrari 5000 computer preloaded with its Vista operating system. The estimated retail value of the computer and software was over $2,000. Microsoft did not require the return of the computer; it merely asked that the recipients review the Vista operating system.[6]

Kmart had an innovative approach to influence bloggers. They gave Chris Brogan (a well-known blogger) and a handful of other bloggers $500 gift cards to spend at Kmart with the request that they write about their experiences. They were also asked to invite their readers to enter a contest to win a comparable giveaway.[7]

Even book publishers participated in paying for blogs. Textbook publisher Reed Elsevier discovered an employee's "overzealous" attempt to generate buzz for its titles. The employee's e-mails announced that anyone writing a "five-star" review of any of Reed Elsevier's new textbooks on either Amazon's or Barnes and Noble's e-commerce sites would get a free copy of the book and a $25 Amazon gift certificate from the publisher.[8] Upon learning of the offer, the publisher immediately withdrew it.

[6] Vaughan-Nichols, "Anatomy of a Blogger Bribe," *Linux-Watch,* December 28, 2009. Retrieved from *http://www.linux-watch.com/news/NS4123497783.html.*

[7] PaulGillan.com, "Ethics and the $500 Gift Card," December 15, 2008. Retrieved from *http://paulgillin.com/2008/12/ethics-and-the-500-gift-card/.*

[8] Bookseller.com, "$25 Offer a Mistake, Admits Reed Elsevier," June 24, 2009. Retrieved from *http://www.thebookseller.com/news/89581-25-offer-a-mistake-admits-reed-elsevier.html.rss.*

Product Recommendations and Undisclosed Advertising

The music industry provided a historic example of undisclosed pay for promotion. In the 1950s, the practice of radio deejays taking payments from record companies to play specific songs was common. Radio listeners could perceive significant airplay as a measure of a song's popularity, which could then lead to higher ratings and additional sales. Deejays did not disclose the fact that they took money to play certain records, and most listeners were unaware that the music choices were not a result of the popularity of a song or artist.

In 1960, as a result of its hearings, Congress amended the Federal Communications Act, specifically sections 317 and 507, to outlaw under-the-table payments and to require broadcasters to disclose if airplay for a song had been purchased. Pay-for-play was legal only if disclosed. Since the year 2000, there had been only 13 Federal Communications Commission (FCC) enforcement actions for undisclosed pay-for-play in the record industry.[9]

Although the FCC was charged with regulating the airways, whether the Internet fell under its jurisdiction was unclear. Other related industries had become the subject of more recent debates. As DVRs and other new technologies allowed viewers to skip traditional TV ads, advertisers looked for new advertising avenues, including paying to have a product used as part of a storyline, either as product placement (use of product as a prop, such as characters drinking a Coke or Pepsi or using an Apple computer) or product integration (use of the product in the dialogue or plot). In 2003, Commercial Alert, a nonprofit organization that sought to "keep the commercial culture within its proper sphere,"[10] petitioned the FCC to require pop-ups announcing "advertisement" in movie or television show scenes where paid product placements appeared.

The Federal Trade Commission (FTC) was charged with safeguarding consumers against false or misleading claims within various media. The FTC, however, had not updated its guidelines since 1980, well before the advent of blogging.[11] As such, no laws existed to regulate payments to bloggers for promotional purposes. The world of blogging and social media had become an unregulated environment with an audience reach that could rival traditional, heavily regulated broadcast media. As a result, lawsuits had been the primary redress for Internet-related grievances; and defamation, product disparagement, and invasion of privacy lawsuits had grown along with the popularity of the blogosphere. In most of these lawsuits, individual judges had to decide the proper balance between protecting individuals and safeguarding free speech.

The Incident

April's primary objective for her mommy blogger approach was to create a buzz about Carolina Pad. She hoped that buzz would lead to positive perceptions of the brand name, as well as positive perceptions of specific Carolina Pad design names. The target market—teenage girls—was very fashion-conscious, with fashion being dictated by peer groups. By generating positive consumer perceptions, Carolina Pad sought to be viewed as attractive to this group.

---

[9] Federal Communications Commission, "Payola and Sponsorship Identification," March 9, 2009. Retrieved from *http://www.FCC.gov/eb/broadcast/sponsid.html.*

[10] Commercial Alert, *http://www.commercialalert.org.*

[11] Elisabeth Eaves, "Marketing's Wild West Gets Civilized," *Forbes,* July 31, 2009.

For nine months her Internet strategy had been building momentum. By July 2009, April had established a good relationship with several mommy bloggers, and they had given Carolina Pad's new product line very positive reviews. The number of positive tweets, Facebook mentions, and blog entries had been growing every month. On March 10, for example, one blogger promoted a Carolina Pad product giveaway contest on the "Just Pure Lovely" blog site:

> Because of my obsession with all things that have to do with "paper" and "writing" and "organizing" (*oh, my!*), I am So. Very. Delighted to host this BIG ($150 value) giveaway from Carolina Pad for one of you. . . . The winner of this giveaway gets to choose which set to call her (his?) own! I know, I know. How can you ever choose? I'll leave that dilemma to the winner. I couldn't choose, so I own parts of both sets.[12]

Less than a week later, another blogger wrote of her experience receiving product supplies from Carolina Pad on the site "This Full House":

> . . . Quite frankly, the girls and I fought tooth and nail over all the awesome stuff inside! My 10-year-old son, not so much.[13]

In late May, another blogger wrote about Carolina Pad on the site "Three Boys and a Dog":

> If you know anything about me, you know I have an honest to goodness addiction . . . ok, a couple of them, but we are only going to address one today. I LOVE office supplies! ALL office supplies! I would rather have paper, pens, notebooks, and binders than shirts, dresses, or shoes! So, when I was given the chance to review Carolina Pad's Eye Candy line, I was super excited. Carolina Pad has a bunch of super adorable things and you can find them everywhere: Walmart & Target both carry their products.[14]

As Carolina Pad moved into the most important part of its selling season—the back-to-school season—the Internet strategy designed to create a buzz seemed to be working. The next conference where a significant number of mommy bloggers would be present was scheduled for September. "A positive response from these women," April thought, "would continue the momentum that Carolina Pad has been generating."

In July, she received e-mails from four mommy bloggers requesting financial assistance ranging from $75 to $1,000 to attend the upcoming bloggers conference. Although these e-mails specifically described how Carolina Pad would benefit in exchange for providing funding, none of the e-mails stated that the blogger would disclose that she had been sponsored for promotional purposes. Exhibit B through Exhibit E provide copies of these e-mails.

"I always thought of mommy-bloggers as women who commented on their lives and the products they used," April thought. "Selling their blogs and tweets seems inconsistent with the concept of blogging." Despite such innocent perceptions, the blogging industry had not adopted any formal code of conduct that would apply to making or receiving payments for

---

[12] Just Pure Lovely, "A BIG Giveaway! $150 Worth of Fashion Office Products," March 10, 2009. Retrieved from *http: //justpurelovely.typepad.com/justpurelovely/2009/03/a-big-giveaway-150-worth-of-fashion-office-line-products.html/*.

[13] This Full House, "Carolina Pad Giveaway: Fashionable School Supplies and Stylish Office Supplies, OH MY!" March 16, 2009. Retrieved from *http://www.thisfullhouse.com/reviews/2009/03/carolina-pad-giveaway.html*.

[14] Three Boys and a Dog, "Carolina Pad Eye Candy Review," May 31, 2009. Retrieved from *http://3boysandadog .com/2009/05/carolina-pad-eye-candy-review/*.

I am attending the Type-A Mom Conference September 24–27th in Asheville, NC. The good news is that I live pretty close so I will be driving and don't need to pay for airfare. I don't, however, live close enough to drive back and forth each day, so I am hoping to find a sponsor for the hotel room while I'm there plus expenses. I am open to more than one company offering partial sponsorships and I will promote however many will contribute. This would be a great venue to promote Carolina Pad to a very specific target audience of Moms/Women. Women who are hip, business oriented and have children of all ages!

Type-A Mom Conference is a unique mom blogging conference designed to help you take it to the next level. The conference will feature some of the most influential, admired and insightful mom bloggers talking about topics like power social networking, branding, blogging, finding your voice, and turning your passion for blogging into a real paycheck.

I'll be blogging/Tweeting live all weekend from the Type-A Mom Conference.

WHAT'S IN IT FOR YOU? GOOD QUESTION!

$100 Sponsors will get:

- Top billing as a [*Blog Site Name*] sponsor in all posts about the conference during the weekend and afterward!
- I'll hand out your business card, flyers, product, etc. during the weekend.
- A blog post about your company and several Tweets about your company during the weekend.

$250 Sponsors will get:

- Top billing as a [*Blog Site Name*] sponsor in all posts about the conference during the weekend and afterward!
- I'll hand out your business card, flyers, product, etc. during the weekend!
- Representation at the Type A Mom Conference in September (I'll pass out cards, wear your tee-shirts, whatever you want me to do to get you noticed)!
- Advertising at [*Blog Site Name*] for one full year (direct link or graphic)!
- A blog post about your company and several Tweets about your company during the weekend.

Sponsors of $500 or more will get:

- Top billing as a [*Blog Site Name*] sponsor in all posts about the conference during the weekend and afterward!
- A blog post about your company and several Tweets about your company during the weekend.
- I'll hand out your business card, flyers, product, etc. during the weekend.
- Representation at the Type A Mom Conference in September (I'll pass out cards, wear your tee-shirts, whatever you want me to do to get you noticed)!
- Advertising at [*Blog Site Name*] for one full year (direct link or graphic)!
- A party hosted by me, sponsored by your company one night during the weekend!

If you are interested in getting your company/product noticed by hundreds of bloggers and companies and being represented by a blogger with a strong background in public relations, promotions and product placement, e-mail me and let's get connected!

[*Blogger Name*]
[*Blog Site Address*]

Exhibit C

Blogger Request B

Hi April!

My name is [*Blogger Name*]. I am the founder and administrator of [*Blog Site Name*], a newly re-vamped women's e-magazine. I received your information from the girls at Blog Friendly PR.

My offer is a bit different than many others you have probably received since posting on Blog Friendly PR. I will be attending the Type-A Mom blog conference in September and am seeking sponsorship in return for several types of compensation. Because of the recent expansion of [*Blog Site Name*], this is a fantastic opportunity for you to be included with one of the newest and most talked about women's blogs on the net. I have included our newest press release and media kit for [*Blog Site Name*].

In return for a FULL sponsorship ($1,000), I will:

- Wear YOUR logo clothing RATHER than my own.
- Hand out samples of YOUR product, business cards, and other promotional products.
- Live Blog for YOU!
- Conduct video interviews of your choice.
- Network on YOUR behalf to exhibitor booths.
- Write five different posts about the Type-A-Mom Conference on [Blog Site Name] linking to YOU.
- For a year, every time I write about the Type-A-Mom Conference I will include a link to YOU.
- Tweet periodically about your product for a month.
- Review of YOUR products featured on my site.

In return for one of five partial sponsorships ($200 each) I will:

- Wear YOUR logo on my clothing along with my own.
- Hand out samples of YOUR product, business cards, and other promotional products.
- Network on YOUR behalf to exhibitor booths.
- Write a post about the Type-A-Mom Conference on [*Blog Site Name*] linking to YOU.
- Review of YOUR product featured on my site.

I am a passionate person who would have to say I have never met a stranger. I am super loyal to the people, companies, products, and services that in return are good to me. Most of all, I feel attending The Type-A-Mom Conference will further bond me with the blogging community making me more relevant and beneficial for a company who understands that **Mom Word of Mouth** is the most power-ful kind of publicity.

Thank you for your consideration and thank you for taking the time to review my bid for sponsor-ship. I am looking forward to your reply and hopefully to the chance of working with you to get to the Type-A-Mom-Conference! ;)

[*Blogger Name*]
Founder/Administrator
[*Blog Site Address*]
Twitter: [*Twitter Link*]
Facebook: [*Facebook Link*]

Hi April,

I love the feedback I'm getting on my giveaway. People really seem to love the products!

I had so much fun with everyone at [*Blog Site Name*] that I'm making plans to attend the Typeamomconference.com in Asheville, NC for September 23–27. I am looking for a few premium sponsors to partner with, and because I have absolutely loved your product, I would love the opportunity to promote this at the conference.

In return, I'd like to offer advertising in the top spots on [*Blog Site Name*] and/or branding on my [*Second Blog Site Name*] page.

I'd like to promote your brand to my 1,000 subscribers, 3,800 twitter followers, and almost 300 friends on facebook before and during the conference, and will be happy to . . .

before the conference:

- Blog, facebook, and tweet about your product at the conference:
- Hand out samples
- Brand my laptop, and phone skins
- Hand out your cards

For $100, I will offer four months' advertising on [*Blog Site Name*] on the top spots above the fold.

For $75, I will offer branding for three months on my [*Second Blog Site Name*] page. Your ad will pop up for every one of my page views, even when I am included in stories of the other bloggers in attendance. ([*Second Blog Site Name*] is a photo, story telling application, check out the sample story here [*Link to Second Blog Site*] and you can see branding on the pages.) I'm looking for up to three sponsors for this spot, and the graphic would hold the logo of all 3.

With both of those advertising options, I will do all the promotions listed before and during the conference.

I'm also willing to brainstorm ideas for additional sponsorship. For my [*Blog Site Name*] sponsor, [*Current Company Sponsor*], we are working on a [*Contest Name Related to Current Company Sponsor's Product*] contest that we started during the conference, and are continuing with voting and prizes after.

Consider me your voice for the conference. Looking forward to hearing your thoughts!

[*Blogger Name*]
[*Blog Site Address*]
www.twitter.com/[*Blog Site Twitter Link*]

promotion within the blogs. Although many blog sites did carry advertising, the fact that they were paid advertisements was clearly disclosed. Promotions within the blogs—and the disclosure of any material relationships with a sponsor(s)—were solely up to the discretion of the blogger.

Despite the absence of an agreed upon industry code of conduct, one independent website offered its own policies for blogging conduct. In evaluating her alternatives, April considered the policies set forth by BlogWithIntegrity.com, a website that sought to promote seven blogging principles deemed to be of high integrity. One of these principles stated that a blogger would disclose any material relationship with a business. The website

Hello,

I found you through the blog friendly companies list. I am currently looking for a sponsor to send me to Type A Mom Conference in Asheville, North Carolina. http://typeamomconference.com/. I work with a lot of websites with large traffic and really think that I could offer you some great promotion. I am currently selling two sponsorship opportunities. One sponsorship for my flight to the conference ($310) and one sponsorship for my hotel stay ($390). I have included a list below of the benefits of being a sponsor. Please take a look and let me know if you have any questions! I would love to work with your company!

- One article write-up/review on [*Blog Site Name*] which receives over half a million views monthly
- One review/giveaway on [*Second Blog Site Name*] which receives over twenty thousand views monthly
- One article write-up/review on my personal blog [*Third Blog Site Name*] as well as free advertising for six months
- Free advertising on [*Fourth Blog Site Name*] for three months. The [*Fourth Blog Site Name*] receives over fifty thousand views monthly
- Wear your logo at Type A Mom Conference as well as pass out promotion materials
- Host a product giveaway at Type A Mom Conference
- Ten tweets about your products and/or promotions (currently have 691 followers)

I would be happy to hear any additional ideas you have for promoting your business. I look forward to hearing from you!

Thanks,

[*Blogger Name*]

had created a "Blog with Integrity" badge that it offered for websites of bloggers who agreed with its principles.[15] (The seven principles and a copy of the badge are presented in Exhibit F.) April had only seen this badge displayed on a few mommy blogger websites. Of the nine websites specifically represented within the four blogger requests she had received, none of them displayed this badge.

Although none of these requests was for more than $1,000, April felt that the amount was not really the issue. April firmly believed the promotional considerations these bloggers were offering could provide a significantly higher rate of return for Carolina Pad than the company could receive from other, more traditional forms of promotion, such as advertising. In addition, she realized that her competitors were likely receiving similar requests from these or other bloggers, and many of them were probably benefiting already from paying such requests. April did not think that the fact that others would make such payments made it inherently acceptable for her to do so. April spoke to Carolina Pad's vice president of marketing who agreed with her on this point, even though no one at Carolina Pad had previously faced this decision.

[15] Blog with Integrity, *http://www.blogwithintegrity.com.*

PRINCIPLES

1. By displaying the Blog with Integrity badge or signing the pledge, I assert that the trust of my readers and the blogging community is important to me.

2. I treat others respectfully, attacking ideas and not people. I also welcome respectful disagreement with my own ideas.

3. I believe in intellectual property rights, providing links, citing sources, and crediting inspiration where appropriate.

4. I disclose my material relationships, policies, and business practices. My readers will know the difference between editorial, advertorial, and advertising, should I choose to have it. If I do sponsored or paid posts, they are clearly marked.

5. When collaborating with marketers and PR professionals, I handle myself professionally and abide by basic journalistic standards.

6. I always present my honest opinions to the best of my ability.

7. I own my words. Even if I occasionally have to eat them.

April was torn as she thought about her decision. The bloggers had not promised favorable reviews, just reviews. So wasn't she just putting forth advertising dollars to get her product visible? And yet, she worried there was something dishonest about this: wasn't it implicit that the reviews would be favorable? Was this ethical? Was it like paying radio disc jockeys to play your records? Would the payments be in violation of Carolina Pad's Mission and Values Statement (see Exhibit G)? And if she declined the bloggers' requests while questioning their ethical standards, would her relationship with any of the bloggers become strained?

Whatever she decided to do, she needed to make a decision soon, as the conference was in September.

We will excite our customers by bringing extraordinary fashion and innovation to everyday products.

At Carolina Pad, our mission and tagline reflect the dedication and care we put in every product we design. We are passionate in our mission to deliver the best product at the best price to the consumer and our customers.

Our core value system defines who we are and what we do every day:

- Build brands that meet the needs and wants of today's consumer.
- Anticipate and exceed consumer and customer expectations.
- Strive for design excellence in every product.
- Deliver products with superior functionality and value.
- Foster and encourage innovation, creativity, and teamwork in our company.
- Promote a healthier and safer workplace, community, and environment.

Discussion Questions

1. What is April Whitlock's dilemma? In your answer, include the relevant facts that Whitlock must consider and the assumptions she has made.

2. What alternative actions could Whitlock take? That is, what are her options?

3. For each of these options, identify which stakeholders would be affected, and how they would be affected.

4. Apply the four methods of ethical reasoning—utilitarianism, rights, justice, and virtue—to this situation. What would each of these methods suggest Whitlock should do?

5. What do you think Whitlock should do, and why?

Moody's Credit Ratings and the Subprime Mortgage Meltdown

On October 22, 2008, Raymond W. McDaniel Jr. raised his right hand to be sworn as a witness before the U.S. House of Representatives Committee on Oversight and Government Reform. The topic of the day's hearing was the role of the credit rating agencies in the financial crisis on Wall Street. McDaniel, 50, was chairman and CEO of Moody's, one of the leading credit rating agencies in the world. The word "credit" came from the Latin verb *credere,* meaning to believe or to trust. Credit rating agencies, such as Moody's, had the job of evaluating bonds issued by governments, companies, and investment banks. The world's financial markets relied heavily on their assurances that various borrowers could be trusted to pay their debts on time. Now, however, Moody's and other credit rating agencies had come under strong criticism, as many questioned the accuracy of their ratings and their role in the widening financial crisis.

In late 2008, the world faced what many believed was the deepest financial crisis since the Great Depression of the 1930s. As the housing bubble burst and home prices began falling across the United States, billions of dollars' worth of securities backed by their mortgages had plummeted in value, straining the balance sheets of venerable Wall Street investment banks. Lehman Brothers, Bear Stearns, and Merrill Lynch had either failed or been sold off. Prominent commercial banks and mortgage lenders, including Washington Mutual, Countrywide, and Wachovia, had collapsed and been sold to the highest bidder. Now credit had seized up, as surviving banks became afraid to lend to businesses and individuals. Consumers were reining in their spending, and jobless rates were rising. Hundreds of thousands of homes bought with easy credit and an assumption of ever-rising values were in foreclosure. In a single year, investors had lost some $7 trillion, as the value of their stocks and bonds fell precipitously.

The causes of the financial crisis were complex, and many parties bore a share of the responsibility. But some analysts pointed to a critical role played by Moody's Corporation and other credit rating agencies. Over the previous several years, Moody's had rated thousands of bonds made up of bundles of "subprime" mortgages—home loans to people with low incomes and poor credit histories, who were buying houses they probably could not afford. Now many of these buyers were failing to make their monthly payments. Their loans were going bad at an alarming rate, and Moody's had downgraded its ratings on

By Anne T. Lawrence. Copyright © 2009 by the author. All rights reserved. This case was presented at the 2009 annual meeting of the North American Case Research Association. The author is grateful to Professors Thomas Nist and James Burnham of Duquesne University for their thoughtful comments on an earlier draft of this case.

many mortgage-backed bonds. Some blamed Moody's for having misjudged the risk inherent in these securities. Henry Waxman, the chair of the oversight committee, was one such critic. He opened the hearing with a broad condemnation. "The story of the credit rating agencies is a story of colossal failure," he told the hearing. "The credit rating agencies occupy a special place in our financial markets. Millions of investors rely on them for independent, objective assessments. The rating agencies broke this bond of trust, and federal regulators ignored the warning signs and did nothing to protect the public. The result," he added, "is that our entire financial system is now at risk."[1]

Moody's Corporation

The company that McDaniel had come to Congress to defend was the oldest credit rating agency in the world. Moody's had been founded in 1909 by John Moody, who got his start as an errand boy at a Wall Street bank. Observing the growing popularity of corporate bonds, the young entrepreneur recognized that investors needed a source of reliable information about their issuers' creditworthiness. Moody's first manual, on the safety of railroad bonds, proved highly popular, and by 1918 Moody and his firm were rating every bond then issued in the United States. By 2008, Moody's had become the undisputed "aristocrat of the ratings business."[2] The company was composed of two business units. By far the largest was Moody's Investors Service, which provided credit ratings; it earned 93 percent of the company's revenue. The other was Moody's KMV, which sold software and analytic tools, mainly to institutional investors. In 2007, Moody's reported revenue of $2.3 billion and employed 3,600 people in offices in 29 countries around the world.[3]

Moody's core business was rating the safety of bonds—debt issued by companies, governments, and public agencies. For example, if a state government issued a bond to build new classroom buildings at a public university, Moody's would evaluate the likelihood that the government would pay back the bondholders on time. (When a bond issuer was unable to make timely payments, this was known as a default.) Then Moody's would rate the bond according to a scale from Aaa—"triple A," with a very low chance of default—to C, already in default, with some 19 steps in between. (Credit ratings were technically considered opinions on the probability of default.) Moody's ratings, along with those of its competitors, enabled buyers to evaluate the risks of various fixed-income investments.

Over the years, Moody's business model had shifted. For many decades after its founding, Moody's had charged investors for its ratings through the sales of publications and advisory services. As a Moody's vice president explained in 1957, "We obviously cannot ask payment [from the issuer] for rating a bond," he wrote. "To do so would attach a price to the process, and we could not escape the charge, which would undoubtedly come, that our ratings [were] for sale."[4] In 1975, however, the Securities and Exchange Commission (SEC) changed the rules of the game. The SEC designated three companies—Moody's, Standard & Poor's (now a unit of the McGraw-Hill Companies), and Fitch (now a unit of Fimalac SA)—as Nationally Recognized Statistical Rating Organizations, or NRSROs. In effect, the government officially sanctioned these three rating agencies and gave them a

---

[1] Congress of the United States, House of Representatives, Committee on Oversight and Government Reform, "Credit Rating Agencies and the Financial Crisis," October 22, 2008, Opening Statement of Rep. Henry A. Waxman, p. 4.

[2] Michael Lewis, "The End," *Portfolio*, December 2008.

[3] *http://ir.moodys.com;* and various annual reports at *www.moodys.com.*

[4] Edmund Vogelius, writing in the *Christian Science Monitor*, quoted in "Debt Watchdogs: Tamed or Caught Napping?" *The New York Times*, December 8, 2008.

quasi-regulatory role. At this time, Moody's and the other two NRSROs began charging bond issuers to rate their products. (In 2008, Moody's market share was about 40 percent; S&P had 40 percent; and Fitch had between 10 and 15 percent.)

The new SEC rules changed the relationship between bond issuers and rating agencies. Because ratings strongly influenced the market value of the bond, issuers had a strong incentive to shop for the best possible ratings. For their part, rating agencies also had a strong incentive to compete for market share by catering to their clients. In 2000, Moody's was spun off from its parent, Dun & Bradstreet (which had acquired Moody's in 1962), becoming once again an independent, publicly owned firm. The spin-off further increased pressure on Moody's managers to increase revenues and improve shareholder returns. A former Moody's executive later recalled that in the early 2000s "things [became] a lot less collegial and a lot more bottom-line driven" as top executives sought to make the firm more responsive to clients.[5]

The Rise of Structured Finance

As Moody's business model was changing, so were the kinds of products the company was asked to evaluate. For many years, Moody's rated mainly plain-vanilla corporate and municipal, state, and federal government bonds. Wall Street investment banks, however, were becoming more innovative. Barriers to the global flow of capital were falling. New techniques of quantitative analysis permitted the creation of increasingly sophisticated financial products, known as structured finance. This term referred to the practice of combining income-producing assets—everything from conventional corporate bonds to credit card debt, home mortgages, franchise payments, and auto loans—into pools, and selling shares in the pool to investors. Instead of buying a simple IOU from a company, say, an investor would buy a share of income and principal payments flowing from a complex financial product made up of many loans.

One structured finance product that became particularly popular in the early 2000s was the residential mortgage-backed security, or RMBS. An RMBS started with a lender—a bank such as Washington Mutual or a mortgage company such as Countrywide Financial—that made home loans to individual borrowers. The lender (or another intermediary) would then bundle several thousand of these loans and sell them to a Wall Street investment bank such as Lehman Brothers or Merrill Lynch. (This gave the lender fresh cash with which to make more loans.) The Wall Street firm would then create a special kind of bond, based on a pool of underlying mortgage loans. Buyers of this bond would receive a share of the income flowing from the homeowners' monthly payments. (The investment banks also held some of these securities on their own books, a fact that contributed to their later difficulties.)

In order to make the RMBS more attractive to investors, the investment bank usually divided them into separate "tranches" (a French word meaning "slice"), with varying degrees of risk. If any homeowners defaulted on their loans, the lowest ("subordinated") tranches would absorb the losses first, and so on, up to the highest tranches. (The lower tranches earned higher interest, commensurate with their higher risk.) This is where the rating agencies, such as Moody's, came in: They were asked to rate the creditworthiness of various tranches of the mortgage-backed securities. Reflecting their greater complexity, Moody's charged more for rating structured products—around 11 basis points, or $11 for every $10,000 in value—compared with traditional corporate bonds (4.25 basis points).

---

[5] Jerome S. Fons, testimony before the House Committee on Oversight, October 22, 2008, p. 4; and Eliot Blair Smith, "Bringing Down Wall Street as Ratings Let Loose Subprime Scourge," *Bloomberg.com*, September 24, 2007.

Year Ended December 31					
	2003	2004	2005	2006	2007
Total revenue	$1,246.6	$1,438.3	$1,731.6	$2,037.1	$2,259.0
Revenue from structured finance	474.7	553.1	708.7	883.6	885.9
Structured finance as % of revenue	38.5	34.1	40.9	43.4	39.2
Operating income	663.1	786.4	939.6	1,259.5	1,131.0
Operating margins (operating income as % of total revenue)	53.2	54.7	54.3	61.8	50.1

Year Ended December 31				
	1999	2000	2001	2002
Total revenue	$564.2	$602.3	$796.7	$1,023.3
Revenue from structured finance	172.4	199.2	273.8	384.3
Structured finance as % of revenue	30.6	33.1	34.4	37.6
Operating income	270.4	288.5	398.5	538.1
Operating margins (operating income as % of total revenue)	47.9	47.9	50.0	52.6

Note: All amounts in millions of dollars, except for percentages.

Source: Moody's Annual Reports, 2001–2008. Where relevant, the most recently corrected figures have been used.

For example, to rate an RMBS worth $500 million, Moody's would receive about half a million dollars in fees.[6]

Credit ratings were especially important to investors in mortgage-backed securities, because these products were so difficult to understand. As a former managing director at Moody's explained,

> First, RMBSs and their offshoots offer little transparency around the composition and characteristics of the underlying loan collateral. Potential investors are not privy to the information that would allow them to understand the quality of the loan pool. Loan-by-loan data, the highest level of detail, are generally not available to investors. Second, the complexity of the securitization process requires extremely sophisticated systems and technical competence to properly assess risk at the tranche level. Third, rating agencies had a reputation, earned over nearly one century, of being honest arbiters of risk.[7]

In other words, investors had almost no way to assess independently the safety or security of these products, so they based their judgment wholly on the agencies' ratings.

Rating structured financial products, such as RMBSs, proved to be a highly lucrative business for Moody's. Exhibit A presents selected financial results for Moody's Investors

---

[6] Estimates of fees for rating various products are drawn from Smith, "Bringing Down Wall Street as Ratings Let Loose Subprime Scourge."

[7] Jerome S. Fons, testimony, p. 2.

Comparison of Cumulative Total Return since December 31, 2001, Moody's Corporation, S&P Composite Index, and Peer Group Index

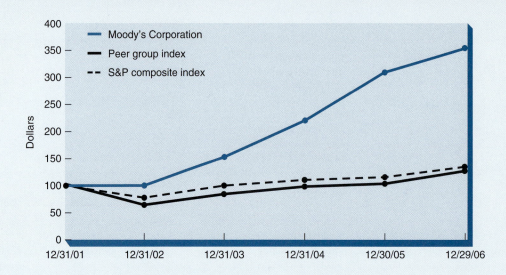

	Period Ending					
	12/31/2001	12/31/2002	12/31/2003	12/31/2004	12/30/2005	12/29/2006
Moody's Corporation	100	104.01	153.07	220.51	313.63	354.23
Peer group index	100	61.80	81.57	96.18	100.97	127.43
S&P composite index	100	77.90	100.25	111.15	116.61	135.03

Source: *Moody's Annual Report,* March 1, 2007, p. 13. The performance peer group is composed of Dow Jones & Company, Inc., The McGraw-Hill Companies, Pearson PLC, Reuters Group PLC, Thomson Corporation, and Wolters Kluwer nv. Figures assume reinvestment of all dividends.

Service for 1999 to 2007. Revenue from structured finance grew as a proportion of Moody's overall revenue throughout much of this period, peaking at 43 percent in 2006, contributing to the company's exceptional profitability. Operating margins (the percentage of revenue left after paying most expenses) during this period ranged from 48 to 62 percent, an unusually high level. In fact, for five years in a row, Moody's had the highest profit margin of any company in the S&P 500, beating even such consistently successful companies as Microsoft and Exxon.[8]

These stellar financial results rewarded Moody's shareholders with an outstanding total return in the early 2000s, relative to the company's peer group and to the broader stock market, as shown in Exhibit B. (Moody's financial results cannot be compared directly to those of S&P and Fitch, since the latter two are both part of larger companies that report consolidated results.)

[8] "Debt Watchdogs"; and Rep. Henry Waxman, statement.

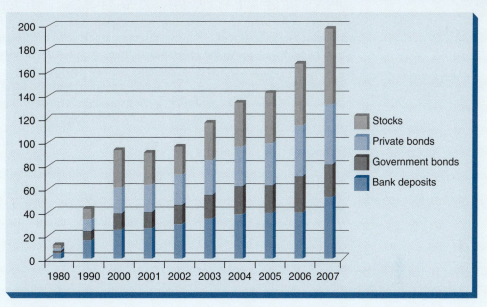

Source: McKinsey Global Institute, *Mapping Global Capital Markets,* 5th Annual Report, October 2008, p. 9. Used by permission.

Reflecting the company's success, Moody's top executives were well compensated. In 2007, for example, Moody's chairman and CEO Raymond McDaniel earned total compensation of $7.4 million, according to *Forbes.*[9]

The Giant Pool of Money

In the 2000s, the total global volume of financial assets—money available worldwide to purchase stocks and bonds, as well as more complex structured financial products created by Wall Street—grew by leaps and bounds. As shown in Exhibit C, global financial assets grew from $94 trillion in 2000 to $196 trillion in 2007. Until the advent of the credit crisis, private bonds (fixed-income securities, including mortgage and other asset-backed securities) were one of the fastest-growing asset classes, growing 10 percent a year between 2000 and 2007, when their global value stood at $51 trillion.

Several factors contributed to the growth of what National Public Radio, on the program "This American Life," vividly dubbed this "giant pool of money." Big pension plans, private hedge funds, individuals saving for retirement, and foreign governments all sought safe investments with good returns. Emerging economies, including China, India, United Arab Emirates, and Saudi Arabia, built up substantial reserves selling oil and manufactured goods to the United States and other developed nations. China grew particularly rapidly; by 2007 it had become the third-largest financial market in the world.

At the same time that the pool of money was growing, many classes of assets were becoming less attractive to investors. In the early 2000s, the stock market was languishing in the wake of the bust of the high-tech bubble and the collapse of Enron and WorldCom.

[9] "Profile: Raymond W. McDaniel," *www.forbes.com.*

Interest rates, driven down by the U.S. Federal Reserve's very accommodative interest policies, were falling to historic lows, reaching 1 percent in 2004. This meant that investors' rates of return in U.S. Treasuries, money market accounts, certificates of deposit, and bank savings accounts were, to many, disappointingly low. In this context, RMBSs, which typically paid well above the federal funds rate, even for the investment grade (Moody's top 10 steps) tranches, became increasingly attractive to the world's investors.

Growing demand for asset-backed securities put pressure on investment banks to create more of them. Mike Francis, formerly an executive director in the residential mortgage trading department at the investment banking firm Morgan Stanley, told a reporter,

> [I]t was unbelievable. We almost couldn't produce enough [residential mortgage-backed securities] to keep the appetite of the investors happy. More people wanted bonds than we could actually produce. That was our difficult task, was trying to produce enough. They would call and ask, "Do you have any more fixed rate? What have you got? What's coming?" From our standpoint it's like, there's a guy out there with a lot of money. We gotta find a way to be his sole provider of bonds to fill his appetite. And his appetite's massive.[10]

No Income, No Jobs, No Assets

As the investment banking firms, such as Morgan Stanley, scrambled to produce enough asset-backed securities to meet global demand, they put pressure on mortgage originators to produce more loans. This, in turn, encouraged lenders to weaken the standards they used to qualify borrowers. Traditionally, when a person applied for a home loan, he or she would be required to have good credit, money for a down payment, and proof of income and assets—all indicators of creditworthiness. Increasingly, in the rush to make loans, lenders began overlooking these requirements—taking on borrowers with poor credit, low-paying jobs, few assets, and no money to put down. These borrowers—and the loans made to them—were known as *subprime*.

Lenders' willingness to weaken their underwriting standards appeared consistent with public policy. The administrations of both presidents Bill Clinton and George W. Bush had pursued policies designed to expand home ownership, particularly among minorities. In an effort to make housing more affordable, the government had helped first-time buyers with down payments and closing costs and allowed borrowers to qualify for federally insured mortgages with no money down. It also encouraged Freddie Mac and Fannie Mae, the two government-sponsored mortgage lenders, to buy RMBSs that included loans to low-income borrowers.[11]

The industry developed tongue-in-cheek acronyms for loans made to poorly qualified borrowers, such as NINAs—no income, no assets—and NINJAs—no income, no assets, and no job. Mike Francis, the former Morgan Stanley executive, described these loans:

> No income no asset loans. That's a liar's loan. We are telling you to lie to us. We're hoping you don't lie. Tell us what you make, tell us what you have in the bank, but we won't verify? We're setting you up to lie. Something about that feels very wrong. It felt wrong way back when and I wish we had never done it. Unfortunately, what happened . . . we did it because everyone else was doing it.

[10] National Public Radio, "The Giant Pool of Money," at *www.thislife.org/extras/radio/355_transcript.pdf.*

[11] "Don't Blame Bankers, It's Down to a Man Called Bill," *The Evening Standard (London),* October 2, 2008; and "White House Philosophy Stoked Mortgage Bonfire," *The New York Times,* December 21, 2008.

The industry also began to write more nontraditional mortgages. Instead of fixed-rate loans, under which a borrower made a stable payment every month for many years, the industry developed products with lower monthly payments to allow less-qualified buyers to get into the market. These included adjustable-rate loans with low introductory "teaser" rates (which reset after three or five years at a much higher rate); interest-only loans (where the borrower was required to pay only the interest, not also a portion of the principal each month); and payment-option loans (where the borrower could choose to make a full payment, an interest-only payment, or a minimum payment that would actually cause the principal owed to increase). From 2003 to 2005, the subprime and low-documentation share of mortgage originations tripled from 11 percent to 33 percent. These loans were particularly popular in states where housing prices were going up the fastest—the so-called "sand states" of Nevada, California, Arizona, and Florida.[12]

Some banks and mortgage companies became particularly aggressive in pushing loans on poorly qualified borrowers. An investigative report for *The New York Times* examined the practices of one such lender, Washington Mutual (which later collapsed in the largest bank failure in U.S. history). WaMu, as it was known, operated a "boiler room" culture in which bank employees were under tremendous pressure to generate loan volume—and were rewarded handsomely if they did. *The New York Times* reported,

> WaMu pressed sales agents to pump out loans while disregarding borrowers' incomes and assets, according to former employees. The bank set up what insiders described as a system of dubious legality that enabled real estate agents to collect fees of more than $10,000 for bringing in borrowers, sometimes making agents more beholden to WaMu than they were to their clients.
>
> WaMu gave mortgage brokers handsome commissions for selling the riskiest loans, which carried higher fees, bolstering profits and ultimately the compensation of the bank's executives. WaMu pressured appraisers to provide inflated property values that made loans appear less risky, enabling Wall Street to bundle them more easily for sales to investors.
>
> "It was the Wild West," said [a founder of an appraisal company that worked with WaMu]. "If you were alive, they would give you a loan. Actually, I think if you were dead, they would still give you a loan."[13]

Of course, on the other side of each of these transactions was a borrower. The producers for *This American Life* interviewed one such individual—who had received a home loan for more than half a million dollars. At the time, this man was working three irregular part-time jobs and making around $45,000 a year. By the time he was interviewed, he had, not surprisingly, fallen behind in his payments, and his home was in foreclosure. The homeowner recalled,

> It's almost like you pass a guy in the street and say, [can you] lend me five hundred and forty thousand? He says, what do you do? Hey, I got a job. OK. It seems that casual . . . I wouldn't have loaned me the money. I know guys who are criminals who wouldn't loan me that and they break your knee-caps. I don't know why the bank did it . . . Five hundred and forty thousand dollars to a guy with bad credit . . . I'm not trying to absolve myself of anything . . . The bank made an imprudent loan. I made an imprudent loan. We're partners in this.[14]

[12] *FDIC Outlook,* Summer 2006, *www.fdic.gov.*

[13] Peter S. Goodman and Gretchen Morgenson, "Saying Yes, WaMu Built Empire on Shaky Loans," *The New York Times,* December 28, 2008.

[14] National Public Radio, *This American Life,* Program #355, transcript.

In many cases, the borrowers knew they were getting in over their heads—or ought to have. But in other cases, borrowers were misled by bank officers or mortgage brokers, did not understand their loan's terms, or simply believed that they would be able to sell or refinance in a year or two when, they assumed, their home would be worth more.

As the quality of mortgage loans deteriorated, some regulators tried to sound the alarm. In 2005, the Office of the Comptroller of the Currency (OCC), the arm of the Treasury Department that oversees most commercial banks, considered new regulations that would have limited risky mortgages and required clearer explanations to borrowers and warnings to buyers of RMBSs. Mortgage lenders and investment banks, however, lobbied strenuously against these rule changes, and federal regulators backed off.[15] Officials in North Carolina, Iowa, Michigan, Georgia, and other states attempted to rein in lenders, but were overruled by federal officials who argued that federal regulation pre-empted state regulation. The OCC brought only one enforcement action related to subprime lending between 2000 and 2006.[16]

The Collapse

In 2006, the market for residential mortgage-backed securities began to unravel. Interest rates began to rise, and housing prices began to drop. As loans began to reset, homeowners found that they were unable to make the new, higher payments—or to refinance or sell their property. Increasing numbers of homeowners realized they were "under water"—that is, they owed more than their home was worth. Lenders coined a new term—"jingle mail"—to describe what happened when borrowers simply dropped the keys in the mail and walked away from their homes. As they did so, their mortgages became worthless—and the value of securities based on them swooned.

In July 2007, Ben Bernanke, chairman of the Federal Reserve, testified in the Senate that he anticipated as much as $100 billion in losses in the market for subprime-backed securities. That month, Moody's stopped rating new RMBSs and began a series of what *Barron's* magazine called "express train downgrades, since there are no stops between Blue Chip Land and oblivion."[17] By the following summer, Moody's had downgraded more than 5,000 mortgage-backed securities, with a value in the hundreds of billions of dollars, including 90 percent of all asset-backed securities it had rated in 2006 and 2007.[18,19]

In April 2008, Roger Lowenstein, reporting for *The New York Times,* took a close look at one of many poorly performing RMBSs that had been rated by Moody's and downgraded around this time. This particular security, which he called Subprime XYZ, was comprised of 2,393 mortgages collectively worth $430 million. A West Coast mortgage lender had issued these loans in early 2006, at the height of the housing bubble. All of the borrowers were subprime—people with poor credit histories and high debt-to-income ratios. Three-quarters of the borrowers had taken adjustable-rate mortgages with low initial rates, and almost half had provided no written proof of their incomes. By early 2007, just a year after this security was created, 13 percent of the loans were delinquent. By early 2008, 27 percent of these mortgage holders were no longer paying.[20]

---

[15] Matt Apuzzo, "Anatomy of the Lending Crisis," *San Francisco Chronicle,* December 2, 2008.

[16] Robert Berner and Brian Grow, "They Warned Us about the Mortgage Crisis," *BusinessWeek,* October 9, 2008.

[17] Jonathan R. Laing, "Failing Grade," *Barron's,* December 24, 2007.

[18] Gretchen Morgenson, "Debt Watchdogs: Tamed or Caught Napping?" *The New York Times,* December 11, 2008.

[19] Eliot Blair Smith, "Race to Bottom at Moody's, S&P Secured Subprime's Boom, Bust," *Bloomberg.com,* September 25, 2008.

[20] Roger Lowenstein, "Triple-A Failure," *The New York Times Magazine,* April 27, 2008.

As Moody's began downgrading bonds like Subprime XYZ, many institutional investors—whose holdings of mortgage-backed securities were suddenly worth much less—became irate. Mary Elizabeth Brennan, a Moody's vice president, got an earful when she called several RMBS investors in the summer of 2007, as the problem was beginning to become obvious. According to internal documents, a portfolio manager at Vanguard, a leading money management company, told Brennan that the rating agencies had "allow[ed] issuers to get away with murder." She added, "Rating agencies aren't helping me make the right decisions." A representative of PIMCO, another money management firm, told her that Moody's "doesn't stand up to Wall Street." "Someone up there just wasn't on top of it," he added. The chief investment officer of Fortis Investments took the initiative to phone Moody's with what the manager who took the call called a "few choice words":

> If you can't figure out the loss ahead of the fact, what's the use of your ratings? You have legitimized these things [subprime mortgage-backed securities] . . . leading people into dangerous risk. If the ratings are b.s., the only use in ratings is comparing b.s. relative to more b.s.[21]

A Slippery Slope

As criticism poured in and the downgrades continued—and Moody's own stock dropped in value—the company's executives began a tough reevaluation of Moody's own practices. On September 10, 2007, McDaniel convened a town hall meeting with his managing directors (top managers). As revealed in a transcript later released to a Congressional investigation, McDaniel started out by acknowledging the criticism that "the rating agencies got it wrong." The CEO offered the following explanation of the subprime mortgage crisis:

> Looking at the subprime crisis specifically . . . We had historically low [interest] rates. We had very easy credit conditions for a number of years. We had official and market-based support for adjustable-rate mortgages. It created what I think is an overdone condition for the U.S. housing [market]. This was a condition that was supported by U.S. public policy in favor of home ownership. And as I once said, once housing prices started to fall, we got into a condition in which people can't refi[nance], can't sell, can't afford their current mortgage.[22]

Later, during the question and answer period, McDaniel reflected on the industry environment in which Moody's had rated many RMBSs:

> What happens is, as long as things are going extremely well, no one cares . . . [It] was a slippery slope . . . What happened in '04 and '05 with respect to the subordinated tranches is that our competition, Fitch and S&P, went nuts. Everything was investment grade. It didn't really matter . . . We rated . . . 20 to 25 percent of that market. We tried to alert the market. We said we're not rating it. This stuff isn't investment grade. No one cared because the machine just kept going.[23]

After the meeting, McDaniel invited attendees to submit any additional comments they wished to make electronically. One managing director commented,

> Really no discussion of why the structured [finance] group refused to change their ratings in the face of overwhelming evidence they were wrong.[24]

[21] Quotations are drawn from internal e-mails, released to Congress on October 22, 2008.

[22] Moody's Investors Service, "Managing Directors Town Hall Meeting," September 10, 2007, transcript, pp. 6–8.

[23] Ibid., pp. 62–63.

[24] "Moody's Managing Director Town Hall Feedback," September 2007, p. 1.

Another managing director asked rhetorically,

> [W]hat really went wrong with Moody's subprime ratings leading to massive downgrades and potential more downgrades to come? We heard 2 answers yesterday: 1. people lied, and 2. there was an unprecedented sequence of events in the mortgage markets. As for #1, it seems to me that we had blinders on and never questioned the information we were given . . . As for #2, it is our job to think of the worst-case scenarios and model them . . . Combined, these errors make us look either incompetent at credit analysis, or like we sold our soul to the devil for revenue, or a little bit of both.[25]

A month later, on October 21, McDaniel made a confidential presentation to his board of directors, also later disclosed to Congress. The subject of his briefing was credit policy—the overall standards governing the rating process. With respect to ratings quality, McDaniel told the board,

> The real problem is not that the market [under weights] ratings quality but rather that, in some sectors, it actually penalizes quality . . . Unchecked, competition on this basis can place the entire financial system at risk. It turns out that ratings quality has surprisingly few friends: issuers want high ratings; investors don't want rating downgrades; short-sighted bankers labor short-sightedly to game the rating agencies for a few extra basis points on execution.

Under the topic heading "rating erosion by persuasion," he commented,

> Analysts and MDs [managing directors] are continually "pitched" by bankers, issuers, investors—all with reasonable arguments—whose views can color credit judgment, sometimes improving it, other times degrading it (we "drink the kool-aid"). Coupled with strong internal emphasis on market share and margin focus, this does constitute a "risk" to ratings quality.

He also noted the inherent tension between market share and ratings quality:

> Moody's for years has struggled with this dilemma. On the one hand, we need to win the business and maintain market share, or we cease to be relevant. On the other hand, our reputation depends on maintaining ratings quality (or at least avoiding big visible mistakes). For the most part, we hand the dilemma off to the team MDs [managing directors] to solve. . . . I set both market share and rating quality objectives for my MDs, while reminding them to square the circle within the bounds of the code of conduct.

Later in the meeting, he reflected,

> The RMBS and derivatives teams are comprised of conscientious bright people working long hours. They are highly desirous of getting the rating right. But a certain complacency sets in after a prolonged period of rating success. . . . Organizations often interpret past successes as evidencing their competence and the adequacy of their procedures rather than a run of good luck.[26]

---

[25] Ibid., p. 3.

[26] "Credit Policy Issues at Moody's," Raymond McDaniel, confidential presentation to the board of directors, October 21, 2007.

What Should Be Done?

Now, on October 22, 2008, the House of Representatives Committee on Oversight and Government Reform had convened a hearing to question executives of the top credit rating agencies about their role in the nation's financial crisis. Testimony at the hearing revealed broad disagreement over the culpability of the agencies, and what if anything should be done about them.

Jerome S. Fons, managing director for credit policy at Moody's until August 2007, testified,

> My view is that a large part of the blame can be placed on the inherent conflicts of interest found in the issuer-pays business model and rating shopping by issuers of structured securities. . . . A drive to maintain or expand market share made the rating agencies willing participants in this shopping spree. It was also relatively easy for the major banks to play the agencies off one another. . . . Originators of structured securities typically chose the agency with the lowest standards, engendering a race to the bottom in terms of rating quality. . . . [T]he business model prevented analysts from putting investor interests first.

Fons recommended a "wholesale change at the governance and senior management levels of the large rating agencies." He also proposed eliminating the SEC's NRSRO designations, an increased reliance on "common sense" in the rating process, and "taming the conflicts posed by the issuer-pays model."[27]

Raymond McDaniel, who addressed the hearing on behalf of Moody's, strongly disputed the view that the business model was to blame. He pointed out the investors—as well as issuers—had an interest in influencing bond ratings. "[J]ust as an issuer has an interest in the rating to improve the marketability of its bonds, investors seeking to improve their existing bond portfolio values or to establish new portfolio positions on more favorable terms have an interest in the rating of a bond," he said. He also noted that bond issuers, such as investment banks, were themselves also often investors, weakening the distinction between the two. Companies such as Lehman Brothers issued asset-backed securities, but also held them on their books. Finally, he argued, switching to an investor-pay model would deprive individual investors of access to ratings, because only big institutional investors could afford to pay.

Rather, Moody's favored various methods of actively managing potential conflicts. The company's code of conduct, McDaniel pointed out, already required that bonds be rated by a committee, rather than by an individual, who might be swayed by personal interest. Analysts were barred from owning stock in companies whose bonds they rated, and compensation was not based on revenue associated with entities analysts rated. McDaniel concluded,

> The events of the past 15 months have demonstrated that markets can change dramatically and rapidly. Such change brings important lessons. The opportunity to improve market practices, including credit analysis and credit rating processes, must be pursued vigorously and transparently if confidence in credit markets and their healthy operation are to be restored.[28]

---

[27] Jerome Fons, testimony, pp. 3–6.

[28] Testimony of Raymond W. McDaniel, House Committee on Oversight and Government Reform, October 22, 2008, p. 19.

Discussion Questions

1. What did Moody's do wrong, if anything?
2. Which stakeholders were helped, and which were hurt, by Moody's actions?
3. Did Moody's have a conflict of interest? If so, what was the conflict, and who or what were the principal and the agent? What steps could be taken to eliminate or reduce this conflict?
4. What share of the responsibility did Moody's and its executives bear for the financial crisis, compared with that of home buyers, mortgage lenders, investment bankers, government regulators, policymakers, and investors?
5. What steps can be taken to prevent a recurrence of something like the subprime mortgage meltdown? In your answer, please address the role of management policies and practices, government regulation, public policy, and the structure of the credit ratings industry.

Merck, the FDA, and the Vioxx Recall

In 2006, the pharmaceutical giant Merck faced major challenges. Vioxx, the company's once best-selling prescription painkiller, had been pulled off the market in September 2004 after Merck learned it increased the risk of heart attacks and strokes. When news of the recall broke, the company's stock price had plunged 30 percent to $33 a share, its lowest point in eight years, where it had hovered since. Standard & Poor's had downgraded the company's outlook from "stable" to "negative." In late 2004, the Justice Department had opened a criminal investigation into whether the company had "caused federal health programs to pay for the prescription drug when its use was not warranted."[1] The Securities and Exchange Commission was inquiring into whether Merck had misled investors. By late 2005, more than 6,000 lawsuits had been filed, alleging that Vioxx had caused death or disability. From many quarters, the company faced troubling questions about the development and marketing of Vioxx, new calls for regulatory reform, and concerns about its political influence on Capitol Hill. In the words of Senator Charles Grassley, chairman of a congressional committee investigating the Vioxx case, "a blockbuster drug [had become] a blockbuster disaster."[2]

Merck, Inc.

Merck, the company in the eye of this storm, was one of the world's leading pharmaceutical firms. As shown in Exhibit A, in 2005 the company ranked fourth in sales, after Pfizer, Johnson & Johnson, and GlaxoSmithKline. In assets and market value, it ranked fifth. However, Merck ranked first in profits, earning $7.33 billion on $30.78 billion in sales (24 percent).[3]

Merck had long enjoyed a reputation as one of the most ethical and socially responsible of the major drug companies. For an unprecedented seven consecutive years (1987 to 1993), *Fortune* magazine had named Merck its "most admired" company. In 1987, Merck appeared on the cover of *Time* under the headline, "The Miracle Company." It had consistently appeared on lists of best companies to work for and in the portfolios of social investment funds. The company's philanthropy was legendary. In the 1940s, Merck had given its

By Anne T. Lawrence. Copyright © 2006 by the author. All rights reserved. An earlier version of this case was presented at the Western Casewriters Association Annual Meeting, Long Beach, California, March 30, 2006. This case was prepared from publicly available materials.

[1] "Justice Dept. and SEC Investigating Merck Drug," *The New York Times,* November 9, 2004.

[2] "Opening Statement of U.S. Senator Chuck Grassley of Iowa," U.S. Senate Committee on Finance, Hearing, "FDA, Merck, and Vioxx: Putting Patient Safety First?" November 18, 2004, *http://finance.senate.gov.*

[3] A history of Merck may be found in Fran Hawthorne, *The Merck Druggernaut: The Inside Story of a Pharmaceutical Giant* (Hoboken, NJ: John Wiley & Sons, 2003).

Company	Sales ($bil)	Profits ($bil)	Assets ($bil)	Market Value ($bil)
Pfizer	40.36	6.20	120.06	285.27
Johnson & Johnson	40.01	6.74	46.66	160.96
Merck	**30.78**	**7.33**	**42.59**	**108.76**
Novartis	26.77	5.40	46.92	116.43
Roche Group	25.18	2.48	45.77	95.38
GlaxoSmithKline	34.16	6.34	29.19	124.79
Aventis	21.66	2.29	31.06	62.98
Bristol-Myers Squibb	19.89	2.90	26.53	56.05
AstraZeneca	20.46	3.29	23.57	83.03
Abbott Labs	18.99	2.44	26.15	69.27

Source: Forbes 2000, *www.forbes.com.* Listed in order of overall ranking in the Forbes 2000.

patent for streptomycin, a powerful antibiotic, to a university foundation. Merck was especially admired for its donation of Mectizan. Merck's scientists had originally developed this drug for veterinary use, but later discovered that it was an effective cure for river blindness, a debilitating parasitic disease afflicting some of the world's poorest people. When the company realized that the victims of river blindness could not afford the drug, it decided to give it away for free, in perpetuity.[4]

In 1950, George W. Merck, the company's longtime CEO, stated in a speech, "We try never to forget that medicine is for the people. It is not for the profits. The profits follow, and if we have remembered that, they never fail to appear. The better we have remembered that, the larger they have been."[5] This statement was often repeated in subsequent years as a touchstone of the company's core values.

Merck was renowned for its research labs, which had a decades-long record of achievement, turning out one innovation after another, including drugs for tuberculosis, cholesterol, hypertension, and AIDS. In the early 2000s, Merck spent around $3 billion annually on research. Some felt that the company's culture had been shaped by its research agenda. Commented the author of a history of Merck, the company was "intense, driven, loyal, scientifically brilliant, collegial, and arrogant."[6] In 2006, although Merck had several medicines in the pipeline—including vaccines for rotavirus and cervical cancer, and drugs for insomnia, lymphoma, and the effects of stroke—some analysts worried that the pace of research had slowed significantly.

Estimating the company's financial liability from the Vioxx lawsuits was difficult. Some 84 million people had taken the drug worldwide over a five-year period from 1999 to 2004. In testimony before Congress, Dr. David Graham, a staff scientist at the Food and Drug Administration, estimated that as many as 139,000 people in the United States had had

[4] Merck received the 1991 Business Enterprise Trust Award for this action. See Stephanie Weiss and Kirk O. Hanson, "Merck and Co., Inc.: Addressing Third World Needs" (Business Enterprise Trust, 1991).

[5] Hawthorne, *The Merck Druggernaut,* pp. 17–18.

[6] Ibid., p. 38.

heart attacks or strokes as a result of taking Vioxx, and about 55,000 of these had died.[7] Merrill Lynch estimated the company's liability for compensatory damages alone in the range of $4 to $18 billion.[8] However, heart attacks and strokes were common, and they had multiple causes, including genetic predisposition, smoking, obesity, and a sedentary life-style. Determining the specific contribution of Vioxx to a particular cardiovascular event would be very difficult. The company vigorously maintained that it had done nothing wrong and vowed to defend every single case in court. By early 2006, only three cases had gone to trial, and the results had been a virtual draw—one decision for the plaintiff, one for Merck, and one hung jury.

Government Regulation of Prescription Drugs

In the United States, prescription medicines—like Vioxx—were regulated by the Food and Drug Administration (FDA).[9] Before a new drug could be sold to the public, its manufac-turer had to carry out clinical trials to demonstrate both safety and effectiveness. Advisory panels of outside medical experts reviewed the results of these trials and recommended to the FDA's Office of Drug Safety whether or not to approve a new drug.[10] After a drug was on the market, the agency's Office of New Drugs continued to monitor it for safety, in a process known as "postmarket surveillance." These two offices both reported to the same boss, the FDA's director of the Center for Drug Evaluation and Research.

Once the FDA had approved a drug, physicians could prescribe it for any purpose, but the manufacturer could market it only for uses for which it had been approved. Therefore, companies had an incentive to continue to study approved drugs to provide data that they were safe and effective for the treatment of other conditions.

In the 1980s, the drug industry and some patient advocates had criticized the FDA for being too slow to approve new medicines. Patients were concerned that they were not get-ting new medicines fast enough, and drug companies were concerned that they were losing sales revenue. Each month an average drug spent under review represented $41.7 million in lost revenue, according to one study.[11]

In 1992, Congress passed the Prescription Drug User Fee Act (PDUFA). This law, which was supported by the industry, required pharmaceutical companies to pay "user fees" to the FDA to review proposed new medicines. Between 1993 and 2001, the FDA received around $825 million in such fees from drug makers seeking approval. (During this period, it also received $1.3 billion appropriated by Congress.) This infusion of new reve-nue enabled the agency to hire 1,000 new employees and to shorten the approval time for new drugs from 27 months in 1993 to 14 months in 2001.[12]

Despite the benefits of PDUFA, some felt that industry-paid fees were a bad idea. In an editorial published in December 2004, the *Journal of the American Medical Association (JAMA)* concluded, "It is unreasonable to expect that the same agency that was responsi-ble for approval of drug licensing and labeling would also be committed to actively seek

---

[7] "FDA Failing in Drug Safety, Official Asserts," *The New York Times,* November 19, 2004. The full transcript of the hearing of the U.S. Senate Committee on Finance, "FDA, Merck, and Vioxx: Putting Patient Safety First?" is available at *http://finance.senate.gov.*

[8] "Despite Warnings, Drug Giant Took Long Path to Vioxx Recall," *The New York Times,* November 14, 2004.

[9] A history of the FDA and of its relationship to business may be found in Philip J. Hilts, *Protecting America's Health: The FDA, Business, and One Hundred Years of Regulation* (New York: Alfred A. Knopf, 2003).

[10] Marcia Angell, *The Trust about the Drug Companies* (New York: Random House, 2004), ch. 2.

[11] Merrill Lynch data reported in "A World of Hurt," *Fortune,* January 10, 2005, p. 18.

[12] U.S. General Accounting Office, *Food and Drug Administration: Effect of User Fees on Drug Approval Times, Withdrawals, and Other Agency Activities,* September 2002.

evidence to prove itself wrong (i.e., that the decision to approve the product was subsequently shown to be incorrect)." *JAMA* went on to recommend establishment of a separate agency to monitor drug safety.[13] Dr. David Kessler, a former FDA Commissioner, rejected this idea, responding that "strengthening postmarketing surveillance is certainly in order, but you don't want competing agencies."[14]

Some evidence suggested that the morale of FDA staff charged with evaluating the safety of new medicines had been hurt by relentless pressure to bring drugs to market quickly. In 2002, a survey of agency scientists found that only 13 percent were "completely confident" that the FDA's "final decisions adequately assess the safety of a drug." Thirty-one percent were "somewhat confident" and 5 percent lacked "any confidence." Two-thirds of those surveyed lacked confidence that the agency "adequately monitors the safety of prescription jobs once they are on the market." And nearly one in five said they had "been pressured to approve or recommend approval" for a drug "despite reservations about [its] safety, efficacy or quality."[15]

After the FDA shortened the approval time, the percentage of drugs recalled following approval increased from 1.56 percent for 1993–1996 to 5.35 percent for 1997–2001.[16] Vioxx was the ninth drug taken off the market in seven years.

Influence at the Top

The pharmaceutical industry's success in accelerating the approval of new drugs reflected its strong presence in Washington. The major drug companies, their trade association PhRMA (Pharmaceutical Research and Manufacturers of America), and their executives consistently donated large sums of money to both political parties and, through their political action committees, to various candidates. The industry's political contributions are shown in Exhibit B.

Following the congressional ban on soft money contributions in 2003, the industry shifted much of its contributions to so-called stealth PACs, nonprofit organizations that were permitted by law to take unlimited donations without revealing their source. These organizations could, in turn, make "substantial" political expenditures, providing political activity was not their primary purpose.[17]

In addition, the industry maintained a large corps of lobbyists active in the nation's capital. In 2003, for example, drug companies and their trade association spent $108 million on lobbying and hired 824 individual lobbyists, according to a report by Public Citizen.[18] Merck spent $40.7 million on lobbying between 1998 and 2004.[19] One of the industry's most effective techniques was to hire former elected officials or members of their staffs. For example, Billy Tauzin, formerly a Republican member of Congress from Louisiana and head of the

---

[13] "Postmarketing Surveillance—Lack of Vigilance, Lack of Trust," *Journal of the American Medical Association* 92, no. 21 (December 1, 2004), p. 2649.

[14] "FDA Lax in Drug Safety, Journal Warns," November 23, 2004, *www.sfgate.com.*

[15] 2002 Survey of 846 FDA scientists conducted by the Office of the Inspector General of the Department of Health and Human Services, *www.peer.org/FDAscientistsurvey.*

[16] "Postmarketing Surveillance."

[17] "Big PhRMA's Stealth PACs: How the Drug Industry Uses 501(c) Nonprofit Groups to Influence Elections," *Congress Watch,* September 2004.

[18] "Drug Industry and HMOs Deployed an Army of Nearly 1,000 Lobbyists to Push Medicare Bill, Report Finds," June 23, 2004, *www.citizen.org.*

[19] Data available at *www.publicintegrity.org.*

Election Cycle	Total Contributions	Contributions from Individuals	Contributions from PACs	Soft Money Contributions	Percentage to Republicans
2006	$5,187,393	$1,753,159	$3,434,234	N/A	70%
2004	$18,181,045	$8,445,485	$9,735,560	N/A	66%
2002	$29,441,951	$3,332,040	$6,957,382	$19,152,529	74%
2000	$26,688,292	$5,660,457	$5,649,913	$15,377,922	69%
1998	$13,169,694	$2,673,845	$4,107,068	$6,388,781	64%
1996	$13,754,796	$3,413,516	$3,584,217	$6,757,063	66%
1994	$7,706,303	$1,935,150	$3,477,146	$2,294,007	56%
1992	$7,924,262	$2,389,370	$3,205,014	$2,329,878	56%
1990	$3,237,592	$771,621	$2,465,971	N/A	54%
Total	$125,291,328	$30,374,643	$42,616,505	$52,300,180	67%

Source: Center for Responsive Politics, *www.opensecrets.org.*

powerful Committee on Energy and Commerce, which oversaw the drug industry, became president of PhRMA at a reported annual salary of $2 million in 2004.[20]

Over the years, the industry's representatives in Washington had established a highly successful record of promoting its political agenda on a range of issues. In addition to faster drug approvals, these had more recently included a Medicare prescription drug benefit, patent protections, and restrictions on drug imports from Canada.

The Blockbuster Model

In the 1990s, 80 percent of growth for the big pharmaceutical firms came from so-called "blockbuster" drugs.[21] Blockbusters have been defined by *Fortune* magazine as "medicines that serve vast swaths of the population and garner billions of dollars in annual revenue."[22] The ideal blockbuster, from the companies' view, was a medicine that could control chronic but usually nonfatal conditions that afflicted large numbers of people with health insurance. These might include, for example, daily maintenance drugs for high blood pressure or cholesterol, allergies, arthritis pain, or heartburn. Drugs that could actually cure a condition, and thus would not need to be taken for long periods, or were intended to treat diseases, like malaria or tuberculosis, that affected mainly the world's poor, were often less profitable.

Historically, drug companies focused most of their marketing efforts on prescribing physicians. The industry hired tens of thousands of sales representatives—often, attractive young men and women—to make the rounds of doctors' offices to talk about new products and give out free samples.[23] Drug companies also offered doctors gifts—from free meals to

[20] "Rep. Billy Tauzin Demonstrates That Washington's Revolving Door Is Spinning Out of Control," *Public Citizen,* December 15, 2004, press release.

[21] "The Waning of the Blockbuster," *BusinessWeek,* October 18, 2004.

[22] "A World of Hurt," p. 20.

[23] In 2005, 90,000 sales representatives were employed by the pharmaceutical industry, about one for every eight doctors. *The New York Times* revealed in an investigative article ("Give Me an Rx! Cheerleaders Pep Up Drug Sales," November 28, 2005) that many companies made a point of hiring former college cheerleaders for this role.

tickets to sporting events—to cultivate their goodwill. They also routinely sponsored continuing education events for physicians, often featuring reports on their own medicines, and supported doctors financially with opportunities to consult and to conduct clinical trials.[24] In 2003 Merck spent $422 million to market Vioxx to doctors and hospitals.[25]

During the early 2000s, when Vioxx and Pfizer's Celebrex were competing head-to-head, sales representatives for the two firms were hard at work promoting their brand to doctors. Commented one rheumatologist of the competition between Merck and Pfizer at the time, "We were all aware that there was a great deal of marketing. Like a Coke–Pepsi war."[26] An internal Merck training manual for sales representatives, reported in *The Wall Street Journal,* was titled "Dodge Ball Vioxx." It explained how to "dodge" doctors' questions, such as "I am concerned about the cardiovascular effects of Vioxx." Merck later said that this document had been taken out of context and that sales representatives "were not trained to avoid physicians' questions."[27]

Direct-to-Consumer Advertising

Although marketing to doctors and hospitals continued to be important, in the late 1990s the focus shifted somewhat. In 1997, the FDA for the first time allowed drug companies to advertise directly to consumers. The industry immediately seized this opportunity, placing numerous ads for drugs—from Viagra to Nexium—on television and in magazines and newspapers. In 2004, the industry spent over $4 billion on such direct-to-consumer, or DTC, advertising. For example, in one ad for Vioxx, Olympic figure skating champion Dorothy Hamill glided gracefully across an outdoor ice rink to the tune of "It's a Beautiful Morning" by the sixties pop group The Rascals, telling viewers that she would "not let arthritis stop me." In all, Merck spent more than $500 million advertising Vioxx.[28]

The industry's media blitz for Vioxx and other drugs was highly effective. According to research by the Harvard School of Public Heath, each dollar spent on DTC advertising yielded $4.25 in sales.

The drug companies defended DTC ads, saying they informed consumers of newly available therapies and encouraged people to seek medical treatment. In the age of the Internet, commented David Jones, an advertising executive whose firm included several major drug companies, "consumers are becoming much more empowered to make their own health care decisions."[29]

However, others criticized DTC advertising, saying that it put pressure on doctors to prescribe drugs that might not be best for the patient. "When a patient comes in and wants something, there is a desire to serve them," said David Wofsy, president of the American College of Rheumatology. "There is a desire on the part of physicians, as there is on anyone else who provides service, to keep the customer happy."[30] Even some industry executives expressed reservations. Said Hank McKinnell, CEO of Pfizer, "I'm beginning to think that direct-to-consumer ads are part of the problem. By having them

---

[24] The influence of the drug industry on the medical professional is documented in Katharine Greider, *The Big Fix: How the Pharmaceutical Industry Rips Off American Consumers* (New York: Public Affairs, 2003).

[25] "Drug Pullout," *Modern Healthcare,* October 18, 2004.

[26] "Marketing of Vioxx: How Merck Played Game of Catch-Up," *The New York Times,* February 11, 2005.

[27] "E-Mails Suggest Merck Knew Vioxx's Dangers at Early Stage," *The Wall Street Journal,* November 1, 2004.

[28] IMS Health estimate reported in "Will Merck Survive Vioxx?" *Fortune,* November 1, 2004.

[29] "With or Without Vioxx, Drug Ads Proliferate," *The New York Times,* December 6, 2004.

[30] "A 'Smart' Drug Fails the Safety Test," *Washington Post,* October 3, 2004.

Exhibit C

Vioxx Sales in the United States, 1999–2004

	U.S. Prescriptions Dispensed	U.S. Sales	U.S. Sales of Vioxx as % of Total Merck Sales
1999	4,845,000	$372,697,000	2.2%
2000	20,630,000	$1,526,382,000	7.6%
2001	25,406,000	$2,084,736,000	9.8%
2002	22,044,000	$1,837,680,000	8.6%
2003	19,959,000	$1,813,391,000	8.1%
2004*	13,994,000	$1,342,236,000	5.9%

*Withdrawn from the market in September 2004.

Sources: Columns 1 and 2: IMS Health (*www.imshealth.com*); column 3: Merck Annual Reports (*www.merck.com*).

on television without a very strong message that the doctor needs to determine safety, we've left this impression that all drugs are safe. In fact, no drug is safe."[31]

The Rise of Vioxx

Vioxx, the drug at the center of Merck's legal woes, was known as "a selective COX-2 inhibitor." Scientists had long understood that an enzyme called cyclo-oxygenase, or COX for short, was associated with pain and inflammation. In the early 1990s, researchers learned that there were really two kinds of COX enzyme. COX-1, it was found, performed several beneficial functions, including protecting the stomach lining. COX-2, on the other hand, contributed to pain and inflammation. Existing anti-inflammatory drugs suppressed both forms of the enzyme, which is why drugs like ibuprofen (Advil) relieved pain, but also caused stomach irritation in some users.

A number of drug companies, including Merck, were intrigued by the possibility of developing a medicine that would block just the COX-2, leaving the stomach-protective COX-1 intact. Such a drug would offer distinctive benefits to some patients, such as arthritis sufferers who were at risk for ulcers (bleeding sores in the intestinal tract).[32] As many as 16,500 people died each year in the United States from this condition.[33]

In May 1999, after several years of research and testing by Merck scientists, the FDA approved Vioxx for the treatment of osteoarthritis, acute pain in adults, and menstrual symptoms. The drug was later approved for rheumatoid arthritis. Although Merck, like other drug companies, never revealed what it spent to develop specific new medicines, estimates of the cost to develop a major new drug ran as high as $800 million.[34]

Vioxx quickly became exactly what Merck had hoped: a blockbuster. At its peak in 2001, Vioxx generated $2.1 billion in sales in the United States alone, contributing almost 10 percent of Merck's total sales revenue worldwide, as shown in Exhibit C. The retail

[31] "A World of Hurt," p. 18.

[32] "Medicine Fueled by Marketing Intensified Troubles for Pain Pills," *The New York Times,* December 19, 2004.

[33] "New Scrutiny of Drugs in Vioxx's Family," *The New York Times,* October 4, 2004.

[34] This estimate was hotly debated. See, for example, "How Much Does the Pharmaceutical Industry Really Spend on R&D?" ch. 3 in Angell, *The Trust about the Drug Companies;* and Merrill Goozner, *The $800 Million Pill: The Truth behind the Cost of New Drugs* (Berkeley: University of California Press, 2004).

price of Vioxx was around $3.00 per pill, compared with pennies per pill for older anti-inflammatory drugs like aspirin and Advil. Of course, Vioxx was often covered, at least partially, under a user's health insurance, while over-the-counter drugs were not.

Safety Warnings

Even before the drug was approved, some evidence cast doubt on the safety of Vioxx. These clues were later confirmed in other studies.

Merck Research: Internal company e-mails suggested that Merck scientists might have been worried about the cardiovascular risks of Vioxx as early as its development phase. In a 1997 e-mail, reported in *The Wall Street Journal,* Dr. Alise Reicin, a Merck scientist, stated that "the possibility of CV (cardiovascular) events is of great concern." She added, apparently sarcastically, "I just can't wait to be the one to present those results to senior management!" A lawyer representing Merck said this e-mail had been taken out of context.[35]

VIGOR: A study code-named VIGOR, completed in 2000 after the drug was already on the market, compared rheumatoid arthritis patients taking Vioxx with another group taking naproxen (Aleve). Merck financed the research, which was designed to study gastrointestinal side effects. The study found, as the company had expected, that Vioxx was easier on the stomach than naproxen. But it also found that the Vioxx group had nearly five times as many heart attacks (7.3 per thousand person-years) as the naproxen group (1.7 per thousand person-years).[36] Publicly, Merck hypothesized that these findings were due to the heart-protective effect of naproxen, rather than to any defect inherent in Vioxx. Privately, however, the company seemed worried. In an internal e-mail dated March 9, 2000, under the subject line "Vigor," the company's research director, Dr. Edward Scolnick, said that cardiovascular events were "clearly there" and called them "a shame." But, he added, "there is always a hazard."[37] At that time, the company considered reformulating Vioxx by adding an agent to prevent blood clots (and reduce CV risk), but then dropped the project.

The FDA was sufficiently concerned by the VIGOR results that it required Merck to add additional warning language to its label. These changes appeared in April 2002, after lengthy negotiations between the agency and the company over their wording.[38]

Kaiser/Permanente: In August 2004, Dr. David Graham, a scientist at the FDA, reported the results of a study of the records of 1.4 million patients enrolled in the Kaiser health maintenance organization in California. He found that patients on high doses of Vioxx had three times the rate of heart attacks as patients on Celebrex, a competing COX-2 inhibitor made by Pfizer. Merck discounted this finding, saying that studies of patient records were less reliable than double-blind clinical studies.[39] Dr. Graham later charged that his superiors at the FDA had "ostracized" him and subjected him to "veiled threats" if he did not qualify his criticism of Vioxx. The FDA called these charges "baloney."[40]

---

[35] "E-Mails Suggest Merck Knew Vioxx's Dangers at Early Stage."

[36] "Comparison of Upper Gastrointestinal Toxicity of Rofecoxib and Naproxen in Patients with Rheumatoid Arthritis," *New England Journal of Medicine,* 2000, p. 323.

[37] "E-Mails Suggest Merck Knew Vioxx's Dangers at Early Stage."

[38] At one of the early Vioxx trials, the plaintiff introduced a Merck internal memo that calculated that the company would make $229 million more in profits if it delayed changes to warning language on the label by four months (*The New York Times,* August 20, 2005). The FDA did not have the authority to dictate label language; any changes had to be negotiated with the manufacturer.

[39] "Study of Painkiller Suggests Heart Risk," *The New York Times,* August 26, 2004.

[40] "FDA Official Alleges Pressure to Suppress Vioxx Findings," *Washington Post,* October 8, 2004.

APPROVe: In order to examine the possibility that Vioxx posed a cardiovascular risk, Merck decided to monitor patients enrolled in a clinical trial called APPROVe to see if those taking Vioxx had more heart attacks and strokes than those who were taking a placebo (sugar pill). This study had been designed to determine if Vioxx reduced the risk of recurrent colon polyps (a precursor to colon cancer); Merck hoped it would lead to FDA approval of the drug for this condition. The APPROVe study was planned before the VIGOR results were known.

Merck Recalls the Drug

On the evening of Thursday, September 23, 2004, Dr. Peter S. Kim, president of Merck Research Labs, received a phone call from scientists monitoring the colon polyp study. Researchers had found, the scientists told him, that after 18 months of continuous use individuals taking Vioxx were more than twice as likely to have a heart attack or stroke than those taking a placebo. The scientists recommended that the study be halted because of "unacceptable" risk.[41]

Dr. Kim later described to a reporter for *The New York Times* the urgent decision-making process that unfolded over the next hours and days as the company responded to this news.

> On Friday, I looked at the data with my team. The first thing you do is review the data. We did that. Second is you double-check the data, go through them and make sure that everything is O.K. [At that point] I knew that barring some big mistake in the analysis, we had an issue here. Around noon, I called [CEO] Ray Gilmartin and told him what was up. He said, "Figure out what was the best thing for patient safety." We then spent Friday and the rest of the weekend going over the data and analyzing them in different ways and calling up medical experts to set up meetings where we would discuss the data and their interpretations and what to do.[42]

According to later interviews with some of the doctors consulted that weekend by Merck, the group was of mixed opinion. Some experts argued that Vioxx should stay on the market, with a strong warning label so that doctors and patients could judge the risk for themselves. But others thought the drug should be withdrawn because no one knew why the drug was apparently causing heart attacks. One expert commented that "Merck prides itself on its ethical approach. I couldn't see Merck saying we're going to market a drug with a safety problem."[43]

On Monday, Dr. Kim recommended to Gilmartin that Vioxx be withdrawn from the market. The CEO agreed. The following day, Gilmartin notified the board, and the company contacted the FDA. On Thursday, September 30, Merck issued a press release, which stated in part,

> Merck & Co., Inc. announced today a voluntary withdrawal of VIOXX®. This decision is based on new data from a three-year clinical study. In this study, there was an increased risk for cardiovascular (CV) events, such as heart attack and stroke, in

[41] "Painful Withdrawal for Makers of Vioxx," *Washington Post,* October 18, 2004. Detailed data reported the following day in *The New York Times* showed that 30 of the 1,287 patients taking Vioxx had suffered a heart attack, compared with 11 of 1,299 taking a placebo; 15 on Vioxx had had a stroke or transient ischemic attack (minor stroke), compared with 7 taking a placebo.

[42] "A Widely Used Arthritis Drug Is Withdrawn," *The New York Times,* October 1, 2004.

[43] "Painful Withdrawal for Makers of Vioxx."

patients taking VIOXX 25 mg compared to those taking placebo (sugar pill). While the incidence of CV events was low, there was an increased risk beginning after 18 months of treatment. The cause of the clinical study result is uncertain, but our commitment to our patients is clear. . . . Merck is notifying physicians and pharmacists and has informed the Food and Drug Administration of this decision. We are taking this action because we believe it best serves the interests of patients. That is why we undertook this clinical trial to better understand the safety profile of VIOXX. And it's why we instituted this voluntary withdrawal upon learning about these data. Be assured that Merck will continue to do everything we can to maintain the safety of our medicines.

Discussion Questions

1. Do you believe that Merck acted in a socially responsible and ethical manner with regard to Vioxx? Why or why not? In your answer, please address the company's drug development and testing, marketing and advertising, relationships with government regulators and policymakers, and handling of the recall.
2. What should or could Merck have done differently, if anything?
3. What is the best way for society to protect consumers of prescription medicines? Specifically, what are the appropriate roles for pharmaceutical companies, government regulators and policymakers, patients and their physicians, and the court system in assuring the safety and effectiveness of prescription medicines?
4. How should the present system be changed, if at all, to better protect patients?

Kimpton Hotels' EarthCare Program

Michael Pace faced a dilemma. He was Kimpton Hotels' West Coast director of operations and environmental programs, general manager of its Villa Florence Hotel in San Francisco, and the main catalyst for implementing its EarthCare program nationally. He was determined to help the boutique hotel chain "walk the talk" regarding its commitment to environmental responsibility, but he also had agreed not to introduce any new products or processes that would be more expensive than those they replaced. They were already successful in introducing nontoxic cleaning products, promotional materials printed on recycled paper, towel and linen reuse programs, and complimentary organic coffee and had made substantial progress in recycling bottles, cans, paper, and cardboard. Now that the initial phase of the program was being implemented nationwide, he and the company's team of eco-champions were facing some difficult challenges with the rollout of the second, more ambitious, phase.

For example, the team had to decide whether to recommend the purchase of linens made of organic cotton, which vendors insisted would cost at least 50 percent more than standard linens. It would cost an average of $100,000 to $150,000 to switch out all the sheets, pillowcases, and towels in each hotel. If they couldn't negotiate the price down, was there some way they could introduce organic cotton in a limited but meaningful way? All linens were commingled in the laundry, so they couldn't be introduced one floor at a time. Maybe they could start with pillowcases—though the sheets wouldn't be organic, guests would be resting their heads on organic cotton. Would it even be worth spending so much on linens? The team would face similar issues when deciding whether to recommend environmentally friendly carpeting or furniture.

There were also issues with their recycling initiatives. The program had been field-tested at Kimpton hotels in San Francisco, a singular city in one of the most environmentally aware states in the United States. Now the eco-champions team had to figure out how to make it work in cities like Chicago, which didn't even have a municipal recycling program in place. In Denver, recycling actually cost more than waste disposal to a landfill, due to the low cost of land in eastern Colorado. Pace knew that the environmental initiatives most likely to succeed would be those that could be seamlessly implemented by the general managers and employees of the 39 unique Kimpton hotels around the country. The last thing he wanted to do was to make their jobs more difficult by imposing cookie-cutter standards. At the same time, he knew that recycling just 50 percent of Kimpton Hotels' waste stream would save over $250,000 per year in waste disposal costs.

Kimpton had recently embarked on a national campaign to build brand awareness by associating its name with each unique property. Pace knew that the success of Kimpton's strategy would rest heavily on its ability to maintain the care, integrity, and uniqueness that customers had come to associate with its chain of boutique hotels. Other hotel companies had begun investing heavily in the niche that Kimpton had pioneered. To differentiate itself, the company had to continue to find innovative ways to offer services that addressed the needs and values of its customers, and EarthCare was a crucial part of its plans. But could Pace find a way to make it happen within Kimpton's budget, and without adversely affecting the customer experience? Would Kimpton be able to keep the promises made by its new corporate brand?

The Greening of the U.S. Hotel Industry

The U.S. hotel industry—with its 4.5 million rooms, common areas and lobbies, conventions, restaurants, laundry facilities, and back offices—had a significant environmental impact. According to the American Hotel and Lodging Association, the average hotel toilet was flushed 7 times per day per guest, an average shower was 7.5 minutes long, and 40 percent of bathroom lights were left on at night. A typical hotel used 218 gallons of water per day per occupied room. Energy use was pervasive, including lighting in guestrooms and common areas, heating and air conditioning, and washing and drying towels and linens. The hotel industry spent $3.7 billion per year on electricity.[1]

Hotels had other environmental impacts, as well. Guestrooms generated surprisingly large amounts of waste, ranging from one-half pound to 28 pounds per day, and averaging 2 pounds per day per guest. Nonrefillable bottles of amenities, such as shampoo and lotion, generated large amounts of plastic waste, and products used to clean bathrooms and furniture contained harmful chemicals. Paints contained high levels of volatile organic compounds. Back office and front desk activities generated large amounts of waste paper. And furniture, office equipment, kitchen, and laundry appliances were rarely selected for their environmental advantages.

Opportunities for reducing a hotel's environmental footprint were plentiful, and many could yield bottom-line savings. Reduced laundering of linens, at customer discretion, had already been adopted enthusiastically across the spectrum of budget to luxury hotels; 38 percent of hotels had linen reuse programs. Low-flow showerheads could deliver the same quality shower experience using half the water of a conventional showerhead. Faucet aerators could cut water requirements by 50 percent. A 13-watt compact fluorescent bulb gave the same light as a 60-watt incandescent, lasted about 10 times longer, and used about 70 percent less energy. Waste costs also could be significantly reduced. For many hotels, 50–80 percent of their solid waste stream was compostable, and a significant part of the remaining waste was composed of recyclables, such as paper, aluminum, and glass.

In addition to bottom-line savings, environmental programs held the potential to generate new business. Governmental bodies and NGOs, corporations, and convention/meeting planners were showing increased interest in selecting hotels using environmental criteria. California, which had an annual travel budget of $70 million, had launched a Green Lodging Program and encouraged state employees to select hotels it certified. The criteria for certification include recycling, composting, energy- and water-efficient fixtures and lighting, and nontoxic or less toxic alternatives for cleaning supplies. State governments in Pennsylvania, Florida, Vermont, and Virginia also had developed green lodging programs.

---

[1] California Green Lodging Program, *www.Ciwmb.ca.gov/epp/.*

CERES, a well-respected environmental nonprofit, had developed the Green Hotel Initiative, designed to demonstrate and increase demand for environmentally responsible hotel services. Some major corporations had endorsed the initiative, including Ford Motor Company, General Motors, Nike, American Airlines, and Coca-Cola. CERC, the Coalition for Environmentally Responsible Conventions, and the Green Meetings Industry Council were encouraging meeting planners to "green" their events by, among other things, choosing environmentally friendly hotels for lodging and meeting sites.

Despite all this potential, environmental progress in the U.S. hotel industry had been very limited. With a few exceptions, most hotels were doing very little beyond easy-to-implement cost-saving initiatives. These hotels had reduced their environmental footprint as a consequence of their cost-cutting efforts, but they were not necessarily committed to a comprehensive environmental program. During a 1998 effort by Cornell University's School of Hotel Administration to identify hotels employing environmental best practices, researchers were "surprised by the dearth of nominations."[2] In contrast to their U.S. counterparts, hotels in Canada and Europe seemed to be embracing the hotel greening process.

Kimpton Hotels

Kimpton Hotels was founded in 1981 by the late Bill Kimpton, who once said, "No matter how much money people have to spend on big, fancy hotels, they're still intimidated and unsettled when they arrive. So the psychology of how you build hotels and restaurants is very important. You put a fireplace in the lobby and create a warm, friendly restaurant, and the guest will feel at home."

Credited with inventing the boutique hotel segment, Kimpton Hotels had built a portfolio of unique properties in the upscale segment of the industry.[3] By 2005, Kimpton had grown to include 39 hotels throughout North America and Canada, each one designed to create a unique and exceptional guest experience. Every hotel lobby had a cozy fireplace and plush sitting area, where complimentary coffee was served every morning, and wine every evening. Guestrooms were stylishly decorated and comfortably furnished, offering amenities such as specialty suites that included Tall Rooms and Yoga Rooms. Every room offered high-speed wireless Internet access and desks with ample lighting. Rather than rewarding customer loyalty with a point program, Kimpton offered customization and personalization. "We record the preferences of our loyal guests," said Mike Depatie, Kimpton's CEO of real estate. "Someone may want a jogging magazine and a Diet Coke when they arrive. We can get that done."

Business travel (group and individual) accounted for approximately 65 percent of Kimpton's revenues, and leisure travel (tour group and individual) the other 35 percent. The selection of hotels for business meetings and conferences was through meeting and conference organizers. Around 35 percent of all rooms were booked through Kimpton's call center, 25 percent through travel agents, and 25 percent through their website, and the remainder "came in off the street." The Internet portion of their business continued to grow, but they didn't cater to buyers looking for the "steal of the century." Rather, they were increasingly being discovered by the 25 percent of customers that market researchers called *unchained seekers,* many of whom used the Internet to search for unique accommodations that matched their particular needs or values.

[2] Cathy A. Enz and Judy A. Siguaw, "Best Hotel Environmental Practices," *Cornell Hotel and Restaurant Administration Quarterly,* October 1999.

[3] Gene Sloan, "Let the Pillowfights Begin," *USA Today,* August 27, 2004.

Historically, Kimpton had prospered by purchasing and renovating buildings at a discount in strategic nationwide locations that were appropriate for their niche segment. The hotel industry in general had been slow to enter the boutique niche, and Kimpton enjoyed a substantial edge in experience in developing value-added services for guests. "All hotels are starting to look alike and act alike, and we are the counterpoint, the contrarians," explained Tom LaTour, Kimpton president and CEO. "We don't look like the brands, we don't act like the brands, and as the baby boomers move through the age wave, they will seek differentiated, experience-oriented products."

Kimpton's top executives took pride in their ability to recognize and develop both undervalued properties and undervalued people. Kimpton's hotel general managers were often refugees from large branded companies who did not thrive under hierarchical, standardized corporate structures. At Kimpton, they were afforded a great deal of autonomy, subject only to the constraints of customer service standards and capital and operating budgets.

This sense of autonomy and personal responsibility was conveyed down through the ranks to all 5,000 Kimpton employees. Kimpton's flexible corporate structure avoided hierarchy, preferring a circular structure where executives and employees were in constant communication.[4] Steve Pinetti, senior vice president for sales and marketing, liked to tell the story of a new parking attendant who had to figure out how to deal with a guest who felt that he had not been adequately informed of extra charges for parking his car at the hotel. The attendant decided on the spot to reduce the charges, and asked the front desk to make the necessary adjustments. He had heard his general manager tell everyone that they should feel empowered to take responsibility for making guests happy, but he fully expected to be grilled by his GM, at the very least, about his actions. A sense of dread took hold as he was called to the front of the room at a staff meeting the very next day, but it dissipated quickly when his general manager handed him a special award for his initiative.

Commitment to Social and Environmental Responsibility

An important part of Kimpton's history was its long-standing commitment to social and environmental responsibility. Staff at each hotel had always been encouraged to engage with local community nonprofits that benefit the arts, education, the underprivileged, and other charitable causes. Kimpton maintained these local programs even in periods of falling occupancy rates and industry downturns. These local efforts evolved into the companywide Kimpton Cares program in 2004, as part of the company's corporate branding effort. At the national level, Kimpton supported the National AIDS Fund (in support of its Red Ribbon Campaign) and Dress for Success (which assisted economically disadvantaged women struggling to enter the workforce) by allotting a share of a guest's room fee to the charity. At the global level, Kimpton embarked in a partnership with Trust for Public Land (TPL), a nonprofit dedicated to the preservation of land for public use. In 2005, Kimpton committed to raising $15,000 from its total room revenues to introduce the TPL Parks for People program, and created eco-related fund-raising events in each of its cities to further support the campaign.

Kimpton also introduced EarthCare, a comprehensive program of environmental initiatives intended for rollout to all the chain's hotels. "As business leaders, we believe we have a responsibility to positively impact the communities we live in, to be conscious

---

[4] Liz French, Americanexecutive.com, December 2004.

about our environment, and to make a difference where we can," said Niki Leondakis, Kimpton's chief operating officer. Kimpton's top executives considered the Kimpton Cares program, and its EarthCare component, essential parts of the company's branding effort. Steve Pinetti noted, "What drove it was our belief that our brand needs to stand for something. What do we want to stand for in the community? We want to draw a line in the sand. We also want our impact to be felt as far and wide as it can. Hopefully, through our good deeds, we'll be able to influence other companies."

Anecdotal evidence suggested that Kimpton's early efforts had already had financial payoffs. Kimpton was receiving significant coverage of its EarthCare program in local newspapers and travel publications. "We've booked almost half a million dollars in meetings from a couple of corporations in Chicago because of our ecological reputation," said Pinetti. "Their reps basically told us, 'Your values align with our values, and we want to spend money on hotels that think the way we do.'" Kimpton believed that companies that identified with being socially responsible would look for partners like Kimpton that shared those values and that certifications like the California Green Lodging Program would attract both individuals and corporate clientele.

However, Pinetti noted, "The cost-effectiveness wasn't clear when we started. I thought we might get some business out of this, but that's not why we did it. We think it's the right thing to do, and it generates a lot of enthusiasm among our employees."

Kimpton's Real Estate CEO Mike Depatie believed that incorporating care for communities and the environment into the company's brand had been a boon to hiring. "We attract and keep employees because they feel that from a values standpoint, we have a corporate culture and value system that's consistent with theirs," he commented. "They feel passionate about working here." While the hotel industry was plagued with high turnover, Kimpton's turnover rates were lower than the national averages.

Rolling Out the EarthCare Program

Pinetti and Pace realized that they were too busy to handle all the planning and operational details of the national rollout, so they turned to Jeff Slye, of Business Evolution Consulting, for help. Slye was a process management consultant who wanted to help small and medium-sized business owners figure out how to "ecofy" their companies. He had heard that Kimpton was trying to figure out how to make its operations greener and integrate this effort into its branding effort. When they first met in October 2004, Pinetti and Pace handed Slye a 10-page document detailing their objectives and a plan for rolling out the initiative in phases. Kimpton's program was to have the following eco-mission statement:

> Lead the hospitality industry in supporting a sustainable world by continuing to deliver a premium guest experience through nonintrusive, high-quality, eco-friendly products and services.
>
> Our mission is built upon a companywide commitment toward water conservation; reduction of energy usage; elimination of harmful toxins and pollutants; recycling of all reusable waste; building and furnishing hotels with sustainable materials; and purchasing goods and services that directly support these principles.

Slye worked with Pinetti and Pace to fill various gaps in their plan and develop an ecostandards program, a concise report outlining a strategy for greening the products and operational processes that Kimpton used. In December 2004, Pinetti asked Slye to present the report to Kimpton's COO, Niki Leondakis. Leondakis greeted the proposal enthusiastically, but noted that it needed an additional component: a strategy for communicating the program both internally (to management and staff) and externally (to guests, investors, and the press). As important as the external audiences were, Slye knew that the internal communications strategy would be particularly crucial, given the autonomy afforded each Kimpton hotel, each with its own set of local initiatives. Getting everyone on board would require a strategy that respected that aspect of Kimpton's culture.

Slye, Pace, and Pinetti decided to create an ad hoc network of eco-champions throughout the company. The national lead (Pace) and colead (Pinetti) would head up the communications effort and be accountable for its success. Each of five geographic regions (Pacific Northwest, San Francisco Bay Area, Central U.S., Washington D.C., and Northeast/Southeast), covering six or seven hotel properties, would also have a lead and colead who would help communicate the program to employees, and be the local point persons in the chain of command. One of their key roles would be to solicit employee suggestions regarding ways to make products and processes greener.

In addition, a team of national eco-product specialists would be key components of the network. These specialists would be responsible for soliciting staff input, and identifying and evaluating greener products as potential substitutes for existing ones. Products would be tested for effectiveness and evaluated on the basis of their environmental benefits, effect on guest perceptions, potential marketing value, and cost. Pinetti and Pace determined that specialists would be needed initially for six product categories: beverages, cleaning agents, office supplies, engineering, information technology, and room supplies. Meanwhile, Pace and Pinetti asked all general managers to report on their existing environmental initiatives, to get baseline feedback on what individual hotels were doing already. They turned the results into a matrix they could use to identify gaps and monitor progress for each hotel.

By February 2005, the network of eco-champions was in place, and everyone had agreed on the basic ground rules for the transition. No new product or service could cost more than the product or service it replaced, nor could it adversely affect customer perceptions or satisfaction. All leads, coleads, and product specialists began meeting via conference call every Friday morning to discuss the greening initiative and share accounts of employee suggestions, progress achieved, and barriers encountered.

To help communicate the program's goals and achievements, and to help motivate employees seeking recognition, the team began to post regular updates and success stories in Kimpton's internal weekly newsletter, *The Word,* which was distributed throughout the organization and read by all GMs. They also ran an EarthCare contest to further galvanize interest, which generated over 70 entries for categories such as Best Eco-Practice Suggestion, Most EarthCare Best Practices Adopted, and Best Art and Humor Depicting EarthCare. The team also communicated the environmental benefits of their activities to the staff. For example, printing on 35 percent postconsumer recycled paper would save 24,000 pounds of wood, and recycling 100 glass bottles per month would save the energy equivalent of powering one hundred 100-watt lightbulbs for 60 days.

The team of eco-champions also quickly learned that the national rollout effort would have its share of potential operational risks and challenges, which would need to be addressed:

- *Potential resistance by general managers (GMs) to a centralized initiative.* A green management program mandated by corporate headquarters might threaten Kimpton's culture of uniqueness and autonomy. GMs might chafe at what they saw as corporate intrusion upon their autonomy and would want the flexibility to adapt the program to local requirements.

- *Potential resistance by hotel staff to new products and procedures.* Kimpton's relatively low turnover meant that some employees had been working there for many years and had become accustomed to familiar ways of doing things. Informal queries by management, for example, revealed that many cleaning staff equated strong chemical odors with cleanliness. Also, many of the service staff did not speak English fluently, and might have difficulty understanding management's reasons for switching to new procedures or greener cleaning products.

- *A slower payback period or a lower rate of return for green investments, relative to others.* The gains in operating costs achieved by installing longer-life and more energy-efficient fluorescent lighting could take years to pay off, while higher acquisition costs could inflate short-term expenses. The same logic applied to water conservation investments. Would corporate executives and investors be patient? What if consumer tastes or Kimpton's branding strategies changed before investments had paid off?

- *Benefits intangible to customers.* Unless informed, guests would not be aware that their rooms had been painted with low-VOC paints. Likewise, organic cottons would likely not feel or look superior to traditional materials.

- *For some products, required investments might exceed existing budgets or fail to meet the cost parity criterion.* For example, the eco-specialists learned that one of Kimpton's vendors did have a Green Seal certified nontoxic line, but the products were selling at a 10–15 percent premium over standard products. They discovered that virtually every product they were interested in was more expensive than those currently used. At the extreme, eco-friendly paper products were priced 50 percent above standard products. Would additional budget be provided? Would savings in other areas be allowed to pay for it?

- *Marketing the program could prove challenging.* How should the EarthCare program be promoted, given customer concerns regarding the impact of some environmental initiatives on the quality of their guest experience? Guests might be concerned, for example, whether low-flow shower heads or fluorescent lighting would meet their expectations. According to the American Automobile Association's Diamond Rating Guidelines, some water-saving showerheads and energy-saving lightbulbs could lower a hotel's diamond rating.[5]

- *Regional variations in customer values.* Environmental awareness and concern varied considerably by geographic region, from very high on the West Coast and in the Northeast, to considerably lower in the South and Midwest.

- *Regional differences in recycling infrastructure and regulatory environment.* California had a mandated recycling program requiring 70 percent recycling of solid waste by 2007, so San Francisco's disposal service provided free recycling containers. Other localities might not be so generous.

Even in the face of these challenges, Kimpton executives believed that the EarthCare program was the smart, as well as the "right," thing to do. According to Tom LaTour, chairman and CEO,

> It's good business. It's not just because we're altruistic, it's good for business. Otherwise the investors would say, what are you guys doing? A lot of people think it's going to cost more. It's actually advantageous to be eco-friendly than not.

---

[5] *AAA Lodging Requirements & Diamond Rating Guidelines* (Heathrow, FL: AAA Publishing, June 2001).

Niki Leondakis, COO, saw the program's impact on marketing and employee retention:

> Many people say we're heading toward a tipping point: If you're not environ-
> mentally conscious, your company will be blackballed from people's choices.
> Also, employees today want to come to work every day not just for the paycheck
> but to feel good about what they're doing. . . . It's very important to them to be
> aligned with the values of the people they work for, so from the employee reten-
> tion standpoint, this helps us retain and attract them so we can select from the
> best and the brightest.[6]

**Discussion
Questions**

1. What are the benefits of Kimpton's environmental sustainability initiatives? What are its costs?

2. How would you justify the EarthCare program to Kimpton's board of directors and stockholders? That is, what is the business case for this program?

3. What challenges face the EarthCare program, and how might Kimpton overcome them?

4. What further steps should Kimpton take to institutionalize its environmental commitments?

5. How would you measure the success of the EarthCare program, and how should it be reported to stakeholders?

[6] Carlo Wolff, "Environmental Evangelism: Kimpton Walks the Eco-Walk," *Lodging Hospitality,* March 1, 2005.

Ventria Bioscience and the Controversy over Plant-Made Medicines

"Ventria is dedicated to leading the development of plant-made pharmaceuticals that promise affordable human health products for the global community."

Scott Deeter, president and CEO, Ventria Bioscience

It was a warm, sunny day in mid-July 2004—perfect conditions for growing rice in California's lushly irrigated Sacramento Valley. But *their* rice was not in the ground, thought Scott Deeter with mounting frustration. Deeter was the president and CEO of Ventria Bioscience, a Sacramento, California–based biotechnology firm. The 20-person start-up had developed an innovative process to produce pharmaceutical proteins in the seeds of genetically modified rice. Ventria believed that its first product—a medicine designed to lessen the severity of childhood diarrhea—held great promise for public health, particularly in the developing world. The company had tested its bioengineered rice in small test plots near its headquarters. That spring, it had sought to plant at least 120 acres to begin commercial-scale production. But in its effort to obtain the necessary permits, Ventria had been stymied at nearly every turn. Facing vigorous opposition from environmentalists, food safety activists, consumer advocates, and rice farmers, the California Secretary of Agriculture had denied the company's request to plant rice on a commercial scale. Now Deeter had to figure out the best way forward for the fledgling, venture capital–backed firm.

 Ventria Bioscience

Ventria Bioscience (originally called Applied Phytologics) was founded in 1993 by Dr. Raymond Rodriguez, a molecular biologist on the faculty of the University of California–Davis. In the early 1980s, Rodriguez and his graduate students had embarked on an ambitious research program aimed at improving the productivity of rice, a crop he recognized as being of great importance to human nutrition worldwide. With the support of a state government grant to encourage the commercialization of basic scientific research, Rodriguez

By Anne T. Lawrence. Copyright © 2008 by the author. All rights reserved. An earlier version of this case was presented at the 2008 annual meeting of the North American Case Research Association. The author is grateful to Dr. Raymond Rodriguez for his assistance in the preparation of this case. The author also gratefully acknowledges research funding provided by the Don and Sally Lucas Foundation.

began to develop techniques to "express" medically useful proteins in rice plants, from which they could be extracted and purified. He explained,

> We were working on expression technology—taking a gene that encodes for a medical protein and using recombinant DNA technology to produce that protein in the plant. The key technology for Ventria was the ability to express a protein abundantly in a harvestable organ or tissue. That was the breakthrough. Roots or tubers like a potato, fruits like a tomato, ears of corn, or grains of rice—those are harvestable. Expressing the protein of interest in stems and leaves is a waste of effort and resources. If you can focus your overexpression technology on a harvestable organ, you are way ahead in terms of efficiency. Very few research labs or ag biotech companies could do this at that time.

In 1993, Rodriguez incorporated Applied Phytologics to commercialize his techniques for producing medical proteins in rice. In his search for funding, he approached Dr. William Rutter, the founder and board chairman of the Emeryville biotechnology firm Chiron, with whom he had earlier worked as a postdoctoral fellow at the University of California–San Francisco. Rutter was immediately attracted to the potential of the new venture. Rodriguez recalled,

> [Rutter and I] both like disruptive technologies. Neither of us was interested in incremental improvements in yield and cost efficiencies. We *were* excited, however, by the prospects of order-of-magnitude improvements—thousand-fold increases in yield with similar fold decreases in costs. For a technology-based industry, that's really critical. We wanted to revolutionize the biopharmaceutical industry by putting production on a metric ton scale instead of a gram or kilogram scale.

With the help of an early "angel" investment from Rutter, Rodriguez opened a lab in Sacramento in 1994 and recruited a small staff of scientists and technicians, including some of his former graduate students. Within a few years, the new company launched research on around 15 different medical and industrial proteins, filed dozens of patent applications, and continued to improve its core technology, which eventually became known as the "ExpressTec System." In the venture's early years, Rodriguez chaired the board, as well as overseeing the company's R&D activities.

As the venture continued its research and development, Dr. Rodriguez gradually built a board of directors of biotech leaders and seasoned entrepreneurs. Early board members included Dr. William J. Rutter and Dr. Pablo Valenzuela, cofounders of Chiron Corporation and early pioneers in biotechnology; William H. Rutter, an attorney and venture capitalist; Ron Vogel, president of Great Western Malting; and bioentrepreneur Dr. Roberto Crea. In 2000, Thomas N. Urban, the former chairman and CEO of Pioneer Hi-Bred International, Inc., a leading agricultural seed company, was recruited to chair the board. Melvin Booth, the former CEO of MedImmune, later became a director. So did William W. Crouse, a general partner of HealthCare Ventures, and David Dwyer, a general partner in Vista Ventures; both venture capital funds specialized in biotechnology. Members of the board and their organizations collectively provided more than 85 percent of the company's financing.

Overseeing the company's day-to-day operations was a management team consisting of Frank E. Hagie, Jr., president and CEO; Dr. Delia R. Bethell, a biologist and Ventria's vice president of clinical development; and Dr. Ning Huang, a molecular biologist and vice president of research and development. (Dr. Huang had received his Ph.D. from Dr. Rodriguez in 1990.) In 2000, Dr. Rodriguez resigned from the board to devote more time to his university research and teaching. As chairman emeritus, Dr. Rodriguez continued to support the company but did not participate directly in its day-to-day operations or governance.

Plant-Made Medicines

Designing plants to produce pharmaceuticals—the work that Rodriguez and his colleagues were pursuing—represented the second wave of agricultural biotechnology. The first wave concentrated on adding traits, such as insect resistance and herbicide tolerance, to edible crops—such as corn, canola, and soybeans—and to fiber crops such as cotton. For example, "RoundUp-Ready" soybeans, developed by Monsanto, were genetically engineered to be impervious to the herbicide RoundUp, allowing farmers to spray the field with weedkiller without hurting the soybean crop. "YieldGuard" corn plants were genetically engineered to resist the corn borer, a common insect pest. The second wave, of which Ventria was part, involved the use of genetic engineering to "phytomanufacture" protein pharmaceuticals and other commercially valuable compounds in plants.

Plant-made medicines, particularly those made in rice, held many real and potential benefits. First, it was too expensive to chemically synthesize anything but the smallest proteins. Most therapeutic proteins, therefore, were produced in mammalian or microbial cell cultures. This was costly and sometimes dangerous, as animal tissues could transmit viruses or prions (such as the infectious agents that caused "mad cow" disease). Second, plant-grown medicines could also be produced much less expensively than they could be using conventional, mammalian cell-culture technology. Third, rice and other agricultural crops could be stored at room temperature from months to years, allowing processing facilities to operate year-round and respond quickly to customer demand. Fourth, the well-established existing infrastructure for harvesting, storing, and milling rice could support the production of rice-based medical proteins. A final advantage of using rice was that medical proteins produced in food crops could be delivered orally without extensive purification. The hypoallergenic and hyperdigestible rice starch served as an ideal natural medium for the recombinant protein.[1]

On the other hand, the technology also carried potential risks. Most plant-made medicines were grown in crops also used for food, posing the danger that pharmacologically active plants might become mistakenly commingled with and contaminate the human or animal food supply. Pharmaceutical plants might crossbreed with wild plants or food crops, creating unwanted hybrids, or pose a threat to insects. Also, since the modified genes being transferred into plants often originated as human or animal genes, the potential ethical issues were profound. The public's reactions to plant-made pharmaceuticals were likely to be extreme, given the high benefits, potential risks, and deep moral quandaries posed by these new technologies.

One earlier incident, in particular, had highlighted the potential risk. In 2001, ProdiGene, a Texas biotech company, had planted a test plot of corn that had been genetically engineered to produce a pig vaccine. The following year, the same field was planted with conventional soybeans, which became contaminated by volunteer corn that had sprouted from the previous season's seeds. By the time this was discovered, the soybeans had been harvested and stored in a silo containing 500,000 bushels. The genetically modified corn tainted the entire lot of soybeans, which had to be destroyed. ProdiGene was fined $250,000 and had to pay for the cleanup. Although the contaminated soybeans never reached the food supply, some saw the incident as a warning of the possible risks of commingling.[2]

[1] Scott Deeter, "Prepared Remarks," House of Representatives, Small Business Committee, Hearing on Different Applications for Genetically Modified Crops, June 29, 2005.

[2] "Pharming Reaps Regulatory Changes," *http://pewagbiotech.org/buzz.*

In 2004, seven companies and research organizations in the United States held permits for field tests of genetically engineered pharmaceutical plants.[3] Most, like Ventria, were small, private firms that relied mainly on venture capital as they worked toward the goal of an initial public offering or acquisition by a larger firm. Many were thinly capitalized. In 2004, according to the Biotechnology Industry Organization (BIO), an industry trade association, 60 percent of all biotechnology firms had less than a two-year supply of cash on hand and 30 percent had less than a one-year supply. Reflecting a high concentration of professionals, wages in the biotechnology industry were relatively high, averaging $65,775 in 2004; top companies invested $130,000 per employee in research and development. With high wages and research costs, many of these firms had high burn rates. A successful product launch, according to BIO, could take 10 to 15 years and cost as much as $1 billion in private investment.[4]

Lactiva and Lysomin

In April 2002, Ventria's board appointed Deeter to succeed Hagie as president and CEO. Born in Kansas, Deeter had completed his undergraduate work in economics at the University of Kansas and had then gone on to earn an MBA at the University of Chicago and a Masters of Science at the London School of Economics. He had begun his career in the technology and life sciences group of the Wall Street investment bank Salomon Brothers. He then took a position with the agribusiness firm Cargill, where he worked on a joint venture with Hoffman LaRoche to make human health products from soybeans. From Cargill, Deeter moved to Koch Industries as vice president for agriculture, where he was involved in negotiations to buy Purina Mills in 1998. In 1999, Deeter left Koch to launch CyberCrops, a venture capital–backed website that hosted an online grain exchange service and provided news, weather, and other information to farmers. Deeter sold the business in April 2001, after the dot-com firm was unable to attract additional capital.[5]

Deeter's first task as the new CEO of Ventria was to help Rodriguez and the board winnow down the professor's long list of projects to one or two that had the greatest likelihood of successful commercialization. Deeter and his team analyzed some two dozen possible medically active proteins. They asked three key questions of each one. Did it meet a demonstrated need? Was another company already working on it? Could it be delivered orally or topically, as opposed to injected? Rodriguez later recalled,

> What we were looking for was a protein that was extremely valuable to human health and in extremely short supply, with no competition, that could be administered orally in a partially purified form.

---

[3] "Regulation of Plant-Based Pharmaceuticals," Congressional Research Service Report for Congress, March 8, 2005, p. 1. Other sources give a higher figure for the number of organizations involved in biopharming. See, for example, "Biopharming: The Emerging World Market of Plant-Based Therapeutics," *Theta Reports,* November 2002; "The Transgenic Plant Market—Profits from New Products and Novel Drugs," Drug and Market Development Corp., August 2002; and "World Agricultural Biotechnology: Transgenic Crops," Freedonia Industry Study, March 2002, cited in the *Federal Register* 68, no. 151 (April 6, 2003), p. 46435.

[4] "Biotechnology Industry Facts" and "Importation of Prescription Drugs," Biotechnology Industry Organization, *http://www.bio.org.* These figures provided by BIO are for the biotechnology industry as a whole, of which plant-made pharmaceuticals represent only a small fraction.

[5] Biographical information on Deeter appears at *http://www.ventria.com* and in press materials released in connection with the Kansas Day of Innovation, September 7, 2006, *http://www.kansasbio.org/news/pdf/8.7_panel.pdf.*

The proteins Deeter and his team selected were *lactoferrin* and *lysozyme*, two compounds naturally found in human breast milk. Medical researchers had long recognized that breast-fed babies suffered less from diarrhea than did bottle-fed babies. They had hypothesized that lactoferrin and lysozyme—both considered "natural antibiotics"—conferred some protection against bacterial gastrointestinal illness. Rodriguez had developed a process for producing these compounds abundantly in the grains of genetically modified rice plants. Since the 1960s, the standard treatment for severe diarrhea had been oral rehydration solution (ORS), a mixture of salts and sugars that had been credited with saving the lives of millions. Ventria's scientists believed that adding lactoferrin and lysozyme to ORS would improve the effectiveness of this commonly used therapy for gastrointestinal illness. The company branded its lactoferrin and lysozyme products *Lactiva* and *Lysomin*, respectively.

The potential market for such a product was huge, the company reasoned. The World Health Organization estimated that the world's children suffered 4 billion episodes of diarrhea each year. Nearly 2 million of these children died annually from complications of the disease, chiefly dehydration and malnutrition. Just 65 acres of pharmaceutical rice could generate 1,400 pounds of lactoferrin, enough to treat 650,000 children with dehydration, the company estimated.[6] It also believed that these compounds might be of value in the treatment of diarrhea suffered by tourists and military personnel and in the treatment of inflammatory bowel disease.[7] The company believed early adopters might include infant formula companies, drug companies that produced oral rehydration solution, and public health organizations like the Red Cross.

Regulation of Farmed Pharmaceuticals

In order to move forward with its plans to commercialize Lactiva and Lysomin, Ventria needed both federal and state regulatory approval. In 2004, the regulatory rules covering plant-made pharmaceuticals were complex and evolving. At the federal level, three agencies held partial jurisdiction over plant-made medicines.

FDA: The Food and Drug Administration (FDA) was responsible for the safety and effectiveness of food and medicines. Normally, a medicine produced in a genetically modified plant was subject to the same mandatory premarket approval procedures as any other medicine. However, Ventria had sought classification of Lactiva and Lysomin as "generally recognized as safe" (GRAS) food additives, which required a lower threshold for approval. A panel of scientific experts commissioned by the company had concluded that Lactiva and Lysomin met the GRAS standard, and the company had submitted these results to the FDA. In 2004, however, the FDA had not yet cleared Ventria's products for commercial sale. The FDA also maintained a "zero-tolerance" standard for pharmaceutical crop products in any food intended for animals or humans; any commingling of pharmaceutical crops and food crops was strictly forbidden. The FDA considered fields in which pharmaceutical crops were grown to be manufacturing facilities, and the agency had a right to inspect them. If necessary, it could condemn contaminated food and enjoin the manufacturer.

---

[6] "Tending the Fields: State and Federal Roles in the Oversight of Genetically Modified Crops," Pew Initiative on Food and Biotechnology, *http://pewagbiotech.com,* p. 97.

[7] Scott Deeter, "Prepared Remarks," House of Representatives, Small Business Committee, Hearing on Different Applications for Genetically Modified Crops, June 29, 2005.

EPA: The Environmental Protection Agency (EPA) was responsible for the environmental safety of food crops genetically engineered to contain pesticides or other substances potentially harmful to the environment. The agency's rules required pesticides—including those engineered into a plant—to have "no unreasonable adverse impact on the environment." Pesticide-containing plants required experimental use permits for most field tests. Because Ventria's rice did not contain pesticides, these rules did not apply to it.

USDA: For its part, the U.S. Department of Agriculture's Animal and Plant Health Inspection Service (known as APHIS) had oversight of genetically modified crops being tested in fields. Plants that were genetically modified to produce pharmaceuticals always required an APHIS permit, which generally specified acceptable field testing, storage, transportation, chain of custody, and auditing requirements. APHIS forwarded its permits to the relevant state agency, which could add its own requirements. The service also conducted its own field inspections; it inspected all pharmaceutical field trials at least annually.[8] Since 1997, Ventria had applied for and received dozens of permits from APHIS to field-test its pharmaceutical crops.

In 1986, the federal government adopted a Coordinated Framework for the Regulation of Biotechnology, which proposed to use existing agencies and laws to regulate the products of biotechnology. Michael Rodemeyer, former executive director of the Pew Initiative on Food and Biotechnology, explained the complexities of this regulatory approach for both regulators and those they regulated:

> On one level . . . the Coordinated Framework is very easy to describe. The FDA is responsible for food safety, the EPA is responsible for microbes and pesticides, and APHIS is responsible for all plants. In practice, however, it is much more complex than that. Why? In part, because some products fall into multiple categories. For example, a corn plant that has been engineered to produce its own pesticide is a plant, a pesticide, and a food, so it falls under the purview of all three agencies. In addition, each of the three agencies uses different laws to govern the products of biotechnology, and most of these laws were passed well before the advent of biotechnology.[9]

The consequence of this system, for biotechnology firms, was a complex regulatory landscape with multiple, overlapping requirements.

California Rice Industry

In California, genetically engineered rice required the approval not only of federal and state regulators, but also indirectly of the rice industry itself.

California was home to a major rice industry. The state was the leading producer of short- and medium-grain rice in the United States and second only to Arkansas in total volume of rice produced. (Other major rice-producing states were Missouri, Texas, Louisiana, and Mississippi.) In 2003, California produced 1.75 million tons of rice on 507,000 acres. Almost all of the state's rice fields lay in a swath of land abutting the Sacramento River, a broad valley that relied on the river and its tributaries for irrigation. The crop generated annual sales of more than $500 million.

---

[8] "Regulation of Plant-Based Pharmaceuticals," CRS Report for Congress, p. 4.

[9] "Opportunities and Challenges: States and the Federal Coordinated Framework Governing Agricultural Biotechnology," Pew Initiative on Food and Biotechnology, May 2006, pp. 9–10.

Forty percent of California rice was exported, mainly to Japan, Taiwan, Korea, and Turkey. The rest was consumed domestically in food, pet food, and beer. Although the United States produced only 2 percent of the world's rice, it accounted for 14 percent of the international rice trade; the nation was second only to Thailand and Vietnam in rice exports.[10] However, the U.S. share of the world rice trade was declining; it had dropped from 28 percent in 1975 to 12 percent in 2003.[11]

Rice producers in California, as in much of the developed world, used highly sophisticated technology. Farmers used laser-guided grading equipment to position perimeter levees and level their fields precisely to enable an even covering of five inches of water during the growing season. From the fourth week in April to the second week in May, weather permitting, skilled pilots used low-flying, small aircraft guided by global positioning systems to deposit pregerminated seeds onto the flooded fields. Within a few days, the plants would emerge above the surface of the water, and within a few weeks the fields would be densely covered with bright green, grasslike stalks. The grains of rice—the plant's seeds—developed in late summer, when the rice was about three feet tall. When the rice matured in September and early October, farmers drained the fields and harvested the crop with combines, which separated the grain from the stalks. After the harvest, the rice was transported to a drying facility and from there to a mill. At the mill, the rice was processed to remove the inedible hull and then either sold as brown rice or further polished into white rice. Many mills used laser sorters to remove broken or immature grains.[12]

The two stages of rice production, farming and milling, defined the two major segments of the industry. California was home to more than 2,000 rice farmers, many of whom continued to operate as family-owned businesses. They were organized through their trade association, the Rice Producers of California. Rice mills, which required significant capital investment, tended to be owned by larger organizations. Leading millers in California included agribusiness giants ADM, Far West Rice, Pacific International, and Sun West. The Farmers Rice Cooperative, owned by a cooperative of 800 growers, also operated several mills.

To protect the interests of its rice industry, the California state government had established a body known as the California Rice Commission (CRC), declaring, "The production and milling of rice in this state is . . . affected with a public interest."[13] The commission's work was supported by an assessment on farmers and millers, based on their volume of production. The CRC was authorized by law to "promote the sale of rice, educate and instruct the wholesale and retail trade with respect to the proper handling and selling [of] rice, and conduct scientific research."[14]

In 2000, California had passed the Rice Certification Act (known as AB 2622), empowering the CRC to appoint an advisory board, which would have the right to review any varieties of rice "having characteristics of commercial impact," except for rice planted for research purposes on 50 or fewer acres. The enabling legislation stated,

There is a growing need to maintain the identity of various types of rice to satisfy increasing consumer demand for specialty rices. This demand requires providing the industry with the ability to establish the terms and conditions for the production

---

[10] California Rice Commission Statistical Report, May 1, 2005.

[11] "Tending the Fields," p. 92.

[12] Information from the California Farm Bureau Federation, the U.S. Rice Foodservice, and personal observation.

[13] California Food and Agricultural Code, Section 71005.

[14] California Legislative Counsel's Digest, *http://www.leginfo.ca/gov.*

and handling of rice in order to minimize the potential for the commingling of various types of rice, and in order to prevent commingling where reconditioning is infeasible or impossible.[15]

By statute, the advisory board was composed of four producers (farmers), four handlers (millers), and four public representatives.[16] The job of the advisory board was to recommend to the Secretary of Agriculture "proposed regulations [on] planting, producing, harvesting, transporting, drying, storing, or otherwise handling rice . . . including, but not limited to, seed application requirements, field buffer zones, handling requirements, and identity preservation requirements." Once the secretary had received a recommendation from the advisory board, he was required within 30 days to issue the proposed regulation, decline and give the advisory board a written explanation, or request additional information.[17] Although the advisory board could not legally prohibit the production of any particular rice, including genetically modified rice, as a practical matter its recommendations to the secretary carried considerable weight. As the CRC itself pointed out, "No other commodity in the U.S. has a similar mechanism to protect its industry."[18]

The CRC Advisory Board Considers Ventria's Protocol

In 2003, as Ventria ramped up to commercial-scale production, Deeter and his team made plans to expand their acreage of rice planted. Their goal was to plant 120 acres during the 2004 growing season, an amount that, for the first time, exceeded the 50-acre rule and therefore fell under the CRC advisory board's authority. Accordingly, the company began discussions with members of the advisory board to develop an acceptable production protocol. During these talks, Ventria stipulated that its rice had a "commercial impact" and agreed to a number of provisions to address the rice industry's concerns. For example, the company agreed to establish buffer zones around its plots, to transport its rice in covered trucks, and to use dedicated processing equipment.

On Monday, March 29, 2004, the advisory board of the CRC held its regular meeting at the Best Western Bonanza Inn in Yuba City, in the heart of the Sacramento Valley rice belt. Heading the agenda was a discussion of Ventria's draft protocol. Discussion was animated. Members who had been involved in the discussions with Ventria recommended that the board approve the draft protocol. Several farmers, however, expressed concern that the presence of genetically modified rice in California posed a serious commercial threat, particularly to the state's export markets. Their concern seemed to be validated by the Japanese Rice Retailers Association, which wrote the advisory board:

> From the viewpoint of rice wholesalers and retailers in Japan, it is certain that the commercialization of GM [genetically modified] rice in the U.S. will evoke a distrust of U.S. rice as a whole among Japanese consumers, since we think that it is practically impossible to guarantee no GM rice contamination in non-GM U.S. rice. As you know, most Japanese consumers react quite negatively to GM

---

[15] Ibid.

[16] The public representatives were drawn, one each, from the California Crop Improvement Association, the California Warehouse Association, the California Cooperative Rice Research Foundation, and the University of California.

[17] Legislative Counsel's Digest.

[18] "California Rice Certification Act," California Rice Commission: *Serving the California Rice Industry* [newsletter], 6, no. 3 (March/April 2004).

crops. If the GM rice is actually commercialized in the U.S., we shall strongly request the Japanese government to take necessary measures not to import any California rice to Japan.[19]

Representatives from Californians for GE-Free Agriculture[20] and the Center for Food Safety both submitted written comments expressing opposition to the protocol.

After further debate and the passage of several amendments to strengthen the protocol—including a provision that Ventria plant its rice in southern California, far from the Sacramento Valley—the advisory board voted 6 to 5 to approve Ventria's protocols. Voting in favor were all four public members, one farmer, and one miller. Most of the farmers and millers voted "nay."[21] Whether for or against, all seemed to agree that the industry was moving into uncharted water. "There's a learning curve here for producers," said Ronald Lee, a farmer. "Some have some knowledge. Some have very little. We're entering new territory here."[22]

At the request of the company, the CRC recommended "emergency status" for Ventria's protocol review. This designation would give the California Secretary of Agriculture 10 days to approve or reject it, without a period of public comment, so the company could move forward in time for the spring 2004 planting season. Over the next 10 days, the Secretary of Agriculture was lobbied from both sides. The Biotechnology Industry Association expressed its support for the emergency status:

> [We] are writing to express strong support for your authorization of a protocol approved by the California Rice Commission. . . . Plant-made pharmaceuticals offer an exciting approach to scalable, economically attractive biopharmaceutical manufacturing, producing broad access to exciting new health products to address many of the most prevalent human diseases.[23]

Several environmental and consumer groups asked the secretary to deny the request for an emergency exemption. A number of rice farmers also spoke out in the press. "Consumers in Japan and many of California's other major rice export markets have already shown strong resistance to GM crops," said Greg Massa, a grower of organic rice. "Approval of this [Ventria] rice could shatter our years of hard work in building these markets and spell trouble for all California rice farmers."[24] Joe Carrancho, a grower and former president of the Rice Producers of California, commented, "If the Japanese have the perception— underline perception—that our rice has [genetically modified organisms] in it, then we're done. You can put a bullet in our head." He and environmentalists "may be apart on some issues, but on this one we're together," he said.[25]

On April 9, the Secretary of Agriculture rejected the recommendation for emergency status for the protocol review, saying, "It is clear that the public wants an opportunity to comment prior to any authorization to plant."[26] He called for more information about federal permits and asked the CRC to consult with affected groups.

---

[19] Quoted in Greg Massa, "Pharmaceutical Rice Is a No-Grow," *Sacramento Bee,* May 14, 2004.

[20] In this context, GE refers to "genetically engineered."

[21] Minutes of the March 29, 2004, AB 2622 Advisory Board, provided to the author by the president of the California Rice Commission.

[22] "State's Rice Farmers Fear Biotech Incursion," *San Francisco Chronicle,* April 8, 2004.

[23] Biotechnology Industry Association, letter to the Honorable A. G. Kawamura, April 5, 2004.

[24] "Plan Calls for Altered Rice Crops in State," *San Diego Union-Tribune,* March 27, 2004.

[25] "State's Rice Farmers Fear Biotech Incursion."

[26] "Modified Rice Won't Be Planted," *San Francisco Chronicle,* April 10, 2004; "Protein Rice Suffers Setback," *Sacramento Bee,* April 10, 2004.

Ventria's Opponents Mobilize

Even after the secretary's decision, the controversy continued to mount. In July, four advocacy organizations—Friends of the Earth, the Center for Food Safety, Consumers Union, and Environment California—produced a detailed report detailing their concerns about pharmaceutical rice in California. The groups submitted their report to the California Department of Food and Agriculture, the California EPA, and the California Department of Health Services, as well as to the public. In the document, the groups called for "a moratorium on the cultivation of Ventria's pharmaceutical rice and other pharm crops."[27]

The activist alliance made four arguments for a moratorium on pharmaceutical rice. First, it argued that contamination of food rice by genetically modified pharmaceutical rice grown outdoors was "inevitable," because of multiple potential pathways:

> Contamination of human foods with plant-made pharmaceuticals can occur through dispersal of seed or pollen. Wildlife, especially waterfowl, can transport seeds for long distances, as can extreme weather events such as floods or tornadoes. Harvesting equipment can carry seed residues to conventional fields, seeds can be spilled from trucks, or unharvested seeds can sprout as volunteers amid the following year's crop. Cross-pollination occurs at considerable distances in high winds or by insect, even with self-pollinating crops such as rice.[28]

The report argued that Ventria's protocols did not offer sufficient protection against contamination:

> The lack of detailed plans to prevent birds from spreading the pharm rice is particularly disturbing. California's Central Valley is one of the most important wintering areas for waterfowl in North America. Viable seed are known to pass through the gut of many waterfowl species, making waterfowl effective dispersal agents for many wetland plant species, including rice. . . .
>
> Ventria's protocol also does not deal with the possibility of seed dispersal through flooding. . . . Historical records show that floods of various magnitude occur not infrequently in the Sacramento Valley. . . .
>
> Ventria's . . . one-year fallow period following cultivation of its pharm rice means a greater likelihood of pharm rice volunteers contaminating a commercial rice crop grown subsequently in the same field. . . .
>
> The 100-foot isolation distance from food-grade rice . . . may not be adequate to prevent cross-pollination.[29]

What would happen if Ventria's rice did contaminate the food supply? Once commingling had occurred, the report continued, the potential for adverse impacts to human health was great. Possible consequences included infections, allergies, and autoimmune disorders:

> While human lactoferrin has antimicrobial properties, it paradoxically poses the potential hazard of exacerbating infections by certain pathogens capable of using it as a source of needed iron. Such pathogens include bacteria that cause

[27] "Pharmaceutical Rice in California: Potential Risks to Consumers, the Environment, and the California Rice Industry," Friends of the Earth, Center for Food Safety, Consumers Union, and Environment California, July 2004, p. 1.

[28] Ibid., p. 6.

[29] Ibid., p. 7.

gonorrhea and meningitis, as well as [those] implicated in causing ulcers and certain forms of stomach cancer. . . . Ventria's rice-expressed lysozyme and lactoferrin have two characteristics of proteins that cause food allergies: resistance to digestion and to breakdown by heat. . . . Pharmaceutical proteins generated by inserting human genes into plants . . . are usually different from their natural human counterparts. These differences may cause the body to perceive them as foreign, resulting in immune system responses.[30]

Finally, Ventria's rice could have serious environmental consequences if it crossbred with existing weed species, creating noxious "super weeds," the report argued:

Ventria's rice-produced pharmaceuticals have antibacterial and antifungal properties. If these traits are passed to related weed species such as wild and annual red rice, they could lend these weeds a fitness boost, promoting their spread.[31]

Moving Forward

In discussions with representatives of the CRC advisory board over the past year and a half, Deeter and his team had offered numerous concessions to address the concerns of rice farmers and others. The company had agreed to grow rice many miles away from any rice grown for food. It had promised to use dedicated equipment for field production, storage, and transportation and to use only processing equipment that was restricted to bio-engineered rice or had been thoroughly sanitized before reuse. The company had agreed to keep detailed logs and to allow third-party inspections. None of this, however, had been enough to satisfy the company's critics. In biotechnology, things always seemed to take longer, cost more, and face hurdles that could not have been anticipated when the company was started. Now another planting season had come and gone, and Ventria's investors appeared no closer to successful commercialization than they had been a year earlier.

Discussion Questions

1. What is the problem facing Scott Deeter and Ventria?
2. What groups have a stake in Ventria's actions? Identify the relevant stakeholders and for each, state its interests and sources of power.
3. What options might emerge from a dialogue between Ventria and its relevant stakeholders?
4. If Ventria chooses to employ a political action strategy, how might it go about influencing relevant regulators?
5. If Ventria chooses not to engage in dialogue or political action (or dialogue and political action are unsuccessful), what other options does the company have?
6. What do you think Ventria should do now, and why?

[30] Ibid., p. 3.
[31] Ibid., p. 3.

The Solidarity Fund and Gildan Activewear, Inc.

In late 2003, officers of the Solidarity Fund, a large pension fund operated by the Québec Federation of Labor (QFL), met to discuss what to do about their investments in Gildan Activewear, a Montreal-based textile and garment company.

Over the previous year, public controversy had swirled around the company's labor practices in its manufacturing plants in Central America. In January 2002, a television documentary aired by the Canadian Broadcasting Corporation (CBC) charged that Gildan's workers in Honduras earned less than a living wage, worked long shifts, had excessively high production quotas, and breathed air filled with fabric dust. Just a few months later, a labor rights group issued a report claiming Gildan had fired Honduran workers who had tried to organize a union. These charges presented the Fund, which owned 14 percent of Gildan, with a difficult dilemma. The textile company had been an excellent investment; its stock had risen in value from just over $2 (Canadian) per share when the Fund first invested in 1995 to nearly $12. However, if the allegations were true, the company's practices would run counter to the basic values of the Fund. Should the pension fund try to influence Gildan's conduct? Should it sell its shares in protest? Or should it do neither?

The Solidarity Fund

The Québec Federation of Labor (QFL), an alliance of unions in the Canadian Province of Québec representing more than half a million workers, founded the Solidarity Fund in 1983. At the time, Québec was mired in a deep recession. High interest rates had put many small and medium-sized businesses into bankruptcy, and nearly a quarter of the province's young people and more than 14 percent of its workforce were unemployed. In an effort to rethink the role of unions in promoting economic development, the QFL launched a new fund designed to invest its members' retirement savings in local companies. With the unionization rate in Québec above 40 percent (compared with around 30 percent in Canada as a whole and around 13 percent in the United States), the federation believed it could have a significant impact.

The Solidarity Fund had two central goals. Its first goal was to democratize access to professionally managed retirement accounts. A network of volunteer local representatives signed up shareholders who directed savings to the Fund. Unionized workers made up close to 60 percent of the Fund's shareholders (the rest were unaffiliated individuals). Participants typically used the Fund as a supplement to an employer-provided pension.

This case was written by Pierre Batellier and Emmanuel Raufflet, HEC Montreal, and abridged and edited by permission of the authors by Anne T. Lawrence. Copyright 2009 © by the authors. All rights reserved.

Under law, savings invested in the Fund were locked in until retirement, except in special circumstances such as job loss or periods of retraining. The Fund's second mission was to support job growth in Québec, either through long-term investment in small and medium-sized local companies or by investing in outside companies whose activities benefited the province.

Although the Fund sought to give its shareholders a fair return, it also used nonfinancial criteria in selecting investments. Its managers looked to invest in companies with good working conditions, positive relations with local communities, and a commitment to environmental responsibility. It also looked for companies that were open to partnering with institutional shareholders, such as the Fund. The Fund did not, however, have an absolute requirement that a company in which it invested be unionized.

As part of its due diligence, when it first invested in a company—and later when it increased its investment or divested—the Fund prepared a social audit. Between 1983 and 2002, the Fund team prepared nearly 2,000 social audits. Fund specialists would visit a company to gather data, observe working conditions, and meet with company managers and employee representatives. The social audits, which were not made public, sometimes identified issues of concern and made recommendations for improvement, which were often addressed in collaboration with the company's management. Once invested, the Fund played an active role in the company as a shareholder, sometimes by placing a member on the board of directors.

Many of the Fund's 400 employees, particularly its development officers and subscription staff, came from a union background and were loyal to the interests of organized labor. The Fund's financial officers, by contrast, were generally trained in the field of finance and saw their main goal as meeting the Fund's financial goals. Major investment decisions often reflected a creative tension between the unionists and the financiers. The final decision, however, rested with the Fund's 17-person board, 11 of whom were union representatives. The president, general secretary, and other executives of the QFL often came from high positions in QFL-affiliated unions, such as those representing metalworkers, Canadian public service employees, and construction workers.[1]

Some two decades after its launch, the Solidarity Fund had 500,000 shareholders and net assets of more than $4.6 billion, making it a crucial financial player in Québec's economy. (This dollar amount, and all others cited later in this case, are given in Canadian dollars, unless otherwise noted.) It had invested in the start-up, development, and growth of 1,800 Québec companies, some of them leading success stories, such as the transport company Transforce, the pharmaceutical company Biochem Pharma, the travel agency Transat, and the insurance firm SSQ. One of its biggest success stories was Gildan Activewear, Inc.

Gildan Activewear, Inc.

Glenn and Greg Chamandy, two brothers from a family of textile entrepreneurs, and their associate Edwin B. Tisch founded Gildan Textiles, Inc., in Montreal in 1984. (The company later changed its name to Gildan Activewear, or—in French—*Les Vêtements de Sport Gildan.*) The company's goal was "to be the world leader in quality knitwear for the North American and international markets, with the lowest operating costs."[2] The company's core business was producing low-cost T-shirts and fleece garments that could

---

[1] Solidarity Fund QFL Board of Directors, *www.fondsftq.com/internetfonds.nsf/vWebTAN/AprCon.*

[2] *www.gildan.com.*

be customized by institutional clients such as schools, universities, and companies with their own logos and designs. Its strategy was to compete on the basis of low prices, good quality, and fast delivery times through vertical integration of its supply chain. In contrast to many textile manufacturers, which relied on subcontractors, Gildan generally owned and operated its own factories. When it did turn to subcontractors, it required that the subcontractor be a dedicated operation, supplying to it alone.

In its early years, Gildan maintained all its operations in Québec, which had been home to a thriving textile industry throughout much of the 20th century. The manufacture of T-shirts required multiple steps: the fabric had to be knitted, washed, and dyed, and then cut and sewn into garments. Gildan operated three factories in Montreal, one each for knitting, dyeing, and sewing, as well as a corporate headquarters; collectively, these operations at their peak employed more than 1,000 workers. But in the early 1990s, in an effort to compete with its main rivals, Fruit of the Loom and Hanes, Gildan began moving some assembly operations, particularly sewing, to subcontractors in Mexico. In addition, the company decided it wanted its own manufacturing capability abroad, and it devised a plan to buy or build several state-of-the art factories in Honduras, a small country in Central America. This was a risky move in the short term, and several banks Gildan approached for financing turned the company down.

In 1995, Gildan contacted the Solidarity Fund for help in financing its expansion. In reviewing this request, the Fund recognized that Gildan's expansion abroad would likely cost some production jobs in Québec, but thought it would also protect and possibly expand Canadian jobs in design, marketing, finance, and other headquarters functions. Some manufacturing would also remain, it concluded. In early 1996, the Fund invested $3 million directly in Gildan stock and lent the company another $3 million.

Gildan's operations, both in North America and Latin America, proved to be extremely efficient, and in the years from 1996 to 2001, Gildan's annual growth ranged from 20 to 30 percent. Very quickly, Gildan took market share from its two leading competitors, Fruit of the Loom and Hanes. Feeling threatened, those companies launched major advertising campaigns to counter their new Canadian rival, but to no avail. Gildan's stack of contracts grew, and in 1998, its sales reached nearly $200 million with a market share of more than 10 percent.

The same year, Gildan was listed for the first time on the Toronto and New York stock exchanges. Hoping to raise an additional $60 million in capital through its initial public offering, Gildan was disappointed to obtain only $30 million. Once again, Gildan turned to the Fund, which provided a loan in 1998 worth $15 million (on top of $12 million in 1997). In 1998 and 1999, Gildan purchased two factories in Rio Nance and El Progreso, Honduras, which were equipped with new equipment and modern technology. Gildan began to transfer jobs from Montreal to Honduras and had soon doubled its production and sales volume.

Gildan pursued a vertical integration strategy, organizing different stages of production to exploit the relative competitive advantages of various locales. The sewing was done in Mexico and Honduras, where labor was cheap; the cutting, in the United States to reduce customs duties; and the dyeing and knitting, in Québec where water and electricity were abundant. The company's acquisition in 2001 of a spinning mill in Long Sault, Ontario, which guaranteed a steady supply of cotton yarn, was the final step in its vertical integration strategy.

By the end of 2001, Gildan was producing 14 million dozen T-shirts annually. The company had 8,000 employees in North and Central America. With sales of more than $500 million, it for the first time surpassed its leading competitor, Fruit of the Loom, which filed for Chapter 11 bankruptcy protection the same year. During the 2002 financial year,

Gildan posted record profits of $42 million, despite closing its factory on Clark Street in Montreal. The same year, salaries of its three top executives collectively rose from $1.5 million to $13.3 million—an increase of more than 800 percent. Gildan's president, Greg Chamandy, earned $5.8 million (mainly in stock options), going from 110th to 6th on the list of best-paid business executives in Québec.[3]

Gildan was proving to be an excellent business partner for the Fund; it repaid principal and interest on the Fund's loans in good time, and its stock continued to appreciate. The Fund felt it had contributed to the growth of a Québec company that was undergoing strong expansion and had a solid financial base characterized by limited debt and significant cash flow.

Honduras

Gildan believed that much of its success hinged on its decision to move a large share of its production to Honduras. In the early 2000s, Honduras, a small nation in Central America with a population of 6 million, remained one of the poorest countries in the Western Hemisphere, with a GDP per capita of less than $1,000 (U.S.) per year. Two-thirds of Hondurans lived below the poverty level, and 44 percent lived on less than $2 (U.S.) a day. In 2000, Honduras ranked 119th (out of 179) in the world on the Human Development Index (HDI).[4]

In the early 1990s, the government of Honduras began to set up export processing zones (EPZs), designated areas in which foreign companies were exempt from import duties, taxes on equipment, property and capital, and national and municipal taxes on revenues for the first 10 years of operation. Companies could return home with no limits on repatriating profits or capital. In 1998, the government extended those advantages across its entire territory. Some 30 industrial parks were built, most of them private, mainly near Puerto Cortes, the leading Caribbean seaport, and in San Pedro Sula, one of the country's major ground transportation hubs. The industrial parks and the EPZs were considered offshore operations, and duties were charged on products made there for sale in Honduras.

The clothing and textile industry was quick to respond to these incentives and, by 2002, accounted for 90 percent of the companies operating in the EPZs. The garment industry created 100,000 jobs in Honduras between 1992 and 2002. Eighty percent of them were held by women, most between 18 and 25 years of age. During this period, Honduras became the third largest exporter of textiles and apparel to the United States.[5] In a country where unemployment reached 28 percent in 2001, the *maquiladoras* (foreign-owned factories) and the more than 125,000 jobs they provided had become a vital part of the Honduran economy.

In 2002, the basic minimum hourly wage was 63 cents (97 cents, all costs included), or $5.58 (U.S.) per day. Under Honduran law, the maximum allowable workday was 13 hours, and the maximum allowable workweek was 44 hours for daytime work. Overtime and night shift work were compensated at a rate that was 25 percent above the regular wage. Employees also received social security contributions, as required by Honduran law, and an extra 13th month's pay (called an *Aguinaldo*), traditional in many Latin American countries.[6]

[3] SEDAR, Circulaire de la direction, Gildan, February 9, 2003.

[4] Panorama de l'espace Caraïbes 2004, INSEE, *www.insee.fr/fr/insee_regions/guadeloupe/publi/pano_economie.htm.*

[5] The investment climate in Honduras is described at *http://strategis.ic.gc.ca/epic/internet/inimr-ri.nsf/fr/gr123052f.html.*

[6] Central American Business Consultants: *http://www.ca-bc.com/zip_internacional.*

Although unions were permitted in Honduras, they were generally weak. In 1954, a general strike had laid the basis for the Honduran union movement and led to a new labor code that guaranteed workers' right to form unions. But in the early 2000s, only about 20 poorly trained inspectors enforced the labor code. The high turnover of both firms and workers in the *maquiladoras* tended to limit union success. Mounting violence associated with youth gangs (*maras*) established a climate of fear and mistrust that also discouraged union organizing. Within the *maquiladoras,* only about 1 in 10 workers were union members (compared with about 25 percent in Honduras as a whole). Many workers had turned to other institutions for protection, including local development agencies, labor support groups, and churches.[7]

By 2002, Gildan had more than 5,000 employees in Honduran factories that it owned directly. Some of those jobs had been transferred from factories in Montreal, including one on Clark Street that shut down permanently in 2002. At the time of that closing, Gildan's management talked publicly about "problems in finding labor to work in [our Canadian] sew[ing] factories. In the South meanwhile, there is a pool of desperate labor."[8] The Canadian workers were more productive, but the difference in salary was enormous: an employee in Montreal earned more in one hour than a Honduran did in one day.

The Solidarity Fund's Social Audits of Gildan

In 1999, Solidarity Fund's management, concerned about the transfer of jobs from Québec to Honduras, asked Daniel Bourcier, one of the Fund's development officers, to undertake a new social audit of the company.

After visiting the Montreal factory on Clark Street as a basis for comparison, Bourcier left for a week's visit to Honduras, accompanied by Gildan's executive vice president, Edwin B. Tisch. Gildan put a car and driver at Bourcier's disposal and gave him full access to its staff, facilities, and books. During that week, the Fund officer visited three Gildan facilities and three subcontractors in the San Pedro Sula area and another in Tegucigalpa and also met with Gildan's local managers.

During his visit, Bourcier was pleasantly surprised by Gildan's newly constructed factories. Located in closed compounds with armed guards at the gate, the modern buildings were equipped with good lighting and up-to-date sewing machines. However, Bourcier identified three issues of concern. The first was dilapidated facilities and substandard working conditions in plants that supplied Gildan. The audit recommended that Gildan cease all dealings with these contractors. The second issue was the high level of cotton dust in the plants—well above standards acceptable under Canadian occupational safety laws.

The third issue involved the production system in the Gildan factories, under which workers were paid based on the productivity of their team of 12 people. The more each team produced, the higher the pay of each member. Each team was responsible for its own discipline. A quick worker would be given a green flag, and one who was slower, an orange flag. If a worker was much slower than her colleagues, the work team could give her a red flag and send her back to the sewing school, causing her a significant loss of income. The social audit found it unacceptable that Gildan had transferred responsibility for discipline from management to the work team.

---

[7] UN Committee on Economic, Social, and Cultural Rights, July 2001.

[8] Katia Gagnon, "Gildan, les rois du t-shirt (Gildan: the T-Shirt Kings)," *La Presse,* March 24, 2001.

After the audit had been completed, the Fund presented its concerns to management. Gildan responded that its production system was completely legal, and sending people for retraining was rare. Gildan also insisted that its system gave workers salaries much higher than the minimum wage. Moreover, the company said, the workers could always form a union if they were dissatisfied. The Solidarity Fund decided after this conversation to maintain its investments in Gildan, at least for the time being, but it remained concerned.

Public Controversy

In 2002, the Canadian Broadcasting Corporation (CBC) television program *Disclosure* ran an exposé entitled "Sewing Discontent." The show's producers had investigated allegedly deplorable working conditions in Gildan's El Progreso factory in Honduras. The report mentioned extremely high production quotas, wages that did not cover even basic needs, wages based on productivity, supervised breaks, 11-hour days, poor air quality in the shops, illegal firings, and forced pregnancy tests. In one scene, the program showed young women working at a furious pace in noisy and dusty conditions.

Mackie Vadacchino, Gildan's vice president for corporate affairs, denied these allegations, saying,

> We do have excellent working conditions. . . . Many people want to work for Gildan because of our wages, because of our benefits, because of our facilities. . . . One of the visions of [the founders] has always been to prove to the world that this industry can be profitable, and not just profitable but very profitable, and maintain excellent working conditions for their employees. . . . We've become an industry leader in a relatively short period of time. However, there are others that aren't so happy about us having gained that market share. . . . I think that [the employees] lied to you. . . . I think that they were coerced by someone, coached by someone, to say things to you to make us look bad.[9]

After the CBC exposé, the Maquila Solidarity Network (MSN), a North American labor rights organization, and Equipo de Monitorio Independiente de Honduras (EMIH), an independent nonprofit monitoring agency in Honduras, undertook a review of Gildan's practices in Honduras. Several months later, MSN gave Gildan its preliminary report and asked for comments. Their findings included

> . . . wages that do not meet basic needs, excessively high production targets, the impact of the 4 × 4 work schedule (4 consecutive 11-hour workdays), and the effects of the intensive pace of production on women workers' health and family life, failure to provide day care and nursing facilities as required by law, lack of freedom of association, and workers' belief that new employees are tested for pregnancy and those found to be pregnant would be fired.[10]

That same month, MSN also received reports from Honduras that 38 workers at the company's El Progreso factory had been fired shortly after applying to the Ministry of Labor to register a union. At MSN's request, EMIH interviewed the workers and drafted a report on the circumstances surrounding the firings. When MSN representatives met with Gildan to discuss the findings, the company denied that union activity had been the

---

[9] "The Gildan Story," *Disclosure*, CBC, *www.cbc.ca/disclosure/archives/0222_gildan/story.html.*

[10] MSN Gildan Campaign Updates Gildan, *http://en.maquilasolidarity.org/gildan.*

cause of any dismissals at the El Progreso plant. It also refused to reinstate the fired workers or to contact the Ministry of Labor to determine if the workers had applied to register their union prior to the firings. MSN called on the company to cooperate with an independent investigation into the firings and other workplace issues documented in the MSN/EMIH report.

Gildan's Social Responsibility Initiatives

Gildan itself—as well as some others in government and the community—held a contrary view that the firm was an exemplary employer.

In 2003, Gildan accepted the Award for Excellence in Corporate Social and Ethical Responsibility. Sponsored by the Nexen Corporation, this award was given to companies that had directly helped developing countries or countries in transition to progress socially and economically. In announcing the award, Susan Whelan, Canada's Minister for International Cooperation, praised the company as

> a prime example of how a company can combine business success with corporate social responsibility. Gildan's employees and business partners benefit from a code of ethics and behavior that values diversity, dignity, fairness, and equal opportunity for all.[11]

Whelan referred to Gildan's own code of ethics, which it attached to contracts given to its business partners and subcontractors. Those partners and sources had to comply with the code or risk the cancellation of their contract. The company had introduced an audit procedure to check for compliance. Gildan management described the process of auditing: "The various factories undergo several inspections a month. We make sure they employ no one under 18 years of age, and that the environment is acceptable and safe and comfortable."[12]

In its 2003 annual report, Gildan emphasized that it offered its employees in Honduras

> well-paying jobs with attractive benefits. . . . Gildan's Honduran employees work in modern air-conditioned and clean facilities and their wages are generally twice the national minimum wage for the apparel sector. The company provides many benefits, such as access to free medical assistance, subsidized transportation to and from work, subsidized meals, and filtered water. The company also empowers workers by providing them the opportunity to upgrade their skill sets and education levels. School classes are offered so employees can earn their diplomas, and extensive on-the-job training is also provided to employees. In addition, Gildan sponsors family days, where employees are encouraged to invite relatives to visit the facility and share lunch with them at the company's expense, in order to foster employees' pride about their jobs and for their relatives to better understand the type of work they do.[13]

Above all, Gildan insisted, it provided jobs in a country with rampant unemployment, especially among women. At the same time, Gildan highlighted its environmental achievements. According to the 2003 annual report, these included

---

[11] Gildan *2003 Annual Report*, p. 23, *http://gildan.com/corporate/downloads/annual_report_2003_en.pdf.*

[12] Campaign Updates.

[13] Gildan *2003 Annual Report.*

the operation of biological wastewater treatment systems in Honduras, the production of environmentally friendly products, and the use of safe, clean, and energy-efficient manufacturing procedures and inputs. . . . All chemicals, dyes, and materials that are used in Gildan production facilities are selected and monitored to ensure that they have been approved for use by the appropriate regulatory authorities, and that they present no adverse effects to health or the environment. In addition, production processes are controlled to ensure reduced energy and water consumption and to minimize effluent discharge.[14]

The Controversy Continues

Even as Gildan touted its own social and environmental responsibility, it continued to attract criticism from NGOs and activists. At the 2003 annual shareholders' meeting, MSN, Oxfam Canada, and Amnesty International publicly accused Gildan of illegally firing employees for union organizing at Gildan's El Progreso factory. They also cited Gildan's failure to give a reason for the firings, threats by supervisors regarding union activities, and failure to respond to three summons from government workplace inspectors. The Solidarity Fund, along with bulk purchasers of Gildan products, including the state of Maine and several universities, joined the NGOs in requesting an independent, third-party investigation of the firings for union organizing, and recommended to Gildan that it speed up its application for membership in the SA8000 (a set of standards developed by Social Accountability International). (Gildan had earlier indicated it planned to do so.)

Under pressure to allow an independent investigation of the allegations at El Progreso, Gildan's management asked the Fund whether, as a longtime partner and investor, it would be willing to conduct the investigation. Although this was not the Fund's preferred approach, it nevertheless agreed to do so. At the end of March 2003, Fund officers Bourcier and Audette left for their week's mission in Honduras. The first few days were devoted to gathering information at meetings with representatives from the union, the main labor federation, EMIH, and the Jesuits (a Catholic religious order), as well as with labor law experts. They collected documentation, including photocopies of the request for unionization filed by the workers with their signatures. The final day was devoted to factory visits and an examination of internal documents, made available by Gildan management. Recalled Bourcier,

> In the documents we obtained, we had the list of fired workers and the list of signatories to the request for union accreditation. The names were the same. So we opened the files, and found copies of the severance checks made out to the workers. I could see they all had the same letter of resignation, almost to the letter.

After checking that the productivity of the workers who had been let go was at least as high as the average, the Fund's auditors were convinced that the workers had been fired for trying to form a union.

Pressure on the company grew even stronger in July 2003, when EMIH and MSN released their report, *A Canadian Success Story? Gildan Activewear: T-Shirts, Free Trade and Worker Rights,* which detailed their evidence of bad-faith practices and abuses of worker rights. The report reiterated the request that Gildan apply corrective measures, including rehiring the fired workers.

[14] Ibid, pp. 24–25.

Gildan categorically denied the charges made by both the Fund and MSN/EMIH, explaining that the firings were the result of a downturn in the industry. In addition, Gildan reiterated that it maintained high social standards and directly challenged the investigative methods used by MSN and EMIH, and threatened to sue the two groups. Gildan argued that local unions were unreliable, and it denounced the labor code as antiquated.

The Solidarity Fund and Gildan

In November 2003, three Solidarity Fund officers, Bourcier, Audette, and Laporte, sat down to talk. The intense media focus on the allegations against Gildan had created a serious dilemma for the Fund, which was heavily invested in a company that appeared not to respect the values that lay at the very core of its operations. The officers needed to make a recommendation to the board and top management of the Fund within the next few days on what to do about their investments in Gildan Activewear.

One option was for the Fund to continue doing what it had been doing—to keep fully invested in the company and to continue its regular social audits. Another option was to divest completely—to sell its stock holdings in the company and to call in its loans. Selling would give the Fund a more than 1,000 percent return on its investment over seven years; but that return could potentially be even higher if it stayed invested. A final option was to keep its shares and to step up its efforts to influence the company's behavior. The officers were aware that the Fund enjoyed significant leverage: it was a major shareholder, had a representative on the board, and had worked closely with the company for many years. But it had already been working for many months to influence the firm's practices. In the Fund's officers' view, they had received, at best, mixed messages from the company—and mixed results in their efforts to shape its behavior.

Discussion Questions

1. What is the purpose of the Solidarity Fund? Do you think it represents an example of social investment? Why or why not?
2. Do you believe the evidence in the case shows Gildan Activewear to be a socially responsible company, or not?
3. What evidence do you find in the case of the benefits and of the costs of globalization?
4. In what ways did the Solidarity Fund attempt to use its position as an institutional investor to try to influence Gildan Activewear?
5. What are the arguments for and against a decision by the Solidarity Fund to divest from (sell its investments in) Gildan Activewear?
6. What do you think the Solidarity Fund managers should do now, and why?

Mattel and Toy Safety

On September 12, 2007, members of Congress, their staff, reporters, prospective witnesses, and curious members of the public gathered in a U.S. Senate hearing room to consider the issue of toy safety. In the weeks leading up to the hearing, Mattel, Inc., one of the world's leading toy makers, had ordered a series of recalls of children's playthings that had been found to be coated with lead paint. Lead—a heavy metal sometimes added to paint to intensify color, speed drying, and increase durability—was a potent neurotoxin and potentially dangerous to children who might ingest bits of paint. The toy recalls had alarmed parents and consumer activists, as well as the toy industry, retailers who marketed their products, and product safety regulators. Now, as the holiday shopping season approached, everyone wanted to make sure that toys—80 percent of which were made in China—were safe. "It's scary," said Whitney Settle, a mother from Petroleum, West Virginia. "I have a 2-year-old boy who chews on everything. I doubt I am going to buy [Mattel toys] anymore—or it's going to make me look twice."[1]

Mattel, Inc.

Headquartered in El Segundo, California, Mattel, Inc., was the global leader in the design, manufacture, and marketing of toys and family products. Mattel toy lines included such best-selling brands as Barbie (the most popular fashion doll ever introduced), Hot Wheels, Matchbox, American Girl, Radica, and Tyco, as well as Fisher-Price brands, including Little People, Power Wheels, and a wide range of entertainment-inspired toys. Mattel had long enjoyed a reputation as a responsible company. *Forbes* magazine had recognized Mattel as one of the 100 most trustworthy U.S. companies, and CRO magazine had ranked the company as one of the 100 Best Corporate Citizens. Mattel employed more than 30,000 people in 43 countries and territories and sold products in more than 150 nations. In 2006, the company earned $592 million on sales of $5.6 billion.

In 2007, Mattel manufactured about 65 percent of its toys in China. When the company first began shifting production to Asia in the 1980s, it used outside contractors. Mattel soon became concerned, however, that outsourcing put the company's intellectual property at risk, as outsiders could learn to make imitation Barbie dolls and other trademarked

By Anne T. Lawrence and James Weber. Copyright © 2008 by the authors. All rights reserved. An earlier version of this case was presented at the 2008 annual meeting of the Western Casewriters Association. The authors developed this case for class discussion rather than to illustrate effective or ineffective handling of the situation. Materials in this case are drawn from testimony at the hearing on toy safety held by the Senate Appropriations Committee, Subcommittee on Financial Services and General Government, on September 12, 2007, and from articles appearing in The *Wall Street Journal, The New York Times, Boston Globe, BusinessWeek, The Guardian, Forbes, Reuters, International Business Times,* and the trade press.

[1] "Amid Recalls, Toy Makers Tout Quality," *Boston Globe*, August 19, 2007.

products. Believing it could handle manufacturing more securely by operating its own factories, in the 1990s Mattel built or acquired production facilities in China, Hong Kong, Indonesia, Malaysia, the Philippines, and Singapore. In 2007, nearly 50 percent of the company's toy revenue came from core products made in these company-run plants, which included five factories in China. Mattel also contracted production to between 30 and 50 Chinese firms, many of which had relationships with other subcontractors. In 2007, production throughout the toy industry was shifting toward China, in part because the weakening Chinese currency made goods manufactured there increasingly cost-competitive.

In 1997, Mattel had developed a detailed code of conduct, called its Global Manufacturing Principles. Covering both Mattel's factories and those of its contractors and suppliers, the principles addressed a wide range of labor issues. These included wages (at least minimum wage or local industry standard, whichever was higher), child labor (workers had to be at least 16 years old or the local minimum, whichever was higher), and health and safety (compliant with the standards of the American Conference of Government Industrial Hygienists). In a move that was at the time unprecedented, the company hired S. Prakash Sethi, a professor at Baruch College in New York, to carry out independent audits to assure compliance with these standards. Mattel gave Professor Sethi a generous budget, access to all facilities and records of the company and its contractors, and permission to make the results of his inspections public. Since 1999, the International Center for Corporate Accountability (ICCA), the nonprofit organization headed by Professor Sethi, had conducted audits of facilities operated by Mattel and its contractors at least once every three years and more often if it found problems. Over the years, Mattel had terminated several dozen suppliers for noncompliance and made numerous changes in its own plants.[2]

Although its Global Manufacturing Principles focused exclusively on working conditions, Mattel also took steps to ensure product quality and safety. In China, Mattel tested products both at its own facilities and in special test labs. The company had specific standards with respect to lead in paint. Robert A. Eckert, Mattel's CEO, described the company's safety protocols for paint:

> For years, Mattel has required vendors to purchase paint from a list of certified suppliers or test the paint that they used to ensure compliance with the established standards; audited the certified paint suppliers to ensure compliance with lead level standards; periodically audited vendors to ensure that they are complying with paint requirements; conducted lead level safety tests on samples drawn from the initial production run of every product; and had protocols for further recertification testing for lead on finished products.[3]

The Toy Recalls

On August 1, 2007, Mattel issued a voluntary recall of 1.5 million Chinese-made, Fisher-Price products, including the popular Big Bird, Elmo, Diego, and Dora the Explorer characters, after the company learned that they contained too much lead. The company had begun a special investigation in July after a European retailer found lead paint on a

---

[2] The ICCA audits are available online at *www.mattel.com/about_us/Corp_Responsibility.*

[3] Testimony of Robert A. Eckert, submitted to the Senate Committee on Appropriations, Subcommittee on Financial Services and General Government, September 12, 2007.

Mattel product. Two weeks later, Mattel recalled another 436,000 toys—the Sarge toy from the Cars die-cast vehicle line—again because of high levels of lead. The second recall also included 18.2 million toys, such as Barbie, Batman, Polly Pocket, and Doggie Daycare play sets, that contained small but powerful magnets that could fall out of the toys and be swallowed by young children. Once ingested, these magnets could attract each other and cause a potentially fatal intestinal perforation or blockage. Mattel's ongoing investigation continued to turn up problems, and in early September the company issued a third recall of 11 different products—eight pet and furniture play sets sold under the Barbie brand and three Fisher-Price toys.

As it issued one recall after another, Mattel sought to reassure its customers. The company told the public that it was aggressively working with the Consumer Product Safety Commission in the United States and other regulatory agencies worldwide that governed consumer product safety. It provided a comprehensive list of all recalled products on its website and a toll-free number to respond to consumer questions regarding the safety of its products. The company also placed full-page ads in *The Wall Street Journal, The New York Times,* and *USA Today.* It also issued many press releases, including one that said, "Mattel has rigorous procedures, and we will continue to be vigilant and unforgiving in enforcing quality and safety. We don't want to have recalls, but we don't hesitate to take quick and effective action to correct issues as soon as we've identified them to ensure the safety of our products and the safety of children."

Mattel instructed customers who had purchased the recalled products to take them away from their children, and it provided them with a prepaid mailing label to return affected toys for a refund or safe replacement product. Although Mattel did not reveal how many toys were actually returned, past recalls of inexpensive toys had yielded return rates below 5 percent, according to product safety experts. The company indicated that it would safely dispose of the returned products and recycle some materials into other products, such as park benches.

What Had Gone Wrong?

In its investigation, Mattel learned that some of its external vendors and their subcontractors were cutting corners to save money and time. Lead paint was at least 30 percent cheaper than unleaded paint, and some thought that it produced a richer color and was easier to apply. Mattel discovered, for example, that the main supplier of the Cars product, the focus of the second recall, was a Chinese contractor called Early Light Industrial. This firm had subcontracted the painting of the toy to another company, Hong Li Da. Although the subcontractor was supposed to use paint provided by Early Light Industrial (which had been inspected and approved for use in toys exported to the United States), instead it substituted lead paint. "Early Light, the vendor, is every [bit as] much the victim as Mattel is," Eckert later commented. "The subcontractor chose to violate the rules."[4] In another instance, Lee Der Industrial, a contractor, had used paint supplied by another firm and had apparently failed to test it for lead. In total, Mattel's investigation uncovered seven contractors that had been involved in making the lead paint–coated products.

In its investigation of the problem with the small magnets, Mattel found that the problem lay in the toys' design, not their production. While the company routinely put its products through rigorous stress tests, it did not anticipate that if two or more high-powered magnets were ingested at once they could close off the intestines if they

---

[4] "What Went Wrong at Mattel," *BusinessWeek,* August 15, 2007.

became attached inside a young child. Once it discovered this possibility, Mattel changed the design of the toy; in the newer versions the magnets were locked into the products so that a child could not break them free and accidentally ingest them. (The Consumers Union reported that one toddler had died and 12 children had been injured as a result of swallowing magnets, but did not say if Mattel toys, in particular, had caused these injuries.)

Regulation in the United States and China

In the United States, the Consumer Product Safety Commission (CPSC) had responsibility for protecting the public from unreasonable risks of serious injury and death from more than 15,000 types of consumer products, including children's toys. The commission's mandate included developing uniform safety standards for various products and, if necessary, issuing a voluntary recall of unsafe products. Some observers believed that the CPSC was underfunded and understaffed, relative to the breadth of its mission. In 2007, the commission had an annual budget of $62 million and employed around 400 people (down from a high of around 900), including about 15 investigators charged with visiting ports of entry to inspect imports and 100 charged with monitoring products on store shelves. According to the Consumers Union, an advocacy organization, Chinese products in 2007 accounted for two-thirds of the products the CPSC regulated and 60 percent of all product recalls, compared with 36 percent in 2000.

When Mattel announced its first recalls in August, the CPSC's acting commissioner, Nancy A. Nord, attempted to reassure the public. She told the press that she was negotiating with representatives from the toy industry to conduct broader testing of imported toys and urged consumers not to overreact to news of the recalls. "In today's environment, it is easy to take recalls out of proportion. By no means is it the largest recall this agency has done, and it represents only a tiny fraction of the hundreds of millions of toys that are sold in the United States every year."[5]

In China, government standards required that paint intended for household or consumer product use contain no more than 90 parts of lead per million. (By comparison, U.S. regulations allowed up to 600 parts per million, although they banned the use of lead paint in toys entirely.) However, enforcement of the lead standard in China was lax, according to some observers. "There is a national standard on the lead level in toys," said Chen Tao, sales manager for a toy factory in Shantou, in southern China, "but no one really enforces it. Factories can pick whatever paint they want."[6] Whether lead-based paint was used or not was generally left up to the customer. "It depends on the client's requirements," explained a manager at another Shantou manufacturer. "If the prices they offer make it impossible to use lead-free paint, we'll tell them that we might have to use leaded paint. If they agree, we'll use leaded paint. It totally depends on what the clients want."[7]

In the wake of the toy recalls, Chinese officials and regulators took several steps. In mid-August, the Beijing government established a cabinet-level committee, headed by Vice Premier Wu Yi, to improve the quality and safety of Chinese products. It suspended the export licenses of two companies, Hanshen Wood Factory (which had made some

---

[5] "Mattel Recalls 19 Million Toys Sent from China," *The New York Times*, August 15, 2007.

[6] "Why Lead in Toy Paint? It's Cheaper," *The New York Times*, September 11, 2007.

[7] Ibid.

lead-painted Thomas & Friends toys recalled by another company) and Lee Der Industrial. Zhang Shuhong, one of the owners of Lee Der Industrial, reportedly killed himself by hanging in a factory warehouse shortly afterward.[8] In September, the government introduced a new food and toy recall system and announced a "special war" to crack down on poor-quality products and unlicensed manufacturers. Beijing's largest state-run television network began broadcasting a special called "Believe in Made in China," featuring interviews with government regulators, reports on China's biggest companies, and segments on foreign buyers of Chinese goods. The government also agreed to prohibit the use of lead paint on toys exported to the United States, to increase inspections of its exports, and to hold regular talks with American safety regulators.

The Senate Hearings

In September 2007, as the hearings commenced, many of the key players in the toy safety crisis gathered to offer their perspectives to members of the Senate. Those testifying included representatives of the Consumer Product Safety Commission, the consumer advocacy organization Consumers Union, the American National Standards Institute, the Toy Industry Association, the retailer Toys "R" Us, and Mattel.

Consumer Product Safety Commission

Acting Commissioner Nancy A. Nord offered the following comments at the hearing:

> I would like to report to you in more detail today on the initiatives that the CPSC has undertaken in recent years to address the growth in imports and to relate to you what actions we are planning for the future. . . .
>
> The issue of Chinese imports cannot be adequately addressed by any one remedy but rather requires a multi-pronged approach to the problem. The CPSC's plan of action includes dialogue and initiatives with the Chinese government; working with the private sector including Chinese manufacturers directly; increased surveillance and enforcement activities at the borders and within the marketplace; and modernization of our governing statutes.
>
> [We are working with Chinese regulators on] specific cooperative actions . . . to improve the safety of consumer products: training; technical assistance; a mechanism to provide for "urgent consultation" when necessary; information exchanges; and the creation of Working Groups to address issues in four priority areas [including toys].
>
> The second prong of our plan to address Chinese imports is to work with the private sector including Chinese manufacturers. One of the commission's first initiatives in responding to the growth in imports was to establish the Office of International Programs and Intergovernmental Affairs to support a comprehensive effort to ensure that imported consumer products complied with recognized American safety standards. . . .
>
> A major emphasis of this program is working with foreign manufacturers to establish product safety systems as an integral part of their manufacturing process. We have found that many overseas manufacturers, particularly those from the developing world, are either ignorant of existing voluntary and mandatory standards or simply choose not to design and manufacture their products to those standards.

---

[8] "Scandal and Suicide in China: A Dark Side of Toys," *The New York Times*, August 23, 2007.

The CPSC has also conducted industry-specific safety seminars and retail and vendor training seminars in China. . . .

The third prong of our plan of action for Chinese imports is increased surveillance and enforcement activities. . . . CPSC obviously attempts to keep dangerous products from entering into the country in the first instance. However, in the event a defective product does enter the stream of commerce, CPSC has been taking stronger measures to effectively remove such products from the marketplace. . . .

CPSC staff is also working with various domestic and international associations and standards groups to assure that a strong message is being delivered to Chinese manufacturers and exporters. . . .

The fourth prong of our plan of action for Chinese imports is the modernization of our governing statutes to better allow us to address the large influx of imports. . . . For example, . . . [we propose to make] it unlawful to sell a recalled product in commerce.

Consumers Union

Sally Greenberg, senior product safety counsel for the Consumers Union, a private consumer advocacy organization and the publisher of *Consumer Reports* magazine, testified,

Unfortunately, the system in place to protect consumers—especially children—from unsafe products has broken down. The recent avalanche of toy recalls, involving Chinese-made toys made with excessive lead levels in the paint, has exposed millions of children to a highly toxic substance and created a crisis of confidence among consumers who feel that they can trust neither the toy industry nor our government to keep their children safe. . . .

Never in its history has the CPSC been so challenged as an agency. . . . [W]e believe the agency's leadership has failed to use the regulatory authority it has to fine companies that violate its rules, has refused to request more funding and resources even while admitting it cannot carry out core functions, and has opposed efforts by consumer groups to provide the commission with the funding and tools it needs to keep consumers safe. In addition, further exacerbating the CPSC's weakened state, the current administration has instead imposed additional cuts on the already woefully underfunded and understaffed agency. . . .

[W]e recommend that Congress set a goal of funding the CPSC at least to reach 700-plus employees, [which] the agency had when its doors opened in 1974. Consumers Union commends the toy industry, including retail giants such as Toys "R" Us, for embracing the idea of third-party testing and inspecting, and for welcoming the federal regulatory involvement in making testing and inspection mandatory.

Greenberg also took the opportunity to press for a proposal backed by her organization to protect consumers from unsafe Chinese-made products.

On July 18 of this year, Consumers Union . . . [proposed] eight steps that should be taken to help safeguard the health and safety of American consumers from the onslaught of unsafe Chinese-produced consumer products and foods. That list included the following steps:

1. Provide increased resources to government safety agencies to prevent unsafe products from crossing our borders.

2. Hold suppliers, importers, distributors, as well as manufacturers accountable for bringing unsafe products to the market by requiring preshipment inspections and testing to ensure product safety.
3. Develop U.S. government–administered, third-party safety certification programs for all products.
4. Develop a product traceability program for country-of-origin labeling for both food and consumer products as well as for all components and ingredients.
5. Require that importers post a bond to ensure they have sufficient resources to recall their products should they prove dangerous or defective.
6. Give all agencies with enforcement authority the power to levy meaningful civil penalties for manufacturers, importers, distributors, and retailers who fail to comply with regulations, and criminal penalties for those who knowingly and repeatedly jeopardize public safety.
7. Authorize mandatory recall authority for all government agencies.
8. Require all government agencies to publicly disclose information pertaining to safety investigations and reports of adverse events.

She later added a comment on recall effectiveness:

Recall notices rarely reach the very people who most need it—parents and caregivers. There is no law requiring manufacturers to try to find purchasers of the product or to notify parents or day care centers if a product proves dangerous and must be recalled. Further, there is no requirement that manufacturers advertise a product recall in the same way they advertised the product in the first place—toys with lead paint and magnets, high chairs, cribs, strollers, infant swings, and carriers often continue to be used for months or years after they have been recalled. In an effort to improve recall effectiveness, consumer groups petitioned the CPSC, asking that the commission require simple registration cards on products intended for use by children. While not a panacea, registration cards are one way to facilitate recalls.

American National Standards Institute

The president and CEO of the American National Standards Institute (ANSI), S. Joe Bhatia, also spoke before the Senate Committee. ANSI is a private nonprofit organization that coordinates the development of voluntary standards to protect consumer safety in a wide range of industries; it collaborates internationally with the International Organization for Standardization (ISO). Bhatia testified,

Standards are important for everyone because they influence the design, safety, manufacturing, and marketing of many products worldwide. Standards are not only developed in response to injuries, hazard, or other identified safety risks, but more often in a proactive manner to prevent injuries from known hazards. . . .

This hearing is necessary not because there is an issue with standards. It is necessary because some suppliers—particularly those who are exporting products to U.S. soil—are not complying with the rigorous standards and regulations that have been established to keep our citizens safe.

Products manufactured in accordance with U.S. toy safety standards provide greater protection to our children. Testing and inspection systems must be strengthened so that compliance with these standards can be verified before unsafe products get into this country. . . .

The system must be efficient, consistent, and sustainable. It must focus on improving how products are evaluated and assessing who is conducting the evaluations. . . .

ANSI wants to help reassure consumers that the products they find on the shelves of their local retailer have been tested and found to be safe—regardless of country of origin. In order for the Institute to accomplish the objective:

- Standards and conformity assessment resources that are already in place must be used more efficiently;
- Government and industry need to work at a single purpose to identify gaps in the current systems of testing and inspection of products imported to the United States;
- New human and financial resources must be brought to bear to strengthen existing systems and fill any identified gaps.

Toy Industry Association

Carter Keithley, president and CEO of the Toy Industry Association—an industry association representing companies that provides 85 percent of the toys sold in the United States—also testified. He said,

At the outset, I would like to note the U.S. has among the strictest, most comprehensive toy safety systems in the world. U.S. toys have, for years, been ranked among the safest of all consumer products in the home. In fact, many nations around the world emulate the U.S. system and understand our toy safety standards to be the premier standards. This is not to say there is no room for improvement. It is our mission to continuously search for new ways to further strengthen our safety systems and standards. . . .

As we entered the summer months and up until as late as last week, toy recalls were in the headlines daily. These recent recalls clearly demonstrated our safety system needed to be strengthened. Although, as I stated, we have some of the best standards in the world, we were left wanting in assuring the application of the standards. This lack of assuring application of standards left our companies, the industry, and most importantly our children exposed. . . .

As companies continue to test current product to clear violative product from their supply chains, TIA has, with the approval of our member companies, set out to provide a long-term program to address the "assurance gap." To that end, I would like to share the framework for our new mandatory testing program for toys sold in the United States.

The new mandatory program will

1. Require all toys manufactured for the U.S. market to be tested to U.S. standards;
2. Standardize procedures that will be used industrywide to verify that products comply with U.S. safety standards;
3. Establish criteria to certify that testing laboratories are qualified to perform testing to U.S. standards using industrywide protocols;
4. Require the development of testing protocols and certification criteria through the cooperation of all stakeholders and apply them consistently;
5. Necessitate that TIA work with Congress, CPSC, and ANSI to implement the legislation, rules, and protocols to ensure industrywide adherence.

It is the toy industry's strong belief that with this new mandatory testing program our industry will be even better equipped to protect the integrity of our products and the safety of American children.

Toys "R" Us

Jerry Storch, chairman and CEO of Toys "R" Us, a toy and baby products retailer operating in 35 countries, with 842 stores in the United States, testified,

> As the recalls this year unfolded, it became clear to us that change was needed. Like many of you, we were frustrated by some of the large recalls earlier this year, especially by what appeared to be an unacceptably long time frame between discovery of a problem and the actual consumer recall. . . .
>
> It is our belief that a combination of strong safety practices when toys are manufactured and reinforcing federal legislation can help provide the answer. We also believe a strong, well-financed Consumer Product Safety Commission (CPSC) is needed, rather than a patchwork quilt of potentially contradictory state legislation.
>
> [W]e believe the recall process itself could be improved in two ways: First, we support legislation shortening the time frames during the period between identification of a problem and the eventual recall of that product. We are troubled by the possibility that we could be continuing to sell toys that someone knows may have a problem, while we remain unaware until we receive word that a recall is coming—usually just a day or two at most before the recall.
>
> Second, we believe that production code stamping of products and packaging would significantly help in tracing potential safety issues. It would make it easier for retailers and parents to identify recalled product, and avoid the guessing game when a mom or dad is trying to remember whether they bought the product before or after the recall date.
>
> To our knowledge, based on the recalls this year, the problem was not that testing wasn't happening, or that testing wasn't being done properly, but rather that testing was not done frequently enough. Prior to recent events, toy makers would test the initial batch of a product, then periodically retest batches to make sure the factory was still complying. What appears to have happened in the recent cases is that someone replaced the compliant paint with noncompliant paint at an unknown point between tests. Therefore, while we have long required testing from our vendors, we are moving to require that our vendors submit to us certification of testing for each batch coming to Toys "R" Us, and we have been told many vendors are already moving to this practice. To reinforce this direction, we strongly support strengthening third-party testing requirements. Specifically, we advocate for legislation requiring accredited certification of testing facilities. It is a sensible way for all of us—including retailers and consumers—to know that the manufacturers have or use quality testing facilities.

Mattel

Mattel also took its message to Capitol Hill. Robert A. Eckert, Mattel's CEO, told the committee,

> Like many of you, I am a parent. I, like you, care deeply about the safety of children. And I, like you, am deeply disturbed and disappointed by recent events. As to lead paint on our products, our systems were circumvented, and our standards were violated. We were let down, and so we let you down. On behalf of Mattel and its nearly 30,000 employees, I apologize sincerely. I can't change the past,

but I can change the way we do things. And I already have. We are doing everything we can to prevent this from happening again.

Eckert continued later in his remarks,

Obviously, we know that parents are looking to us to see what we're doing to improve our system to make people live up to their obligations and meet our standards. We have acted quickly and aggressively by implementing a strengthened 3-point safety check system to enforce compliance with all regulations and standards applicable to lead paint. . . .

I would like to conclude by reiterating my personal apology on behalf of Mattel and to emphasize our commitment to parents. The steps we have taken will strengthen the safety of our products. Parents expect that a toy carrying the Mattel brand is safe. Ensuring safety is crucial to the long-standing trust this company has built with parents for more than 60 years. There is simply nothing more important to Mattel than the safety of children.

Discussion Questions

1. Do you believe that Mattel acted in a socially responsible and ethical manner with regard to the safety of its toys? Why or why not? What should or could Mattel have done differently, if anything?

2. Who or what do you believe was responsible for the fact that children were exposed to potentially dangerous toys? Why do you think so?

3. What is the best way to ensure the safety of children's toys? In responding, please consider how the following groups would answer this question: government regulators (in the United States and China); consumer advocates; the toy industry; children's product retailers; and standard-setting organizations. What might explain the differences in their points of view?

4. What do you think is the best way for society to protect children from harmful toys? Specifically, what are the appropriate roles for various stakeholders in this process?

This glossary defines technical or special terms used in this book. Students may use it as a quick and handy reference for terms that may be unfamiliar without having to refer to the specific chapter(s) where they are used. It also can be a very helpful aid in studying for examinations and for writing term papers where precise meanings are needed.

A

acid rain   Rain that is more acidic than normal; occurs when emissions of sulfur dioxide and nitrogen oxides from utilities, manufacturers, and vehicles combine with water vapor in the air.

ad hoc coalitions   The bringing together of diverse groups to organize for or against legislation or regulation.

advocacy advertising   A political tool used by companies to promote their viewpoint through the media.

affirmative action   A positive and sustained effort by an organization to identify, hire, train if necessary, and promote minorities, women, and members of other groups who are underrepresented in the organization's workforce.

air pollution   When more pollutants, such as sulfur dioxide or particulates, are emitted into the atmosphere than can be safely absorbed and diluted by natural processes.

alternative dispute resolution   A method for resolving legal conflicts outside the traditional court system, in which a professional mediator (a third-party neutral) works with the two sides to negotiate a settlement agreeable to both parties.

anti-Americanism   Opposition to the United States of America, or to its people, principles, or policies.

antitrust laws   Laws that promote competition or that oppose trusts, monopolies, or other business combinations that restrain trade.

auditing process   Systems used by a business to ensure compliance with an industry or global set of standards.

B

B corporation   A business that is certified by an external organization to verify the blending of its social objectives with its financial goals.

behavioral advertising   Advertising that targets particular customers based on their observed online behavior.

biodiversity   The number and variety of species and the range of their genetic makeup.

biotechnology   A technological application that uses biological systems or living organisms to make or modify products or processes for specific use.

blogs   Web-based journals or logs maintained by an individual containing commentaries, descriptions, graphics, and other material.

blowing the whistle   (See whistle-blowing.)

board of directors   An elected group of individuals who have a legal duty to establish corporate objectives, develop broad policies, and select top-level personnel for a company.

bottom line   Business profits or losses, usually reported in figures on the last or bottom line of a company's income statement.

bottom of the pyramid   The world's poor; also refers to creative business actions to develop products and services that meet the needs of the world's poor.

boundary-spanning departments   Departments, or offices, within an organization that reach across the dividing line that separates a company from groups and people in society.

bribery   A questionable or unjust payment often to a government official to ensure or facilitate a business transaction.

bundling   The collection of political contributions made by an organization's stakeholders to increase the organization's ability to influence a political agent.

business   An organization that is engaged in making a product or providing a service for a profit.

business and society   The study of the relationship between business and its social environment.

business ethics   The application of general ethical ideas to business behavior.

C

campaign finance reform   Efforts to change the rules governing the financing of political campaigns, often by limiting contributions made or received.

cap-and-trade   Allows businesses to buy and sell permits that entitle the bearer to emit a certain amount of pollution. The government or international agency issues these permits and caps the total amount of pollution that may be produced.

carbon neutrality   When an organization or individual produces net zero emissions of greenhouse gases.

carbon offsets (carbon credits)   Investments in projects that remove carbon dioxide or its equivalent from the atmosphere.

carrying capacity   The maximum population that the Earth's ecosystem can support at a certain level of technological development.

cellular telephones (or cell phones)   Mobile devices using wireless technology that enable users to place calls from anywhere.

central state control (system)   A socioeconomic system in which economic power is concentrated in the hands of government officials and political authorities. The central government owns the property that is used to produce goods and services, and most private markets are illegal.

CERCLA   (Comprehensive Environmental Response, Compensation, and Liability Act) The major U.S. law governing the cleanup of existing hazardous-waste sites, popularly known as Superfund.

chief information officer   Manager who has been entrusted with the responsibility to manage the organization's technology with its many privacy and security issues.

chief sustainability officer   Manager responsible for the organization's sustainability activities and performance.

child care   The care or supervision of another's child, such as at a day-care center; offered as a benefit by some employers to working parents.

Citizens United   A U.S. Supreme Court ruling that allowed corporations and unions to directly contribute to political campaigns.

citizenship profile   Choosing a configuration of citizenship activities that fits the setting in which the company is working.

civic engagement   The active involvement of businesses and individuals in changing and improving communities.

civil society   Nonprofit, educational, religious, community, family, and interest-group organizations; social organizations that do not have a commercial or governmental purpose. See also nongovernmental organization.

clean economy   Sectors of the economy that produce goods and services with an environmental benefit.

climate change   Changes in the Earth's climate caused by increasing concentrations of carbon dioxide and other pollutants produced by human activity.

codes of conduct   Codes of conduct that seek to define acceptable and unacceptable behavior for corporations or their partners.

collaborative partnerships   Alliances among business, government, and civil society organizations that draw on the unique capabilities of each to address complex social problems.

command and control regulation   A regulatory approach where the government "commands" companies to meet specific standards (such as amounts of particular pollutants) and "controls" the methods (such as technology) used to achieve these standards.

commons   Traditionally, an area of land on which all citizens could graze their animals without limitation. The term now refers to any shared resource, such as land, air, or water, that a group of people use collectively.

community   A company's area of local business influence. Traditionally, the term applied to the city, town, or rural area in which a business's operations, offices, or assets were located. With the rise of large, complex business organizations, the meaning of the term has expanded to include multiple localities.

community relations   The organized involvement of business with the communities in which it conducts operations.

community relations manager (or community involvement manager)   Manager delegated to interact with local citizens, develop community programs, manage donations of goods and services, work with local governments, and encourage employee volunteerism.

competition   A struggle to survive and excel. In business, different firms compete with one another for customers' dollars, employees' talents, and other assets.

competitive intelligence   The systematic and continuous process of gathering, analyzing, and managing external information on the organization's competitors.

Comprehensive Environmental Response, Compensation, and Liability Act (CERCLA)   (See CERCLA and Superfund.)

computer hackers   Individuals often with advanced technology training who, for thrill or profit, breach a business's information security system.

conflicts of interest   Occur when an individual's self-interest conflicts with acting in the best interest of another, when the individual has an obligation to do so.

constructive engagement   When transnational corporations guided by strong moral principles become a force for positive change in other nations where they operate.

consumer affairs officer Manages the complex network of consumer relations.

consumer movement A social movement that seeks to augment the rights and powers of consumers. (Also known as consumerism.)

consumer privacy A consumer's right to be protected from the unwanted collection and use of information about that individual for use in marketing.

consumer protection laws Laws that provide consumers with better information, protect consumers from possible hazards, encourage competitive pricing, protect privacy, or permit consumer lawsuits.

consumer rights The legitimate claims of consumers to safe products and services, adequate information, free choice, a fair hearing, competitive prices, and privacy.

consumerism (See consumer movement.)

corporate citizenship This term broadly refers to putting corporate social responsibility into practice through stakeholder partnerships, serving society, and integrating financial *and* social performance.

corporate crisis A significant business disruption that stimulates extensive news media or social networking coverage.

corporate culture A blend of ideas, customs, traditional practices, company values, and shared meanings that help define normal behavior for everyone who works in a company.

corporate foundations Organizations chartered as nonprofits, and funded by companies, for the purpose of donating money to community organizations, programs, and causes.

corporate giving (See corporate philanthropy.)

corporate governance The system of allocating power in a corporation that determines how and by whom the company is to be directed.

corporate philanthropy Gifts and contributions made by businesses, usually from pretax profits, to benefit various types of nonprofit and community organizations.

corporate political strategy Those activities taken by an organization to acquire, develop, and use power to achieve a political advantage.

corporate power The strength or capability of corporations to influence government, the economy, and society, based on their organizational resources.

corporate social reporting The public reporting of information collected by the organization or another party during a social audit.

corporate social responsibility The idea that businesses should act in a way that enhances society and their stakeholders and be held accountable for any of its actions that affect people, their communities, and their environment.

corporate volunteerism A program wherein a company engages its employees in community service as a way to improve the company's image as well as serve the communities in which the business operates.

corporation Legally, an artificial legal "person," created under the laws of a particular state or nation. Socially and organizationally, it is a complex system of people, technology, and resources generally devoted to carrying out a central economic mission as it interacts with a surrounding social and political environment.

cost-benefit analysis A systematic method of calculating the costs and benefits of a project or activity that is intended to produce benefits.

crisis management The process organizations use to respond to short-term or intermediate-term, unexpected, and high consequences shocks, such as accidents, disasters, catastrophes, and injuries.

cyberchondriacs People who leap to the most dreadful conclusions while researching medical matters online.

cyberspace A virtual location where information is stored, ideas are described, and communication takes place in and through an electronic network of linked systems.

D

dark site A website developed and uploaded with critical information but remains dormant or "dark" until activated by the firm when needed in response to a crisis.

debt relief The idea that the world's richest nations should forgive poor nations' obligation to pay back loans.

deceptive advertising An advertisement that makes false or misleading claims about the company's own product or its competitor's product, withholds relevant information, or creates unreasonable expectations; generally illegal under U.S. law.

democracy A form of government in which power is vested in the people and exercised by them directly or by their elected representatives.

department of corporate citizenship A department created in a business to centralize under common leadership wide-ranging corporate citizenship functions.

deregulation The removal or scaling down of regulatory authority and regulatory activities of government.

digital divide   The gap between those that have access to technology and those that do not.

digital medical records   The electronic storing of a patient's medical records so that they are accessible by other medical providers.

Digital Millennium Copyright Act   The U.S. law that made it a crime to circumvent antipiracy measures built into most commercial software agreements between the manufacturers and their users.

directors   (See board of directors.)

discrimination (in jobs or employment)   Unequal treatment of employees based on non–job-related factors such as race, sex, age, national origin, religion, color, and physical or mental handicap.

diversity   Variation in the characteristics that distinguish people from one another, such as age, ethnicity, nationality, gender, mental or physical abilities, race, sexual orientation, family status, and first language.

diversity council   A group of managers and employees responsible for developing and implementing specific action plans to meet an organization's diversity goals. (See also diversity.)

divestment   Withdrawing and shifting to other uses the funds that a person or group has invested in the securities (stocks, bonds, notes, etc.) of a company. Investors sometimes have divested the securities of companies doing business in countries accused of human rights abuses.

dividend   A return-on-investment payment made to the owners of shares of corporate stock at the discretion of the company's board of directors.

Dodd-Frank Act   Legislation passed in the U.S. in 2011 in response to the financial crisis; extensively reformed the regulation of financial institutions such as banks and credit rating agencies, established a new consumer financial protection bureau, and changed corporate governance and executive compensation rules.

drug testing (of employees)   The testing of employees, by the employer, for the presence of illegal drugs, sometimes by means of a urine sample, saliva, or hair follicle analyzed by a clinical laboratory.

E

e-business   Electronic business exchanges between businesses and between businesses and their customers via the Internet.

ecological footprint   The amount of land and water an individual or group needs to produce the resources it consumes and to absorb its wastes, given prevailing technology.

ecologically sustainable organization (ESO)   A business that operates in a way that is consistent with the principle of sustainable development. (See also sustainable development.)

economic leverage   A political tool where a business uses its economic power to threaten to relocate its operations unless a desired political action is taken.

economic regulation   The oldest form of regulation in the United States, aimed at modifying the normal operations of the free market and the forces of supply and demand.

ecosystem   Plants and animals in their natural environment, living together as an interdependent system.

egoist   (See ethical egoist.)

elder care   The care or supervision of elderly persons; offered as a benefit by some employers to working children of elderly parents.

electronic monitoring (of employees)   The use by employers of electronic technologies to gather, store, and monitor information about employees' activities.

emissions charges or fees   Fees charged to business by the government, based on the amount of pollution emitted.

employee assistance programs (EAPs)   Company-sponsored programs to assist employees with alcohol abuse, drug abuse, mental health, and other problems.

employee ethics training   Programs developed by businesses to further reinforce their ethical expectations for their employees.

employment-at-will   The principle that workers are hired and retained solely at the discretion of the employer.

enlightened self-interest   The view that holds it is in a company's self-interest in the long run to provide true value to its stakeholders.

environmental analysis   A method managers use to gather information about external issues and trends.

environmental intelligence   The acquisition of information gained from analyzing the multiple environments affecting organizations.

environmental justice   The efforts to prevent inequitable exposure to risk, such as from hazardous waste.

environmental partnerships   A voluntary, collaborative partnership between or among businesses, government regulators, and environmental organizations to achieve specific environmental goals.

Environmental Protection Agency (EPA)   The U.S. federal government agency responsible for most environmental regulation and enforcement.

environmental scanning   Examining an organization's environment to discover trends and forces that could have an impact on the organization.

environmental standards   Standard amounts of particular pollutants allowable by law or regulation.

equal employment opportunity   The principle that all persons otherwise qualified should be treated equally with respect to job opportunities, workplace conditions, pay, fringe benefits, and retirement provisions.

Equal Employment Opportunity Commission (EEOC)   The U.S. federal government agency charged with enforcing equal employment opportunity laws and executive orders.

ergonomics   Adapting work tasks, working conditions, and equipment to minimize worker injury or stress.

ethical climate   An unspoken understanding among employees of what is and is not acceptable behavior.

ethical egoist   A person who puts his or her own selfish interests above all other considerations, while denying the ethical needs and beliefs of others.

ethical principles   Guides to moral behavior, such as honesty, keeping promises, helping others, and respecting others' rights.

ethical relativism   A belief that ethical right and wrong are defined by various periods of time in history, a society's traditions, the specific circumstances of the moment, or personal opinion.

ethics   A conception of right and wrong conduct, serving as a guide to moral behavior.

ethics audit   An assessment used by an organization to target the effectiveness of their ethical safeguards or to document evidence of increased ethical employee behavior.

ethics and compliance officer   A manager designated by an organization to investigate breaches of ethical conduct, promulgate ethics statements, and generally promote ethical conduct at work.

ethics policies or codes   A written set of rules used to guide managers and employees when they encounter an ethical dilemma.

ethics reporting mechanisms   A program that enables employees, customers, or suppliers to report an ethical concern directly to someone in authority in an organization.

European Union (EU)   The political and economic coalition of countries located in the greater European region.

executive compensation   The compensation (total pay) of corporate executives, including salary, bonus, stock options, and various benefits.

extended product responsibility   The idea that companies have a continuing responsibility for the environmental impacts of their products and services, even after they are sold.

external stakeholder   Individuals or groups that make important transactions with a firm but are not directly employed by the firm, such as customers or suppliers.

F

fair labor standards   Rules that establish minimum acceptable standards for the conditions under which a company's employees (or the employees of its suppliers or subcontractors) will work. For example, such standards might include a ban on all child labor, establishment of maximum work hours per week, or a commitment to pay wages above a certain minimum level.

family-friendly corporation   A company that fully supports both men and women in their efforts to balance work and family responsibilities.

family leave   A leave of absence from work, either paid or unpaid, for the purpose of caring for a family member.

Federal Communications Commission   The U.S. federal government agency created in 1934 to regulate interstate and international communications; specifically regulates business advertisement.

fiscal policy   The patterns of taxing and spending adopted by a government to stimulate or support the economy.

527 organizations   Groups organized under section 527 of the Internal Revenue Service tax code for the purpose of donating money to candidates for public office and influencing elections.

flextime   A plan that allows employees limited control over scheduling their own hours of work, usually at the beginning and end of the workday.

focal organization   The organization central to the stakeholder analysis being conducted.

foreign direct investment   When a company, individual, or fund invests money in another country.

fraud   Deceit or trickery due to the pursuit of economic gain or competitive advantage.

free enterprise system   A socioeconomic system based on private ownership, profit-seeking business firms, and the principle of free markets.

free market   A model of an economic system based on voluntary and free exchange among buyers and sellers. Competition regulates prices in all free market exchanges.

G

general public   Broadly defined as individuals or groups in society.

general systems theory   A theory that holds that all organisms are open to, and interact with, their external environments.

genetic engineering   The altering of the natural make-up of a living organism, which allows scientists to insert virtually any gene into a plant and create a new crop, or an entire new species.

genetically modified foods   Food crops grown from genetically engineered seeds or food processed from such crops.

glass ceiling   An invisible barrier to the advancement of women, minorities, and other groups in the workplace.

glass walls   An invisible barrier to the lateral mobility of women, minorities, and other groups in the workplace, such as from human resources to operations, which could lead to top management positions.

global action network   A collaborative, multisector partnership focused on particular social issues or problems in the global economy.

global corporate citizenship   Refers to putting an organization's commitment to social and environmental responsibility into practice worldwide.

global warming   The gradual warming of the Earth's climate, believed by most scientists to be caused by an increase in carbon dioxide and other trace gases in the Earth's atmosphere resulting from human activity, mainly the burning of fossil fuels.

globalization   The movement of goods, services, and capital across national borders.

greenhouse effect   The warming effect that occurs when carbon dioxide, methane, nitrous oxides, and other gases act like the glass panels of a greenhouse, preventing heat from the Earth's surface from escaping into space.

greening of management   The process by which managers become more proactive with respect to environmental issues.

green marketing   A concept that describes the creation, promotion, and sale of environmentally safe products and services by business.

greenwashing   When an organization misleads consumers regarding the environmental benefits of a product or service.

H

hacktivist   Individual or group that invades a secure computer network and releases the information stored there.

harmonization   The coordination of laws and enforcement efforts among nations.

hazardous waste   Waste materials from industrial, agricultural, and other activities capable of causing death or serious health problems for those persons exposed for prolonged periods. (See also toxic substance.)

honesty tests   Written psychological tests given to prospective employees that seek to predict their honesty on the job.

human genome   Strands of DNA developing a unique pattern for every human.

human rights   An ethical approach emphasizing a person or group's entitlement to something or to be treated in a certain way, such as the right to life, safety, or to be informed.

I

ideology   A set of basic beliefs that define an ideal way of living for an individual, an organization, or a society.

image advertisements   Used by businesses to enhance their public image, create goodwill, or announce a major change, such as a merger, acquisition, or new product line.

industrial ecology   Designing factories and distribution systems as if they were self-contained ecosystems, such as using waste from one process as raw material for another.

information phase   The fifth phase of technology; emphasizes the use and transfer of knowledge and information rather than manual skill.

in-kind contributions   Corporate charitable contributions of products or services, rather than cash.

innovation   Creating a new process or device that adds value.

insider trading   Occurs when a person gains access to confidential information about a company's financial condition and then uses that information, before it becomes public knowledge, to buy or sell the company's stock; generally illegal.

institutional investor   A financial institution, insurance company, pension fund, endowment fund, or similar organization that invests its accumulated funds in securities offered for sale on stock exchanges.

institutionalized activity (ethics, social responsiveness, public affairs, etc.) An activity, operation, or procedure that is such an integral part of an organization that it is performed routinely by managers and employees.

intangible assets Nonphysical resources of the organization that enable it to achieve its goals and objectives, including intellectual property and corporate reputation.

integrity capital Return when ethical performance is linked with financial performance.

intellectual property Ideas, concepts, and other symbolic creations of the human mind that are recognized and protected under a nation's copyright, patent, and trademark laws.

interactive social system The closely intertwined relationships between business and society.

internal stakeholder Individuals who are employed by the firm, such as employees and managers.

international financial and trade institutions Institutions, such as the World Bank, International Monetary Fund, and World Trade Organization, that establish the rules by which international commerce is conducted.

International Monetary Fund An international financial institution that lends foreign exchange to member nations so they can participate in global trade.

Internet A global network of interconnected computers, enabling users to share information.

iron law of responsibility The belief that those who do not use their power in ways that society considers responsible will tend to lose their power in the long run.

issue advertisements A technique used by businesses to influence the public's opinion of a political or legislative issue of concern to the company.

issue management The active management of public issues once they come to the attention of a business organization.

issue management process A five-step process where managers identify the issue, analyze the issue, generate options, take action, and evaluate results.

J

justice An ethical approach that emphasizes whether the distribution of benefits and burdens among people are fair, according to some agreed-upon rule.

K

Kyoto Protocol An international treaty negotiated in 1997 in Kyoto, Japan, that committed its signatories to reduce emissions of greenhouse gases, such as carbon dioxide.

L

labor force participation rate The proportion of a particular group, such as women, in the paid workforce.

labor standards Conditions affecting a company's employees or the employees of its suppliers or subcontractors.

labor union An organization that represents workers on the job and that bargains collectively with the employer over wages, working conditions, and other terms of employment.

laws Society's formal written rules about what constitutes right and wrong conduct in various spheres of life.

leadership PAC (political action committee) Organization that collects political contributions on behalf of a politician and uses them to support others' campaigns, showing the politician's leadership within the political party.

legal challenges A political tool that questions the legal legitimacy of a regulation.

legal obligations A belief that a firm must abide by the laws and regulations governing the society.

license to operate The right to do business informally conferred by society on a business firm; must be earned through socially responsible behavior.

life cycle analysis Collecting information on the lifelong environmental impact of a product in order to minimize its adverse impacts at all stages, including design, manufacture, use, and disposal.

living wage The moral obligation for a company to pay its employees enough to achieve a decent family standard of living.

lobbying The act of trying to directly shape or influence a government official's understanding and position on a public policy issue.

M

marine ecosystems Oceans and the salt marshes, lagoons, and tidal zones that border them, and well as the diverse communities of life that they support.

market-based mechanism A form of regulation, used in environmental policy, that uses market mechanisms to control corporate behavior.

market failure Inability of the marketplace to properly adjust prices for the true costs of a firm's behavior.

market stakeholder A stakeholder that engages in economic transactions with a company.

M-commerce Commerce conducted by using mobile or cellular telephones.

media training The education of executives and employees, who are likely to have contact with the media, in how to communicate effectively with the press.

microfinance Occurs when financial organizations provide loans to low-income clients or a community of borrowers who traditionally lack access to banking or related services.

military dictatorship A repressive regime ruled by a dictator who exercises total power through control of the armed forces.

monetary policy Government actions that affect the supply, demand, and value of money in the economy.

monopoly Occurs when one company dominates the market for a particular product or service.

Montreal Protocol An international treaty limiting the manufacture and use of chlorofluorocarbons and other ozone-depleting chemicals. (See also ozone.)

moral development stages A series of progressive steps by which a person learns new ways of reasoning about ethical and moral issues. (See stages of moral development.)

morality A condition in which the most fundamental human values are preserved and allowed to shape human thought and action.

N

nanotechnology The application of engineering to create materials on a molecular or atomic scale.

natural monopolies Where a concentration of the market is acquired by a few firms due to the nature of the industry rather than because of company practices.

negative externalities (or spill-over effects) When the manufacture or distribution of a product gives rise to unplanned or unintended costs (economic, physical, or psychological) borne by consumers, competitors, neighboring communities, or other business stakeholders.

nongovernmental organizations (NGOs) Organizations that do not have a governmental or commercial purpose, such as religious, community, family, and interest-group organizations. Also called civil society or civil sector organizations.

nonmarket stakeholder A stakeholder that does not engage in direct economic exchange with a company, but is affected by or can affect its actions.

nonrenewable resources Natural resources, such as oil, coal, or natural gas, that once used are gone forever. (See also renewable resources.)

O

Occupational Safety and Health Administration (OSHA) The U.S. federal government agency that enforces worker safety and health standards.

occupational segregation The inequitable concentration of a group, such as minorities or women, in particular job categories.

ownership theory of the firm A theory that holds that the purpose of the firm is to maximize the long-term return for its shareholders. (Also called the property or finance theory of the firm.)

ozone A gas composed of three bonded oxygen atoms. Ozone in the lower atmosphere is a dangerous component of urban smog; ozone in the upper atmosphere provides a shield against ultraviolet light from the sun. (See also Montreal Protocol.)

P

parental leave A leave of absence from work, either paid or unpaid, for the purpose of caring for a newborn or adopted child.

pay gap The difference in the average level of wages, salaries, and income received by two groups, such as men and women (called the gender pay gap) or whites and persons of color (called the racial pay gap).

performance-expectations gap The perceived distance between what a firm wants to do or is doing and what the stakeholder expects.

philanthropy (See corporate philanthropy.)

phishing The practice of stealing consumers' personal information by using fake e-mails.

political action committee (PAC) An independently incorporated organization that can solicit contributions and then channels those funds to candidates seeking political office.

pollution prevention (See source reduction.)

predatory pricing The practice of selling below cost to drive rivals out of business.

privacy (See right of privacy.)

privacy policy Business policies that explain what use of the company's technology is permissible and how the business will monitor employee activities.

privacy rights Protecting an individual's personal life from unwarranted intrusion by the employer.

private property   A group of rights giving control over physical and intangible assets to private owners. Private ownership is the basic institution of capitalism.

privately held corporation   A corporation that is privately owned by an individual or a group of individuals; its stock is not available for purchase by the general investing public.

product liability   The legal responsibility of a firm for injuries caused by something it made or sold.

product recall   Occurs when a business firm, either voluntarily or under an agreement with a government agency, removes a defective or sometimes dangerous product from consumer use and from all distribution channels.

profits   The revenues of a person or company minus the costs incurred in producing the revenue.

proxy   A legal instrument giving another person the right to vote the shares of stock of an absentee stockholder.

proxy statement   A statement sent by a board of directors to a corporation's stockholders announcing the company's annual meeting, containing information about the business to be considered at the meeting, and enclosing a proxy form for stockholders not attending the meeting to vote.

public   (See general public.)

public affairs management   The active management of an organization's interactions with government at all levels to promote the firm's interests in the political process.

public issue   An issue that is of mutual concern to an organization and its stakeholders, sometimes called a social or sociopolitical issue.

public policy   A plan of action undertaken by government officials to achieve some broad purpose affecting a substantial segment of the public.

public-private partnerships   Community-based organizations that have a combination of businesses and government agencies collaborating to address important social problems such as crime, homelessness, drugs, economic development, and other community issues.

public relations   A program that sends a constant stream of information from the company to the public and opens the door to dialogue with stakeholders whose lives are affected by company operations.

public relations department   Manages the firm's public image and, more generally, its relations with the public.

public service announcements (PSAs)   Advertisements that address critical social issues.

publicly held corporation   A corporation whose stock is available for purchase by the general investing public (as contrasted with a privately held firm).

Q

QR code   An abbreviation for "quick response"; a square consisting of black and white spaces that transmits information to the user when scanned by a smartphone.

quality management   Measures taken by an organization to assure quality, such as defining the customer's needs, monitoring whether or not a product or service consistently meets these needs, analyzing the quality of finished products to assure they are free of defects, and continually improving processes to eliminate quality problems.

questionable payments   Something of value given to a person or firm that raises significant ethical questions of right or wrong in the host nation or other nations.

R

racial harassment   Harassment in the workplace based on race, such as ethnic slurs, derogatory comments, or other verbal or physical harassment that creates an intimidating, hostile, or offensive working environment or that interferes with an individual's work performance. (See also sexual harassment.)

rain forest   Woodlands that receive at least 100 inches of rain a year. They are among the planet's richest areas in terms of biodiversity.

regulation   The action of government to establish rules by which industry or other groups must behave in conducting their normal activities.

renewable resources   Natural resources, such as fresh water or timber, that can be naturally replenished. (See also nonrenewable resources.)

reputation   The desirable or undesirable qualities associated with an organization or its actors that may influence the organization's relationships with its stakeholders.

reregulation   The increase or expansion of government regulation on activities where regulatory activities had previously been reduced.

return on social investment   Benefits of a business's social actions that accrue to both business and society.

reverse discrimination   The unintentional discrimination against an individual or group in an effort to help another individual or group.

revolving door   The circulation of individuals between business and government positions.

right (human)   A concept used in ethical reasoning that means that a person or group is entitled to something or is entitled to be treated in a certain way.

right of privacy   A person's entitlement to protection from invasion of his or her private life by government, business, or other persons.

S

salience   Causes a stakeholder to stand out as important and to receive managers' attention; based on the stakeholder's power, legitimacy, and urgency. (See stakeholder salience.)

Sarbanes-Oxley Act   U.S. law enacted in 2002 that greatly expanded the powers of the SEC to regulate information disclosure in the financial markets and the accountability of an organization's senior leadership regarding the accuracy of this disclosure. (See also Securities and Exchange Commission.)

say-on-pay   U.S. regulation requiring public companies to hold an advisory shareholder vote on executive compensation at least once every three years.

Securities and Exchange Commission (SEC)   The U.S. federal government agency whose mission is to protect stockholders' rights by making sure that stock markets are run fairly and that investment information is fully disclosed.

semantic phase   A phase of technology that began around 2000; characterized by the development of processes and systems that enable organizations and people to navigate through the expanding amount of information on the Internet.

sexual harassment   Unwanted and uninvited sexual attention experienced by a person, and/or a workplace that is hostile or threatening in a sexual way. (See also racial harassment.)

shareholder   (See stockholder.)

shareholder lawsuit   A lawsuit initiated by one or more stockholders to recover damages suffered due to alleged actions of the company's management.

shareholder resolution   A proposal made by a stockholder or group of stockholders and included in a corporation's notice of its annual meeting that advocates some course of action to be taken by the company.

social assistance policies   Government programs aimed at improving social welfare in such areas as health care and education.

social audit   A systematic evaluation of an organization's social, ethical, and environmental performance.

social capital   The norms and networks that enable collective action; goodwill engendered by social relationships.

social contract   An implied understanding between an organization and its stakeholders as to how they will act toward one another.

social enterprise   A business that adopts social benefit as its core mission and uses its resources to improve human and environmental well-being.

social entrepreneur   An individual driven to create and sustain social value rather than solely economic value in business.

social entrepreneurship   The identification of a social need and using entrepreneurial skills to address this need.

social equity   Determined by assessing the company's social benefits and costs, as revealed by a social performance audit.

social investment   The use of stock ownership as a strategy for promoting social objectives. (Also called socially responsible investing.)

social networking   A system using technology to enable people to connect, explore interests, and share activities around the world.

social regulation   Regulations intended to accomplish certain social improvements such as equal employment opportunity, on-the-job safety and health, and the protection of the natural environment.

social responsibility   (See corporate social responsibility.)

social responsibility shareholder resolution   A resolution on an issue of corporate social responsibility placed before stockholders for a vote at a company's annual meeting, usually by social activist groups.

society   Refers to human beings and to the social structures they collectively create; specifically refers to segments of humankind, such as members of a particular community, nation, or interest group.

soft money   Unlimited political contributions made to a political party by individuals or organizations, but not by businesses or labor unions, to support party-building activities.

software piracy   The illegal copying of copyrighted software.

sound bite   Information, often 30 seconds or less, used by the media in its broadcast to the public.

source reduction   A business strategy to prevent or reduce pollution at the source, rather than to dispose of or treat pollution after it has been produced. (Also known as pollution prevention.)

spam   Unsolicited e-mails (or junk e-mails) sent in bulk to valid e-mail accounts. (See unsolicited commercial e-mails.)

spirituality (personal)   A personal belief in a supreme being, religious organization, or the power of nature or some other external, life-guiding force.

stages of moral development   A sequential pattern of how people grow and develop in their moral thinking, beginning with a concern for the self and growing to a concern for others and broad-based principles.

stakeholder   A person or group that affects, or is affected by, a corporation's decisions, policies, and operations. (See also market stakeholder and nonmarket stakeholder.)

stakeholder analysis   An analytic process used by managers that identifies the relevant stakeholders in a particular situation and seeks to understand their interests, power, and likely coalitions.

stakeholder coalitions   Alliances among a company's stakeholders to pursue a common interest.

stakeholder dialogue   Conversations between representatives of a company and its stakeholders about issues of common concern.

stakeholder engagement   An ongoing process of relationship building between a business and its stakeholders.

stakeholder interests   The nature of each stakeholder group, its concerns, and what it wants from its relationship with the firm.

stakeholder map   A graphical representation of the relationship of stakeholder salience to a particular issue.

stakeholder networks   A connected assembly of concerned individuals or organizations defined by their shared focus on a particular issue, problem, or opportunity.

stakeholder power   The ability of one or more stakeholders to achieve a desired outcome in their interactions with a company. The five types are voting power, economic power, political power, legal power, and informational power.

stakeholder salience   A stakeholder's ability to stand out from the background, to be seen as important, or to draw attention to itself or its issue. Stakeholders are more salient when they possess power, legitimacy, and urgency. (See salience.)

stakeholder theory of the firm   A theory that holds that the purpose of the firm is to create value for society.

stem cell research   Research on nonspecialized cells that have the capacity to self-renew and to differentiate into more mature, specialized cells.

stockholder   A person, group, or organization owning one or more shares of stock in a corporation; the legal owners of the business. (Also known as shareholder.)

stock option   A form of compensation. Options represent the right (but not obligation) to buy a company's stock at a set price for a certain period of time. The option becomes valuable to its holder when, and if, the stock price rises above this amount.

stock screening   Selecting stocks based on social or environmental criteria.

strategic philanthropy   A form of corporate giving that is linked directly or indirectly to business goals or objectives.

strict liability   A legal doctrine that holds that a manufacturer is responsible (liable) for injuries resulting from the use of its products, whether or not the manufacturer was negligent or breached a warranty.

Superfund   A U.S. law, passed in 1980, designated to clean up hazardous or toxic waste sites. The law established a fund, supported mainly by taxes on petrochemical companies, to pay for the cleanup. (Also known as the Comprehensive Environmental Response, Compensation, and Liability Act [CERCLA].)

super PAC (political action committee)   An organization that raises and spends money focusing on political issues but is not directly affiliated with any political campaign; also called an independent expenditure-only committee.

sustainability report   A single report integrating a business's social and environmental results.

sustainable development   Development that meets the needs of the present without compromising the ability of future generations to meet their own needs.

sweatshop   Factories where employees—sometimes including children—are forced to work long hours at low wages, often under unsafe working conditions.

T

technology   A broad term referring to the practical applications of science and knowledge to commercial and organizational activities.

technology cooperation   Long-term partnerships between companies to transfer environmental technologies to attain sustainable development.

The Business Roundtable   Founded in 1972, an organization of chief executive officers from leading corporations involved in various public issues and legislation.

tissue engineering   The growth of tissue in a laboratory dish for experimental research.

toxic substance   Any substance used in production or in consumer products that is poisonous or capable of causing serious health problems for those persons exposed. (See also hazardous waste.)

tradable permits   A market-based approach to pollution control in which the government grants companies "rights" to a specific amount of pollution (permits), which may be bought or sold (traded) with other companies.

trade association   A coalition of companies in the same or related industries seeking to coordinate their economic or political power to further their agenda.

transnational corporation   Corporations that operate and control assets across national boundaries.

transparency   Clear public reporting of an organization's performance to various stakeholders.

triple bottom line   The measurement of an organization on the basis of its economic results, environmental impact, and contribution to social well-being.

U

undocumented immigrant workers   Noncitizens employed by businesses without having the legally required work documents.

United Nations Global Compact   Voluntary agreement of business, labor, and nongovernmental organizations to work for sustainable development goals.

unsolicited commercial e-mails (or junk e-mail)   Unrequested e-mail messages sent in bulk to valid e-mail accounts. (See spam.)

U.S. Corporate Sentencing Guidelines   Standards to help judges determine the appropriate penalty for criminal violations of federal laws and provide a strong incentive for businesses to promote ethics at work.

U.S. Foreign Corrupt Practices Act   Federal law that prohibits businesses from paying bribes to foreign government officials, political parties, or political candidates.

utilitarian reasoning   An ethical approach that emphasizes the consequences of an action and seeks the action or decision where the benefits most outweigh the costs.

V

values   Fundamental and enduring beliefs about the most desirable conditions and purposes of human life.

virtue ethics   Focuses on character traits to define a good person, theorizing that values will direct a person toward good behavior.

vlogs   Video web logs produced by a digital camera that captures moving images and then transferred to the Internet.

volunteerism   The uncompensated efforts of people to assist others in a community.

W

Wall Street   A customary way of referring to the financial community of banks, investment institutions, and stock exchanges centered in the Wall Street area of New York City.

water pollution   When more wastes are discharged into waterways, such as lakes and rivers, than can be naturally diluted and carried away.

whistle-blowing   An employee's disclosure of alleged organizational misconduct to the media or appropriate government agency, often after futile attempts to convince organizational authorities to take action against the alleged abuse.

white-collar crime   Illegal acts committed by individuals, employees, or business professionals, such as fraud, insider trading, embezzlement, or computer crime.

workforce diversity   Diversity among employees, a challenge and opportunity for business. (See also diversity.)

World Bank   An international financial institution that provides economic development loans to member nations.

World Trade Organization   An organization of member nations that establishes the ground rules for trade among nations.

Z

zombie   A hijacked computer that can be remote-controlled by the attacker to respond to the attacker's commands.

BIBLIOGRAPHY

Part One: Chapters 1–3

Ackerman, Robert. *The Social Challenge to Business*. Cambridge, MA: Harvard University Press, 1975.

Albrecht, Karl. *Corporate Radar: Tracking the Forces That Are Shaping Your Business*. New York: American Management Association, 2000.

Bakan, Joel. *The Corporation: The Pathological Pursuit of Profit and Power*. New York: Free Press, 2004.

Barth, Regine, and Franziska Wolff, eds. *Corporate Social Responsibility in Europe—Rhetoric and Realities*. Cheltenham, UK: Edward Elgar Publishing, 2009.

Boutilier, Robert. *Stakeholder Politics: Social Capital, Sustainable Development, and the Corporation*. Sheffield, UK: Greenleaf Publishing, 2009.

Bowen, Howard R. *Responsibilities of the Businessman*. New York: Harper, 1953.

Chamberlain, Neil W. *The Limits of Corporate Social Responsibility*. New York: Basic Books, 1973.

Clarkson, Max B. E., ed. *The Corporation and Its Stakeholders: Classic and Contemporary Readings*. Toronto: University of Toronto Press, 1998.

Frederick, William C. *Values, Nature, and Culture in the American Corporation*. New York: Oxford University Press, 1995.

———. *Corporation Be Good!* Indianapolis, IN: Dog Ear Publishing, 2006.

Freeman, R. Edward. *Strategic Management: A Stakeholder Approach*. Cambridge, UK: Cambridge University Press, 2010.

Isaacs, William. *Dialogue: The Art of Thinking Together*. New York: Doubleday, 1999.

Kolb, Robert W., ed. *Encyclopedia of Business Ethics and Society*. Thousand Oaks, CA: Sage, 2008.

McElhaney, Kellie. *Just Good Business: The Strategic Guide to Aligning Corporate Responsibility and Brand*. San Francisco: Berrett-Koehler, 2008.

Phillips, Robert. *Stakeholder Theory and Organizational Ethics*. San Francisco: Berrett-Koehler Publishers, Inc., 2003.

Phillips, Robert A., and R. Edward Freeman, eds. *Stakeholders*. Northampton, MA: Edward Elgar Publishing, 2010.

Post, James E., Lee E. Preston, and Sybille Sachs. *Redefining the Corporation: Stakeholder Management and Organizational Wealth*. Palo Alto, CA: Stanford University Press, 2002.

Prahalad, C. K. *The Fortune at the Bottom of the Pyramid: Eradicating Poverty through Profits*. Philadelphia, PA: Wharton School Publishing, 2006.

Reich, Robert B. *Supercapitalism: The Transformation of Business, Democracy, and Everyday Life*. New York: Alfred A. Knopf, 2007.

Scofield, Rupert. *The Social Entrepreneur's Handbook: How to Start, Build, and Run a Business That Improves the World*. New York: McGraw-Hill, 2011.

Svendsen, Ann. *The Stakeholder Strategy: Profiting from Collaborative Business Relationships*. San Francisco: Berrett-Koehler Publishers, 1998.

Visser, Wayne. *The Age of Responsibility: CSR 2.0 and the New DNA of Business*. Chichester, UK: John Wiley & Sons, 2011.

Vogel, David. *The Market for Virtue: The Potential and Limits of Corporate Social Responsibility*. Washington, DC: Brookings Institution Press, 2005.

Waibel, Piera. *Putting the Poor First: How Base-of-the-Pyramid Ventures Can Learn from Development Approaches*. Sheffield, UK: Greenleaf Publishing, 2012.

Wall, Caleb. *Buried Treasure: Discovering and Implementing the Value of Corporate Social Responsibility*. Sheffield, UK: Greenleaf Publishing, 2008.

Yankelovich, Daniel. *The Magic of Dialogue: Transforming Conflict Into Cooperation*. New York: Simon & Schuster, 1999.

Yunas, Muhammad. *Building Social Business: The New Kind of Capitalism that Serves Humanity's Most Pressing Needs*. Philadelphia: Perseus Books Group, 2010.

Zakhem, Abe J., Daniel E. Palmer, and Mary Lyn Stoll. *Stakeholder Theory: Essential Readings in Ethical Leadership and Management*. Amherst, NY: Prometheus Books, 2008.

Part Two: Chapters 4–5

Ariely, Dan. *The Honest Truth about Dishonesty—How We Lie to Everyone—Especially Ourselves*. New York: HarperCollins, 2012.

Callahan, David. *The Cheating Culture*. Orlando: Harcourt, 2004.

Cavanaugh, Gerald F. *American Business Values: With International Perspectives*, 6th edition. Upper Saddle River, NJ: Prentice-Hall, 2009.

Colby, Anne, and Lawrence Kohlberg. *The Measurement of Moral Judgment: Volume I, Theoretical Foundations and Research Validations*. Cambridge, MA: Harvard University Press, 1987.

Comer, Debra R., and Gina Vega. *Moral Courage in Organizations: Doing the Right Thing at Work.* Armonk, NY: M.E. Sharpe, 2011.

Cortright, S.A., and Michael J. Naughton, eds. *Rethinking the Purpose of Business: Interdisciplinary Essays from the Catholic Social Tradition.* Notre Dame, IN: University of Notre Dame Press, 2002.

Donaldson, Thomas, and Thomas W. Dunfee. *Ties That Bind: A Social Contracts Approach to Business Ethics.* Cambridge, MA: Harvard Business School Publishing, 1999.

Fluker, Walter Earl. *Ethical Leadership: The Quest for Character, Civility, and Community.* Minneapolis, MN: Augsburg Fortress, 2009.

Gentile, Mary C. *Giving Voice to Values; How to Speak Your Mind When You Know What's Right.* New Haven, CT: Yale University Press, 2010.

Giacalone, Robert A., and Carole L. Jurkiewicz, eds. *Handbook of Workplace Spirituality and Organizational Performance.* Armonk, NY: M.E. Sharpe, 2003.

Hamington, Maurice, and Maureen Sander-Staudt, eds. *Applying Care Ethics to Business.* New York: Springer, 2011.

Jackall, Robert. *Moral Mazes: The World of Corporate Managers.* New York: Oxford University Press, 1988.

Kochan, Nick, and Robin Goodyear. *Corruption: The New Corporate Challenge.* New York: Palgrave Macmillan, 2011.

Leipziger, Deborah, ed. *SA8000: The First Decade.* Sheffield, UK: Greenleaf Publishers, 2009.

McLean, Bethany, and Peter Elkind. *The Smartest Guys in the Room: The Amazing Rise and Scandalous Fall of Enron.* New York: Penguin Books, 2003.

O'Brien, Thomas, and Scott Paeth, eds. *Religious Perspectives on Business Ethics: An Anthology.* Lanham, MD: Rowman & Littlefield Publishers, 2007.

Payne, Brian K. *White-Collar Crime.* Thousand Oaks, CA: Sage, 2012.

Price, Terry L. *Leadership Ethics, An Introduction.* New York: Cambridge Press, 2008.

Rawls, John. *A Theory of Justice.* Cambridge, MA: Harvard University Press, 1971.

Stone, Christopher D. *Where the Law Ends: The Social Control of Corporate Behavior.* Prospect Heights, IL: Waveland Press, 1975.

Vagelos, Roy, and Louis Galambos. *The Moral Corporation, Merck Experiences.* New York: Cambridge University Press, 2006.

Werhane, Patricia H., and R. Edward Freeman. *The Blackwell Encyclopedic Dictionary of Business Ethics.* Malden, MA: Blackwell, 1997.

Zak, Paul J., ed. *Moral Markets: The Critical Role of Values in the Economy.* Princeton, NJ: Princeton University Press, 2008.

Part Three: Chapters 6–7

Bhagwati, Jagdish. *In Defense of Globalization.* New York: Oxford University Press, 2007.

Burke, Edmund M. *Managing a Company in an Activist World: The Leadership Challenge of Corporate Citizenship.* Westport, CT: Praeger, 2005.

Coicaud, Jean-Marc et al., eds. *The Globalization of Human Rights.* New York: United Nations University Press, 2003.

Crane, Andrew, Dirk Matten, and Jeremy Moon. *Corporations and Citizenship.* Cambridge, UK: Cambridge University Press, 2008.

Elkington, John. *Cannibals with Forks: The Triple Bottom Line of 21st Century Business.* London: Thompson, 1997.

Epstein, Mark J. *Making Sustainability Work: Best Practices in Managing and Measuring Corporate Social, Environmental, and Economic Impacts.* San Francisco: Berrett-Koehler, 2008.

Fombrun, Charles. *Reputation.* Boston, MA: Harvard Business School Press, 1996.

Friedman, Thomas L. *The Lexus and the Olive Tree.* New York: Anchor Books, 2000.

————. *The World Is Flat: A Brief History of the Twenty-First Century.* New York: Farrar, Straus and Giroux, 2005.

Googins, Bradley K., Philip H. Mirvis, and Steven A. Rochlin. *Beyond Good Company: Next Generation Corporate Citizenship.* New York: Palgrave Macmillan, 2007.

Kiggunda, Moses N. *Managing Globalization in Developing Countries and Transition Economies.* New York: Praeger, 2002.

Korten, David C. *When Corporations Rule the World,* 2nd ed. San Francisco, CA: Berrett-Koehler, 2001.

Margolis, Joshua Daniel, and James Patrick Walsh. *People and Profits? The Search for a Link between a Company's Social and Financial Performance.* Mahwah, NJ: Erlbaum, 2001.

McIntosh, Alastair. *Soil and Soul: People versus Corporate Power.* London: Aurum Press, 2004.

Orlitzky, Marc, and Diane Swanson. *Toward Integrative Corporate Citizenship: Research Advances in Corporate Social Performance.* New York: Palgrave Macmillan, 2008.

Porter, Michael. *The Competitive Advantage of Nations.* New York: Basic Books, 1991.

Savitz, Andrew W., and Karl Weber. *The Triple Bottom Line: How Today's Best-Run Companies Are Achieving Economic, Social, and Environmental Success—And How You Can Too*. San Francisco: Jossey-Bass, 2006.

Scherer, Andreas Georg, and Guido Palazzo, eds. *Handbook of Research on Global Corporate Citizenship*. Northampton, MA: Edward Elgar Publishing, 2008.

Sethi, S. Prakash. *Setting Global Standards: Guidelines for Creating Global Codes of Conduct in Multinational Corporations*. New York: John Wiley & Sons, 2003.

Soros, George. *On Globalization*. New York: Perseus Books, 2002.

Stiglitz, Joseph E. *Making Globalization Work*. New York: W.W. Norton, 2007.

Waddell, Steve. *Global Action Networks: Creating Our Future Together*. New York: Palgrave Macmillan, 2011.

Williams, Bob. *The Sustainability Advantage: Seven Business Case Benefits of a Triple Bottom Line*. Gabriola Island, British Columbia: New Society Publishers, 2002.

Williams, Oliver F., ed, *Peace through Commerce: Responsible Corporate Citizenship and the Ideals of the United Nations Global Compact*. South Bend, IN: University of Notre Dame Press, 2008.

Yaziji, Michael, and Jonathan Doh. *NGOs and Corporations: Conflict and Collaboration*. New York: Cambridge University Press, 2009.

Part Four: Chapters 8–9

Coen, David, Wyn Grant, and Graham Wilson, eds. *The Oxford Handbook of Business and Government*. New York: Oxford University Press, 2011.

Epstein, Edwin M. *The Corporation in American Politics*. Englewood Cliffs, NJ: Prentice-Hall, 1969.

Foundation for Public Affairs. *The State of Corporate Public Affairs 2011–2012*. Washington, DC: Foundation for Public Affairs, 2012.

Harris, Phil, and Craig S. Fleisher, eds. *Handbook of Public Affairs*. Thousand Oaks, CA: Sage, 2005.

Lodge, George C. *The New American Ideology*. New York: Alfred A. Knopf, 1978.

———. *Comparative Business–Government Relations*. Englewood Cliffs, NJ: Prentice-Hall, 1990.

———, and Ezra F. Vogel, eds. *Ideology and National Competitiveness*. Boston: Harvard Business School Press, 1998.

Miller, Brian, and Mike Lapham. *The Self-Made Myth: And the Truth about How Government Helps Individuals and Businesses Succeed*. San Francisco: Berrett-Koehler, 2012.

Parker, Christine, and Vibeke Lehmann Nielsen, eds. *Explaining Compliance: Business Responses to Regulation*. Northampton, MA: Edward Elgar Publishing, 2011.

Sachs, Jeffrey D. *The End of Poverty: Economic Possibilities for Our Time*. New York: Penguin Press, 2005.

Schier, Steven E. *By Invitation Only: The Rise of Exclusive Politics in the United States*. New York: Random House, 2001.

Sorkin, Andrew Ross. *Too Big to Fail: The Inside Story of How Wall Street and Washington Fought to Save the Financial System—and Themselves*. New York: Viking, 2009.

Vogel, David. *Kindred Strangers: The Uneasy Relationship between Politics and Business in America*. Princeton, NJ: Princeton University Press, 1996.

Wilson, Gregory P. *Managing to the New Regulatory Reality: Doing Business under the Dodd-Frank Act*. Hoboken, NJ: John Wiley & Sons, 2011.

Woodstock Theological Center. *The Ethics of Lobbying: Organized Interests, Political Power, and the Common Good*. Washington, DC: Georgetown University Press, 2002.

Yadav, Vineeta. *Political Parties, Business Groups and Corruption in Developing Countries*. New York: Oxford University Press, 2011.

Part Five: Chapters 10–11

Anderson, Ray C., with Robin White. *Business Lessons from a Radical Industrialist*. New York: St. Martin's Griffin, 2011.

Arnold, Matthew B., and Robert M. Day. *The Next Bottom Line: Making Sustainable Development Tangible*. Washington, DC: World Resources Institute, 1998.

Cline, Elizabeth L. *Over-dressed: The Shockingly High Cost of Cheap Fashion*. New York: Penguin, 2012.

Daly, Herman E. *Beyond Growth: The Economics of Sustainable Development*. Boston: Beacon Press, 1996.

Dunphy, Dexter, Suzanne Benn, and Andrew Griffiths. *Organisational Change for Corporate Sustainability*. New York: Routledge, 2003.

Esty, Daniel C., and Andrew S. Winston. *Green to Gold: How Smart Companies Use Environmental Strategy to Innovate, Create Value, and Build Competitive Advantage*. Revised edition. Hoboken, NJ: John Wiley & Sons, 2009.

Foreman, Christopher H., Jr. *The Promise and Perils of Environmental Justice*. Washington, DC: Brookings Institution, 2000.

Frederick, William C. *Natural Corporate Management: An Evolutionary Interpretation*. Sheffield, OK: Greenleaf Publishing, 2012.

Friedman, Frank B. *Practical Guide to Environmental Management*, 11th ed. Washington, DC: Environmental Law Institute, 2011.

Friedman, Thomas L. *Hot, Flat, and Crowded: Why We Need a Green Revolution—and How It Can Renew America*. New York: Farrar, Strauss and Giroux, 2008.

Hammond, Allen. *Which World? Scenarios for the 21st Century*. Washington, DC: Island Press, 1998.

Hart, Stuart L. *Capitalism at the Crossroads: The Unlimited Business Opportunities in Solving the World's Most Difficult Problems*. Philadelphia, PA: Wharton School Publishing, 2005.

Hawken, Paul, Amory Lovins, and L. Hunter Lovins. *Natural Capitalism: Creating the Next Industrial Revolution*. Boston: Little Brown, 1999.

Hoffman, Andrew J. *Competitive Environmental Strategy: A Guide to the Changing Business Landscape*. Washington, DC: Island Press, 2000.

Holliday, Charles O., Jr., et al. *Walking the Talk: The Business Case for Sustainable Development*. Sheffield, UK: Greenleaf Publishing, 2002.

Long, Frederick J., and Matthew B. Arnold. *The Power of Environmental Partnerships*. Fort Worth, TX: Dryden Press, 1995.

Russo, Michael V. *Companies on a Mission: Entrepreneurial Strategies for Growing Sustainably, Responsibly, and Profitably*. Stanford, CA: Stanford University Press, 2010.

Sharma, Sanjay, and J. Alberto Aragon-Correa, eds. *Corporate Environmental Strategy and Competitive Advantage*. Northampton, MA: Edgar Elgar Academic Publishing, 2005.

Schendler, Auden. *Getting Green Done: Hard Truths from the Front Lines and Sustainability Revolution*. New York: Foundation for Public Affairs, 2009.

Speth, James Gustaveth. *The Bridge at the Edge of the World*. New Haven, CT: Yale University Press, 2008.

Stead, Jean Garner, and W. Edward Stead. *Management for a Small Planet*, 3rd edition. Armonk, NY: M.E. Sharpe, 2009.

Stoner, James A. F., and Charles Wankel, eds. *Managing Climate Change, Business Risks and Consequences: Leadership for Global Sustainability*. New York: Palgrave Macmillan, 2012.

Waddock, Sandra, and Malcolm McIntosh. *SEE Change: Making the Transition to a Sustainable Enterprise Economy*. Sheffield, OK: Greenleaf Publishing, 2011.

Winston, Andrew S. *Green Recovery*. Boston: Harvard Business Press, 2009.

Worldwatch Institute. *State of the World 2012: Toward Sustainable Prosperity*. New York: W.W. Norton, 2012.

Part Six: Chapters 12–13

Andrews, Lori. *I Know Who You Are and I Saw What You Did: Social Networks and the Death of Privacy*. New York: Free Press, 2011.

Auplat, Claire. *Nanotechnology and Sustainable Development*. London: Routledge, 2011.

Baram, Michael, and Mathilde Bourrier. *Governing Risk in GM Agriculture*. New York: Cambridge University Press, 2011.

Bynum, Terrell Ward, and Simon Rogerson. *Computer Ethics and Professional Responsibility*. Malden, MA: Blackwell, 2003.

Done, Adrian. *Global Trends*. New York: Palgrave Macmillan, 2011.

Heinberg, Richard. *Cloning the Buddha: The Moral Impact of Biotechnology*. San Juan Capistrano, CA: Quest Books, 1999.

Horn, Tom, and Nita Horn. *Forbidden Gates: How Genetics, Robotics, Artificial Intelligence, Synthetic Biology, Nanotechnology, and Human Enhancement Herald the Dawn of Techno-Dimensional Spiritual Warfare*. Crane, MO: Defender Publishing, 2010.

Larquin, Paul. *High Tech Harvest*. Cambridge, MA: Westview Press, 2008.

Levy, Steven. *Hackers: Heroes of the Computer Revolution*. Sebastopol, CA: O'Reilly Media, 2010.

McClure, Stuart, Joel Scambray, and George Kurtz. *Hacking Exposed: Network Security Secrets and Solutions*. New York: McGraw-Hill, 2009.

Micek, Deborah, and Warren Whitlock. *Twitter Revolution*. Las Vegas, NV: Xeno Press, 2008.

Muller, Hunter. *The Transformational CIO*. Hoboken, NJ: John Wiley & Sons, 2011.

Paarlberg, Robert. *Starved for Science: How Biotechnology Is Being Kept Out of Africa*. Cambridge, MA: Harvard University Press, 2008.

Park, Alice. *The Stem Cell Hope: How Stem Cell Medicine Can Change Our Lives*. New York: Hudson Street Press, 2011.

Rader, William C. *Blocked in the USA: The Stem Cell Miracle*. Malibu, CA: Nanog Publishing, 2010.

Rosen, Larry D. *Understanding Our Obsession with Technology and Overcoming Its Hold on Us*. Hampshire, UK: Palgrave Macmillan, 2012.

Safko, Lon, and David K. Brake. *The Social Media Bible: Tactics, Tools, and Strategies for Business Success.* New York: John Wiley & Sons, 2009.

Shaw, Michael J., ed. *E-Commerce and the Digital Economy.* Armonk, NY: M.E. Sharpe, 2006.

Straub, Detmar, Seymour Goodman, and Richard Baskerville, eds. *Information Security: Policy, Processes, and Practices.* Armonk, NY: M.E. Sharpe, 2008.

Weasel, Lisa H. *Food Fray: Inside the Controversy over Genetically Modified Food.* New York: American Management Association, 2009.

Zook, Matthew. *The Geography of the Internet Industry.* Malden, MA: Blackwell, 2005.

Part Seven: Chapters 14–19

Andvliet, Luc, and Mary B. Anderson. *Getting It Right: Making Corporate-Community Relations Work.* Sheffield, UK: Greenleaf, 2009.

Bainbridge, Stephen M. *Corporate Governance after the Financial Crisis.* New York: Oxford University Press, 2012.

Bebchuk, Lucian A., and Jesse M. Fried. *Pay without Performance: The Unfulfilled Promise of Executive Compensation.* Cambridge, MA: Harvard University Press, 2004.

Bugg-Levine, Antony, and Jed Emerson. *Impact Investing: Transforming How We Make Money While Making a Difference.* San Francisco: Jossey-Bass, 2011.

Carter, Colin B., and Jay W. Lorsch. *Back to the Drawing Board: Designing Corporate Boards for a Complex World.* Boston: Harvard Business School Press, 2004.

Cohan, William D. *House of Cards: A Tale of Hubris and Wretched Excess on Wall Street.* New York: Doubleday, 2009.

Coombs, W. Timothy. *Ongoing Crisis Communication.* Thousand Oaks, CA: Sage, 2012.

Davidson, Kirk D. *Selling Sin: The Marketing of Socially Unacceptable Products.* New York: Praeger, 2003.

Dine, Philip M. *State of the Unions: How Labor Can Strengthen the Middle Class, Improve Our Economy, and Regain Political Influence.* New York: McGraw-Hill, 2008.

Edley, Christopher, Jr. *Not All Black and White: Affirmative Action and American Values.* San Francisco: Noonday Books, 1998.

Eichenwald, Kurt. *Conspiracy of Fools: A True Story.* New York: Broadway Books, 2005.

Fagan, Colette, Maria Gonzalez Menendez, and Silvia Gomez Anson, eds. *Women on Corporate Boards and in Top Management.* New York: Palgrave Macmillan, 2012.

Ferracone, Robin A. *Fair Pay, Fair Play: Aligning Executive Performance and Pay.* San Francisco, CA: Jossey-Bass, 2010.

Gehrt, Jennifer, and Colleen Moffitt. *Strategic Public Relations: 10 Principles to Harness the Power of PR.* Bloomington, IN: Xlibris Publishing, 2009.

Gordon, Averill Elizabeth. *Public Relations.* New York: Oxford University Press, 2011.

Grant, Peter. *The Business of Giving.* New York: Palgrave Macmillan, 2011.

Greenhouse, Steven. *The Big Squeeze: Tough Times for the American Worker.* New York: Anchor Books, 2009.

Grunig, Larissa A., James E. Grunig, and David M. Dozier. *Excellent Public Relations and Effective Organizations.* Mahwah, NJ: Erlbaum, 2002.

Hilts, Philip J. *Protecting America's Health: The FDA, Business, and One Hundred Years of Regulation.* New York: Alfred A. Knopf, 2003.

Jordan-Meier, Jane. *The Four Stages of Highly Effective Crisis Management.* Boca Raton, FL: Taylor & Francis Group, 2011.

Kelly, Marjorie. *The Divine Right of Capital: Dethroning the Corporate Aristocracy.* San Francisco: Berrett-Koehler Publishers, Inc., 2003.

Lakin, Nick, and Veronica Scheubel. *Corporate Community Involvement: The Definitive Guide to Maximizing Your Business' Societal Engagement.* Sheffield, UK: Greenleaf, 2010.

Leana, Carrie, and Denise Rousseau. *Relational Capital.* New York: Oxford University Press, 2000.

Lewis, Michael. *The Big Short: Inside the Doomsday Machine.* New York: W.W. Norton, 2010.

Lorsch, Jay W. *The Future of Boards: Meeting the Governance Challenges of the Twenty-First Century.* Boston, MA: Harvard Business Review Press, 2012.

Miceli, Marcia P., Janet Pollex Near, and Terry M. Dworkin. *Whistle-Blowing in Organizations.* London: Routledge, 2008.

Mitroff, Ian I. *Managing Crises before They Happen.* New York: American Management Association, 2005.

Monks, Robert A. G., and Nell Minow. *Corporate Governance,* 5th ed. Hoboken, NJ: John Wiley & Sons, 2011.

Rosen, Jeffrey. *The Unwanted Gaze: The Destruction of Privacy in America.* New York: Random House, 2000.

Schepers, Donald. *Socially Responsible Investing.* Florence, KY: Routledge, 2007.

Schlosser, Eric. *Fast Food Nation: The Dark Side of the All-American Meal.* New York: Perennial, 2002.

Siegel, Lucy B., ed. *Public Relations around the Globe: A Window on International Business Culture*. New York: Bridge Global Strategies, 2012.

Smallen-Grob, Diane. *Making It in Corporate America.* New York: Praeger, 2003.

Stout, Lynn. *The Shareholder Value Myth: How Putting Shareholders First Harms Investors, Corporations, and the Public.* San Francisco, CA: Berrett-Koehler, 2012.

Whitman, Marina, V.N. *New World, New Rules: The Changing Role of the American Corporation.* Boston: Harvard Business School Press, 1999.

A

Adams, Amanda, 369n
Adelson, Sheldon, 198
Adler, Paul S., 406n
Adler, Roy Douglas, 386n
Adoboli, Kweku, 95
Agle, Bradley R., 16n
Akalp, Nellie, 60n
Albrecht, Karl, (fig.) 29n, 29, 29n
Altman, Barbara W., 139n
Anderson, Ray C., 249, 249n
Anderson, S. Cathy, 467n
Andrews, Lori, 343n
Angell, Marcia, 495n
Apuzzo, Matt, 488n
Aquinas, St. Thomas, (fig.) 84
Aragon-Correa, Alberto, 252n
Aristotle, (fig.) 84
Arneault, Ted, 199
Arnold, Matthew B., 250n
Ayala, Anna, (exh.) 438
Azcuenaga, Mary L., 436n

B

Baase, Sara, 98n
Babchuk, Lucian A., 319, 320n
Bakar, Joel, (exh.) 59
Baker, Drew, 273
Barber, Alison E., 56n
Barnett, Jonathan, 220n
Barr, Bob, (exh.) 194
Bartlett, Christopher A., 25n
Bass, Carl, 253
Batellier, Pierre, 522n
Baum, Bob, (exh.) 435
Bear, Larry Alan, 96n
Beauchamp, Tom L., 76n
Beaupre, Ryan, 204n
Benn, Suzanne, 248n
Bentley, R.W., 215n
Berenbeim, Ronald C., 100n
Berman, Marc, (exh.) 270
Berner, Robert, 488n
Berners-Lee, Tim, 263n
Bewkes, Jeff, 434
Bhagwati, Jagdish, 126n
Bhatia, S. Joe, 537–538
Biden, Joseph, 106
Birleffi, Bobbie, 459n
Black, Stephanie, 121n
Blair, Margaret M., 6n

Blair, Natasha, 203n
Blankenship, Donald L., 449–452, (exh.) 452, 454
Block, Walter, 280n
Blomstrom, Robert, 49n
Blumenthal, Neil, 61
Boatright, John R., 77n, 84n, 96n
Boggs, Carl, 48n
Bonardi, Jean-Philippe, 187n
Bornstein, Robert, (exh.) 270
Boss, Allen D., 55n
Boss, R. Wayne, 55n
Boutilier, Robert, 17n
Bowen, Howard R., 50n, 147n
Bowie, Norman E., 76n
Brammer, Stephen, 324n
Branson, Richard, 62n
Brennan, Mary Elizabeth, 489
Brooks, Bradley W., 467n
Brooks, Leonard J., 94n
Brotatzky-Geiger, Jeugen, (exh.) 149n
Brown, Gordon, 286
Bryant, Bunyan, 241n
Buchholz, Rogene, 32n
Bullard, Robert D., 241n
Burke, Edmund M., (fig.) 404n
Burkett, Genesis, 270
Burns, Ursula, 385–386
Bush, George H.W., 177
Bush, George W., 177

C

Cameron, Andrew, 279
Campbell, Tom, 439
Carlson, Curtis L., 459
Carter, Colin, 315, 315n
Carter, Jimmy, 177
Caulfield, Brian, 470n
Chou, Dorothy, 276
Civita, Roberto, 139
Clapp, Jennifer, 54n
Clarkson, Max B.E., 7n
Clinton, Hillary Rodham, (exh.) 197
Coburn, Tom, 177
Cody, Doug, 464
Cohan, William D., 326n
Cohn, D'Vera, 401n
Colby, Anne, 82n
Connerly, Ward, 391n
Conyon, Martin J., (fig.) 319n
Corbett, Tom, 200
Corbyn, Peter, 219n

Cox, Christopher, 328
Cox, Steven M., 467n
Crain, Mark, 176
Crain, Nicole, 176
Cramer, Ann Wilson, 407
Crane, Andrew, 139n
Cullen, John B., (fig.) 92n

D

Dalton, Dan R., 73n
Daly, Herman E., 219n
Darcy, Keith, 100
Davenport, Kim, 139n, (exh.) 141n
David, Eugen, 257
Davidson, D. Kirk, 97n
Davidson, Julie O'Connell, 461n
Davies, Kert, 224n
Davis, Julie, 3n
Davis, Keith, 49n
Davis, Rob, (exh.) 438
Deal, Terrence E., 91n
Deeter, Scott, 511, 513n, 514, 515n
DeGeorge, Richard T., 83n
De la Cruz, Gabrial, 22
DeRugy, Veronique, (fig.) 175n, (fig.) 176n
DesJardins, Joe, 76n, 83n
Dessain, Vincent, 25n
Diamond, Jared, 258n
Dillon, Robin L., 437n
DiMaio, Andrea, 274
Dimon, Jamie, 181
Doh, Jonathan, 41n
Donaldson, Thomas, 6n, 7n
Donna, Rose, 60
Dunfee, Thomas W., 418n
Dunford, Benjamin B., 55n
Dunn, Paul, 94n
Dunphy, Dexter, 248n
Duska, Brenda, 94n
Duska, Ronald, 94n

E

Eaton, Adrienne E., 359n
Eaves, Elisabeth, 472n
Eccles, R.G., 251n
Eckert, Robert A., 532, 532n, 539–540
Eichstaedt, Peter, 135n
Eisenbeis, H. Richard, 16n, 458n
Elkington, John, 153n
Enz, Cathy A., 505n

Epstein, Edwin, 48n, 201n
Erickson, Markham, 207

F

Farrell, Michael B., 461n
Fiet, James O., 79n
Fishman, Charles, 254n
Fleisher, Craig S., 203n, 433n
Fombrun, Charles J., 55n, 140, 140n
Fons, Jerome S., 482n, 483n,
    491, 491n
Ford, Gerald, 177
Foreman, Jr., Christopher H., 241n
Foster, Gary, 76
Fox, Steven, 293n
Fralin, Roy, 423–424
Frank, Barney, 181
Frank, Loven, (exh.) 270
Franklin, Benjamin, (fig.) 84
Freda, Fabrizio, 320
Frederick, J. Norris, 467n
Frederick, William C., 50, (fig.) 51n
Freeman, Morgan, 198
Freeman, R. Edward, 7n, 11n, 50n
French, Liz, 506n
Fried, Jesse M., 319, 320n
Friedman, Frank B., 245n
Friedman, Milton, 56, 56n, 57n, 58n
Friedman, Thomas, 117, 117n, 119, 119n,
    (www) 133, 220
Frooman, Jeff, 52n

G

Gagnon, Katia, 526n
Gardberg, Naomi A., 140, 140n
Gary, Elbert, (exh.) 101
Gat, Azar, (exh.) 129n
Gavales, Lisa, 431
Gentile, Mary, 79, 79n
Gillespie, Janet, 82n
Gingrich, Newt, 198
Githua, Moses, 270
Glaser, Mark, 470n
Goldstein, Jerry D., 49n
Goodell, Jeff, 450n, 452n, 454n
Goodman, Peter S., 437n, 487n
Googins, Bradley K., 143, 143n,
    (fig.) 145n, 421n
Gossling, Tobias, 52n
Greenberg, Sally, 536–537
Griffiths, Andrew, 248n
Grossman, Lawrence, 278
Grossman, Lev, 470n
Grow, Brian, 488n
Grunig, James, 429, 429n

H

Hackman, J. Richard, 80n
Hall, Jr., Joseph K., 467–468
Hammond, Allen, 124, 124n
Hanks, Sue, 16n
Hanna, Sherman D., 311n
Hansen, Duane, 55n
Hanson, Gordon, 401n
Hardin, Garrett, 221n
Harrison, Jeffrey S., 79n
Hart, Stuart L., 61n, 248n, 252n
Hartman, Laura P., 76n, 83n
Hawken, Paul, 219n
Hawley, Jack, 80, 80n
Hawthorne, Fran, 493n, 494n
Heald, Morrell, 50n
Heath, Robert, 32n
Hemphill, Thomas, 177n
Hendler, James, 263n
Herford, Mark, 440n
Hersman, Deborah, 165
Hess, David, 418n
Hilfer, Joelle, 268
Hilfer, Tom, 268
Hill, John W., 73n
Hillman, Amy J., 56n, 187n, (fig.) 188n
Hilts, Philip J., 495n
Hitt, Michael A., (fig.) 188n
Hoffman, Lou, 433n
Holleyman, Robert, 294
Hollinger, Richard C., 369n
Hoog, Andrew, 292
Horowitz, Sara, 364
Hsieh, Tony, 431
Hubbard, Brian, 181
Husted, Bryan, 54, 54n

I

Ilioipulp, Andrei, 100
Isaacs, William, 40n
Issa, Darrell, 27n
Izraeli, Dove, 73n

J

Jobs, Steven, 134
Johnson, Bobbie, 265n
Johnson, Fisk, 434
Johnson, Simon, 181
Jones, Adrian, 31
Jones, David A., 415
Joseph, Joshua, 104n
Josephson, Matthew, 50n
Joy, Bill, 265, 265n, 287, 287n,
    298, 298n

K

Kanter, David, 224n
Karpoff, Jonathan M., 73n
Katzenberg, Jeffrey, 198
Keim, Gerald D., 187n
Keithley, Carter, 538
Kennedy, Allan A., 91n
Kennedy, Anthony, (exh.) 197
Kenneth-Hensel, Pamela A., 55n
Kerry, John, 283
Khera, Mandeep, 305
Kim, Peter S., 501
Kirkpatrick, Grant, 317n
Kleinfeld, Klaus, 113n
Kochan, Thomas A., 359n
Kohlberg, Lawrence, (fig.) 81n, 82n
Kopf, Beverly, 459n
Korten, David C., 48n, 220, 220n
Kozlowski, Dennis, 76
Kramer, Mark R., 50n, 417n
Krell, Eric, 104n
Kurtz, Justin, 272
Kwon, S.W., 406n

L

LaBerge, Myriam, 41n
Lacey, Russell, 55n
Laczniak, Gene R., 97n
Laing, Jonathan R., 488n
Lassila, Ora, 263n
LaTour, Tom, 509
Lawrence, Anne T., 27n, (fig.) 39n, 40n,
    143n, 448n, 467n, 480n, 493n, 511n,
    522n, 531n
Le, Vananh, 17n
Ledbetter, Lilly, 389
Lee, D. Scott, 73n
Leisinger, Klaus M., (exh.) 149n
Leondakis, Niki, 507, 509
LeVeness, Frank P., 86n
Levine, Diana, 347
Levine, Ronald J., 440n
Levy, Paul, (exh.) 365
Lewellyn, Patsy G., 139n
Lewis, Arthur, 127n
Lewis, Michael, 481n
Lichtenstein, Nelson, 3n
Lindamood, Suzanne, 311n
Linde, Robyn, 458n
Lockhart, Joe, 207
Loden, Marilyn, 379n
Lodge, George, 164n
Logsdon, Jeanne M., 139n, 324n
London, Ted, 250n
Long, Frederick J., 250n
Lorsch, Jay, 315, 315n

Lovins, Amory, 219n
Lovins, L. Hunter, 219n
Lowenstein, Roger, 488, 488n
Luce, Rebecca A., 56n
Lynch, Denny, (exh.) 438

M

MacDonald, Chris, 153n
MacLaury, Bruce K., 6n
Madoff, Bernard, 328
Madson, Peter M., 437n
Mahon, John F., 55n, 187n
Maldonado-Bear, Rita, 96n
Malone, Patricia, 204n
Mamic, Ivanka, 100n
Mandel, Michael, 262n
Margolis, Joshua, 52n
Martin, Gerald S., 73n
Mate, Janos, 224n
Matten, Dirk, 139n
McCain, John, (exh.) 194, 283
McConnell, Ryan, 74n
McDaniel, Jr., Raymond W., 480–491
McDonald, Bob, 250
McGowan, Richard A., 187n
McIntosh, Alastair, 48n
McKersey, Robert B., 359n
Meade, Paul, 31
Melani, Kenneth, (exh.) 435
Metzger, Michael B., 73n
Milliman, John F., 80n
Minnis, Perry, 113n
Mirvis, Philip H., 143, 143n,
    (fig.) 145
Misser, Sunny, 154
Mitchell, Ronald K., 16n
Moody-Stuart, Mark, 27
Moon, Ban Ki, 127
Moon, Jeremy, 139n
Moore, John, (fig.) 287n
Moreland, Eric, 74n
Morgenson, Gretchen, 487n, 488n
Moynihan, Patrick, 164
Murphy, Patrick E., 97n
Mvistendahl, Mara, (exh.) 350n

N

Nader, Ralph, (exh.) 194
Nasir, Adnan, 299
Neal, Alfred C., 48n
Neck, Christopher P., 80n
Nelson, Marilyn Carlson, 458–466
Nest, Michael, 135n
Nielsen, Bill, 428, 428n
Nooyi, Indra, 382

Nord, Nancy A., 534–536
Norman, Wayne, 153n

O

Obama, Barack, (exh.) 173, 177, (exh.) 194,
    198, 200, 264, (exh.) 300, 389
Obama, Michele, 170
O'Daniel, Adam, 468n
O'Hara, Jerome, 98
Oldham, Greg, 80n
Olson, Kim, 460
O'Neal, Stanley, 318
O'Neill, Paul, 111–123, 113n
Orlitzky, Marc, 52n
Orsato, Renato J., 252n
Otterbourg, Susan, 421n

P

Pace, Michael, 503
Paine, Lynn, 99, 99n
Palmer, Daniel E., 7n
Pandit, Vikram, 330–331
Passel, Jeffrey S., 401n
Perez, George, 98
Peslak, Alan R., 288n
Phillips, Robert, 7n
Pinetti, Steve, 507
Plascencio, Jaime, (exh.) 438
Plato, (fig.) 84
Polski, Tom, 464
Porter, Michael E., 50n, 252n, 417n
Post, James E., 6n, 37n, 139n, 363n
Prahalad, C.K., (exh.) 61, 61n
Presley, Clay, 468
Preston, Lee E., 6n, 7n, 37n
Primeaux, Patrick, 86n
Putman, Robert D., 201n, 406n

Q

Quilty, David, 441

R

Rajaratnam, Raj, 69, 327
Rands, Gordon P., 143n, 249n
Ransler, Chip, 60
Rauch, Maggie, 459n
Raufflet, Emmanuel, 522n
Reagan, Ronald, 177
Reder, Melvin W., 80n
Reding, Vivlane, 387
Rehbein, Kathleen, 324n

Reich, Robert, (exh.) 59
Ricardo, David, 122
Ricci, Frank, 391
Roberts, David, 451n
Rochlin, Steven A., 421n
Rockness, Howard, 74n
Rockness, Joanne, 74n
Rodemeyer, Michael, 516
Rodriguez, Raymond, 511–512
Rogovski, Nikolai, 418n
Romney, Mitt, (exh.) 194
Rondinelli, Dennis A., 250n
Roth, Eldon, 444–445
Rowley, Timothy J., 10n
Rudd, Kevin, 437
Rutter, William, 512
Rynes, Sara, 52n

S

Saba, Sally, 395
Sachs, Sybille, 6n
Saiia, David, 17n
Salazar, Jose de Jesus, 54, 54n
Sandberg, Sheryl, 434
Sanyal, Rajib, 105n
Savarese, John F., 440
Schmidt, Eric, 192
Schmidt, Frank, 52n
Schumacher, Tom, 102
Schumer, Charles, 165
Schwartz, Jonathan, 431
Schwartz, Mark S., 73n
Scott, Lee, 3
Seidman, Dov, 75
Sethi, S. Prakash, 532n
Sharfman, Mark, 411n
Sharma, Sanjay, 252n
Shnayerson, Michael, 450n, 451n
Siguaw, Judy A., 505n
Silverman, Murray, 503n
Simpson, Anne, 316n, 331n
Singer, Andrew, 102n, 104n
Sinha, Manoj, 60
Sjoman, Anders, 25n
Sloan, Gene, 505n
Smith, Eliot Blair, 482n, 483n, 488n
Smith, Lamar, 208
Snyder, Jim, 451n
Solomon, Robert C., (fig.) 84, 84n
Song, Susan, 461n
Sopow, Eli, 32n
Soros, George, 198
Speth, James Gustave, 219n
Spinello, Richard, 98n
Spitzner, Lance, 292, 292n
Starik, Mark, 143n, 249n
Steinhafel, Gregg, 195

Stevens, Betsy, 100n
Stiglitz, Joseph E., 126n
Stoll, Mary Lyn, 7n
Storch, Jerry, 539
Sundar, Mario, 431n
Svendsen, Ann, 40n, 41n
Swartz, Jeff, 65, 66n
Swartz, Nathan, 65

T

Tao, Chen, 534
Tapia, Andres, (exh.) 381, 381n
Taylor, Jacqueline Sanchez, 461n
Thomas, Tom, 503n
Tinsley, Catherine H., 437n
Toffler, Alvin, 262, 262n
Trevino, Linda Klebe, 100n

V

Vadacchino, Mackie, 527
Valenti, Alix, 74n
Van Burden, Pieter, 52n
VanBuren III, Harry J., 324n
Van der Linde, Claas, 252n

Varney, Christine A., 172
Vasella, Daniel, (exh.) 149
Velasquez, Manual G., 84, 84n,
    85n, 372n
Victor, Bart, (fig.) 92n
Vidaver-Cohen, Deborah, 139n
Vogel, David, (exh.) 59
Vogelius, Edmund, 481n
Volker, Paul, 181
Vollmer, Christopher, 281
Votaw, Dow, 48n

W

Waddell, Steven, 131n, (fig.) 132n, 132n
Waddock, Sandra, 37n, 148n, 421n
Wahab, Suraj, 232–233
Walsh, James P., 52n
Walton, Clarence C., 54n
Walton, Sam, 406
Warren, Melinda, (fig.) 175n,
    (fig.) 176n
Wasieleski, David, 82n
Waxman, Henry, 481, 481n, 484n
Weaver, Gary R., 100n
Weber, James, 79n, 82n, 93n, 531n
Wells, Tina, 387–388

Wettstein, Florian, 49n
Whelan, Susan, 528
Whitcomb, Robert, 9n
White, Robin, 249n
Whitlock, April, 467–479
Wicks, Andrew C., 49n
Williams, Oliver, 100n
Williams, Wendy, 9n
Winkenwerder, William, (exh.) 435
Witzel, Jay, 464–465
Wood, Donna J., 16n, 147n
Woodford, Michael, 93
Woods, William John, 163
Wu, Meng-Ling, 52n

Y

Yager, Christine, 165
Yaziji, Michael, 41n
Yunus, Muhammad, (exh.) 62, 62n

Z

Zadek, Simon, 143n, 147, 147n
Zakhem, Abe J., 7n
Zivan, David, 351n

A

Aaron's, 391–392
Abbott Laboratories, 397
Absolut Vodka, 432
Accenture, 140
Acid rain, 238, (exh.) 239
Acxiom, 343
Ad Council, 433
Ad hoc coalitions, 186
Advanced Micro Devices, 171
Advocacy advertising, 200–201
Affirmative action, 390–391
Affordable Care Act, (exh.) 173
AFL-CIO, (www) 375
African Institute of Corporate Citizenship, (exh.) 144
A.I.G. International, 309
Ajinomoto, 146
Alburnus Maior, 257
Alcoa, 111–113
Alliance Boots, 143
Alternative dispute resolution (ADR), 348
American Arbitration Association, 348
American Business Collaboration for Quality Dependent Care, (www) 399
American Business Ethics Awards, 104
American Civil Liberties Union (ACLU), (www) 375
American Eagle Outfitters, 272
American Institute for Certified Public Accountants (AICPA), (exh.) 94
American Legislative Exchange Council (ALEC), 184
American Lung Association, 236
American Marketing Association (AMA), (exh.) 97
American National Standards Institute (ANSI), 537–538
American Petroleum Institute, 434
Americans with Disabilities Act (ADA), (exh.) 390
Anti-Americanism, 125
Anti-Phishing Working Group, 275, (www) 282
Antitrust laws, 171–172
Apple, 147, 155–157, 334
APPROVe, 501
Arab Spring, 127
Arbitration Fairness Act, 348
Asea Brown Boveri (ABB), 145
Asian Forum on Corporate Social Responsibility, (exh.) 144, (www) 155

Association for Computing Machinery (ACM), (exh.) 97
Association of Certified Fraud Examiners, 109–110
As You Sow Foundation, (www) 65
AT&T, 172, 409, 432
Auditing process, 150–151
Autodesk, 253
Automobile emissions and mileage standards, 172–173
Avon, 51–52

B

Bangladesh, 361
Bank of America, 324–325
Barlow et al. v. A.P. Smith Manufacturing, 54
Barrick, 92
Baxter International, 346
Bayer, 286
B corporation, 60–61
Bear Stearns, 326
Beef Products Inc., 444–445
Behavioral advertising, 343
Beth Israel Deaconess Medical Center, (exh.) 365
Better Business Bureau, (www) 352
Better Regulation, (www) 180
Big Data R&D Initiative, 264
Biodiversity, 224–226
Biotechnology, 263, 300
Biotechnology Industry Organization, (www) 282, 514
Bioterrorism Biodefense, (www) 304
Bipartisan Campaign Reform Act, 198
Bloggers, 467, 470–479
Blogs, 261, 272–273
Blog with Integrity, 477, (exh.) 478
Bloomberg BusinessWeek, (www) 22
BlueScope Steel, 36
BMW, 393, (exh.) 412
Board of directors, 313–315
Boeing, 292
Bottom of the Pyramid, 61–62, (exh.) 62
Boundary-spanning departments, 18–19, (fig.) 18
BP, 238–239, 427
Bribery, 105–109, (exh.) 107
Bromium, 275
BSR, (www) 65, 142, (exh.) 144, (www) 155
Bundling, 202

Business and government:
    at arm's length, 163–164
    collaborative partnerships, 162
    influencing the relationship, 187–188
    legitimacy issues, 164
Business and society:
    dynamic environment, 19–21
    forces, (fig.) 19
    a systems perspective, 5, (fig.) 5
Business Charter for Sustainable Development, 230
Business ethics, 70–71, (fig.) 70
Business Fights Poverty, (www) 423
Business political action, global, 204–205
Business Roundtable, 192, (www) 206
Business Software Alliance (BSA), 294, (www) 304
Business USA, (www) 180

C

California Public Employees Retirement System (CalPERS), (www) 329, 331
California Rice Commission, 517–519, 521
Canadian Broadcasting Corporation (CBC), 520, 527
Canadian Business for Social Responsibility, (www) 65, (exh.) 144
Canadian Public Relations Society, (www) 443
CAN-SPAM Act, 274
Cap-and-trade, 243
Carbon Disclosure Project, (exh.) 225
Carbon neutrality, 228
Carbon offsets, 228
Carlson Company, 458–466
Carolina Pad, 467–479
Carrying capacity, 219
Casis Bahia, 61
CA Technologies, 251
Cato Institute, (www) 180
Cell phone regulation, 165–167
Cellular telephones, 269
CEMEX, 138, 409
Center for Corporate Citizenship at Boston College, (www) 423
Center for Democracy and Technology, 344
Center for Media and Democracy, (www) 443
Center for Responsible Nanotechnology, (www) 304
Center for Responsive Politics, (fig.) 189n, 190, (fig.) 196n

Centers for Disease Control, 341
Central state control, 128
CERES Principles, 230, 505
Chartered Financial Analysts (CFA), (exh.) 195
Chesapeake Energy, 324
Chevron, 434
Chief Information, Security, Technology Officer, 292–293, (exh.) 293, (www) 304
Chief Sustainability Officer, 250–251
Child care, 396
Children's Online Privacy Protection Act (COPPA), 291, (www) 304, 339, 436
China, (exh.) 107, (exh.) 129, 204, 218, 266–267, 275, 295, 346
Chipotle Mexican Grill, 400–401
Chiquita Brands, 88–89
Chronicle of Philanthropy, (www) 423
Chrysler, 161, 349
Cisco Systems, 417
Citibank, 286
Citigroup, 305–306, 330–331
Citizen Schools, 423–425
Citizens United, (exh.) 197, 200
City Newsstand, 290
Civic engagement, 405–406
Civil society, 131, (fig.) 132
Class Action Fairness Act, 347
Clean economy, 247
Climate change, 222–224, (fig.) 223
Cloning, 301–302
CNN Money, (www) 22
Coca-Cola, 43–44
Codes of environmental conduct, 229–230
Collaborative partnerships, 420–422
Coltan, conflict, 134–135
Committee Encouraging Corporate Philanthropy, (www) 423
Common Cause, (www) 206
Commons, 221 (*See* Natural Environment, Global Issues)
Community:
    business involvement in the, 405–407
    business relationship, 404–405, (fig.) 404, (fig.) 404, (exh.) 405
    relations, 407–410
Community Action Partnerships, (www) 423
Community relations manager, 407
Competitive intelligence, 31–32
Comprehensive Environmental Response Compensation Liability Act (CERCLA) (*See* Superfund)
Computer hackers, 289, (exh.) 289
Computer World, (www) 282
Conflicts of interest, 77–78
Constructive engagement, 130
Consumer Action, (www) 206, 352
Consumer affairs departments, 350–351
Consumer affairs officer, 350–351

Consumer Federation of America, 334, (www) 352
Consumer Financial Protection Bureau, (www) 180, (fig.) 340, (exh.) 342, 342
Consumer International, 334, (www) 352
Consumerism:
    achievements, 351–352
    advocacy for, 334–335
    business responses to, 348–351, (exh.) 350
    government protection, 336–342, (fig.) 337, (exh.) 338, (fig.) 340, (exh.) 342
    privacy in the digital age, 342–345
    product liability, 345–348, (exh.) 347
    reasons for, 335–336
    rights, 336
Consumer movement, 334–335
Consumer Product Safety Commission, 163, (fig.) 340, 351, (www) 352, 533–539
Consumer Product Safety Improvement Act, 163, 339
Consumer Reports, 334–335, (www) 352
Consumers Union (CU), 335, 536–537
Convoy Solutions, 237–238
Co-operative Bank, 71–72
Corporate citizenship,
    assessing, 147–151, (fig.) 148
    department of, 142
    global, 139–143, (exh.) 141
    management systems, 142–143
    principles, (exh.) 141
    professional associations, (exh.) 144
    profile, 140–142
    stages of, 143–146, (fig.) 145
Corporate crisis, 437
Corporate culture, 92
Corporate Executive Board, 72
Corporate foundations, 413
Corporate giving, 410–420, (fig.) 410, (fig.) 411, (exh.) 412, (exh.) 416, (fig.) 416, (fig.) 420
Corporate governance, 313
Corporate philanthropy, 410, (fig.) 410, (exh.) 412
Corporate political strategy, 187–188, (fig.) 188
    constituency-building, (fig.) 188, 199–201
    financial-incentive, (fig.) 188, 192–199, (exh.) 193, (exh.) 194, (fig.) 195, (fig.) 196, (exh.) 197
    information, (fig.) 188, 189–192, (fig.) 189, (exh.) 191
Corporate power, 47–49, (fig.) 48
Corporate Responsibility Magazine, 111, (www) 155
Corporate Responsibility.Net, (www) 155
Corporate social reporting, 151

Corporate Social Responsibility, 49–51, (fig.) 51
    award-winning practices, 63–64
    balancing multiple responsibilities, 51–53
    debate, 53–58, (fig.) 53
    limits, (exh.) 59
    role of business in society, (fig.) 59
Corporate Social Responsibility Europe, (exh.) 144
Corporate Social Responsibility Newswire, (www) 65
Costa Rica, 461–466
Council of Foreign Relations, (www) 43
Council of Institutional Investors, 322, (www) 329
Countrywide, (exh.) 338, 370
Covalence, 92
Crisis management, 437–440, (exh.) 438, (exh.) 441
Cruise ships, pollution, 227
CSR Asia, (exh.) 144
CSR Europe, (www) 65, (www) 155
CSR News, (www) 65
Cyberchondriacs, 279
Cyberspace, 263

D

Daimler AG, 107
Dark site, 439
Data Privacy Day, 291
Debt relief, 121
Deceptive advertising, 337–338
Defense Industry Initiative on Business Ethics and Conduct, (www) 111
Democracy, 127, (exh.) 129
Democratic Republic of the Congo (DRC), 134–135
Department of Justice, (fig.) 340
Department of Labor, 360, 364
Deregulation, 177
Derivatives, 180–182
Diageo, 185
Digital Advertising Alliance, 344
Digital Divide Network, (www) 282
Digital divide, the, 280–281
Digital medical records, 279
Digital Millennium Copyright Act, 295
Direct-to-consumer (DTC) advertising, 498–499
Disaster, terrorism and war relief, 409–410
Diversity, 379 (*See* Workplace diversity)
Diversity council, 394
Diversity, Inc. (www) 399
Diversity policies and practices, 393–398, (exh.) 398
Dodd-Frank Act, 170–171, 181, 319, 321, 326, 330, (exh.) 342, 342

Domestic partner benefits, (exh.) 398
Dow Corning, 232
Drug-Free Workplace Act, 367
Drug testing, 367, (fig.) 369

E

EarthCare program, 503–510
Earth Charter Initiative, (www) 231
Earthtrends, (www) 231
E-business, 267–268, (fig.) 268
E. coli bacteria, 333
Ecological challenges (*See* Natural
    environment)
Ecological footprint, 219
Ecologically Sustainable Organization
    (ESO), 249–252
E-commerce Times, (www) 282
Economic development, 408
Economic leverage, 199
Economic regulations, 170
Economist, The, (www) 22
Economy Watch, (www) 180
Ecosystem, 213
Elder care, 396
Electronic Communications Privacy
    Act, 366
Electronic Privacy Information Center
    (EPIC), 356
Eli Lilly, (exh.) 371
Employee assistance programs (EAPs), 369
Employee Polygraph Protection Act, 369
Employment-at-will, 362
Employment relationship, 357, (fig.) 357
Energy Management Inc., 18–19
Enlightened self-interest, 52
Environmental analysis, 28–31, (fig.) 29
Environmental audits, 251–252
Environmental Defense Fund, 235
Environmental intelligence, 29
Environmental justice, 241
Environmental management as a competitive
    advantage, 252–255, (exh.) 253
Environmental management in practice,
    250–251
Environmental partnerships, 250
Environmental Protection Agency (EPA),
    (www) 231, 236, 238, (www)
    256, 516
Environmental regulation:
    alternative policy approaches, 242–245,
        (fig.) 245
    costs and benefits of, 246–247, (fig.) 247
    greening of management, 248–249
    major areas of, 236–242, (fig.) 237,
        (exh.) 239, (exh.) 240
Environmental standards, 242–243, (fig.) 245
Equal employment opportunity, 388–393,
    (fig.) 389, (exh.) 390

Equal Employment Opportunity
    Commission (EEOC), 389, 391,
    (www) 399
Equality and Human Rights Commission
    (U.K.), 384
Equator Principles, 230
Ergonomics, 360
Ethical character, core elements of, 78–82,
    (fig.) 81
Ethical climates, 91–93, (fig.) 92
Ethical egoist, 76
Ethical principles, 69
Ethical problems, analyzing, 83–87
Ethical problems occur in business, why,
    75–78
Ethical relativism, 70
Ethical Trading Initiative (ETI), (exh.) 374,
    (www) 375
Ethics:
    in accounting, 93–94, (exh.) 94
    audits, (fig.) 99
    awards and certifications, 104–105,
        (fig.) 105
    in a global economy, 105–109,
        (exh.) 107
    in finance, 95–96, (exh.) 95
    in information technology, 97–98,
        (exh.) 97
    and law, 109–110
    in marketing, 96–97, (exh.) 97
    meaning of, 69–75, (fig.) 70, (fig.) 71,
        (fig.) 72, (exh.) 74
    officers, (fig.) 99, 101
    policies or codes, (fig.) 99, (exh.) 100,
        100–101
    reporting mechanisms, (fig.) 99, 102
    safeguards, 99–100, (fig.) 99
    training programs, (fig.) 99, 103
Ethics and Compliance Officers Association,
    101, (www) 111
Ethics and Policy Integration Centre,
    (www) 111
Ethics Resource Center, (fig.) 70n, 71,
    (www) 88, 92–93, 102, 104,
    (www) 111
Ethisphere Institute, (fig.) 72n, 72, (fig.)
    105, (www) 119
Ethisphere Magazine, 104
European Consumer Organization,
    (www) 352
European Corporate Governance Institute,
    (www) 329
European Parliament, 190
European Public Relations Confederation,
    (www) 443
European Social Investment Forum, 323
European Union, 178, 387, 392
Executive compensation, 317–321,
    (fig.) 319, (fig.) 320, 330–331
Extended product responsibility, 228

F

Facebook, 199, 271–272, 434
Fair Labor Association, 155–157
Fair labor standards, 373–374
False Claims Act, U.S., 372
Families and Work Institute, (www) 399
Family-friendly corporation, 397–398
Family leave, 396
Family Smoking Prevention and Tobacco
    Control Act, 201
Fannie Mae, 27
Farm subsidies, (exh.) 123
Federal Communications Commission
    (FCC), 280, 436, (www) 443, 472
Federal Reserve Bank, 168
Federal Reserve System Board of
    Governors, (www) 180
Federal Trade Commission, (www) 180,
    (www) 304, 337, 339, (fig.) 340,
    344, (www) 352, 436, 472
FedEx, 235
Fidelity Investments, 423–425
Financial Times (London), (www) 22
Fiscal policy, 167
527 Organizations, 198
Food and Drug Administration (FDA), 333,
    (fig.) 340, 341, (exh.) 371, 493–502,
    515
Foreign direct investment, 118
Foresight Institute, (www) 282
Fortune, (www) 22
Forum Empresu, (exh.) 144
FosterHyland, (exh.) 441n
Foundation Center, (www) 423
Foundation for Public Affairs, 36,
    (exh.) 203n
Foxconn, 155–157
Fracking, (exh.) 240
Freddie Mac, 27
Free enterprise systems, 128
Freelanchers Union, 364
Freeport-McMoran, 151–152
Free trade, (exh.) 123
Fuji Industries, 235

G

Galleon Group, 69
Ganges River, 215
Gap, 150
Geisinger Health System, 376–377
General Electric (GE), 242, 248, (exh.) 350
General Mills, 397–398
General Motors, 161
General systems theory, 5
Genetically engineered/modified foods
    (GM foods), 302–303
Genetically modified organisms (GMO), 54

Genetic engineering, 302
Genome Projects (U.S. Department of
        Energy), (www) 304
Germany, 241
Gilden Activewear, 522–530
Giving Institute, (www) 423
Giving USA Foundation, (www) 423
Glass ceiling, 386
Glass walls, 387
GlaxoSmithKline, 46, 96, 318–319
Global action networks (GAN), 131
Global Alliance for Clean Cookstoves, 232
Global corporate citizenship, 138
Global Electoral Organization Conference,
        205
Global Issues, (www) 43
Globalization:
    acceleration of, 119–120
    benefits and costs of, 122–126,
        (exh.) 123, (fig.) 126
    business in a diverse world, 126–131,
        (exh.) 129
    collaborative partnerships, 131–133,
        (fig.) 132
    international institutions, 120–122,
        (exh.) 122
    major transnational corporations,
        118–119, (fig.) 119
    process of, 117–121
Global Policy Forum, (www) 133
Global Reporting Initiative, (fig.) 148,
        (www) 155
Global warming, 169, 222, (fig.) 223,
        (exh.) 225
Goldman Sachs, 95
Gold mining, 257–258
Google, 28, 49, 192, 199, 261, 263–265,
        271, 276, 333
GovernanceMetrics International, 317
Government Made Easy,
        (www) 180
Government regulation:
    continuous reform, 177–178
    effects, 175–177, (fig.) 175, (fig.) 176
    global context, 178–179
    of business, 168–170
    types of, 170–175, (exh.) 173, (exh.) 174
Grameen Bank, 62
Grameen Foundation, (www) 65
Grameen Group, (exh.) 62
Grassroots strategy, 208
Greece, 161
Green Business Network, (www) 256
Greenhouse Gas Protocol, 230
Green marketing, 253–254
Green Mountain Coffee Roasters, 415
Greenwashing, 254
Groupe Danone, (exh.) 62
GT Nexus, (exh.) 221
Gun violence, (exh.) 357

H

Hackers, computer (*See* Computer hackers)
Hacktivists, 290
Henry Ford Health Systems, 349
Herman Miller, 252
Hewlett-Packard, 46
Highmark, (exh.) 435
Home Depot, 415
Honda Motors, 403
Honduras, 525–526
Honesty tests, 370
Housing, 408–409
Human genome, 299–300
Human rights (*See* Rights reasoning)

I

IBM, 254, 396, 421
IKEA, 25, 359–360
Image advertisements, 434–435,
        (exh.) 435
Immigration and Customs Enforcement
        (ICE), 400–401
Imperial Sugar, 356
Industrial ecology, 228
Information phase of technology, 263
ING, 403
In-kind contributions, 414
Insider trading, 326–328
Institute for Business Ethics,
        (www) 88
Institute for Crisis Management, 438
Institute for Drug-Free Workplace,
        (www) 375
Institute for Global Ethics, (www) 111
Institute for Public Relations (IPR),
        (www) 443
Institute for Social and Ethical
        Accountability (ISEA), (fig.) 148,
        (www) 155
Institute for Supply Management (ISM),
        98–99
Institutional investors, 310–311
Institutional Shareholder Service (ISS),
        (www) 329, 331
Integrity capital, 72
Intel, 171, 413, 419–420
Intellectual property, 294
Interactive Digital Software Association, 109
Interactive social system, 5
Interface, 249
Interfaith Center on Corporate
        Responsibility (ICCR), 324
Intergovernmental Panel on Climate
        Change, 222
International Association of Business
        Communicators (IABC), (exh.) 430,
        (www) 443

International Association of Machinists and
        Aerospace Workers, 359–360
International Business Ethics Institute,
        (www) 88, (www) 111
International Coal Group, 439
International Council for Local
        Environmental Initiatives (ICLEI),
        (www) 231
International Federation of the Phonographic
        Industry (IFPI), 296
International financial and trade institutions
        (IFTIs), 120
International Forum on Globalization,
        (www) 133
International Integrated Reporting Council
        (IIRC), 153
International Intellectual Property Alliance,
        (www) 304
International Labour Organization (ILO),
        (www) 375
International Monetary Fund (IMF),
        120–121, (www) 133
International Organization for
        Standardization (ISO), (fig.) 148,
        (www) 155, 230
International Panel on Climate Change,
        (www) 231
International Public Relations Association
        (IPRA), (exh.) 430, (www) 443
International Service for the Acquisition of
        Agri-biotech Applications (ISAAA),
        303
International Society for Stem Cell
        Research, (www) 304
Internet, 265–267, (fig.) 266
Internet Society, (www) 282
Investor Responsibility Research Center
        (IRRC), (www) 329
Iron law of responsibility, 49
Issue Management Council, (www) 43
Issues management, 32–35, (fig.) 32
    organizing for effective, 35–37, (exh.) 37

J

Jamaica, 120–121
Japan, 363
Johnson & Johnson, 54–55, 350–351
John Wiley and Sons, 297
Josephson Institute, (www) 88
JPMorgan Chase, 180–182
Justice reasoning, (fig.) 83, 86

K

KaBOOM!, 415
Kaiser Permanente, 359, 500
Kalundborg (Denmark), 228

Kiedanren, 204
Kimberley Process, 132
Kimpton Hotels, 503–510
KPMG, (fig.) 152, 152–153, 394
Kyoto Protocol, 224

L

Labor unions, 358–359
Leadership in Energy and Environmental
    Design (LEED), (exh.) 253
Leadership PACs, 198
Lebanon, 204–205
Legal challenges, 201
License to operate, 406
Life-cycle analysis, 227–228
Lilly Ledbetter Fair Pay Act, 389
LinkedIn, 271
Living wage, 373, (exh.) 374
Lobbying, 189–191, (fig.) 189,
    (exh.) 191, 204
Lobbying Disclosure, (www) 206
LRN Corporation, 75

M

Malcolm Baldrige National Quality
    Award, 349
Maquiladoras, 525–526
Maquila Solidarity Network, 527–528
Marine ecosystems, 226
Market-based mechanisms, 243, (fig.) 245
Market failure, 169
Marks & Spencer, 228–229
Marriott, 379, 418, 462
Masdar City, (exh.) 214
Massey Energy, 244, 448–457
Mattel Toy Company, 531–540
McDonald's, 33–35, 146, 345–346
M-commerce, 269–270, (exh.) 269
Media training, 440–442
Medtronics, 102
Mercatus Center, (www) 180
Merck, 169, 493–502
MF Global, 95
Microfinance, 62
Microsoft, 408
Military dictatorships, 127–128
Millennials, 380, (exh.) 381
Mine Safety and Health Administration,
    452–455
Minha Casa, Minha Vida, 168
Minnesota Forward, 195–196
Mitsubishi, 16
Monetary policy, 168
Monsanto, 302–303, 513
Montreal Protocol, 222
Moody's Corporation, 480–492

Moral development, stages of, 81–82,
    (fig.) 81
Motion Picture Association of
    America, 296
Mylan, 98
MySpace.com, 271

N

Namaste Solar, 184
Nanotechnology, 298–299
National Center for Policy Analysis,
    (www) 180, (www) 206
National Federation of Independent
    Businesses, (www) 206
National Highway Traffic Safety
    Administration (NHTSA), 165,
    (fig.) 340, 341
National Issues Forum, (www) 43
National Nanotechnology Initiative,
    (www) 304
National Transportation Safety Board
    (NTSB), (fig.) 340
National Whistleblowers Center,
    (www) 375
National White Collar Crime Center,
    (www) 111
National Workrights Institute, (www)
    375, 377
Natural environment,
    Earth's carrying capacity, 219
    forces of change, 216–218, (fig.) 217,
        (fig.) 218
    global issues, 221–227, (exh.) 221,
        (fig.) 223, (exh.) 225
    international community response,
        227–230
    sustainable development, 213,
        (exh.) 214
    threats to the Earth's ecosystem,
        214–216
Natural monopolies, 169
Negative externalities, 169
Network World, (www) 282
Neuromarketing, 333
Newmont Mining Group, 117
News Look, (exh.) 374
New York Stock Exchange,
    (www) 329
New York Times, The, (www) 22
New Zealand, 235
Nike Corporation, 41, 211, 356
Nokia, 413
Nongovernmental organizations (NGOs),
    131–132
Novartis, (exh.) 149, (exh.) 374
Novo Nordisk, 138
Novozymes, 252
Nutrition labeling, 170

O

Obesity, 353–354
Occupational Safety and Health
    Administration (OSHA), 359,
    (exh.) 360, 361, (www) 375
Occupational segregation, 383
Olympus, 93
One Million Acts of Green, 219
Online privacy, 282–284
Open cookstoves, 232–233
Opensecrets.org, (www) 206
Open Security Foundation, (www) 304
Organization for Economic Cooperation and
    Development (OECD), 106, 317
Ownership theory of the firm, 6
Ozone, 221–222

P

PacificCorp, 40
Pakistan, 276
P & G, 432
Parental leave, 396
Pay gap, 383, (fig.) 383
PayPerPost.com, 471
Pepsi-Cola, (exh.) 47
Perfect Citizen program, 291
Performance-expectations gap, (fig.) 26
Pershing Square Capital Management, 322
Pew Internet and American Life Project,
    (www) 282
Pfizer, 142, 414
Pharmaceutical Researchers &
    Manufacturers of America (PhRMA),
    496–497, (exh.) 497
Phishing, 274–275
Pink slime (lean finely textured beef),
    444–445
Pitney Bowes, 394
Pittsburgh Penguins, 199
Plant-made medicines, 511–521
Points of Light Foundation, (www) 423
Political action committees (PACs),
    193–198, (exh.) 194, (fig.) 195,
    (fig.) 196, (exh.) 197
Political environment:
    arguments for and against business
        involvement, (fig.) 185
    participants in the, 185–187
Political involvement, levels of, 202,
    (fig.) 212
PoliticsOnline, (www) 206
PPG Industries, 78
Predatory pricing, 171
Prescription Drug User Fee Act, 495–496
PricewaterhouseCoopers, 80, 394
Privacy in the workplace:
    alcohol abuse, 368–369

Privacy in the workplace—*Cont.*
    drug use and testing, 367–368, (fig.) 369
    electronic monitoring, 365
    romance, 367
    theft and honesty testing, 369
Privacy rights, 364
Product liability, 345–348, (exh.) 347
Product recall, 351
Professional sport franchises, (exh.) 405
Project Honey Pot, (www) 304
Proxy, 312
Public Affairs Council, (www) 206
Public affairs department, 203–204,
    (fig.) 203
Public Disclosure Commission, (www) 206
Public issue, 25–28
    issue ripeness, (exh.) 27
Public policy:
    elements of, 165–167
    role of government, 164–165
    types of, 167–168
Public relations,
    crisis management, 437–440, (exh.) 438,
      (exh.) 441
    department, 429–432, (fig.) 429,
      (exh.) 430
    emerging digital world, 428–429
    global, 432–433
    government regulation, 435–437
    influencing public opinion, 433–435,
      (exh.) 435
    media training of employees, 440–442
Public Relations Society of America
    (PRSA), (exh.) 430, (www) 443
Public service announcements (PSAs),
    433–434
Public, the general, 427–428
PVH Corporation, 361

Q

QR codes, (exh.) 269
Quality management, 348–349
Quebec Federation of Labor (QFL), 522–523

R

Racial harassment, 392–393
Radio Frequency Identification (RFID), 288
Raytheon, 103
Regis Corporation, 12
Regulation, 168
Regulations.gov, (www) 180
Republic Windows and Doors, 362
Reputation, 55
Reregulation, 177–178
Research In Motion, 275–276
Return on social investment, 419

Reverse discrimination, 391
ReviewMe.com, 471
Revolving door, 190–191
Rights reasoning, (fig.) 83, 85–86

S

Sahz Holdings, 211–212
SAI Global, (www) 111
Samsung, 335
Sanford Limited, 154
Sarbanes-Oxley Act, (exh.) 74, 74–75,
    (www) 88
Saudi Arabia, 275
Say-on-pay, 327, 330–331
Schneider Electric, 229
Schwab Foundation, (www) 65
S.C. Johnson, 396, 434
Securities and Exchange Commission
    (SEC), (exh.) 323, 325, 327, (www)
    329, 436
Semantic phase of technology, 263
Sex trafficking, 458–466
Sexual harassment, 391–392
Shareholder activism, 321–324
Shareholder lawsuits, 324–325
Shell Oil, 130–131, 200
Siemens Building Technologies, 251
Smoking in the workplace, 376–377
Social Accountability International,
    (fig.) 148, (www) 155
Social and environmental reporting,
    151–153, (fig.) 152
Social assistance policies, 168
Social audit, 147–151, (fig.) 148
Social capital, 406
Social contract, 363, (exh.) 365
Social enterprise, 59
Social entrepreneurs, 60
Social entrepreneurship, 60
Social equity, 147
Social investment, 322–324
Social Investment Forum, 323, (www) 329
Social Media Today, (www) 282
Social networking, 271–275
Social regulations, 172–175, (exh.) 173,
    (fig.) 174
Social responsibility shareholder resolutions,
    323–324
Society for Corporate Compliance and
    Ethics, (www) 111
Society of Consumer Affairs Professionals,
    (www) 352
Sodexo, 56
Software piracy, 294–297, (fig.) 294, (fig.) 297
Solidarity Fund, 522–530
Sound bite, 442
Source reduction, 241
Source Watch, (www) 443

Spam (unsolicited commercial e-mail),
    273–274
SpeechNow.org, 197
Spinwatch, (www) 443
Spirituality in the workplace, 80–81
Stakeholder:
    analysis, 10–17
    coalitions, 14–16
    concept of, 7–8
    dialogue, 40
    engagement, 37–42, (fig.) 39
    interests, 11–12, (exh.) 14–15
    internal and external, 9–10
    are managers, (exh.) 9
    market and nonmarket, 8–10, (fig.) 9
    power, 12–13, (exh.) 14–15
    salience and mapping, 16–17, (fig.) 17
    theory of the firm, 6–7
Starboard Value, 12
Starbucks, 250, 269–270, 432
Stem-cell research, 300–301, (exh.) 300
Stockholders:
    and corporate governance, 313–317
    and the corporation, 328
    defined, 309–311, (fig.) 310, (fig.) 311
    government protection of, 325–328
    legal rights and safeguards, 312–313,
      (fig.) 313
    objectives of ownership, 312
Stock options, 318
Stop Online Piracy Act, 207–208
Strategic and Competitive Intelligence
    Professionals, (www) 43
Strategic philanthropy, 417
Strategic radar screens, (fig.) 29, 29–30
Strict liability, 345–346
Subprime mortgage meltdown, 480–492
Sun Microsystems, 40
Superfund, 241–242
Super PACs, 197–198
SustainAbility, (www) 256
Sustainability report, 251–252
Sustainable agriculture, (www) 304
Sustainable development, 213, (exh.) 214
Syria, 276

T

Target, 195–196
Technology:
    defined, 262
    digital divide, the, 280–281
    fueling technological growth, 264–265
    government censorship, 275–276,
      (exh.) 277
    management of information security,
      291–293, (exh.) 293
    managing scientific breakthroughs,
      298–303, (exh.) 300

phases of, 262–263, (fig.) 263
powerful force in business, 265–270, (fig.) 266, (fig.) 268, (exh.) 269, (exh.) 270
privacy violations, 287–291, (fig.) 287, (exh.) 289
protecting intellectual property, 294–297, (fig.) 294, (fig.) 297
socially beneficial uses of, 277–280, (exh.) 278
Technology cooperation, 229
Technorati, 272, (www) 282, 470n
TeleTech Customer Case, 368
Telstra, 441
Timberland, 65–66
Time Warner, 434
Tissue engineering, 300
T-Mobile, 172
Tobacco advertisement, 437
Top Dog Daycare, 268
Toy Industry Association, 538
Toyola Energy, 232–233
Toyota, 26–27, 255
Toy safety, 531–540
Toys "R" Us, 539
Trade associations, 201
Transnational corporations, 118, (fig.) 119
Transparency, 151
Transparency International, 105, (www) 111
Triple bottom line, 153–154
Truth In Lending Act, 336–337

U

UBS, 95
Ukraine, 295
Undocumented (unauthorized) immigrant workers, 380, 400–401
UNICEF, 25, 25n
United Airlines, 427
United Arab Emirates, 275
United Auto Workers, 197–198
United Food and Commercial Workers Union, 272
United Kingdom, 274
United Kingdom Bribery Act, 108
United Mine Workers, 455–456
United Nations, 179
United Nations and Civil Society, (www) 133
United Nations Environmental Program, (www) 231
United Nations Framework Convention on Climate Change, (www) 231

United Nations Global Compact, (www) 133, (fig.) 148, (exh.) 149, (www) 155
United Nations Global Issues, (www) 43
United Nations International Law, (www) 180
United States Steel Corporation, (exh.) 101
University of Pittsburgh Medical Center (UPMC), (exh.) 435
Unocal, 13
Unsolicited commercial e-mail (*See* Spam)
Upper Big Branch Mine, 448–457
U.S. Chamber of Commerce, 201
U.S. Corporate Sentencing Guidelines, 73–74
U.S. Department of Agriculture, 444, 516
U.S. Federal Election Commission (FEC), 193–194, (www) 206
U.S. Federal Trade Commission (*See* Federal Trade Commission)
U.S. Foreign Corrupt Practices Act (FCPA), 107–108
U.S. Green Building Council, (exh.) 253
U.S. Office of Government Ethics, (www) 88
U.S. Office of Information and Regulatory Affairs, (www) 180
U.S. Sentencing Commission, (www) 88, 245
U.S. Small Business Administration, (www) 399
U.S. State Department, (www) 375
U.S. v. O'Hagan, 327
Utilitarian reasoning, (fig.) 83, 84–85

V

Value Line, 91
Values, manager's, 78–79
Ventria Bioscience, 511–521
Verizon, 359
VIGOR, 500
Violence in the workplace, (exh.) 360
Vioxx, 493–502
Virtue ethics, 83–84, (fig.) 83, (fig.) 84
Vlogs, 273
Volunteerism, 414, (exh.) 416
Vulture find, (exh.) 122

W

Wall Street Journal, The, (www) 22
Walmart, 3–4, 324, 406
Walt Disney Company, 22–23
Washington Mutual (WaMu), 487
Wells Fargo, 415

Wendy's, (exh.) 438
Western Growers Association, 349
Whistle-blowing and free speech in the workplace, 370–372, (exh.) 371
White-collar crime, 109
Whole Foods Market, 403
Worker Adjustment Retraining Notification Act (WARN), 362
Workforce, the changing face of, 379–380, (exh.) 381
gender and race at work, 380–382, (fig.) 382
gender and racial pay gap, 383–384, (fig.) 383
glass ceiling, breaking the, 385–387
women and minorities ownership, 387–388
women and persons of color, 384, (fig.) 385
Working conditions around the world, 372–374, (exh.) 374
Working Mother magazine, (www) 399
Workplace rights:
to a safe and healthy workplace, 359–362, (exh.) 360
to a secure job, 362–364
to organize and bargain collectively, 358–359
Workplace Spirituality, (www) 88
World Bank, 120, (www) 133
World Business Council for Sustainable Development (WBCSD), (www) 231
World Future Society, (www) 43
World News, Public Issues, (www) 43
World Resources Institute, (www) 231
World Summit on Sustainable Development, 211
World Trade Organization (WTO), 121, (exh.) 123, 125, (www) 133
Worldwatch Institute, (www) 231
Wyeth v. Levine, 347–348

X

Xcel Energy, 251

Y

Yahoo!, (www) 43
YRC/Roadway Express, 392

Z

Zombie, 288–289